Figured tapestry

Textile Mills, Kensington, lithograph by Herschel Levit, 1937. (Courtesy of the Atwater Kent Museum.)

Figured tapestry
Production, markets, and power in Philadelphia textiles, 1885–1941

PHILIP SCRANTON
Rutgers University

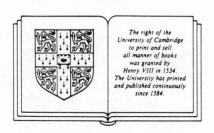

The right of the
University of Cambridge
to print and sell
all manner of books
was granted by
Henry VIII in 1534.
The University has printed
and published continuously
since 1584.

CAMBRIDGE UNIVERSITY PRESS

Cambridge
New York   Port Chester   Melbourne   Sydney

Published by the Press Syndicate of the University of Cambridge
The Pitt Building, Trumpington Street, Cambridge CB2 1RP
32 East 57th Street, New York, NY 10022, USA
10 Stamford Road, Oakleigh, Melbourne 3166, Australia

© Cambridge University Press 1989

First published 1989

Printed in the United States of America

Library of Congress Cataloging-in-Publication Data
Scranton, Philip.
Figured tapestry : production, markets, and power in Philadelphia
textiles, 1885–1941 / Philip Scranton.
p. cm.
Includes index.
ISBN 0–521–34287–2 hard covers
1. Textile industry – Pennsylvania – Philadelphia – History.
I. Title.
HD9858.P5S34   1989
338.4′7677′00974811 – dc19   88-32215
                                                                    CIP

British Library Cataloguing in Publication Data
Scranton, Philip
Figured tapestry: production, markets, and power in Philadelphia textiles, 1885–1941.
1. Pennsylvania. Philadelphia. Textile industries, 1885-1941
I. Title
338.4′7677′00974811

ISBN 0-521-34287-2 hard covers

In memory of William McIntosh, gentleman of New Bedford, and Gladys Palmer, Philadelphia scholar

Contents

Figures

Tables

xi

Philadelphia: neighborhoods, waterways, and principal streets. (Courtesy of Temple University Press.)

Preface

In the spring of 1985, our elderly neighbor sold her home and moved in with her daughter's family, leaving on the curb, among other things, a battered wooden trunk. For no good reason at all, I dragged the thing up our steps, opened it, and discovered a peculiar treasure, a hoard of salesman's samples. Folded neatly, and untouched for sixty years, they comprised lengths of tapestries made at Philadelphia's renowned Orinoka Mills, brilliantly colored hangings and upholsteries, crowded with mythological figures, hunters and horses, Poussinesque nymphs, rendered in rayon, silk, and cotton. All but a few of them are now in the fabric collection of the Paley Design Center at Philadelphia College of Textiles and Science, but their arrival as the research for this book was gathering momentum is now memorialized in its title. Not only did the fineness of those fabrics epitomize the stylish, technically demanding character of seasonal goods made in the Quaker City, their ornamentation suggested a metaphor for its elaborate social relations, an ever-moving "figured tapestry" of production and exchange, contest and accommodation, likewise lying silently for over half a century awaiting inquiry. Though the Orinoka samples have survived intact, the tapestry of production frayed with use and was discarded. Hence the goal of this study is to reconstitute it in a fashion that will restore its vibrance, mark its flaws, and account for its decay.

Like the making of any product, creation of this book was a collective project. The research and writing were supported by grants from the National Science Foundation, Geography and Regional Science Division (SES 84-14703), the New Jersey Historical Commission, and the Rutgers University Research Council. A National Endowment for the Humanities/Mellon Foundation fellowship enabled me to spend six privileged months at the Hagley Museum and Library, Greenville, Delaware, and a sabbatical leave from Rutgers speeded the writing and rewriting of the present text. With regard to these grants, I would like to acknowledge the valuable assistance of Henry Williams, George Demko, Mary Murrin, Glenn Porter, and my department chair, Andrew Lees. Research assistance was provided by Julie Johnson, Gail Farr, Margaret Sobczak, Karen Mittleman, Nancy Kerns, and

Elizabeth Fox, with crucial advice on data management offered by Walter Licht. Invaluable help was given by the library and archives staff at Hagley, the National Archives in Washington, Suitland, Maryland, and Philadelphia, the Free Library of Philadelphia, the Philadelphia College of Textiles and Science, the Historical Society of Pennsylvania, the University of Pennsylvania's Van Pelt and Lippincott Libraries, Temple University's Urban Archives, and the now-dismembered Franklin Institute Library. Special thanks are gratefully offered to Walter Licht and Alice Miller for making possible access to Gladys Palmer's unprocessed papers.

For their counsel and support, the following veterans of Philadelphia textile families deserve special mention: Elizabeth Doak Tarnay, Jean Blum Seder, Lester Blankin, Patricia Bromley Crowell, Dobson Schofield III, and Charles Webb. Richard Bromley kindly opened portions of the Quaker Lace Company's business papers for my use. For critical discussions of manuscript drafts and help in formulating approaches to the work, I thank Howell Harris, Patricia Cooper, Robert Fishman, Jonathan Zeitlin, Neil Smith, Michael Storper, and Steve Fraser. Opportunities to present portions of work in progress were cordially made available by the Harvard Business School's Business History Seminar, the Mellon Seminar on Technology and Culture at the University of Pennsylvania, and the program committees of the American Historical Association and the Association of American Geographers. Typing was managed skillfully by Monica deCarlo and Eleanor Pulice. For their reservoirs of patience and timely wit, I could have had no better companions on this journey than my spouse, Virginia McIntosh, and my son, Christopher.

None among this crew are responsible for the faults in what follows, but all have contributed to whatever merit it is found to possess.

1

Introduction

"The interesting story of the rise, growth and decline of Philadelphia's many textile trades is still to be written."

Gladys Palmer, 1939.

"Textiles . . . are nothing to depend on for a living, with conditions what they are in Philadelphia."

Plush weaver interview, 1936. (Both quotes from Palmer Papers, Box 135, "Textiles," Urban Archives, Temple University, Philadelphia.)

In the pages that follow, the course of the Philadelphia textile industry will be traced across six decades, from the 1880s through World War II, completing a chronicle of regional economic development and decline that commenced with *Proprietary Capitalism: The Philadelphia Textile Manufacture, 1880–1885*. Together, these two volumes serve to answer a set of questions with which research began nearly a decade ago, thereby raising others which will motivate related inquiries in the years to come. From the outset, it seemed important to explore why it was that a rapidly growing and ultimately massive network of industrial establishments in the Quaker City seemed so poorly to fit the traditional image of textile industrialization drawn from the New England experience. What distinguished Philadelphia's format for production and accumulation from the integrated, corporate, bulk output, staple goods mills of Lowell, Lawrence, and Fall River? What was the significance of these contrasting approaches for the shape and character of American industrialization? How might an appreciation of Philadelphia's pattern alter and enhance our portrait of urban and economic growth, our understanding of entrepreneurship, labor–capital relations, and the social, political, and spatial contexts for industrial conflict and collaboration?

Briefly, the findings presented in *Proprietary Capitalism* indicated that Philadelphia mill owners, chiefly immigrants from working-class backgrounds, had erected a coherent alternative manufacturing system, applying their craft talents in individual, partial process firms reliant on skilled labor to generate a diverse array of seasonal specialties rather than staple textiles. These separate establishments clustered in urban industrial districts and were linked sequentially (spinning, dyeing, weaving, knitting, etc.) to meet variable demand through batch output of fashionable intermediate and final goods (cloths vs. carpets or hosiery). Proprietors both owned and managed their plants, engaged in contentious but mutualistic relations with workers, and regarded their family and partnership enterprises as personal projects and legacies as much or more than as investments. This proprietary capitalism differed from the better known corporate and bureaucratizing form along virtually every parameter of comparison and exemplified a penchant for flexibility and product differentiation that secured a national reputation for Philadelphia goods, fueled profitability and expansion, and underwrote high earnings for thousands of veteran craftsmen. Parallel with the evolution of an industrial capitalism based on speedy, routinized bulk production, there had developed a format centered on timely, specialized batch production. Where Lowell's advantages lay in scale, Philadelphia's stemmed from scope and versatility. By the 1880s, both approaches to textile industrialization were solidly grounded.

Such conclusions immediately spawned fresh queries. More narrowly, how did the flexible format fare in the ensuing era of mergers and trusts, in the depression of the 1890s and the ferment of World War I? How did the growing role of the state affect Philadelphia proprietors? What of labor? the "new" immigration? the rise of southern textiles? Where else did flexible textile manufacturing take root, and how did its course at other sites mirror or depart from the Philadelphia experience? As both Yankee and Quaker City industries were plainly in decline by the 1930s, what had undercut each successful format, and were the two slides related? As the Philadelphia trades contracted much more gradually than their staple counterparts, what accounted for their relative durability as prospects dimmed? What weaknesses inherent in the proprietary pattern were exposed? In what context of shifts in the larger industrial and commercial environment? What strategies were implemented by capital and by labor to deal with short-term crises and longer-term erosion of opportunities for profit and employment?

More broadly, how rare or general was flexible manufacturing in the post-bellum American economy? What were its relations to emergent mass production? Given that staple and specialty/seasonal/stylish goods evidently targeted different markets, how was competition between the two formats possible? How adequate are our customary notions of competition, based on price, factor costs, and assumptions of product homogeneity, perfect information, etc., for such an inquiry? What hidden rigidities and costs might be involved in achieving product flexibility? What role did private and governmental institution building (trade associations, unions, vs. bureaus, commissions, and services) play in the eclipse of flexible firms? How was their decline related to urban decay? How might mass distribution and mass consumption on the basis of rising real incomes have been involved? Was there a breaking point after which former assets of flexible firms were transformed into growing liabilities? If thousands of firms across dozens of sectors relied on such a format for three generations after the Civil War, how might acknowledgment of their durable industrial role alter the texture of American business, labor, and economic history?

In a study of one industry and one region, however carefully linked to national matters, only the roster of "narrow" questions can be fully addressed. In attempting this task, glimpses of the larger picture may be had, shadows that will be soon pursued in a more wide-ranging study of batch manufacturing.[1] Yet this "Philadelphia story" may have the potential to do more than document the latter days of a major city's chief industry. It is hoped that the present work will also: (1) suggest that the dynamics of decline are fully as complex and significant as those of growth, meriting close empirical research and theoretical reflection; (2) provide some historical background and cautionary thoughts for advocates of a revitalized flexible format; (3) indicate the utility of an interdisciplinary industrial history; and (4) lead toward construction of an alternative narrative of American industrialization that will take fuller account of diversity and Charles Tilly's "large processes, huge comparisons" than does the prevalent Lowell-to-General Motors-by way-of-the-railroads tale.[2]

At the close of a decade during which the erosion of American industrial preeminence has been confronted, debated, and analyzed, a reassessment of the nation's industrial history may be peculiarly timely. The structural rather than cyclical character of recent reverses has brought decline onto the agendas of essayists and social scientists, but the topic has hardly been magnetic among mainstream historians conditioned to celebrating innovation, growth, and achievement.[3] Yet as regional industrial crises multiply, as

---

[1] This study, tentatively entitled "Endless Novelty: The Other Side of Industrialization," will examine flexibility and batch manufacturing in various American industries ca. 1860–1950.

[2] Charles Tilly, *Big Structures, Large Processes and Huge Comparisons*, New York, 1984.

[3] Among a wide variety of assessments, see Barry Bluestone and Bennett Harrison, *The Deindustrialization of America*, New York, 1983; Robert Reich, *The Next American Frontier*, New York, 1983; Robert Reich and John Donahue, *New Deals*, New York, 1985; David Bensman and Roberta Lynch, *Rusted Dreams*, New York, 1987; and Stephen Cohen and John Zysman, *Manufacturing Matters*, New York, 1987. For a collection of policy overviews, see David Obey and Paul Sarbanes, eds., *The Changing American Economy*, New York, 1986. Labor historians, given the twenty-five-year fade of the American labor movement, have taken the issue of decline most seriously. See Christopher Tomlins, *The State and the Unions*, New York, 1985, and David Montgomery, *The Fall of the House of Labor*, New York, 1987. Given Great Britain's longer experience with industrial decline, historians of the British economy have recently initiated vigorous reassessments

core mass-production industries stagnate, restructure, or decay, and as tariff wars shoulder their ominous way onto the political stage, those seeking a historical perspective on such matters will find precious few resources available.[4] The Whiggish cast of business and labor history from Cole and Commons to Chandler and Taft entailed a double disability. Incidents of decline, whether in particular sectors or among regionally independent unions, were viewed unproblematically as the naturalistic outcome of competition informed by growing organizational and technical sophistication, creative destruction in the service of efficiency, and progress. This "winners' " history, attuned to tracing the paths to the present of "big business" and "big labor," has passed over the histories of those whose differing approaches to accumulation and work lay outside the territory of mass production or national unionism. Such omissions make it difficult to appreciate the means by which winners are transformed into losers.

The notion of ceaseless, cumulative advance has been often enough questioned in the last generation that a benevolent, "ever forward" industrial history is no longer tenable. Yet the character of its replacement is still unclear; orthodox and revisionist Marxist frameworks, however suggestive, have been repeatedly found inadequate in both theory and application by scholars committed to their development and use. Meanwhile, essential neoclassical concepts and methods in economics have been judged severely deficient by critics both within and beyond the professional "guild." Noting the "fundamental internal contradiction" between the assumptions of micro- and macroeconomics, Lester Thurow rests "convinced that accepting the conventional supply-demand model of the economy is rather like believing the world is flat...you can make a rigorous case, on paper, for both prop-

of older neoclassical and cultural interpretations, studies that in part parallel the findings presented below. Arguing for the crucial role of "rigidities in the economic and social institutions that developed in the nineteenth century," a group of scholars led by William Lazonick and Bernard Elbaum are concerned to portray the constraints on adaptation to changing circumstances that were inherent in "[e]ntrenched institutional structures." See Elbaum and Lazonick, eds., *The Decline of the British Economy*, Oxford, 1987 (quotes from p. 2).

[4] The roster of regional and industrial studies from the 1930s through the 1950s is not generally cited in recent work, as they were chiefly focused on the "sick" sectors of an earlier era: coal, textiles, agriculture, railroads. On textiles, see Daniel Creamer and Charles Coulter, *Labor and the Shut-Down of the Amoskeag Textile Mills*, WPA National Research Project, Report L–5, Philadelphia, 1939; Gladys Palmer, *Union Tactics and Economic Change*, Philadelphia, 1931; S. L. Wolfbein, *The Decline of a Cotton Textile City*, New York, 1944; Commonwealth of Massachusetts, *Report of the Special Committee Relative to the Textile Industry*, Boston, 1950; R. C. Estall, *New England: A Study in Industrial Adjustment*, London, 1966; Seymour Harris, *The Economics of New England: Case Study of an Older Area*, Cambridge, MA, 1952; and State of Rhode Island, *Report of the Commission to Investigate Problems of the Cotton Textile Industry*, Providence, 1935.

ositions, but hard evidence is more than a bit scarce."[5] Thus as a goal of generating scientific appraisals of society and history recedes, and epistemological issues in the social sciences become, in Charles Sabel's phrase, "radically open," the historian's artful efforts to display values, pattern, and movement, to convey an inclusive sense of conflict and context, and relate tales and tables to intelligible and accessible concepts, become all the more relevant. In restoring contingency, culture, and "nonoptimal" behavior to industrial history, and reconstituting the experiences of firms, workers, districts, and sectors excluded from reductionist or hypothesis-testing agendas, we may develop accounts rich enough empirically to provoke new, eclectic initiatives in theory formation. Certainly, what follows will be eclectic enough to annoy purists of all persuasions, yet, with any luck, plausible enough to illuminate persuasively a significant dimension of the process of industrialization.[6]

Distant from these abstract concerns, but no less relevant to the present study, are the policy debates surrounding calls for a revival of flexibility as a part of the remedial "search for excellence" by American corporations. The advocates of institutional flexibility and a renewed personalism as tools to correct the perceived rigidity of bureaucratized organizations have lacked perspective on the benefits and hazards of similar approaches practiced in American economic history. Work by Sabel, Michael Piore, and Jonathan

[5] See Jon Elster, *Making Sense of Marx*, New York, 1985; idem, *Explaining Technical Change*, New York, 1983; John Roemer, ed., *Analytical Marxism*, New York, 1986; and William Reddy, *Money and Liberty in Modern Europe*, New York, 1987, for extensive critiques of Marxism and other theoretical perspectives. Rational-choice substitutes have come under heavy return fire, and Elster is somewhat cautious in his introduction to a recent collection (John Elster, ed., *Rational Choice*, New York, 1986, pp. 2–4, 17–27). The Thurow quotes are taken from Lester Thurow, *Dangerous Currents*, New York, 1983, pp. xvii, xviii, 4. For insightful efforts at moving beyond the static frameworks of traditional economic theorizing, see Burton Klein, *Dynamic Economics*, Cambridge, MA, 1977, and idem, *Prices, Wages and Business Cycles: A Dynamic Theory*, New York, 1984. Klein's notions of static and dynamic flexibility, informed by mass-production dilemmas (*DE*, pp. 194–200), both draw on Stigler (George Stigler, "Production and Distribution in the Short Run," *Journal of Political Economy* 47 (1939):305–27) and have been adopted by Cohen and Zysman as ways of appreciating industrial rigidities and their sources (Stephen Cohen and John Zysman, *Manufacturing Matters*, New York, 1987, Chapter 9). For key elements in the critique of marginalism and the neoclassical paradigm, see Arthur Young, "Increasing Returns and Economic Progress," *Economic Journal* 38(1928):527–42; Nicholas Kaldor, "The Irrelevance of Equilibrium Economics," *Economic Journal* 82(1972): 1237–55; A.P. Thirlwall, ed., "Symposium: Kaldor's Growth Laws," *Journal of Post-Keynesian Economics* 5(1983):359–429; and Albert Arough, "The Mumpsimus of Economists and the Role of Time and Uncertainty in the Progress of Economic Knowledge," *Journal of Post-Keynesian Economics* 9(1987):395–423.

[6] Charles Sabel, "Opening Statement," Working Group on Historical Alternatives to Mass Production, Paris, December 1986.

Zeitlin has probed secondary sources of largely European origin, while other studies attempt to draw lessons from the Japanese ascent, hoping to infuse American capitalism with a new resilience. However, enthusiasm for re-creating flexible industry in the absence of a detailed appreciation of its history of efficacy and breakdown risks substituting a romanticized simplification for a creative alternative. The critical debate may be sharpened both by review of the Philadelphia example and by a heightened awareness of the ways in which flexibility may be achieved at the cost of exposure to other hazards.[7]

The term "industrial history," used frequently here, reflects more than my agreement with geographer Richard Peet's view that manufacturing is "*the* significant economic activity in advanced societies."[8] It expresses as well my continuing faith in interdisciplinarity as a pathway for historical understanding and consequent distress at the fragmentation of industrial studies among business, labor, and economic history and the history of technology, each of which has moved in differing directions over the last few decades. Devotees of the Chandler managerial synthesis find the labor process uninteresting, while other business historians may well follow Thomas McCraw's concern for state–corporate relations. Labor historians who had shifted their focus from national unions to study communities, workplaces, and conflict so scattered their energies that a return toward institutionalism and biography has surfaced, rather than a concern for markets, technology, and finance. Economic historians, for the most part, are still chasing machine-translatable aggregate data, despite pervasive critiques of their neoclassical assumptions and the flattening of historical process they entail. Historians of technology have so focused on innovation and diffusion as to have, with rare exceptions, ignored their socioeconomic context and the workers who activated the mechanisms. None seem to find spatial questions of more than passing interest, though industrial geographers have been exceptionally active in conceptualizing and researching patterns of production restructuring over the past generation. By contrast, an "industrial" historian undertakes to assess the evolution of manufacturing in an integrative fashion, encompassing value conflicts and value added, language and location, production technologies and distributive relations, organization and outputs, all in their shifting

---

[7] Charles Sabel, *Work and Politics*, New York, 1982; Michael Piore and Charles Sabel, *The Second Industrial Divide*, New York, 1984; Charles Sabel and Jonathan Zeitlin, "Historical Alternatives to Mass Production: Politics, Markets, and Technology in Nineteenth-Century Industrialization," *Past and Present* 108(August 1985):133–176; Larry Hirschhorn, *Beyond Mechanization*, Cambridge, MA, 1984; Morton Schoolman and Alvin Magid, eds., *Reindustrializing New York State*, Albany, 1986.

[8] Richard Peet, ed., *International Capitalism and Industrial Restructuring*, Boston, 1987, p. 288.

political, social, and cultural environments. The ensuing evaluation of a regional industrial complex, elaborated in the context of the sector's national experience and its political/ideological currents, is intended to underscore the potential of interdisciplinary industrial history. Its shortcomings will doubtless also highlight the risks involved in such a scholarly high-wire act. Nonetheless, this treatment of Philadelphia textiles aims to help lay the foundation for an inclusive reconsideration of the American industrial achievement that intertwines diversity, skill, and flexibility with standardization, speed, and routinization.[9]

1.1. A textile scenario

The remainder of these introductory remarks will consist of a preliminary overview of the course of American textile manufacturing from the 1880s through the Great Depression, a short assessment of the scholarly literature that has influenced the study, and the customary preview of chapters to come.

For a generation after the Civil War, the textile trades in the United States contained two complementary divisions. A substantial group of firms, initially concentrated in New England, manufactured staple cotton and woolen fabrics, the standard goods whose constancy of form permitted the erection of long price series for sheetings or print cloths. A second array of mills aimed at batch production of goods whose style and composition changed seasonally. These enterprises developed on either flank of the great central fashion market, New York City, from Providence through Connecticut and New Jersey to Philadelphia. Whereas competition among firms within each division was often intense, competition between the two was scarcely imaginable. Although bulk and batch producers operated in the same industry, for each section the logic of accumulation was distinctive, involving price versus product rivalry, fast versus flexible machinery, capital-intensive versus skill-demanding manufacturing, etc. Bulk-output mills sought economies of scale and speed, where batch specialists thrived on economies of scope and timing, their ability to shift production readily to match the vagaries of differentiated demand.

---

[9] The seminal texts in business history include Alfred Chandler, *The Visible Hand*, Cambridge, MA, 1977; Alfred Chandler and Herman Daems, eds., *Managerial Hierarchies*, Cambridge, MA, 1980; Thomas McCraw, *Prophets of Regulation*, Cambridge, MA, 1984. On labor history and the history of technology, see Philip Scranton, "None-Too-Porous Boundaries," *Technology and Culture* 29(1988):722–43, and for strongly integrative work, David Noble, *Forces of Production*, New York, 1984; Judith McGaw, *Most Wonderful Machine*, Princeton, NJ, 1987; and Patricia Cooper, *Once a Cigar Maker*, Urbana, IL, 1987.

When markets contracted, the two sorts of firms responded differently. Bulk mills continued to run full for as long as possible, accumulating stock, shading prices in order to protect shares of a homogeneous demand, a strategy in part derived from their need to pay dividends and cover high fixed costs. Batch firms had a horror of running stock, for style goods were made to order and were perishable. Inventories might well prove unsalable when markets revived. Hence, when buyers faded away, these operations promptly went on short time, defended their prices by filling only such orders as had been booked or trickled in, and set to fashioning samples of new designs for the coming season. For workers, bulk production involved a trade-off between monotony and steady work at modest pay, whereas batch labor, though more varied and better compensated, carried the surety of irregular employment, both seasonal and recession-driven cutbacks being common. Finally, while integrated production characterized bulk mills and created openings for routinization and scale economies, batch manufacturers relied on others for processing steps not connected with their particular sphere of expertise and versatility, generating an interlaced network of separate establishments. This divergence informed the former's higher fixed-cost, run-full strategy as well as the latter's ability to throttle back to half or three-quarters capacity in wobbly markets.

In the two decades after 1885 both segments of the textile industry expanded and shuddered with movements in the national economy. In cotton staples, the basic outlines are familiar: dramatic growth at Fall River and New Bedford, print cloth capacity there reaching 180,000 pieces weekly by the 1893 break; gradual development of southern coarse staple and yarn fabrication, pressing Yankee companies toward middling grades of standard cloths; technical advances toward near-continuous weaving linked to the battery loom; growing concern about the prospect of excess capacity; hopes for the China trade mixed with speculations about trust formation, ventures into specialty manufacture, or the potential for more comprehensive forward and backward integration. Batch operations were similarly energetic, but moved along quite different trajectories. Assisted by tariff protection, about which they were obsessive, proprietors established branches of textile manufacturing entirely new to the United States: laces, plush, fancy upholstery and draperies, silk hosiery. New firms multiplied, particularly in the knitting trades, where the pace of technical development was dizzying. Travelers commenced carrying seasonal samples to distant points, seeking the orders that would spur the mills into action, and established firms staffed permanent New York offices to keep a finger on the market's pulse. For these flexible specialists, the threat to prosperity seemed to lie not in southern hands but in the wily maneuvers of importers who shouted for free trade, plotting to bring low-wage, high-reputation European novelties into ruinous competition with domestic seasonal output. Different risks attended each format, different problems confronted operators in each division, and in the new century separate crises would first transform the structure of bulk textile production and then undercut the viability of the batch system.

Between 1900 and the Great Depression, textiles became a "sick" industry in the United States, a negative reference point against which the rapid development of the auto and electrical sectors could be charted. The fading fortunes of New England bulk production centers caused concern before World War I and liquidations mounted thereafter, idling tens of thousands in Lowell, Fall River, and New Bedford. By the 1930s, when the gigantic Amoskeag closed, crippling Manchester, New Hampshire, mill cities seemed to be being transformed inexorably into ghost towns. The elements contributing to this reversal were varied and widely bemoaned. Many corporations had been slow to adopt the high-output battery looms, disbursed reserves to buoy up dividends and protect share values, or self-consciously set aside surpluses in holding companies, starving the operating units. Unionization enhanced wage differentials with southern rivals and impeded stretchout and speedup of the labor process; taxes were higher in built-up cities, progressive legislation restricted hours, and multistory mills were aging, their very structure impeding more efficient production flows. A devotion to maximum output yielded fierce price competition that depressed margins to ever lower levels; wage cuts proved but temporary and ineffectual expedients.

Yet there was another little-noted dimension to the bulk system's crisis. In the last decade of the nineteenth century, the two-division categorization of textile production must be modified to take account of a creative strategy implemented by a segment of the bulk-oriented mills, some in cotton and more broadly in the woolen and worsted sectors. To evade the rigors of staple production, a group of companies gradually mixed specialty lines into their output plans, making, for example, seasonal styles in men's suitings or women's dress goods alongside basic overcoatings and serges. The development of the ready-to-wear clothing industry, meeting the apparel needs of increasing numbers of office and commercial workers, created sufficiently consolidated demand (for changing, if conservative stylings) to sustain the trend. For large firms, this "mixed-output" strategy had clear benefits. Sizable sales to major clothiers in New York, Rochester, or Philadelphia could bring higher per yard returns than staples, and opened the way to additional savings and better information gathering if direct marketing could be accomplished, bypassing the commission houses that handled bulk goods. Second, an element of flexibility was thereby introduced into the factories, for experienced workers could be assigned to make styles that had "taken" and yielded repeat orders, then returned to running staples in slack periods between seasonal peaks. Ultimately, the blending of staple and specialty lines promised to optimize use of a firm's capacity, enabling it to run full with lowered stock accumulations. In cottons, similar diversification was undertaken at New Bedford, and even a casual glance at Lowell entries in a 1913 trade directory confirms that several of its pioneer corporations had adopted a mixed-output approach.[10]

These developments brought such firms for the first time into direct competition with Philadelphia-type batch operations, the lifeblood of which was the introduction of seasonal novelties. Ominously, by 1905 the merged American Woolen Company assumed price leadership across the broad middle range of menswear grades soon known as semistaples, linking the close costing and aggressive selling that sustained its bulk lines with cautiously varied seasonal patterns that dodged the hazards of fashionable novelty. Price began to displace styling and quality, an encroachment of bulk mill practices into the specialists' territory that was reinforced in this sector by trends toward set price laddering in retail merchandising and its feedback effects on apparel and textile production. Flexible firms found themselves compelled to "make for the price" or forced to meet the offering figures established grade by grade at American Woolen's openings. Within the affected sectors, the mixed-output strategy and the "big company's" leadership combined with distributional shifts to create a squeeze. Simply matching American's prices was hardly an adequate response, for the Lawrence giant could shade them readily or offer clients credit terms that only comparable financial strength could support. To restore profitability, some flexible firms resorted to manipulating their goods, sacrificing quality for short-term gains; but most continued to play from their strong suit, spinning out novelties at the extremes of fashion, gradually giving ground in lines invaded by the "down East" crowd. To be sure, the impact of this restructuring was confined to one segment of flexible manufacturing (wool/worsted), but in Philadelphia this division of the weaving trades had lost its earlier dynamism by World War I, as had carpets, in which a northern price leader had emerged by a different route. However, as no comparable pattern materialized in other sectors, the profound reversals specialists experienced in the 1920s stemmed

---

[10] *Official American Textile Directory for 1913*, New York, 1913, pp. 157–9. For example, the Massachusetts Cotton Mills had branched out to making "Denims, Chambrays, Flannelettes, Ginghams and Miscellaneous Goods," and the Boott Mills were running semistaples and various grades of "White Goods in the Gray." The split is evident at Fall River where the 13,767 looms of the Fall River Iron Works Company were committed to print cloths, but Granite Mills's 2,969 looms were devoted to "Plain and Fancy Cotton Goods on order and for commission houses" (p. 151). Larry Gross of the Museum of American Textile History has undertaken a study of the Boott Mills that reveals a good deal about output diversification at Lowell in the late nineteenth century.

not from mergers or encroachment but from a decisive reshaping of distribution relations at which these early tremors had only hinted.

The war carried a demand surge that vitiated the threat lowered tariff barriers posed for style-centered producers. Emergency demand activated a seller's market in which mills could allot goods among eager bidders and brought both rapid inflation and state interventions after 1917. When the sharp "inventory" depression struck in 1920, textile jobbers and retailers were left holding huge stocks accumulated during the feverish market conditions of 1919. Sudden deflation brought painful losses, especially on seasonal goods, confirming the wisdom of a tight inventory, rapid turnover, hand-to-mouth purchasing format for distribution. Advocated during the preceding decade, this piecemeal buying strategy was adopted by flagship retailers and generalized through trade association publicity, firmly displacing previous patterns of advance ordering at seasonal openings. Demands for quick delivery of style goods pressed flexible manufacturers to run and hold stock or lose clients.

Together with the establishment of trade terms wholly advantaging buyers and the blossoming of collaborative and chain store purchasing, the hand-to-mouth system displaced risk onto producers, helped hammer down prices and profits, and generated a persistent realization crisis for batch textile manufacturers. Their trade associations proved useless as means to create a unified response, whereas union busting and rate cuts simply furthered a spreading demoralization. Strategies to accommodate to or evade buyers' market power were indeed devised; but well before the Crash, Philadelphia textile districts featured more failures than fresh starts. Employment trended steadily downward. Furthermore, a parallel crunch among southern staple-goods operations drew regional capital in the 1920s toward replicating two of Philadelphia's last vital trades, first furnishings fabrics then full-fashioned hosiery. Meanwhile near Reading, Pennsylvania, the open-shop Berkshire Mills became the industry pacesetter for bulk production of silk, full-fashioned stockings, the era's final textile seller's market. When the post-1929 slump afforded hosiery buyers the same advantages enjoyed for years in other sectors, Berkshire waded into deflation with stunning price and wage cuts, successfully resisted spirited unionization drives, and displaced much of the contraction's impact onto style-oriented Philadelphia mills, which soon began to go belly up.

The Depression was grim in specialty textile centers, and New Deal programs did little to alleviate their difficulties. Though widely welcomed as a move toward stabilization, the NIRA proved incapable of reversing the structural asymmetry in distribution relations that plagued batch manufacturing. Reflating wages and prices, however urgent or important, addressed only one dimension of a problem far more complex and poorly perceived.

Available concepts (overproduction, excess capacity) drawn from the experience of bulk sectors and mass-production industries grossly oversimplified the conditions facing specialty operations. Nonetheless, their owners scrambled for survival, victimizing workers, hunting for niches, dumping maintenance and equipment updating overboard, running down capitals, and taking home salaries rather than surpluses. Ensconced by the 1930s on the industrial periphery, hundreds of firms stumbled toward the long, slow death of specialty production, busy during the new war, slack and crumbling into the 1950s. Their dogged perseverance is a testament to the durability of the proprietary motif, the ambiguous mixing of firm and individual identity, and the refusal to embrace or master the "scientific" techniques of "rational" cost management. It contrasts neatly with the corporate surgery repeatedly performed by investors' boards who far sooner emptied mills in the old New England centers. Gutted by or in the 1930s, these areas retained enough wool-using capacity to share in wartime vigor but saw the lion's share of cotton procurement flood southern sites, as did postwar investment in development of synthetic fabrics.

Though interregional restructuring brought temporary revival to textile manufacturing, a persistent inability to defend prices or overcome blocks to forward integration yielded, by the 1960s, an industry notable for small profits, gloomy prospects, and the marked vulnerability of its standardized operations to duplication by lower-waged international rivals. In a bitter irony, the tariffs that once facilitated the industry's elaboration are presently seen as essential to preventing its eradication. In the 1980s, textile mills must look abroad for technical innovations and draw strength not from skill and entrepreneurship but from the protection of a state whose willingness to shelter them is far from certain. Foreign producers provide American markets with acres of cheap but well-made fabrics whose entry threatens to give back the triumph wrested from the importing merchants of the early republic by Lowell, Coxe, Hamilton, and the promoters of domestic manufacture.

This schematic reprise of a century-long industrial process of necessity has compressed a great deal of activity into a few paragraphs. More important, it has been framed chiefly from a business and old-fashioned economic history perspective, glossing issues of labor process and conflict, state action at all levels, technical change, profitability and productivity, style, culture, and institutional development. Each of these dimensions of the industrial process could provide the foundation for a parallel or interlocked scenario, successive passes across the same ground from differing angles that might topically reconstitute the tapestry of experience. Done here, such an effort would utterly overload an introduction. Nor has the main text been structured in this fashion, changing lenses chapter by chapter across the whole era, for this would defeat the integrative intentions noted earlier. Instead, the narrative preserves the sequences of gain and loss as they were temporally encountered by the participants, emphasizing different aspects of the relations of production and distribution as they become more salient to shaping the overall process. In consequence, the resulting text is more cinematic than architectural, jump-cutting from close-ups to aerial views, from strike action to reflections on language, all in the service of advancing the story line. Ultimately, there is a story here that needs telling, a tale of independence, skill, personalism, and place being devalued, of flexibility under strain revealing underlying limits and human rigidities, of the defeat of prowess and the advance of rationalizing order. The players struggle for advantage, betray one another, misconstrue their circumstances, fashion alliances, and discover once-potent values and practices becoming useless baggage strangely difficult to discard. In the largest sense, the drama concerns the definition and impact of "modernism" (as did memorable theatrical offerings in the same era), here in an industrial setting. The secular triumph of procedure and price, achieved and applauded elsewhere, spelled disaster for textiles, for Philadelphia, and for proprietary capitalism.[11]

This view of industrial process in Philadelphia has been shaped by a congeries of influences. Inspiration has flowed in from the writings of scholars in half a dozen disciplines, but the present work is in no way intended as a test of their hypotheses or conceptualizations. Among recent works, Naomi Lamoreaux's timely reconsideration of the great merger movement (1895–1904) calls for special mention. Presenting a fully specified treatment of the distinctions between bulk and batch production within industries, Lamoreaux used case studies to illustrate the imperatives conditioning divergent strategies in response to the market reverses of the 1890s. In paper manufacturing's technically advanced newsprint division, high fixed costs drove dispersed manufacturers to maximize output, running full in crisis times to protect market shares even if price slashing yielded losses. By contrast, batch-oriented premium paper mills were both geographically concentrated and accustomed to varying demand levels. Without evident collusion, they dealt with downturns by reducing production to match orders, protecting the price of their goods by adjusting supply, practices that resonate with the textile experiences in staple and specialty sectors.[12]

Michael Burawoy likewise attends to contrasting formats for production,

[11] For cultural perspectives on this process, see T. Jackson Lears, *No Place of Grace*, New York, 1981; and David Shi, *The Simple Life*, New York, 1985. On related business and industrial issues, see Roland Marchand, *Advertising the American Dream*, Berkeley, CA, 1985; John Heskett, *Industrial Design*, New York, 1980; and Bevis Hillier, *The Style of the Century, 1900–1980*, New York, 1983.

[12] Naomi Lamoreaux, *The Great Merger Movement in American Business, 1895–1904*, New York, 1985, chapter 2.

but from a neo-Marxist perspective. Noting wide variation in "production apparatuses" in nations and periods, he urged investigators to take account of "considerable variation within countries, occasioned by market factors, the labor process and the differential relations of factories and their employees to the state." Criticizing Harry Braverman for assuming that Fordism and scientific management represented the "expressive totality" of twentieth-century industrialism, Burawoy added that "it would be of interest to examine the changes in the labor process of some competitive industry during the period of monopoly capitalism."[13] Geographers such as Richard Walker and Michael Storper have expressed related sentiments, stressing the need for spatial and sectoral disaggregation and the thinness of historically detailed studies.[14] It is plausible that this study will intersect with a number of scholarly agendas in useful and perhaps unanticipated ways.

Among the various fields to which it is connected, labor history is especially prominent. David Montgomery's probes into metalworking and shop floor relations helped frame questions for the study of textile labor processes, and Susan Benson's analysis of department stores opened important windows on issues and conflicts in distribution. Work on Paterson by Steve Golin, David Goldberg, and Philip McLewin stimulated thinking about similar phenomena in Philadelphia, while Ardis Cameron's study of Lawrence enhanced such alertness to gender as is present in what follows. From business history, the sequence of Harvard monographs from Melvin Copeland to Alfred Chandler provided a scholarly context to which this study is related simultaneously as an appreciation and a reaction. Both the content and the silences in David Hounshell's treatment of the technical evolution of mass production proved stimulating in the struggle to characterize batch manufacturing, while David Noble's books illuminated both the institutional and factory-based contests over technical knowledge and technological change. For theoretically challenging eclecticism, one could hardly ask for better than Dietrich Rueschemeyer's ruminations on *Power and the Division of Labour*, whereas the reflections of Theda Skocpol, Fred Block, and Gordon Clark on state, society, and economy forced a serious effort to convey the problematic relation between state interests and the actions and goals of

---

[13] Michael Burawoy, *The Politics of Production*, London, 1985, pp. 15, 58.

[14] Michael Storper and Richard Walker, "The Spatial Division of Labor: Labor and the Location of Industries," in Larry Sawers and William Tabb, eds., *Sunbelt/Snowbelt: Urban Development and Regional Restructuring*, New York, 1984, pp. 19–47; Richard Walker, "Technological Determination and Determinism," in Manuel Castells, ed., *High Technology, Space and Society*, Beverly Hills, CA, 1985, pp. 226–64; and Michael Storper, "Technology and Spatial Production Relations," in ibid., pp. 265–83. For a stimulating cluster of recent work, see Derek Gregory and John Urry, eds., *Social Relations and Spatial Structures*, New York, 1985.

capital and labor in Philadelphia. Whatever sense there is in later discussions
of language stems from the author's contact with work by Raymond Williams
and Gareth Steadman Jones on one side of the Atlantic and by Joan Scott
and Daniel Rodgers on the other.[15]

For broadly integrative considerations of industrial history, the disparate
views of David Landes, Jonathan Zeitlin, Charles Sabel, and Michael Piore
have set out the guideposts for a continuing debate over the course and
meanings of industrialization. William Reddy's equally contentious critiques
of markets, motivation, and various species of historical theorizing cautioned
against grandiose model building, yet David Harvey's persistent sifting of
ideas and evidence was sufficiently provocative to rekindle the dying embers.
Finally, parallel inquiries by Howell Harris, published and in progress, indicated that it could be productive to dig deeply into place and practice as
a means to explore much larger processes in economy and society. With all
these participants, the production of this text has been, like the production
of fabrics, both a social and an individual phenomenon.[16]

[15] David Montgomery, *Workers' Control in America*, New York, 1979; Susan Benson, *Counter Cultures*, Urbana, IL, 1986; Steve Golin, "The Unity and Strategy of the Paterson Silk Manufacturers in the 1913 Strike," in Philip Scranton, ed., *Silk City*, Newark, NJ, 1985, pp. 73–98; David Goldberg, "The Battle for Labor Supremacy in Paterson, 1916–1922," in ibid., pp. 107–34; Philip McLewin, "Labor Conflict and Technological Change: The Family Shop in Paterson," in ibid., pp. 135–58; Ardis Cameron, "Bread and Roses Revisited," in Ruth Milkman, ed., *Women, Work and Protest*, Boston, 1985, pp. 42–61; David Hounshell, *From the American System to Mass Production*, Baltimore, 1984; David Noble, *America by Design*, New York, 1977; and *Forces of Production*; Dietrich Ruesche-meyer, *Power and the Division of Labour*, Stanford, CA, 1986; Peter Evans, Dietrich Rueschemeyer, and Theda Skocpol, eds., *Bringing the State Back In*, New York, 1985; Fred Block, "Beyond Relative Autonomy: State Managers as Historical Subjects," *Socialist Register: 1980*, London, 1980, pp. 227–42; Gordon Clark and Michael Dear, *State Apparatus*, Boston, 1984; Raymond Williams, *Culture and Society, 1780–1950*, New York, 1958; idem, *Keywords*, New York, 1983; Gareth Steadman Jones, "Rethinking Chartism," in *Languages of Class*, New York, 1983, pp. 90–178; Joan Scott, "On Language, Gender, and Working-Class History," *International Labor and Working-Class History* No. 31(1987):1–12; idem, "A Reply to Criticism," *ILWCH* No. 32(1987):39–45; and Daniel Rodgers, *The Work Ethic in Industrial America*, Chicago, 1978.

[16] David Landes, *The Unbound Prometheus*, Cambridge, UK, 1969; idem, "Small is Beautiful, Small is Beautiful?" in *Piccola e Grand Impresa: Un Problem Storico*, Milan, 1987, pp. 15–28; Jonathan Zeitlin, "Shop Floor Bargaining and the State: A Contradictory Relationship," in Steven Tolliday and Jonathan Zeitlin, eds., *Shop Floor Bargaining and the State*, New York, 1985, pp. 1–45; Steven Tolliday and Jonathan Zeitlin, "Between Fordism and Flexibility," in idem, eds., *The Automobile Industry and Its Workers*, Oxford, 1986, pp. 1–25; Sabel and Zeitlin, "Historical Alternatives"; Piore and Sabel, *Second Industrial Divide*; William Reddy, *The Rise of Market Culture*, Cambridge, UK, 1984; idem, *Money and Liberty*; David Harvey, *The Limits to Capital*, Chicago, 1982; idem, *Consciousness and the Urban Experience*, Baltimore, 1985; idem, *The Urbanization of Capital*, Baltimore, 1985; Howell Harris, *The Right to Manage*, Madison, WI, 1982; idem, "The

A preview of the road ahead will complete these introductory remarks. Chapter 2 charts the development of Philadelphia textile manufacturing from the Knights of Labor era through the slump of the general economy in 1893. The reader is invited in Chapter 3 "inside the mill" for a close look at the mechanics of batch manufacturing and later a portrait of manufacturers' activism regarding their beloved tariff. Chapter 4 treats the effects of contraction in the 1890s, the activities of highly visible proprietors, and the revival of craft unionism, leading toward the great general strike of 1903. Between 1904 and 1918 the flexible array of batch producers approaches full maturity, though the first indications of sectoral decay also appear (in Chapter 5). Comparisons with the state of other textile centers will lead toward discussions of labor solidarity, federal activism, the bustle and complications of war demand, shortages, inflation, and conflict.

The fifteen years following the armistice become crowded with falling indicators. Chapter 6 commences with a round of postwar strikes, continues with the assertion of buyer's power, and concludes with the Depression's contribution to gathering demoralization. The New Deal sparks exaggerated hopes, grounded in genuine fears, but the later 1930s, explored in Chapter 7, feature unrelenting decline amid unionization efforts whose success only reinforces the dynamics of contraction. By 1941 it is plain that Philadelphia's textile trades, having become ever more marginal and vulnerable, will find the wartime revival only a deferral of impending liquidation. The Conclusion, in summarizing the arguments advanced in the body of the text, sketches out their implications for a more inclusive understanding of American industrial history.

Snares of Liberalism?" in Tolliday and Zeitlin, *Shop Floor Bargaining*, pp. 148–91; and idem, "Reassessing the Open Shop Movement: The Metal Manufacturers' Association of Philadelphia, ca. 1900–1930," unpublished discussion paper, 1987.

2

Advantage, proprietors,
1886–1893

Philadelphia, January 9, 1886
Textile manufacturers enter upon the new year with every evidence in their favor
for a year of great activity... The feeling of genuine confidence has not been so
deep and general for many days. The favorable condition of trade is largely due
to the enterprise which is displayed in bringing out new lines of goods, keeping
abreast of the popular taste and in finding new markets.

Manufacturers' Review and Industrial Record (New York), January
1886, p. 778.

Philadelphia, February 10, 1886
The striking spirit that has been so general in this city has done less harm than
might have been expected... Wages have been advanced about ten per cent.
The manufacturers do not apprehend any further trouble this season.

Manufacturers' Review and Industrial Record, February 1886, p. 101.

As the Philadelphia textile trades entered the second half of the 1880s,
manufacturers expressed buoyant hopes for expansion and prosperity. Orders were coming in "very liberally," stocks in dealers' hands were "low
everywhere," and recent advances in the prices mills asked for their goods
had been accepted with little more than routine grumbling on the part of
merchants and retailers. In the city, production rolled along in some eight
hundred firms, with another hundred mills active in the four Pennsylvania
counties abutting Philadelphia. Together, they employed about sixty-five
thousand workers and represented the largest single element in the regional
industrial base.[1] Their skills generated not only seasonal novelties aimed at

---

[1] *Manufacturers' Review and Industrial Record* 19(1886): 778–9 (hereafter cited as *MRIR*);
Philip Scranton, *Proprietary Capitalism: The Textile Manufacture at Philadelphia, 1800-
1885*, New York, 1983, chapter 9 (hereafter cited as *PC*). These figures are estimates
based on the city manufacturing census of 1882 and an 1880 compilation of textile
firms that included the suburban counties (Lorin Blodget, *Census of Manufactures of
Philadelphia [1882]*, Philadelphia, 1883; Lorin Blodget, *The Textile Industries of Philadelphia*, Philadelphia, 1880, pp. 61–8). In the 1880 listing, Blodget noted 121 outlying
firms in Bucks, Delaware, Montgomery, and Chester counties, estimating the largest
concentration (in Delaware County) as employing 8,200 workers.

capturing "popular taste," but also entirely new classes of textiles, introduced under the tariff umbrella since 1880. Prominent among the recent additions to Philadelphia's diversified fabric output were, in woolens, mohair plushes for upholstery and, in cottons, damasks and curtains for table and drapery uses. In these subsectors, and in the burgeoning knitting trades, each month fresh partnerships reported commencing operations. Moreover, the great family firms built in the Civil War years hardly rested on their laurels. In the mid-1880s, James and John Dobson added a plush factory to their twenty-building complex at the Falls of Schuylkill, the Bromleys entered the curtain market, and James Doak, Jr., brought machinery for creating knitted fabrics into his Kensington worsted mills. The flexibility that had brought Philadelphia textile manufacturers to national prominence continued to invigorate both new ventures and veteran firms. Representing 10 percent of national textile employment and a quarter of regional industrial jobs, the Philadelphia textile sectors held a clear and firm place in the structure of American manufacturing a decade after the centennial of the republic.[2]

How did this differentiated urban manufacturing complex come into being? For readers of *Proprietary Capitalism*, what follows will be redundant; but rather than presume familiarity with that work, I will summarize its account of Philadelphia's textile development across the nineteenth century. Though both contemporary writers and later scholars celebrated the achievement of integrated, corporate textile manufacturing at Lowell and other New England cities after 1820, a parallel but distinctive process of industrial growth was under way in the Quaker City. There, by 1820, the first generation of largely immigrant British, Irish, and German shop and mill masters had commenced "in a small way" the production of textile specialties. In that year, William Horstmann and Henry Korn reported their manufacture of braids to the census and the Austrian silkweaver Joseph Ripka had arrived by way of Lyon to set up his handlooms in a warehouse north of Market Street. Other proprietors indicated their activity as producing fine white flannels, fashionable paisley shawls, or more mundane cotton checks and stripes.

Over the next twenty years, three districts in the county surrounding the two square miles of Philadelphia's Old City became centers for textile ventures. Kensington, a mile north of the Delaware River docks, emerged as a locale for hand loom weaving, sporting scores of workshops staffed by Irish

---

[2] For background on the Dobsons, Bromleys, and James Doak, Jr., see Scranton, *PC*, chapters 3, 7, 9, 10. Share estimates are drawn from Census Office, Department of the Interior, *Report on Manufacturing Industries at the Tenth Census: 1880*, Washington, D.C., 1883. "Atlantic corridor" refers to the belt of manufacturing cities from Lowell and Worcester, Massachusetts, southwest to Baltimore.

Figure 1. James Dobson, partner in the Falls of Schuylkill Mills, circa 1890. (Courtesy of the Free Library of Philadelphia.)

arrivals who often boarded with masters. Outwork and subcontracting arrangements were a constant feature of Kensington entrepreneurship. Masters had but small capitals and thus secured yarn from a nearby water-powered mill or from dealers who handled Paterson's products, had it dyed at one of the small, nearby works and ran up goods on their own looms or those of weavers who worked in their own backyard sheds. As power looms were fashioned for making Kensington's multicolored cottons, the hand loom trades shifted to ingrain carpets, a flat double-weave "floorcloth" whose patterning became more elaborate as jacquard attachments were adopted. Germantown, in the hills six miles northwest of Old City, re-created its eighteenth-century specialty, the knitted stocking, upon the arrival of English hosiers and knitters in the 1830s. Initially a hand-frame product, the wool and cotton stocking and other fancy knit goods were the objects of considerable tinkering, as John Button, Charles Spencer, and others undertook to apply first water and then steam power to the knitting process. Manayunk, alongside the Schuylkill River west of Germantown, became in the 1820s Philadelphia's only canalside mill center. Using for power waterflow through the trench dug by the Schuylkill Navigation Company so its coal barges could evade the adjacent falls, Charles Hagner, Captain John Towers, and other speculators erected factories for rent by "apartments." They leased space to masters like Joseph Ripka who sought to make cotton checks with the new power looms Kensington machinist Alfred Jenks had constructed. Successful, Ripka rented additional floors for expansion, then bought the mill he occupied and erected others. This pattern of gradual extension through plowing back profits became a staple of the local format for accumulation by the 1840s.

By midcentury, Philadelphia held about twelve thousand textile workers, a force roughly the size of that employed by the ten major Lowell corporations, but in the Quaker City spread across 326 separate establishments. The three main textile districts accounted for three-fifths of firms and workers in the county, but some level of activity was present in all its townships and boroughs. By 1850 as well, the cadre of specialist spinning and dyeing firms had become solidly implanted, generalizing the early Kensington pattern. A few proprietors were tempted toward integration and bulk production, but the fate of the Ripka Mills during the Civil War was an object lesson. Ripka had gravitated into running vast quantities of cotton "pantaloon stuffs," which like many local firms he sold direct to the cutting-up trade. Focused on a single class of goods, his mills closed with the wartime cotton famine and went bankrupt. Other proprietors who routinely shifted from cotton to woolen goods with the seasons prospered in the war years, making blended fabrics with recycled cotton, running blankets and hosiery on government contracts, building new facilities and adding to their fortunes. In 1870, 464 firms and 26,000 workers filled the Philadelphia textile landscape. Many of the new starts were operated by shop floor "graduates," former workers or room bosses who took their skills in dyeing or knitting, rented a room or floor "with power," bought machinery "on time," and commenced "on their own account." For example, James Doak, Jr., who had run looms in Ripka's mill, used his war enlistment bonus as the stake for a partnership with a fellow Scotch-Irish immigrant, William Arrott, and began carpet manufacturing in 1866.

At the same time, a number of family and partnership firms that had profited handsomely from war demand and had significantly expanded their mills grew to proportions only Ripka had earlier reached. James and John Dobson and Sevill Schofield at Manayunk, the former pair married to the latter's two sisters, Thomas Dolan, and John Bromley and his sons in Kensington, each would engage a thousand or more workers by the 1880s. Each would as well offer the market a diverse array of seasonal products, whose manufacture necessitated the same quality of skilled labor employed by smaller neighborhood competitors. Indeed the demand for talented workers with the capacity to adapt to changing styles and novel machinery, together with an industrial structure that fostered the transition to proprietorship, made Philadelphia textiles "the paradise of the skilled workman" after the Civil War.

Through the 1880s, Philadelphia mill owners and workers were still predominantly western European immigrants and their children. The relations between them blended mutual respect and episodic antagonism over trade and craft customs and the uneven prerogatives of master and men. To distinguish it from the formal system of company houses and invasive supervision found elsewhere, I have described this relationship as fraternal paternalism, a pattern of bounded conflict and mutuality founded on shared histories of industrial labor. It must be noted that through the late nineteenth century few Philadelphia textile proprietors came from commercial backgrounds, though increasing numbers of sons succeeding their fathers in persistent firms had had a bourgeois upbringing that threatened to distance them from the earlier dynamic. Proprietors reared on the shop floor could recognize themselves in their workers, and vice versa; thus the social relations of production included rituals of regard. Workers elected shop committees, prepared bills or schedules of prices for the various goods they created, and presented them to proprietors, who regularly drafted their own schedules. Complex compromises averted strikes in many instances, but stiffness in the process led to walkouts or lockouts. Shop delegates toured the factory district, comparing rates and conditions at other firms, and by the 1870s convened general sessions to establish common prices throughout Kensington. Manufacturers, too, shared notes and at times groups of a dozen or more midsize

firms selected representatives to confer with a committee of shop delegates
and arrived at a schedule for the ensuing six months or year. If agreement
could be had on a bill, delegates from shops outside the manufacturers'
group would press for its acceptance generally. Through 1880, little of this
customary activity was lodged in formal organizations; it was an element of
a factory culture that encompassed a variety of other practices: weavers'
rights to "their" looms, hiring of kin, summer excursions, and reciprocal
testimonials. In its language and its informal democracy, this pattern echoed
key elements of artisan republicanism from the antebellum era. It was however fragile, vulnerable to betrayals, actions that implied rejection of the
values that underlay the established relations.

In a flexible production system that matched skilled labor with seasonal
markets, workers could exert tremendous pressure for concessions once
orders were booked and the busy months were at hand. A strike at the
season's outset could lead to buyers' cancellations, shifting demand to other
firms, wrecking a proprietor's expectations. In a falling market, a mill owner
could at the season's beginning push for reductions, informing the "hands"
that should they reject a lowered bill, closing for a time did not fill him with
anxiety. This gamelike exchange was legitimate; its ebb and flow accounts for
the prevalence of six-month agreements. In the maneuvering, it should be
evident, Philadelphia textile workers stood on considerably more even terms
with their employers than did Fall River staple-goods operatives whose
bosses warehoused a hundred thousand or more bolts of plain print cloth.
Yet the very openness of the process and its connection to a tissue of social
relations and values allowed perceived violations, evidences of bad faith, to
blossom into escalating antagonisms. The arbitrary exercise of authority by
an overseer, refusing to follow up weavers' complaints that poor-quality yarn
was breaking in the loom and lowering their earnings, could lead to a shop
stand-down and a demand for the replacement of the room boss. If the
proprietor had resorted to lower-quality yarn to save a penny a yard in a
competitive market and pledged to return to a better grade, the situation
(and the overseer's position) might be secured. If he balked at this and
backed his supervisor, the protest became a strike. Should the firm attempt
to "place" its booked orders with other mills and this be discovered, the
strike would spread. Should the millman, furious, undertake to hire replacements, neighborhood crowds would shame them from the factory door
through the streets to their homes. Should he import new workers, as
Thomas Leedom did in the mid-1880s (from Lowell), full-blown riots might
ensue. For their part, manufacturers might feel genuine betrayal when workers filed out in the rush season over some triviality, and as in one dyeworks
case, left hundreds of pounds of yarn steeping in their tubs, ruined.

As conflicts of this character recurred in the early 1880s, it is little wonder that arbitration, put forward as a valuable tool by the Universal Peace Society, the Knights of Labor and others, should appeal both to workers and proprietors in Philadelphia textiles. Yet with arbitration, and the initiation of many workers into the Knights, came new complications, the most problematic of which was the entry of outsiders into the relations between masters and operatives. Neither attempts at mediation by District Assembly representatives nor the selection of "disinterested" arbitrators was a simple matter. Manufacturers were discomfited that men who knew little of their trade's complexity should propose to settle disputes over the price of work or the composition of shop rules. Shop committees resisted the Knights' efforts at centralizing authority and its respectable rejection of the strike weapon's primacy. By the close of 1885, it was an open question whether the lengthening series of brushfire conflicts would lead to creation of durable and formal links between the Knights and the growing membership of the Philadelphia Manufacturers' Association, a return to the old face-to-face exchanges between shop delegates and proprietors, or to a generalized test of strength and a leap into the abyss. With the city industry having more than doubled in size since 1870, over eight hundred firms and fifty thousand workers occupying hundreds of brick and stone factories surrounded by acres of row houses, there was more than a little understatement to yarn manufacturer Theodore Search's observation that "The textile industry in Philadelphia is passing through a transition period."[3]

By the 1880s, the flexible production system in Philadelphia textiles was experiencing a set of transformations that became highly visible in the labor–capital controversies sketched above. Beneath the tattoo of strikes and tense conferences there were significant changes afoot in other quarters, both individual initiatives at the firm level and collective moves toward institution building by groups of proprietors. Through a brief survey of shifts in production techniques and relations, marketing and credit, and developments related to the supply of labor and the political environment, the breadth of the transition in motion in the 1880s may be appreciated.

Incremental technical change and the dramatic crisis in factory social relations altered the social relations of production in the Philadelphia textile trades. On the first count, the installation of thousands of power ingrain

---

[3] Scranton, *PC*; idem, "Varieties of Paternalism: Industrial Structures and the Social Relations of Production in American Textiles," *American Quarterly* 36(1984): 235–57: idem, "Learning Manufacture: Shop-Floor Schooling and the Family Firm," *Technology and Culture* 27 (1986): 40–62; idem, *The Philadelphia Textile Manufacture: 1884–1984*, Philadelphia, 1984. On games in production, see Michael Burawoy, *The Politics of Production*, London, 1985, pp. 38–9. Search's remark was printed in Pennsylvania Secretary of Internal Affairs, *Eleventh Annual Report, Part 3: Industrial Statistics*, Harrisburg, PA 1884, p. 42.

looms and introduction of a power loom for Smyrna rugs wiped out the last preserve of workshop hand loom weaving in the carpet trades. Of the 330 local carpet firms counted in 1882, 70 percent vanished by 1893 as powered production increased output, intensified competition, raised the capital stake necessary to remain in business, and brought the employment of women weavers.[4] The invention of dozens of simpler, cheaper and yet more versatile knitting machines by Philadelphia machinists Nye and Tredick, William Wrightson, James Branson, and others triggered a wave of new starts, "garret" firms seeking a place in the expanding knitwear sector.[5] Further, dyers in the 1880s began to shift from reliance on traditional organic dyestuffs (e.g., logwood) and "rule of thumb" methods as a new world of formal chemistry arrived with the dawn of the aniline revolution. With the widespread adoption of synthetic German colorants, craft knowledge passed down through generations of master dyers to apprentices was steadily devalued.[6] The installation of electric lighting in Philadelphia mills, an accelerating process spurred by the Franklin Institute's Electrical Exposition of 1884, displaced gas illumination and thus reduced the hazards of running mills into the night during the busy season. These technological developments intersected with the dramatic running battles between textile manufacturers and their workers as fundamental questions about the prerogatives of capital and the rights of labor were contested.

In the marketplace, in the distributional relations of the textile trades, Philadelphia firms adopted noticeably more assertive selling practices in the 1880s. In earlier years, direct sales rather than the use of New York commission houses had been usual in the Quaker City. This was a conservative approach, bordering on a contented passivity, as the flow of country merchants and agents for urban clothing cutters and retail stores into Philadelphia long enabled proprietors to receive buyers either at the mill or at offices in the business district along Market or Chestnut streets. In this fashion, local firms

---

[4] Scranton, *PC*, p. 321; *Textile Manufacturers' Directory of the United States and Canada (1894–95)*, New York, 1894, pp. 130–51; Susan Levine, *Labor's True Woman*, Philadelphia, 1984. Hand loom carpet weaving was a physically demanding craft; women had been by custom excluded from learning the trade, though they had worked in carpet mills preparing warps, winding yarn on cops for insertion in shuttles, and as "burlers," inspecting finished work and repairing flaws.

[5] *MRIR* 19 (1886): 101, 229.

[6] Though the English chemist Perkin made breakthroughs in the synthesis of dyes from coal tar, it was German chemical firms that routinized and exploited their commercial production. The Philadelphia trade journal *Textile Colorist* inveighed relentlessly against by-guess and by-golly dyers throughout the 1880s, calling for the application of science to textile processing and an end to craft secrecy. Dyers' power in the workplace, of course, had depended on their monopoly of practical knowledge, which steadily eroded in the late nineteenth century.

in style-dominated markets achieved direct contact with customers, and could work from orders rather than running diverse patterns in advance and risking the accumulation of dead stock at season's end. This goal remained intact, but the means to achieve it altered. First, prosperous local mills opened New York offices to reach the heart of its wholesale nexus, an extension of direct selling that was initiated in the previous decade. In time, firms announced formal New York openings at which their new seasonal designs and colors were revealed. In addition, the practice of "sampling" became general, that is, firms set up and wove or knit short runs of each fabric variation that was to be introduced to the trade in the coming season. Ten- or twelve-yard sample "blankets" would show a new design filled out sequentially in several color combinations. A score of these blankets was cut up and assembled into sample "books" that became concrete selling tools. (Earlier, firms had collected swatches of European goods that they would show at the office and pledge to copy for so much a yard, but buyers could hardly know in advance whether the facsimile would match the original.) Partners or their sons next commenced taking their samples on the road, especially the western road, as Chicago rebounded from its catastrophic fire to become the nation's second central distributional point.

This extension of marketing efforts soon outran the personnel resources of family and partnership firms, leading to the engagement of professional "travelers" who rode the rails for months at a time in search of orders, telegraphing back calls for carpets or curtains as they proceeded from Cleveland to Toledo to Detroit. Reversing this flow, local manufacturers clubbed together to sponsor eastern trips for trainloads of western buyers, fought for free stopover privileges for rail passengers en route to New York, and ultimately sponsored erection of a massive central display space, the Bourse, as a magnet for those visitors who could no longer be expected to tramp through Kensington from mill to mill. Competition within and beyond Philadelphia was thus both intensified and transformed before the Panic of 1893.

A second development also was directly related to the market competitiveness of local mills. Credit and working capital shortages had long vexed Philadelphia proprietors. Banks were generally loath to provide loans to manufacturers oriented toward volatile markets. Eschewing the services of commission houses also meant that the advances such agents provided for goods delivered and not yet sold were unavailable. Direct sales to East Coast or Chicago jobbing houses that purchased for further distribution brought reliable but not always timely payments, whereas collections from distant retailing accounts proved considerably more erratic. Frequently, the practice of forward dating further stretched manufacturers' financial resources. Forward or advance dating was the competitive extension of credit to a customer in order to secure a sale, delivering goods on March 1, dating the bill May

1, with a discount of several percent if paid in thirty days, the full sum due
not less than sixty days after the invoice date. In such a case, four months
could elapse after shipment before the mill saw the first dollar of return on
its production. Seasonality meant additional pressure, as needs for working
capital were concentrated rather than spread across the full calendar. Two
customary mechanisms had regularly been employed to bridge the credit
gaps this pattern entailed. First, raw-materials suppliers routinely extended
long credits to manufacturers who were steady customers for wool or yarn.
Given the disaggregated structure of production at Philadelphia, weaving or
knitting firms could also defer paying invoices from their spinners or dyers,
displacing part of the credit tension in two directions at the price of modest
interest payments. Second, commercial paper in the classic form of acceptances and promissory notes circulated among firms to settle accounts,
ultimately being presented to their original maker for cash payment on the
due date, three or four months after their initial use. These hodgepodge
arrangements were systematized in the 1880s through textile manufacturers'
establishment of a set of industrial banks in Kensington, Frankford, and
Manayunk. As directors and members of loan committees, prominent carpet
and worsted men restructured the credit system to fit the eccentricities of
flexible production, easing their former dependence on suppliers and making it simpler to avoid "embarrassments" through refinancing current
obligations.

A thread that runs through the first two elements of this transition is the
pattern of formalization and institutional creation in the labor process and
the market, a pattern that was one element in the general "search for order"
during the Gilded Age.[7] From the systematic application of chemistry to
dyeing, through the reorganization of direct selling, creation of the Bourse
and manufacturers' banks, new ways of handling information and regular-
izing the untidy processes of production and accumulation were sought
energetically. These efforts may be seen as an interactive counterpoint to
the perennial risks and uncertainties of flexible production and as evidence
that a sufficient critical mass of successful capitalists had emerged for ventures at collective agency to enter the realm of the possible. Eighty or ninety
proprietors became the active center for institutional development, moving
beyond the production focus that their own factory origins had once mandated to grapple with credit, marketing, and, in the Textile School project,
with the reproduction of the labor force. The link between inaugurating
American technical education in textiles and enhancing accumulation

[7] Robert Weibe, *The Search for Order*, New York, 1967; Daniel Nelson, *Managers and
Workers: Origins of the New Factory System in the United States, 1880–1920*, Madison, WI
1975.

through flexible production was direct and essential. Theodore Search, the school's chief promoter, believed that only through the education of creative designers could American textile stylings escape their reputation as cheap derivatives of British and Continental fashions. The latter brought the greatest note and the highest profits; facsimiles trailed the trends, with the time lags carrying the risk that a shift in Paris would undercut the bundled samples local copyists had labored to create. For Search, the next generation of American fabric designers had to rise above stealing ideas to shape a genuinely American creative style that would match the technical prowess being achieved in textile manufacturing. Other school supporters had less visionary reasons for backing technical education. They envisioned an institution in which men could be trained in industrial techniques counterposed to the shop-floor culture that constrained proprietary prerogatives. While the full-time day course was largely filled by sons of manufacturing and commercial families in the textile trades, the much larger evening school was a testing ground for aspiring overseers and superintendents, whose tuition was often paid by their sponsoring companies. Technical education built a proprietary alternative to worker-centered apprenticeships, which "in the light of scientific application, ... being found unsatisfactory, have to a large extent been abandoned."[8] Thus this novel Philadelphia textile institution of the 1880s was concerned with intervening in the reproduction of labor power in a fashion conducive to the reproduction of capital.

The Textile School, with its commitment to "intelligent industrial training,"[9] had little to do with the masses of textile workers and the sociohistorical process of renewing the labor supply. In this regard, home ownership had far more importance in Philadelphia's industrial districts. In the Quaker City, far more commonly than in New York or other major urban sites, working people bought their own houses at modest prices, a practice facilitated by the multiplication of tiny building and loan associations and the "custom of ground rent," through which purchasers bought only the building they would live in while leasing for long periods the land underneath it. Two- and three-story Kensington and Manayunk rows sold steadily in the 1880s for one thousand to twenty-five hundred dollars, with 10 percent

---

[8] Charles H. Hutchins, "Industrial Education," *First Annual Report of the Alumni Association of the Philadelphia Textile School*, Philadelphia, 1902, p. 16. Apprenticeship systems were, however, preserved in the most skilled textile crafts (loom fixing, jacquard weaving) through World War I at least, and were established in the newest craft, full-fashioned knitting, through the 1920s. The class distinction between students was noted by Samuel Butterworth, a manufacturers' son and 1886 graduate, who referred to "the night student, with coarse exterior; the day student, with polished manners." (*Third Report, 1904*), p. 34.

[9] Ibid., p. 19.

down and the rest held on mortgage through one of the more than four hundred building associations that dotted the city. Whereas by the centennial Philadelphia counted 147,000 buildings within its limits, in the fifteen years after 1887, 102,000 more were erected, an unprecedented construction boom which carried through the long downturn of the 1890s. Of these new structures, 92 percent were two- and three-story residences, principally row houses occupied by working-class families.[10] Though home ownership did not likely exceed 25 percent of the labor force, the numerical increase in such purchases helped divide workers into groups manufacturers regarded as "responsible" versus "unreliable." The former, settled, stable house-holders, might expect preference in slack seasons, be less likely to strike, find ready acceptance of kin or children for places at the mill, etc. Though few textile manufacturers followed the lead of John Stetson and Henry Disston, who set up "captive" building and loan associations for their work-ers, they were vocal supporters of the stabilizing influence of home ownership as an element reinforcing the ideology of harmonious interests between capital and labor.[11]

Last, Philadelphia textile proprietors' relations with government were also transformed in the 1880s. In earlier decades, the textile men had been a negligible political force. However, in 1881, allied with other industrialists and merchants, they successfully promoted a reform city administration in which a West Philadelphia fabric printer was elected receiver of taxes and a retired Quaker manufacturer acceded to the mayoralty. Though periodic efforts to restrain corruption followed, and individual manufacturers sought and gained seats on the city council, the main arena for continuing mobi-lizations was national not local. Area textile activists pursued tariff questions relentlessly after 1880, most consistently through their major collective in-stitution, the Philadelphia Textile Association. Formed early in 1880 by about thirty owners of middling to large mills, the association sent first memorials and then committees to Washington responding to every political tremor concerning duties on woolens, worsteds, carpets, or hosiery. They remained independent of the national associations of woolen and cotton

---

[10] Russell Weigley, ed., *Philadelphia: A 300-Year History*, New York, 1982, pp. 421–2; John F. Sutherland, "Housing the Poor in the City of Homes," in Allen Davis and Mark Haller, *The Peoples of Philadelphia*, Philadelphia, 1973, p. 181; Kenneth Jackson, *Crabgrass Frontier: The Suburbanization of the United States*, New York, 1985, pp. 51, 130.

[11] Philadelphia's near-obsession with the building association continued through the Great Depression. In 1929, the state Department of Banking reported on the 3,800 building and loans operating within its borders. Of the total, 2,830, three-quarters, were Phil-adelphia institutions, at least half of which were chartered during the post-World War One housing boom (Pennsylvania Department of Banking, *Annual Reports of Pennsylvania Building and Loan Associations: 1929*, n.p., n.d.).

manufacturers, for these were dominated by New England bulk-production firms whose interests were not congruent with those of Philadelphia specialists. Local recruitment was pressed through personal solicitations and the publication of a bimonthly *Bulletin*, which commenced in 1883. Facing the challenge of the Knights of Labor, the textile proprietors created the Philadelphia Manufacturers Association, whose membership reached nearly a hundred firms in late 1886. Recognizing that ever broader fronts were necessary to defend the tariff and confront the Knights, the PMA opened its doors to all local manufacturers and in 1887 began raising funds for establishment of a splendid Manufacturers' Club (located on Pine Street near quarters soon occupied by the expanding Textile School). The *Bulletin* shortly was succeeded by *The Manufacturer*, a monthly high-tariff journal; influential congressmen were lauded in its pages and invited to address the club at festive banquets. Nothing comparable had been achieved previously; every call for proprietary organization had been a short-term response to crisis. As the carpets were laid and the draperies hung in the clubrooms, as the legislative committee sent its regular deputations off to congressional hearings armed with reams of statistics, it was plain that the "factory regime" characterized by flexible production in Philadelphia was reaching a new level of organizational sophistication.[12]

Relations with the state government of Pennsylvania were of marginal interest to Philadelphia's textile men until legislation for factory inspection was enacted in 1889. Thereafter, their opposition to threatened invasions of the property rights of manufacturers was voiced through persistent lobbying and testimony in Harrisburg. When in 1909 it became evident that "do-gooders" were gaining undue influence over the General Assembly, a cluster of Philadelphia-area textile manufacturers set in motion formation of the Pennsylvania Manufacturers' Association. In so doing, they brought in representatives from a number of local textile groupings (the Turkish Towel, Upholstery, Worsted Spinners, and Hosiery Manufacturers' associations) that had been established in or after the 1880s and had retained their individual identities. Thus the institutionalization of business–government relations through the PTMA and the Manufacturers' Club also was paralleled by the creation of permanent and separate subsectoral bodies that promoted their specific interests vis-à-vis the politics of labor and the tariff.[13] That this aspect of the story extended into the new century indicates that

---

[12] *PC*, pp. 396–405; *Bulletin of the Philadelphia Textile Association* 1–5 (1883–7); *Business Classification of the Members of the Manufacturers' Club of Philadelphia*, Philadelphia, 1895.

[13] *Fourth Annual Report of the Factory Inspector of the Commonwealth of Pennsylvania*, Harrisburg, PA 1984, pp. 5–12, 20–30, 58–61; J. Roffe Wike, *The Pennsylvania Manufacturers' Association*, Philadelphia, 1960, pp. 17–21.

the transition toward industrial maturity was gradual and uneven. The wave of institutional development that appeared in the 1880s did not homogenize the interests of local textile proprietors so much as provide topical focal points for their concerted action.

As much as labor conflict, credit, and politics exerted centripetal pressures for unity, to which many firms responded, competition as well as technical and product changes pushed all the mills toward individualistic behavior. Thus the various elements of the transition had contradictory implications. The inherent volatility of flexible production and the multidimensional conflicts necessary to the accumulation process limited all alliances, frustrated all grand schemes. At any point, Philadelphia firms were quite differently placed in the search for profit, divided by age, scale, sector, and location. The risks that plagued new or small operations were more intense than those facing larger, veteran businesses. Hence the area within which common policies could be fashioned was relatively narrow; when overproduction threatened or markets collapsed in depression, Philadelphia textile firms neither collectively limited output nor merged into multiplant corporations. Individually they shut down, cut back, or ran stock, praying for orders to materialize. Market-sensitive, they were also vulnerable to import dumping, cutthroat pricing, fashion shifts, tariff fiddles, cancellations, duplication of their best-selling designs, labor agitation, and even bad weather.[14] Local manufacturers may have entered 1886 with a "feeling of genuine confidence," but they well knew that the unexpected could advance on them suddenly, and from any quarter.

Two days after the *Manufacturers' Review*'s Philadelphia correspondent filed his glowing report on the prospects for 1886, a dozen Kensington proprietors awoke to the news that their factories had burnt to embers. The fire had begun about 4 A.M. in the dyehouse of Joseph Greer's gingham mills, part of an eight-building complex owned and rented out (with power) by fellow manufacturer and insurance broker William Arrott. Greer had leased the bulk of the space, but two spinners and two upholstery operations also occupied one or more floors of the Arrott Steam Power Mills, which had been built in the mid-1870s. Though three alarms were rapidly sounded, "the firemen were delayed somewhat by reason of the snow and frozen conditions of some of the fire-plugs." Within half an hour, walls of the Arrott mills toppled and wind-borne flaming fragments ignited the adjacent factories of William and Robert Beatty, wherein their ginghams, cotton yarn, and tenant John Blood's cotton hosiery had been made. In turn, a nearby wool

---

[14] A long winter frustrated sales of spring lines, whereas a warm fall could slow sales for "winter weights." Snow balked the itineraries of travelers and, locally, floods could inundate Manayunk's riverside factories.

machinery works (James Smith) and independent dyehouse (Firth and Foster) were consumed, though firemen were finally able to prevent the blaze from setting afire row houses across Coral, Adams, Taylor, and Letterly streets. By dawn eighteen buildings were a mass of crumbled wreckage and nine hundred workers were jobless.[15] The following day the *Public Ledger* reported the losses of the ten companies amounted to $750,000. Their insurance, totaling $573,000, covered about 70 percent of the buildings, machinery, and stock destroyed. William Arrott had placed this coverage for his tenants, James Smith and Firth and Foster, spreading the risk across more than forty companies in parcels of $1,000 to $10,000,[16] an indication of contemporary practice regarding placement of industrial insurance.

The Arrott fire and its aftermath highlight several aspects of the contemporary textile scene. Though Greer had partially integrated by adding a dyehouse to his 520 looms, the other victims were specialized single-function firms clustered in adjacent mills in the close-packed Kensington district. Their proximity facilitated ready provision of goods and services among neighbors in related sectors. Yet the close juxtaposition of factories heightened their exposure to fire, and in labor conflicts their openness to the contagious strike virus. In multistory buildings, separate firms operated literally right on top of one another, as shared tenancy was common not only in purpose-built industrial space (Arrott) but also in family-firm mills (the Beattys).

In the wake of the conflagration, several companies relocated elsewhere in the district. Two proprietors took a step up in the industrial hierarchy, investing their insurance payments in construction of their own mills. John Blood, the Beattys' tenant, erected his factory away from the main concentration at Seventh and Somerset, and spinner Thomas Henry moved into his new facilities at Trenton and Tioga in the early summer. Robert Beatty rebuilt on his own ground and by May was reported "getting a considerable amount of machinery from England," while Firth and Foster were back in business in eight weeks.[17] Joseph Greer was equally eager to resume. He leased temporary quarters in a portion of Archibald Campbell's Manayunk plant and additional space on the third floor of another of Arrott's buildings, somehow getting three hundred looms running by mid-March.

Greer's troubles were not over, however; for on the first Monday in April, 150 weavers in the Manayunk mill struck "because four of their number

---

[15] *The Public Ledger* (Philadelphia), January 11, 1886 (hereafter cited as *PL*).
[16] *PL*, January 12, 1886. Firth and Foster's dyehouse was insured with 32 firms, Joseph Greer with 22. Insurance for the other manufacturers was brokered through Creth and Sullivan and placed at an equally wide range of companies in the U.S. and Great Britain.
[17] *PL*, January 11, 1886; *MRIR* 19(1886): 229, 230, 293.

were . . . unjustly discharged." The proprietor quickly took three of them back, but his manager, a Mr. Kelly, declared the fourth was incompetent. The strikers demanded proof of this allegation, and Greer agreed to provide it. Thus the Ledger detailed:

> a committee of the strikers held a friendly conference with the propri-
> etor, during which a piece of gingham said to have been made by the
> discharged "incompetent" weaver was shown. The committee admitted
> that it was an "imperfect, unsalable fabric" and so reported to a general
> meeting of the strikers held late in the afternoon at Temperance Hall.
> The weavers agreed to submit to the action of their employer and
> declared the strike at an end.[18]

The sequence here is classic. Workers' solidarity and concern for justice was displayed in their unified response to the firings. The three Kelly dismissed for lateness and absence were promptly returned to work after the first day, Greer rescinding his manager's decision; but the issue of bad work involved workers' values and pride. They stayed out two more days, chose delegates for the "friendly conference," received their report, and accepted the results. In arranging the fabric evaluation, Greer had acknowledged his participation in a factory culture that rejected the arbitrary use of authority. He had to demonstrate, not just assert, that his action was correct. That most of the strikers were "young women" further indicates that solidarity and the rituals of shop democracy were not solely a male preserve.

Joseph Greer did not long remain in Manayunk. Like Blood and Henry, he secured his own mill properties in 1887, succeeding C. J. Milne in a south Philadelphia factory and erecting a second plant in Frankford, northeast of Kensington. In the process, he extended his capacity two hundred looms beyond the machinery lost in the fire and added lines of fashionable cheviots and mixed-fiber goods, moving away from his former reliance on ginghams.[19] Thus the Kensington fire proved to be an instance of creative destruction, setting off ripples of relocation, expansion, and product development.

The Arrott fire cost nine hundred workers their jobs, but no lives were lost in the silent mills the predawn blaze gutted. Had the flames begun their course during working hours, the story would have been more tragic, repeating the horrors of Kensington's fatal mill fire of October 1881. Public reaction to the multiple deaths on that and other recent occasions did prod the Pennsylvania legislature into passing a mandatory fire escape law for

---

[18] *MRIR* 19(1886): 165; *PL*, April 9, 1886.
[19] *Textile Manufacturers Directory of the United States and Canada (1885)*, New York, 1885, p. 386; ibid. (1888), pp. 135, 147, 256 (hereafter cited as *TMD*).

factories in which work was done on the third story or above. That statute, however, had been signed only in June 1885 and wrangles over whether tenants or owners were responsible for erecting "permanent external" escapes, a matter of particular relevance to Philadelphia's occupancy pattern, continued into the 1890s.[20] Yet though the timing of the Arrott fire spared their lives, the impact of job losses on the displaced workers is worth considering. Nowhere in the press accounts was this discussed, but reports of another winter night's conflagration five years later give a fuller picture.

On January 16, 1891, eight buildings of the Dobson mills at Falls of Schuylkill near Manayunk burned spectacularly, idling an estimated 4,800 workers. The new plush factory was saved, as was a great deal of finished stock, as hundreds of the Dobson workers raced through the mills, heaving carpets, woolens, and yarn out their windows "while the fire raged furiously behind them." By the following Monday, cleanup was under way with the removal of debris "furnish[ing] work to many of the men thrown out of their regular employment." This continued for two months at least, with five hundred to a thousand "male employees removing and assorting the burned machinery and aiding in other ways the work of rebuilding." The rescue of the plush mill meant work for another thousand, but over half the Dobson workers, chiefly women, went jobless. Though some of these were absorbed by Germantown and Manayunk firms, their numbers were too great for all to find work readily. Hence most waited at home until reconstruction opened the mills one by one during the summer. In this situation, requests were quickly made "that the building societies suspend the payment of dues for six months," many Dobson operatives "having borrowed money" to secure "their properties."[21]

The outline of a network of social bonds, social relations in and beyond production, is visible here. Though the Dobsons were well known as hard masters, hundreds of workers risked injury to rescue yarn and fabrics from the flames. Dobson in turn employed his men as far as possible in the clearing and rebuilding process, but this was not women's work and their support was left to their families. Protection of home investments through deferring payments at the building associations was immediately undertaken, and doubtless rent collection was sporadic for the next six months as well. Still, the high, if temporary, level of unemployment did not restrain weavers in the surviving buildings from demanding an increase in the price of work six weeks after the fire. Refused, they struck, including "the women...who

---

[20] *Fourth Annual Report... Factory Inspector (1893)*, pp. 27, 61–5; on the 1881 fire see *PL*, October 14, 19, 1881.

[21] *PL*, January 17, 18, 1891; *Manayunk Sentinel*, January 22, February 5, March 5, 1891.

Figure 2. The Dobson brothers' mills along the Schuylkill, with insets of other factories operated by the partnership.

appear not to have any complaint to make, but joined the strike in order to give moral support to the men." Perhaps dumbfounded, the Dobsons made "satisfactory arrangements" and work resumed the next day.[22]

The two big mill fires help illuminate both the vulnerability and the resilience of the production system in Philadelphia textiles. Yet for this sort of catastrophe, manufacturers could at least ready an individual defense through insurance. For the other, more comprehensive disaster that the rise of the Knights of Labor portended in the 1880s, a collective counterthrust would be mandatory.

2.1. The Knights of Labor in Philadelphia textiles, 1880–1889

In the spring of 1886, *Textile Record*'s editorial writer observed with some alarm that "there is going on a process of organization and concentration of the power of the laborers which can best be expressed by the word colossal."[23] In a few short years after 1880, the Knights of Labor had become a major force. Though there is evidence of textile workers forming Local Assemblies in Philadelphia a decade earlier, the order reached its point of greatest membership and influence in 1885–6. In those years, some 25,000 area spinners, dyers, weavers, and knitters filled twenty-five assemblies in the city, accounting for roughly half the textile workforce.[24] Though the informal system of shop committees, delegates, and conferences with pro- prietors over schedules of the price of work had long been practiced, the Knights' appeal in the early 1880s materialized along three supplementary dimensions, as Judy Goldberg has rightly argued. First, the Knights func- tioned as an association of trade unions in a period of rising conflict between laborers and "increasingly organized employers." Kensington textile workers could hardly ignore the leverage that Knights' members had possessed during conflicts between organized shoemakers and associated manufacturers in the adjacent Northern Liberties district. Entry into the Knights promised to enhance solidarity, smooth the flow of information, and formalize through permanent institutions customary practices and relations under threat from technical change and market competition. Second, the Knights were a neigh- borhood organization that reinforced the proximity of industrial workers in

---

[22] *Manayunk Sentinel*, March 5, 1891.

[23] *Textile Record of America* 7(1886): 67 (hereafter cited as *TRA*). *Textile Record* was published in Philadelphia through the turn of the century, then merged with New York's *Textile World*.

[24] *PL*, March 16, 1889.

different trades and had the potential for creating citywide linkages within individual trades, a goal that had eluded earlier union efforts. Third, the order rapidly achieved national scale, facilitating ready comparison of working conditions and evaluations of manufacturers' claims about wages and competition in other regions. For example, in the carpet trades, Philadelphia assemblies tracked events at the major New York and "down East" firms through communication with fellow Knights in Amsterdam and Yonkers, Thompsonville and Lowell.[25] Moreover, while the Knights surely offered the chance to show that strength flowed from unity, their concern for shaping alternatives to raw struggle (particularly arbitration and cooperative enterprise) presented for some workers a timely vision, as the tempo and intensity of industrial conflict increased in the early 1880s.

The multiplication of textile assemblies was not without its contradictions. The image of strength and assumption of unity doubtless encouraged new assemblies to press demands and strike for them in haste. The introduction of "outsiders" from District Assembly No. 1 into the dynamics of settling disputes annoyed, then enraged, proprietors. Faced with labor's consolidating power, Philadelphia textile manufacturers created institutions of alliance as had the local shoe factory masters. As important, the progressive centralization of authority at regional and national levels of the Knights' hierarchy violated the custom of shop and craft autonomy, generating internal struggles that together with manufacturers' collective resistance brought collapse to the textile assemblies. Both arbitration and cooperatives failed to live up to their billing, and experiments with them barely outlasted the effective presence of the organization that had brought them to labor's attention. Surveying in some detail the interaction of the Philadelphia Knights and their proprietary antagonists in the year of crisis (1886) and thereafter is now the task at hand.[26]

A few weeks after the devastating Kensington mill fire, contention emerged over the price of work in both the oldest and the newest textile trades organized in the Knights of Labor. Hand loom carpet weavers, claiming that a succession of rate cuts had reduced their earnings to a bit over six dollars

---

[25] Judy Goldberg, "Strikes, Organizing and Change: The Knights of Labor in Philadelphia, 1869–1890," Ph.D. dissertation, New York University, 1984, chapter 2 (quote from p. 2). Six major firms formed the eastern competition in this era: Alexander Smith of Yonkers, NY; E. S. Higgins and Company, New York City; S. Sanford and Sons, Amsterdam, NY; the Hartford Carpet Company, Thompsonville, CT; the Bigelow Carpet Company, Clinton, MA; and the Lowell Company, Lowell. Through a series of mergers, the last five of these were brought together into the Bigelow-Sanford Carpet Company by 1929 (see Arthur Cole and Harold Williamson, *The American Carpet Manufacture*, Cambridge, MA, 1941, p. 147).

[26] For fuller discussion of the development of the Knights in Philadelphia textiles, see Scranton, *PC*, pp. 353–96.

per week, called for an advance of one to one and a half cents per yard, which would net them an additional one to two dollars weekly. At 75 shops, about 1,500 ingrain hand looms were still in place, down from 5,000 in the 1870s. John Boggs voiced the manufacturers' view that a prolonged strike would end handwork entirely, but the determined weavers rejected arbitration and shut down all the firms that operated hand looms, excepting a handful that conceded the advance immediately. As the ingrain crew sent its delegates on their rounds and expressed their thanks for offers of financial support from other carpet weavers, workers in the rising upholstery and curtain trades presented new rate scales to their employers and prepared for conferences.[27]

Knights were involved in all three disputes, but in three different ways. Although hand loom ingrain weavers' Local Assembly (LA) 23 was one of the first groupings established by Philadelphia Knights, the decline of manual weaving had eroded its strength considerably. Thus it was necessary for an order member to propose at a January 1886 delegates meeting that all handworkers join the Knights in a body, a motion tabled for lack of general support. The curtain weavers were composed both of Knights in the recently formed LA 4172 and of German-speaking members of the separate Textile Workers Union. Smooth cooperation between the two organizations proved to be one key to their success in this fray, but the unbounded ambition of the Knights as a universal labor formation led to serious tangles later in the year. Only in the upholstery branch were the Knights of Labor alone responsible for the union side of the debate about advancing prices. The five hundred Kensington and West Philadelphia weavers in LA 3574 could not agree among themselves on a uniform scale and referred the matter to the executive board of District Assembly 1 (DA 1), the governing body for assemblies in seventy Philadelphia trades. DA 1 resolved their differences and selected seven weavers for a February 2 meeting with a committee of seven manufacturers. After two unsuccessful sessions, the weavers called for help from DA 1's executive board. Three of its members reached a compromise February 19 with three proprietors, all signing an agreement running through the end of November and thus averting a strike.[28]

Seasonality was central to the dynamics of all three conflicts. January and February were the heaviest production months for ingrain mills, as orders taken from fall samples were run up for spring delivery.[29] The differential placement of firms with both power and hand looms versus those reliant

[27] *PL*, January 23, 25, 26, 28, 29, 30, February 1, 1886.

[28] Ibid., January 23, February 1, 3, 8, 9, 20, 1886; March 16, 1889.

[29] John Gay's Sons, Park Carpet Mills, "Daybook, 1876–1916," Historical Society of Pennsylvania, January–February 1886, January–February, 1887 (hereafter cited as Gay Daybook).

entirely on hand looms gave ingrain weavers direct leverage over the latter. These small shops could lose a whole season's production through a six- or eight-week stoppage, and they accepted the new scale in quick succession. Yet the larger mixed-equipment factories, which had booked a full roster of orders, also needed the 120 yards a week that each of their 50 to 100 hand looms dutifully yielded. Running their power looms overtime each day would just not fill the gap. Thus they too succumbed, a prominent user of hand looms, Ivins, Dietz and Magee, agreeing to the advance on February 24, a month after the shutdown began. The weavers' triumph was ephemeral, however. Within a few years, most of the small handwork shops were but a memory, and the larger firms phased out manual weaving with considerable speed. Ivins, Dietz and Magee, which had 125 hand looms in 1884 and 87 at the time of the strike, reported but 50 remaining in 1887, having increased its complement of power looms from 46 to 100 in three years. By 1890, only a few ingrain hand looms were still actively used, reportedly by several manufacturers who kept them going to provide work for aged weavers.[30]

The seasonal alternation of intense and slack periods was a focal point in the upholstery settlement, which provided advances in the schedule ranging from 3 to 12 percent on different grades of goods. In the busy season overtime work was common, but the new "bill" set a limit of five hours per week to such additional required labor. Each extra weekday hour would now also cost proprietors a flat ten cents in addition to regular yardage earnings. Moreover, when samples were run in the slack season, piecework rates framed for regular production would be set aside in favor of a simple day rate ($2.10). This figure indicates upholstery weavers' pay expectations for a five-and-a-half-day week were about $11.55, nearly double that of ingrain hand loom men. The city's 300 curtain weavers made appreciably more ($12–$20 per week), but could anticipate only seven months' work a year, instead of the ten months usual in the more established carpet sector. The day rate that accompanied their schedule for six categories of fabrics compensated for this by providing for earnings of $15 over a sixty-hour week; but they accepted longer hours during the rush period by omitting all mention of overtime. The recent introduction of curtain manufacture had also resulted in "many different scales of wages" in the area. The proffered bill had, the operatives said, been assembled "at the expressed wish of most of our employers who, from time to time, have requested some one or more of their weavers to provide them with some kind of general scale of prices to be paid for the

---

[30] *PL*, February 5, 12, 25, 1886; *TMD (1885)*, p. 211; *TMD (1888)*, p. 140. See also James Kendrick, "The Carpet Industry of Philadelphia," Pennsylvania Bureau of Industrial Statistics, *Seventeenth Annual Report (1889)*, Harrisburg, PA, 1890.

various kinds of work."[31] When conferences failed and a strike commenced, tiny firms were the first to settle on their weavers' terms; for if they could ill afford the advanced rates, they could less afford to be idle in the season.

In the first days of the strike, ten proprietors who "manufactured nine tenths of the...curtains" made in Philadelphia met to form "a permanent organization to protect their interests," hoping to enlist their smaller brethren in a common cause. Three days later, the strikers reported fifteen firms had accepted their list, including three of the big ten (Hoyle, Harrison and Kaye; Davenport and Hepworth; H. Roth and Co.).[32] If manufacturers' solidarity was porous, the weavers were hardly rigid in their demands. Before the walkout, shop committees had interviewed firm owners who "declined to sign the schedule" but averred they would pay its rates nonetheless. At first, this would not do; "a mere promise to pay the prices without signing will not be satisfactory." Yet the workers soon realized that this requirement overreached the boundaries of the possible within the social relations of proprietary capitalism. As reports accumulated that manufacturers who could accept the bill "did not relish the idea of being forced to sign the paper drawn up by their employees," the delegates' committee relented. On the strike's third day, it announced that "hereafter we will accept the verbal promise of a manufacturer to pay the prices asked." A week after this symbolic obstacle was removed, all but three of the twenty-seven firms affected had started up under the new scale of prices. Yet in reporting this success, the failure of the drive for uniformity was acknowledged. The West Philadelphia curtain weavers, whose initial discontent with the schedule drafted by their Kensington colleagues was noted above, had refused to join the strike at all, settling on their own terms with their employer, George Brooks and Sons. As the curtain strike illustrates, for both labor and capital, there was a genuine tension between the custom of shop or entrepreneurial autonomy and calls for united action, a tension that would persist through the next five decades of flexible production in Philadelphia textiles.[33]

At the close of the curtain strike, a committee of weavers and proprietors confirmed that the new scale would be in force through July 1 and that future lists would "be drawn up by joint committees," in hopes of avoiding renewal of the February exchanges. By this device, both the Knights and the residuum of the Curtain Manufacturers' Association sought as well to seize the high ground for future dealings with their balky confreres. A few

---

[31] *PL*. February 1, 8, 11, 13, 20, 1887 (quoted passage from February 8). The use of both "wages" and "prices" in this and other contemporary documents may be another linguistic outcropping of the 1880s transition, here from artisanal to wage-worker forms of expression.

[32] Ibid., February 19, 22, 1886.   [33] Ibid., February 13, 15, 16, 17, 27, 1886.

days later, Hammond Miller of the German Textile Workers Union and
the Knights' Thomas Wylie trooped off together to visit the newly started,
outlying curtain mill at Hulmeville in Bucks County, each seeking to build
on their joint achievement in the city. Workers at Markgraf and Henry, a
twenty-one-loom shop, promptly formed a chapter of Miller's German
union, no surprise if the leading partner's name be any indication of the
ethnic composition of his weavers. Wylie went home empty-handed. In
Philadelphia, grumpy curtain manufacturers accepted back all the strikers,
but leaders of the latter's executive committee were given unacceptable tasks
in two mills, an attempt at retribution which was withdrawn when it provoked
an immediate threat of a fresh walkout.[34]

"Stimulated by recent advances gained by other weavers," textile workers
in the Brussels carpet subsector in Kensington and Germantown, cotton
weavers in South Philadelphia and Frankford, and dyers from Kensington
and Manayunk presented employers with new price scales in March. All but
the South Philadelphia cluster had the same organizational character (price
schedules, delegates, and conferences) as had the earlier trio, a pattern
characteristic of the shop traditions and close lines of communication in the
dense textile districts. South Philadelphia was spatially different, for a dozen
sizable fabric plants were scattered across several square miles below South
Street. This dispersion and the fact that textiles were but a small part of
that district's employment base inhibited the close and continuing contact
among workers that facilitated the orchestration of Kensington militance
and its support in the streets, clubs, and saloons. Hence there was no
coordination in the South Philadelphia activities, but instead a sequence of
independent demands, strikes, and settlements a few days apart, commencing
March 8 and spiraling out through April as word of gains and compromises
spread.[35]

The enthusiasm for action infected Manayunk at midmonth, reaching into
the district's largest mills, those of Sevill Schofield and Son and the Dobson
brothers. The vanguard of the Manayunk disturbers was certainly an unlikely
group, lowly picker and cardroom "boys" paid a flat $5.25 per week for their
unskilled but hazardous task of assisting the boss carders. On March 15,
sixty of Schofield's teen-aged helpers demanded an increase to $6.00, were
offered $5.50, but refused this and quit. Their example set off pressure for
raises in nearby mills; by the eighteenth, strikes by "boys and girls," the
"minor" hands, had surfaced in most Manayunk factories. Small increases
were granted by employers, who attributed the rash of diminutive insur-

---

[34] *TMD* (1888), p. 161; *PL*, February 23, 27, March 1, 1886.
[35] *PL*, February 27 (Brussels); March 1, 9, 10, 11 (Frankford); March 16, 17, 20, 22, 24
(dyers); March 8, 11, 13, 15, 16, 17, 19, 29, April 17, 19, 1886 (South Philadelphia).

gencies to "pleasant weather." Schofield soon recognized that something more substantial was afoot; on the twentieth, a hundred men and boys in the finishing department of his integrated woolen plant struck. Together with the dye-house and fabric-drying workers, they had asked that $1.00–$1.50 be added to their weekly rates of $5.25–$7.50. Schofield offered 50 cents, which the dyers accepted and the finishers turned down. The affair ended a week later, when the proprietor upped his ante to $1.00 for the adult finishers and 75 cents for the boys.

Where the children had led, much of Manayunk followed. In the week after March 20, textile workers voiced calls for advances in at least ten other mills, several of which were struck. Increases of roughly one dollar per week were reported by April 1. However, when Manayunk millmen chose to stiffen their necks, proximity was an ally. For example, Richard Hey sent over some raw stock for spinning at C. W. Preston's factory while his own spinners stood out. When the news of this stratagem leaked to Preston's employees, a dozen of them struck in protest. Their solidarity did little good, for Hey replaced his strikers with new workers a week later.[36]

Perhaps Hey was inspired by the equally tough response of the Dobsons to their dyers' demands for increases to the pay levels achieved in Kensington. On March 12 dyers LA 4018 (which had in six months grown from 40 to 1,000 members), presented a nine-point program for review by masters of independent works and owners of fabric mills with attached dyeing operations. It was far and away the most comprehensive schedule to blossom that spring. Among other provisions, it called for a closed shop, only boys and learners permitted to be non-Knights, and their numbers restricted to one for each ten qualified "Kettlers or scourers." Wages, which had sunk to an average of seven dollars weekly for piece dyers and eight dollars for yarn and warp dyers, would rise to ten and twelve dollars, with twenty and twenty-five cents an hour for overtime, not to exceed five hours a week. Refusal to work overtime would be no cause for dismissal, and in slack times, rather than individual layoffs "the working time shall be apportioned among all the hands as far as practicable." A proprietors' committee representing independent job dyers adopted the "general shop regulations" and wage list March 19, the full text being printed in the *Bulletin* of the Textile Association so that partly or fully integrated firms would have complete notice of the schedule. The *Public Ledger* indicated that such firms had generally signified their "willingness to go along,"[37] but the Dobsons entirely rejected acquiescence.

---

[36] Ibid., March 16, 19, 22, 25, 27, 30, April 1, 1886.
[37] *Bulletin of the Philadelphia Textile Association* 3(April 1, 1886): 6–7; *PL*, March 13, 20, 1886. See also *Textile Colorist* 8(1886): *passim*, for its separately paginated "Manufac-

On Saturday, March 22, forty-five dyers at the carpet mill section of the Dobson complex asked not for the full schedule but simply that their rates be increased from $8.50 to $10.00, the low end of the Kensington scale. The firm offered $9.00, pointing out that unlike many others, Dobson's dyers were "employed all year round." This was rejected. The men held out for their initial figure, struck, and only at this point voted to petition for inclusion in LA 4018. Certainly the Kensington list most aggressively aimed at responding to seasonality, attempting to spread work out through controlling overtime and calling for work sharing rather than selective layoffs in dull periods. Dobson's diversified factories – blankets, worsteds, carpets, and plushes – bridged seasons internally. Carpet-mill dyers could readily be shifted from coloring yarns for Brussels looms to handling the overflow work in busy times at the plush or blanket mills, giving them twelve months' labor where job dyers might have but ten. It is plausible that the Schuylkill dyers recognized this difference in calling for the lower piece-dyers' rate, but they also realized that a year's work to achieve earnings Kensington men made in ten months was still an unlovely bargain.[38] Though expressions of sympathy were forthcoming from LA 4018, the craft boundaries to solidarity were evident in the fact that none of Dobson's spinners or weavers joined the dyers' strike or put forward claims of their own. After waiting two days for their return and laying off 130 carpet weavers for want of tinted yarn, the firm began replacing the dyers, a process completed by the end of the week.[39]

These episodes reveal several things about Manayunk in contrast with Kensington. Though spinoff strike patterns were not unusual in the Schuylkill district, it never evinced the vigorous labor activism characteristic of the crosstown wards, neither in the Knights years nor in later waves of union upheaval. Two large enterprises, linked by marriage, dominated the Manayunk area; yet even though the Bromley clan employed thousands in Kensington, they played no comparable role there. Moreover, whereas the goal of uniform rates energized labor leaders, distance and varied conditions of

turers' Department" that tracked controversies in dyeworks at Philadelphia and Paterson, and included an elaborate review of the Knights' major 1887 strike in the New Jersey silk center (*TC* 9 [1887]: 81–2).

[38] Under the schedule, LA 4018 yarn dyers would earn in ten months (43 weeks) $516, piece dyers $430. At $8.50 weekly for 50 weeks, two weeks being set aside for stock-taking and repairs, Dobson's men earned $425, which could rise to $500 at the $10 weekly they sought. Were their demand conceded they would still labor seven weeks longer for less pay than the Kensington yarn dyers (yarn dyeing being the main task at Dobsons' for all but plain blankets and solid worsteds which were dyed as cloth, "in the piece").

[39] *PL*, March 24, 25, 26, 27, 30, April 1, 1886. The dyers gave up April 2; Dobson rehired only eleven of those who asked for their places (*PL*, April 3, 1886).

work obstructed its achievement even within Philadelphia, much less beyond its borders. Further, replacing fired workers in Manayunk infrequently brought the explosive street scenes common in Kensington since the 1840s. It was in Kensington that socialists and anarchists spoke to crowded halls; Manayunkers quietly clung to their hillside, their homes, and their jobs.

In the latter part of March, Terence Powderly responded to the national flurry of Knights of Labor strikes with an order to suspend organizing of new Local Assemblies for forty days and a circular letter condemning walkouts. He advised his comrades: "You must submit to injustice at the hands of the employer in patience for a while longer . . . do not strike but study – not only your own condition but that of your employer – find out how much you are justly entitled to and the tribunal of arbitration will settle the rest." DA 1 fell in line quickly and tried to consolidate its hold on the reins by issuing a decree "that no 'local' shall have the authority to order a strike in any shop or factory without having the supposed grievance before the District Assembly."[40] This attempt to put a spoke in the wheels of shop insurgencies foreshadowed a crisis of authority which in a year's time would shatter the labor movement in the textile trades. "Interference" would become a word angrily used not just by mill masters but also by shop delegates and craft assemblies, as the gap between unruly workers and leaders seeking order and respectability steadily widened.

The DA 1 leadership soon initiated quick interventions in textile walkouts. When Dobson's plush mill manager instituted a technical change in gearing to increase output on fifty looms and then cut weavers' piece rates from eight to seven and one-half cents, two hundred women walked out in support of those affected. The next day, April 9, district executive board member James A. Wright hastened to Manayunk and persuaded them all to resume work immediately. By the summer, the board was simply ordering strikers back when it judged they had acted in a hasty or inappropriate fashion. Textile Knights, for their part, came to feel that district leaders rarely understood the mechanics of their trades, and put forward several times the demand that a separate textile assembly be formed so that independent self-regulation could be achieved.[41]

Issues centered on the labor process proved to be as important to textile workers as price schedules or formal recognition of the union. Beyond their centrality to the dyers' program, labor process matters were evident in the quick strike at Stead and Miller's curtain mill over poor-quality yarn (the firm pledged to improve it), or the challenge to weavers' pay being calculated by the cut in many mills, rather than by the yard. A "cut" or "piece" was

---

[40] Ibid., March 29, 31, 1886. The order was often ignored by textile assemblies.
[41] Ibid., March 8, April 9, 10, 27, June 18, 26, August 30, November 1, 1886.

a single, continuous strip of cloth whose length was governed by the number of yards of warp thread wound onto the "beam" at the back of a loom. Cut lengths varied from trade to trade, 125–130 yards in ingrain carpet, 50 yards or less for fancy damasks or worsteds. In April, weavers from seven Local Assemblies sent delegates to confer on shifting to payment by the yard, a shift that "will prevent the manufacturers ... from lengthening the warps so as to require an employee to weave a cut 45 yards in length and receive payment for but a few yards." Evidently, some firms had been doing just this, a clever form of stretch-out in response to the March rounds of rate hikes under the cut system. Here the workers' aim was not to advance prices but to achieve justice and fair compensation.[42]

Social relations also provided triggers for shop action. When proprietor G. F. Jones ended his loom fixers' power to hire weavers at Frankford's Calcutta Mills, they struck and by six that June afternoon "179 looms got out of order, or stopped," perhaps a quiet show of weavers' support. Nonetheless, Jones hired new fixers within a week and the Knights condemned the walkout. In Manayunk, David Wallace declined to hire a helper for his loom boss, who "resigned" and was followed out the door by his forty weavers. All were replaced. At about the same time, W. T. Smith introduced three "learners" into his Kensington Orianna Mills, breaking the custom of carpet weavers' choosing their own learners (who were not infrequently kinsmen). After two weeks, the workers pressed for their discharge. Smith perceived this as a demand for a closed shop. The exchange that followed epitomized the generally mounting tensions. After meeting with the shop committee, Smith wrote them a scathing, yet curiously defensive reply. It read, in part:

> In response to your demand to declare this mill a place where no capable mechanic can get employment unless he belongs to certain orders which are banded together to compel men of honor and principle, men ... with independence enough not to be dictated to by certain men who demand that their opinions and principles shall rule, ... my answer is as follows:
> First, I cannot and will not ever consent to such an act of injustice against myself and against honest, independent workmen who are in

[42] Ibid., April 19, 22, 28, 1886. Six of seven LA's approved the change, but its implementation was not further treated in the *Ledger*. One long strike in which cut length was the issue did take place. At Wall and Stewart in south Philadelphia, workers went out in late April and did not return until early July when the firm agreed to count 720 yards as constituting twelve rather than eleven cuts. The firm evidently had added five yards to its warps, but had initially not paid for the additional weaving this entailed. After the strike, all weaving would be compensated though Wall and Stewart retained the old system of calculating earnings by the cut, an awkward compromise.

my employ (which includes my brothers and son) to discharge them because they do not belong to your orders...

Second, it is against all reason, common sense, rules of society, and the law of the land and it is a conspiracy on your part to demand such discharges...

Fifth, this is not a question of wages; it is a question of my rights and principles, and I will not sink my manhood so low as to consent to such injustice.

Sixth, I hope you will look at the utter foolishness of the measure, and the injustice to yourself and to all others in compelling me to close this mill for such a trifling cause as you present.

Smith's outrage was total; his "manhood" would be compromised should he accept this "injustice." The *Ledger* printed a worker's cool reply, to the effect that as their earnings were on piecework, "when teaching a 'learner' they lose time and money." Wages were indeed involved, but they were not the main issue. Nor had the weavers asked Smith "to make the factory a union establishment." They would teach "all the 'learners' the trade can stand, provided we select them," a right they felt was fully theirs since "each one of us is compelled to give thirty cents per week to pay their wages." Thus Smith's choleric reply was "far-fetched and void," and all trouble would have been avoided if "he had given us the same privilege as is granted in the factories of such employers as John Bromley and Sons, where the greatest satisfaction prevails." But it was Smith who prevailed, and satisfaction at the Bromleys was short-lived, for they quickly followed his example, hired learners on their own, and set off a strike of four hundred rug weavers that idled several hundred workers in other sections of their factories.[43]

In the course of this conflict, the links among workers and manufacturers that engendered the major confrontations of fall 1886 surface clearly. What had initially been a question of shop customs escalated into a perceived challenge to proprietary rights which could only be preserved by tough action. The root of the Smith struggle lay in the effort of the carpet assemblies to control the supply of labor by placing a moratorium on learners. In March they had declared that none were to be accepted until August 10; Smith's weavers had asserted their customary privilege to implement this "rule." They failed and the initiative passed to the Bromleys. There workers struck July 11 to defend their position, returning to the mill the next day in order to work "under protest" while the grievance was debated, only to find "the doors of the manufactory closed." A committee waited upon the Messrs. Bromley and were told the company had come to three decisions:

[43] Ibid., June 3, 4, 8, 18, July 3, 5, 12, 1886 (quotes from July 3 and 5).

...to reserve the right to discharge anyone who was on strike at any
other manufactory whom the firm had employed whilst ignorant of that
fact; to take on learners at any time, no matter what the condition of
the trade is; and that it shall not hereafter recognize the Knights of
Labor nor the grievance committee of their employees."[44]

The manufacturers' counterattack was well and fully under way. How had
this come to pass?

In the wake of serial setbacks, crowned by the Kensington dyers' March
coup, the Philadelphia Manufacturers' Association was formed, largely by
members of the Philadelphia Textile Association, which continued to confine
its concerns to tariffs and education. The PMA, on May 17, elected officers,
three of the four being textile men, and selected eight committees, seven
for trade divisions and an aid committee charged with handling labor difficulties referred to it by the association. A fund was begun "for the benefit
of any member who may get into trouble by his laborers striking against
him." Modeled on the Rhode Island Slater's League, the PMA adopted two
of its powerful tactics. First, through an orderly procedure, a sectorwide
lockout would be authorized when an "unjustified" strike was judged to be
in process, "closing...all establishments in the same line of industry, for
the purpose of preventing their employees from assisting the strikers." Second, the besieged owner would draw as needed from the aid fund, to which
members contributed a set percentage of their monthly payroll. The Philadelphia group reportedly set this figure at 5 percent; in six months, given
that the initial textile members employed over twenty thousand workers, this
sum would foot up to six figures quite rapidly.[45]

Within days, textile proprietors began to take a firmer stance toward
members of the Knights. Weavers of damask carpets (used for halls and
stairs), struck Bromley Brothers on May 14; Thomas Bromley essentially
told them to stay out. George Callaghan announced that strikers returning
June 1 to his West Philadelphia mills must renounce the Knights or leave
their places to others. The Bromley Brothers walkout was still going in July
when the Smith/John Bromley and Sons episode commenced. The latter's
reference to firing workers who had taken jobs while on strike from their
"home" firm was no solitary maneuver. On July 19, W. T. Smith learned
that three Bromley Brothers strikers had been working cheerfully along at
his own Orianna Mills, and dismissed them, posting a notice on his gate

[44] Ibid., July 12, 13, 14, 1886 (quotes from July 14).
[45] *Textile Colorist* 8(1886): 41(Manufacturers' Department, separate pagination). The fund
estimate is based on a rough annual wage of $300, dyers appreciably higher and doffers
and bobbin boys lower. Five percent of $150 (six months) times 20,000 workers would
build a fund of $150,000.

that "no strikers need apply for work." How did he discover that he was unwittingly aiding the order? Strikers averred that Bromley Brothers had circulated a "printed list" of names to other carpet men, a blacklist. Though a PMA officer denied having seen it himself, he added that "he had no doubt that a firm whose hands were out would be willing to furnish others in the same line with the names of the strikers." Working elsewhere during a shutdown was a key weapon in the arsenal of shop autonomy, one that was steadily used. Few individual mills had the Bromleys' resources to stand on their own while their rooms were silent, the season running along, and their strikers sustained by sharing the earnings of those among their number who had been taken on by rival mills. For this the carpet men were now ready.[46]

These tactical innovations did not all at once produce rigidity on the part of proprietors, as the settlement of the Bromley Brothers dispute indicated. The PMA Rug and Carpet Section investigated the strike, beginning July 27, its five representatives meeting a committee of weavers twice in the next week. Six winders had struck when told to supply yarn to a group of non-union weavers Thomas Bromley had hired in early July; the weavers would not return without them, but Bromley did not want them back at all. The stalemate seemed to have been broken August 2 with a compromise that two of the six would be rehired immediately, the rest "as needed," for four of them had been replaced. This the full group of weavers rejected, at which point the PMA delegates turned up the heat. They called upon Bromley Brothers to hire a full complement of new weavers and pledged that "to those who are engaged police protection will be given by the association," anticipating the likelihood of "violence, intimidation or threats" that would follow such a course of action. The next day Thomas Bromley stepped in with a neat compromise that married family resourcefulness with a clear demonstration that the strike had been quite ineffectual. The weavers would all be taken back, but those who had been replaced would be set to learning to run a different variety of carpeting; that is, their old looms had been passed on to the new non-union workers. Two of the winders also returned, the other four were "given employment at John Bromley and Sons' mill." To reemphasize the point that the scabs stayed on, the last clause of the brief agreement read: "all non-union employees to continue at work." The weavers accepted this, with its tiny, clever concession regarding the winders and no mention of the issue that had provoked the initial walkout some eleven weeks before. As disappointing settlements accumulated, as press reports noted that relations between the Knights and other Philadelphia unions were very troubled, as antagonism built between the textile assemblies

[46] *PL*, June 1, July 20, 1886.

48 Figured tapestry

and DA 1 over the latter's antistrike stance, the manufacturers began to take command.[47]

Proprietary resistance was not a consequence of market troubles. Indeed, the prosperity anticipated early in the year had shaped up quite satisfactorily. One millman, questioned by the *Manufacturers' Review* correspondent in April, did not expect that the "agitations" would have an adverse effect on trade.

> If demand keeps up, no harm will be felt; the people generally are well employed and more profitably so than for years, and are living cheaply; new markets are being developed all the time; ... there is no reason why we should not safely get over this little advance, for, in truth, it is but a restoration of wages [lowered] by the general depreciation of values a year or two ago.

Nor was the upheaval experienced in all sectors; in the booming knitting division, manufacturers had "comparatively little trouble with their operatives." There the flurry of new-starting firms had intensified competition, leading to "useless complaint" by the larger firms about the incursions made by "the tenement house people, who get a few machines in a garret and start a factory."[48] Local companies knitting underwear could at least take heart from the miseries their rivals in New York's Mohawk Valley were enduring, as major strikes by Knights there brought three-quarters of their sizable capacity to a halt, easing the situation of Philadelphia and New Hampshire competitors.[49] In hosiery, a subsector "composed of a large number of small makers," firms were by April actively engaged in getting out their fall styles and news of expansions dotted the monthly trade reports. The vogue for organization caught hold in knitting after the PMA was formed in May, when a new assembly of hosiery workers submitted a schedule of prices calling for dramatic increases, in some lines doubling or tripling the rate previously in force. Forty proprietors, most of whom were not PMA members, created the Association of Manufacturers of Hosiery and Knit Goods of the City of Philadelphia, which held together long enough to blunt the Knights' hosiery drive, then merged with the PMA.[50]

Meanwhile the Textile School held its commencement exercises at which prizes for designing went to the sons of manufacturers (Ivins, Butterworth, Platt, Holt) and to Emily Uhlinger, daughter of jacquard machinery maker W. P. Uhlinger (a $20 award for the finest jacquard pattern). A few weeks

[47] Ibid., August 2, 3, 4, 5, 1886.
[48] *MRIR* 19(1886): 229. [49] *TRA* 7(1886): 114.
[50] *PL*, May 25, 27, 28, June 1, 2, 15, 1886; *TRA* 7(1886): 179. Though the assembly threatened a strike of 10,000 hosiery workers for June 1, no walkouts occurred upon the manufacturers' rejection of their list and the hosiery assembly faded rapidly away. The AMHKGCP merger with the PMA is reported in *PL*, August 27, 1886.

later, having secured donations of damask and jacquard looms for expansion of the school's facilities, Theodore Search departed on a European tour to survey practical textile education in the state-sponsored schools of Germany, France, and Britain.[51] School enthusiast James Doak, Jr., announced that Westinghouse had been charged with installing a 200-light electric illumination system in his Kensington Standard Worsted Mills. Factory construction was booming with a dozen mills in progress by late spring; a brisk demand for land had driven prices of Kensington acreage skyward. The centerpiece of district building activity, Arrott's burnt-out blocks, was renovated by August, two new five-story, fire-resistant factories ready for fresh tenants.[52]

If these initiatives indicated that local manufacturers were hardly paralyzed by the Knights' advances, they had had to adjust business practices in response to the strike waves. Every order booked now contained "a proviso that in case of a strike the manufacturer has the privilege of cancelling the contract." More generally, the fear that production would suddenly be suspended had spawned "a disinclination to shoulder any large contract for fear something will happen."[53] The rush to the Knights had generated strikes outside the rubric of seasonal or annual conferences over the price of work, an older routine that had introduced some measure of predictability to the patterns of labor–capital exchanges. That proprietors bore a good deal of responsibility for this irruption (e.g., in disregarding customs about learners so as to expand production quickly) may be more apparent to us than it was to them. Marshaling their forces in new organizations, generating funds and the interpersonal familiarity necessary for unity in a confrontation, they prepared to meet a colossus whose weak points, already hinted in the summer's conflicts, would become major fractures in the fall.

A controversy at William Troth's Frankford gingham mills provided the trigger to the ultimate denouement through its combination of a traditional scale-increase demand with a call for firing an obnoxious loom fixer, the latter directly challenging proprietary prerogatives. On September 4, ninety weavers at Troth's Wingohocking Mills struck, nominally for a 10 percent increase in their rates, but more centrally over issues of shop authority. Claiming that loom fixer and overseer Robert McGowan was disregarding an earlier agreement to hire only union members and among them, a certain number of men, the workers called for his discharge. LA 3516 authorized the strike at its September 7 session and ten days later expelled nine members

---

[51] *MRIR* 19(1886): 164: *TRA* 7(1886): 172, 215, 234. The new jacquard loom was not a quid pro quo for Ms. Uhlinger's prize; it was donated by a different local jacquard builder.
[52] *TRA* 7(1886): 78, 114, 234.   [53] *PL*, July 28, 1886.

who had returned to the mill on their own. This act of breaking faith, scabbing, promptly occasioned a fracas at the factory, completing the second cycle of escalation.[54] One of the returnees had bowed out, but the other eight faced a rowdy crowd at the mill doors when work ended September 17. Before they emerged from the factory, eighteen policemen drove the jeering hundreds into the cemetery of the nearby St. Joachim's Catholic Church. Soon there was no stillness amid the stones, however, for the appearance of the scabs brought much hissing and hooting. As pairs of bluecoats escorted each of the workers toward their homes (two of the eighteen being assigned to McGowan, the rest to weavers), they were "followed by at least one thousand men, women and children, some of whom threw pieces of bricks, decayed fruit, & c." Intimidation and shaming, a ritual element of conflict in working-class industrial districts, was however not the strikers' responsibility, "the crowd consisting of sympathizers and others who gathered out of curiosity." That this response was bounded is plain; for had the mob, which grew to "several thousand" by the time McGowan came out, wanted to club and clobber their targets, a handful of policemen would have been hard pressed to prevent it.[55]

When the offensive overseer was tucked safely within his doors, a cry went up, "Now for Henry Dale's," and some hundreds trooped off to his turkish-towel mill, also on strike, also running with scabs to counter the shutdown. As in the two carpet cases, the Dale conflict had surfaced over the question of taking on learners, but DA 1 had ordered the strikers back in late July. Few had complied, being increasingly dissatisfied with the judgment of the Knights' district leadership; but their cause had provoked no significant demonstration until the Troth affair. Dale was intensely unpopular in Frankford; when he opened a window to harangue the crowd, a "piece of stone narrowly escaped hitting his head." Dale's reply to this was challenging as well as ethnically specific. He shouted, "All the Mollie Maguires in Frankford, and out of Frankford, can't shut my mill." Certainly the Irish were a considerable presence in the northeastern textile wards and their activism went beyond factory matters. For example, at Stinson Brothers, a solidly organized carpet mill, seventy-five workers in family groups – Donahue, Costello, O'Donnell – had gathered $128.25 for the Irish Parliamentary Fund. When the question whether membership in the Knights violated Catholic religious principles was raised in the summer of 1886, following a

----

[54] Ibid., September 8, 17, 18, 1886. Escalation cycles may be conceived as serial actions and responses that intensify conflicts, here initially "demand – rejection – strike," then "some workers return – expulsion from Knights – continue at work – crowd intimidation."

[55] Ibid., September 18, 1886. For other examples of these crowd patterns, see Scranton, *PC*, pp. 385–7, 392–3.

Canadian edict that so argued, Philadelphia's Archbishop Ryan tried to pick his way through the brambles. "So far as I know, the order does not affect the United States, and I do not anticipate the promulgation of any bull prohibitive to the Catholics joining our order in this country." "*Our* order" – perhaps a misquote, but it seems far more likely that Ryan's phrasing revealed accidentally his sympathy for the organization of Philadelphia's heavily Irish Catholics, expressing a political position certainly in harmony with the contemporary spirit of church leaders like Baltimore's Cardinal Gibbons and Pope Leo XIII. The Knights were certainly aware of this ethnic/religious climate, for when the issue surfaced, DA 1 "sent a committee, accompanied by a competent stenographer, to a number of prominent priests, who all united in favor of organized labor. We have certified copies of these decisions, on which numbers have joined our ranks."[56]

In or out of their ranks, whether Irish or not, the numbers of Knights and supporters roaming Frankford's streets demonstrated the spontaneous and traditional character of the neighborhood base for an escalating response to manufacturers' and workers' violations of customary values, here scabbing. Evidently satisfied with this show of strength, the gingham strikers called that evening for quiet in the district, asking their backers to stay away from the mills. This news traveled fast that Friday night, and when the Wingohocking Mills stopped at their usual noon hour for the Saturday half-holiday, "comparatively few people gathered" in front of the building for token heckling of the scabs, whom police shepherded home quickly. Troth, for his part, had appealed to the PMA's Narrow Loom Branch for assistance. A four-man PMA team promptly contacted the strikers, inviting their committee to a joint session September 24, at which eight weavers and representatives from two Local Assemblies presented their grievances. Shortly before the manufacturers' committee delivered its evaluation to the PMA, one of its members described the strike as "unjustifiable," as "no employer could conscientiously concede" several of the propositions in the workers' "bill of grievances." If the rest of the PMA concurred, "decisive steps will be taken, which may affect the employes in other mills." The same day dyers at Greenwood and Bault walked out on discovering that their employers

---

[56] For the origins of the Dale strike, see *PL*, July 29, 30, 1886. The Stinson contributions were listed in full in ibid., February 15, 1886, and Ryan's and DA1's comments appeared August 16, 1886. The favorable attitudes of Cardinal Gibbons and Pope Leo XIII toward the Knights are noted in *The Catholic Encyclopedia*, New York, 1910, Volume 9, p. 171. The latter's seminal encyclical "Rerum Novarum" followed in 1891 (ibid., Volume 12, p. 783.). Later in 1886, Archbishop Ryan announced at a synod meeting that "no secret society can hereafter be denounced, either by a bishop or a priest, unless it has already been named or denounced by the Supreme Pontiff." (*PL*, November 5, 1886.)

were processing yarn for William Troth's scab weavers, but it was not this
spinoff solidarity to which the manufacturers' spokesman was referring. The
PMA mechanisms borrowed from Slater's League were about to be tested.[57]

The Narrow Loom group reported October 1 to the PMA Aid Committee,
chaired by Thomas Dolan, a worsted goods manufacturer who would later
head the National Association of Manufacturers. Rejecting three of the
workers' five grievances, the committee affirmed that McGowan was a "careful, trustworthy and energetic" employee, that firing the returnees was un-
seemly and that the wage demand was faulty in that Troth's rates were up
to area standards. In response, the aid committee issued an ultimatum: If
Troth's hands did not resume work by Thursday, October 7, all Frankford
mills that were members of the PMA would close. Resolving to stay out,
the weavers secured a statement from their LA 3516 that the strike "was
justifiable when it was inaugurated, [and] it is justifiable now." A member
of their committee observed: "The contest had to come at some time and
we are perfectly willing to have it now and to make this a test case.... Our
Assembly will be supported liberally by members of the Order and we are
prepared for a long fight, which we think we will win." One proprietor
expressed his disappointment with the whole situation: "We have expected
this for some time. Things had come to such a pass that our people struck
for the most trivial causes without regard for the state of our business....
We are forced into this action to protect ourselves." As each side geared up
for the lockout so as to coerce justice from the other, word spread that dyers
at Kedward and Thorp had joined those at Greenwood and Bault, stopping

[57] *PL*, September 20, 23, 25, 30, 1886 (quotes from September 20 and 30). It may be
apposite here to note the brief flowering of labor initiatives in politics (both reformist
and revolutionary) in the months surrounding the major crisis of 1886. As Henry George
was pressing the single tax in his campaign for the New York mayoralty, his views were
presented at heavily attended meetings in Kensington and Old City. The United Labor
League, in which the Knights were much involved, contended with the Greenbackers
for third-party honors. Socialist Labor Party No. 1 joined several German trade unions
in bringing William Liebknecht to the city for a speech one day after Edward Aveling
had addressed 800 English-speaking workers on socialist principles (*PL*, August 14, 16,
September 9, 30, October 1, 1886). British-born residents of Kensington formed an
association to promote naturalization and thus full political participation (September 4).
At the height of the Troth escalation, Lucy Parsons spoke on behalf of the condemned
Haymarket anarchists to a Kensington crowd of 1,200–1,500, and was introduced by a
well-known K. of L. dyer (November 1). For a thoughtful evaluation of this burst of
political activity, see Goldberg, "Strikes, Organizing and Change," chapter 10, and for
the more explosive results of the mixture of the Knights and politics in Cincinnati,
Steven Ross, *Workers on the Edge*, New York, 1985, chapters 11 and 12. The broadest
analysis of these matters is Leon Fink, *Workingmen's Democracy*, Urbana, IL, 1983.
Finally, "employee" was commonly spelled with a single final "e" at least through World
War I.

work because their firm had taken orders to color yarn for Henry Dale's scab operation.[58]

Frankford assemblies created a Joint Executive Board (JEB) to manage the spreading crisis. The group selected as its chairman Henry Lowe, a Troth striker, voted to provide cash support of nine dollars weekly to men from the Wingohocking Mills, six dollars to the women, and issued a circular calling for peaceable behavior by "members and friends." Yet their most serious immediate problem was the dyers' sympathy strikes, which illuminated the functional network of local single-process firms. Within days of the two walkouts, over five hundred workers at other factories from Kensington to South Philadelphia were laid off due to the exhaustion of their stocks of dyed yarn. Since the lockout shut down Troth's (and nine other Frankford mills), the Knights' emergency JEB ordered Greenwood and Bault's dyers back to work on October 12, for none of their labor would be feeding looms at that shop for the foreseeable future. This brushfire fought, the focus could be kept on Troth and Frankford. Soon the JEB's plan became clear. Though Troth's strikers wanted a trial of wills, the LA leaders sought to initiate an arbitrated settlement. Once the dyers were back, the JEB met the aid committee and harmony was quickly achieved. All the mills would reopen, workers would be taken back without discrimination, and the Troth grievances would be settled by an arbitration committee, one member chosen by the JEB, the second by the aid committee, those two to pick a third. The arbitrators' decision would be final. This was evidently accepted all around. The lockout was ended, work to recommence Monday, October 18.[59]

The most obvious question at this juncture is: Why did the PMA settle so quickly? The answer is simple. In its first test, manufacturers' solidarity had not proved so mighty as first expected. Of the thirty or so Frankford textile firms, eighteen belonged to the PMA in 1886, and of these just half had joined the common front on Troth's behalf. Major non-participants included Caleb Milne, S. J. Campbell and the Whitakers, mills which together held well over five hundred workers, whereas just six hundred were idled by the lockout team. When a settlement was offered, the aid committee took it before their exposed position could deteriorate. Next, why did the JEB act as it did, sending everyone including Troth's workers back without any concrete gains? Given the DA 1 pattern evident since the late spring, I suspect that the confrontational phrases spoken when the lockout ultimatum was issued set ears tingling in leadership circles, and that the JEB was firmly urged to seek arbitration. As the most telling demand, to fire McGowan,

---

[58] *PL*, October 2, 3, 6, 1886.
[59] *Textile Colorist* 8(1886): 73–4; *MRIR* 19(1886): 591–2; *PL*, October 7, 8, 11, 12, 15, 1886.

went well beyond the Knights' gathering focus on wages and hours issues, it is perhaps surprising that DA 1 did not simply order the strikers back, as had happened repeatedly in similar cases over the previous six months. The JEB proposal, all back to work while arbitration proceeded on the Troth dispute, looked like a compromise that would, with luck, defuse the crisis.

It did not work, however. When Monday rolled around, resumption was accomplished everywhere but the Troth mill. There a tangle arose, the workers claiming that they were not all taken back in a body, as promised, the proprietor countering that men discharged well before the strike arrived to claim back their positions and were turned away, leading their comrades to refuse employment. The JEB urged the strikers to return to their looms, but they met and reiterated the decision to stay out. Though two arbitrators had been chosen, the PMA aid committee convened on Tuesday and called off the process. Arbitration had been "nullified" by the strikers' disinclination to follow the terms of the preliminary settlement. The pendulum swung back toward coercion, for the PMA announced that were the Troth matter not settled to the proprietor's "satisfaction" by November 3, two weeks hence, "a lockout of all employees in the mills of the members" would "be ordered." The aid committee resolved to have "no further dealings with the strikers." When a reporter asked a committee member whether the PMA "proposed to make a general contest against the recognition of the Knights of Labor in this City?" the response was plain enough: "It certainly does." Other employers indicated that as they were amid the slack season, with most orders for fall and winter goods having been delivered, shutting down would cause them no great hardship.[60]

This bombshell produced a great flurry of activity. The JEB appealed for the restoration of the arbitration mechanism; the strikers announced they did not believe the PMA would carry out its new threat. Troth's workers also distributed a circular putting the best light on their case, averring that McGowan was a man "whose language to the female help would not be fit for publication." Getting rid of him "was the only issue when we went out," they continued, and the 10 percent advance was but a restoration of an earlier rate cut. This had been requested in June but nothing was done, "owing to the absence of the senior member of the firm in Europe." Since all firm partners had to approve the change, they had worked "under protest

---

[60] *PL*, October 16, 18, 19, 21, 1886. The *Ledger* printed firm names of 49 of the nearly 100 PMA members, estimating that 50,000 workers would be idled if the general lockout was set in motion. This was far too generous a guess. Although most of the city's largest firms were in the printed group, their total employment in 1882 was slightly over 20,000. As doubtless the less sizable and prominent members were omitted by the paper, an estimate of 30,000 total employees for the hundred firms would be more appropriate (*PL*, October 21, 1886; Blodget, *Census of Manufactures of Philadelphia: 1882*).

until his return," then reiterated the rate demand after the strike for McGowan's dismissal. Rejecting any resort to arbitration at this stage, aid committee head Thomas Dolan posted notice of the impending lockout in his mills. Though five hundred of his workers met Saturday, October 23, to register their "indignant... protest" at the PMA threat, the manufacturers seemed resolute.

Events moved quickly in the final week before November 3. Sharpening its tactics to isolate the Knights, the PMA let it be known that only order members would be locked out. Framing this stratagem in terms that emphasized the conserving role of proprietary authority, one manufacturer explained:

> Many of our workers... fear to withdraw their support from the Order, no matter how much they may desire to work in harmony with their employers. We will not only make this fight against the Knights of Labor as a body, in order to sustain authority over our own mills, but to relieve many of the members of the Order who are now restive and as anxious to escape the lash of their [union] masters as we are to resent this dictation. This is not a question of class against class, nor of capital against labor, but it is a question of the intelligent husbandman of labor against the improvident and ignorant. The manufacturers of this city and of other cities have been harassed by Knights of Labor until business has become unsettled in the industries concerned to an alarming extent.[61]

Unimpressed, the Troth workers vowed they would return only if the few dozen replacements he had secured were dismissed. The JEB modified this position slightly in a letter October 29 to the aid committee, again encouraging the PMA to restart the wheels of arbitration. That was ultimately done, but in a fashion which helped wreck the Knights in the textile trades and gave the "husbandmen" a clear victory.

Two critical events sealed the fate of the Troth strikers Friday, October 29. First, "General Master Workman" Terence Powderly and his colleague on the General Executive Board (GEB), John Hayes, arrived in Philadelphia to meet with the aid committee, announcing that the national body had taken direct charge of the strike. Though a representative from DA 1 was included, neither the JEB nor the Troth workers were present. Second, after some consultation, Hayes issued an order that officially called off the strike, instructing the militant weavers to return without further quibbling. Lowe, for the JEB, "indignantly handed back the order to Mr. Hayes, and declared that they would not be bound by it." Later at a strike meeting, it was realized that within the boundaries of the Knights, there was no alternative to ac-

---

[61] Ibid., October 22, 25, 27, 1886.

cepting Powderly's intervention and the consequent decree as "binding." Though some strikers had already "obtained situations elsewhere" and others said they would never walk into Troth's mills again, all did look forward to the arbitration sequence. Here the Knights' centralization of authority became yet more clear. The PMA had suspended its lockout order once Hayes's decree was promulgated, and the aid committee received a November 4 delegation from the national GEB headed by Powderly to discuss the scope of the arbitration. The Frankford JEB was excluded from the session, even though its members had come to the Continental Hotel to see that all five of the original grievances were processed. Refusing them admission was quite "productive," for the GEB promptly withdrew all but the wage grievance, which it determined was "the only fair question for arbitration." The aid committee was happy to comply, for the issue of proprietary authority was accepted now as undebatable.[62]

When this resolution was communicated to the Troth crew by JEB's Henry Lowe, together with Troth's list of sixteen of the ninety strikers he would consider rehiring, their defeat was apparent. Troth later announced he had plenty of workers; given this, arbitrating the wage issue was irrelevant and the effort was suspended November 16. Manufacturers shortly broadcast the news that hereafter only wage questions would be arbitrated, clear evidence that they felt able again to claim the full range of their prerogatives. Workers' bitterness was general, especially at the role of the GEB in engineering a flaccid retreat rather than accepting a test of power in the streets of the industrial districts. The textile assemblies renewed their demand for a separate organization outside DA 1, but this would little alter the power of the GEB to force settlements for the good of the order, even if they shattered individual assemblies. Rival Philadelphia unions circled like buzzards over Frankford and Kensington. Both the Central Labor Union and the German Textile Workers Union sponsored mass meetings after the Troth debacle, criticizing the Knights and offering the merits of, respectively, craft organization and socialism to crowds of five hundred and more. Rumors spread of defections from the order.[63]

Again following in the path of the fabric firms, a group of seven hosiery manufacturers locked out their employees in a scale dispute November 1. Though three of these capitulated, accepting the workers' list within a week, the others held on until the affair was referred to DA 1 on November 28.

---

[62] *TRA* 7(1886): 330; *PL*, October 30, November 1, 2, 4, 5, 1886.

[63] *PL*, November 6, 8, 9, 11, 13, 16, 1886. Parallel with the Frankford struggle was a long strike sequence at Sevill Schofield's Manayunk mills, in which Schofield delayed settlement until the course of the Troth affair was clear (*PL*, September 8, 20, October 19, 20, 27, 28, 29, November 2, 1886).

Instantly, the district leadership ordered the workers at those firms to return on the proprietors' terms, even though the owners would rehire only half of those locked out, keeping on the partial forces they had recruited. Compounding this betrayal, in December DA 1 concluded a general agreement with the PMA that further distanced union authority from the shop committees and craft assemblies. To be ratified by the Philadelphia LA's, it provided that all conflicts over wage lists and shop grievances would be immediately directed to the executive board of DA 1 and the PMA aid committee, work to continue under existing conditions and schedules until a decision was reached by the two bodies or by disinterested arbitrators. Retroactive bonuses or deductions would follow a scale decision. In addition, employers' absolute control over hiring and firing was conceded.

The Troth settlement had served as a template for a general abandonment of the tools through which workers had exercised shop-floor power at the firm level. With a token show of unity, the PMA had faced down the Knights' leadership, transferred to a new bureaucracy the customary institutions of shop and subsectoral conferences, erased the strike weapon, and eradicated shop autonomy. The textile assemblies made a terrific fuss. Delegates from their twenty-five LA's assembled December 28 and rejected each of the eight sections of the agreement, demanding their own district organization be chartered. Though this was granted by the GEB in January, the damage was permanent. After their own nasty fight with the GEB, the carpet workers were expelled from the order and their locals soon began to deteriorate. Philadelphia assemblies in fabrics, hosiery, and dyeing folded serially throughout 1887 and 1888, reconstituting themselves in some cases as independent craft unions, as did the rug weavers, or as sections of the Progressive (formerly German) Textile Workers Union. By March of 1889, Samuel Gompers appeared in Kensington to urge reorganization of the textile trades, finding only a half-dozen Knights' assemblies still active, membership having dropped by 95 percent in three years (from 25,000 to 1,200). Reviewing this disaster, one worker traced it directly to the Troth strike and the PMA's threatened general lockout:

> All the organizations were preparing themselves to meet this when General Master Workman Powderly stepped in and ordered the Frankford strikers back to work. So disappointed were a large majority of the Knights that they commenced to drop out and gradually the assemblies were compelled to turn in their charters for want of membership.[64]

[64] Ibid., November 2, 5, 6, 9, 11, 29, 30, December 6, 8, 17, 25, 28, 1886; January 22, May 2, 17, June 1, 24, August 1, December 9, 14, 1887; March 16, 1889. The new textile body (District Assembly 190) formed in January 1887 did not authorize a single strike by May of that year. Its cooperativeness with proprietors and general conservatism were "appreciated" by the manufacturers (PL, May 2, 1887).

The Knights' effort to gain managerial control of the labor movement in textiles had led to an organization of leaders without members. Yet this collapse in no way meant the death of the laborist spirit among Philadelphia textile workers, for they would mobilize major challenges to the mill operators at roughly eight-year intervals after 1887 (viz., 1895, 1903, 1910, 1919). Still, there is little question that the PMA had mastered the scene in the crisis year. What is worth some further speculation are two matters: How fortunate was the PMA that the Knights folded their cards in the Troth escalation and what might be the most effective form of labor organization for workers in a flexible production format such as that in place in Philadelphia textiles?

On the first count, the PMA directors must have been enormously relieved that their members were never called upon to follow through on the plan for a citywide lockout. The weak showing in the first round Frankford stoppage, combined with the quick collapse of hosiery proprietors' solidarity in early November, indicates that collective action was as problematic in labor confrontations as it had been in the struggle to establish the Textile School in 1884.[65] Though the aid fund project was much discussed in early summer, there is no further reference to it – odd that a weapon of such power would remain unmentioned in the fall propaganda barrage. More significant, in discussing the origins of the Manufacturers' Club, formed in March and April 1887, Joseph Truitt pointed out that by the end of 1886, "strikes in the textile mills of Philadelphia and vicinity almost entirely ceased, and interest in the Association began to lessen, so much so that there was danger of a discontinuance of the organization." This decay had reached such proportions in the four months after the general lockout was cancelled that PMA officers met, not to revive the association, but to form a social club that would continue the contacts it had stimulated among proprietors. The PMA had never drawn more than a handful of nontextile manufacturers; the club would successfully bring in scores of them for food, drink, the occasional business deal over dinner, and resolutions on behalf of high tariffs and Republican wisdom. Just as the Knights never claimed more than half of the city's textile workers, so too the PMA never pushed much past that limit. Conceived in a crisis, it folded itself into a textile section of the club in 1888, along with the PMA, whose concerns for protection and technical education were expressed by the continuation of its *Bulletin* as *The Manufacturer*. Surely the PMA leadership was as uncertain about maintaining its fragile unity in the Troth crisis as were the order leaders, but the Knights flinched and were lost.[66]

---

[65] Scranton, *PC*, pp. 405–11.

[66] *Business Classification of the Members of the Manufacturers' Club of Philadelphia*, Philadel-

Another indication that the PMA was a soft-edged alliance may be found in W. T. Seal's mocking essay, "The True Way to Run 'Model' Mills," published in the *Bulletin* as Truitt and Dolan were reshaping the association into a club. In this rare piece of industrialist humor, the activities of Theophilas Spriggans, a worthy, upstanding but fictional Philadelphia textile proprietor, were lampooned in a caricature that revealed the lines of strain between organized capital and individualistic manufacturers. Spriggans has simply charming relations with his workers:

> His rules must be obeyed, and as they are not harsh, the work people are only too glad to observe them, and do all in their power to make things agreeable; in fact they are very fond of Mr. Spriggans, and will, he claims, do anything for him; ... It is true that occasionally an unruly person is employed, who endeavors to raise a disturbance, but the argus eye of Theophilas soon finds him out, and he has to go, of course, as nothing but perfect harmony is allowed.

The women he employs are always clean and tidy, and "as for his men they are all gentlemen to the manor born." They do not shout or loaf about, and after work, his hands may be found either at home or in "some library or reading room" where they repair "to improve their minds."

More remarkable are Spriggans's relations with his proprietary colleagues:

> He is probably the only manufacturer who ever kept to a bargain with his fellow manufacturers. He used to belong to a number of organizations for promoting the welfare of owners and operators of mills, but he was never able to find a fellow-member who would do as he agreed. They would all attend meetings, fix price lists, make wage lists, agree to stand firmly together, etc., etc., but he was the only one who ever lived up to the agreements; all the rest broke them; in fact, they never intended to keep them.

Theophilas cast scorn upon those who would band together for defense against strikes and boycotts for he has a pact with his workers, "that if they do not join any organization neither will he." Of late there had been some troubles, but his earnest flexibility resolved them all. When a walkout came due to his employment of a learner, he sent "the girl away" for he had forgotten that "he had as many learners as his people desired." In another case, he at first failed to discharge a man not liked by other workers, but after his factories were idle for several weeks, he relented. "No one could expect him to keep his mills closed forever, simply on account of one man."

phia, 1895, unpaged; *PL*, April 26, May 18, December 14, 1887; February 1, 1888. Truitt's recollections were fairly accurate; Philadelphia textile strikes numbered nearly 100 in 1886; in 1887, only eleven took place, seven of those in the first half of the year.

Then, determining "that he was making too much money, more than he needed," Spriggans's workers struck for a raise. Eventually he conceded the justice of their demand; but he had to fumigate his mills to erase the pestilential traces of "scabs" who had worked during the dispute before his loyal hands would resume their customary posts.

Seal continued in this vein at considerable length, giving his readers a portrait of a genial fool whose workers at last took the business off his hands to run it themselves, allowing him "6 percent interest on his capital and a certain share of the profits." As secretary of two of the Philadelphia associations and the *Bulletin*'s editor, Seal had an axe to grind with the Sprigganses of Philadelphia. Their naive individualism and commitment to a fraternal paternalism was both an embarrassment to forward-thinking manufacturers and the source of repeated depredations by clever and aggressive workers. Worse, it was the key to the perennial weakness of serious alliances among the millmen. Yet in this caustic view of one who "goes through his mills frequently, and knows personally every Tom, Jack and Pete," Seal ignored the logic of competition in seasonal and specialty trades that reinforced Spriggans-like values. The Manufacturers' Club endured, hosting gatherings of sectoral associations for two generations, but the format for accumulation in Philadelphia textiles firmly obstructed creation of permanent and general organizations. It is well that the projected mass lockout was withdrawn, for the Sprigganses would soon have broken away to get their samples out and on the road for the coming season.[67]

If the industrial structure set limits on the organization of manufacturers' interests, the problem for textile workers was even more severe. The bureaucratic control initiatives the Knights attempted were not simply premature, along some putative time line of progressive development of labor institutions. They were profoundly inappropriate for workers involved in flexible production of specialty goods in the context of market volatility. Hierarchical authority may have been attractive to DA 1 and the GEB, but it compromised the force of shop and sectoral autonomy and substituted the calculation of organizational welfare for the periodic tests of workers' and proprietors' resources under the pressure of seasonal opportunities. Both interdependent and antagonistic, workers and firms engaged in episodic

---

[67] *Bulletin of the Philadelphia Textile Association* 4(May 2, 1887): 5–6. The reference to 6 percent and a share of the profits had a concrete local basis. In April 1887, James Magee installed a profit-sharing plan at his Kensington carpet mill, "irrespective" of the means of payment in force at other firms. After six months, Magee would allot the mill's income to wages, expenses, and 6 percent on his own invested capital. The residual, which was termed profit, was to be divided between Magee and all workers in a ratio of capital to wages earned, individual employees' shares being proportional to their percentage of the wage pool over the six months (*PL*, April 25, 1887).

cycles of bluff and shove that neither could afford to win too thoroughly, generating a pattern of erratic conflicts ill suited to institutionalization. Thus as the aid committee dropped from sight and DA 1 faded away, the old ways proved resilient. For years after 1886, neighborhood shop delegates convened to press both price lists and labor process matters (e.g., sharing work in slack times) upon committees of upholstery, carpet, curtain, and dyehouse proprietors. Spot strikes over the quality of yarn or excessive overtime popped up. The role of milling sympathizers remained a potent element in strike escalations through the 1930s. However, the centrality of the shop and its network of relations to the reproduction of factory culture in Philadelphia textiles made formal union membership a low priority for thousands of operatives. Indeed, most regional textile workers were terrible unionists. They alternated between periods of deep conservatism, which the *Manufacturers' Review* credited to home ownership, times during which they wore ruts in the sidewalks between their looms and their row houses, and periods of intense activism and community mobilization which in manufacturers' eyes approached near-insurrectionary proportions. Durable unions did function in a few trades where skilled workers undertook to regulate the labor supply through apprenticeship (loom fixing, jacquard weaving), but those that joined the AF of L were at times expelled for their defiant, autonomous behavior. Except in a general crisis, these craft organizations showed little interest in linking with one another or in reaching out to the female half of the textile workforce. In a way, the absence of a single focus for organizing, there never being a Philadelphia analogy to U.S. Steel or Ford, combined with a tradition of shop and sectoral independence to render the puzzle of unity insoluble for labor (and for capital) in the Philadelphia textile industry.[68]

---

[68] *MRIR* 19(1886): 595; *PL*, May 12, 13, November 21, 1887; April 30, July 10, 1888. On later craft unions see Sol Selig Papers, Archives, Pastore Library, Philadelphia College of Textiles and Science, and Gladys Palmer, *Union Tactics and Economic Change*, Philadelphia, 1932.

3

Inside the mill: flexible production and the family firm

June 21st. Arose before 7. Ate badly fried eggs like Soft Leather and a little ham with tea. Out through the Park with my Wife (who was going to see her Sister) as far as Strawberry Hill then in by way of Diamond and Norris Streets. Reached the Mill 8.45. Ed was in, had been drinking this morning...Had a very plain talk with him...

Journal of James Doak, Jr., proprietor of Standard Worsted Mills,
Kensington, June 21, 1888

Trade journals and newspaper accounts can reveal the contours of public encounters between labor and capital in Philadelphia textiles; but to move from visible conflict to the quotidian processes of production and distribution, one must go "inside the mill." To identify the everyday patterns and problems of flexible production, access to records of individual firms is essential. Fortunately, though surviving materials of this character are few, several quite detailed sources have been preserved, opening the door to the interior life of Kensington textile specialists. When accounts of activity in a carpet factory and a worsted mill are linked to printed materials, we will have a suggestive sketch of firm dynamics in the years before the 1893 Panic, a narrative which will lead toward a rough portrait of profitability of the local textile sectors a decade after the national and city censuses of 1880 and 1882.

John Gay's Sons' Park Carpet Mills stood at the corner of Howard and Norris Streets in the heart of Kensington. The founder, John H. Gay, had carefully arranged his sons' succession to the helm, and having restyled the company name, James and Thomas Gay were in general charge by 1886. The elder Gay, an English immigrant, accompanied Thomas on a sales trip to Boston early in the year, but his spring departure for a western pleasure tour the day their carpet weavers went out on strike indicates that the new generation was expected to handle both routine and troublesome affairs. For thirty years after they assumed control, James and Thomas Gay kept a daybook in which they recorded significant happenings and into which they pinned and pasted newspaper clippings and broadsides relevant to their

Figure 3. James Doak, Jr., proprietor of Standard Worsted Mills, circa 1900. (Courtesy of the Philadelphia College of Textiles and Science.)

carpet business. Through the prism of these jottings and cuttings the operations of a midsize family firm are revealed.

Park Carpets was a steadily growing enterprise in the late 1880s, running eighty-six power looms in 1885, to which twenty-two were added in 1887 and another twenty-two in 1889. An additional mill was erected along Howard Street in 1892, expanding capacity to 160 looms just as the brothers incorporated their firm, the stated capital being $300,000. The operations were partially integrated, for the Gays bought their yarns and dyed them in their own attached works before winding and weaving. In the 1890s, when running full this complex held 300 workers, two-thirds of whom were women winders, burlers, and power loom weavers. Men also tended power looms, but the dye and engine houses were exclusively male domains. This force dropped by half in dull periods. As orders ran out, layoffs followed the production sequence, first dyers, then winders, weavers, burlers, packers and shippers, until recalls commenced after idleness that lasted from a week to a month or more in slack markets.[1]

The brothers rarely recorded these arrivals and departures in their mill journal, taking special note only when the chief engineer quit, a new female office clerk was hired, and when "Charles Sweeney severed his connection with us as Loom Boss by eloping with one of the weavers in our employ."[2] Requests by the hands for holidays were inscribed, and usually refused unless the workers pledged to make up the lost hours by adding them to subsequent days. In the busy season, even this rearrangement of work was unacceptable to the Gays. An entry for January 2, 1888, reads: "Weavers requested to stop at noon, but were refused – worked to 7 o'clock p.m." The mills' regular sixty-hour week had been extended to sixty-five to get out the orders for the spring trades, a situation that lasted six weeks from mid-December to early February. When the rush was nearing its end, the proprietors were a touch more responsive. In September 1887, they posted notice of a special Thursday holiday so their workers could attend the grand parade celebrating the centennial of the Constitution. The "employees then requested us to stop on Friday also, and they would work one-half hour overtime each day after Monday until the 10 ½ hours were made up, we agreed to it." On Christmas Eve, 1889, the operatives appealed for early closing "in order to

---

[1] John Gay's Sons Park Carpet Mills, "Daybook, 1876–1916," Historical Society of Pennsylvania, April 10, 29, December 31, 1886; December 9, 1889; May 30, 1892 (hereafter cited as Gay Daybook); *Textile Manufacturers Directory of the United States and Canada (1888)*, New York, 1888, p. 145 (hereafter cited as *TMD*); *TMD*(1894–5), p. 138; Pennsylvania Secretary of Internal Affairs, *Eighteenth Annual Report (1890), Part 3: Industrial Statistics*, Harrisburg, PA, 1891, p. 38; idem, *Twenty-Fourth Report (1896)*, p. 120.

[2] Gay Daybook, May 10, 1886; January 9, 1890; April 27, 1891.

see Christmas sights." Making certain the lost production hours would be rescheduled, the partners shut down at 3 P.M., an hour or so before dark on one of the shortest days of the year. If images of Scrooge push their way forward, they are surely reinforced by the quiet satisfaction contained in notations of holidays not observed: "Nov. 25, 1886 – Thanksgiving Day – Hands asked to stop at noon, refused them on a/c of stopping soon to take a/c of stock . . . May 30, 1887 Decoration Day, worked all day. No one asked . . . February 22, 1890 Washington's Birthday (Saturday) – Mill did not stop . . ."[3] The Gays were at best distant kin of Theo Spriggans.

At times, however, the proprietors made unreasonable demands and were forced to retreat. When the flywheel on the mills' main steam engine cracked, causing the loss of thirteen working hours before repairs were completed, "the weavers were ordered to work until 7 o'clock p.m. for 13 evenings to make up time lost." This they refused to do. No one was fired for this, but the Gays did decline the next request for a half-holiday, Easter Monday.[4] The cause of the 1886 strike was an analogous "push." The six-month price list expired when committees could not come to agreement about the carpet manufacturers' appeal for a one-half cent per yard reduction across the board. As the issue was referred for arbitration, the Gays told their weavers that as of April 29 their rates would be fixed at whatever level the impartial outsiders ultimately set. How earnings would be calculated in the interim was unclear. Assuming that the ambiguity would in the short term be resolved by the proprietors paying *their* proffered schedule, the weavers walked. After three days, the firm "agreed to pay the old rate . . . until the price was settled." Seven weeks passed before the arbitrators' judgment was issued; the carpet men gained their reduction, which was implemented June 22. This maneuvering over a half-penny seems trivial until one does the sums. Had the weavers acceded to the April ploy, Park Mills would have saved one hundred dollars a week on its labor bill while the arbitration proceeded, in seven weeks amounting to more than enough to pay for one of the new power looms then on order.[5] Full shutdowns were not frequent; more common were shop floor squabbles. Late in 1890, for example, the firm set up a number of looms for a fine grade of carpeting, but refused the workers' request for a six cent rate. Receiving this news, "they put on their hats and coats to walk out, and we told them to go to work and took the 16 pair work out of

[3] Ibid., November 25, 1886; May 30, September 12, 1887; January 2, 1888; December 24, 1889; February 22, 1890.

[4] Ibid., February 6, April 11, 1887.

[5] Ibid., April 29, 1886. The calculation is as follows: 86 looms × 240 yards output weekly per loom × $.005 × 7 weeks = $722.40, or about $103 per week savings. The new looms cost $500 each, and were installed in December 1886. Loom price is given in *Manufacturers Review and Industrial Record* 19(1886): 594 (hereafter *MRIR*).

loom."[6] Whether the Gays cancelled the order or relented on the price was not recorded.

The reference to "16 pair work" brings us to Park's products, technology, and working conditions. John Gay's Sons ran ingrain carpets along ten lines of goods, from top-grade, all-worsted Delhis (the 16-pair, sold at 63 ½ cents a yard in 1890) down to cheap cotton-wool Unions (9-pair, 29 cents). Their most successful variety was the midprice Park worsted (13-pair, 53 ½ cents), which together with Park cotton chenilles (12-pair, 44 cents) constituted four-fifths of production in 1888–91. These fabrics were woven on four varieties of power looms. Perhaps twenty-six old Babbits that dated to the 1870s and were junked beginning in 1891, and sixty classic Murkland jacquards, made in Philadelphia by Merrill Furbush under license from the patentee, were in place in 1886. The two batches of new looms installed in 1887 and 1889 were "fast" Cromptons, built in Worcester, Massachusetts, by Furbush's former partner, George Crompton. These sales were one of the benefits reaped after the Worcester firm opened a Philadelphia agency in 1886, at which manufacturers could see its "looms in working order, one of each kind built" having been set up in quarters at 526 Arch Street. Such a step made quite good sense, for the ingrain carpet loom market was heavily concentrated in Philadelphia. By the mid-1890s, 3,400 of the nation's 4,800 power looms on ingrains rested in local mills. The Murkland/Furbush folks did not take the Crompton competition lying down. They redesigned their product to match or exceed its rival's capacity and took it directly to the factories. Thus the Gays recorded in the summer of 1892 that "M. A. Furbush del[ivere]d their new high speed loom for trial and if we like it, we to buy same – price $400. Complete." Six weeks later, they ordered thirty-four of them, the first arriving "painted Red" August 24.[7]

The adoption of these technical advances had problematic results, however. At the sectoral level, they exaggerated a trend toward excess production and price cutting led by down East major firms that sought to run full, liquidating at small prices patterns that failed to take during the season. The most notorious of these companies was Alexander Smith, which sold its surplus at immense auctions that whetted dealers' taste for lowered prices. Facing the November 1891 Smith auction, Park stopped each of its looms when it ran out its warp. "We concluded best to wait and see what the whole

---

[6] Ibid., November 25, 1890. The "pair" unit referred to the fineness of the fabric construction, higher numbers indicating more paired threads per inch of this double cloth, i.e., a fabric woven with two sets of warp and filling yarns.

[7] Ibid., October 21, 1888; January 9, 1890; January 29, November 13, 1891; June 22, August 9, 24, 1892; *Textile Record of America* 7 (1886): 48 (hereafter, *TRA*); James Dobson, "The American Carpet Industry," in *Jubilee Number of The Dry Goods Economist*, New York, 1896, p. 85.

thing means before continuing to run the mill full...the Smith sale may cause the price on ingrains to be made so low that we culd not run at a profit." Unloading 60,000 pieces (over seven million yards) under the hammer, Smith did indeed glut the short-term market, as the Gays observed late in November that the "business is in bad shape." *Manufacturers' Review* credited arrival of the second generation of faster power ingrain looms to the decreasing margins of the mid-1880s, which "compelled inventors to introduce looms that would do better and more work." If they were to stay in the hunt, proprietors had little choice other than to adopt the speedier machines, some three hundred of which were set going in Philadelphia carpet mills the summer before Park's second complement of Cromptons was delivered.[8]

At the level of the firm, technical progress and intensified competition put pressures on production and marketing. When the new model Murklands were started up, the Gays set the price for weaving on them at $\frac{1}{4}$ cent below the 5 cents per yard paid for Crompton work, reasoning that total earnings would not diminish and might well increase if per loom output rose over 5 percent. Weavers accepted this for a month, but soon found that they were not making out, as the faster looms used filling yarn more quickly than the available winders could prepare it, forcing them to stop and wait. Agitated meetings ensued, and strikes as well at other firms where, once the Murkland rate was established, proprietors tried to lower all rates to that level. The squeeze was being passed along and workers resisted. Manufacturers replied that carpet weavers were quite well paid as it was, and calculations based on the Gay Daybook suggest that this was the case. A close record of total shipments was kept during 1891, showing the firm sold 6,160 rolls of carpet in the spring season and 4,326 for the fall. In the spring, the mill ran 24 of 26 possible weeks, with 65 hours overtime, a total of just over 1,500 hours yielding 6,160 rolls, or 47 rolls from each of the 130 looms then in place. As a roll was 125 yards long, at 5 cents a yard, each weaver earned just under $300 for the season, or about 20 cents an hour. The fall was less hectic, about 20 weeks' work for 4,326 rolls, yielding just over $200 for each weaver, or $500 for 10 months' labor. This figure is 60 percent above the 1890 average for textile workers in the Northeast and 12 percent above the average earnings of all adult carpet operatives in Philadelphia that year ($447).[9] Such numbers are really quite impressive, particularly remembering

[8] *MRIR* 22(1889): 437,600; Gay Daybook, November 2, 6, 14, 26, 1891.
[9] Carroll D. Wright, "Workmen and Wages in the Textile Industry," in *Jubilee Number, DGE*, p. 47; Gay Daybook, June 1, October 1, 1891; Census Office, Department of the Interior, *Report on Manufacturing Industries in the United States at the Eleventh Census: 1890, Part II: Statistics of Cities*, Washington, D.C., 1895, pp. 438–41 (hereafter *Report: 1890, Part II*). Earnings of children included in the Census *Report* were excluded to

Figure 4. James W. Gay, partner in Park Carpet Mills, circa 1910. (Courtesy of the Philadelphia College of Textiles and Science.)

that an increasing proportion of skilled ingrain carpet weavers were women for whom few industrial occupations offered comparable returns. Though working weeks of sixty hours and more hardly were a source of cheerfulness, carpet workers resisted rate cuts not to keep the wolf from the door but to protect a good thing, insofar as Gilded Age factory work was concerned. The Gays got their Murkland rate solidified by the spring of 1893, just at the point when their new departure in marketing fell flat.

Like most Philadelphia firms, Park Mills sold direct, avoiding commission houses and relying on face-to-face dealing with customers. In the late 1880s, partners still received buyers at the Kensington mill, but these visits accounted for an ever smaller share of sales (not more than 15 percent, 1888–91). After taking charge, James and Thomas Gay twice yearly entrained for Boston and Chicago to visit offices of the two major wholesale jobbing houses that purchased roughly two-thirds of their production. On these April and October journeys, they hauled along heavy trunks containing samples of patterns introduced for the coming fall and spring seasons, respectively. The shipping weight of the four sample trunks for spring 1887 was 1,116 pounds; selling carpets had its physical demands. Midway in each production period, one of the brothers would make an additional trip to New York, Boston, or Chicago "for new ideas," secured in consultation with jobbers who tried to anticipate trends in color and design. Jobbers purchased goods outright from their makers and redistributed them to retailers. Thus the sale price was clear in advance, which was not the case for commission houses. John Pray of Boston and New York made a specialty of carpeting, buying from many firms including the grand old Lowell Company which had erected the first of Erastus Bigelow's ingrain looms in the 1840s. Marshall Field, the Chicago connection, bought textiles of all sorts for its own department store and for its extensive western wholesale accounts, combining jobbing and retailing operations. As steady as these two accounts were, the Gays could well fear that depending on them too heavily would put the mill in the buyers' hands, unable to defend its pricing for want of alternative outlets.[10]

Events in 1891 and 1892 convinced them that these hazards were real. First Pray announced a five cent a yard reduction in the most popular grades

arrive at an average for adult carpet workers in Philadelphia. The "all adults" category includes the lower earnings of winders and inspectors (burlers). To earn enough to offset the ¼ cent lower rate on the Murklands, weavers would have to generate 13 yards over the 240 yards per week that the Cromptons averaged in 1891, hence the 5 percent figure. This production was about double that of hand looms whose 125-yard weekly capacity in turn accounts for the customary roll length.

[10] Gay Daybook, April 11, 18, July 21, October 9, 1886; April 11, 21, October 12, 21, 1888; January 23, 1889; Arthur Cole and Harold Williamson, *The American Carpet Manufacture*, Cambridge, MA, 1941, pp. 56–7, 199–201.

of Lowell carpets and turned to Park with demands for a comparable cut. When the Gays demurred, Pray's New York office pushed a pawn. "They have not ordered any goods forward without playing a waiting game." Early in the new year, Thomas Gay trundled to Manhattan, to find that instead of 53 or 52 cents for Park worsteds, they "wanted them at 48 cents or 49 ... nothing was done." The next day Pray's William Chipman stopped down to Philadelphia and "gave us his best figure, 50 cents. We refused this and said 51 cents," a price that was accepted the following morning in a telegram that also placed an order for 260 rolls of carpet. More pressure followed. Understanding that "our jobbers could not live under our price, 51 cents," the firm reluctantly shaved another penny in March 1892. Hardly had this tangle been resolved when Field notified the Gays that they planned to "pay only for goods sold, not to buy outright commencing in the fall of 1892." Though the Chicago house backed away from this assertion when James Gay arrived there to contest it, the ground on which their marketing strategy was based was evidently giving way beneath their feet, just as the firm was starting construction on a new building that would further increase its output capacity.[11]

In this context, the Gays confronted the limitations of a family enterprise. Activity by their father appears less and less frequently in the daybook after 1886; the two brothers were facing the downside of self-reliance, for they were quite on their own in addressing the multiple demands of creating seasonal lines, getting out production, and placing their goods. Where were they to find the time to reach other outlets beyond their two main jobbers? Certainly the thought of hauling half a ton of samples from city to city in hopes of piling up individual orders to replace Field's thousand-roll purchases must have been staggering. In previous years when orders had lagged two tactics were attempted that were not repeated in 1892–3. On several occasions, Park had simply shipped the sample trunks to potential buyers, no member of the firm traveling with them. This had poor results, yielding orders that would occupy their looms for but three or four days. At other times, one of the brothers made one-day runs up to New York to show samples to other jobbing houses. Though the first effort with H. Claflin and Co. generated a six-thousand-dollar sale of their cheapest goods, a return trip was completely wasted. On James Gay's arrival, Claflin's representative informed him that one and a half cents would have to be cut from the mill's price before he would open the sample trunks to examine the styles. Refusing

[11] Ibid., October 6, November 24, December 9, 31, 1891; January 7, March 12, 21, April 9, 1892. The Field move would have pushed Park's account toward commission house vulnerability, here the risk being that at season's end the Chicago firm would return goods ordered but not sold, passing the problem of their disposal back to the mill.

this, James departed, ending Park's brief connection with one of the most famous New York houses. Relations begun with several Philadelphia jobbers did realize modest returns (100–200 rolls), but no avenue opened in this direction that would substitute for Field and Pray's large demand.[12] A fresh departure was called for.

Shortly after the squabbles with their major clients, the partners contacted Messrs. Riefsnyder and Dutcher, a firm which sent out commercial travelers, about taking their goods on the road. In late May 1892, an agreement was reached whereby the middling and lower grades would be shown by these salesmen to retailers, compensation to be 3 percent on twelve-pair shipments and 4 percent on the cheaper nine-pairs. Ten days later, Riefsnyder complained that Park's prices were too high, the Gays declined to reduce them and by mid-June had "not rec'd a single order." That fall a second effort was initiated when Theo Steenson was engaged on terms far better for the firm. Working by himself, rather than for a selling group, Steenson accepted 3 and 2 percent commissions on the same grades Riefsnyder was handling. The Gays noted: "We to furnish trunks and stationery only. All else at his expense." The eager salesman had an announcement printed and "addressed *himself* 300 envelopes and mailed his circulars to the trade." Riefsnyder had evidently had some success in the summer and fall, for arrangements were made in November for defining the territories to be coverd by Park's two representatives. This done, Steenson set off confidently. In Boston, he "did not show samples as no one wished to buy," and soon headed west toward better opportunities. By the time he reached Kansas City December 19 (by way of Pittsburgh), after three weeks on the road, Steenson had sold but thirty-four rolls of carpet. His commission could not amount to much over forty dollars; given that all his expenses came from his own resources, Park's road man was seriously out of pocket. Still he persevered. The day after Christmas he telegraphed a ten-roll order from Des Moines, earning another twelve dollars. Steenson's return to Philadelphia January 9, 1893, was barely noted; his resignation a month later was hardly a surprise.[13]

The disappointing attempt to corral retail clients exposed Park's weakness before the demands of their major jobbers. Though they remained determined to take selling in their own hands eventually, for the immediate season they had no means to defend their prices. For the past seven years at least, the firm had pegged its best seller (Parks worsted, 13-pair) at 5 cents a yard below the wholesale price of the Lowell Company's comparable grade, a

[12] Ibid., July 1, October 25, November 1, December 31, 1889; May 1, 5, November 4, 10, 1890.

[13] Ibid., May 25, June 6, October 25, November 14, 24, December 19, 29, 1892; January 9, February 15, 1893.

sign of price leadership appearing in the ingrain branch of the carpet trade. At the end of January 1893, they were forced to accept terms for the fall season at 7 ½ cents below the Lowell scale, thereby securing orders of 2,000 pieces each for Field and Pray. Field also negotiated a price 10 cents below the Lowell list for 500 rolls of "High Grades" (16-pair). These concessions stiffened the partners' resistance to the Murkland weavers' request for a ¼ cent advance on the new fast looms, for together they represented a loss of nearly $16,000 in revenue that would have been realized under the old pricing scheme. Reliable orders from Field and Pray had produced the profits that fueled the Gays' expansion. Now the tables had turned; to keep running the Park Mills had to accept substantially tightened margins until they could through trial and error establish their own direct links to retail markets.[14]

The general increase in productive capacity since 1880 had created a buyer's market for ingrains in which price was becoming steadily more significant. To protect their prices, Philadelphia firms sought to reach retailers who potentially could be sold goods at figures just below those offered by wholesalers, thus preserving the mills' overall returns. This would work only if the additional costs incurred to secure the store trade were modest, and if sufficient orders could be taken in small lots to substitute adequately for the consolidated demand that jobbers' massive buys represented.

Another possible strategy to enhance the proprietors' position was collective action to limit production, starve demand, and force prices to advance. Philadelphia's ingrain proprietors knew one another well; the principal Kensington manufacturers had for decades gathered to deal with labor's price lists. By the 1890s, thirty-five of them were members of the Manufacturers' Club, as were the Dobsons and Alexander Crow, whose factory in the Spring Garden district operated not far from those of Theodore Search, the Fleishers, and the Woods. When a movement for restricting output appeared in 1890, owing to the problem of securing "satisfactory prices," four of the five committee members were club men. The plan was simple. If signatures of manufacturers running 2,500 Philadelphia looms could be secured, all firms would confine themselves to forty hours a week from April 1, 1890, through the end of the year. This move would cut output by one-third, or about 20 percent industrywide. On March 15, the committee visited Park Mills and was rebuffed. A second call on the seventeenth got no positive response from the Gays. However, committee head Robert Dornan returned

---

[14] Ibid., January 28, 1893. The cost of the concessions is derived as follows: 4,000 rolls × 125 yards/roll × .025 reduction/yard = $12,500; 500 rolls × 125 × .05 = $3,125, totaling $15,625. Price leadership by the eastern majors was first noted in the late 1880s and continued through the 1930s (Arthur Cole and Harold Williamson, *The American Carpet Manufacture*, Cambridge, MA, 1941, p. 231).

on the twentieth. Dornan was an old colleague; his mills and their 158 looms were but a block away. He had just that winter made his winding machinery available to them to run three tons of yarn onto cops for Park's weavers during a busy spell. Their resistance wilted. After telegraphing both Field and Pray and getting from the latter a recommendation to "join...by all means," they signed. The effort collapsed, however, ten days later.[15]

On March 31, the committee circulated a statement that the Gays affixed to a daybook page admitting that the drive had failed. Though initially it had seemed that "the necessary 2,500 looms could be secured without difficulty," the visiting proprietors had come up against "a manufacturer whose signature was indispensible [sic] to the successful issue of the plan proposed, whom they utterly failed to convince..." His refusal led them to abandon "the canvas [sic] of those...who had not yet been interviewed." The goal set represented 70 percent of the ingrain looms in Philadelphia factories, 58 percent of total national capacity in 1890. The five promoters owned 15 percent of this total among themselves. How could one proprietor's obstinacy defeat the whole project? Our consternation is briefly increased by the Gays' scrawled addendum: "Robert Carson is the person meant in the circular." Carson ran but sixty-two looms in his Kensington mill; he was no James Dobson with millions in plant and machinery, with bluster, clout, and authority to match. However, he *was* typical of the other end of the spectrum, the striving proprietor of a smallish establishment. The committee, together with all the other Philadelphia firms having one hundred or more looms, could account for only half the looms needed to put the agreement into action. To top the mark, they would have to enlist dozens of Carsons, each with ten to seventy-five looms. Carson, like the rest of the small operators, sought individual gain, not a restrictive collaboration with bigger firms that surely would benefit the latter but would cut deeply into *his* narrower base. If the committee could not win him, what use trying to convince the ten-loom men for whom every yard carried its tiny contribution toward an ac-cumulation of capital that would build *their* firms as Dornan, Bromley, and the others had built theirs in the 1870s? The scheme was abandoned; a more ambitious design for an ingrain trust in 1893 was similarly stillborn. Manufacturers' unity was even more difficult to forge in a trade crisis than in a labor one.[16]

Quick responsiveness to opportunities as they surfaced was a defining

[15] *Kendrick's Directory of the Carpet and Upholstery Trades (1890)*, Philadelphia, 1890, p. 207–9; Gay Daybook, January 31, March 15, 1890; *Business Classification of Members of the Manufacturers Club of Philadelphia*, Philadelphia, 1895.

[16] *Kendrick's Directory (1890)*, pp. 207–11; Gay Daybook, March 31, 1890; Cole and Williamson, *American Carpet*, pp. 207–8. The committeemen were Dornan, George Bromley, Alex Crow, William Henderson, and Philip Doerr.

characteristic of proprietary, flexible firms; accepting voluntarily any constraints on this capacity was rare for Philadelphia mills. A cadre of established, veteran carpet manufacturers might have a larger vision, but their
ability to realize it was bounded on one side by the eastern majors and on
the other by the ambitions and greater insecurity of their smaller local
competitors.

Both fast response to special orders and the careful timing of styling
changes were essential to flexible production for seasonal markets. The ability
rapidly to turn orders into shipments is illustrated at Park Mills by a daybook
entry for March 1891. Experiencing heavy resales, Field telegraphed late in
the production season for a second look at samples of the low-grade Unions,
calling for the Gays to send the trunks "by Express and name price." An
order for 140 rolls was wired March 16. Patterns were set up as soon as
looms became available, and in ten days the carpet went out the door to
Chicago. More routine but critically important was the firm's close timing
in running up its samples for each new season. From scattered details, this
sequence can be roughly reconstructed. After getting "ideas" from their
jobbers in midsummer (or midwinter for the next fall's styles), the Gays very
likely consulted with an outside designer who worked up an array of new
patterns. By early September, designs had been chosen and the contractor
brought the mill jacquard card sets for each of the patterns. As this was the
point at which the tail-end orders from the previous season were running
out, idle looms were set up to run sample blankets of each pattern, the design
effects being worked sequentially in different color combinations every few
yards along the same warp. These "strip samples" were laid out "on the
sample room floor" for the selection of "shadings" that seemed to the proprietors most likely to catch the buyers' fancy. This process, which took
from three days to a week, occurred as more and more looms grew silent
with the exhaustion of orders. The decisions made, a few weavers created
a full set of "trial or show samples" for each grade of carpeting, a job
completed in two weeks' time. Immediately thereafter, James or Thomas
Gay set out to solicit the jobbers, returning in a week at most with their
selections. Cards for those patterns in heavy demand were duplicated in the
mill on a "repeater," so that they could be run simultaneously on several
looms in different color sets. Dyers, winders, and weavers not involved in
sampling were all called back after several weeks' layoff and production
resumed.[17]

---

[17] Gay Daybook, December 31, 1888; March 15, 22, 27, 1889; March 24, 1890; September
26, October 12, 1892. There were fifteen Philadelphia card cutting and designing firms
active in 1890, employing 113 workers (90 percent men) at an average of $566 yearly.

However, other than one reference to choosing "50 samples to be made up," the Gays left no information about the numbers of different patterns introduced for a season. Certainly if novelty and design innovation are to be presented as a key dimension of industrial flexibility, evidence concerning the extent of seasonal changes must be advanced. To discover that firms put forward a dozen new patterns and simply added them to strong sellers from previous seasons would be disappointing, for it would suggest a mixed-output strategy (both staples and specialties) rather than a fundamental orientation to fresh designs. Happily, production ledgers from the Whitaker family's Tremont Carpet Mills in Frankford fill this gap, and underscore as well a number of related elements in the flexible production format.

William Whitaker and Sons was one of the oldest Philadelphia textile operations, founded in the War of 1812 period as a cotton mill, switching over to blanket manufacturing during the Civil War then back to cotton goods in the 1870s. By the time of Lorin Blodget's 1880 survey, the firm had branched out to join the carpet surge, placing forty ingrain power looms and equipment for spinning cotton and worsted yarns in Foster's Mill at Adams and Sellers Streets. Their dyeing was handled by Greenwood and Bault, the city's major yarn dyer. The Whitakers sold direct, indeed nearly their entire output was taken up by the Philadelphia retail store Boyd, White and Co. in the years surrounding 1890. As at Park, the firm ran samples in slack weeks between seasons, sent them down to Boyd's store at 1216 Chestnut Street, and wove the retailer's selections as ordered. This certainly simplified the sales end of the business, but the result was a considerably lower per loom output than Park Mills achieved. The Gays in 1891 averaged 80 rolls from each of their 130 looms, whereas Tremont that year sent out but 48 rolls for each of the 38 looms then available. This figure rose to 58 in 1892, still not three-quarters of Park's yield. It is unlikely that Tremont ran full for more than seven months a year, leaving its weavers with earnings a good one-quarter below those at Park Mills.[18]

Despite the absence of aggressive or diversified marketing, novel designs were introduced twice yearly, succeeding rather than supplementing previous styles. For the fall 1891 season, Tremont introduced forty-eight new patterns, any of which could be woven in one or another of nine color com-

---

Few firms hired their own staff designers by 1890, though Hardwick and Magee, successors to Ivins, Dietz and Magee, would do so after 1900.

[18] Scranton, *Proprietary Capitalism*, New York, 1983, pp. 102, 143, 284–5; Whitaker Papers, Accession 1471, Volume II, Hagley Library, Wilmington, Delaware (hereafter, Whitaker Papers); Lorin Blodget, *The Textile Industries of Philadelphia*, Philadelphia, 1880, p. 37; *Kendricks Directory (1890)*, p. 209; *Historical and Commercial Philadelphia: 1892*, New York, 1893, p. 117.

binations. For the following fall, sixty new designs were created in eight color effects. The patterns were individually numbered and color selections letter-coded in the production register, simplifying tracking the extent to which earlier styles were reproduced and new ones ordered. Of 500 rolls woven in the summer of 1891, only 25 represented re-use of old card sets. This figure rose to 61 of 500 rolls for the summer of 1892, but 35 of these were due to continued demand for No. 3188H, the best-selling item from the previous year. For the two sessions, over 90 percent of shipments reflected sales of novel patterns. Samples for seasonal patterns were routinely recycled through sale to one of the outside spinners the Whitakers used to supplement their frames' capacity. Tremont wrote John Gardner at the close of spring 1891 production offering "about 2000 lb. of new carpet samples... Are you working stock of this sort? If so, what would you give for what we have?" Gardner would shred these fabrics and bleach their fibers, creating shoddy for mixing with new wool in spinning.[19]

In each of the two seasons here examined, between four and five hundred new carpet possibilities were put forward by the Whitaker mill. Though it is doubtful that samples for all new patterns were woven in each of the eight or nine color sets, a review of the two summers' production shows satisfying differentiation. The five hundred 1891 rolls were spread across 105 pattern-color pairs, those the next year across 124 pairs. In only three cases in the two periods were more than twenty rolls of a single pair produced, and across all colors, only four designs totaled more than thirty rolls in sales. On the other hand, a fifth of the new patterns each year failed to land a single summer order, though a few of these might have been adopted late in the season. Whereas the mean production for samples that did sell was thirteen and nine rolls respectively in 1891 and 1892, the increased number of designs in the second year led to a flurry of small orders, spreading output more thinly across the wider range of choices. Though this might at first seem wasteful,

[19] Whitaker Papers, Volume II, June 15–August 31, 1891; June 17–August 30, 1892. Cards for discontinued patterns were evidently dumped. When Boyd White called for three rolls of #331A (an 1890 design) in the summer of 1891, the firm replied, "the cards for weaving that pattern were destroyed. Consequently, we cannot make it." (July 10, 1891; see also July 31.) One additional aspect of Tremont's operation further highlights its versatility and the links among Philadelphia firms. The spinning machinery in Foster's Mill was not only used to make carpet yarn for the firm's own products. It was also often committed to running a variety of cotton yarns for fabric firms and worsted yarns for other carpet mills. In the summer of 1891, Tremont sold 38,000 pounds of cotton yarn to six local mills and 6,000 pounds of worsted carpet yarn to John Gay's Sons and Robert Carson. When John Carruth asked to increase his orders for yarn in the fall, the Whitakers replied that they had had "a mule on for you" for some time, "but find we must change it to our own work in a day or two" and thus regrettably could not comply with his request (Whitaker Papers, Volume 11, October 9, 1891).

Table 3.1. *Tremont deliveries to Boyd White and Co., June 15–December 31, 1891, and 1892, at half-month intervals, in rolls (about 125 yards)*

	1891	1892
June (second half)	96	93
July (first half)	103	91
(second)	145	125
August (first)	98	99
(second)	72	108
September (first)	126	119
(second)	101	87
October (first)	62	109
(second)	45	81
November (first)	13	13
(second)	3	0
December (first)	3	0
(second)	4	30[a]
	871	955

[a] First delivery of new patterns for spring 1893 season.
Source: Whitaker Papers, Accession 1471, Volume 11, Hagley Library, Wilmington, Delaware.

total shipments for the fall 1892 season increased 6 percent over 1891 and overall production rose 20 percent for the year as a whole.[20]

In Table 3.1, the force of seasonality and its variation are nicely illustrated. At Tremont, 1891 was far from a banner year. Orders dipped briefly in August and essentially collapsed after September 30. Only 14 percent of shipments for the fall season took place in the final quarter of the year. Certainly Whitaker's weavers, other than those running samples, endured a layoff of two or more months before Christmas. The next year (1892) proved more rewarding, for the fall production run continued through late October, and early calls for the 1893 spring patterns sent looms back into motion in the last part of December. Consequently, the slack period fell from twelve to

[20] Ibid. The spring 1892 season was quite successful for Tremont. (It was also the busiest period at Park.) For the year 272 rolls were shipped for spring markets, 925 in the fall, and 30 rolls at the end of December for the coming 1893 season. The spring 1892 performance was 32 percent above that for spring 1891, yielding the 20 percent increment over 1891 when the two falls are included and the advance shipment of December 1892 is set aside. Standard deviations for the new patterns among the summer 1891 sales: 7.9; for 1892: 9.9; variance 1891: 62.4; 1892: 98.2.

roughly seven weeks, as the new range of designs enjoyed better success than had the 1891 cluster. The experience of Tremont Mills in sampling resonates with the *Manufacturers' Review*'s observation: "Everything the manufacturer shows the trade will not sell. The buyers know their needs and they must be met or there will be no sale."[21] By expanding the number of their patterns, the Whitakers enhanced their market chances, shortening the mill's idle time considerably.

Outside the carpet trades, nowhere was the "cry for something new" more persistent than in the hosiery sector. Though the tremendous popularity of staple "fast black" stockings encouraged German and British importations and sustained the initial flutterings of local fledgling firms, Philadelphia's distinction lay in the novelty end of the trade. Thus the *Review* expressed no astonishment when the Germantown Hosiery Mills of Charles Chipman presented "about 220 styles" for the fall 1892 market, "representing Balmorals, a new line of mixtures,... a full line of seamless; also something extremely loud for their South American and Mexican trades." Such regional stylistic differences were generally acknowledged – muted colors in the North, flashy ones for the South as well as for Latin America. The various grades of hose also showed rural–urban geographical variations: "For the far Western and Southern trade, cheap hosiery is in extremely active demand, while in the larger cities and towns, the tendency is toward the higher priced goods." To reach these differentiated national and (to a small degree) international markets, an extremely wide range of products was required. At Chipman too these had to change with the season; for spring 1893, the firm focused on specialties. As the *Review* correspondent reported, "Their sample room is stocked with about 200 designs. In staple goods they are importing from Germany and finishing themselves, and find this about the only way to make any money." The same month, Taylor and Hawthorne also unveiled its seasonal innovations: "Their line is entirely new and in which there are over 200 designs. This concern never run the same lines two seasons." The situation in woolens was similar. In late spring of 1892, making for the fall clothing trade, "manufacturers find themselves well loaded with orders.... Samples for overcoats are simply legion, and there seems to be no difficulty in suiting all classes of trade."[22]

As woolens were largely sold to clothing cutters, who in turn sold to wholesale and retail outlets, their manufacturers were insulated to a degree from the problem changing styles posed for retailers still holding aging stock as fashion moved along. This was a more immediate issue for Philadelphia hosiery firms, for they sold direct to jobbers and stores. However, local

[21] *MRIR* 23 (1890): 282.
[22] Ibid., 22(1889): 610; 24(1891): 45; 25(1892): 338, 395, 605.

proprietors were encouraged when stores were stuck with cases of low-priced imported stockings amid a wave of demand for specialties. "So many new styles of goods are constantly coming out that retailers frequently find themselves caught with stocks of unsalable goods; it then occurs to them that cheapness is a very small consideration in comparison with freshness, attractiveness and novelty." Where fashion ruled, Philadelphia goods found a "quick sale," a lesson retailers rapidly appreciated. In the 1890s, specialties and fancies were pushing back the tide of plain black hose; and the same tale was told in cloths, where "the call has been for loud effects, some of which are positively 'alarming.' " Philadelphia's surging prosperity was linked to the rage for ornament and newness. One stylist captured the moment in 1891: "One does not tire so quickly of novelties as of plain goods, since one may select from an almost infinite variety of designs." Assuredly, with the exception of the southern taste for flamboyant hose, much of this demand was urban and middle class. As the growing masses of conveyancers, managers, and lawyers followed the "tendency to ornament" while avoiding the "gewgaw tack" of extremism, Philadelphia mills annually and eagerly fed their demand for suitings, socks, upholstery, draperies, laces, and carpetings until the parlors and drawing rooms of the Gilded Age fairly burst with color and curlicue.[23]

Supplying hundreds of designs for hundreds of firms was a task essayed by three sorts of providers in late-nineteenth-century Philadelphia. For the fancy end of the spectrum, fifteen jacquard-designing and card-cutting firms were in place by 1890, supplemented by a number of independent, contract artists and a small group of "house" drafters engaged by the largest mills. Second, the Textile School graduated annually from five to twenty men with the essentials of design training in hand, and its fabric construction instructor took on work from local firms for a time before leaving to launch his own design periodical, *Posselt's Textile Review*. Such publications were useful as a third line of resource, especially for smaller firms, as the *Manufacturers' Review*, *Textile Record of America*, and others issued pattern details each month for what were expected to be the coming ideas. Consistent with the Phila-

---

[23] Ibid., 23(1890): 130, 290; 24(1891): 554. The very wealthy seem to have retained a taste for imported fabrics and were developing a delight in oriental rugs, but "the great middle class, if that term be permitted, are satisfied with the product of your own mills," (*MRIR* 24 [1891]: 111). This, as with virtually all citations from the *Review*, is drawn from its monthly Philadelphia Interests report, which was supplemented by a separate column on the Quaker City hosiery and knitting trades. These two regular features make the *Review* an invaluably focused source. How prosperous the Philadelphia textile industry was will be evaluated later in this chapter. On southern taste for fancy hose see ibid., 24(1891): 265; for more on "pronounced effects, . . . combining uneven yarns and strangely wrought weaves," see ibid., 24(1891): 626.

delphia tradition of producing "facsimiles" of the most striking European fashions, local firms continued to copy from British and Continental fabrics secured through importers and previewed in the reprinted fashion reports featured in the trade press. Some manufacturers were themselves able designers; Robert Dornan went so far as to patent a number of his creations. But the output of commercial designers was frankly prodigious. One of the Philadelphia veterans celebrated his twenty-fifth year in the business shortly after 1910 with release of his 25,000th carpet pattern, a landmark passed by another local independent "dots-and-spots" man a few years later. By 1892, the *Review*'s Philadelphia correspondent could report "less copying of European patterns and more originality in our work" than ever before, a result which flowed from the novelty that centered in Kensington and splayed outward to the county lines. The individual manufacturer still guarded fabric ideas "zealously...lest some base competitor reproduce his styles" before he marketed them. Occasions on which importing agents sold their sample books to drooling proprietors still occurred. Yet tariff protection, technical advance, a skilled labor base, and the development of a cadre of creative and subtly imitative designers had combined by the early 1890s to extend the reach of the local product scheme. Put simply, "fabrics which a decade ago it was thought impossible to produce [here] are now made to perfection."[24]

Through the foregoing review, we have assessed the mechanics of flexible production before the 1893 depression in terms of labor relations, technology, seasonality, marketing, sampling, and designing, stepping in and out of Philadelphia carpet mills as the occasion afforded and venturing briefly beyond that sector to other regions of the textile economy. Still there are more components in the operations of a flexible production system at the level of the firm, questions of credit and finance, of the social relations among manufacturers and with workers, of politics and profits. To reach into these quarters, we must turn toward James Doak, Jr., and Kensington's Standard Worsted Mills, where through the medium of Doak's journal we shall encounter a drunken manager, a bankrupt manufacturer, another incompetent salesman, and, once again, the irascible James Dobson.

James Doak, Jr., like many Kensington proprietors, was the son of an English immigrant textile worker. In his youth he joined his father in Joseph Ripka's Manayunk cotton mills, becoming a power loom boss there by 1860.

---

[24] Frederick Zenke, "The Designers Position in the Commission House," *Third Annual Report*, Alumni Association of the Philadelphia Textile School, Philadelphia, 1904, 54–59; L. M. Dillon, "The Designer in the Mill," *Fifth Report*, 1906, p. 46–51; *MRIR* 21(1888): 919; 22(1889): 429, 530; 23(1890): 290, 522, 852, 926; 25(1892): 395; *American Carpet and Upholstery Journal* 30 (September 1912): 84.

During the Civil War, Doak served in both the army and navy, drawing a $525 bonus from the latter upon his enlistment in 1864. This sum he put in the hands of William Arrott, to be invested after $15 was disbursed to his father. As his war letters home reveal, Doak was an aggressive reader, a thorough autodidact who wrote with wit and compassion of the grim scenes he witnessed. At the war's end, he joined Arrott's insurance office as a clerk for a year, then with his own small capital and additional backing from Arrott commenced manufacturing carpets in a modest way. The partners began with sixteen hand looms in rented Frankford quarters, moving twice to larger spaces in the next five years. Burnt out in Christmas week 1872, they invested their insurance returns in the purchase of the ruined property and construction of a factory to hold both spinning and weaving machinery. At first running worsted yarns for their carpet looms, Doak and Arrott chose not to buy ingrain power looms as the local industry began the transition away from handwork. Instead they moved laterally, feeding their yarns into a new set of worsted cloth power looms while keeping their hand carpet looms active at least through 1880. In that year, Standard Worsted Mills operated 120 looms on worsted coatings and 2,100 spindles supplied with "tops," the long staple fibers which make worsted yarn, produced from four "combs" in the factory on East Norris Street. In a Cumberland Street annex, eight hand loom weavers still thumped their treadles, but the shift to clothing fabrics was evident.[25]

During the 1880s, Doak succumbed to the temptation of integrated production, adding a dyehouse to the plant, introducing knitting machinery for the manufacture of fashionable jersey cloths, and in a step rare for textile proprietors, beginning to cut and stitch apparel from his own goods. These ambitious maneuvers added layers of complexity to the firm's operations just when Arrott's death in 1888 forced the reorganization of its ownership arrangements. Settling with William Arrott, Jr., on a figure of $80,000, Doak bought his late partner's half share of the enterprise, and perhaps to help keep track of his affairs in a confusing period, commenced recording his daily activities in a journal.[26]

Doak stated the purpose he had in mind for his journal in an entry for June 18, 1888, several months after he had begun his daily summaries.

[25] Scranton, *The Philadelphia System of Textile Manufacture, 1884–1984*, Philadelphia, 1984, pp. 38–9; Charles Doak Papers, Archives, Pastore Library, Philadelphia College of Textiles and Science; Blodget, *Textile Industries*, p.11.

[26] James Doak, Jr., Journal: 1888–91, Archives, Pastore Library, Philadelphia College of Textiles and Science (hereafter, Doak Journal). Doak family folklore has it that James Doak, Jr., kept journals in later years as well, but to date only this volume has come to light, along with a collection of his Civil War letters in the possession of his granddaughter, Elizabeth Doak Tarnay.

Having recounted in some detail his amazement at finding in his suit pocket a streetcar transfer dated exactly one year earlier and his embarrassment in presenting it to a baffled conductor, he continued:

> I have written so fully about this trifling incident for the purpose of seeing how much I could recall of it, in fact that is my chief reason for keeping this book. The majority of the incidents noted are of no importance but I wish to Strengthen my Memory and acquire the habit of rehearsing at length the details of any trifling incident. As it is now I can never talk unless I have something to say and there are occasions when it is convenient to be able to talk about nothing.[27]

Thus for a time his entries were encyclopedic, but after the first six months, the journal steadily became a record of business problems. Concern for the unrelieved flow of blunders and glitches soon outweighed his commitment to improving his parlor conversation through more effective recall. These upsets fell into four general categories that will be treated in turn: managing the labor process, marketing, finance and credit, and politics, chiefly tariff issues. Those that overlap with questions addressed by the Park Mills daybook allow a second angle of approach to the daily challenges of flexible production, whereas those that are newly exposed here will help round out this sketch of late-nineteenth-century firm dynamics.

James Doak resided in a fine house on Spring Garden's Green Street, well across the city from his factory at the eastern edge of Kensington. Most days, he left home a bit after 7 A.M. and drove his carriage north through Fairmount Park to Diamond Street, then east into the textile districts across Broad Street, a journey that lasted roughly an hour. After checking in with the room bosses and his "Super" or manager, Doak reviewed the state of production on the varied orders booked by his two salesmen, Sam Hepburn and Louis Gilroy. Late in the morning, he returned home, napped for an hour or more, then departed by horsecar for the firm's office at 233 Chestnut Street. Doak consulted with his road men about the quality of samples, the lines that were selling and those that were dead, and in their absence, debated related matters with his distribution manager, Sam Irwin. In the late afternoon, he generally circulated along Chestnut Street, chatting with wool men, jobbers, and manufacturers, eventually strolling west to the Manufacturers' Club, or less frequently, the Union League, for his evening meal and hours of conversation about trade and tariffs. Somewhere between eight and eleven, he rode the trolley home, where, were it still early enough, he played checkers with his eldest son or listened as his wife read aloud from Pepys's *Diary* or Young's *Tour of Ireland*. James Doak had traveled some distance from Ripka's

---

[27] Doak Journal, June 18, 1888. Doak's grammar and spelling are reproduced in all citations.

Manayunk weave-rooms, but the easy pace of his days conceals their constantly nettling content.[28]

Rarely did he enter the mill to find everything serene. Coope, his spinning boss, "generally runs to extremes." First he rushed through combing white stock, "taking no pains whatever to keep it from getting mixed with the black," wrecking the dyeing. Upbraided for his casualness, now "he is putting four times as much labor on it as is necessary." Next came the news that warps from Beswick and Kay, outside spinners who supplied cotton yarn for mixed goods, were so badly spun that double the set price for weaving had to be paid in order to get them used up. Meanwhile some of the yarn spun inside "will answer for nothing but corkscrews," rather than being good enough for finer coatings. Meanwhile the stock account of knitted jersey cloth for the garment section failed to jibe with what was actually in the storeroom. Johnson, head of the fashionable jersey department, was taking home a fancy forty dollars weekly, but could not seem to estimate how much cloth was required to cut a dozen of the new styles. His calculations were consistently low, with the result that prices were established from them, goods ordered, made, and shipped only to discover that 15 percent more yardage had been used than expected, evaporating any hope of profit.[29]

Jerseys were "close fitting upper garment[s] or jacket[s] made of elastic woolen or silk material," somewhat like present-day sweaters, "made popular by Mrs. Langtry, the 'Jersey Lilly' " in the 1880s. Ornamented with braid, sold as vests or with sleeves, their sales rocketed after 1885, drawing dozens of Philadelphia knitters into their production, and in Doak's case, enticing a lifelong woven-goods man as well. For fall 1888, Standard would offer 101 styles, its numbering series having passed 500 in the short time since their introduction. However, shipping big orders for small or no profits was hardly reassuring. Johnson's errors were not confined to cloth estimates; he evidently mixed up pattern numbers and "insists on keeping on an unnecessary force when there is very little work being done." At the close of June, Doak put the matter to himself: "We find Johnson very inaccurate. The question is can we get along without him." When Morris, from the mill office, asked "in a mysterious way" that his employer come up to the mill on the 28th, the balance tipped. Morris thought Johnson hopeless; his assistant Mary "does all the work...and Johnson could be dispensed with and no loss result." Doak moved quietly, sending Sam Hepburn to "make

[28] *Gopsill's Philadelphia Directory for 1888*, Philadelphia, 1888, p. 477; *Boyd's Business Directory of Philadelphia City (1890)*, Philadelphia, 1890, p. 213; Doak Journal, June 11–18, 1888.

[29] Doak Journal, June 12, 15, 29, 1888.

a contract with Mary for a year at $15 a week" before ousting the department head. Sam delayed a few days, "reluctant to push the matter," but by July 3 had arranged for the yearlong contract (at only $13.50 weekly) without mentioning that Johnson was poised for the drop. Doak did not record the substance of his parting conversation with the failed jersey boss, but by July 17 Mary was solidly in charge, the situation smoothing out. In making a woman his department chief, Doak was advancing his interests, not taking a step toward feminism. The cutters and sewers Mary would supervise were also women, her competence was obvious, and he was saving two-thirds of Johnson's wage in the bargain.[30]

If Doak acted cautiously before dumping Johnson, taking a month to reach a final decision, he was virtually frozen before the problems caused by his factory superintendent, Ed Magner. Magner had taken the post in the spring of 1888, coming to Kensington from some distance without his spouse and taking up residence in a mill district hotel. His special talent was in the dyeing end of the business, but he was to oversee all the room bosses with Morris's assistance. A clear sign of trouble bubbled up Monday, June 18, when Magner failed to appear for work. Though he had been "all right" when one of the mill boys had seen him the previous evening outside his rooms, Doak noted that "as long as he lives at that hotel, there can be no reliance placed on him." Indicating that this was not the first of Magner's absences, he wrote: "this is getting to be a very serious business and it is time to consider whether we wont be compelled to run the place without him." Doak considered the question for nearly a year.

Magner's invisibility continued on Tuesday; Doak arrived at the factory to find "everything going wrong." Tom, the super's assistant in the dyehouse, "made several abortive attempts to dye a pc. of Jersey Cloth," samples needed immediately "are neglected," and production of serges "is not started although Coope has the yarn ready." Vowing to advertise for a replacement if there were no satisfactory explanation for Magner's disappearance, Doak charged Coope with tracking him down after work. This brought him in Wednesday, but the next day the proprietor noticed that Ed "had been drinking this morning" and "had a very plain talk with him." Magner promised he would "drink no more" and told an involved story about trying to find a house for his wife and their furniture. Doak reflected that the tale "does not hold together well. It looks as if he and his wife had a dispute." Instructing himself to "follow him up closely," the mill owner made daily notes on Magner's state for a week, then turned to other concerns. In late July, the super again fell off the wagon, went missing for three days, then

[30] George S. Cole, *A Complete Dictionary of Dry Goods*, Chicago, 1892, p. 210; Doak Journal, June 5, 29, July 2, 3, 5, 17, 18, 19, 1888.

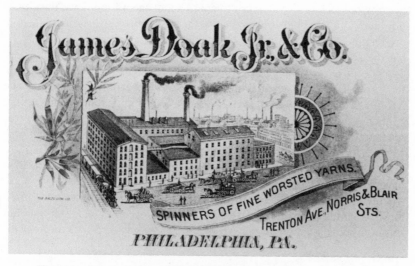

Figure 5. Standard Worsted Mills, trade card, circa 1900, issued after James Doak discarded integrated manufacturing for a focus on worsted spinning. (Courtesy of the Philadelphia College of Textiles and Science.)

wandered in with his face a mass of cuts and bruises. His "story this time is that he was going into his room and his toe caught on the rug his face Striking the bed and blacking his eyes." Though Magner was "Straighter" by the fall, his continuing binges, perhaps either the cause or the consequence of his marital discord, were disruptive. He was at last let go in the spring of 1889, and after some searching was hired by Doak's colleague Joseph Truitt, partner with Thomas Dolan in the Quaker City Mills, another worsted firm. Magner's "habits have not improved," but Truitt "values him highly for his knowledge of Dyeing." There was evidently little rancor in the parting, for Doak and Magner shared a dinner at the Kensington Hotel that fall, talking of ways to eliminate "brown patches" that spotted cotton yarns.[31]

Why did the master of Standard Mills avoid firing his reprobate manager for so extended a period? First, between sprees, Magner was generally competent in his duties, as other journal entries testify. He was a master dyer, skilled in the trickiest part of the production process. More important, unlike the Johnson case, Doak here had no obvious alternatives. He had created an integrated plant that, with the addition of apparel construction, was more complex and less routinized than the larger New England staple firms. Doak

[31] Doak Journal, June 18, 19, 20, 21, 22, 23, 26, July 27, 28, August 1, 21, September 6, October 16, 1888; August 19, October 7, 1889.

never wrote of considering recruitment of a mill agent from down East; their tidy hierarchical systems were a poor fit for the fluctuating disorder of flexible production. Some local textile companies might have adequate managers, but the scarcity of integrated, flexible mills in the city (Dobson, Schofield, and a dozen others), meant that the pool of men who had experience handling the tortures of synchronizing inside operations was agonizingly small. Since Arrott's death, Doak had to keep watch on both production and marketing; neither was proceeding smoothly. His eldest son was still in his early teens. No help from that direction could be expected for some years. Sticking with Magner for as long as he could stand it, Doak was forced after his departure to spend more time with the production end, though this at least provided him "the satisfaction of getting my knowledge at first hands."[32]

The problem of effective oversight and coordination was not solved through pirating a manager from a mill like Dobson's. In fact it was not solved at all. Six months after Magner left, Doak looked back beyond his tenure.

> We have been running for a number of years without a Skilled Manager, we have tried several but in every case they have been failures. This state of affairs has had many disadvantages. Each man in charge of a room manages or mis-managed [sic] in his own way ... [I] had not the technical knowledge required to warrant in contradicting them on any technical question. I have now resolved to try Our Spinner, "John Vogelman" as Manager. He will have charge of the Drawing, Spinning, Twisting, Spooling, Reeling, etc., and in J. Rogers absence of the Combing. also of the Engineer.

The "etc." leaves an ambiguity as to Vogelman's span of control, but as major departments (dyeing, weaving, knitting, cutting, and sewing) are omitted whereas the new manager would have charge of combing *only* in that overseer's absence, it seems his job was confined to supervising the yarn division. Vogelman was quite up to this task. In time he became superintendent of all activity at Standard, but not by mastering the mill's other sections. Instead, Doak after 1892 eliminated all but the spinning department, first dropping jerseys, then cutting the number of looms and increasing spindlage. By 1898, the dyehouse was gone. Standard Worsted Mills had experimented with integration, found it beyond the capacity of proprietary resources, and returned to the classic Philadelphia pattern. As a producer of specialty yarns, it established its niche within the flexible production system, bridged the generational succession, and survived the Great Depression.

---

[32] Ibid., June 22, July 19, August 28, 1888; October 7, 1889.

Snarls in managing production contributed to Doak's decision, but the miseries of the selling process added pressure from another quarter.[33]

In distributing his goods, James Doak had twice the task the Gays struggled with, for his cloakings were aimed at cutters and fabric jobbers whereas jerseys as finished goods brought him into the wholesale and retail clothing market. In the journal's first entry, Doak recorded his personal selling effort on both accounts, April 16, 1888. While at the Manufacturers' Club the previous evening he had received a note from Mr. Weeks, buyer for the Cincinnati house Rockfellow and Sheppard, who introduced him to Mr. Sonneborn, a Baltimore jobber. Meeting the pair in the morning, Doak sold Sonneborn "250 pc. @ 85 cents." For setting up the deal Weeks was "to be paid 2% and R & S to have no knowledge of it." Satisfaction was had all around, as Standard had a quick $10,000 worsted sale and Weeks netted $200 for steering Sonneborn.[34] The jersey picture looked equally bright. Doak next called on Wanamaker and Brown, clothiers at Sixth and Market streets, "by appointment." Jersey manufacturer Joseph McKee had recently failed and was thus "out of the race." Wanamaker needed a new supplier. This prospect soured the next day, at their second conference. Doak examined a sample of the goods they wished made, but soon found himself in deep waters. A clever kickback scheme was revealed and Doak wrote with feeling:

> This thing is all off. It transpires [that] Mr. Wm. H. Brown must be paid 6% on the goods we sell Wanamaker . . . [who] said he could not do much business with us unless we made a satisfactory arrangement with Brown. I wrote Brown . . . that we would not pay him 6% for the privilege of selling goods to Wanamaker – he is now trying to get the goods from Godshalk . . . J. D. McKee had been making for them but

---

[33] Ibid., October 10, 1889 (this entry is out of order and may be located on p. 124 of the Journal); *TMD(1894–5)*, p. 150; *Official American Textile Directory (1898)*, New York, 1898, p. 211 (hereafter, *OATD*). For the dyeshop, Doak also promoted from within. "Tom," who had made a botch of jersey work in 1888 when Magner was out, the next year was running the department adequately with Morris's advice (Doak Journal, August 19, 1889). In a sense, Doak's integrated setup had the worst of both worlds, for with all its internal troubles, the mill was not free from needs for outside contractors as well. Both the trouble with the Beswick and Kay warps and recurring difficulties with braiders who added ornament to the jerseys show that integration would not realize entire control of production unless Doak added cotton spinning and braiding machinery to his plant.

[34] Estimating piece length at 50 yards, the transaction would have involved 12,500 yards or a gross of $10,625. The terms were "10% in 10 days," meaning prompt payment would save Sonneborn $1,062. Weeks's 2 percent of the gross would be $212 (Doak Journal, April 16, 1888).

as they with others have ruined him they want to try their hands on some one else.[35]

These slick operators were not again mentioned in the journal.

If the results of his personal salesmanship were mixed, the returns brought in by his two travelers were sharply different. Lou Gilroy, who oscillated between New York and Baltimore, was a steady producer, but Sam Hepburn, who was to cover "the West," looked to be a dead loss. Gilroy and Doak felt that western sales could effectively be handled from a "desk in New York," catching visiting buyers as they migrated through. Hepburn insisted that he go to Chicago directly. This was agreed. As Hepburn left the night of June 10, Doak observed: "Our course in the future will [depend] greatly on Sam's success on this trip." At week's end, Sam telegraphed an order for "1 doz. jerseys, gave no shipping instructions." His journey was having no better effect than Steenson's pathetic trip for Park Mills. Late in the second week, Johnson implored Doak to advertise for more help in the jersey department, but was rebuffed "until Gilroy returns from New York and Hepburn from the West." He arrived over the weekend, and put up a brave front at the store. Doak had his doubts: "Hepburn talks of his Orders but he has not entered any of them in the Order book." The truth was soon out. Sam was "putting in his time" at the mill "to avoid coming to the office. He has had such ill success in Selling that he would like to drop it. He is very easy discouraged and then loses all interest."[36]

Once again, the proprietor refrained from cashiering a problematic employee. At first, he mused about having Sam take over the mill's jersey department which he could learn to run "with the help of a good woman." It was soon clear that the "good woman" could run it just as well without either Johnson or Hepburn. Instead, he sent Sam to New York to secure desk space and after the Johnson succession was settled, kept him there making the rounds of jobbers, while Gilroy worked the Philadelphia and Baltimore markets. When Doak tired of the frustrations of direct selling a year later, and moved to engage commission houses to distribute Standard's output, Hepburn would be drawn into the plan. Though Doak, like other millmen, readily laid off production workers in slack periods, or for incompetence, he was more reluctant to dismiss supervisors or office/selling staff. Both Vogelman and Hepburn remained with the firm into the new century.[37]

Like the Gays, James Doak struggled to defend the prices he set on his

---

[35] Doak Journal, April 17, 1888.

[36] Ibid., June 10, 15, 22, 25, 26, 1888.

[37] Ibid., June 26, July 21, August 2, 1888; Charles Doak, Journal, 1902–06, Archives, Pastore Library, Philadelphia College of Textiles and Science. This journal was kept by Doak's youngest son during the years when he was learning the family business.

products. Buyers' efforts to squeeze them down at times took on comic-opera proportions. Louis Kessel, a New York jobber (330 Church Street) who often bought Standard's worsteds, sent his brother to Philadelphia in June 1889 to talk about a dead stock lot of seventy-four pieces, offering sixty-three cents a yard for the dropped styles. This was refused and Sam escorted Kessel back to his train at the Kensington depot. The New Yorker "waited until the minute bell had rung. As soon as Sam had gone Kessel left the train and came over again raising his offer to 65 cents." Doak rejected this too and accompanied him to the Broad Street depot, where the price was again presented for the manufacturer to consider. Telegraphing another no to sixty-five cents in the morning, the firm "rec'd an answer raising it to 67 ½ cents. Sam declined[;] that got another telegram asking us to ship the goods at our price 70 cents net cash." Holding out for one's price took a certain delicacy and nerves of steel, but the rewards were tangible. The seven cent difference between the first and final prices netted Standard $250 literally overnight.[38]

Less satisfying was the steady trickle of claims and demands for rebates or refunds from dissatisfied customers. Worse were sizable jersey orders placed so that a bulk price could be gotten, a few items be picked out, perhaps for imitation, and the rest returned. Twice in 1888, Doak smelled a rat in such jersey orders, having likely been previously burnt. He refused them both, the second time telling Gilroy "when the offer was reported that they wanted 100 pc. that they might select from them the few that they really did want."[39] These annoyances were not enough by themselves to drive Doak away from direct selling, but combine them with Hepburn's weak showing, Magner's dismissal, the consequent increased production demands on his energies, and the proprietor's decision to give it up in July 1889 becomes sensible. Personally stretched too thin, short on talented "white-collar" employees, he negotiated with Bacon, Baldwin and Co. of New York to handle all selling of woven goods. Their Mr. Dunn would "represent us," Standard paying commission of 7 percent, "which is to cover everything – we deliver the goods FOB in Philadelphia and are at no farther expense connected with them..." The other shoe dropped in October, when the jersey trade was placed with M. Brown's Son and Co. of Philadelphia, Gilroy going along with the bargain. Gilroy was guaranteed $1,800 per annum plus 1 percent of all sales over $100,000 as Standard's agent with the commission house. "We are to pay 7 ½% Com. and Guar[antee] and deliver goods... in Phila." In the interim between the arrangement with Bacon and that with

---

[38] Doak Journal, June 13, 14, 1889. The calculation here is 74 pc × 50 yards × .07 = $259.
[39] Ibid., July 20, 23, 1888 (the July 23 entry is out of chronological sequence and may be found on p. 82 of the Journal).

Brown, Bacon's Mr. Dunn had been found unsatisfactory and Hepburn substituted in his place. Dunn shared Magner's fondness for fortification and with the commission house's consent, Hepburn took his position in September at a "guarantee" of thirty-five dollars weekly, the same base from which the more proven Gilroy was operating.[40]

Within six months, Doak was clearly dissatisfied with the new marketing arrangements. He was at first hopeful; "they are not selling many goods but the sales are growing." By spring 1890, the situation looked glum: "Sam was here last Friday 14th March and I told him we would have to make other arrangements for disposing of our goods as at present it was not paying any person connected with it." Yet as with staffing, Doak was slow to move. Even though he complained in August that the "largest houses are buying one or two pcs. at a time," he kept his ties with Bacon, Baldwin and later sought to transfer to them the jersey account that Brown had failed to handle effectively. The journal ends at that point, but following the serial cutbacks to specialize in yarn production, Standard returned to direct selling exclusively in the mid-1890s. Few flexible firms operating in unpredictable seasonal markets could to good effect adopt the integrated production format and the commission house marketing style of bulk-oriented staple mills. Doak's experiments along both lines were disappointments and he terminated them, returning to characteristic Philadelphia strategies for manufacturing and accumulation.[41]

James Doak's activities beyond the mill and store reflected his involvement with the financing of textile production and its defense through political organization and lobbying. Doak was a director of the National Security Bank, located on Girard Avenue along Kensington's lower edge. Four other directors were textile proprietors – William Allen (yarns), Philip Doerr, C. G. Berlinger, and John Hamilton (carpets). Doak, Doerr, and Allen served on the loan committee, which met early every Tuesday morning to evaluate the state of the bank's paper and requests for credit. On the political side, the owner of Standard Mills was active in Republican politics, visiting Wash-

---

[40] *TMD (1880)*, p. 426; Doak Journal, July 13, August 29, 30, 31, September 4, October 30, 1889. "Guarantee" referred to a portion of the fee that purchased a form of insurance coverage through the commission house. If a customer defaulted on payment, the house would make full restitution to the firm whose goods were involved. In selling direct, mills were responsible for collecting late or defaulted accounts themselves, or had to resort to paying others to do so for them.

[41] Doak Journal, October 7, 1889; March 18, August 22, December 1, 1890; *TMD (1894–5)*, p. 136; *OATD (1898)*, p. 211. As early as July 1889, Doak expressed his concern about the fabric operations and the marketing difficulties: "Serious question where this thing is going to stop. It does not seem worth our while to give much attention to woven goods as we never know" (July 6, 1889). The sale of his weaving plant was announced in *TRA, 15* (1894): 337.

ington on behalf of the worsted schedules and being offered a delegate's seat at the 1888 Chicago nominating convention, a post he declined. Through these "outside" roles, Doak exemplified the mature proprietor, a man recognizing that continued industrial success depended on maintenance of a reliable credit system and a congenial political environment as buttresses to quality production and effective selling.[42]

The National Security Bank was founded in 1870, "mainly by German residents of the northern section of the city." Two decades later it held assets of $1.8 million, including $183,000 in surplus and undivided profits, and retained something of its immigrant character, as half the twelve board members had German surnames. Yet its operations, if Doak's reports be a guide, were entwined with the functioning of the textile industry, for the loan committee regularly financed the short-term capital needs of local millmen. At its June 12, 1888, meeting, the bank picked up a $5,000 note signed by Thomas Leedom, a decision Doak and Doerr favored but Allen opposed. Leedom was the carpet manufacturer who had moved to Bristol, Bucks County, after being embroiled in bitter controversies during the 1885 Kensington strikes. Allen "also objected to repeatedly renewing J. McConnell's paper, we have $2400 of it." McConnell had a cotton yarn factory in the adjacent Northern Liberties section, and as he kept a bank balance of $1,500 or more, Doak saw little difficulty in keeping his credit open. A more serious problem dominated the next week's session.[43]

Joseph McKee, "ruined" by his commercial contacts in the Wanamaker jersey fiasco, had defaulted on a $3,500 note to National Security. William Montague, a Manayunk carpet yarn manufacturer, acted as the "assignee" in rounding up McKee's creditors, assessing his liabilities, and arranging distribution of available assets proportionally. Meanwhile, McKee had approached Doak with an offer to retire the past-due note for $2,000, the bank to take the loss on the residual. This proposal Doak put before his fellow directors, who settled on $2,500 as a more suitable figure. When he arrived at the mill, Doak found Widdis, McKee's clerk, waiting for news from the board. Widdis "seemed pleased that the bank would accept $2500 but did not say whether McKee would give it." The failed proprietor had assured Doak that all but four creditors and the bank had signed voluntary agreements to clear his debts, but this fiction dissolved the next day. While discussing the bankruptcy with Montague on Chestnut Street, Doak en-

[42] *Philadelphia and Camden National Bank Returns (1891)*, Philadelphia, 1891, p. 30; Doak Journal, June 15, 16, 1888.

[43] J. T. Holdsworth, *Financing an Empire: The History of Banking in Pennsylvania*, Chicago, 1928, Vol. 4, p. 331; *National Bank Returns (1891)*, p. 30; Doak Journal, June 12, 1888; *TMD (1888)*, p. 257.

countered the more hard-headed of the two Dobson brothers. "Jas. Dobson joined us who said that at least ten creditors had not signed. He said they would never sign and if Montague did not close the concern P[retty] D[amn] Q[uick] he would do it himself."

It was common for an "embarrassed" firm to continue running under the assignee's supervision, turning raw stock into more valuable finished products while the proprietor negotiated terms of payment with his creditors. If this could be accomplished, the firm would recover gradually or would be slowly liquidated when its stock was exhausted; if not, if creditors had little faith that its prospects would revive, they could force prompt liquidation through the courts. This was Dobson's threat, given his view of McKee as a wastrel and his recognition that the jersey trade was increasingly crowded. Doak's faith in McKee was shaken: "It is impossible to believe anything he says." He related this tale at the next loan committee gathering; thereafter McKee dropped from sight. Though Doak could for a time tolerate Magner's dissimulations, he could not accept dishonorable behavior by a fellow manufacturer. Their contacts ended once McKee's tactical lie was exposed.[44]

Whereas National Security was by the late 1880s an experienced and successful bank serving industrial interests (its stock was selling at double its initial $100 par value), it was joined in the decade after 1882 by ten new Philadelphia national banks aimed at similar purposes. In 1888 the *Manufacturers' Review* observed this movement in midstream: "Our uptown people now have improved banking facilities. Three or four banks have opened their doors under Kensington smoke, and they are doing a good discounting business. They are supported by manufacturing capital." By 1891, forty textile manufacturers were directors of twelve city national banks whose assets totalled $28 million. While it is hardly surprising to find them at the Kensington, Manayunk, Germantown, and Ninth Nationals, the last formed almost entirely by textile capital, three of the millmen were board members at the grand old Bank of North America (Search, his partner Fiss, and Eddystone printworks's William Simpson), a signal of manufacturing's growing significance within the local financial network. The multiplication of enterprises that would facilitate "discounting" proprietors' notes eased the seasonal working capital pressures for already successful mills, but this institutional development was of little value to newly begun firms whose risky courses would add little to bankers' profits. Larger veteran capitals had

---

[44] Doak Journal, June 11, 12, 19, 20, 22, 1888. Banks in which manufacturers were "interested," i.e., shareholders, clearly served a valuable credit function in this era, but the older pattern of personally lending funds to reliable colleagues through acceptances and short-term notes continued. William Arrott, Jr., had lent worsted manufacturer Nathan Folwell money in this fashion in the summer of 1888, then brought the note to Doak who took it "at 5%" (July 21, 1888).

created financial mechanisms to service their needs, giving them a freer hand vis-à-vis suppliers, jobbers, and agents, but small capitals were as vulnerable as ever.[45]

Textile manufacturers were directly involved in another Kensington bank, the Ninth National, from its beginnings in 1885. Ten of its thirteen directors were millmen who held a third of the capital stock, while another 30 percent was in the hands of textile veterans and families not represented on the board. The Gay brothers, together with John Dickey and Charles Porter, partners in a cheviots and cottonades enterprise, were the largest investors, each tandem holding over 300 shares (of 3,000 total). James Doak , along with five other textile men serving on bank boards, expressed their support by buying a nominal five or ten shares, which Doak, like many others, retained until his death.[46] Both steady dividends (6–8 percent through 1906, more thereafter) and ease of access to the loan committee encouraged the leaders to continue their board roles, though loss of committee records renders invisible the details of their portfolio management. Nevertheless, as Table 3.2 indicates, while individual holdings changed, nine of the ten textile directors retained an interest until after the turn of the century. None of these men had visions of financial grandeur. They, like others of their colleagues, simply erected a modest bank to remedy their credit difficulties, shared ownership among the "family" of family firms, and operated it at a profit for a generation.[47]

3.1. Tariff politics and sectoral profitability

The politics of the 1888 Republican convention may have been gripping for those who rode the rails to Chicago, with Blaine and Sherman giving way before the colorless but safe General Harrison; but for James Doak, political discussion began and ended with the tariff. He talked of it on the street, arguing with cotton manufacturer Robert Garsed for "¾ of an hour," at-

---

[45] William Post, *The Text-Book of Banking: Philadelphia*, Philadelphia, 1893, unpaged; *MRIR* 21(1888): 360; *National Bank Returns (1891)*, pp. 5, 8, 12, 16, 18–20, 22, 24–6, 28–32.

[46] *Historical and Commercial Philadelphia* (1893), p. 145; *Textbook of Banking*, Philadelphia (1891), unpaged; Dividend Book, Ninth National Bank, 1889–1923, Philadelphia National Bank Collection, Accession No. 1658, Hagley Library, Wilmington, Delaware.

[47] Dividend Book, Ninth National, and Stock Ledger, Ninth National 1885–1917, Hagley Library. Ownership was divided among 115 to 120 individuals for the first thirty years. With the death of most of the founders, ca. 1910–20, and the expansion of stock to 5,000 shares in two steps after 1917, ownership was further dispersed to above 250 after 1920. The bank continued to prosper, in 1922–3 paying $10 per share twice a year. In the later 1920s, it merged with the Philadelphia National Bank.

Table 3.2. *Shareholdings of 1891 directors, Ninth National Bank, 1889, 1895, and 1902*

	1889	1895	1902
John Dickey (cottons)	285	290	296
James Mitchell (yarns)	77	149	186
John R. White (carpets)	30	10	0
James Butterworth[a] (txtl. machinery)	105	105	6
Thomas Gay[a] (carpets)	290	210	210
James Pollock (carpets)	45	10	10
John G. Carruth (cottons & woolens)	50	94	94
Adolph Woll (hair cloth)	50	50	50[b]
Robert Pilling (knits)	50	50	50
Charles Kurlbaum[a] (carpets)	8	23	20
Philip Ritter (conserves)	10	10	0
Edward McCaulley[a] (coal)	30	30	30
James Gillinder (glass)	10	0	0
	1,040	1,031	952
Percent of total shares	(34)	(34)	(32)

[a]Includes shares held by family members
[b]estate
Source: Dividend Book, Ninth National Bank, 1889–1923, Philadelphia National Bank Collection, Hagley Library.

tended meetings to endorse high and higher protection at the Manufacturers' Club, and worked out fine points of the schedule in table talk over dinner there and at the Union League. There is no gainsaying the obsession of wool, hosiery, and fine-goods proprietors with holding the tariff line against the free-traders. Their arguments, indefinitely rehearsed, put the low wages of European textile workers in Bradford, Belfast, and Chemnitz at the center of the transatlantic rivalry. First-rate textiles could be shipped to the United States at small prices because operatives across the water were paid sums that would dishonor an American citizen. Protectionist manufacturers stood up for the American standard of living, not just for their own prosperity. They reminded their critics that though workers might have now to pay more for many goods than they would under free trade, they now had jobs with which to earn the necessary cash, jobs which would vanish in short order if mills were forced to close under an avalanche of imports. Alternately under a free-trade system, proprietors would be required to cut wages to Continental levels to compete with ill-treated European labor, wrecking the promise of America for those who had come here with such high hopes.

This rhetoric represented an energetic burning of straw men. Though free-trade advocates were just numerous enough to present ideal targets, the real question over which manufacturers sweated was precisely how much protection they could reap from political maneuvering before the tide reversed toward reductions. Wrangling was always over the *level* not the substance of protection. In the early 1880s, deft gambits by the wool men secured quite solid advantages, as the Tariff Commission, appointed to provide an impartial evaluation of rates and scales, was chaired by the head of the National Association of Wool Manufacturers, John Hayes. Even Frank Taussig, perennial critic of the protectionists, had to admire the aplomb with which textile and steel producers manipulated congressional procedure and trade diplomacy to achieve satisfying results in the tariff act of 1883. However, Hayes's close calculations had erred with regard to worsteds, "which were admitted at specific duties not sufficient to compensate for the duties on [raw] wool." As a worsted producer, Doak joined with Dolan, Search, and his Philadelphia colleagues in that sector in attempting to remedy this inadequacy. The first Cleveland administration would not tolerate a reading of the act that would classify worsteds under the advantageous schedules provided for regular woolens, hence the Philadelphians' enthusiasm for Harrison who was reportedly "sound" on the matter, given his support for the Republican platform of 1888 that regional power broker Joseph Grundy had had a role in creating. (Indeed, Grundy left the convention once the platform was settled, returning to Philadelphia and his worsted plant at Bristol while the standard bearer was being selected.)[48]

Once the election was favorably resolved, commuting to Washington soon became routine for Philadelphia textile manufacturers, as during the months before Harrison's inauguration, the Senate Finance Committee continued its long series of hearings on tariff revision. On December 19, 1888, Doak, Search, Dolan, and Grundy were accompanied by their colleagues George Campbell, Charles Salmon (a Dolan partner), Rudolf Blankenburg (later mayor of Philadelphia), dyers Thomas Firth and H. B. Thompson, and John Bottomly of the Camden (N.J.) Woolen Mills. Making clear his application of the presidential vote to the worsted cause, Dolan announced: "We feel now that we have a right to ask for a protective tariff. I do not believe there should be any compromise about it. If there is, then, in my judgment, the election was a failure." Philadelphia textile proprietors, particularly Dobson and Grundy, had been active in building the Republican war chest, and were calling in their debts.[49]

---

[48] Frank Taussig, *The Tariff History of the United States*, New York, 1899, pp. 231–3, 242–3; Doak Journal, June 21, 23, 1888.

[49] U.S. Senate, Finance Committee, *Testimony Taken by the Subcommittee on the Tariff*, Washington, 1888, pp. 1613–14.

Search and Dobson presented horror stories of their persistent losses on sales of worsted yarn in the face of cheaper imports. The textile educator claimed he had recently sold a large quantity and had "lost 10 cents a pound by doing so." Dobson bluntly added his two cents. "We have had a worsted mill to spin worsted yarn for three years and we have dropped about $25,000 every year in it, and think it is time to stop." Search portrayed himself as the benevolent proprietor, keeping the mills going "rather than send the organization on the street." He continued:

> We have done the very best that we could, and the result was that I had 100,000 pounds of yarn on hand...that I had to carry, in order that the men I had employed for years should be kept at work doing something. When I came to unload that yarn, which I had to do in the last sixty days – and I am sorry to say that I transferred some of my profits to the pockets of gentlemen here present [weaving proprietors] – of course I was obliged to sell it for what I could get...Unless you have pretty good backing, you can't stand such business as that. You get tired and sick and disgusted.

Search may well have run his mill in slack times on yarn numbers normally most in demand, but his sense of injury was overdrawn. William Arrott, Jr., reported to Doak that "Search said to him that they consider it a bad year if they did not make $100,000." The textile industries of Philadelphia were profitable and prosperous; public poormouthing was a tactic to make them more so through effecting a rise in tariffs that would inhibit foreign competition and elevate price levels.[50]

In the course of the hearings, Doak and the senators struggled hilariously to get their arithmetic right so as to draw conclusions about the mass of statistics paraded before the committee. But despite this stumbling about, the Philadelphia men stressed their claim to the top end of the trade. Speaking of Doak's jersey group, Search averred that "we make no finer yarns in our business than are consumed by these men..." Dobson was drawn into discussing his advances into mohair plushes, which were flowing from the Falls of Schuylkill mills at the rate of 140 forty-yard pieces daily. None of these goods were made in the United States before the 1880s.

> Up to 1881,...there were not more than 5,000 pieces of mohair plush imported. The industry was entirely French. The merchants had to give their orders probably more than a year in advance before they could get them filled. In 1881, we commenced to make the goods, both silk and mohair. The price of an ordinary mohair plush at that date was about $160 landed; $75 a piece for the very poorest quality...Since

---

[50] Ibid., p. 1631; Doak Journal, January 15, 1890.

the introduction of the industry here, you can import the goods that
[once] cost...$120 for 40 yards...for $45 and do not have to give
your order more than two weeks in advance in order to get them.

Dobson's motive in relating this tale of innovation was to ask that the tariff
on silk-hat plushes be raised so that imports could be vanquished in this
quarter as well. When a senator pointed out he had "a lot of hatters to deal
with," Dobson replied crisply, "I do not see why you should not have your
hats on as favorable terms as the ladies get their bonnets."[51]

Presenting the industry's side of tariff debates was not a task confined to
hearing rooms. Once the new executive was in place, Doak and Camden's
Bottomly traveled to the capital in order to brief Colonel Tickenor, assistant
secretary of the treasury, and W. P. Hepburn, the department's solicitor, on
the "processes employed in making wool into woolen or Worsted goods."
As Doak reviewed twenty-six steps in the sequence summarized in his journal
entry, his presentation outlasted the morning hours and the pair were invited
to return at 4 P.M. Upon arriving, they overheard the tail-end of a plea by
the (former?) U.S. attorney from the New York City district, a man who
eloquently "claimed fees and allowances" of $45,000 in addition to his salary
of $6,000 per annum. Solicitor Hepburn rejected these inflated figures, turn-
ing to Doak and Bottomly after the paunchy attorney had departed.

> [He] asked if we had had any experience of those New Yorkers, they
> think he said that the Sun rises and Sets only for the benefit of N.Y.,
> that the rest of the people of this country have no rights which a citizen
> of that highly favored locality is bound to respect.

After imagining how his disappointed visitor would relate this experience
"to the members of his Club," Hepburn discussed trade issues with the
Philadelphia team, arranging that he and Tickenor would join them for the
evening at the Riggs House. The new treasury leaders responded far better
to representatives of Philadelphia enterprise than they had to an imperious
gouger from Tammany's New York.[52]

The following January, as the process that resulted in the McKinley tariff

---

[51] *Testimony...on the Tariff*, pp. 1635–6. Dobson and a clutch of carpet men returned
January 17, 1889, in a different voice, arguing for reduction of tariffs on coarse raw
wools used in their mills and not produced in the U.S. This was a touchy matter, for
"free wool" was favored by some manufacturers who felt tariffs on behalf of American
sheepmen were a hindrance. Dobson was treading a fine line, arguing that the low-
grade wools were not worth raising here, given the far better returns from merinos; and
thus lower tariffs on these varieties would help manufacturers without injuring herders.
The decade-long truce between wool growers and millmen was under considerable
strain (ibid., pp. 2016–27, 2067–72; for a sharp exchange between Dobson and Columbus Delano, the growers' spokesman, see pp. 2082–3).

[52] Doak Journal, May 16, 1889.

act of 1890 was beginning with hearings before the House Ways and Means Committee, Doak attended a session at which Frank Bennett, editor of the *American Wool Reporter*, delivered petitions on behalf of "free wool." This proposal would end all duties on imported raw wools, a disadvantage to American husbandmen, but a move that would lower materials costs and goods prices and thus ease criticism of textile manufacturers as robbers of the public. For decades, the wool millmen had staked out a reliable alliance with sheep farmers through a system of compensatory and ad valorem tariffs. It worked this way. Imported wool was taxed eleven cents a pound to encourage expansion of merino herds and keep domestic raw wools high. To shield manufacturers from imported fabrics made abroad with lower-cost materials, all imported woolens were first hit with a specific, compensatory duty of forty-four cents per pound, on the principle that four pounds of raw wool yielded one pound of finished goods, given wool's sizable weight loss when grease, sticks, etc., were removed from baled fleeces. This was not protection for *manufacturers*; it simply figured in the differential cost of raw materials that protection for *farmers* entailed. To this compensatory duty, a range of *ad valorem* charges were attached for the varieties of woolen imports, providing a barrier for manufacturers that both underwrote higher American wages and made possible sufficient profitability to spur investment in domestic mill capacity. This system and the unity of factory and farm was threatened by Bennett's advocacy of "free wool."[53]

Most of the 530 signers of Bennett's petition were from New England, New York, or the Midwest; only 28 Philadelphia names could be gathered. To compensate for this underwhelming support from the nation's greatest textile city, Bennett in his opening remarks called attention to the signature of "Mr. James Kitchenman, a large manufacturer, and a leading Republican of the city of Philadelphia, and one of the men who helped raise the celebrated Philadelphia campaign fund in the last Presidential campaign." James Doak took umbrage at this statement. He broke into Bennett's testimony:

Mr. DOAK: Mr. Kitchenman never was a Republican, and did not contribute anything toward the Republican campaign expenses. He has been a life-long Democrat. I know him very well.

The CHAIRMAN: Do you live near him?

Mr. DOAK: Yes, sir; Mr. Kitchenman was a Democratic candidate for sheriff in Philadelphia.

Mr. BENNETT: This Mr. Kitchenman?

Mr. DOAK: Yes, sir; this Mr. Kitchenman.

---

[53] Taussig, *Tariff History*, 196–200; idem, *Some Aspects of the Tariff Question*, Cambridge, MA, 1915, pp. 322–3; U.S. House of Representatives, Committee on the Ways and Means, *Revision of the Tariff*, Washington, D.C., 1890, p. 164.

Mr. BENNETT: I am ready to stand corrected in regard to any error…There
may be two James Kitchenmans.

There were not. Doak knew whereof he spoke; Kitchenman, an active Democrat, was a Kensington carpet mill owner known for his independence of
mind, and was not a member of the Manufacturers' Club. Despite Bennett's
surprise at this embarrassing moment, he plunged ahead with his doomed
presentation. "Free wool" was not included in the McKinley tariffs.[54]

Doak returned to Washington twice again before the tariff bill was passed
in October, meeting with "Major McKinley" and Columbus Delano (of the
wool-growers' association) to discuss final adjustments in the schedules. The
McKinley tariff was "entirely satisfactory" to Philadelphians, for it raised
specific duties from 10 to almost 40 percent, the highest levels in the nineteenth century. More critically for specialists, the biggest hikes came in fine
goods classes; as NAWM leader S. N. D. North put it, the "law was successfully framed to promote the higher forms of textile industry." In consequence, by 1892, both migrations of European firms and domestic new
starts blessed either the expansion or inauguration of quality work in lace
curtains, velvets, "novelties" in wool and worsteds, and new lines of silk
goods. Moreover, woolen imports that in 1889 represented roughly 21 percent of domestic output fell by 1892 to 13 percent, dropping from $57
million to $36 million. Though Taussig would fulminate about the alliance
of manufacturers and Republicans against the interests of consumers and
the prod of international competition, the political and economic outcomes
of the 1890 tariff deals made it plain that Philadelphia textile industrialists
had become skilled at work in shops quite different from those in which
they had learned their trades.[55]

Through this review of James Doak's many activities, we gain a perspective
on the cultural prism through which a textile proprietor's enterprise is re-
fracted. Self-educated, Doak was not a man of nice refinement; he attended ·
no concerts, read the *Ledger* as did his workers, lived in a world of men in
business. He cherished his family, yet was rarely at home in the evenings,
which were spent with colleagues at one of his clubs. Honesty might not be
scrupulously expected of his factory hands, but it was an essential in business
relations. His rejection of McKee, blunt contradiction of Bennett, and distress at the machinations of sly buyers indicate expectations of fair dealing,
but he was probably unperturbed at Search's touching performance before
the Senate Finance Committee. Tariff relief would aid the worsted trade,

---

[54] Ibid., pp. 164–5, 176–9. There was but one James Kitchenman in *Gopsill's Philadelphia
City Directory (1890)*; the carpet manufacturer's entry may be found on p. 1023.
[55] Doak Journal, April 2, September 4, 1890; *MRIR* 23(1890): 595,758; *Bulletin of the
National Association of Wool Manufacturers* 22(1892): 271–3.

in which (as Doak's jottings reveal) business could well be better. The level of a firm's profits was a private affair, and on this particular topic, Philadelphia was a decidedly private city. At the mill and office, though gaffes by his employees were frequent, Doak was hardly quick to fire, nor did he crowd journal pages with recriminations about clumsy spinners or craft-proud dyers. Instead, such temper as he vented was directed toward other businessmen, for he did not suffer fools gladly.

On the occasion of his birthday in 1888, Doak gave a dinner at the Manufacturers' Club for a few friends.

> Ellis Hey was there and I of course invited him to join the party. Ellis is a fool and will sometime or other disgrace his friends unless all Signs fail. McKeown says he has a power of attorney from his father [a Manayunk textile manufacturer], it would be better if his father appointed a care taker for him ... Vandegrift took one of his odd notions and to show the strength of his grip crushed a tumbler in his hand which was cut badly with the broken glass. He left at 8 o'clock. Could not say whether it was on account of his hand.

The dry irony and sociability, the quiet conservatism that speaks from his journal suggest James Doak's Scots-Irish working-class roots, as do his weekend teas with fellow manufacturers, his penchant for rubbing himself down with whiskey (and salt), and his habit of "plain talk." Like so many of Philadelphia's Anglo-American millmen, he had come from the shop floor to a position of substance, one in which Standard Worsted possessed him as much as he possessed it. From the cultural centrality of the firm to the lives of its proprietors flowed much of the strength and resilience in the regional system of flexible production. Ultimately, its very rootedness in place and practice would contribute to its demise as well.[56]

One of the last entries in the Doak journal blends issues of family succession, privacy, and firm profitability in a fashion that leads usefully toward an attempt to assess the relative success of Philadelphia's accumulation strategy against the record of staple centers down East. On December 6, 1890,

> Allen, Wm. F. called this morning, he is very anxious that his Father should retire. The Store and the Mill although run so far as the public know as entirely independent concerns are in reality One. Their capital is about $180,000 their profits after each man receives interest on his money are divided ⅓ to Will, ⅓ to Charlie, ⅙ to Allen Senior, ⅙ to George. Their profits this year after interest is paid will be about $50,000, $40,000 for the store and $10,000 for the mill.

---

[56] Ibid., June 13, 1888.

The Allen Senior referred to was Doak's fellow board member at National Security. In 1890 he was 66 years of age, having emigrated from his native Manchester to Philadelphia in 1848. A journeyman cabinetmaker, William C. Allen after two years joined Manayunk's J. C. Kempton as a "machine carpenter and pattern maker," progressing to foreman at Archibald Campbell's nearby mills, then to a partnership with Saxon Warren for the manufacture of cotton goods in 1858. This firm dissolved early in the Civil War, Allen serving various mills as superintendent, most notably those of Sevill Schofield. He departed Manayunk for Kensington in 1869, commencing yarn production with his son George. Burnt out after three years, Allen joined with Henry Morris, returned to lease a section of Schofield's old Blantyre Mill, and there made mixed cotton and wool goods ("Doeskins and jeans") until March 1880, when they closed out the partnership and transferred their machinery to their landlord. William Allen and Son was shortly again established in Kensington, running carpet yarns in a small way (1,000 spindles).[57]

By 1890, when his younger son called on Doak, Allen Senior had branched out into the recycling of wool waste, setting up his namesake William F. Allen in a partnership with Charles Cole at 132 N. Front Street. Buying and selling "Rags, Wool and Hair" at the "Store" and producing yarns at the mill were the two interlocked businesses which the public thought to be separate concerns. Allen's elder son George was the official partner at the yarn factory, rounding out the foursome mentioned in Doak's entry. Given the small scale of the mill's operations, its proportion of total profits, and the fact that Cole and young William were entitled to two-thirds of the $50,000 the combination earned, it is likely that the bulk of the capital was tied up in their wholesale enterprise. Whatever the exact balances, the profitability of the linked firms is little short of staggering. The partners drew interest on their $180,000 before calculating trade profits; at a conservative 5 percent, this would realize $9,000 plus the $50,000, a total return to capital of 32 percent in a single year. The major partners could expect a distribution of $20,000 each, the minor, $10,000, unless a portion of the net were set aside as a reserve for machinery, bad debts, etc.[58]

How typical were such prodigious returns on investment in Philadelphia's textile manufacture? Given the commercial source of much of the Allen-Cole gains, what profits attended the activities of strictly industrial com-

[57] Ibid., December 6, 1890; Daniel Robson, *Manufactories and Manufacturers of Pennsylvania in the Nineteenth Century*, Philadelphia, 1875, pp. 514–15; Lorin Blodget, *The Textile Industries of Philadelphia*, Philadelphia, 1880, p. 1; *TMD (1888)*, p. 129.

[58] *TMD (1888)*, p 370; *Gopsill's Philadelphia City Directory* (1890), pp. 97, 99; *Boyd's Business Directory of Philadelphia (1890)*, p. 177. Allen Sr. resided at 167 West Susquehanna Street in Kensington; his two sons lived next door at 169.

panies? Though Search's expectations are also suggestive, analysis of financial data for Philadelphia firms presented in the published 1890 census of manufactures reveals the striking yields local proprietors achieved in 1889, returns that take on additional significance when it is recognized that they reflect business done *before* implementation of the McKinley tariff hike for yarns, woolens, and worsteds. Table 3.3 presents information on capital, workforce, profits, and rates of return on sales and to capital for eight sectors in the city and county of Philadelphia. Clearly Allen's gain was above average for Philadelphia firms, but not spectacularly so. The entire knit-goods sector reported comparable profitability, and earnings were about the same or better in the smaller upholstery and silk-goods trades. Relatively, carpets, worsteds, and wool lagged behind, making the tariff determination of Dobson, Doak, Search and company understandable. Dyeing as a contract business yielded lower returns than sectors marketing finished goods; I suspect that spinning firms also had lower rates than hosiery or upholstery operations, but the mixing of these specialists with fabric producers masks this effect. In any event, the lower returns were compensated for by lessened risk, which always accompanied the seasonal markets of style-conscious fabric and knitwear firms. There is here also good evidence of why so much excitement attended the expansion of knitting and jacquard work in silk and upholstery, for one's entire investment might be recouped in two or three years. Overall, Philadelphia's textile sectors generated products worth $98 million in the census year (14 percent of the national total), employed nearly 58,000 workers (11 percent), and earned profits of $13.8 million on their goods (17 percent).[59] These gross figures suggest that the city industry was more effective in its use of labor and more profitable than its share of national output would indicate. More specific sectoral and city comparisons are presented in Table 3.4, which contrasts Philadelphia's performance with data from other textile centers.

What emerges from a review of Philadelphia's sectoral profitability is as close to a clean sweep as can be expected. In every category, both earnings and accumulation were at or above the average for urban manufacturing (the five "all cities" lines) in the United States. Its focus on high-value damasks and curtains pushed the local cotton sector far ahead of returns in staple centers. Dobson's plushes and others' specialties from tapestries to braids outpaced even Paterson's record, though her dyeworks, all committed to silk, did appreciably better than Philadelphia's more diverse colorists. In knits, the Quaker City was the national leader, supporting 20 percent of the sector's workers nationally with but 15 percent of total capital, yet reaping

[59] Calculated from figures in *Report: 1890, Part II*, pp. 434–53, and *Report: 1890, Part III: Selected Industries*, pp. 4–5.

Table 3.3. *Profitability by sectors for Philadelphia textile industry, 1890*

Sector	Firms	Total capital (000)	Total workers	Return on sales (%)	Return to capital (%)
Carpets	133	14,458	12,124	13	20
Cotton goods[a]	123	7,942	7,080	16	23
Dyeing/finishing	78	4,378	2,710	14	14
Hose & knits	178	7,830	12,637	17	32
Silk goods[a]	43	4,748	4,145	27	46
Upholstery	17	899	627	22	31
Woolen goods[a]	115	14,270	10,583	13	20
Worsted goods[a]	32	12,064	7,904	11	14
Aggregates	719	66,589	57,810	14	24

Note: The detailed breakdown of firm expenditures and investments provided in this volume makes calculation of profits fairly straightforward. The tables give under "capital" both fixed (land, buildings, machinery) and working capital figures, the latter labeled "Live Assets" and including raw materials on hand, stock and work in progress, cash and accounts receivable. Product value is provided both for main lines and auxiliary goods (here yarns within fabric sectors). Costs of production are represented by figures for principal materials, other materials, mill supplies, fuel and power, while labor costs are broken down between "operatives" and "pieceworkers" in male, female, and child categories. Miscellaneous expenses specify "rent paid for tenancy, taxes, including internal revenue, insurance, repairs, amount paid to contractors, interest paid on cash used in the business," and "all sundries not elsewhere reported." Value of product is value at the factory, expenses of selling being reported under all sundries in the miscellaneous category. (See *Report*, "Introduction," pp. ix–xliv.) Deducting all costs from product value yields approximate profit. Two ambiguities cannot fully be resolved – whether product value equals sales and whether product value is partly double-counted in the stock-on-hand category of live assets. If sales are less than product value, profits and return to capital are lowered, but if the difference was reported as stock/assets, then capital ought to be less as well, perhaps offsetting the effect. Reducing both product value and capital by the amount given as stock yielded losses in every sector, suggesting that the two were kept apart in accounting and not double-listed, and that sales and product value were roughly interchangeable. For a similar use of this data source on cotton staple-goods firms, Massachusetts and North Carolina, see Nancy Kane, *Textiles in Transition*, Westport, CT, 1988, Ch. 3.

[a]Includes both fabrics and yarn for sale. No separate category for spinning mills was established.

Source: Department of the Interior, Census Office, *Report on Manufacturing Industries in the United States at the Eleventh Census: 1890, Part II: Statistics of Cities*, Washington, 1895, pp. 434–53.

Table 3.4. *Profits and return to capital, Philadelphia and selected cities, six sectors, 1890 (in percentages)*

Sector	Profit[a]	Return to total capital[b]	Sector	Profit	Return to total capital
Cotton Goods			*Dye-finish*		
Philadelphia	16	23	Philadelphia	14	14
Lowell	8	6	Lowell	12	8
Lawrence	10	7	Lawrence	2	1
Manchester, NH	5	4	Fall River	18	8
Fall River	12	9	Paterson	14	24
All cities[c]	10	8	All cities	14	12
Hosiery & Knit Goods			*Silk & Silk Goods*		
Philadelphia	17	32	Philadelphia	27	46
Cohoes, NY	11	14	New York City	13	22
Milwaukee	12	16	Paterson	15	27
All cities	15	24	All cities	16	29
Woolen Goods			*Worsted Goods*		
Philadelphia	13	20	Philadelphia	11	14
Lowell	16	13	Lawrence	7	6
Holyoke, MA	10	10	Providence, RI	14	22
All cities	12	14	All cities	na	na

[a]Residual after all costs are deducted from product value.
[b]Profit divided by total of fixed investment and "live assets."
[c]Represents total for 165 U.S. cities with populations of 20,000 and over, including those individually given here. No all-cities data available for worsted sector.

27 percent of all profits from the trade.[60] The area worsted group had more satisfying earnings than the staple-oriented Lawrence mills, but lagged behind Providence, another specialty textile center. Part of the differential between the Pennsylvania and Rhode Island cities may be traced to the different composition of their worsted production. In Philadelphia, 58 percent of output was yarns, not fabrics, whereas at Providence, spinning accounted for but 29 percent of production for sale. The greater profitability

---

[60] The national figures are capital − $50.6 million; products − $67.2 million; workers − 61,209; profit − $9.5 million. In Philadelphia total capital was $7.8 million, products $14.9 million, workers 12,637, and profit $2.5 million. National data was drawn from *Report: 1890, Partk III*, pp. 128–33; Philadelphia figures are from *Report: 1890, Part II*, pp. 442–5.

of finished goods and their greater role in Providence's output account for its relative advantage.[61] Philadelphia was in 1890 not only the most diversified textile district in America; it was the most prosperous as well.

Also of real significance in Table 3.4 are the relationships between the profit and capital return items. For those centers with capital-intensive orientations that so often went hand in hand with bulk production, the return to capital was lower than the profit on production, as the total volume of relatively low-value goods represented less than one full "turn" of a heavy investment. Thus for Lowell, Lawrence, Fall River, and Manchester the capital return percentage was consistently below that for profit on sales. In contrast, batch-production centers like Philadelphia, Providence, Paterson, and New York were oriented toward labor-intensive production, featuring on average firms with more modest investments, which together with their higher-value outputs resulted in consistently higher returns to capital than to sales. Here investment was turning over at a greater velocity, a sign of rather more efficient use of capital within the flexible production systems than in the bulk arenas. For example, in the three sectors in which both Philadelphia and Lowell are present in Table 3.4, cottons, woolens, and dyeing, the ratio of production value to capital is 1.42 at the former and .82 at the latter. Where Philadelphia and Lawrence share sectors, in cottons, worsteds, and dyeing, the ratios are 1.26 and .73 respectively.[62] In both cases, capital turned over more than half again as fast in the Quaker City as in the major New England centers, certainly a salient element in the greater productivity of capital at flexible centers more generally.

It has already been hinted that Philadelphia workers were more productive than their counterparts in staple-oriented centers. Table 3.5 expresses this in monetary terms, exhibiting value added per worker, average wages, and profit per worker comparatively. In the cotton sectors, Philadelphia firms paid the highest wages, secured the highest value added and profit per worker of any city, the last category standing at more than double the figure for all urban cotton production. Elsewhere in cottons, Fall River showed the best effect of devotion to standardized cloths, in this case gray goods for printing. The linkage between this finely tuned weaving system and Fall River's massive printworks is evident in the dyeing category, as is the importance of cotton printing at Lowell. High per worker value added was consequent

---

[61] *Report: 1890, Part II*, pp. 450–3, 470–3. Providence yarn represented $5.1 million of its total output of $17.6 million; at Philadelphia, $8.5 million of $14.7 million.

[62] Ibid., pp. 286–9, 310–17, 434–53. Lowell capital in the three sectors was $27.9 million, production, $22.9 million; for Philadelphia, capital, $26.6 million, production, $37.8 million. In the Lawrence case, capital in cotton, worsted, and dyeing amounted to $23.4 million, production, $17.1 million, and for Philadelphia, capital, $24.4 million, production, $30.6 million.

Table 3.5. *Wages, profit, and value added per worker, Philadelphia and selected cities, six sectors, 1890*

Sector	Avg. wages[a]	Profit/ worker	Value added/ worker[b]	Sector	Avg. wages	Profit/ worker	Value added/ worker
Cotton goods				*Dye-finish*			
Philadelphia	$407	$260	$714	Philadelphia	$528	$225	$886
Lowell	322	92	524	Lowell	520	174	935
Lawrence	343	127	566	Lawrence	455	23	590
Manchester	355	57	467	Fall River	329	322	921
Fall River	345	153	580	Paterson	570	249	879
All cities	333	114	549	All cities	494	203	838
All rural	292	na	na	All rural	460	na	na
Hose–knit				*Silk*			
Philadelphia	$319	$201	$571	Philadelphia	$395	$525	$1091
Cohoes	335	135	547	New York City	438	186	706
Milwaukee	171	78	289	Paterson	433	285	802
All cities	298	163	517	All cities	409	236	763
All rural	298	na	na	All rural	341	na	na

Woolens			
Philadelphia	$375	$270	$730
Lowell	358	320	822
Holyoke	382	141	630
All cities	358	205	664
All rural	359	na	na

Worsteds			
Philadelphia	$376	$205	$675
Lawrence	378	115	621
Providence	371	278	774

*a*Includes overseers and office workers.

*b*Value added represents product value less materials costs, which include mill supplies, power, and fuel, but not miscellaneous expenses (insurance, taxes, etc.).

*c*Average rural wages could be calculated from tables in the "Introduction to Statistics of Cities," which gave sufficient rural data for this category, but not for assessment of profits and value added.

Source: Department of the Interior, Census Office, *Report on Manufacturing. . .1890, Part II: Statistics of Cities*, Washington, 1895.

on the intensive mechanization of drum printing, clearly more successful as a business proposition at Fall River, where wages were lowest and per worker profits the highest in the nation. Independent dyeing languished at Lawrence, a city dominated by integrated manufacturing, but it flourished in the climate of separate establishments to be found in Philadelphia and Paterson. There, wages were the highest, and value added, despite reliance on spoon dyeing and tubmen, was 95 percent of the level achieved in Yankee printworks, and profit per worker above all but the driving Fall River operations.

In hosiery and silk a different pattern is evident. Here Philadelphia firms paid above-average rates for labor but not the highest, yet due to their dominance of seasonal knitgoods markets and silk specialties, had the top value added among comparable sites. Both New York and Paterson firms combined staple and fashion output in silks, whereas Cohoes and Milwaukee produced common-grade knitted underwear, not the multicolored hose and decorated jerseys that flowed from Philadelphia. In wool and worsted, Philadelphia's returns show the effect of mixing independent spinners with single-function weaving mills and partly integrated firms. Lowell, whose woolen mills were led by the venerable Middlesex Company, had in 1888 fewer than 5,000 independent spindles on wool and worsted combined, whereas Philadelphia had eight firms in this category operating above 100,000 spindles.[63] With the single exception of wages for silk workers, Philadelphia was above the all-cities average in every category of the five sectors for which a national mean could be calculated. The bulk centers, Lowell, Lawrence, Manchester, Holyoke, and Fall River, appear nine times in Table 3.5. Of these twenty-seven figures, ten are above the all-cities average, one duplicates it, and sixteen fall below. On balance, Philadelphia textile workers contributed more to value and profit and were among the best paid factory operatives in the industry nationally.

By way of reinforcing the claim that capital in the textile trades' flexible sectors and sites was more productive in 1890 than investments in bulk-oriented cities and mills, Table 3.6 presents an additional measure, the ratio of production value to fixed capital (i.e., land, buildings, and machinery). This latter calculation represents a simple effort to exclude the possible effects of double-counting stock (finished and in process) both as output and as a component of the live-assets division of capital invested in the firm (see Note to Table 3.4). Again, the bulk centers, with much larger commitments in plant and technology yielding staple goods of small wholesale value, lagged well behind successful flexible specialists in Philadelphia, Paterson, Providence, and New York.[64]

[63] *TMD (1888)*, pp. 64–5, 129–53.
[64] *Report: 1890, Part II*, pp. 744–5.

Table 3.6. *Ratio of product value to fixed capital, Philadelphia and selected cities, six sectors, 1890*

Sector	Product Value/ Fixed Capital	Index Phila. = 100	Sector	Product Value/ Fixed Capital	Index
Cotton goods			*Dye finish*		
Philadelphia	2.51	100	Philadelphia	1.58	100
Lowell	1.58	63	Lowell	.69	44
Lawrence	1.13	45	Lawrence	1.18	75
Manchester	1.48	59	Fall River	1.06	67
Fall River	1.00	40	Paterson	2.63	166
Hose-knit			*Silk*		
Philadelphia	3.94	100	Philadelphia	4.25	100
Cohoes	2.69	68	New York City	4.30	101
Milwaukee	3.47	88	Paterson	4.36	103
Wool			*Worsted*		
Philadelphia	3.44	100	Philadelphia	3.08	100
Lowell	1.89	55	Lawrence	2.05	66
Holyoke	1.86	54	Providence	3.00	97

Source: Department of the Interior, Census Office, *Report on Manufacturing. . .1890, Part II: Statistics of Cities*, Washington, 1895.

In situating major sectors of the Philadelphia textile trades in the context
of comparable production centers, nothing has been yet presented with
regard to the carpet division. The main reason for this is that eastern competitors were generally the only carpet plant in cities like Hartford or Lowell.
Census reports lumped sectors with fewer than three firms with "All other
industries" to preserve confidentiality. In only one case is there printed data
concerning one of the giant firms, but that data (for Yonkers, New York,
the home of the auction-crazed Alexander Smith company and two other
tiny mills) illustrates why Philadelphia carpet men were anxious for the
future. Smith led the carpet business toward a version of the mixed output
strategy that would so threaten Philadelphia's format for production. The
company ran full year after year, stopping only for the customary semiannual
week to make repairs and take stock. In 1890, on a capital of just under $3
million, Smith achieved 2.7 turns with nearly $8 million in output versus
the 1.5 turns accomplished in Philadelphia ($22 million product, $14 million
capital). Its return to total capital (51 percent) was more than double the
Philadelphians' 20 percent, and profit on production was likewise sharply
higher (19 percent vs. 13 percent). In the composition of their workforces
and wage structures lay one key to this differential. At Philadelphia over half
the carpet workers were adult men, earning on average $501 yearly, whereas
Smith's employees were only one-third male and were paid a higher rate,
$543. It was with women workers that the Yonkers firm solidified its route
to accumulation. Over two thousand women were there engaged at $283
yearly income; women workers in the Philadelphia carpet trades took home
a third more ($371). This wage gap and Smith's increasing focus on the
higher grades of carpeting (Brussels, moquettes, Wiltons), gradually eliminating the cheaper ingrains, brought its wage costs down to 18 percent of
product value versus 23 percent in Philadelphia. Going upscale in product
lines at a savings of several hundred thousand dollars over what a comparable
output would have cost at Philadelphia wages redoubled the returns to
Alexander Smith while its periodic auctions both cleared the warehouses
and leveled pricing pressures at its eastern rivals and Philadelphia mills
alike.[65]

So long as population expanded at a considerable rate fed by immigration,
housing construction followed apace, and the national trend toward rising
real income led new buyers into the carpet retailers' rooms, the troubling
implications of the Smith strategy would produce grumbling, but not serial
bankruptcies. However, in the depression that followed the 1893 economic
crisis, a third of Philadelphia's carpet firms would topple over. Those survivors most sensitive to the movements of the trade pushed out from ingrains

[65] Ibid., pp. 630–3.

into new classes of goods; those who stuck to their familiar tasks exhausted themselves by chasing falling prices and shrinking markets through recourse to cheaper materials and wage cuts. Flexible production in the carpet trades was not undercut by standardized bulk goods, circa 1890–1920, but by an adaptation toward "flexible mass production" in David Hounshell's apt phrasing. Markets and tastes remained heterogeneous; the era of plain floor coverings for suburban developments and office complexes was a generation away. But in the Yonkers mills lay the germ of ruin.

Despite the troubling implications of the carpet situation, the rest of Philadelphia's textile sectors saw only a rosy-hued horizon in the early 1890s. Profits were strong, tariffs high, markets expanding. A rising level of sophistication in dress and in the use of furnishing textiles on floors, walls, windows, and sofas expanded demand for Philadelphia plushes, curtains, upholstery, and lace. Labor was "quiet and silent." The manufacturers were "fraternizing as they never did before."[66] Yet the Philadelphia system of flexible production would shortly be put to the test of depression with the return of the despised Grover Cleveland to the presidency, the financial crisis of the following year, and the renewal of attacks, this time successful, on the tariff structure local proprietors had so carefully helped craft. Between the Columbian Exposition and the St. Louis World's Fair, the industry would lurch from crisis to crisis before emerging from conflict and confusion into its era of greatest achievement.

[66] *MRIR* 21(1888): 440.

4

From crisis to crisis, 1893–1904

Spring business has been of a most cautious and conservative character, buyers feeling their way; not anticipating wants to any extent until the wants of the trade are more generally disclosed . . . It is generally conceded that . . . orders placed in 1893 for spring goods now in hands of manufacturers have been less than 50 per cent of the previous year . . . No special lines or makes will have the call for this year's trade.

Textile Record of America, January 1894, p. 57.

Manufacturers are in a sea of bewilderment and are drifting along like derelicts.

Manufacturers' Review and Industrial Record, May 1894, p. 267.

Gloom settled over the Manufacturers' Club when the outcome of the 1892 presidential race became clear. Low-tariff Grover Cleveland again assumed the leadership position that had slipped from his grasp four years earlier, and worse, a "radical" majority hostile to manufacturing interests now controlled the House of Representatives. Though the lull in business that generally accompanied national elections had not occurred that fall, the textile trade's response to the Democratic victory was immediate. A "feeling of uncertainty" was most marked in the knitting sectors, where by December the *Manufacturers' Review* reported mills "countermanding orders for machinery" and buyers cancelling "orders for goods for future delivery." Philadelphia hosiers suffered from "the blues" for they much feared "the results of a probable change in the tariff" to the advantage of fiercely competitive German imports. Were these political auguries not dismal enough, the rising price of cotton added its measure of woe to the scene. Fabric and knitting firms had booked orders for spring, basing their prices on a September cost of just over seven cents per pound for "middling upland," a common grade of cotton around whose price the values of finer or coarser varieties fluctuated. By December, middling upland was selling at 9⅜ cents, having touched ten amid a rash of speculation. Increasing by one-third in three months, "high cotton" spelled losses for firms who had not bought supplies well ahead for their spring lines. Integrated firms that had secured a year's cotton through dealings at or before the harvest would profit by the inevitable rise in goods prices, unless they too were sold ahead, in which case only normal margins

Figure 6. Kensington, looking north from the roof of the Bromley Carpet Mills, 1912. (Courtesy of the Pennsylvania Historical and Museum Commission.)

could be expected. But for companies (like most of those active in Phila-delphia) that bought yarn as needed or, having their own spindles, called for raw cotton a few bales at a time, the implications were ugly. They could not anticipate that jobbers and retailers would accept changes in prices previously negotiated. As the *Review* commented, "somebody undoubtedly will be the loser..., and it will not be the buyers."[1] Thus in Philadelphia, before the spring gold outflow signaled the 1893 depression's onset, many a discouraging word was muttered by those local millmen disappointed with the electorate and "middled" by the price squeeze that loomed ahead.

The new year brought a temporary brightening. The market for goods quickly recovered from the election drawback; retailers had experienced a

---

[1] *Manufacturers Review and Industrial Record* 25(1892): 589, 725, 727, 787, 793, 797, 807 (hereafter *MRIR*). The Senate was thought to be more amenable to high rates, an assumption that proved only partly correct.

record "holiday trade" that exhausted their stocks and precipitated a rush of new orders. Though importers were supplying a good portion of the hosiery demand, in the fabric division prospects had "never been more favorable" with both Philadelphia woolen and Fall River cotton mills sold well ahead "through March and April." Moreover, a flurry of short strikes in carpet firms were settled without serious difficulty. Spinners of both cotton and woolen yarns advanced their prices more than enough to compensate for increased rates for materials, seeking to enhance profitability, which they claimed had not been satisfactory "for some years." Fears about immediate changes in the tariff were also allayed by March, for no substantive action could be foreseen for at least another year. Yet just as the effects of these adjustments were being savored, distressing news from the money markets began to accumulate.[2]

The first tremor came with the announcement that the January 1893 international gold account was negative to the tune of $13 million, information that caused "some disquietude in speculative circles." February bank clearings were well above those for 1892, but "considerable anxiety was felt in regard to the continuance of heavy gold shipments." In March collections began to be "a trifle slow," credit commenced to tighten, Charles Spencer's venerable Germantown hosiery firm failed, and the Gays' carpet mills sought the protection of incorporation. By late April, it was plain that the gold drain had made inroads on the treasury reserve, a development that "had a somewhat demoralizing influence on business in general." As interest rates rose, cotton fell back below eight cents, the money market "fluctuated wildly and the tone of nervousness" spread from speculative to the more respectable channels of trade. Others followed Spencer into bankruptcies whose "immediate causes...are too great expansion of business and the unexpected tightness in the money market." Observers assured one another that no crash was impending: "The time for panics has long since passed. We may and do have depression in business, but no panic."[3]

With the credit contraction came a "sudden" falling off of orders, a closer scrutiny of acceptances, and word that local banks were "protecting" only their regular, well-known customers, taking very little outside commercial paper. By mid-May, Germantown was "extremely quiet," half the workers having been laid off. Renewed complaints about being forced to issue long credits to secure orders surfaced among manufacturers who sold direct. Meanwhile, outlying firms that had run stock were rumored to be sacrificing their staple goods to raise cash, depressing price levels. The early summer brought a deepening of the decline. Philadelphia mills closed for a long

[2] Ibid., 26(1893): 35, 101, 111, 169; Gay Daybook, January 1893.
[3] MRIR 26(1893): 97, 167, 241, 287, 315, 325.

holiday (Decoration Day). "The day was perhaps never so generally observed, which clearly indicates that business is not very pressing." As call
loan rates soared toward 25 percent and commercial paper became "at times
practically unsalable," millmen struggled "to avert the suspension of their
entire plants by laying off the employees one room at a time, hoping that
trade will take a change."[4]

Local charities geared up their modest resources to ameliorate the worst
cases of privation in the Kensington district, for "the idleness of so many
thousands . . . was not anticipated by the workers themselves, and being taken
unawares, they soon found themselves in want." As a bitter winter unfolded,
buyers proved "indifferent" to the new styles for spring 1894, leaving the
Philadelphia trades "somewhat crippled" while imports, especially of knits,
seemed less affected. Earlier efforts to minimize the crisis gave way to
exaggerated statements and sharp hostility to foreign producers and tariff
meddlers. At year's end, the *Review's* Philadelphia correspondent estimated
100,000 regional textile workers were idle. Nine-tenths of all textile machinery was "absolutely at a standstill." In a characteristic proprietary formulation, the strain this collapse put on the social relations of production
was expressed thus:

> It is certainly a disheartening condition of things for a manufacturer
> who has built up a large business and has established around him a
> hundred or more families, to be obliged to shut down his mills in order
> that a foreign manufacturer and his poorly paid workmen may find a
> market in this country.[5]

Worse, the draft tariff reform bill had at last appeared with provisions
"sweeping and radical enough . . . to justify the apprehensions" of the most
fearful protectionist. The long siege of the mid-1890s had opened. For the
next four years, every harbinger of revival was closely attended, every failure
mourned. The toll was heavy, particularly on textile workers, whose earnings
suffered from the downward spiral of defensive competition and for whom
the steady swings of seasonality were replaced by long stretches of under-
and unemployment.[6]

The importance of the 1890s depression to the restructuring of American
manufacturing has long been recognized, especially as a spur to the intense
merger movement that commenced after the middle of the decade and lasted
through 1902. For Naomi Lamoreaux, the great consolidation was not simply
a natural result of heavy investment, circa 1880–93, in "large scale industry,"
a rational effort to increase sectoral efficiency. Rather, "a particular con-

[4] Ibid., 26(1893): 315, 325, 383, 393, 395, 445, 457.
[5] Ibid., 26(1893): 521, 587, 593, 653, 723, 733, 790.
[6] Ibid., 26(1893): 593, 719, 785.

junction of circumstances – specifically the simultaneous rapid expansion of many capital-intensive industries in the early 1890s followed by the deep depression of 1893 – gave rise to abnormally serious price wars and consequently to the great merger movement."[7] Examining specifically the tin-plate and paper industries, Lamoreaux found by 1890 a group of firms in each division that "were large, mass-production enterprises whose heavy capital investments gave rise to new forms of competitive behavior – an emphasis on 'running full' and a neglect of product differentiation."[8] Whereas specialty tin-plate and fine-writing-paper firms responded to the crisis by attempting to protect prices and scale back output, the bulk-oriented firms, burdened with high fixed costs, hammered at one another by cutting prices and struggling to preserve their individual shares of a contracting market. These competitive forays collectively wrecked profitability and cleared the path for mergers that would rationalize competition, markets, and production. As her interest lay with the consolidators, Lamoreaux did not follow the later activities of the flexible specialists in plate and paper, a task that will be taken up here with regard to the textile trades. Her findings – that in specialty subsectors "output declined in accordance with demand; prices fell, but not excessively . . . ; and the burdens of curtailment were spread throughout the industry" – suggest lines of inquiry for a parallel review of depression responses by batch and bulk components of the textile industry, in and beyond Philadelphia.[9]

Neo-Marxist scholars also are concerned with the structural ramifications of crises like that of the 1890s. David Harvey views them as the product of "underlying contradictions" in the accumulation process, "irrational rationalizers" that can transform not only production, exchange, distribution, and consumption practices but also "institutional structures." Harvey conceptualizes them as "partial," "switching," and "global" crises of growing scale. The first are essentially local or confined to a sector or region, and like the mid-1880s Philadelphia contests are "capable of being resolved" through expedient institutional development of the sort that yielded the Manufacturers' Club and the Textile School. Switching crises are more general, like the 1893 collapse, and generate "a major reorganization and restructuring" of the sort Lamoreaux details. Global shocks, like the 1930s depression, seem to threaten the very roots of capitalism as a system.[10] Though as we shall see, the Great Depression served to deepen the difficulties of Philadelphians already in trouble, it is here worth considering the impacts of a

---

[7] Naomi Lamoraux, *The Great Merger Movement in American Business, 1898–1904*, New York, 1985, p. 12.

[8] Ibid., p. 46.   [9] Ibid., pp. 26–7.

[10] David Harvey, *The Urbanization of Capital*, Baltimore, 1985, pp. 11–13.

second-order crisis on their flexible production system. In what ways were production, exchange, distribution, and consumption altered in the region's textile trades? What institutional shifts, relocations, or reorganizations represented responses to economic gloom?

4.1. The regional textile system in 1893

To begin with an outline of Philadelphia textiles' sectoral and locational pattern before the crunch may be useful. Table 4.1 presents the distribution of firms for 1893. Note the diminished number of active firms since Lorin Blodget's city census of 1882. Two-thirds of the shrinkage occurred in carpets, signaling the extinguishing of several hundred hand loom shops. In the other sectors, the smaller 1893 numbers may well reflect the more comprehensive coverage of census enumerators versus trade directory compilers. Blodget was obsessively thorough in his 1882 effort, as it was a response to a serious undercount of industrial firms during the 1880 federal census. The 1890 census reported above seven hundred textile companies in Philadelphia; doubtless some of the smaller firms were not included in the 1894 textile directory. Still the numerical shrinkage in carpets accentuates the solidity of the fabric sector, revitalized by the developing plush, upholstery, curtain, and lace subdivisions.

Geographically, Kensington stands out as even more the focal point of city textile production than it had been in 1882 (56 percent vs. 45 percent of all firms). It had successfully negotiated a reorientation toward the rising novelties, as increases in firms handling weaving, spinning, and dyeing partly offset the loss of over a hundred carpet hand shops. Intensified commercial use had pressed manufacturers out of the Old City business district and the end of hand frame work had reduced Germantown's complement of knitting firms. Similarly, all but five of the seventy-one carpet shops in Spring Garden and the Northeast had expired, accounting for most of the change in these areas. Manayunk, on the other hand, had long been a power mill center, and little alteration was there observable. The overall decline in firm numbers did imply an increase in average firm size, at least insofar as this may be estimated from returns to the 1890 manufacturing census. Total 1882 employment was nearly identical to the 1890 count, a bit over 57,000, but mean employment per firm rose from 63 to 80 in eight years, substantial but still a far cry from the average of 929 workers per firm for Lowell and 697 for Lawrence in the latter year.[11]

---

[11] Calculated from figures given in Department of the Interior, Census Office, *Report on Manufacturing Industries in the United States at the Eleventh Census: 1890, Part II: Statistics of Cities*, Washington, D.C., 1895, pp. 286–91, 310–17; and Table 3.3, *supra*.

Table 4.1. *Textile firms, by sector and district, Philadelphia, 1893, with 1882 totals*

	Woven goods	Carpets	Hose-knit	Dye-finish	Spinning	Misc.	Total 1893	Total 1882
Kensington	105	85	62	55	32	12	351	410
Manayunk	15	1	2	3	16	2	39	42
Germantown	6	1	37	1	12	3	60	101 [a]
Frankford	19	1	2	9	5	2	38	(187) [a]
North Central	18	4	10	6	4	2	44	
S. & W. Phila.	23	4	2	1	6	1	37	69
Northern Liberties	6	2	9	6	2	0	25	29
Old City	14	1	12	0	2	2	31	72
Total 1893	206	99	136	81	79	24	625	
Total 1882	204	316	167	95	96	32		910

[a] In *Proprietary Capitalism*, the districts here represented by Frankford and North Central were differently bounded as Northeast Philadelphia and Spring Garden. For this study, all of North Philadelphia below Frankford Creek and east of Kensington was added to Spring Garden, forming the North Central area. Totals of the two cover the same area in 1893 as in 1882.

Sources: *Textile Manufacturers' Directory of the United States and Canada: 1894*, New York, 1894; Scranton, *Proprietary Capitalism*, Table 9.1. (Information for 1894 Directory was collected in 1893.)

To ascertain the distribution of this employment across the city districts, directory listings were linked with the reports of Pennsylvania's factory inspectors for 1893, the results of this effort being offered in Table 4.2. Though only 61 percent of firms could be matched with employment data issued by the state, they accounted for over 50,000 workers, certainly four-fifths or more of those engaged in 1893. As might be expected, the missing group were quite small firms, as was evident from inspection of machinery listings in their textile directory entries and from the fact that average employment at those mills visited by inspectors was 133, well above the 1890 mean. The very poor linkage in dyeing (12 of 81, or 15 percent) reflects the inspectors' mandate to guard the working conditions of women and children under sixteen. In 1890, adult males comprised 94 percent of dyehouse workforces; having no employees in the critical categories, most dyeworks fell outside the law's provisions.[12]

The spatial specificity of sectors and districts is plain from Table 4.2's figures, as are certain continuities. Manayunk focused on fabrics from its antebellum beginnings, and as the century's end neared, 97 percent of its textile workers produced woven goods or the yarns to weave them. Germantown's knitting tradition continued to dominate there, whereas nine-tenths of the city's carpet jobs lay in Kensington, the district in which the trade's origins lay. Kensington had far outpaced Germantown in knitting, as its nexus of spinners and dyers eased the entry of the "garret" competitors about whom veteran millmen complained. In the years since Blodget's 1882 count, Kensington's share of local textile employment had advanced from 41 percent to above 50 percent, as continuing agglomeration in the area's most vital factory district yielded a greater concentration of firms and jobs than in previous decades. The melange of new starts and midsize operations in curtains and other fancy work, together with older worsted companies, made Kensington the leader in woven goods as well as the other six divisions portrayed in the table.

Two aspects of the accumulation strategy practiced in Philadelphia textiles emerge from the 1893 data – information on the extent of integration and the use of commission agents by local firms. Table 4.3 offers a spatial view of the distribution of mills and workers that were involved in fully integrated production (spinning, dyeing, and fabrication) and those engaging "houses" for selling their goods. As might be expected, integration was infrequent, representing but 5 percent of linked and 3 percent of all firms in the directory. These companies were vastly larger than average (mean employment = 497)

---

[12] *Fourth Annual Report of the Factory Inspector of the Commonwealth of Pennsylvania* (1893), Harrisburg, PA, 1894, pp. 58–61; *Report on Manufacturing at the Eleventh Census, Part II*, pp. 438–41.

Table 4.2. Employment in textiles by sector and district, Philadelphia, 1893

	Woven goods	Carpets	Hose-knit	Dye-finish	Spinning	Misc.	Total	N_f Link	N_f Tot.
Kensington	7,111	10,491	5,360	604	1,491	967	26,024	208	351
Manayunk	5,712	69	12	81	1,105	38	7,017	38	39
Germantown	565	60	1,840	0	385	0	2,850	35	60
Frankford	977	373	360	218	776	430	3,134	25	38
North Central	940	464	1,381	15	1,473	15	4,288	30	44
S.&W. Phila.	2,937	0	0	0	946	530	4,413	24	37
Northern Liberties	779	23	408	60	138	0	1,408	9	25
Old City	392	0	450	31	439	12	1,324	11	31
Total Workers	19,413	11,480	9,811	1,009	6,753	1,992	50,458	380	625
Total firms link	134	72	85	12	65	12		380	
Total firms TD	206	99	136	81	79	24			625
% Linked	65	73	63	15	82	50		61	

Note: N_f = number of firms.
Sources: Fourth Annual Report of the Factory Inspector of the Commonwealth of Pennsylvania, 1893, Harrisburg, PA, 1894; Textile Manufacturers' Directory of the United States and Canada: 1894–95, New York, 1894.

Table 4.3. *Integration and agency selling, Philadelphia textiles, 1893, firms and workers, by district*

	Integration		Agents		Both
	N_f	N_w	N_f	N_w	N_f
Kensington	4	1,900	32	7,544	2
Manayunk	6	4,938	5	4,852	5
Germantown	1	60	6	783	—
Frankford	3	484	3	291	—
North Central	—	—	6	1,214	—
S. & W. Phila.	4	1,567	8	1,585	3
Northern Liberties	—	—	1	23	—
Old City	—	—	2	275	—
Totals	18	8,949	62	16,567	10
Linked f.& w. (%)	5	18	16	33	
All firms (%)	3		10		
Average workforce		497		269	

Note: N_f = number of firms, N_w = number of workers.
Source: *Fourth Annual Report of the Factory Inspector of the Commonwealth of Pennsylvania, 1893*, Harrisburg, PA, 1894; *Textile Manufacturers' Directory of the United States and Canada: 1894–95*, New York, 1894.

and were most likely to be found in Manayunk (Dobson, Schofield) or in outlying districts where independent contractors were few or absent (South and West Philadelphia, the Northeast beyond Frankford). If the 245 small firms not linked are kept in mind, it appears that roughly 85 percent of textile employment was located in "separate establishments" citywide, over 90 percent in the Kensington heartland. These figures provide a late-nineteenth-century benchmark against which later to examine stability or shifts in production orientation through twentieth-century data.

Considerably more common was marketing through commission agents, an arrangement present in 16 percent of linked firms representing a third of the fifty thousand workers included in the factory inspectors' tours. Ten integrated firms used agents, which, given Doak's experience, was perhaps a consequence of the production demands on proprietors that multidepartment operations entailed. There was no dramatic spatial or sectoral concentration of this choice of sales technique; several spinners and one dyeworks contracted with agents to solicit trade for their goods and services outside the network of Philadelphia opportunities. However, agency selling did attract firms appreciably larger than the 1893 average (269 workers vs. 133), it again being a plausible technique for relieving the strains of scale in a context of family and partnership management. Direct sales to jobbers, retailers, and downstream users of intermediate products and services were far more general in Philadelphia than in bulk-production centers like Lowell or Lawrence. There in the same year, thirty of fifty-five cotton and woolen companies relied on selling agents, a group representing over 80 percent of the workforce.[13] Flexible production, direct selling, and partial-process manufacturing went hand in hand in Philadelphia's urban textile districts in the 1890s, just as a bulk orientation, commission agents, and integration were complementary elsewhere. A processual question immediately arises. As information on integration and marketing by Philadelphia firms is fragmentary before 1880, does the 1893 snapshot represent a moment in a trend toward or away from comprehensive production and agency selling? Twentieth-century information, which will be developed in later chapters, will indicate the direction and the character of such change.

Thus far, this study has undertaken comparisons between Philadelphia and other urban textile centers along the Atlantic corridor, but has rarely strayed beyond the city borders into the immediate region surrounding the metropolis. As issues of capital relocation and the suburbanization of both population and industry are hardly tangential to the long-term course of flexible production in Philadelphia, a parallel sketch of textile manufacturing in Bucks, Chester, Delaware, and Montgomery counties in 1893 may be inserted here. Though much of the nineteenth-century industrial activity in these largely rural environs was located along rushing streams whose waterpower drove the mills of Rockdale and similar hamlets, three riverside towns gradually developed as the focal points for textile and other manufacturing: along the Delaware, Bristol, in Bucks County to the north of Philadelphia, and Chester, in Delaware County to the south; and on the Schuylkill, Norristown in Montgomery County to the northwest. Across the narrow Schuylkill from Norristown lay Bridgeport, with which it formed an economic if not a political partnership. These centers held half the textile firms visited by inspectors (42 of 81) and 56 percent of the workers documented in 1893. The rough employment balance between town and country mills reflects the continued operation of sizable rural firms like Rhodes Brothers at Aston (Delco), 414 workers, and David Trainer and Sons at Trainer (Delco), 477 workers. The older country mills were family-based like their city cousins, but they rarely were oriented to specialty production, competing instead with bulk corporate enterprises generating similar "Tickings, Stripes,

---

[13] *Textile Manufacturers' Directory of the United States and Canada: 1894–95*, New York, 1894, pp. 63–5, 226–8 (hereafter *TMD*).

Table 4.4. *Outlying textile manufacturing, Bucks, Montgomery, and Delaware Counties, 1893, firms and workers*

	N_f Total	N_l Total	Bucks	Workers Montgomery	Delaware	Total
Woven goods	53	44	620	3,002	5,658	9,280
Carpets	4	3	473	157	0	630
Knit goods	23	13	601	710	68	1,379
Dye-finish	1	1	0	0	915	915
Spinning	22	17	275	221	1,229	1,725
Misc.	8	4	29	0	50	79
Totals	111	82	1,998	4,090	7,920	14,008

Note: N_f = number of firms. N_l = number of firms linked.
No factory inspector returns for Chester County in 1893; directory listings give eleven small firms located there.
Source: Fourth Annual Report of the Factory Inspector of the Commonwealth of Pennsylvania, 1893, Harrisburg, PA, 1894; *Textile Manufacturers' Directory of the United States and Canada: 1894–5*, New York, 1894.

Denims," or "Plaids, Checks, Shirtings, and Osnaburgs," low-priced, long-run staple cotton goods. Factories in the satellite centers presented a more mixed picture. Those that stemmed from the *urban* reinvestment of *rural* mill capital, like the Trainers' Patterson Mills in Chester, kept to staple lines, in this case bed tickings. Others that drew on city capital accumulations sent *outward* remained consistent with the specialty character of their Philadelphia origins, as with Thomas Leedom's carpet and William and Joseph Grundy's worsted mills at Bristol.[14] Yet as a whole, the textile industry in the suburban counties resembled that of Manayunk or South and West Philadelphia far more than the formations of Kensington or the Yankee corporate cities, as Table 4.4 suggests.

Two-thirds of all workers in outlying towns and townships produced woven goods (vs. 37 percent for Philadelphia), the main concentration for which was Chester and its adjacent townships. None of the new subsectors that were invigorating Kensington were present; nor were there many giant mills of the Lowell or Dobson type; only James Lees's Bridgeport woolen mills and the Eddystone Printworks, the single entry in the dyeing and finishing sector, had over 750 workers. The principal carpet mill was Leedom's transplant from Kensington, accounting for three-quarters of sub-

[14] *Fourth Annual Report, Factory Inspector: 1893*; *TMD (1894–95)*, pp. 152–5, 266–70; Anthony Wallace, *Rockdale*, New York, 1978.

urban jobs in that sector. A group of spinners sold yarn to the city, especially those devoting their attention to worsted and carpet yarns in nearby Darby and upriver at Bristol and Norristown. Montgomery County held a modest cluster of new hosiery and underwear knitters, running staple rather than fashion goods. Overall, textile employment in the neighboring counties represented 22 percent of the regional total, but average firm size (173) was appreciably larger than in Philadelphia.

One reason for this scale difference was the greater incidence of full integration outside the city, necessitated by the lack of sufficient spatial concentration to support independent spinners and dyeworks, and once in place inhibiting their establishment. Of the forty-three linked woven-goods firms, twenty-seven (63 percent) were integrated, more than in all of Philadelphia. They, together with Leedom's full-process carpet plant, employed 55 percent of all textile operatives in the four counties beyond the city (vs. 18 percent within it). Again conditioned both by the staple character of their product and their location, marketing for three-quarters of the weaving plants was through commission houses. Of all suburban mills, half used agents; their operations involved 9,007 employees (64 percent), or about twice the city proportion of the workforce. Finally, both absolutely and relatively, more outlying mills had incorporated by 1893 than had city firms. Whereas even major Philadelphia figures like Sevill Schofield and James Doak continued to rely on proprietary and partnership organization, the Trainers, Croziers, and Rhodeses all took advantage of Pennsylvania's 1874 incorporation act. One-third of the eighty-one linked outliers were closely held public companies in 1893, reporting above $5 million in capital and employing 40 percent of the four-county workforce, whereas in Philadelphia only twenty-three firms had taken the same step, listing capital of $3.5 million and engaging 12 percent of the urban operatives.[15] Without making the facile assumption that incorporation automatically signals "progressive" business practices, and in the absence of detailed research into the leading families of Delaware and Montgomery counties, it is possible to suggest that the ready acceptance of incorporation by these veteran family firms had to do both with earlier experiences of failure or near-bankruptcy and their possession of considerable nonindustrial holdings, especially land, which after 1874 could be shielded from creditors under the provisions of incorporation. Urban manufacturers in Philadelphia usually had few possessions outside

[15] All calculations from *TMD (1894–95)* and *Fourth Annual Report, Factory Inspector: 1893*. The Eddystone Printworks, removed by the Simpson family from its location along the Schuylkill when Fairmount Park was formed in the 1870s, was not a contract or job dyer. The firm, like others in Fall River or Providence, handled the printing of gray goods on large drum printers and was eventually joined with the Bancroft family mills of Wilmington, Delaware.

their businesses other than their homes, as bankruptcy files reveal.[16] (The family home was often held in the wife's name to separate it from assets of firm members.) Until the 1893 contraction, the lure of incorporation was weak, for flexible firms in the city had well-tried and distinctive mechanisms to protect themselves from crises (piecemeal materials buying, running on orders, seasonal layoffs, etc.). These different approaches to accumulation and differing contexts for production help account for the gap between urban and outlying rates of incorporation.

In sum, Philadelphia textile capitalism in the 1890s may readily be distinguished both from the production format in Yankee corporate cities and from the family corporations in staple trades arrayed beyond its county lines. Some out-migrating local millmen carried Philadelphia's seasonal market responsiveness to their exurban locations, but in its continuous embarkation on new lines of production and alertness to fashion trends, Philadelphia textiles had more in common with the manufacturing styles of Paterson and Providence than with its immediate periphery. The jacquard loom was as valued by Paterson's silk firms as it was by Quaker City carpet and damask mills; Paterson fortunes were erected on its proprietors' anticipation of demand for ribbon silks, brocades, and dress goods and on the skills of its weavers and dyers. Providence, already a center of profitability for worsted suitings and dress fabrics, would soon become the second pole of the developing American lace manufacture, which would not become rooted in Lawrence or Fall River. Flexible production was an urban phenomenon, but not one common to all urban textile complexes.

Bulk-production commitments in the northern crescent from Fall River to Manchester led most cotton firms to envision the advantages of southern annexes or of weaving finer grades of print cloths, not the risks of curtain, damask, or lace manufacture. The wool-using corporations in the great New England centers could reap little from southern developments. They would, as the 1890s crisis matured, speculate about mergers to limit competition in staple goods; or more troubling for Philadelphia, they would move steadily toward adding lines of fancies to their basic overcoatings and plain goods. In carpets, where what Lamoreaux terms "dominant firm" price leadership was already in evidence before the slump, the next decade would feature the first two in a series of stepwise mergers that enhanced the power of eastern competitors vis-à-vis smaller individual firms. These developments form the shifting scenery against which movements in Philadelphia generated a range of restructurings within the batch components of the textile industry.

---

[16] U.S. District Court, Eastern District of Pennsylvania, Bankruptcy Docket and Case Files, 1898–1902, National Archives and Records Service Branch, Philadelphia. Specific use of individual files will be made later in this and following chapters.

In the balance of this chapter, we shall first view the impact of the depression at the firm level in Philadelphia textiles. Then topically, we will proceed to assess the indications of spatial and sectoral restructuring in the years surrounding the turn of the century. After a pause to contrast the Philadelphia pattern with short sketches of developments in Paterson and New England, a second structural portrait of regional textile sectors will be brought forward, using data for 1899, one year after the signs of economic revival ceased to be tentative. With the recovery, Philadelphia workers were quick to find their voices, pressing a series of demands that, when resisted, culminated in new bursts of organizational activism and eventually in the general textile strike of 1903, an extended and extraordinary struggle whose roots may be traced to the depression-induced shifts.

That labor turmoil should attend such efforts is understandable for, in Harvey's phrasing, "accumulation and class struggle . . . are integral to each other and have to be regarded as different sides of the same coin – different windows through which to view the totality of capitalist activity."[17] We shall glance through these windows, and through assembling fragments of the jigsaw from disparate sources, will set out the dynamic sequence through which flexible production in the Philadelphia textile system proceeded from a market crisis in 1893–4 through an era of reorientation to a labor crisis in 1903.

4.2. Depression and the family firm:
Park Carpets, 1893–1894

Late in February 1893, James Gay noted in his daybook: "Every loom running full of orders. The consumption is so great that DH [dye-house] cannot keep up." Though he little suspected at the time, Gay would not be able to make such an observation again for nearly two years. His brother had just returned from a winter week's vacation at Atlantic City; the mill had run all day through Washington's birthday, and the partners looked forward to hiking the price of their products in the near future. After an effort by several Kensington carpet mills to secure a one-quarter cent cut in weavers' rates had failed, the Gays and seven other millmen gathered to discuss an advance of ingrain prices for the coming season. Their dependence on the eastern majors taking the lead was clear. The group "agree[d] if Lowell and Hartford would [advance] to have 28 manufacturers bind themselves to advance under oath 2 ½ cents per yard." Notwithstanding the fractured syntax, the situation here described was the inverse of that

---

[17] Harvey, *Urbanization of Capital*, p. 1.

which had provoked the failed 1890 attempt to gain broad assent to a reduction in output. Even if the big mills down East put out an increase, individual proprietors felt they could not rely on one another to follow, as their individual interests in booking orders to keep their looms occupied would be enhanced by enlarging the gap between their charges and those of the majors, even if unit profits would not be swelled. No formal pool existed, but recurrent ad hoc committees tried to create working arrangements that would coordinate responses to movements by their giant rivals. In this case, the market break intervened; at the end of May, the Lowell list appeared, no advance having made made, and the coalition vaporized as each firm scrambled after diminishing opportunities.[18]

Consistent with the pattern Lamoreaux presented for the fine paper sector, the reaction of Philadelphia carpet specialists was a gradual cutback as orders dwindled. Though more ragged than it would have been had they colluded, the slowdown by manufacturers "acting individually" in response to slackening demand was little different from what might have been expected had they "acted in concert."[19] In July, Park went on three-quarter time (45 hours weekly) as 42 of its 160 looms were idle, thus spreading the remaining orders across a longer span. James Gay added that "Ivins, Dietz and Metzger, Judge's, Sam'l White and a few others also running on ¾ time." At month's end, both Alexander Smith and the Lowell Company shut down entirely, having operated at full capacity as long as possible before cutting the steam and sending everyone home.

The orders being completed that summer had been secured in April from Marshall Field and John Pray and Co., the jobbers who had accounted for most of Park's sales in recent years. Once it became plain in June that no price increase could be anticipated and that indeed profitability might be severely impaired, the Gays made another attempt to reduce the rate for weaving on Crompton looms to the four and three-quarters cents paid on the faster Murklands. "Called Crompton weavers together and told them on and after Monday 5th inst., beginning a new 'Pay,' we proposed to make the price of weaving . . . 4 ¾ cent in place of 5 cent. They objected and in order to have not strike or trouble, we withdrew our proposition." These traditional interchanges with their hands not having gained the proprietors' object, the Gays framed a fall-back strategy. "We intend to stop that floor entirely when each loom's warp is out, and then start it up and offer each weaver individually 4 ¾ cent per yard."[20] This failed as well, for when the

[18] John Gay's Sons, Park Carpet Mills, "Daybook, 1876–1916," Historical Society of Pennsylvania, February 20–5, March 2, May 26, 1893 (hereafter cited as Gay Daybook).
[19] Lamoreaux, *Merger Movement*, p. 26.
[20] Gay Daybook, June 3, 1893 (both quotes).

last of the Cromptons was shut down June 26, none of the weavers would break with his or her fellow workers and accept fresh work at the reduction. Word of the dispute reached the daily press, but the *Ledger* reported the Gays' denying there was really anything devious going on. They asserted that the layoff of thirty-four employees "was simply caused by overproduction and the unsatisfactory condition of the money market." Credit was surely tight (Marshall Field refused to advance Park anything against the booked orders unless 8 percent interest was paid), but the Gays' defensiveness reflected an effort to conceal their individualizing stratagem. Referring to the early June conference at which a cut was spurned by the weavers, one of the brothers explained self-righteously:

> As we were very busy nothing more was said of the matter, now that trade is so dull and we were forced to reduce the production they imagine, I suppose, that we are taking revenge, but such is not the case. When I tell you that we have men here that started with the firm in 1868 and never lost a day through any fault of the firm, and others who came as boys and have risen to the head positions in the different departments, you will see that we have treated them fairly and still intend to do so.[21]

This ringing of the changes on proprietary virtue was a face-saving smoke-screen. Through it, the perceptive observer could see that a standoff had resulted from this round in the continuous fencing between capital and labor, a routine of contest basic to the dynamic of the accumulation process. Before their orders ran out, Park's owners had tried to force the rate down for the present and the future, but the Crompton weavers had defended their price, just as the mill masters had tried to defend theirs in the product market.

By early August, prospects for any additional sales for the fall season had evaporated. When Field wrote "asking us to cancel everything" ordered but not yet woven, the Gays determined to stop each of the fifty-five looms still operating "when their marks come up," when the roll in process was completed. Three days later, all but two looms had run out; the mill closed midmorning Friday, August 11. Trouble soon materialized at the marketing end of the business. Two weeks after the general shutdown, Park shipped John Pray the balance of his fall carpets, some six hundred rolls. Receiving them, Pray replied that as he had not "ordered them forward" just as yet, no payment would be made to the mill until there was some call for the

---

[21] *Public Ledger*, June 28, 1893. The reason for the long gap between the Gays' decision June 3 and the shutdown of the last of the looms June 26 is that their warp beams generally held about 1,000 yards of "ground" yarn, enough for eight rolls of carpet, or roughly four weeks' production. Field's interest charges are noted in Gay Daybook, July 24, 1893.

goods from the jobbers' clients. Little wonder that James Gay described the carpet trade as "demoralized." By mid-September, Kensington grew silent, Park and "every other mill in town closed of any size. The Lowell Co. is shut tight." Still, the spring season lay ahead and its possibilities had to be probed. Park Mills cut back the range of its new patterns, selecting "only 277 samples, . . . 48 designs," then called back the Crompton weavers who, after nearly three idle months, accepted the quarter-cent reduction. With labor more tractable and the samples completed after a week's work, the mill stopped again.[22]

Between August and early October, Pray had called forth only a fifth of the stalled rolls, leaving the Gays fearing that "they intend to cancel them on us." This concern was allayed October 20 when the jobber agreed to take the balance of his commitment, but only if the bill was dated ahead to December 1, further delaying the flow of funds to the factory. Orders from the Boston and Chicago trips were a cause of serious disappointment, for Field's and Pray's requirements for spring 1894 together were less than a thousand rolls, enough to keep the mill running full for less than a month. Quickly, James Gay tried to explore other avenues for sales, visiting Arnold Constable in New York and Hecht and Son in Baltimore within the week. Amid rumors that the majors were preparing to lower their price lists, Park started twenty-eight looms on spring orders in early November, roughly one-sixth of the firm's capacity. Both deterioration of their once-reliable marketing contacts and downward pricing pressures threatened the Gays' accumulation strategy. As other carpet men were facing a similar misery, another convocation of manufacturers assembled to discuss means by which part of the slump's effects could be displaced through additional labor rate reductions.[23]

The results of the meeting were far from satisfactory to the Gays, as "it was agreed to not change the prices of weaving" except for a quarter-cent cut on cheaper grades. To their minds, this was far too feeble an action, and their accord with the group's decision lasted but five days. On November 18, they called in enough workers to staff fifty-one looms, offering rates one-half to three-quarters of a cent below the revised scale. Only six weavers appeared, perhaps representing the rest, and declined to accept these terms. Three days later, "a Committee of Weavers" returned to find the Gays sticking to their scale, thus work was suspended "indefinitely." Room bosses

---

[22] Gay Daybook, August 2–27, September 18–20, 1893. Parallel with the Park stoppage, James Gay noted the closing of Dornan's and Judge's mills "and many others" and the failures of two small firms (Daybook, September 4, 11, 1893).

[23] *MRIR* 26(1893): 725; Gay Daybook, September 29, October 9, 22–31, November 1, 1893.

and the head dyer were kept on at full or partial salaries to preserve the production supervisory team, but in early December the partners "discharged" their office clerk, saving eight dollars a week thereby.

The December 9 release of the Lowell list made such expense reductions seem trivial, for the Massachusetts corporation lowered its basic ingrain line by five cents a yard, (from sixty to fifty-five cents) and offered an additional five-cent cut to clients ordering forty or more rolls at a time. Again the Kensington carpet proprietors assembled, this time launching a signature campaign to secure owners' bonds that they would install a 15 percent across-the-board pay reduction in response to Lowell's 8–16 percent drop. As total labor costs were but one-fourth of the price of a fifty cent per yard carpet, this maneuver would compensate for only two cents of the Lowell reduction; falling yarn prices would have to be counted on for three cents or more if any semblance of profitability was to be achieved. Even so, the effort, like its predecessors, failed to gather in the two thousand looms its promoters believed would make it effective. "Joe Taylor, Caves, Jackson and Holmes would not sign and it was abandoned."[24]

Whether due to "possessive individualism" or sheer cussedness, gathering a critical mass sufficient to experiment with common trade or labor policies was extravagantly difficult in flexible sectors like carpets in which neither product nor technology were uniform, in which labor rates and marketing practices varied as did capital and credit accessibility and the character of raw materials (there being at least two dozen varieties of carpet wools). Yet each crisis led some manufacturers to confront collectively the contingency enveloping their operations and to repeat these frustrating exercises, attempting to convince their brethren that unity would bring greater control over their fates. To their dismay, except when labor tensions mounted or the tariff was threatened by blackguards, Philadelphia textile capitalists strove "to sail on their own bottoms," acting self-consciously but individually to advance the interests of their enterprises. In their inability even in crisis to bridge the conflict between the goals of separate capitals and the collective consequences of individual actions (excess capacity, overproduction) we may perceive a fundamental contradiction in the accumulation process for flexible producers. In other industries, the merger movement would address this contradiction through standardization of process and products, managerial reorganizations, rationalization of operations, liquidation of surplus capacity,

[24] Gay Daybook, November 13, 27, December 2, 9–20, 1893. The manufacturers' visiting committee consisted of Robert Dornan, James Gay, William Henderson, John Hamilton, and several of the Bromley brothers. Costs of a 50 cent carpet in 1890 were roughly as follows: materials – 30 cents; wages and salaries – 13 cents; power, supplies, insurance, et al. – 2 cents (leaving a profit of 5 cents). Calculated from figures on *Report on Manufacturing (1890) Part II*, pp. 438–41.

and oligopolistic pricing. In the bulk staple section of the textile industry (cotton duck, thread) mergers attempted to achieve an analogous transformation. But virtually every element of the batch, flexible system militated against such drives: uneven and unpredictable demand, relative ease of entry, the absence of significant scale economies, mind-boggling product differentiation. Like members of a fraternity, Philadelphia textile men shared social, economic, and cultural bonds, talked out their difficulties with one another, but ultimately were left to struggle with them alone, preserving an autonomy they cherished and clung to.

Given the collapse of collective action, and beyond carpets the utterly depressed state of knitting and fabrics, dyeing, and spinning, the *Manufacturers' Review* correspondent in Philadelphia soberly reported in December 1893 that "quiet talks . . . at the Manufacturers' Club in this city are not of a kind calculated to fill the mind with hope." Christmas was certainly bleak at Park Mills; the Gays even reduced their annual holiday gifts to room bosses from five to three dollars. Given the dispute about rates for weaving, which fits neither the standard strike or lockout formula, little had been accomplished on the meager orders that had been harvested. Significantly, though thousands were unemployed in Kensington, the Gays made no attempt to hire new weavers willing to accept their terms. Instead, once Robert Dornan had held a factory assembly the day after Christmas and persuaded his employees to accept a 10 percent reduction, the brothers copied his offer, which represented roughly a half-cent shrinkage in the price list for weaving, yielding a one to one and a half cent selling price reduction. (Winders, dyers, and loom fixers worked by the hour, burlers and spoolers by the piece and pound respectively, complicating the figuring somewhat.) Exempted from the reduction were the office staff, the four room bosses, and the machinist, fireman, and watchman. All but the most critical workers accepted the new deal immediately, the weavers, dyers, and loom fixers objecting. The day after New Year's the first two groups "called" to accept the proposal; the fixers counterproposed a one dollar weekly reduction. This being refused "they retired to the wareroom to talk it over and came into the office again" agreeing to the 10 percent. The mill promptly started on a forty-hour basis (two-thirds time); within a week, sixty-six looms were activated. Park was running again, but at 40 percent of its capacity.[25]

The Gays had not been able to avoid pressure from their jobbers to match Lowell's five cents; 13-pair Park ingrains were soon shipped at forty-seven and a half cents per yard, two and a half cents beneath Lowell's bulk rate. "Fearing countermands" for its pitiful pile of orders, the firm got ninety-eight looms in action January 20 and commanded they be operated the full

[25] *MRIR* 26(1893): 793; Gay Daybook, December 23–31, 1893, January 2, 3, 10, 1894.

sixty-hour week. No additional demand for ingrains trickled in during February; six looms were stopped March 1, thirty-four were down a week later. In a pickle, the Gays departed from their customary path, deciding "to make up a stock of about 100 Rolls in order to keep a certain number of looms running, picking out the good sellers of this Spring Season and making 3 pc. each." Their resolve soon failed, though, as an appended note records that Park "only made abt. 20 pc." By late April, a mere fifteen looms were still filling warps.[26]

What are we to make of this depression sequence? First and most obviously, their actions in the winter of 1893–4 suggest that the Gays adhered to the customs of proprietary relationships with their factory force. Even in the crisis months, they offered terms for work, grumbled when they were refused, but did not treat their operatives as interchangeable parts by seeking replacements, although volunteers could be expected to be eager for recalcitrant workers' places in the 1893 situation. Burned by their first attempt to make a separate peace in mid-November, disgruntled at the failure of the coalition effort in December, they waited for someone else to find a settling point, then echoed the form and content of his arrangement. Like Dornan, the Gays called a mill meeting to "talk over the trade." (How was this done? Some two hundred Kensington workers were involved; whether notices were posted and idle workers who routinely visited the mill saw them, or whether room bosses were sent off to chase after their respective charges, was not recorded.) Their proffered terms were less draconic than the November set; and after two further days of discussions and meetings, ending in the fixers' wareroom conference, they were accepted with dignity if not enthusiasm. On the other hand, some favoritism may well have operated in the owners' selection of those who would staff the mill; for even with a hundred looms running, its capacity was little over half utilized.

The abrupt and short-lived entry into making stock is here particularly intriguing. Running full to get rolls out the door and avoid cancellations was of value to proprietors and workers alike, but the departure into weaving without orders was a move that worked to labor's advantage at the risk of proprietary losses. That this was stopped even before the modest total of a hundred rolls was completed expresses the Gays' ambivalence in the face of new risks on one side and their publicly stated concern for their workers' welfare on the other. The struggle to realize a profit was not an indifferent market transaction, but was infused with social meaning and personal history that added ambiguity to the Gays' calculations. Crusty as they were, the brothers were forced in the crisis to operate on the soft boundary turf between self-interest and a risk-laden mutuality. They ventured briefly into a novel

[26] Gay Daybook, January 20, March 2, 9, 10, 1894.

production tactic, then backed away and tried to provide work for their employees and profits for themselves by revolutionizing their marketing strategy, an effort which we will review shortly.

The carpet market was so wretched in spring 1894 that on reflection, making stock seemed more foolish than beating the bushes for orders. How bad was it? Though detailed production records for Park Mills have not survived, the Daybook contains summaries of spring season orders as of April 1, 1891, and March 16, 1894, clearly good and terrible years. Table 4.5 reproduces these entries, illustrating that sales for spring 1894 were barely one-quarter of what they had been for the same season in 1891 (27.5 percent). Reports of the depression emphasized its severe effects in the West; bank failures were heavily concentrated beyond Pittsburgh, but were infrequent in the Northeast. This pattern was echoed in the near-total collapse of sales to Chicago's Marshall Field, a difference of over 2,800 rolls or about $140,000 in values, in the two years. By contrast, the Boston connection fell off only by half, a relatively good showing considering the western sag. Equally deflating, deliveries to clients outside the big two had collapsed both absolutely (from 625 to 119 rolls) and relatively (from 11 to 8 percent of sales). Though three new buyers had been enlisted, including Constable but not Hecht, four of the old accounts had been closed. Moreover, half of the ten grades sold in 1891 found no takers in 1894, the cheapest lines being wiped out as working-class and rural demand vanished. The reference to Field's high interest rates for advances against orders booked suggests that Park at times had used this channel for working capital, and no mention of promissory notes appears in the daybook. Park Mills was not likely in financial danger; bankruptcy did not loom ahead, but the company was stuck in as deep a trough as it had ever experienced.

The way out was far from clear, but as looms were shut down in March and April, the Gays made four assertive moves to regain their momentum. Screwing up their courage, believing that "the bottom has been reached on yarns of all kinds," they contacted their spinners to order supplies ahead for the fall. As Field had selected but 444 rolls for the coming season, Park informed the midwestern giant that they would fill the order if these carpets were "confined to ... the City of Chicago *only*." This tactic interlocked with their third gambit, engaging Theo Steenson, terminated in February 1893, and F. G. Rogers "to travel as salesmen for us." Finally, the firm pulled a power play on their Boston jobbers, who had given the Gays such an anxious time the previous fall. On April 17, they wrote Pray and Co. severing their "connection" summarily. This brought immediate results, a telegram the 19th "to come to Boston to fix up the trouble." Thomas Gay promptly complied, bringing back "a contract signed by them to use 2500 pc. in the Fall 1894" and an order based on available samples for "771 pc. Park Wors.

Table 4.5. *Park Mills order book, spring season, 1891 and 1894, number of rolls by client and type of carpet*

	1891	1894	
Marshall Field (Chicago)			
Parks, 13-pair	1,590	560	
Leicestershire, 13	336	—	
Cotton chenille, 13	447	31	
Parks, 12-pair	452	154	
Cotton chenille, 12	429	—	
Fine, 16-pair	96	1	
Plain (no pair given)	77	50	
Plain cotton chenille	6	—	
9-pair	1	—	
Union B, 10-pair	140	—	
	3,574	796	
John Pray and Co. (Boston)			
Parks, 13-pair	1,221	562	
"customers" (?)	47	12	
Cotton chenille	4	17	(16-pair)
	1,272	591	
Boyd Harley (unspecified)	149	—	
Boyd White & Co. (")	124	—	
F. van S.	260	—	
Gimbel	41	—	
Stark	51	27	
	625	27	
Finch		60	
Taft Weller and Co.		8	
Arnold Constable		24	
		92	
Totals	5,471	1,506	
Shipped already	(4,086) (Apr. 1)	(1,313)	(Mar. 16)
To be made	(1,385)	(193)	

Source: Park Mills Daybook, Historical Society of Pennsylvania.

Extras." Their actions between May and November strongly suggest that the Gays had taken a decision to plunge into more direct selling to escape their crippling dependence on the two jobbing houses. They opened their own New York office, hiring "Mr. Van Deventer," whose New Jersey carpet business had failed in 1893, to represent them as of May 22. When Pray returned fifty rolls rejected as "greasy," Park "refused to sell [to] them hereafter," negotiating with Boston's W. W. Corson to send travelers through New England visiting retailers with samples "on a 3% basis." They added to their own sales force Mr. A. C. Green "formerly of Pray's," Fred Senior, and P. K. Riefsnyder, dividing up the territory outside New England. Thus in November, Steenson started out from Louisville and Senior from Dubuque to cover the Midwest and Green commenced a westward tour across New York from Binghamton just a few days after Van Deventer opened the line for spring 1895 in New York. The results were gratifying. By the end of the month, warps were installed in 120 looms "and orders coming in so fast will start on full time 12/3." Two weeks later, Park Mills reached full capacity (160 looms and 60 hours) for "the first time since the panic struck the country in June 1893." Hearing a report that Field's wholesaling agents were offering Park ingrains to midwestern stores at a penny less than the mill's own salesmen, the Gays dropped Field entirely and entered 1895 wholly reliant on traveling road men for its marketing.[27]

Here at the firm level is evidence of the restructuring to which Harvey refers. The standard maneuvers employed in slipping markets (rate cuts, output restriction) were understood after some false starts to be inadequate steps. The Gays' machinery was for the most part less than eight years old; switching to another branch of the carpet manufacture through acquiring looms for tapestry or Wiltons would entail a serious capital sacrifice. Relocating to some low-wage district outside Philadelphia was even more laughable; skilled carpet weavers were not to be had in the anthracite districts where Paterson silk throwers were establishing annexes and employing miners' wives and daughters. Further, the resale value of their Kensington plant was diminished in depression markets. Less radical options – becoming rentiers by leasing buildings and machinery to some eager superintendent who sought to commence on his own account – were foreclosed by the tight credit environment. Who in his right mind would supply working capital to such a venture? Thus the Gays scrapped their previous marketing strategy, even though their experience with Steenson and Riefsnyder's direct selling to retailers had been a disappointment two years earlier. If other firms shared Park's evaluation, that marketing was the weakest link in their struggle to realize a surplus, salesmen would become progressively more visible in the Philadelphia textile trades and the use of commission houses might decline. Yet it should not be presumed that there would be a singular response to the general crisis. Reactions may take diverse forms: changing subsectors, adding to or subtracting from integration, driving for fresh novelties through technological adoptions or innovations, abandoning textiles or manufacturing

[27] Ibid., March 31–April 28, May 17–30, July 14, 16, September 15, November 12, 27, December 13, 14, 18, 1894. The Field cutoff indicates Park was selling to retailers at prices higher than those quoted to jobbers.

generally to reinvest capital in more fertile fields, relocation to low-skill, cheap-labor sites with a consequent reorientation toward simple staples rather than demanding specialties. All these and perhaps other shifts beyond the routine of seasonal adjustments may be expected as indicators of a diffuse but general reaction to the extended crisis of the 1890s and will bear comparison with the contemporary initiatives taken by bulk producers in New England and fellow flexible batch operators in Paterson's silk trade.

4.3. Crisis responses in Philadelphia textiles

A. Production and distribution

Though they are valuable touchstones, Harvey's main categories of "production, distribution, exchange and consumption" do not exhaust the set of areas in which manufacturers may fashion restructuring, responsive strategies. In addition, some attention needs to be given to matters "external" to factory and market, yet impinging on them. As he notes, politics and institutional development are collective activities, entwined both with one another and with production relations. "Departures" of various sorts also reflect reactions to both opportunities and frustrations within the industrial system. From relocations and creation of branch plants to passively attending the gradual failure of long-established firms, they are consequences of diverse responses at the individual and firm level to the long crisis. Through surveying shifts along this roster of possibilities during the 1890s, the character and extent of developments in proprietary Philadelphia may be sketched as a new century draws near.

In production, the most emphatic reorientation was undertaken by the Bromley carpet clan. Despite declining markets and unfavorable tariff conditions, the Bromleys determined that their entry into the lace curtain manufacture (ca. 1891) should be pursued, not abandoned. During the depression, they added machinery to the existing plant and embarked on production of bobbinet, a finer quality of lace goods than had hitherto been produced in the United States. By 1899, the family had both devoted the entirety of one of its several firms to lace curtain production and had spun off a second lace company (Lehigh Manufacturing) in a newly erected five-story factory at Fourth Street and Lehigh Avenue.[28] As late as 1894, there

---

[28] *Official American Textile Directory, 1899–1900*, New York, 1900, pp. 193, 204 (hereafter *OATD*); *American Wool and Cotton Reporter* 12(1898): 5 (hereafter *AWCR*). Both carpets and curtains had been made at W. H. Bromley in 1894 (*TMD 1894–95*, p. 131), as the Bromleys purchased lace curtain equipment from the failing Horner Brothers (*AWCR* 13[1899]: 491).

were but nine lace manufacturers in the nation, a field far less crowded than their customary carpet trade. Given the Bromleys' considerable resources, purchasing lace machines from Britain for three to five thousand dollars each (ten times the cost of an ingrain power loom) was a step they could confidently feel few others would be able to imitate. This strategy was both consistent with and an ornament on earlier Bromley patterns. Since the 1870s, the family had pursued a diversified approach to carpet production, adding Brussels and Wilton machinery to their basic ingrain lines. When power looms for much-demanded Smyrna carpets were developed in the late 1880s, the Bromleys adopted them readily. However, a major commitment to the technically demanding lace business was their first step beyond floor coverings. Significantly, in the crisis years, they did not draw back from the venture, but instead deepened their investment in it.[29]

Other local carpet manufacturers recognized their ingrain specialty was threatened by more than the immediate contraction and put fresh capital into adapting their mills. At John Gay's Sons, a group of looms were fitted for production of a "Flemish Tapestry" carpet; at least a dozen firms phased out their ingrain looms, replacing them with machinery for higher-grade Wiltons or "taps." The introduction of a Crompton loom to weave wide "Art Square" ingrain rugs, rather than twenty-seven to thirty-six inch rolls that had to be stitched together, brought quick Philadelphia adoptions in the later 1890s. Moreover, several table cover and chenille curtain firms, notably Barnes and Beyer and David Stroud, moved *into* carpet production by 1899, running fine "Khorasan" imitation orientals as a supplement to their previous lines. In hosiery, the Philadelphia Knitting Mills added machinery for full-fashioned cotton and silk stockings to their seamless capacity, a harbinger of things to come. Facing tariff revision in 1894, and having evidently studied the schedules closely, William Bilyeu, its proprietor, explained that under the new bill he would "be able to throw [our] banner to the breeze and defy the Germans." The strategy worked, as the firm reported capital of $100,000 and 125 workers five years later, but declined to reveal its capacity. Another indication that Bilyeu had installed the multisection German full-fashioned machines, introduced in the late 1880s, was that nearly half his employees were men. In seamless mills, women outnumbered male workers three or four to one, but the new and technologically complex equipment was assigned to male knitters supposedly more skilled and mechanically more proficient than their female colleagues.[30]

[29] *The Manufacturer*, 7(March 31, 1894), p. 7.
[30] *TMD, 1888*, p. 146; *TMD 1894–95*, p. 313; *Davisons Blue Book for 1899–1900* (New York, 1900), pp. 214, 225; *OATD, 1899–1900*, pp. 189, 208, 211; PA. Factory Inspector, *Report: 1899* (Harrisburg, 1900), p. 100; *MRIR* 27(1894): 423; *AWCR* 12(1898): 157.

These switches within and across sectors were shifts among specialty lines, each being facilitated by a technical advance and a personal reading of the future course of the firm's present product area against the political backdrop of tariff alteration. These same components were present in the enthusiasm with which new devices for "automatic" knitting of seamless hosiery were received in the mid-1890s, but here the innovation led toward bulk production of staple hosiery rather than seasonal fancies. Imports of German plain goods, which had had the advantages of low-wage labor and longer familiarity with fast dyeing, drove wholesale prices for black cotton half-hose down from about one dollar twenty-five cents per dozen pairs (1885) to nearly a dollar by 1893. The depression promised further deflation, but adoption of three-quarter or fully automatic knitting machines provided an escape hatch for domestic hosiers concentrated in Philadelphia. The older half automatics used in the 1880s were assigned two to a worker and each yielded five to six dozen pairs daily (240–288 stockings) at a per dozen labor cost of eight to nine cents. The "full" automatics brought forward in the early 1890s stretched out the labor force to six machines per worker, but did not perform a number of "time-consuming" hand operations. Thus though total per worker output rose to twenty-one dozen pairs daily, and labor cost fell to five cents per dozen, output per machine actually dropped from about five to three and a half dozen daily. With the introduction of the Branson Automatic in 1894, built by one of Philadelphia's many knitting machinery works, a further advance was made. The hand steps were embodied in a set of adjusting devices, activated briefly by the operative in the course of machine knitting. With this "three-fourths" system, a worker could tend only five rather than six machines, but incorporation of the detail steps in machine attachments smoothed the flow of work, increasing total production. With the Branson, a day's work yielded thirty dozen pairs at a labor cost of three and a half cents per dozen. As Branson averred in announcing this device in June 1894, it was a knitter created "to meet the exigencies of the times."[31]

The appeal of these highly productive knitters was quickly acknowledged. At summer's end, the *Manufacturers' Review*'s Philadelphia correspondent explained: "Two years ago German hosiery at $1.05 drove us out of the market, for do what we would we could not get below $1.25. Our mechanics, however, have perfected machines that are quick producers." Though there was naturally a lag in purchase and activation of Branson's and competing automatics, by 1897 the German tide had been stemmed. Well before the

Brown Brothers and Aberle also moved into full-fashioned hosiery, spending $150,000 for new machinery in 1894 (*MRIR* 27[1894]: 577).
[31] *The Manufacturer* 7(June 16, 1894): 10. It was reported in 1895 that Branson had sold 27,000 knitting machines since 1880 (*Textile World* 8 [February 1895]: 19).

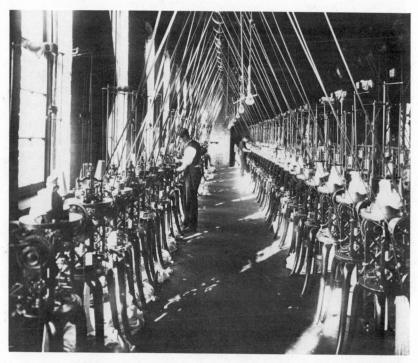

Figure 7. "Automatic" knitters running seamless hosiery, with overhead shaft drive, at the Brown-Aberle Company, Kensington, circa 1910. (Courtesy of the Pennsylvania Historical and Museum Commission.)

Dingley tariff was enacted, providing more satisfactory duty schedules under the new McKinley administration, trade observers reported that the quantity of German hosiery imported had become "insignificant." The short-run cost involved in this push to meet and best German competition on plain goods was a neglect of fancies. Indeed depression demand for high-style, expensive hose was somewhat muted. The market dominance achieved by plain and steadily more inexpensive hose "narrow[ed] the scope of manufacturing." The consequence of the output explosion was a further, downward rush in prices, aided in no small way by the continuing drop of cotton (to five cents in the late 1890s), and an intensification of competition. Writing of fast blacks in 1897, a columnist exclaimed:

> And how cheap they are turned out for the populace who expect today (and their expectations do not fail), to get as good value for a half-dime as they once obtained for two and a half times the money. One would think that fast black seamless cotton, full hose (seamless

toe) at 67 ½ cents per dozen, was a bargain for the million. But think of the fast black seamless (cut toe) at 47 ½ cents.[32]

Fast black hose, an unsteady novelty in the early 1880s given the erratic quality of then current dyeing skills, had become a staple little more than a decade later. Manufacturers who would pursue the staple lines had to cut costs closely, as the wide market and simplified manufacturing process brought on by technical advance encouraged rural new starts as well as extraurban relocations. The majority, remaining in Philadelphia, welcomed the return of prosperity, and renewed interest in fancies. In that sphere, "the multitude of designs ... stripes, plaids, checks, etc. – gives a great opportunity for diversified production."[33]

Another production-centered shift inspired by the deflationary trend was the dramatic increase in the use of shoddy – fibers derived from shredding woolen garments, rags, and carpets – in place of new wool. During the wool boom that flourished in tandem with the Civil War cotton famine, shoddy was heavily relied on to stretch available raw material supplies, and at times to defraud government contractors.[34] Due to the rapid deterioration of such goods, postwar American use of shoddy was soon confined to the lowest grades of blankets and similar cheap stuffs. Europeans continued skillfully to blend modest amounts of shoddy in spinning yarns for their fabrics, a tactic which helped them breach protectionist barriers. The 1890s depression again brought Americans into the hunt for cheapness. As Philadelphia's Channing Smith put it in 1903:

> The great success of the English and German manufacturers have [*sic*] been that they knew how to work shoddy better than we did, and even with the tariff their goods had the call, for it was impossible for any customs official or expert to determine what is old and what is new wool in a fabric. But times have changed, and the one benefit the American manufacturer gained from the hard times of 1893, was how to work shoddy. He had to do it to survive.[35]

In the midst of the slump, a manufacturer growled, "There never before was one half the shoddy used in any one year that has been used ... in 1895. The fact is, that we find our European neighbors teaching us one lesson – namely, how to make a most miserable piece of goods." Steady pressure

---

[32] *MRIR* 27(1894): 423; *AWCR* 11(1897): 154, 213.

[33] *AWCR* 11(1897): 213.

[34] See Philip Scranton, "An Immigrant Family and Industrial Enterprise," *Pennsylvania Magazine of History and Biography* 106(1982): 365–92, and idem, *Proprietary Capitalism*, New York, 1983, chapter 8.

[35] Channing Smith, "Shoddy: Its Use and Abuses," *Second Annual Report of the Alumni Association of the Philadelphia Textile School*, Philadelphia, 1903, p. 38.

came from distributors, jobbers, and clothiers demanding goods "they could sell at a price (a price below what [they] could be made for)." This forced a "deterioration of quality"; the goods delivered "were, in fact, shoddy." This cycle reinforced itself. By 1897, sellers' complaints about buyers' disdain for quality were legion: "You tell him that a certain fabric is an honest piece of goods – no shoddy, good in every respect – he will say; 'I don't care a rap for that... I can buy goods that *look* as well as yours ten cents a yard less.' "[36]

The drive to cheapen goods, through shoddy or other substitutions, spread from woolen fabrics and hosiery to the carpet trades. By 1899, a Philadelphia correspondent reported that 70 percent of all ingrain looms were running on cotton-wool mixed carpets, only 15 percent on the pure wool finer grades that had composed nine-tenths of Park Mills' production before the depression. It was regrettable that most new design ideas were in "the line of cheaper materials... made more largely than ever before of jute yarn." This had to be done in order "to meet the buyers' low offers." Even though better times had dawned, price rigidities remained a severe problem for manufacturers. Raw wool prices had bounded upwards in 1898, but both clothiers and department stores were reluctant to hike prices as yet, thus continuing "the incentives for manipulation." Apart from ruining the reputations of heavily adulterated goods (e.g., Kentucky jeans, which were replaced by heavy cotton denims for work clothes), the shoddy trick could rebound savagely were it played on government contracts.

In 1900, George Campbell's Dingley Mills in South Philadelphia received a surprise visit from two Quartermaster Corps inspectors that plunged the firm into bankruptcy within three weeks. Campbell had secured a contract for 15,000 blankets for the military, all new wool, at $3.23 each. Upon inspection of the delivered goods, the military detected a heavy admixture of shoddy, contrary to specifications. Despite his plea that "[t]here was absolutely no attempt to defraud the government," Campbell was exposed and soon "embarrassed." Local wool men estimated that the employment of shoddy would have added $10,000 to the profits from the $48,450 contract. Campbell had been low bidder on a federal call for 50,000 more blankets, but the quartermaster declined to confirm the award, and Campbell "assigned" a few days later. An emergency shift by embattled manufacturers in depressed markets, the adulteration of materials and production of "trash" goods had become a nagging sore point that would remain troublesome for

---

[36] *The Manufacturer* 8(November 9, 1895): 10; *AWCR* 11(1897): 411, 474 (emphasis added). The volume of imported shoddy rose from 1.1 million pounds for the first ten months of 1894 to 17.8 million pounds for the same period in 1895 (*Textile World* 9[January 1896]: 31).

decades. More important, it represented a production response to the growing role of clothiers and big stores as price setters, reflecting a subtle erosion of bargaining position by flexible manufacturers, some of whom were, as we shall later see, simultaneously facing an emerging encroachment from the bulk-production end of the trade.[37]

The foregoing discussion indicates that important aspects of production shifting were linked to market changes stemming from the depression. In focusing now more consciously on the distribution process, we will survey thematically the alterations in mills' selling practices and buyers' behavior across four main sectors – wool and worsted fabrics, carpets, upholstery and related specialties, and knit goods. Buyers' usual response to a tightening of consumers' purses had been to cut orders and sell out their current stock gradually, to avoid having incoming goods piling up in storerooms or jobbers' warehouses. As the depression extended, with only periodic spurts of revival in late 1894 and early 1896, a general change in their practices emerged. Before the Panic, Park Mills had long relied on sizable initial orders soon after showing its new samples each season; two-thirds or more of the rolls to be made were regularly booked through the Gays' Boston and Chicago trips in April and October. This too had been the experience of fancy woolen and worsted manufacturers, who expected to record as much as 90 percent of their orders in the first weeks after their seasons opened in August and February. (The longer lead times here, for spring and fall goods respectively, were necessary to provide several months for clothing cutters to work up garments for sale.) By the later 1890s, however, each season had been broken into two segments, the opening and the duplicate periods. At the openings, buyers of clothing fabrics, upholstery, furnishing goods, and knits rushed about ordering sample pieces of styles that took their fancy. These were gathered, compared, and among clothiers, turned into sample garments that were shown to reliable customers for their verdict. Only after this sequence had run its course, a process that took a month or two, did sizable orders

---

[37] *AWCR* 13(1899): 104, 151, 1465; 14(1900): 1512, 1571. Frank Bennett, the *AWCR*'s editor, observed in 1901 that "competition ... in wool products will be so keen as to place the mills constantly under the temptation to adulterate" (15[1901]: 1596). Worsted manufacturers had no shoddy option as the shredding of fabrics yielded only short-fiber wool, not the long-fiber staple needed for worsted yarn. Their response to calls for cheapness in the depression was an emphasis on cotton warp-worsteds, usually so labeled. However, at times long-staple combed cotton yarns were mixed with worsted yarn and the resulting fabric was sold as an all-worsted product. Cheapening the quality of chenille bedspreads was also credited with losing this line its middle-class trade in the 1890s (*AWCR* 11[1897]: 232). In fancy goods, samples were dyed with top-quality colorants, but goods ordered were dyed with cheaper ones, producing nasty controversies (*AWCR* 11[1897]: 345; also 13[1899]: 83). On Kentucky jeans, see *AWCR* 13(1899): 115.

appear for "duplication" of the styles that had at last been selected. In the process, manufacturers could do little but chew their nails and try to defend themselves from pricing pressures ("Take five cents off this suiting and I'll order thirty pieces").[38]

Apart from increasing the vulnerability of flexible manufacturers, this shift forced a change in selling practices. No longer were twice-a-year trips to New York sufficient to harvest a season's trade; instead a constant presence there was essential during the entirety of the duplicate period. If the firm could manage it, road men could snare orders in Cleveland and Peoria from retailers of piece goods, hose, and carpets as the New York scenario played along. Samples could as well be sent to sales agents ("reps") in major market centers such as Boston and Chicago, to men who worked on commission for a number of firms seeking to place goods in their regions. Jobbing houses followed the retailers' depression-era trend toward cutting the scale of stocks they were willing to hold for resale, relying instead upon manufacturers' eagerness for duplicate orders to yield rapid production of styles that found a ready demand. If placing one's goods in the hands of commission houses paved the royal road to ruin, as their goal was to move the goods at prices that might prove fatal to manufacturers, selling direct rapidly became more complex and trying for Philadelphia textile proprietors and their colleagues in Paterson or Providence. In knits, jobbers' panicky reluctance to buy for stock led manufacturers to rely on salesmen's visits to scattered retailers. In the carpet and upholstery sectors, trade journals by 1900 published long lists of salesmen and reps at the outset of the seasons, just as they began lugging their samples from station to store. But for firms oriented to the clothing trade, effective alternatives to New York and its anxieties were elusive.[39]

There was one clear benefit to this restructuring of buying patterns – it dramatically favored domestic producers over importers of European products. The latter were placed in a squeeze, for they were in no position to fill rush orders in the duplicate period unless they had already providentially imported just the right quantities of styles called for. Outside of the latest Lyon silks and Bradford high-line worsteds, which were sure to sell to the carriage trade, importers were drawn into a dangerous guessing game. The choice between stockpiling large deliveries or showing samples and cabling English mills to make goods for a transatlantic passage was an unwelcome

[38] *AWCR* 11(1897): 38; 13(1899): 241–2. Persistent market uncertainties triggered this commodity version of "hot potato," as all parties sought to avoid the risk of holding stocks when news of fresh economic disaster evaporated demand.

[39] *The Manufacturer* 9(August 9, 1896): 9; *Textile World* 8 (March 1895): 51; 9 (September 1896): 31; *AWCR* 11(1897): 38.

Figure 8. Direct selling of woolen and worsted fabrics, central Pennsylvania, circa 1910. Note the salesman's two trunks at center, the client sitting on one of them examining fabrics for use in overcoats of the style being modeled at left. (Courtesy of the Atwater Kent Museum.)

novelty. The increasing competence of American mills in styling and production of medium and fine goods, together with intensified time pressures, worked against the importers' interests. By late 1894, American firms poised for quick production were gathering the lion's share of duplicate orders.

The new buying patterns also spawned abuses that added other difficulties, but these were faced by all purveyors of seasonal textile styles.[40]

By 1897, millmen and agents expressed annoyance with several new marketing problems derived from the opening and duplicate sequence. Instead of purchasing full pieces (forty to fifty yards) at the initial style offering, clothiers and upholsterers had begun requesting yardage samples, just enough to make one suit or cover a chair. This maneuvering eventually reached bizarre proportions. A New York sales representative related this tale in 1899:

> I had a man come into the store the other day, . . . who wanted me to sell him a yard each of the various pieces of goods. I, of course, refused to consider such a thing. Goodness knows a sample piece order is small enough, but when it comes to buying or trying to buy a yard at a time, things have come to a pretty pass.[41]

Often in the opening weeks, so few sample pieces were ordered of a particular style that manufacturers could not run out a full warp of the goods. They thus notified the buyers through their sales office that the shortfall in demand precluded making up the sample lot. To guard against this, "clothiers have in many instances placed small orders with a number of agents for fabrics that are very similar in construction and appearance; thus, if one mill cannot give them the sample pieces desired, they hope to be able to satisfy themselves with one of the other fabrics." Another issue developed as a consequence of customers' diminished willingness to buy and hold stocks. Both sample and duplicate calls increasingly became "rush" orders. Manufacturers' rapid responsiveness to depression calls for any of their styles had reinforced a pattern which persisted even as business conditions improved.[42]

Not all clothiers, jobbers, and stores embraced the new buying techniques. Some continued to place sizable early orders, but adopted a new practice which brought bitter denunciations from manufacturers and their friends in the trade journals. Often just as a proprietor had gotten his looms running on a big lot of fancy worsteds or floral carpets, a telegram would arrive cancelling all or part of the contract. In 1896, a writer in the *Textile Manufacturers' Journal* explained:

> The cancellation of orders began in a small way a few years ago, and with some excuse or apology, or even request, in each case, but it soon became a regular and understood plan to which only feeble objection was made. One result . . . is that [salesmen and] agents are often misled

---

[40] *MRIR* 27(1894): 525; *AWCR* 11(1897): 154.
[41] *AWCR* 11(1897): 75; 13(1899): 358.   [42] Ibid., 11(1897): 214; 12(1898): 1009.

at the start of the season as to the probable demand and tendency of style, for buyers order freely, expecting to later revise their entire purchases.[43]

By 1898, this crippling counterpart to the sample and duplicate strategy had become "a crying evil," in the view of the *American Wool and Cotton Reporter*. An order was a contract after all; how could one party go back on a lawful agreement with impunity? The answer lay in the "scramble for business" since the onset of the depression. "The policy is for a mill to keep on the best of terms with every one who is, or may become a buyer of its products, submitting to present loss in the hope of future profit." Though the *Reporter* might suggest boards of arbitration or a blacklist of abusers, the reality of "keen" competition made it implausible that mills would "stand shoulder to shoulder." Thus as the decade closed, it became common to observe that early orders for woolens "will not be worth the paper they are written on if later better lines are shown by competitors for the same money." In combination, the two shifts in buyers' practices made salesmen gun shy. As duplicate purchases grew more dominant, large, early orders become so "infrequent that when [salesmen] do get one of moment, there is awakened within their breasts a fear of possible cancellations." Worse, once goods were finally delivered, buyers all too often filed claims for refunds on grounds that the quality of fabric or dyeing failed to match that of samples. This practice, also occasional in the previous decade when it annoyed James Doak, developed into a "menace"; for it was used as an end-of-season tactic by clothiers and stores that had bought goods beyond their needs. Allowing the claims only ensured that they would become routine; disregarding them hazarded the next season's business with the client.[44]

One result of these complications was that for mills using commission agencies, critical decisions in an unsteady marketing environment were being

[43] *Textile Manufacturer's Journal*, quoted in *The Manufacturer* 9(April 4, 1896): 11. In recent years, major research libraries have deaccessioned (dumped) hundreds of volumes of trade and technical journals from the late nineteenth and early twentieth century, evidently without realizing they held the last surviving long runs of these periodicals. In the course of research for this book, I found sadly that a half-dozen textile journals cited in the Union List of Serials had been discarded by libraries at major research universities. At this writing the extraordinary collection of the Franklin Institute Library has been disassembled, and a consortium of regional libraries has purchased thousands of its journal volumes on industrial and scientific affairs. The aforementioned losses make economic and labor historians' tasks the more difficult as rich and irretrievable sources disappear without a trace, but the preservation efforts of the Hagley Library, the Library Company of Philadelphia, and their consortium partners are thus made all the more praiseworthy.

[44] *AWCR* 12(1898): 466; 13(1899): 76, 270, 297, 358, 390. Goods were not returnable except for "cause," a matter of great importance in style-related sectors.

taken far from the mill among parties who often were not directly "inter-ested" in its prosperity. Though fresh designs fared badly early in the depres-sion, commission houses soon took the initiative and urged "their" mills to generate wide arrays of samples in hopes that a few would catch on. The costs of expanding design ranges nettled manufacturers, bringing angry re-sponses that urged mills to take selling into their own hands.

> Commission houses which have become fossilized must get out of the business... many of the mills have become disgusted with the selling agents, on account of the unreasonable demands for the large number and lines of samples which they ask the mill to make regardless of expense, decreased production or whether they will ever sell or not. The live mill... can sell its own goods direct, as most of the successful mills are now doing.

In carpets, the shift away from agents was most pronounced, and jobbers as well were discarded. Whereas ten Philadelphia carpet firms with some 4,350 workers marketed through commission houses in 1893, only five (with 767 workers) still did so six years later.[45] The chief defectors were the Bromleys, who dismissed their agent in order to form an "alliance" with the Worcester Carpet Company, opening a joint office in New York to take charge of the selling tasks of both firms. Department stores' growing com-mercial prominence played a role in this shift, for they began buying direct from the mills so as to "purchase at wholesale prices just the same as the jobber." In 1899, John Wanamaker placed a $40,000 duplicate order with Kensington's Stinson Brothers; making the 90,000 yards of carpet would keep the mill running full for a month or longer. Clothiers too sought to evade the jobbers' and commission houses' share of the wholesale price of piece goods. When a tailor wrote the *Reporter* in 1897 asking for a list of woolen and worsted firms that sold direct, the journal prepared one, sent it along, and promised in its columns to supply a duplicate to any other buyer seeking to contact manufacturers handling their own accounts.[46]

Several observations may be added about the implications of the trend toward direct selling and the new characteristics of buying. First, for makers of seasonal goods, taking direct responsibility for distribution was not nec-essarily cheaper than employing a "house." Textile School graduate Robert Francis explained that "to market... novelty patterns... may cost as high as 7 percent" of the sale price, equal to the top rate quoted for commission

---

[45] Figures drawn from linkages between Pennsylvania Factory Inspector's *Reports*, 1893, 1899 and *TMD* (1894–5); and *OATD* (1899–1900); *AWCR* 13(1899): 372.

[46] *AWCR* 11(1897): 75; 13(1899): 38, 248, 1214. Comprehensive urban department stores were reportedly forcing many independent carpet retailers to the wall by 1900 (*AWCR* 12[1898]: 5, 98).

house services.[47] The important difference was achieving control over pricing and immediate contact with customers (retailers, cutters) who might be two removes from the millmen if their goods passed from agent to jobber to "final hands." Second, direct selling was beyond the reach of small firms that could not sustain the expenses of their own New York offices and travelers. Here, particularly in knits and upholstery, the jobber remained prominent as an alternative to commission houses, along with independent "reps" who sold the lines of several firms at the manufacturers' prices. For the "reps' " efforts, 3 percent of order values was paid by the mill, which received neither the cash advances against goods delivered or the guarantees against bad accounts that commission houses provided their clients. These latter services, in tight credit markets, had drawing power for some Philadelphia firms during the depression, despite the risks of falling "into the hands" of commission houses. Still in 1899, firms with a sharply smaller proportion of the city textile workforce than in 1893 (20 vs. 33 percent) listed commission houses in the marketing category of trade directory entries. The consolidation of carpet demand in the hands of major jobbers and department stores had enabled mill operators in that sector to move firmly into direct selling. But the absence of a comparable development in upholstery, woolens and worsteds, and hosiery brought about forty new Philadelphia firms in these sectors to an expedient reliance on agents. Nonetheless, all observers acknowledged that by 1900 direct sales "represent[ed] the prevailing tendency" in textile marketing.[48]

Looking back to the predepression years in 1905, John Wood, owner of Spring Garden's Pequa Worsted Mills, pithily summarized the changes in distribution.

> Those were the days of ten-case orders, and now it is the three-yard sample piece. In those days the entire mill output would be sold in two days, and then one could go to Europe for the rest of the season, where now the entire sales force is sent forth to every crossroad and town – and with different results.[49]

Of the buyer, H. H. Bosworth added: "This gentleman's stomach is gradually getting weaker and weaker, and the manufacturer has to assume more risk every year. This is not right, and will not always continue, but the fact

---

[47] Robert Francis, "Marketing Textiles," *First Annual Report of the Alumni Association of the Philadelphia Textile School*, Philadelphia, 1902, pp. 46–8.

[48] Ibid.; figures drawn from linkages between Pennsylvania Factory Inspector's *Report (1899)*, Harrisburg, 1900, and *OATD* (1899–1900), Boston, 1899; see also John B. Thickeris, "The Selling Agency as a Factor in the Disposal of Textiles," *Fourth Annual Report, AAPTS* (1905), pp. 43–4.

[49] John P. Wood, "Remarks," *Fourth Annual Report, AAPTS* (1905), p. 36.

exists to-day and must not be ignored."[50] Bosworth was correct in his assessment of the early-twentieth-century situation, but his forecast was wrong. Heightened risk and increased vulnerability would plague flexible manufacturers in the ensuing decades. Pre-World War I prosperity masked for a time structural shifts in distribution relations that would cripple profitability and imperil the Philadelphia textile trades in the "buyer's market" of the 1920s.

B. *Exchange and consumption*

Issues of credit and finance, the terms of exchange, were another aspect of the manufacturing system that underwent alterations during the 1890s. The extension of long credits by Philadelphia manufacturers was halted by the 1893 money market contraction. The following spring, "instead of dating ahead six months, the rule now is two to four weeks." Proprietors had for years passed "big-worded resolutions" against long dating, but these condemnations had proven to be "ropes of sand." Thus "it was left to this depression to bring about a change." The shift to short dating put such business as could be had on a much firmer footing, as revenues would follow shipments in close order. However, in their individual desperation to chase any glimmers of fresh demand, local millmen gradually broke ranks. In midsummer 1894, "with the first favorable symptoms of the revival of business, postdating is heard of on a large scale." As orders were taken for immediate production, with invoices to be dated November 1, payment due in January 1895, "the old evil" was back in full force, "there being nothing to help or prevent it." By 1902, the terms of trade had further shifted to the buyers' advantage, as woolens selected for the fall season in January and delivered in March were not invoiced until July 1, with a 7 percent discount applying through November 1, when the full bill came due. From dating ahead four months in 1894, with the bill due in 60 days, the terms had advanced to dating ahead five or six months, with an additional 120 days available to settle the account at discount.[51]

More encouraging developments materialized on the other side of the credit front, collection. Under the commission house system, mills were forwarded advances covering two-thirds or more of the value of delivered goods, easing cash flow, though firms were charged interest on these sums until the account was cleared. Moreover, for an additional fee, agents guar-

[50] H. H. Bosworth, "Marketing the Product of the Small Mill," *Fifth Annual Report, AAPTS* (1906), p. 53.

[51] *MRIR* 27(1894): 213, 369; Francis, "Marketing," p. 46.

anteed collection and remittal of amounts owed for all goods sold through their efforts. Prices might be uncertain, but the flow of funds was sure. Although the coming vogue of direct selling represented a means to protect prices, cash-poor manufacturers needed real alternatives to the commission houses' financial backing. During the 1890s, as Philadelphia's Robert Francis detailed, firms selling direct contracted for replacement services with "banking concerns" that specialized in managing collections. For a fee of 2 ½ percent of invoice values, manufacturers secured from them both "guarantees" of payment as well as "advances when required . . . as in the case of the commission houses." Alternately, mills could arrange with "a credit indemnity company" for insurance against bad debts. Upon payment of $400 the company received a policy that covered losses up to $10,000, though the mill did have to absorb the first $1,800 of uncollectable accounts as a deductible. Such steps were taken "by many manufacturers selling direct."[52]

The use of promissory notes as a source of credit and working capital for manufacturers evidently resumed after the most worrisome days of 1893– 4, without serious loss to local banks. The Ninth National in Kensington, after all, never missed a dividend payment to its mill-owning shareholders during the decade. However, the needs of some large firms for working capital went beyond the ten to twenty thousand dollar levels acceptable to neighborhood and center-city banks. George Campbell, for instance, engaged the services of note brokers Bodine and Altemus (Philadelphia), Dix and Phyfe (New York), and Gartenlaub and Company (Chicago) to tap the national funds market. Such "commercial paper houses" had begun to appear in the 1880s, but no evidence of their use by Philadelphia textile proprietors has come to light before the late stages of the 1890s. Their role was to place unsecured promissory notes with distant banks holding idle funds. Such "single-name" paper was disproportionately taken up by midwestern and western banks, a "regional variation" that John James, a student of post-Civil War banking practices, has dubbed "a mystery." Campbell's borrowings in 1900 were recounted in the bankruptcy schedules he filed June 20, 1901. His Philadelphia broker had found takers for $315,000 in notes, his Wall Street agent had distributed $140,000 worth, and Gartenlaub in Chicago, $150,000. With regard to the $455,000 in paper distributed by his eastern brokers, Campbell stated that "the present holders therof are unknown to me." However, he did submit a list from Gartenlaub, showing that nine $5,000 notes had been absorbed by four Chicago banks and that twenty-one others were held by eighteen national banks scattered from LaCrosse, Wisconsin, to Mattoon, Illinois. The articulation of a national capital market made such interregional transfers readily available by 1900,

[52] Francis, "Marketing," pp. 47–8.

but Campbell's failure and the enormous losses it entailed showed the wisdom of W. S. Witham's 1898 warning to "country" banks: "Do not permit any loans to be made to anyone on single-name paper."[53]

It is impossible to say how extensive was manufacturers' involvement with the note-brokering function. None of the other major local textile firm failures recorded in the four years following the federal Bankruptcy Act involved comparable extraregional borrowing.[54] Still, given the presence of an important commercial paper house in Philadelphia, it would be surprising if other enterprises, more successful than Campbell's, had not availed themselves of the opportunity to draw on an increasingly fluid capital market. In sum, by the turn of the century, though the terms of exchange extended to buyers by Philadelphia textile firms had become, if anything, more unfavorable to flexible producers, they at least had begun to take advantage of an array of financial services which both made selling direct more secure and widened their potential access to short-term capital funds.[55]

The depression caused an immediate shift not *in* consumption, but *away from* consumption, as all but the privileged classes stretched out the use of their present stocks of clothing and home-furnishing textiles. When replacements were unavoidable, price and quality declines interacted to stimulate further demand. As the cheaply constructed goods Philadelphia firms reluctantly made had followed the market trend, they also wore out rapidly, soon necessitating another round of replacement purchases. In design terms, buyers' tastes psychologically mirrored the depressed economy, as plain and drab goods carried the day against fancy cloths through much of the decade. Fast blacks dominated the hosiery trade, though the bicycle craze (ca. 1894–7) and increasing interest in golf hose provided some outlet for colorful patterns. This demand was limited, to be sure, for bicycle prices had only recently dropped below a hundred dollars, and golf was a sport for gentlemen

---

[53] U.S. District Court, Eastern District, Pennsylvania, Bankruptcy Case File #979, Schedule A-3, National Archives and Records Service, Philadelphia Branch; John James, *Money and Capital Markets in Post-Bellum America*, Princeton, NJ, 1978, pp. 41, 54–8, 183. Campbell's notes to five Philadelphia banks amounted to $70,000, a tenth of his total borrowings at the time of bankruptcy. Witham's warning came at the 1898 American Bankers' Association convention.

[54] These were the heirs of Sevill Schofield and William Brown's Phoenix Mills, another worsted spinning mill (Bankruptcy Case Files #387, 388, and 775–6).

[55] Jones notes that against the dictate of banking canons (the "real-bills doctrine"), 60- and 90-day promissory notes were often indefinitely renewed upon payment of interest due, thus turning them into sources of longer-term capital resources (*Money and Capital Markets*, pp. 62–3). In such recycling, brokers provided key services that would have allowed proprietary firms to widen their effective investment pool without diluting ownership through adding partners or incorporating and attempting to market shares publicly.

and ladies. For their parts, carpet retailers attempted to restore sales of rugs by offering them on the installment plan, even as the price of a room-sized ingrain or tapestry grade dipped below eight dollars.[56]

Of longer-term significance to Philadelphia woolen, worsted, and hosiery firms was the steep decline in importations of competing European goods. The trade in German hosiery fell from $11.4 million (1890) to $4.2 million (1898), a reduction far greater than the average one-third lowering of unit prices during the period. Similarly, woolen and worsted imports in 1890 were above $50 million; by 1899 they failed to reach $20 million, a level that would be achieved only three times in the first fifteen years of the new century.[57] Both technical productivity and the ventures by flexible firms into specialties previously imported (lace, Turcoman curtains, fine upholstery) contributed to this shift, as did the restoration of favorable tariff rates through the 1897 Dingley bill that followed renewed Republican political ascendancy. Thus encouraged, Philadelphia textile mills replicated further lines of European finery, most notably producing the first American "Gobelin tapestries" in 1898 (by the Philadelphia Tapestry Mills and its rival, New York Tapestry, both in Kensington). Knitters were stimulated by the increasing consumption of sweaters, previously a rough overgarment favored by teamsters and dockers, now being demanded in varied colors and styles by middle-class consumers increasingly active in outdoor leisure. In 1898 as well, the wool and worsted markets turned firmly toward fancies again, away from the plain staples that were so closely competitive. This cheered local specialists, for in fabrics and knit goods alike, fancy styles paid a far better profit than piece-dyed goods. European events soon churned the recovering clothing markets. The death of Queen Victoria brought a rush toward black-and-white effects, fashion's seasonal version of mourning. In short order, the coronation of Edward VII brought reds and purples into vogue, quickly followed by calls for shades linked to the armistice that ended the Boer War, "blue and dark orange or gold." The "discovery" of oriental rugs, which with Axminsters formed 90 percent of imports, 1898–1903, spurred designers to produce sheafs of new patterns incorporating Asiatic effects, and further stimulated the shift toward mill-made "area rugs." The long drought was over at last.[58]

[56] *MRIR* 27(1894): 101, 317; *Textile World* 8(April 1895): 47; *AWCR* 11(1897): 44; 13(1899): 869.

[57] *AWCR* 13(1899): 154; Paul T. Cherington, *The Wool Industry*, Chicago, 1916, pp. 129–30.

[58] *AWCR* 12(1898): 375, 1346, 1374, 1578; 13(1899): 326; *Textile World* 9(November 1896): 50; Richard Strong, "Styles and Styling in Men's Wear Fabrics," *Eighth Annual Report, AAPTS (1909)*, pp. 36–7; George F. Hargh, "Ten Years of Evolution in Men's

Batch manufacturers of textile specialties responded to the crisis of the 1890s in ways that exposed their strengths and their vulnerabilities. In production terms, both aggressive and defensive strategies were employed, the former indicated by lateral movements within and among specialty sectors and by adoption of technical advances that increased productivity, though at times at some cost to flexibility. Shoddy use and substitution of cheaper raw materials (cotton, jute) represented a retreat from quality in the face of sliding prices and a buyer's market, but manufacturers' proficiency at fiddling their goods' composition ironically demonstrated their versatility. Both the inclination toward direct selling and the development of means by which modest-scale firms could evade the pricing risks of commission house trading represented efforts to take fuller control of distribution. However, the general shift on buyers' parts to the sample and duplicate sequence proved an unmanageable disruption of the earlier purchasing pattern. The escalation of cancellations and claims, along with firms' inability to sustain the short credit terms established in the first crisis year, suggest that the balance of market control swung toward the buyer's advantage, enhancing the risks borne by flexible manufacturers. The erosion of imports' role in key Philadelphia sectors, reemergence of demand for fine and fancy textiles, and rising interest in new product lines in whose manufacture local mills would play a major part buoyed proprietors' hopes in the first years of the twentieth century.

C. Institutions and departures: mergers, failures, and moves

At the same time, the depression years had been dotted with portentous disappointments and losses that underscored the limitations of individual and flexible firms. Institutionally, every local effort to participate in the general merger movement (which brought forth William Wood's American Woolen Company in New England) failed dismally. Second, a group of major firms and figures departed from the Philadelphia textile scene in the decade after 1893. Some were caught by the hazards of the changing industrial context. Others folded their tents rather than endure the risks any longer, taking their capital with them to other enterprises or locations. Together, these events illuminate the weakest elements of the proprietary system, the paradoxical underside of the personalism that had contributed to its distinctiveness and success.

The first effort at industrial combination in Philadelphia came naturally enough in the troubled ingrain carpet sector. In the spring of 1893, before

Wear Fabrics," ibid., p. 50; Arthur Cole and Harold Williamson, *The American Carpet Manufacture*, Cambridge, MA, 1941, pp. 254–5.

the downturn accelerated, W. W. Law, a member of the New York commission house W. & J. Sloane, issued invitations to local ingrain mill owners to assemble at the Bellevue Hotel with a view toward "amalgamat[ing] the Ingrain Industry into one Company." The Gays inserted Law's engraved message in their daybook without comment; as only fifteen manufacturers attended and markets soon collapsed, the notion was stillborn. Hard times brought Kensington ingrain proprietors closer together. Initially unable to reach accord on wage lists and reductions, as noted earlier, they tried again in 1895 collectively to resist workers' demands for restorations amid apparently stabilizing markets. Proprietary solidarity fractured once a strike was launched that summer, weavers gaining their object first at firms eager to run such orders as they had on hand and then generally once the manufacturers' front had broken. The following May, Park Mills and nine other ingrain firms tried a more modest effort at unity, agreeing to offer common prices and selling terms for their various grades at the market opening for the fall 1896 season. The "Manufacturers' Syndicate" operated for two years, confining its activities to distribution issues, avoiding labor matters entirely. No new firms were added, no shared sales representatives were chosen; its sole purpose was to establish and defend prices in the face of Lowell's and Alexander Smith's leadership market position and pressures for shaving by store buyers.[59]

Though the composition of the ten-firm group was not recorded, it is likely that the midsize independents who had earlier attempted to curtail output were at the heart of the alliance, together running 1,200–1,500 of the 3,200 ingrain looms present in 1898 Philadelphia. Their experience in working together on one issue may have emboldened these firms to contemplate mergers, for a plan to unify Philadelphia's ingrain factories into a single $10 million company was announced in February 1898. The *Reporter* immediately put its finger on the sticking points. Would the small firms come in, and how would the down East majors respond? After a brief flurry, during which the hope was expressed that combination would "check the ruinous price-cutting now carried on by the large department stores," the scheme lay idle for the balance of a difficult year. Led by reductions at the Lowell Company, prices for extra-supers slipped to forty-two and a half cents per yard "to the trade on the road." At the same time, Philadelphia firms' return to "striving... after new effects" increased their costs. When to this squeeze was added the news that the American Woolen Company had been formed (March 1899), the ingrain consolidation drive resumed under the guidance

---

[59] Cole and Williamson, pp. 207–8; Gay Daybook, April 13, 1893; January 30, April 16, July 17, August 21, 1895; May 15, November 13, 1896; July 27, October 19, November 13, 1897.

of New York's Charles Flint and Boston's S. W. Janes. Options were reportedly collected from a dozen Philadelphia firms in April, including Dornan, Henderson, Stinson Brothers, Carson, the McCallums, Ivins, Dietz and Metzger, and John Gay's Sons. Though the claim that all these and several eastern giants (Smith, Hartford) would combine to create the $40 million National Carpet Company was soon denied by several of the firms, the Gays clearly had given in their option, for its details were inscribed in their daybook.[60]

William Ivins, speaking for the Philadelphia group in early May, averred that the envisioned trust, managed by "only thoroughly practical men" would maintain current prices and achieve profits through economies in buying materials and selling products. Manufacturers would receive half cash and half stock for the worth of their mills, with all goods, stock, and guaranteed receivables purchased at value. Six weeks later, the merger was "deferred," dead for all practical purposes. The text of the Gays' option gives two clues to its rapid demise. First, the brothers valued their business, incorporated at $300,000 in 1893, at three times that figure, though it had staggered through the depression, had added no new machinery in six years, and had taken only minimal steps toward diversifying beyond ingrains. Second, the terms of their option were "net cash," not an acceptance of the half-and-half proposition Ivins presented. Even starry-eyed promoters would flinch at such figures and terms. Beyond these financial concerns, the *Reporter* made it clear that some proprietors were reluctant to participate as they "believe that the individuality of the manufacturer as well as the young man growing up in the business would be at a discount under a trust." For such men, the image of the family firm both as an extension of the proprietor's self and as a legacy had little diminished. Others also clung to their individualism, arguing that markets had begun to improve and that "they are willing to take their chances." Finally, the promoters had erred in announcing Smith's commitment to the trust; this falsehood, quickly exposed, damaged their credibility and raised doubts about the entire project. Several large eastern firms *had* been eager to amalgamate, however; the Lowell and Hartford Companies moved into mergers (with Bigelow and E. S. Higgins respectively) within the next two years. No such bilateral combinations appeared in proprietary Philadelphia; for their part, the Gays bought forty used looms from bankrupt Samuel White's Centennial Mill in the fall of 1898 and plowed along on their own.[61]

---

[60] *AWCR* 12(1898): 252, 306, 1484, 1606; 13(1899): 278, 391, 424, 447, 553, 583, 603, 746; Gay Daybook, April 8, 1899.

[61] *AWCR* 13(1899): 447, 746; Gay Daybook, April 8, September 30, 1898; Cole and Williamson, p. 147.

The textile trust fever materialized the same year in other less beleaguered Philadelphia sectors. In knitting and upholstery, carpet yarn and worsted spinning, plans were laid for massive consolidations, all of which came to naught. Of these the most interesting and fully developed was the drive toward a worsted spinners' trust, originating in the fertile brains of Philadelphia's George Campbell and the Boston merchants who simultaneously were promoting the ingrain trust. Their scheme was immediately linked to the forging of Wood's American Woolen, which despite its name was principally a merger of worsted weaving firms. The week that the New England combine was completed, Campbell broadcast invitations to worsted spinners for an organization meeting March 14, 1899, at the Manufacturers' Club. Chairing both the meeting and the continuing committee, Campbell listened as S. W. Janes proposed a $30 million combine to include for a start three New England spinners and twelve firms from Philadelphia and vicinity. The ultimate aim was to "unite" with American Woolen to create a "general concern, the result of which cannot but be beneficial to the industry." American Woolen quickly let it be known that they were unopposed to the fashioning of an "independent organization" that would correct "trade abuses," but had no interest in adding a mass of spinning mills to their roster.

More grandiose than the carpet trust, the worsted promoters pledged to offer participating mills either full cash for the valuation of their plants, or a like sum of 7 percent preferred stock in the United States Worsted Company *plus* an equal denomination of common stock in the new trust. They soon announced that options had been secured on "90 percent of the worsted spinning machines" making yarn for sale, exclusive of American Woolen and the Arlington Mills of Lawrence, Massachusetts. However, major Philadelphia firms (Doak, S. B. & B. W. Fleisher, Wolstenholme, Grundy) had not attended the session, and did not join. The unraveling was gradual, but irresistible. Underwriters, responsible for disposing of the combine's stock to the public, hiked their fees "more than the proprietors [were] willing to grant." Again, firms were observed valuing their properties far above what they would bring in a straight sale. Howland Croft, who had graduated from Campbell's mill to start Camden, New Jersey's first worsted spinning mill in 1880, had developed a business worth about $500,000 that was to be "taken in on the basis of two millions of dollars." Despite claims that the first $11 million in preferred stock had been doubly subscribed and that important figures in American Woolen had taken a $4 million block, the project collapsed in the last week of June.[62]

Several unnamed "large mills whose cooperation was looked for drew out at the last moment," said the *Reporter*. Why? Some sour rumors, which later

[62] *AWCR* 13(1899): 279, 286, 299, 329, 496, 520, 553, 583, 724.

proved of substance, had made the rounds. The entire effort to create the combine, it appeared, "grew out of the fact that certain parties had made extensive sales of raw materials to various mills whose resources subsequently failed to permit as prompt payment as might have been desired." In the wrangling that surrounded Campbell's bankruptcy in 1900 and that of William Browne, who served on the continuing committee with him, the foundation for these misgivings was laid bare. The two firms had bought heavily in combing wools in 1897 and 1898 through Boston merchants, expecting a rise in raw stocks and anticipating a sizable increase in yarn prices toward the Dingley tariff line (up from $.90 to about $1.10 a pound). They soon were stuck, as raw wool prices did rise rapidly but market resistance to goods advances kept yarn prices from moving upward significantly. Both Browne and Campbell began running losses, which they hoped would be washed away in a sale of their properties to the trust at figures above their actual worth. Suspicions about Campbell had appeared before the project was balked, for when the "promoters made a request to examine his books," he refused it and "was dropped out of the combine." Campbell's earlier brashness obstructed sympathy for him when his problems deepened into bankruptcy. When the trust had first blossomed, he had charged that middlemen had "made too much money on the spinners in the past, and drank too much champagne and smoked good Havana cigars" at their expense, extravagances which would stop once the spinners banded together. At his failure, such remarks were "remembered and commented on accordingly."[63]

As their presence at the center of the worsted trust effort suggested, Campbell and Browne were intimate colleagues. Their bankruptcies in 1900 came ninety days apart. Both were immigrants, Campbell a Scots-Irish orphan who toiled in Philadelphia mills until starting on his own in 1861, Browne a Welshman who arrived in 1890 after a successful career as a Manchester wool dealer. Initially, Browne confined his activities to importing and marketing raw wool. Campbell was likely one of his customers, for when Browne determined to venture into production of worsted yarns, he leased a mill that Campbell owned at nearby Chester (1896). Expanding rapidly as the worsted market recovered, Browne added a branch mill in lower Germantown, then consolidated his operations through purchase of a large, idle Manayunk factory. For two years, trade seemed satisfactory, but the 1898 squeeze brought him severe losses. Having borrowed heavily through his trade contacts, Browne by 1899 had accumulated obligations of $1 million, but had a cash investment of only $70,000. Though with rising wool prices each new lot of wool cost more than had been realized by sales of previously

[63] Ibid., 754, 14(1900): 1571; U.S. District Court, Eastern District, PA, Bankruptcy Case Files #775, 776 (Browne), 979 (Campbell), NARS, Philadelphia Branch.

manufactured yarn, he had little choice but to keep running and hope for
a miracle. The trust beckoned and Browne leapt. To improve the appearance
of his books, he altered them to show a sizable profit for 1898, then added
a fictitious entry that increased by $600,000 the firm's apparent raw wool
stocks. This creative accounting added just under $1 million to assets and
profits, a clumsy attempt at deception only revealed when auditors reviewed
the Phoenix Mills' records during the bankruptcy proceedings. Campbell's
refusal to permit the trust promoters access to his books suggests he too
may have done some juggling.[64]

Campbell's and Browne's affairs were further entwined both before and
after the trust campaign. When Campbell incorporated a weaving plant in
1897, reaching full integration in order to pursue government contracts,
Browne became an officer in the new firm. At Browne's failure, Campbell
was initially appointed as a representative of his Philadelphia creditors, for
the Corn Exchange National Bank, on whose board Campbell served, had
helped finance Browne's quick expansion. Campbell's subsequent assignment brought his immediate replacement on the Browne creditors' committee. Negotiations with creditors in contentious hearings continued
through the following year. Revealed as a maker of fraudulent goods on his
military contracts, Campbell was forced to the wall. Though Campbell's
businesses were liquidated amid angry exchanges, Browne escaped relatively
unscathed. His contemplated fraud in the spinning trust had not been con-
summated, and in bankruptcy, perhaps chastened, he endeavored to keep
scrupulously to the procedural letter. Thus no criminal actions ensued.
Moreover, his creditors were ultimately persuaded that liquidating Browne's
raw wool supply, the bulk of his assets, would bring a lesser return than the
yarn into which it could be transformed by running the mill. Thus in May
1901, a "composition" settlement was arranged through which over the next
eighteen months, creditors would receive one-third of the sums due them,
the mill being operated by a trustee's committee. Thereafter, Browne would
be released from all obligations toward his creditors, such assets as remained
being returned to him so that he could form a new company and resume
business. This plan, accepted by a majority of the creditors both in "number"
and "amount" due, was certified by the court, bringing this sleazy episode
to a close.[65]

---

[64] *Textile World* 9(September 1895): 20–1; *AWCR* 14(1900): 1182; Bankruptcy Case Files
#775–6.

[65] Bankruptcy Case Files #775–6, 979; *AWCR* 14(1900): 1182, 1571. One reason for
acceptance of the "composition" was that the raw-wool market had broken downward
sharply in 1900, combing wools dropping from 60 cents/lb. to 40 cents or thereabouts.
Dumping Browne's stock into a falling market seemed senseless (*AWCR* 15[1901]: 95),

The collapse of the worsted spinning combine and its aftermath ended the merger craze in Philadelphia textiles, and as well induced several substantial "departures." Though regional manufacturers had been able to create institutions to take action on business-related matters (technical education, tariff politics, social contacts) or to respond to specific labor or marketing crises, amalgamation of production units was exceedingly rare. (Indeed, the spinners' trust may be seen as one more crisis activity, given the Browne-Campbell revelations.) The standard economic blockages were surely of major relevance here – diverse products, relatively low entry costs, etc. But as well proprietors' reluctance to enter combines stemmed from their immersion in a personalistic factory culture characteristic of the Philadelphia production format. Manifested in images of families settled around the mill, in expectations that young men would grow up in the business, in practices like the "manufacturing apprenticeship,"[66] in social and trade dealings at the Manufacturers' Club, this habit of mind and manner ill suited proprietors for entry into the "modern business organization." Striving to remain in command of their enterprises, and thereby to remain in command of their fates, they either shunned promoters' visions of giant mergers, or participated for a time only to express misgivings, then relief when the project fell through.

Perhaps a mix of greed and genuine ambivalence fed into proprietors' placing astronomical valuations on their mills as the schemes matured and options were solicited. To sell out and take direction from executive management, to become a hireling operating one's own plant was to invite humiliation. To take the money and walk away? Toward what? The lure of amassing a competence and entering a retirement spent in comfortable efforts at service and good works had faded, and in any event, handing along one's business to the coming generation had always given meaning to a proprietor's withdrawal. I suspect that most Philadelphia proprietors were in 1900 as married to their mills as they were to their wives, and that the "death" of the mill was as frightening a prospect as the death of a loved one.

In this lay a deep vulnerability. As they hovered over stylings and fretted about prices, or alternately speculated about their sons' capacities for succession, Philadelphia millmen clearly lacked the rationalizing distance between self and enterprise that would distinguish the modern corporation. Theirs was the world of the educated, short-term guess, not that of production cost

---

as 2-40s worsted yarn for dress goods and menswear was bringing $.95–$1.05/lb. at the time (ibid., 162).

[66] Philip Scranton, "Learning Manufacture: Shop-Floor Schooling and the Family Firm," *Technology and Culture* 27(1986): 40–62.

accounting and capital assets depreciation.[67] Their long-term imagination
was fixed on adding "and Sons" to their stationery, not on career ladders
or shifting their capital into fields beyond textiles of which they knew next
to nothing.[68] This incapacity for high abstraction bound the masters to their
mills, to their workers, to their machinery, even as they moved to or built
new quarters, replaced "hands," and installed fresh technical devices. Enterprises so framed were fundamentally constrained when forced to compete
directly with more keenly "rational" rivals that gradually encroached upon
their industrial "turf." Though shifting to new product lines was a feasible
and often successful tactic, crossing the border from weaving to knitting was
infrequent and problematic. Promulgating deep rate cuts to overcome interregional wage differentials both provoked stiff worker resistance and damaged proprietors' self-esteem, for they were compelled to present themselves
as hapless victims of market trends. Speedup and stretch-out wounded
quality; narrowing product ranges and stylings imperiled sales efforts, and
so forth. Standing their ground as it crumbled underneath them, in the
1890s as well as the 1920s, proprietors tended to run out their capitals rather
than act rationally, according to the rules of an unfamiliar calculus of rationality. Only rarely did any of them liquidate and invest funds in transit
shares or bank stocks.[69]

To flesh out the personal dimension of the hazards, bonds, and options

[67] John Wood, in 1911, referred back to a P.T.S. Alumni Association meeting "held some
years ago for the purpose of discussing cost-finding." The school "had three distinguished managers of Philadelphia mills and myself present to enlighten you on that
subject...I did not know anything about it and I did not dare to tell you so. The only
thing I could do was talk. The other three gentlemen, much more experienced than I,
finding that I had sized up the question, absolutely refused to talk about it. They told
me afterwards that they did not know where to begin studying the questions of com-
parative costs." John P. Wood, "Impromptu Remarks," *Tenth Annual Report, AAPTS*,
Philadelphia, 1911, pp. 40–1.

[68] Browne was ridiculed at his hearings for having squandered $10,000 to secure an option
on a Venezuelan asphalt mining venture in 1899. His explanation of this speculation
was halting and apologetic.

[69] This final option was available even theoretically only to owners of roughly the hundred
largest Philadelphia firms, mills that employed 100 or more workers, representing
$50,000 or more in assets. For several hundred firms with 40–100 employees and
comparably smaller assets, departure from proprietorship would necessitate a search for
work as a mill manager or sales representative. For fledgling entrepreneurs, quitting
business, or more routinely, simply failing might well mean a return to labor as an
overseer or boss dyer. Reluctance to take these steps down or backward was surely
great; lacking the option of clipping coupons, these proprietors also stayed the course.
Had large numbers of firms voluntarily liquidated in a short period, the value of their
plant and machinery would have fallen precipitously. Similarly, as liquidation became
inevitable in later contractions, exhausted machinery and deteriorating buildings had
precious little value.

that accompanied proprietary manufacturing, bankruptcy cases contemporaneous with the Browne and Campbell failures may be probed profitably. Sevill Schofield and Sons, the large Manayunk firm linked by marriage to the Dobson Brothers, collapsed several times in the 1890s. On the first occasion, in 1895, the Dobsons helped reorganize the partnership's debts, so the business could be "reassigned" to the aging founder and his two sons, John Dobson Schofield and Seville Junior. A year later, the partners again suspended, finally filing for bankruptcy under the new federal statute in 1899. They then reported $494,000 in liabilities, a quarter of which were secured by a second mortgage on the mill properties, and but $54 in other assets. In the sequence of creditors' meetings that continued through 1901 and generated hundreds of transcript pages, the family and business affairs of the Schofield–Dobson clan were painstakingly uncovered.

Sevill Schofield may well have been a fair-minded employer, a benefactor of local churches and charities, but he horribly botched the process of taking his younger sons into the family mill. In 1894 the partnership between the senior Sevill and William M. Somerset, son of his wife's brother, was dissolved so that Somerset could commence his own yarn firm in Manayunk. Seville Junior and J. Dobson Schofield had been working at the factory since they left school in the late 1880s, clerking and generally learning manufacturing. Their father promptly created a new partnership, Sevill Schofield and Sons, by fiat. Responding to a question about this reorganization, Seville Junior explained: "Well, Father merely told us he was going to take us into the firm, there were no signed arrangements or agreements made in any way, but from what I understand, we were merely taken in as interested in the stock in the manufactory." J. Dobson was slightly more frank:

Q: At the time you were taken into the firm, were there no written articles of partnership?
A: Yes, but it was never agreed to and never signed.
Q: There were articles of partnership drawn up ... but they were not signed?
A: He drew up articles of partnership and submitted them to us and we were not satisfied with them and they were never signed. That was just after we were advertised as partners ... It was a one-sided affair.

Expanding on these remarks, J. Dobson added that he and his brother had been paid "a small wage ... $18 or $20 a week" both before and after their elevation to partnership, received no share in company profits, had no "authority" and had objected to the manner in which his father ran the business.

Q: What was your objection to being a member of the firm? (Witness laughs in reply; Mr. Levin then remarks, "I do not see any fun in it, Mr. Schofield") ...
Q: What was the character of the objections?

A: Well, in goods; take for illustration, he would say that we ought to make certain
    kinds of cloth, and I would say that I did not think we ought to make such
    kinds of cloth, and he would lay out a certain manner in which they should
    be made and I would not approve [of it] and there was a clash of authority...
Q: Were you consulted by your father at any time about any business affairs?
A: He would probably tell me that he was going to do such and such a thing...
Q: Did he ask your advice?
A: It did not make any difference whether he did or not.[70]

The senior Schofield retained complete control of the firm, its finances,
marketing, styling, purchasing.[71] His peremptory treatment of his sons left
them piqued and powerless; stoic in bankruptcy, neither of them expressed
the slightest regret that the family firm had gone "up the spout."[72]

Given the scale of his operations and his lack of confidence in his sons,
who were just reaching their majority in 1890, Sevill Schofield could hardly
copy the Gays' semiannual selling trips. Instead, he placed his varied cloth
output through three commission houses, while marketing yarns direct from
a Front Street office in Philadelphia. The results of the distributors' efforts
evidently proved unsatisfactory as markets slumped, for by 1894 all three
had been discharged and replaced by two other agencies. In the final two
years, three additional houses were tried, to no better effect. Schofield had
become heavily reliant on advances against goods delivered, usually receiving
about three-quarters of their estimated value upon receipt. Collecting the
residual 25 percent was chancy. Not only was it diminished by commissions
and interest against the advances, it might be nearly erased by price reductions houses made in order to move the fabrics, which in Schofield's case
at times lay in the agents' hands "two or three years." For example, when
Schofield failed in 1896, he had delivered to three of his new houses goods
nominally valued at $111,500 and had been advanced some $83,800 (75
percent) in anticipation of their sale. These accounts were "assigned" to
several preferred creditors, the balance expected being about $28,000 less
charges. When the houses cleared out these cloths, a task undertaken in no
great rush, only $10,000 was returned to the creditors, the shrinkage of
$18,000 being due to fees, interest, and price reductions deemed necessary

---

[70] U.S. District Court, Eastern District, PA, Bankruptcy Case File #387, Hearing Tran-
     script, pp. 8–25, 132. When Schofield first assigned in 1895, his idled workers received
     their full last pay and creditors accepted 50 percent of the bills owing (*Manufacturer*
     8[1895], April 27: 5; May 4: 5; June 1: 9). At the second assignment, the mill was
     reported "unlikely to resume" (ibid., 9[1896] May 23: 10). Though the elder Schofield
     spelled his surname without a terminal "e," Seville, Jr.'s signature adds this extra letter,
     a distinction reproduced here.
[71] Clarence Whitman, "The Field for Textile Graduates in the General Textile Industry,"
     Fourth Annual Report, AAPTS (1905), Philadelphia, 1905, pp. 21–2.
[72] Bankruptcy Case File #387, Hearing Transcript, p. 112.

in uncertain markets. In no position to defend his prices, dependent on advances for his working capital, receiving successively more disappointing settlements from a series of commission houses, Schofield still had to keep getting goods out to secure cash for wages and bills, chasing his tail in a downward spiral. As everything began to unravel in 1896, the firm, which had $1 million in annual sales, possessed only $648 in cash.[73]

Family relationships and tensions were entwined throughout the Schofield collapse. At the bankruptcy hearings, the sons' attorney was their cousin Charles Schofield, namesake of Sevill's brother, who withdrew from the original partnership near the end of the Civil War boom that had initially built the family firm. One George Schofield "of New York" bought a quantity of the finished stock auctioned at the 1896 sheriff's sale. Some $71,000 had been borrowed by Seville from his wife, Catherine Somerset Schofield, $40,000 before 1892 and additional sums as the company's fortunes declined. Both sons reported her discontent that no income was forthcoming on these obligations.[74] The receiver appointed after the 1895 embarrassment was Seville's son-in-law, Charles Cox. Yet most critical to the final days of the Economy, Blantyre, and Eagle Mills were his brothers-in-law James and John Dobson. In the two years after the 1893 Panic, they loaned Sevill $45,000 to help keep the firm afloat. Always aggressive technically and in product development, they may have lost patience with his plodding ways, for in 1895 it was the Dobsons who triggered the first assignment in alliance with Sevill's aggrieved spouse. Through ·this maneuver, they secured her loans to a second mortgage on the mill property, but left their own exposed as a simple promissory note. When evidently the shock of this family power play had altered neither Sevill's approach to manufacturing nor the deteriorating course of the firm, a full halt was called and the mills put up at auction. James Dobson "bought in" most of the stock in process together with the entire plant and machinery and commenced to operate the factories "individually." He soon rid the mills of their looms, tooled up the spinning frames, and confined their product to worsted yarns, sold direct.[75]

James Dobson had no interest in directly supervising this addition to his

---

[73] *TMD (1888)*, p. 135; *TMD (1894–5)*, p. 146; Bankruptcy Case File #387, Hearing Transcript, pp. 89–91, 195–6, 200–2, 217. The same results of commission house selling were evident in the bankruptcy of A. L. Robertshaw, a Germantown worsted cloth firm (Bankruptcy Case File #1444).

[74] Catherine Schofield's dowry had been placed in her own name by her father upon her marriage to Seville in 1860. Their sons referred to her other "properties," which may have represented an inheritance after her manufacturer father's death. See Scranton, "An Immigrant Family and Industrial Enterprise," *PMHB* 106(1982): 365–92.

[75] Bankruptcy Case File #387, Hearing Transcripts, pp. 96, 118, 125, 146, 160, 162, 165, 176, 209–11. For an insightful treatment of crisis patterns in family firms, see Harry Levinson, *The Great Jackass Fallacy*, Cambridge, MA, 1973, chapter 8.

IMPERIAL WOOLEN COMPANY
————————MANAYUNK, PHILADELPHIA————————

Figure 9. Imperial Woolen Mills, Manayunk, 1904, the renamed Eagle, Blantyre, and Economy Mills of Sevill Schofield, after James Dobson's postbankruptcy reorganization. (Author's collection.)

sprawling holdings. He had engineered this rescue as a family obligation, and lacking sons of his own, perhaps also as a means of liberating J. Dobson and Seville Junior from their father's harness. His first personnel action was to hire the three failed partners and John Morton, the bookeeper, the sons and Morton at the wages previously paid them. The Schofield sons were well satisfied with the new arrangement, but Sevill Senior's thoughts at being placed on his brother-in-law's wage list went unrecorded. In 1900, Dobson incorporated his acquisition as the Imperial Woolen Company, capital $1 million. J. Dobson Schofield became treasurer and secretary in the new firm, acting as the resident manager; his father was excluded from the roster of officers. Through this awkward and extended process, the baton at last was passed from one generation to the next. Sevill Schofield did not live to witness the successful outcome of Dobson's interventions. He died from a heart attack, aged 68, in Christmas week, 1900. Though the bankruptcy hearings continued well into the following spring, his passing went unremarked.[76]

The depression-era failure of Sevill Schofield's enterprise may be subjected to two opposed yet complementary readings. A firm that had won notice at the Centennial Exposition for its novel "facsimiles" of fashionable

[76] Ibid., pp. 26, 119–22, 178–9, 181–2, 210–11; *AWCR* 14(1900): 1563. Seville Jr. was appointed a director; he and J. Dobson Schofield each were stockholders (one $100-share each), but their father neither held stock nor served on the board.

European styles had two decades later gone under the sheriff's hammer, a victim of its proprietor's willful individualism. As the founder aged, his business underwent a hardening of its once-flexible arteries, that creeping sterility of practice recently discussed by Michael Piore and Charles Sabel.[77] Unwilling to relinquish control of style selection or any other element of day-to-day decision making to his sons, unwilling even to transfer a portion of the book capital to them as partners and prospective heirs, he slipped into the hands of his commission houses. As his products sat for years in storerooms only to be sold at a loss, Schofield's rigidity increased, the mill technology stagnated, while the fruitless search for the right selling-house combination confirmed the company's fading dynamism. Viewed thus, flexible production and the proprietary personalism that facilitated it are self-blocking and self-liquidating. Lacking a managerial approach, awkward at infusing new talent, deficient in capacities for *organizational* flexibility and self-renewal, such firms generate underlying rigidities that contradict and undermine their advantages. While this is plausible at the level of the firm, the contemporary incidence of new product initiatives and newly starting firms that pursued them indicates that the broad vitality of the industrial district must be appreciated. Failed firms leave behind substantially devalued plant and equipment for others to activate; mill space is readily occupied and old machines may be so cheaply bought as to be profitably operable or sufficiently adaptable to be modified for new purposes that eluded their former owners. So long as this sequence is viable, a species of non-kin succession recurs; collapses may open the way for new starts as much as successes offer examples for them to emulate. In Manayunk, for example, the now gigantic Collins and Aikman Company installed its first twenty plush looms in mill space vacated by an 1890s failure.[78]

Yet even at the level of the firm, the Schofield case may be viewed as a quirky triumph of family capitalism. Though it took six years after Sevill Senior's 1894 gaffe, and involved a family upheaval through which an uncle assumed effective authority, the generational transition and reorientation of the firm were both at last accomplished. If Sevill Schofield seems to have been pitilessly shouldered aside, the designated successor played his new role well. With his uncle's fresh capital invested in up-to-date worsted combs, J. Dobson Schofield managed Imperial Woolen adequately for the next thirty years. Scores of other families had less rocky experiences drawing sons into

---

[77] Scranton, "Immigrant Family," p. 385; Michael Piore and Charles Sabel, *The Second Industrial Divide*, New York, 1984, pp. 263–7.

[78] *TMD* (1894–5), p. 135. The firm increased to sixty-one looms by 1898 and expanded to control five factories in Manayunk and west Philadelphia by the 1920s [*OATD (1898)*, p. 209; *OATD (1928)*, pp. 467, 495].

partnership. As Doak's journal revealed, the Allens had worked out their shares of the business's income well before concern developed to press their father into full retirement. In his own case, James Doak routinely had his sons work their way through each room of his worsted mills before they were admitted to the firm. Similar were the experiences of the Buttons, Bairds and Meyers (hosiery), the Greenwoods and Fosters (dyeing), the Wolstenholmes and Fleishers (yarns). Nor was stagnation necessarily a product of continuity; indeed, sons' entry in a context of shared authority could precipitate experiments in marketing, styling, or technology. The proprietary firm was more erratic than its bureaucratized counterpart, for it centered on people rather than procedures. Yet even after 1900 as incorporations multiplied, limiting liability and covering one of its weak points, the partnership or closely-held family firm remained the predominant format for textile manufacturing in the Philadelphia textile trades.

The informal orderliness of partnership successions is confirmed in other bankruptcy files. The James Martin and Company dyeworks was a family firm founded before the Civil War, failing ultimately in 1900 after running losses for six years after 1894. Sons of the two Martin brothers who founded the concern were "given an interest in the firm," but formal agreements lapsed and were not recast. "It was a family affair and we never considered it worth while to have written articles of partnership." Nonetheless, the accounts of the company were adjusted to reflect these admissions. "When anyone would come into the firm it would be designated on the books... the exact proportion and amount of their holdings." When the older Martins died, their wills provided that their widows should no longer share in profit and loss risks. Instead their portions were transformed into a variety of life annuity, paying the widows 6 percent on the capital their spouses had invested by the time of their deaths. Additionally, in a personalistic touch that wreaked eventual havoc on the firm, the survivors also had the right to draw against that capital account such sums as they needed, the balance remaining at their deaths being inherited by their sons and daughters. Until the depression, the dyeworks had been prosperous, reporting a 28 percent return to capital in 1892. However, thereafter, family obligations entailed that "living expenses" for various active partners and inactive heirs continued to be disbursed despite slack trade. As these payouts were "taken from the cash assets, or cash capital," the company's reserves were bled dry, leading to bankruptcy at the turn of the century.[79]

The same emphasis on succession and the firm as a legacy was present in the simpler transfer that created August and Adolph Lessig's tiny (eight looms) coverlet enterprise. Their father "abandoned" his business "and the

[79] Bankruptcy Case File #844, Hearing Transcript, pp. 24–6, 29, 39, 65–71.

boys took over" in 1894, agreeing to operate in the small factory he had managed to purchase on North Sixth Street, at the edge of Kensington. The sons would pay $900 a year rent, which would provide a competence for their parents in retirement. At the father's death in 1897, ownership of the mill passed to his widow, and quarterly rent payments, usually in cash set aside from the brothers' receipts, continued to her. Again the arrangements were all verbal; other than the will, no formal documents were prepared or filed. Adolph reported his father saying: "I want you boys to move back there...You take that and I hope you boys can in a few years buy the property and save any future dispute which may arise." His expectations went unrealized. Eighteen months after the senior Lessig's death, his sons made their last rent payment to their mother, and assigned three months later. The "boys" had kept primitive books, had tried to expand in recovering markets (buying upholstery machinery), and overreached themselves. As a creditor, Mrs. Lessig secured $145 toward the rent delinquency and could seek new tenants, but her sons were compelled to search for employment until such time as they might make a fresh start. Despite the tidy succession processes achieved in these two cases, fidelity to family commitments and eagerness to "increase the business" were fatal to the firms involved. Though hundreds of similar firms more ably negotiated the hazards of succession in a flexible production system, failures (like crises) emphasized the values and practices that constituted the cultural dimension of manufacturing, and highlighted as well the perennial economic risks that menaced individual mills.[80]

Two other sorts of departures are noteworthy in closing this extended review of Philadelphia responses to the 1890s depression: withdrawal from textile manufacturing and relocation outside the city or region. On the first count, two significant figures in the events of preceding decades ended their association with textile production. In 1892, Theodore Search left Erben, Search and Co., taking a management post as treasurer of the Stetson Hat Company upon the retirement of John B. Stetson from service as "the head of the corporation." The demands of executive responsibility must have been modest, for Search soon committed much of his attention to the outside interests whose claims on his energies had been mounting ever since he spurred the Textile School project in the mid-1880s. In 1894 he assumed the presidency of the "newly organized Colonial Mutual Fire Insurance Co." Two years later he became both vice-president of the Manufacturers' Club and president of the National Association of Manufacturers, taking the place of his old friend Thomas Dolan in the latter post. In 1898, Dolan too announced his withdrawal from textiles, leaving Kensington's Keystone Mills in order to take the presidency of the scandal-ridden United Gas

---

[80] Bankruptcy Case File #598, Hearing Transcript, pp. 1–11; *OATD (1898)*, p. 217.

Improvement Company. His listing in the 1900 Philadelphia directory of financiers ran several inches, including posts on traction companies, banks, etc., but no textile connections remained.

Two comments are in order. Both Search and Dolan came to textile manufacturing not from the mill floor but from commercial backgrounds. Neither had that intense and perhaps confining identification with factory life that possessed so many of their industrial colleagues. Having reached the summit of proprietary influence and prosperity and lacking sons in their middle age, they sought new challenges beyond the mills, making quite "modern" career shifts to other branches of enterprise and public influence. Though other proprietors entered politics and became involved in education and charitable efforts, few copied Search and Dolan's example. Second, the firms that they left behind promptly reorganized and pushed ahead. The new Erben, Harding and Co. expanded its branch plant at Tacony, whereas Dolan's former partners incorporated their concern as the Keystone Spinning Company, and replaced his integrated format for making worsted cloths with a special focus on yarns, echoing Doak's decision a few years earlier. Meanwhile, the Bromleys were setting up their third lace firm (North American Lace) at the west end of Allegheny Avenue, and James Dobson was happily sold far ahead on "frieze overcoatings and ulsterings." The resilience of the local textile complex was little affected by the departure of two of its most visible figures.[81]

Though more common than proprietors' shifts into corporate leadership, physical removals from Philadelphia were still comparatively rare in the 1890s. Trade journals were regularly informed of relocations, as firms reported them in order to publicize their new situations and, often, increased capacity. Very few such "notes" were printed in the slump years, as the uncertainties attending starting in a new location only added to the problems presented by depressed markets. However, with the breath of recovery that stirred in 1895, three midsize regional firms pulled up stakes. One city hosiery mill removed to Reading, Pennsylvania, and two outlying companies headed south. Not surprisingly, the largest of the three, the Thurlow Cotton Company of Chester, was a producer of coarse cotton warps, not a manufacturer of skill-demanding specialties. Reestablished in Birmingham, Alabama, and incorporated at only $75,000, Thurlow was no great loss to the regional textile system. Its removal spawned no imitators among local op-

---

[81] *Textile World* 10(April 1896): 15–16; *AWCR* 12(1898): 1545, 1576; 13(1899): 69; 446; *Textile Record of America* 18(1896): 83; *TMD (1894–5)*, p. 136; *OATD (1898)*, p. 211; *The Financiers of Philadelphia*, Philadelphia, 1900, p. 47. After Search left his firm, the new partners sold off all their wool-spinning machinery to concentrate on worsted yarn only (*TRA* 18[1896]: 765).

erators.[82] With the eventual recovery, a half-dozen more Philadelphia firms departed the city proper in 1898–9. Certainly others may have been overlooked, but the *American Wool and Cotton Reporter*'s weekly coverage of starts, shutdowns, relocations, and enlargements seems to have been close to exhaustive. Each case was slightly different. T. Birken and Company moved its lace curtain equipment from Kensington to Chester to secure added space at small cost, as several failed Chester cotton mills were then vacant. Oliver Wilson's small cotton hosiery plant was lured to Warsaw, New York, by "inducements" offered by local businessmen. Frederick Rumpf did not abandon his Kensington damask cloth factory in 1899; he simply built a branch plant in Langhorne, Bucks County, in order to install seventy-two new looms for making bedspreads. Still, in these few actions were the germs of later restructuring. Both Birken and Rumpf contributed a bit to what would become a more general suburbanization of manufacturing in the twentieth century. They did not go far, but they did escape the periodic labor turmoil of Kensington and were likely to enjoy slightly reduced labor costs in outlying locations. Wilson's distant site was made attractive by the investment of local funds in building a "three story mill" filled with "the best machinery" for his use. Technical advances in staple hosiery production had made it possible for low-waged, inexperienced operatives to learn the rudimentary skills quickly and generate profits in this closely competitive line. Problems with machine maintenance and repair, however, were acute in isolated locations. Later hosiery relocations from Philadelphia rarely chose sites so distant from centers of mechanical expertise as Wyoming County, New York.[83] Branch planting, evident in the Rumpf and Erben, Harding cases, also began to appear in the 1890s, but again few firms strayed far from the city industrial districts, unlike Paterson silk companies that placed their "annexes" in the anthracite region of Pennsylvania or major New England corporations that launched southern extensions of their mills.

---

[82] *The Manufacturer* 8(October 26, 1895): 11; *TMD (1894–5)*, p. 266; *OATD (1898)*, p. 83. The other two firms were Wallace Wilson (to Reading) and Lewis Jones of Bristol, who relocated to Winchester, Virginia. Chester's Trainer Manufacturing Company did investigate a site in Rome, Georgia, but decided against relocation [*TRA* 17(1895): 789].

[83] *AWCR* 12(1898): 213; 13(1899): 801, 1156. Warsaw lay over 200 miles west of Cohoes and the Mohawk Valley centers of upstate New York knitting. Though the promoters of Wilson's removal expected a "large number" of workers would be employed, in 1903, the New York factory inspector reported a workforce of only seventy-eight hands, a disappointing figure after four years (New York State Department of Labor, *Eighteenth Annual Report on Factory Inspection*, Albany, 1904, pp. 522, 708–9). One of the other relocators reached out toward the Paterson annexes in northeastern Pennsylvania. Lotte and Mazeres, silk dyers, removed to Allentown in 1899; their Philadelphia plant was immediately restarted as a branch of Stead and Miller's fancy upholstery works [*OATD (1899–1900)*, pp. 205, 211].

In fleshing out this portrait of continuities and shifts in the 1890s both the adaptive capacities and the contradictory rigidities of Philadelphia textile enterprises have been detailed. In order more fully to situate these phenomena in the context of the industry at large, the contemporaneous movements at a similar flexible center (Paterson) and among firms at the bulk-production end of the trades need attention. Although it shared many characteristics with Philadelphia industrial practice, Paterson's textile system was focused on a single fiber, silk, and was in distribution wholly dependent on sales through the nearby central New York market. In consequence, the 1890s contraction struck Paterson a paralyzing blow, one from which recovery was never quite total. By contrast, the depression drove major New England firms and centers toward innovations that seemed to strengthen their production and marketing power. Some of these, like textile education and direct selling, echoed Philadelphia ventures; others, like the American Woolen merger, went beyond them, facilitating an encroachment on flexible specialists in wool/worsted production that would press them toward the industrial periphery.

4.4. Silk, cotton, and wool: Paterson and New England

By the 1880s, Paterson, New Jersey, had matured into the American center of silk manufacturing, as a complex of separate specialists firms founded by immigrant mill "graduates" grew around an antebellum core of family enterprises. Both tariff walls and decline in Britain's Macclesfield aided this development; and by 1890 the city held nearly one hundred companies employing over twelve thousand workers in the trade's three divisions: staple and fancy broad goods and ribbons. As in Philadelphia, successful firms moved up the ladder from renting to erecting quarters; personal relations between millmen and craft-proud operatives were the rule. Similar too was the mid-1880s pattern of Knights' activism, which led to an 1886 confrontation with parallel results: a brief proprietary alliance, defeat and decay for the union, and a rapid return to rivalry among the mills.[84]

Unlike Philadelphia, however, Paterson's trades lived and died with silk. This focus had a technical benefit, for local mechanics specialized in devices that enhanced productivity in working the "queen of fibers," but the drawbacks were substantial. Not only could Paterson not shift to other materials when raw silk prices soared and buyers resisted advances, local firms also

---

[84] Richard Margrave, "Technology Diffusion and the Transfer of Skills," in Philip Scranton, ed., *Silk City: Studies on the Paterson Silk Industry, 1860–1940*, Newark, NJ, 1985, pp. 9–34; Philip Scranton, "An Exceedingly Irregular Business," in ibid., pp. 35–72.

shunned silk uses beyond their chief lines, ignoring knitting, plushes, and upholstery. Different too was the trade's utter dependence on credits and advances from New York agencies, both raw silk suppliers and commission houses. Even the largest mills refrained from selling direct, whereas cash-poor new companies often had to continue production even in bleak periods in order to secure advances on deliveries that cobbled their precarious finances together. Veteran firms were better placed to cut back output, hoping quietly that smaller competitors would run aground, a not infrequent outcome.[85] Labor relations, prickly in the 1880s, showed signs of strain before the Panic. During an 1890 dyeworks fray, a worker slugged the company president; the same month, a weaving mill partner was convicted for battery on a woman employee. The depression further unsettled relations in both market and factory, triggering a series of problematic responses. Examining these changes will suggest why Paterson became seriously troubled just when Philadelphia was entering its era of prominence.[86]

Two depression-spawned technological "gains" created conflicts in production and consumption, respectively. First, Paterson and Philadelphia machine builders created an array of faster, sturdier, and larger devices which accelerated output, saved space, and aggravated labor. Protesting an 1898 rate reduction of "from 5 to 20 percent," weavers complained that "the Schaum and Uhlinger high-speed loom has served to introduce women and girls into this branch of the silk trade, and they are gradually routing out the old-time craftsmen." Machinery firms, eager to place their innovations, offered easy credit terms, which in turn encouraged supervisors to start out on their own accounts.[87] Second, in dyeing, weighting or "loading" silk fibers ran riot, cheapening dress goods in price and quality and hazarding their high standing with consumers. Where it was once common only to add sufficient chemicals to offset weight lost in "degumming" raw silk, much heavier loading could produce thicker yarns that ran out far more yards of fabric per pound of raw material.[88] The ghost in the process was that in adulterating and stretching the yield of silk yarn the resulting goods were prone to rapid decay. "Very brief wear reveals the deception. It will crack and grow rusty in a night." Before the depression, importers were charged with bringing in cheap adulterated stuffs, while American mills claimed to produce "the most honest fabrics in the world." A decade later, loaded silks

[85] Scranton, "Irregular Business," pp. 43–53. [86] Ibid., p. 61.

[87] Morris Garber, "The Silk Industry of Paterson, N.J., 1840–1913," Ph.D. dissertation, Rutgers University, 1968, pp. 180–7; AWCR 12(1898): 1411.

[88] Scranton, "Irregular Business," pp. 66–7; George Cole, A Dictionary of Dry Goods, Chicago, 1892, p. 328; TRA 17(1895): 719–20.

from Paterson "rotted" in closets across the land, their reputation wounded by the trend toward cutting costs by making "trashy goods."[89] This dual dynamic led to multiplication of the number of firms in Paterson – 91 in 1896 but 174 in 1901. Cheaper dress silks broadened demand and opened the way for "mushroom" shops (they seemed to spring up overnight) to grasp machinery credits and try to establish themselves at the low end of a sinking market. Their inexpensive, "inferior fabrics undercut sales of pure, high quality, durable silks," leading even major mills to begin weighting, which spurred the "mushrooms" to run more heavily loaded goods in attempts to regain a price advantage.[90] Shortly after 1900, the chief trade journal blamed the quality decline largely on "the almost insane competition in retail merchandising" and sponsored a fruitless "crusade for better silks." In Paterson, however, the damage was severe.[91]

A series of increasingly violent strikes had commenced after 1894, polarizing owners and workers in camps whose internal divisions were as sharp as their mutual antagonisms. Ethnic and ideological rivalries beset workers; harried mill veterans despised the "mushrooms." Leading manufacturers dropped integration to focus on weaving or spun off "annexes" for staple work in Pennsylvania's coal districts, while leaguing together to "reform" city government, which had been too often neutral or favorable to labor in strikes. However, on economic issues, they were incapable of unity. When a merger scheme surfaced at a 1900 session of the local manufacturers' association, it "created only smiles from those present."[92] The same year, two of the city's largest older firms failed, as did efforts to obstruct design piracy. "Unscrupulous buyers of silk goods" took the major firms' samples to competitors who quickly duplicated novelties created by those "who go to great expense and trouble to produce new and desirable styles." Big mills in Paterson were in disarray; the future lay with the hordes of scrambling shops. Within a few years, only two of its first-generation firms remained intact, as the local complement crept steadily toward three hundred enterprises, a figure reached in 1914 and more than doubled by 1923, with roughly constant overall employment.[93]

We will return to Paterson later, but here several brief points will distinguish its course from that of Philadelphia. Clearly the latter's diversity was

---

[89] Scranton, "Irregular Business"; Cole, *Dictionary*, p. 329.

[90] Scranton, "Irregular Business," p. 67.

[91] *American Silk Journal* 25(February 1906): 48–9; (June 1906): 34.

[92] Scranton, "Irregular Business," pp. 61–5; *American Silk Journal* 19(August 1900): 31; (December 1900): 41–2.

[93] *AWCR* 14(1900): 612, 869, 1445; Philip McLewin, "Labor Conflict and Technological Change," in Scranton, *Silk City*, p. 140. Average employment per firm dropped from 151 in 1891 to 58 by 1914 (ibid., p. 78).

an asset, enhancing individual mills' flexibility. Philadelphia's dull machine Republicanism made the city rocky ground for the radicalism that marked Paterson. Industrial wards voted "correctly," and textile workers assembled protariff petitions with satisfying regularity. More important, labor relations were less volatile and firms selling direct were better situated to protect prices and prevent their fates resting "in the hands" of commission houses. Paterson strikes in 1901–2 took an insurrectionary hue, ultimately triggering intervention by the militia. Philadelphia's major contests in these years, more fully treated shortly, were a successful drive for rate restorations in 1895, to levels that generally held through the subsequent hard years, and the 1903 general strike for shorter hours. Philadelphia textile workers manifested their grievances in a fashion that accepted rather than challenged the fact of capitalism. As crucially, while Paterson millmen became increasingly the prisoners of distributors, Philadelphia proprietors devised and adapted selling techniques that gave them a greater purchase on market relations, as road men fast-talked retailers in Sioux City, "reps" circulated through clothiers' offices in Chicago, and partners or new-style 3 percent agents received their New York clients in showrooms along Broadway or Franklin Street.[94] The implications of these differences, had they been perceived at the time, might have chilled Paterson's staunchest boosters and perhaps heartened Philadelphia's. But the parallel reorientation of segments of the New England textile industry were, in their own way, another cause for pause.

The impact of the 1893 Panic on New England bulk-production mills was serious and widespread. Stocks piled up as offering prices slumped. By August, Lowell mills went on half-time, and the Amoskeag in Manchester shut down entirely, as did eastern carpet majors Smith, Bigelow, and Sanford. Print cloth prices dropped a third in 1893, precipitating ragged curtailments at Fall River.[95] Even so, most large firms could not remain long shuttered. One Massachusetts woolen operator explained:

> It is better policy for a mill to run without profit on its output, or even at a slight loss for a time, rather than shut down. The help scatter, the moths get into the partly finished goods, the machinery rusts, and the

[94] *Philadelphia Public Ledger Almanac for 1897*, Philadelphia, 1896, p. 75; Fredric Miller, "Philadelphia: Immigrant City," in Gail Stern, ed., *Freedom's Doors: Immigrant Ports of Entry*, Philadelphia, 1985, pp. 13–25. For election returns by ward, see *Public Ledger Almanacs, 1890–1901*, in which local, state, and federal returns were broken down by political subdivisions. In Philadelphia during the 1890s, from 3 to 6 of the 157 posts in city councils were held by textile manufacturers. Others served on the school board, including Edward Steel who was its president in the mid-1890s. The *Almanacs* also give these rosters annually.

[95] *The Manufacturer* 6(August 5, 1893): 6–7; (September 2, 1893): 7; (November 11, 1893): 7; 7(January 6, 1894): 7; *MRIR* 27(1894): 31.

watchman's pay goes on with the insurance rates and the interests on the investment.

Thus by mid-1894, despite "piling up goods" or selling at "absolutely no profit," the Arlington, Atlantic, Pacific, and other Lawrence corporations were again feeding yarn to their thousands of looms, though the continuing price slide brought rate cuts for labor. Fall River print cloths that stood at four cents a yard early in 1893 fell to two and five-eighths cents by summer 1894. The leading mills installed 10–11 percent reductions and increased loom assignments (from four to five), setting off an extended, futile strike that merely allowed firms to liquidate overhanging stocks. Similar efforts at resistance in New Bedford and Lowell likewise failed, and by 1900 Fall River's stretch out reached eight to sixteen looms per weaver.[96]

The "Spindle City" corporations' collective action in the 1894 piece rate cuts introduces the question of the different routes bulk staple mills charted in the depression. As the center of gravity in Yankee cottons shifted toward southeastern Bristol County, Fall River by 1900 assumed informal leadership, particularly in wage movements. Its corporations, operating three million spindles and 70,000 looms, created a common institution to govern marketing, while each firm retained control over internal matters (workloads, technical and product choices). These expedients, and the evident distrust most millmen had for local magnate "Matt" Borden, insulated Fall River from merger-mania, but few deviations from staple production emerged.[97] By contrast, in wool and worsteds, a single corporation, and in a way, a single person, seized center stage and introduced pivotal innovations: the mixed-output strategy, close costing, direct selling, and tactical pricing. William Wood's Washington Mills (Lawrence) became the linchpin of the one great textile merger, the 1899 formation of American Woolen, the giant that assumed price leadership in short order, driving dozens of competing mills to the wall, then selectively acquiring some thirty of them by 1920. Whereas Fall River developments offered few threats to Philadelphia firms, Wood's shift toward flexibility and fancy goods, plus American's market power, was considerably more troublesome.[98]

---

[96] *The Manufacturer* 7(June 9, 1894): 6; (August 11, 1895): 6–7; (October 20, 1894): 7; *MRIR* 27(1894): 97, 519, 623. During the strike, the backlog diminished from 1.3 million pieces to 133,000 pieces, the latter figure representing less than one week's output for the Fall River print-cloth mills. See also T. R. Smith, *The Cotton Textile Industry of Fall River, Massachusetts*, New York, 1944, p. 117; and John Cumbler, *Working Class Community in Industrial America*, Westport, CT, 1979, pp. 192–4.

[97] Smith, *Fall River*, pp. 106, 109; Louis Galambos, *Competition and Cooperation: The Emergence of a National Trade Association*, Baltimore, 1966, p. 37. A $150 million scheme for a print-cloth combine was briefly floated in 1899 (*AWCR* 13[1899]: 1000, 1023, 1030).

[98] *A Sketch of the Mills of the American Woolen Company*, Boston, 1901; *American Woolen*

In the 1890s, Fall River, New Bedford, and nearby Rhode Island firms represented about three-fifths of the national print cloth industry and a third of its capacity for imprinting patterns on the plain fabrics.[99] At mid-decade forty-one Fall River corporations employed over 23,000 workers; staple cottons accounted for 92 percent of total output, just the goods George Draper and Sons' remarkable new loom was designed for. Their Northrop automatic or battery loom would become the most significant technical advance in plain weaving of the generation. It featured a "hopper" which sequentially fed fourteen yarn bobbins into the shuttle, as well as devices for immediately halting weaving when yarns broke, improvements that, as the Drapers proclaimed, "relieve...the weaver of all responsibility." Protected by over fifty patents, the Northrop was extensively tested on print cloths for eighteen months before its formal unveiling. The results showed not great speed, but a capacity for self-regulation that permitted dramatic stretch out and reduction of unit labor costs by half or more. In addition, the automatic stops lessened the quantity of faulty goods woven (seconds), further enhancing profitability.[100] The response was enthusiastic everywhere but Fall River, which took none of the 9,000 looms Draper customers ordered within a year. Yet local mills did add 10,000 looms by 1900, chiefly nonautomatics made by regional firms whose principals were long allied with the textile corporations. Only the Bourne Mill departed from these comfortable interlocks, in 1900 buying 2,000 Northrops at a crack. Many other firms spent twenty-five dollars per loom to add a stop motion, used larger quantities of yarn on bobbins to lower the number of manual changes, then stretched out their weavers to "ten, twelve, and even sixteen ordinary looms" and cut piece rates. These maneuvers embittered workers and set the stage for a disastrous six-month strike in 1904–5. Meanwhile, the "progressive" Bourne spread out its Northrops and modified plain looms twenty to a weaver, provoking a walkout that was met by wholesale hiring of new hands. As heavy southern Northrop installations helped double that region's print cloth market share (to 33 percent, 1899–1905), the technical misjudgment of corporate directors steered Fall River toward an industrial blind alley.[101]

Company Mills, Boston, 1920; American Wool and Cotton Reporter, *History of American Textiles*, Boston, 1922, pp. 138–40.

[99] Smith, *Fall River*, pp. 50–65, 72; J. H. Burgy, *The New England Cotton Textile Industry: A Study in Industrial Geography*, Baltimore, 1932, pp. 37–42.

[100] Cumbler, *Working Class Community*, p. 113; Smith, *Fall River*, p. 109; *TRA* 17(1895): 302–3; *AWCR* 12(1898): 880.

[101] Smith, *Fall River*, pp. 84, 102, 106, 113–16; Cumbler, *Working Class Community*, pp. 201–8. Both Smith and Cumbler, relying on Smith, charge the local industrialists with cheese paring, arguing that the cheap improvements on existing looms and expectations that real profits were made by sharp cotton purchasing were crucial to avoiding the Northrop. Neither stresses the 8,000 ordinary looms that were purchased, 1895–1900, an expense of perhaps two to two and a half million dollars that increased total capacity

Elsewhere, major firms like the Amoskeag also found it impossible to change course, even when pressed by hard times and querulous shareholders. In his 1896 report, its treasurer acknowledged losses of $100,000 in six months, while the company held "a heavy stock of 25,000,000 yards which can only be disposed of at less than cost." He added defensively that the directors considered "that we could have changed from the goods we made," but seeing other staple markets "already overstocked," they stood pat. The silence with regard to contemplating even modest experiments with new lines, say cotton-worsted blends, curtains, or corduroys, expresses the then-current boundaries of the bulk mill imagination. What the Amoskeag directors "very wisely" did was simply to shut down for seven weeks, unloading some goods while making none, before resuming "in full."[102]

While the above actions reflected and reinforced rigidities within the bulk-production system, in marketing at least, the Fall River crew tried something new. In the spring of 1898, print cloth prices dipped to an unbelievable one and three-fourths cents per yard, and even "at the reduced price, there has been but very little demand and the stock of goods...is now larger than ever." Individual mills had bid one another down to unload endlessly accumulating inventory, wrecking profits and depressing share values. After quiet summer discussions, the mills stunned clients with an October announcement that two men had been named as a "selling committee" for the entire standard print cloth output at Fall River. One agent would buy raw materials; one house would sell the cloths in an attempt to drive prices back to sensible levels. The *Reporter* noted approvingly: "The time has arrived when agreements of various kinds are necessary to keep the industry from being done to death by overcompetition."[103]

Between 1893 and 1897, average dividends paid by thirty-four local cotton corporations had fallen by half to under 4 percent; nine companies passed dividends in 1897. With the 1898 price slide, the average tumbled to a pitiful 2.2 percent. The committee posted a two and one-fourth cent price, and firms elsewhere followed. By summer 1899, as demand recovered broadly, the duo added another half-penny, and though pattern printers "scoured the markets of New England and the south...rather than yield" to the increase, their search only drew prices upwards. In August, lots of 100,000 pieces were being sold at the stated price, stocks were vanishing, and advance

by 13 percent. Given this expenditure, the close links with local machine builders seem more central to the industrialists' refusal to buy Draper's innovation.

[102] Smith, *Fall River*, pp. 102–3; Cole, *Dictionary*, p. 161; *Textile World* 9(October 1896): 21. The New Hampshire firm also considered making drillings and sheetings for export, but this also was dropped. By 1905, the Amoskeag cotton fabrics range had expanded, however, to include "many varieties of goods." (*AWCR* 19[1905]: 1179).

[103] *AWCR* 11(1897): 44, 238; 12(1898): 3, 603, 1292.

orders for two months' work were generally in hand. When a three cent level was reached in October, mill shares rebounded. In 1898, stock in only six of the thirty-four mills was quoted as high as par. Late in 1899, only seven were not being offered at par or above. The selling committee was not to be permanent, however, for it was phased out when markets became shaky and irregular in the summer of 1901. Desperate three years earlier, corporations had been willing to relinquish a measure of control in order to find a way out of the slump. Having recovered only to face a new contraction, they were not ready to accept central direction when decline threatened, for the committee failed to demonstrate "its efficiency as a means of averting hard times."[104]

Limited collaboration among Fall River firms had been evident since at least the mid-1880s when they gathered and published figures on weekly output and inventories, a practice unimaginable in Philadelphia with its product diversity and closely guarded proprietary privacy. Fall River mills, through their local association, also moved as a body in successive piece-rate cuts and rises during the 1890s. The city's regional leadership in these matters was obvious by 1898, for when its mills promulgated a reduction on January 3, about one hundred fifty other cotton companies echoed the action within two weeks with cuts that affected 125,000 workers. Debates there over an 1899 restoration were closely monitored throughout New England, as its outcome would direct "in large measure the course to be taken in other places." Fall River workers twice won increases (totaling 22 ½ percent) that year, and twice did waves of comparable adjustments spread across neighboring counties and states.[105] These advances held for four years, until reductions in 1903 and 1904 brought about the long strike. Despite Portuguese workers' solidarity with long-hostile English and native-born com-

---

[104] Ibid., 13(1899): 131, 250, 942, 1234; 15(1901): 998–9. Stocks rose to 2.5 million pieces in March 1901 and the selling committee urged a "general curtailment," a four-week shutdown during April and May. This was achieved by circulating "a paper" that was approved by thirty corporations. However, the overall situation was little improved by late May when an effort at a second four-week shutdown met stony rejection. Divided over the issues of wage cuts and reorganizing the selling committee, the associated manufacturers initially fragmented, then dissolved the committee in August, posting a 15 percent wage reduction a week later (ibid., 330, 344, 644, 1028). The powerful M. D. C. Borden spiked this move by announcing two 5 percent wage increases in his Fall River Iron Works, which *was* a cotton mill notwithstanding its name. As this sally failed to "coerce the other manufacturers to make an advance" or to "precipitate a strike" to achieve one, he withdrew the increases after several weeks, but the general reduction was averted for the moment (ibid., 1083, 1092–3, 1247, 1352–3, 1416–17, 1424).

[105] Ibid., 12(1898): 80; 13(1899): 143, 257, 276, 676, 1454, 1474, 1481; Cumbler, *Working Class Community*, p. 202.

rades, defeat wrecked the effort to create industrial unionism, for the skilled crafts thereafter distanced themselves from unskilled recent immigrants. There were, however, two aspects of Fall River's labor situation that were germane to attempts at achieving greater productive flexibility at the close of the depression decade.[106]

First, in 1898, the Loom Fixers' Association began organizing a school in order to educate themselves to "perform any class of work, from the plainest to the most difficult." Faced with wages lower by a third and expanding responsibilities, the fixers had a vision of change and revival. "They want to see the manufacturers in Fall River throw out the old plain work, with which the market is continually glutted, and run on special lines, or goods requiring a higher order of workmanship."[107] Of the six looms first installed in the union hall, four were set for fancy weaving, of open-work lenos and "nineteen-harness dress goods." As the union secretary explained, fixers' self-education on fine work would make it easier for industrialists to "go into the manufacture of damasks or other fancy goods." Yet the union's project was soon overshadowed by a grander plan, sponsored by politicians and local worthies. Whereas Lowell and New Bedford had taken advantage of state largess and opened textile schools in part modeled on the Philadelphia scheme, Fall River had let its option lapse. Between 1899 and 1901, the state's offer to match $25,000 from the city for startup costs was renewed, downtown land donated, and the Bradford Durfee Textile School erected, memorializing an investor in the early cotton corporations. As it was agreed that the school would well serve the staple goods interests of the area, its orientation signaled that the fixers' dreams of damasks would slip into the mists along Mount Hope Bay.[108]

As technical education was shaped into a symbol of what was rather than what might be, more direct attempts at stepping out of the staple track had little success. The problem of recruiting and retaining sufficiently skilled labor to create more specialized goods was a sizable obstacle. Bourne attempted to develop a line of cotton flannels, but failed, "one reason being the difficulty in securing the right kind of help." For the purpose of "attracting and keeping" quality workers, the firm adopted an effective and applauded profit-sharing plan in the 1890s, and by 1897 had a workforce "competent to produce the best of goods, including specialties, which require much skill." Even as Bourne paid its shareholders an 18 percent dividend and 4 percent bonuses on wages to workers, its practices were not duplicated by other Fall River corporations. Other mills did try their hand at fancy work, but in a fashion that was self-blocking. Weavers shunned the new

---

[106] Cumbler, *Working Class Community*, pp. 202–11.   [107] *AWCR* 12(1898): 555, 582.
[108] *AWCR* 12(1898): 1524; 13(1899): 135, 620; 15(1901): 463; Smith, *Fall River*, p. 33.

jobs, for as a unionist explained: "The manufacturers will not pay the money they should for such work, and weavers prefer to work on print goods. Another reason . . . is . . . that mill men expect them to run as many looms as they do on plain work." Cheap rates and stretch out dominated managerial strategies, obstructing efforts to achieve versatility. Even Bourne, with its later purchase of 2,000 Northrops, moved away from specialties and toward aggressive intensification and cost cutting.[109]

Fall River represents the extreme of staple rigidity. Elsewhere, a cluster of large firms was experimenting with the mixed-output approach in New Bedford and Lowell cottons. At Waltham, the venerable Boston Manufacturing Company, still flanked by boarding houses and company "tenements," had added "lenos, fancy colored dress goods, fine colored silks and knit underwear" to its staple sheetings, employing 1,200 workers. The fancies were run on "dobbies and jacquards, as good machinery" handled by "as skilled operatives as New England contains." Having roasted the trade's major cities and firms in a series of 1898 exposés, the *Reporter*'s correspondent, "Textile Worker," found a healthy vigor at Waltham. The mill's treasurer paid top wages, secured up-to-date machinery, and declined to cut wages simply to "supply a dividend." Rental properties were well kept and the boarding houses served ample meals including "pastry . . . of the genuine old-fashioned New England kind that pleases the eye and tickles the palates of all pie lovers." Retaining social relations long abandoned by others and blending them with a diversified product mix, the Boston company combined conservatism and venturesomeness in a novel way. Whereas, to my knowledge, no other firm offered both such a broad range of goods *and* great pie, it is clear that here and there in the cotton sector, diversification had sprouted, while at Fall River and in most of the other staple-driven corporations deviation from bulk output was virtually unthinkable.[110]

Among the wool men, the depression of the 1890s brought "without any reservation . . . the most disastrous period in the history of the American wool manufacture."[111] A Yankee survivor noted: "New England was like the

---

[109] *AWCR* 12(1898): 70; 13(1899): 1120; Smith, *Fall River*, p. 109.

[110] *OATD (1898)*, pp. 134–5; *AWCR* 12(1898): 756–7. Marketing print cloths was handled directly by firms specializing in them, but sales were often made through the Providence and New York brokers who issued the regular statistics on production and inventories. Coarse-staple producers became excited about exporting, especially to China, in the 1890s, but watched Japanese textile growth fearfully. The Boxer Rebellion deranged the China market in 1900, leading to new calls for making fine and stylish cottons in New England. New Bedford accelerated along these lines, but Fall River did not. (*AWCR* 15[1901]: 219; Patrick Hearden, *Independence and Empire: The New South's Cotton Mill Campaign, 1865–1901*, DeKalb, IL, 1982, chapter 7.)

[111] Quoted in Arthur Cole, *The American Wool Manufacture*, Vol. 2, Cambridge, MA, 1926, p. 230.

shores of the ocean after a mighty storm. The wrecks of the woolen mills were strewn all over it."[112] Yet beneath the general distress was developing a permanent shift in the balance between woolen and worsted output. In 1894 the *Manufacturer* reported business "dragging and unsatisfactory" for all lines but worsteds, in which "the demand is as unsatisfied" as ever. Two years later, as Schofield failed and Lowell's Middlesex woolen mills closed for the entire summer, William Browne began his move from wool brokering to worsted yarn production. By 1900 woolen goods' total value had dropped 11 percent from 1890 levels, whereas worsteds rose 52 percent, surpassing woolens in nominal values. Thereafter, especially in menswear and coatings, "the worsted output steadily drew away from its elder competitor."[113]

What brought this shift? Arthur Cole suggested that the typical weight of cloths used for winter and summer wear dropped appreciably after 1880, perhaps in tandem with early installations of central heating at the homes and offices of suit wearers. This was a boon for worsted makers, who could produce the "required . . . yarns of finer diameter" more readily than could woolen mills. Worsteds are composed of long-staple fibers ("tops"), separated from shorter lengths through "combing," spun to finer counts than ordinary wools to yield thin, yet sturdy and warm fabrics. Moreover, the rapid growth of the ready-made clothing industry created a "demand for large quantities of homogeneous goods" for large lots of "garments of identical fabric as well as identical cut." As worsted raw materials had a "limited range" and finishing was simpler, the "standardization" of suiting lines like serges and clays gave "the worsted branch a material advantage."[114] Finally, worsteds were immune from the shoddy blight, for shredding broke the necessary longer fibers. Only new wool could be used, ensuring that an all-worsted fabric could not be fiddled, a matter of importance in the depression years.[115]

Philadelphia, Providence, and Lawrence developed as the three urban centers in woolens and worsteds, the first pair known for their diversity, the last for its two giants, the Washington and the Arlington mills. The Washington entered worsted production in 1870, three years after one of its

---

[112] Edward Mott Wooley, quoted in Edward Roddy, *Mills, Mansions and Mergers: A Life of William M. Wood*, North Andover, MA, 1982, p. 40.

[113] *The Manufacturer* 7(August 4, 1894): 6; 9(September 19, 1896): 8; Cole, *Wool Manufacture*, Vol. 2, pp. 157, 230.

[114] Cole, *Wool Manufacture*, Vol. 2, pp. 157–9, 271; for definitions of "serge" and "clay," see Cole, *Dictionary*, pp. 76, 310–11.

[115] The price squeeze in the depression years led some worsted manufacturers to weave cotton-worsteds either cotton-warp with worsted filling or with both yarns made by blending "tops" with long-staple cotton before spinning. Though some of these were doubtless sold as all-worsteds, no outrage comparable to the shoddy scandals appeared.

directors was impressed by Roubaix goods shown at the Paris Exposition. Using a long-staple Ohio wool and imported machinery, it wove its first worsted coatings, "sold in the market as French goods." Others soon followed, but a Washington venture into fancier goods failed to pay and was dropped. Lawrence mills concentrated on plain work; the style-conscious found Providence and Philadelphia congenial locations. Indeed, by 1891 the Arlington credited its success to "a persistent adhesion to the production of standard grades of goods, which have received the popular approval." Trade observers agreed that staple mills had "a strong inducement to integrate" whereas those oriented to style had "every inducement to specialize."[116]

William Wood's trek toward prominence began in 1870 when the orphaned twelve-year-old secured an office boy's post at New Bedford's Wamsutta mills. By 1880, after a stint as a railroad bookkeeper, Wood became paymaster at a Spindle City print cloth plant. Six years later, while soliciting "subscriptions" for investment in a new Fall River corporation, he encountered the new general manager of the Washington, recently rebuilt by patent-medicine millionaire Frederick Ayer, and was quickly offered $1,800 a year to remove to Lawrence and direct the firm's cotton department.[117] Ayer and his brother James had repeatedly invested in textile corporations, and had been repeatedly stung since the 1850s. When the Washington went belly up in 1885, he suspected the collapse had been "engineered" by its commission house, attended the auction, found the agents placing the only bid, and enraged, bought the mills on the spot. After pouring $2 million into new plant and machinery, Ayer found his mills losing money by the bucket, yet his engagement of Wood seems similarly impulsive and mysterious. Wood was never a "practical manufacturer"; his experience was in financial and marketing matters. His inability to direct production was soon apparent, but Wood averted discharge by offering to sell yarns direct, nicely gauging Ayer's hostility to commission agents. Booking $2 million in orders his first year, he married the owner's daughter the next, and by 1889 became general manager, assuming both control over production and sales and his predecessor's $25,000 salary.[118]

The depression stymied Wood's efforts to put the Washington on a profitable course. By 1895, when he was appointed treasurer, its debts had mounted to a formidable $3 million. To this Wood responded by applying his bookkeeping background, demanding weekly "meticulous cost accounting reports from every branch of the firm" and introducing a bonus and speedup production system to spread fixed costs over expanded output.

---

[116] *The Arlington Mills*, Boston, 1891, pp. 89–91, 96–7, 104; Cole, *Wool Manufacture*, Vol. 2, 160, 163; Paul Cherington, *The Wool Industry*, p. 105.
[117] Roddy, *Mills*, chapter 2. [118] Ibid.

Salesmen received weekly quotas; trade journal advertising puffed the quality
and durability of Washington staples. Wood sponsored splashy openings and
against the trend toward caution, scored major early-season sales. Just after
the January 1898 opening, the *Reporter* commented:

> the Washington Mills have transacted an enormous volume of business
> ... The clothing trade bought the goods as quickly as shown, and not-
> withstanding the [price] advance, bought with a freedom and liberality
> that betokened their belief that they were getting fully their money's
> worth. There is no question but that ... their product is considered by
> many the standard by which all other goods are gauged.[119]

Wood had used what he knew best, costing and marketing, to carve a leadership position in worsteds. In 1898 the company turned a profit for the
first time in years; for the workforce, steady employment was available,
though the intensification of work brought a lingering bitterness toward
Wood that did not abate.

Arlington adopted a different strategy to meet the depression. Headed by
Boston merchant William Whitman, it led the way in stretch outs and rate
cuts; weavers' earnings fell 40 percent or more by 1898. The firm also
experimented with flexibility, selling combed tops to yarn spinners, a move
that permitted the mill to run its combing sections "night and day" in 1894–
5, and led to construction of a separate "top mill." This however did not
address the question of how to achieve full capacity use plantwide in shaky
cloth markets. Here the answer was to copy Smith's carpet practice – run
for stock and sell the accumulated residuals at periodic auctions. The composition of the goods offered in the 1898 sale indicates the firm had as well
adopted a mixed-output format, with initially disappointing results. Of the
75,000 pieces offered, only a fifth was "really desirable and readily saleable
stuff ... staple goods." The rest, about three million yards, were "out of
date" fancies that Arlington had made "in quantities far beyond the requirements of the market." Dumping them would wreck prices and was
termed "wicked and unfortunate" by trade observers. Still, after the well-
attended sale, Whitman was "perfectly satisfied with the results, notwithstanding that the prices were very low." However despised, his low-road
predatory strategy was manifestly profitable, for Arlington shares rose steadily
above par, reaching 117 ½ by 1902.[120]

---

[119] Ibid., pp. 39–40; *AWCR* 12(1898): 4, 49. Speedup spread capital charges across a larger
output, permitting price reductions. If per yard rates for weaving were also reduced,
this effect was enhanced.

[120] Cole, *Wool Manufacture*, Vol. 2, p. 201; *AWCR* 12(1898): 776, 784, 1043, 1050, 1082;
16(1902): 1288. The fancies realized from 40 to 60 percent of their "agent prices,"
bringing roughly $600,000 or $10 a piece; the staples sold at 80 percent of their regular

Wood's crafty pricing tactics brought the Washington its share of op-probrium. It regularly pegged opening prices on staples at breathtakingly low levels (the 1898 "advance" was exceptional). The first 1899 quotes were so sharply cut "as to stand many [competing] agents on their heels, so to speak."

> To the average agent the Washington people have been a "thorn in the flesh" for some seasons past. These mills have, however, continued to undersell their previous season's prices, and have been a very potent factor in the market...Now that prices have been established by the Washington people, and the suiting men know something of what they have to contend with, they will adjust themselves to...the situation as best they can.[121]

A better example of effective price leadership without oligopoly would be difficult to find, but Wood also intended pushing back buyers' advantages. In February 1899, after doing an "enormous amount of business at the opening prices," Wood raised his entire list 5 percent. The *Reporter* quickly noted this as a tactic to "guarantee that first orders will remain uncancelled," thereby frustrating clothiers' shopping for better deals and signaling other mills that the Washington was a benevolent leader. Having filled its order books, it bumped up prices to levels less ruinous for competing, less efficient firms. Moreover, it as well served advance notice on buyers that in later seasons the stalling to which they had grown accustomed would be unwise. To secure Washington's best price, they would have to buy early and heavily.[122]

Scarcely a month later, Wood created the greatest stir in the industry's history by announcing the formation of the American Woolen Company. With Ayer's backing, he had contacted James Phillips, Jr., and Charles Fletcher, each of whom owned several mills, the latter's Providence group being experienced with the fancy fabrics Wood had thus far avoided. During merger planning discussions, with the establishment of common manage-ment practices in mind, Wood quizzed the other owners on their costing techniques. "One...produced a paper bag covered with a maze of illegible figures. Another had [his] on the flyleaf of a ledger." In the new corporation, such sloppiness would end. Retaining promoter Charles Flint, who had been involved in failed Philadelphia and successful "marriages" elsewhere, Wood soon assembled the twenty-six mills of American Woolen, in the process

---

prices, $17.50 a piece yielding $260,000. Buyers were determined "not to bid too strongly against each other so that they might all participate in some bargains" (p. 1082).

[121] *AWCR* 13(1899): 125.

[122] Ibid., 107, 135. The reductions were about 20 percent from the spring 1898 prices for "fall goods," quite a sharp drop.

wrecking plans by Arlington's Whitman for a similar merger.[123] Incorporated at a plant value of $40 million, American's claimed capital per loom was more than double the sectoral average. All observers agreed this figure "was seriously inflated," that the stock issue was part "water." This was hardly novel, but of greater note was the firm's pledge to "sell its own goods." Indeed, at the root of proprietors' willingness to join Wood was "the high cost of marketing goods and the abuses which have crept into commission house methods." At least fourteen houses were dismissed; the combine's output would be handled by the Washington's experienced direct sales manager, J. C. Woodhull. Wood, committed to running full, wished to avoid accumulating stock of fancies; thus four of the firm's five selling divisions were concerned with fancy woolens and worsteds, nicely concentrating the sales force in lines where aggressive canvassing was crucial. Further, the corporation established common dating, discount, and credit rules and announced that "preventing cancellations" was a key goal. In all this, Wood's experience and influence dominated.[124]

Consolidated materials buying was quickly adopted; American was soon reported buying four million pounds weekly at Boston when a busy week there counted ten million pounds in total sales. Its position nationally was less commanding, for the company operated only 8.5 percent of all wool/worsted looms (5,400 of 63,300). Nevertheless, it was the biggest player on the scene, even better fitted to assert leadership than had been the Washington. Other firms now showed samples privately, awaiting release of the lists of the "pretty generally acknowleged leader" before affixing prices. Yet despite its cost-consciousness, American was willing to spend to gain an advantage. In 1900 it shipped buyers fancy samples by express (rather than regular freight) and absorbed the extra charges. Later that season, when rumors circulated that American had overbooked, yielding short shipments and delays, Wood confidently countered that every yard was going out on time, adding that cancellations were rare, amounting to but 4 percent of total orders.[125]

Usually hostile to mergers, the *Reporter* commended American for bringing order to the trade and dampening cancellations, but the situation of firms outside the combine was dicey. Weaving firms had to match or best its prices,

---

[123] Cole, *Wool Manufacture*, Vol. 2, pp. 232, 233n; Roddy, *Mills*, pp. 41–2; *Sketch of the Mills of the AWC*, (1901): unpaged.

[124] Cole, *Wool Manufacture*, Vol. 2, p. 245; Roddy, *Mills*, p. 42; *AWCR* 13(1899): 285, 329, 419. The new trade terms were published May 11, cutting discounts and the time given to enjoy them. The *Reporter* added, "it seems probable that a few wholesale clothiers will have to readjust their books to meet the requirements of the new order of events" (p. 802).

[125] *AWCR* 13(1899): 285, 406, 496, 905, 1115.

American Woolen Company,

WILLIAM M. WOOD, Treasurer,

Ames Building, Boston, Mass.

EDWARD P. CHAPIN, General Agent, W. H. DWELLY, Jr., Asst. Treas.
AMES BUILDING, BOSTON, MASS.

MANUFACTURERS OF

Beavers, Kerseys, Friezes, Meltons, Thibets, Wool and Worsted, Plain and Fancy Overcoatings, Coverts, Broadcloths, Venetians, Granites and Vicunas. Piece Dye and Mixed Clay Diagonals. Fancy Weave Piece Dyes and Mixtures. Serges, Wool and Worsted Cheviots. All Grades of Worsted and Wool Fancy Trouserings and Suitings, and Wool and Worsted Mercerized Fabrics.

HIGHEST AWARD, GOLD MEDAL,

PAN-AMERICAN EXPOSITION.

Selling Agent, American Woolen Company of New York.

J. CLIFFORD WOODHULL, Selling Agent,
66-72 LEONARD STREET, NEW YORK.

Spinners of Worsted Yarns, English and French Systems.

Yarn Dept., H. C. JEALOUS, Mgr., Ames Bldg., Boston, Mass.

Transfer Agents, Old Colony Trust Co., Boston, Guaranty Trust Co. New York. Registrars, International Trust Co., Boston, Knickerbocker Trust Co., New York.

Figure 10. American Woolen Company advertisement, 1902, showing the array of staple and fancy wool/worsted fabrics offered through the firm's mixed output strategy. (Courtesy of the Philadelphia College of Textiles and Science.)

and two sizable Lawrence spinners who had spurned Wood's invitations went bankrupt. Both had had "practically but one customer," a company that did join. Coolly assessing their plants in dissolution, Wood bought one and let the other vanish under the auctioneer's hammer. American soon announced its profits for the first seven months of 1900 as $2.15 million, enough to leave a $750,000 surplus after paying a full year's dividend on preferred stock. A thousand new high-speed Knowles looms were added, "materially reducing the cost of production," and the first day's orders at the January 1901 openings mounted up to 30,000 pieces. Fancies sold so well that the firm teased buyers with the news that only "a moderate number of orders can yet be taken care of." At American's founding, a selling agent remarked: "The manufacture of fancies is an entirely different thing from ...piece dyes [the Washington's chief staple line] and I doubt if they can get as strong a hold on the fancy goods market as they have on plain goods." Two years later, the verdict was evident. Provided with an effective selling system, American's fancy mills were kept fully occupied on orders and avoided disposal auctions. By 1904, American's sales had risen a third over their 1900 level (to nearly $40 million), Ayer's financial gambles were redeemed, and Wood had arrived as an industry power. Everyone else, including the Philadelphians, watched and wondered what it all might mean.[126]

4.5. The Philadelphia system in 1899: a structural portrait

While Wood maneuvered, the Philadelphia textile trades were again expanding by 1899. The region's 800 firms (Table 4.6) represented an 11 percent increase over 1894 figures, with gains both spatially and sectorally concentrated (twelve of seventeen suburban additions were in knitting or hosiery). In the city, sectorally, the number of woven goods mills remained nearly stable, as did carpet and dyeworks operations. However, net gains were recorded in hosiery and spinning (forty-two of sixty-two), indicating the rising regional prospects of these sectors. The jump in the number of "miscellaneous" specialists was due to the finer subdivision of the production sequence, as small firms preparing fancy beams for weaving or reprocessing waste and rags multiplied. Several of these located in Germantown, near

---

[126] Ibid., 542, 838, 1087, 1134, 1315; 14(1900): 1078, 1571; 15(1901): 43, 61; Cole, *Wool Manufacture*, Vol. 2, p. 235; Roddy, *Mills*, p. 62. American spun off a wholly owned corporate subsidiary in 1900 to control selling from a sixteen-story office building in lower Manhattan (18th Street and Fourth Avenue). In its first five years, the corporation spent $6 million on new machinery (Roddy, *Mills*, chapter 2).

Table 4.6. *Textile firms by sector and district, Philadelphia and suburban counties, 1899*

	Woven goods	Carpets	Hose-knit	Dye-finish	Spinning	Misc.	Total
Kensington	96	92	73	49	32	11	353
Manayunk	13	0	1	4	24	6	48
Germantown	10	2	49	1	11	9	82
Frankford	25	3	7	13	9	7	64
North Central	23	1	11	6	7	3	51
S.&W. Phila.	16	1	1	1	4	4	27
Northern Liberties	6	1	9	2	5	1	24
Old City	16	0	13	5	2	2	38
City totals	205	100	164	81	94	43	687
Bucks Co.	6	1	8	0	1	2	18
Chester Co.	4	0	7	0	1	0	12
Delaware Co.	27	0	3	2	14	5	51
Montgomery Co.	16	4	13	1	10	3	47
Suburban totals	53	5	31	3	26	10	128
Total	258	105	195	84	120	53	815

Source: Official American Textile Directory (1899–1900), Boston, 1899.

the Pennsylvania Railroad's Wayne Junction; they, with a dozen new hosiery starts, helped account for a textile resurgence in the district. Kensington held its own, a slight drop in wovens more than compensated for by an increase in knitting. South and West Philadelphia suffered the loss of a set of older and more staple-oriented firms. Outside the main concentration, their relative importance was fading. Adjacent to increasingly crowded Kensington, Frankford and the North Central areas were choice sites for both relocation and initiation of textile manufacturing. New worsted and upholstery operations surfaced in North Central; the Bromley's North American Lace plant would soon be built there as well. Frankford experienced a burst of tiny shops, especially in damask weaving and the associated "Turkey red" dyeing that was then fashionable in table coverings.

Most of these additions were quite new, having commenced in 1898 or 1899. Hence their employment impact was minimal, as Table 4.7 suggests. Overall, city textile workforce figures had increased about three thousand over the 1893 reports, but by 1899 factory inspector coverage was vastly improved. Remembering the earlier wide exclusion of dyeworks, two-thirds of the apparent gain in employment is attributable to their inclusion in 1899 (compare with Table 4.2). Nonetheless, the depression's lingering effect on the carpet industry is plain: 4,000 jobs present in 1893 were vacated six years later, over a third of the total. This collapse was temporary, however, representing idle looms rather than a serious reduction in capacity. When the recovery reached the carpet trade, employment levels rapidly rose to predepression levels.[127] The innovations in lace and growth of upholstery

---

[127] The 1900 Census report on manufactures gave Philadelphia carpet employment as 12,190. Two details help reconcile these figures with Tables 11 and 12. First, it is well known that 1900 industrial data reflect firm accounts for the period preceding June 1, 1900. (The agents' work in Philadelphia actually began May 1.) Thus some portion of 1899 is covered. It is less well known that the factory inspectors' 1899 year began November 1, 1898, with most inspections being taken before June 1, 1899. The carpet "year" always began in the fall and ended in the summer; spring season sales were lighter than those from each preceding fall. Hence, carpet inspections given in the 1899 factory inspectors' report reflect visits in the winter 1898-9 production period. Reports provided the 1900 census agents reflected the 1899-1900 winter activities. Second, the extra thousand above the 1893 figures most likely represents Dobson's carpet mill, which was lumped together with his plush mill in the FI Report (pp. 92-3) in 1899 and earlier, and could not be separately tabulated. If the census took and totaled these separately, and half the 2,267 Dobson plush and carpet workers fall in the carpet column, the figures square. Total Philadelphia carpet employment for 1899 would then be about 8,600 rising to 12,190 with the resurgence of carpet demand. See *Tenth Annual Report of the Factory Inspector (PA): 1899*, Harrisburg, 1900, p. 5; *Census Reports, Volume 7, Manufactures (1900), Part I*, Washington, D.C., 1902, p. xvii.

Table 4.7. *Employment in textiles by sector and district, Philadelphia and suburban counties, 1899*

	Woven goods	Carpets	Hose-knit	Dye-finish	Spinning	Misc.	Total	N_f Link	N_f Total
Kensington	8,777	6,595	6,336	2,414	2,078	669	26,869	300	353
Manayunk	2,993	1,790	20	107	1,789	112	6,811	47	48
Germantown	875	285	2,442	56	395	185	4,238	71	82
Frankford	1,424	197	548	347	742	301	3,559	62	64
North Central	2,851	251	604	290	1,382	11	5,389	49	51
S.&W. Phila.	1,921	2	50	24	1,075	705	3,777	21	27
Northern Lib.	660	82	29	6	0	0	777	18	24
Old City	926	0	374	41	556	6	1,903	21	38
City totals	20,427	9,202	10,403	3,285	8,017	1,989	53,323	589	687
% linked	(88)	(72)	(79)	(96)	(87)	(91)		(85)	
Bucks Co.	1,125	300	163	0	418	34	2,040	14	18
Chester Co.	222	0	532	0	94	0	848	12	12
Delaware Co.	5,475	0	84	1,050	1,053	66	7,728	48	51
Montgomery Co.	2,105	85	1,549	28	357	15	4,139	43	47
Suburban totals	8,927	385	2,328	1,078	1,922	115	14,755	117	128
% linked	(100)	(60)	(97)	(100)	(81)	(70)		(93)	
Total	29,354	9,587	12,731	4,363	9,939	2,104	68,078		
% city	(70)	(96)	(82)	(75)	(81)	(95)	(78)		

N_f = number of firms.
Sources: OATD (1899–1900); Tenth Report of the Factory Inspector (PA), 1899, Harrisburg, PA, 1900.

weaving are reflected in the rise of woven goods figures, especially in Kensington and North Central. Schofield's fall is visible both in wovens' drop at Manayunk and in the rise in spinning employment, as his mills were devoted to yarns after Dobson's intervention. Spatially, Kensington, Manayunk, and Frankford had returned to roughly their 1893 employment levels, but the Northern Liberties' largest hosiery mill had relocated to Kensington and failures in South and West Philadelphia cost that area a net 600 textile jobs. Increases of over 1,000 "places" in North Central and Germantown derived from the growth of their woven and knitting divisions respectively.

In the hinterlands, aggregate employment had likewise recovered to just about the 1893 level, or perhaps a bit less, as 1893 inspectors' tours had omitted Chester County and surveyed only 81 percent of firms elsewhere (vs. 91 percent for the three other counties in 1899). Though the sectoral balance in Delaware County was little altered, shifts had taken place in Bucks and Montgomery. In the first, hosiery work had declined, but wovens, especially at Edward Steel's Bristol worsted mill, had nearly doubled, more than making up the loss. Montgomery County was moving in the opposite direction, knitting growth offsetting a slide in fabrics. There and in neighboring Chester County, the knit-goods corridor between Reading and Philadelphia was taking solid form. Reading was becoming a satellite center for knitting machinery builders and knit-goods mills, over thirty of which were located there in 1898. Towns northwest of Philadelphia were already starting to fill with similar shops, a pattern that would continue in these two counties for decades, but which would not materialize northeast of the city (Bucks) or to the south (Delaware).[128]

With regard to production format and marketing approaches, the sharp distinction between the core city and its surrounding counties persisted (Table 4.8). In Philadelphia, the proportion of textile workers engaged by integrated plants had dropped only slightly, but two of the seventeen firms in this category were on the verge of bankruptcy (Campbell's Dingley Mills and McCallum carpets). As the depression wrecked a number of outlying staple-goods mills, the integrateds' suburban share shrank somewhat more, yet still represented about half of all employment, triple the level in Philadelphia. The impact of the drive toward direct selling was far more dramatic. In both areas, firms using commission houses employed a much smaller share of all textile operatives as the region began climbing out of the depression trough, reduced since 1893 from a third to a fifth in the city and from nearly two-thirds to two-fifths in the four counties. Despite this shift, firms in satellite towns and rural hamlets remained twice as likely to rely on "houses" in 1898 as were their metropolitan colleagues. Interestingly

[128] *OATD (1898)*, pp. 72, 238–9.

Table 4.8. *Integration and agency selling, Philadelphia and suburban counties,*
1899, firms and workers, by district

Philadelphia	Integration N_f	N_w	Agents N_f	N_w	Both N_f
Kensington	8	3,664	49	6,725	3
Manayunk	2	2,943	5	1,540	2
Germantown	2	639	11	549	—
Frankford	2	277	10	978	—
North Central	1	241	6	623	—
S.&W. Phila.	2	853	—	—	—
Northern Lib.	—	—	1	26	—
Old City	—	—	2	71	—
Totals	17	8,617	84	10,512	5
% linked f. & w.	3	16	14	20	
% all firms	2		12		
Average workforce		507		125	
Suburban	Integration N_f	N_w	Agents N_f	N_w	Both N_f
Bucks County	2	906	2	22	—
Chester County	1	25	7	146	1
Delaware County	18	4,465	17	4,052	13
Montgomery County	11	1,787	13	1,656	9
Totals	32	7,183	39	5,876	23
% linked f. & w.	27	48	33	40	
% all firms	25		30		
Average workforce		224		151	

N_f = number of firms; N_w = number of workers.
Source: *OATD (1899–1900)*; *Tenth Report of the Factory Inspector (PA), 1899*, Harrisburg, PA, 1900.

enough, incorporation was not among the "switches" essayed by Philadelphia
textile mills in dealing with the 1890s crisis. In six years, the number of
incorporated companies grew only from twenty-three to thirty-seven, employing 12 percent of city textile workers, a figure unchanged from 1893.
Outside Philadelphia, chartered coarse goods mills were among the decade's
casualties. Their replacements were evidently in no hurry to file incorporation
papers, for corporations employed 34 percent of textile hands in the nearby
counties in 1899, down six points from their 1893 showing.[129]

[129] Incorporation workforce shares result from linkage of *OATD (1899–1900)* and *Tenth*

Table 4.9. *Profitability by sectors in textiles, Philadelphia, Chester, and Norristown, 1899–1900*

	Firms	Total Capital (in thousands)	Total Workers	Return on Sales (%)	Return to Capital (%)
Philadelphia					
Carpets	88	16,867	12,190	9	11
Cotton goods	143	14,380	10,695	14	17
Dyeing & finishing	91	4,981	3,455	17	19
Hose & knits	142	10,025	11,944	11	15
Jute & cordage	13	4,833	1,787	19	27
Silk goods	28	3,813	2,506	20	25
Upholstery	22	2,580	1,282	13	14
Woolen goods	93	12,874	9,438	9	13
Worsted goods	36	14,080	7,407	10	12
All sectors	656	84,433	60,704	12	15
Chester					
Cotton goods	11	3,444	1,906	11	8
Woolen goods	3	521	385	17	23
Worsted goods	3	455	369	11	22
Norristown					
Hose & knits	5	488	678	14	22
Woolen goods	4	541	465	15	19
Suburban sectors (two towns)	26	5,449	3,803	12	13

Source: Calculated from data in United States Census Office, *Census Reports, Volume 8, Manufactures (1900): Part 2*, Washington, D.C., 1902, pp. 774–5, 784–91. See also Note to Table 3.

If employment was rebounding and soon to surpass even the earlier 1882 peak, profitability did not mimic this performance. Contrasting the information in Table 4.9 with that from Table 3.3 offers a glance at the overall situation. Citywide, return on sales had dropped 2 percent since 1890, return to capital slid 9 percent, though at 12 and 15 percent per annum the figures

Report, Factory Inspector (1899). The increase in the number of Philadelphia firms using selling houses reflected the decisions of small newly started firms, as the sharp drop in average employment at such firms (1893–9) indicates. A third of these eighty-four firms had fewer than fifty workers in 1899.

were still quite respectable. They reveal that manufacturers' complaints that they were making no money despite the turn of the century boom were moonshine, but they do give weight to reflections that the years before the Panic were something of a golden age for proprietors. Certainly the falloff in capital return was related to the sizable increase in reported investment (20 percent, 1890–1900).[130] This increase did not reflect a shift in the proportions of capital represented by fixed versus working assets ("live" or "quick" assets), nor were there major disproportions in the components of fixed funds (plant versus machinery). Why did this added investment fail to keep returns high? First, at least part of the increase may be illusory, if firms both revalued their plant upwards and failed to depreciate their machinery on the books, a practice revealed in several local bankruptcy cases. Second, and more significant, as goods prices and qualities were lowered, the dollar return per machine-year would be lessened. This was surely the case in carpets, in which product value was almost identical ten years apart, while profit had fallen a third despite a 17 percent increase in capital and the partial adoption of faster looms. Resistance to price advances was widely noted and may be visible in the overall product value statistics. Technical improvements installed before the Panic and on the upswing after 1897 meant that the total volume of goods turned out by 60,000 workers in 1899–1900 well surpassed that of 1890. However, the value of this output was only 1 percent above the 1890 total ($100.1 million vs. $98.8 million, jute and cordage excluded as not in the 1890 group). The depression had driven qualities and prices downward and they had not recovered to 1890 levels, as the Bureau of Labor Statistics textile products index also indicates. If 1890 be taken as 100, general textile prices in 1900 stood at 92 and would not surpass the base level until 1906. City textile profits in the eight sectors noted above were $11.3 million in 1900, $2.5 million below 1890, or 82 on a comparable 100 scale for profits.[131]

As disappointing prices squeezed profitability from the market end, were changes on the production cost side adding to the problem? In 1900 neither

---

[130] Jute and cordage, not included in 1890 figures, are excluded from this calculation. In the other sectors the increase was $13 million or 19.5 percent over 1890.

[131] U.S. Department of Commerce, *Historical Statistics of the United States: Colonial Times to 1970, Part I*, Washington, D.C., 1975, p. 200. These profit dollars in 1900 had roughly the same purchasing power as in 1890, for the all-commodity index was at the same level in both years (56.2 vs. 56.1, 100 = 1926). This of course accentuated the impact of the profit slippage, as other goods had returned to their pre-Panic levels faster than had textiles. The gap, however, also spurred workers' demands for wage increases, for other commodities were becoming more expensive quite rapidly. The all-commodities index rose from 46.6 to 56.1, 1897–1900, a 20 percent upward movement.

labor nor material costs per dollar of product were appreciably different from 1890 proportions, nor were salaries to proprietors and office staff. Miscellaneous expenses had, however, climbed enormously, from five cents to eight cents of every value dollar. Taxes, rent, interest, and "other" categories had little role in this, when "miscellaneous" is broken down into its components. The difference largely is attributable to the vague heading, "contract work," where spending rose $2.3 million over 1890 (when only $61,000 was reported), accounting for three-quarters of the 3 percent increase. As this line was to reflect payments to other firms "to whom were let certain portions of the work," and as partly finished materials (i.e., yarn) had their own entry in a separate section, it is most likely that this sum represents contract dyeing, beaming, and jacquard card-cutting services, along with fees paid outside fabric designers. Clearly this subcontracting was going on in 1890, but was not reported separately. The figures cannot be lumped with either labor or materials, for is a design a product or is designing a service? The best that can be said is that overall production costs had risen to above 1890 levels and that the city textile trades were thus being pressed from both sides, for prices failed to advance fast enough while manufacturing costs crept upward.[132]

These effects were not mapped equally across the various sectors in and about Philadelphia. Well below average returns were recorded in carpets, woolens, and worsteds in both categories (sales and capital earnings). Near the averages were knitting, cottons, and upholstery, with the best performances falling to dyeworks, silks, and the jute and cordage group. Several points follow. First, by mixing independent spinners with fabric weavers in its classes, the census obstructs further analysis of the relative performance of these different divisions of the local trades. Second, the relatively strong showing by cotton, silk, and upholstery firms indicates the success of the new product lines, for from these mills came the damasks, laces, and curtains for which the city had become the national production center by 1900. Third, dyeing was the one sector that showed an absolute increase in profitabilty; its capital base changed but little whereas average wages dropped from $528 to $457 (13 percent). Though dye chemistry had been radically altered since 1880, labor process breakthroughs that would replace manual vat dyeing were just being introduced and adopted at the turn of the century.[133] A

---

[132] The breakdowns are as follows: wages 21 percent and salaries 2 percent at each date, materials 58 percent in 1890, 57 percent in 1900, miscellaneous 5 percent and 8 percent, profit 14 percent and 12 percent. The definition of contract work is in U.S. Census Office, *Census Reports, Volume 7, Manufactures (1900), Part I*, Washington, D.C., 1902, p. cxxxiv.

[133] Wage figures calculated from the 1890 and 1900 census tables. The technological reference here is to the closed "dyeing machine," one version of which was created by

larger wage reduction in silk work (16 percent) kept it near the top of the list, but the equally satisfying statistics from the jute and cordage business had less to do with wages than with the degradation of qualities and technological innovations in the carpet sector. In 1890, the local cordage firms alone (jute data was not given) made 10 percent on sales and returned 14 percent to a collective investment of $2.2 million. In 1900 cordage and jute capital neared $5 million and returned a handsome 27 percent, realizing the profit potential of jute yarns and carpet backings. Cheap ingrains were made by substituting jute for wool warps, covered with wool or cotton fillings, and the new cut weft insertion process, used in pile carpets, tucked segments of wool into a heavy jute backing cloth to form a vertical pile, demanding far less woolen yarn than an all woven carpet. Low-price carpets to satisfy depression demand meant prosperity in the jute mills, just as it rewarded recyclers in the woolen business.[134]

Although the aggregates for Chester and Norristown sectors differ little from Philadelphia's data on profitability, inspection reveals that the large role of Chester's fatigued staple cotton mills weighed down much stronger activity in wool, worsted, and hosiery. The numbers of noncotton firms are small (fifteen), but their capital return averaged above 20 percent, hinting at the attractiveness of suburban locales. The wage differential was noticeable, if not massive, 6 percent below Philadelphia's mean for the most profitable trio.[135] It is tempting here to repeat the interregional contrasts done for 1893, but this comparison will be saved for the next chapter, using 1905 data and allowing time for the general recovery to accumulate some momentum. Instead we shall have a look at one other aspect of industrial structure, the composition of the workforce, men, women, and children under sixteen in 1890 and 1900.

Were male workers displaced by women as a depression expedient or in response to simplified and accelerated textile technologies? The sectoral picture is mixed, but overall the shift between 1890 and 1900 was more toward child labor than gender substitution (Table 4.10). Over 1,700 more youths were employed in city mills at the turn of the century than had been recorded ten years before. Indeed, the absolute number of women's positions was little altered, resulting in a share loss, whereas the number of jobs for

Philadelphia's Klauder and Weldon and Camden's Joseph Hussong in the 1890s. Adoption of these machines to displace open wooden-vat dyeing was a bone of serious contention after 1900 in Philadelphia. (See *Dyers' Trade Journal* 4[1898]: 216–217.) Later advances would yield the pressurized steel kettle for rapid, effective large-scale dyeing of yarns.

[134] *Census Reports, Manufactures, (1890)* Pt. 2, pp. 438–41; *Census Reports, Manufactures (1900), Pt. 2*, pp. 784–91.

[135] *Census Reports, Manufactures, (1900), Pt. 2*, pp. 774–5, 784–91.

Table 4.10. *Workforce in Philadelphia textiles, by sector, 1890 and 1900 (percent)*

	1890				1900			
	% Men	% Women	% Child	N_w	% Men	% Women	% Child	N_w
Carpets	52	40	8	11,881	51	43	6	12,190
Cotton goods	40	52	8	6,865	44	47	9	10,695
Dyeing & finishing	93	6	1	2,515	88	6	6	3,455
Hose & knits	21	68	11	12,231	19	63	18	11,944
Silk goods	30	61	9	4,018	26	62	8	2,506
Upholstery	60	39	1	576	35	59	6	1,282
Wool goods	53	39	8	10,289	54	38	8	9,438
Worsted goods	39	52	9	7,797	38	44	18	7,407
Cordage (& jute – 1900)	53	29	18	930	43	43	14	1,787
All sectors	43	49	9	57,102	43	46	11	60,704
N_w	24,331	27,770	5,001		25,895	28,069	6,740	

Note: Three-digit percentages for *All sectors* are: 1890: Men, 42.6; Women, 48.6; Children, 8.8. 1900: Men, 42.6; Women, 46.2; Children, 11.1.

N_w = number of workers.

Sources: Same as Tables 3.3 and 4.9.

men increased enough (1,664) to duplicate their 1890 workforce proportion. The increase in youth employment was most substantial in knitting and worsteds. In the former, youths likely were increasingly assigned to tend batteries of automatic knitting machines; the roles for teen workers in spinning, the largest portion of Philadelphia's worsted activity, were the time-honored and dreary tasks of changing yarn packages on vertical frames or piecing for mule spinners. Though children ("back boys") were usually involved with mules, they might replace adult women in ring spinning of medium or coarse yarns. Both men and women were displaced in some trades where employment held static or declined (worsteds, silk), but as in strike times, weavers could readily shift into expanding sectors (upholstery, cotton specialties). Women burlers, dressers, and winders were likewise far more skilled and flexible than their pay levels reflected, and could switch with relative ease into all sectors but dyeing, which remained a male bastion.[136] Youth work had occasioned little comment as it increased; but it developed as a topic for heated dispute in the 1903 general strike, during which Mother Jones set off from Philadelphia leading a children's crusade to secure industrial justice. The conflict that spawned that quixotic trek had its beginnings in renewed skirmishing between mill workers and proprietors that quickly surfaced at the end of the depression. Money was at first a natural issue, but by 1902 workers made the call for shorter hours their main priority. The manufacturers refused, in a manner that showed their understanding of the necessities of accumulation, a decision that triggered walkouts on an unprecedented scale. Having set aside labor–capital relations in order to focus on other issues and other regions, we return to them so as to address the second major crisis in Philadelphia textiles within a decade.

4.6. Prosperity and struggle: labor and capital, 1895–1903

As Alexander Keyssar has aptly phrased it, the 1890s depression was "double-dipped," for economic strains "eased in late 1894 and 1895" before contraction again appeared. In February 1895, some months after this apparent recovery had settled in, Philadelphia's Ingrain Carpet Weavers Union sent forward a schedule of prices that would largely restore the cuts established in the previous year. Like the Power Loom Body Brussels Carpet Weavers' Mutual Defense and Benefit Association, the ingrain union was a carryover from the Knights' era. In addition, the Dyers' Union and fourteen other local associations of textile workers constituted the District Council

---

[136] C. C. Balderston, R. P. Brecht, et al., *The Philadelphia Upholstery Weaving Industry*, Philadelphia, 1932, p. 15.

of Textile Unions, an independent unbrella organization to which each member group sent three delegates. Though they had been relatively quiet for some years, area textile operatives had reshaped the Knights' overbearing centralization of authority into an institution better suited to Philadelphia labor customs. Respecting shop and trade autonomy, the district council was a forum for debate, a source of resolutions mobilizing "moral, and if necessary, financial support" for strikers, not a body that intervened to settle disputes. Both the council and the separate carpet unions were descended from the textile sections of the Philadelphia Knights of Labor, the assemblies that had had such contentious relations with the order's regional and national leadership.[137]

The ingrain weavers' initial request was declined as manufacturers had set prices for the present season on the basis of the reduced scale. Pledges were made that an upward revision would be forthcoming in May, but after several conferences, the firms decided against making any adjustments. Hence in June, the carpet workers resubmitted their schedule and set a July 10 date for a strike were it not implemented. The familiar routine of delegates and shop meetings, proprietors' committees haggling with the strikers' representatives at the Manufacturers' Club, failed attempts to reopen the mills, etc., was followed during July. The mill owners offered to adopt the new rates as of December 1, but their credibility was low. Strikers affirmed they would return with an advance or stay out. Orders for fall delivery had accumulated; the weavers had been alert to seasonal timing, and facing the prospect of lost business, smaller proprietors began defecting week by week. The strike remained orderly, for the millmen had announced they would not "import" workers to replace their hands and the union discouraged rowdiness.

As so often, leadership exercised by one division of the Philadelphia textile workforce encouraged others to raise their own grievances. Twelve hundred dyers from forty-three firms assembled July 14 to voice support for the weavers and soon got around to expressing an old demand, that dyers employed by inside shops (Bromley, Dobson, et al.) be paid the higher rates in effect at independent firms. Brussels and chenille weavers met to create new price lists and sought affiliation with the district council, which the ingrain workers reportedly had now joined. Blanket weavers secured advances and gingham weavers demanded them. Nine hundred silk workers filled the Labor Lyceum in Kensington to organize a branch of the International Silk Ribbon Workers, a division of the United Textile Workers.

[137] Alexander Keyssar, *Out of Work: The First Century of Unemployment in Massachusetts*, New York, 1985, p. 47; Gladys Palmer, *Union Tactics and Economic Change*, Philadelphia, 1932, p. 23; *Public Ledger* (Philadelphia), July 3, 15, 20, 1895 (hereafter *PL*).

Fifteen bobbin boys at James Doak's spinning mills struck for an increase; George Campbell's 200 weavers walked out for "an advance on clay worsted goods" in distant South Philadelphia. Ordered to weave carpets, two Bromley Brothers' loom fixers refused and were fired; the fixers supported them and all were discharged. The ingrain strikers' determined stance had emboldened textile workers across the city to rebuild an older solidarity and to push for comparable restorations.[138]

Carpet manufacturers who operated the larger factories kept up a brave front into early August, but when Judge Brothers offered a compromise dating of the advance (October 1), the workers sensed victory was near. At Park Mills on August 13, the Gays tried a second time to reopen, putting an announcement "in 4 dailies. No weavers showed up. We sent for the loom fixers but they refused to weave by our even paying them their regular wages." During the next week, several major firms conceded defeat. James Gay, in the longest sentence entered in the daybook, described the proprietors' final meeting at the club.

> On a/c of Messrs. Jos. Taylor, Keefer and Coon, Sam'l White, John Boggs, and Thos. Boggs giving in to the weavers promising the advance in wages Sept. 16th and from the fact of Judge Bros. notifying the manufacturers in session that they would also give in, the Manufrs. tho't best to give up the struggle and make best terms possible with their weavers, we notified our weavers at once and compromised the matter by agreeing to advance all wages Sept. 16th, 1895 to the rate paid prior to the reduction of Jan. 3rd, 1894.

The mill started up the next morning; Park mills added two and a half cents to the prices of all their carpet lines the following day and by the end of the week every loom in the factory was clacking away.[139]

If manufacturers had failed to stand together, labor's gains beyond ingrains were far from general. To avert a strike, Joseph Grundy voluntarily advanced his rates as did the Bochmann worsted mills, but Campbell fired his striking weavers and replaced them. When the chenille weft weavers went out at two of the Bromleys' companies in the fall, they too were discharged. The return of depressed conditions early in 1896 dampened labor's enthusiasm. The failure of two ingrain firms paying the restored schedule plus news of a 10 percent rate cut by Alexander Smith led to scattered reductions that September. Distress in Kensington soon threatened to approach the miseries of 1893–4; the Society for Organizing Charity again broadcast an appeal for relief funds over the signature of dry-goods merchant Joshua Baily. Inter-

---

[138] *PL*, July 15, 16, 17, 18, 19, 20, 24, 25, 26, 27, August 7, 1895.
[139] Gay Daybook, August 13, 21, 22, 23, 26, 1895; *PL*, August 3, 5, 1895; *Manufacturer* 8(July 27, 1895): 7.

viewed by a newspaper, John Bromley admitted he was operating four days, providing work on alternate days for three-quarters of his regular force. Revealing perhaps intentionally a touch of the paternalist ethos, he added, "We are doing this solely to keep our hands employed, and the goods thus produced are 'piled up' in the hope that we can sell them later." The accumulation would not be great for the mill was running at one-quarter of its capacity. For their part the Gays cut their burlers' rates, but like many others, did not attempt a reduction in weaving. Manufacturers consoled themselves by blaming the slippage on election year nerves and "the Free Silver agitation"; labor, once again, fell silent.[140]

Meanwhile, a legal case was making its way through the Pennsylvania courts, a battle over property rights in knowledge and craft customs that was followed assiduously in the trade press. *Dobson* v. *Dempsey*, twice set before the state supreme court, concerned the encroachment of proprietary authority on the craftsman's realm and exemplified dyers' struggle to defend their prerogatives against manufacturers who claimed ownership of their personal coloring formulas and secrets. John W. Dempsey had learned the dyer's trade in Britain before coming to Philadelphia and the Dobson mills in 1873. He was at that time an accomplished color mixer, for his initial wage was twenty dollars weekly, plus a two hundred dollar bonus at the end of a year's employment, fully double the rate paid a journeyman dyer. His job involved working with the carpet designer to match pattern colors, creating batch lots of dyes in "pitchers" labeled for each design and used in tinting yarns for both initial and repeat orders. Each of these formulas was entered by Dempsey in his "color books" along with notes and comments that would make for ready duplication of the shade at a later time.

Dempsey worked at the Falls of Schuylkill factories for nearly twenty years, his earnings climbing to a remarkable $2,260 in 1891. The following August, he gave the Dobsons notice of his intention to leave their employ in September 1892. Though he had routinely taken his books home with him for study and updating, Dempsey was stopped August 30 by the mill watchman and was "informed that he could not quit the mill until he gave up his recipe books . . . by order of the Dobsons." Though he proposed to stay the night with his books, he was after a few hours forced out of the factory, the books remaining behind. The Dobsons retained them for twenty-seven days, until they could be completely copied for the firm's use; and even then, only a portion of the volumes were returned. In December, Dempsey filed a complaint in Philadelphia Common Pleas Court No. 1, setting off what became known as the "famous color formula case."[141]

[140] *Manufacturer* 8(May 18, 1895): 8; 9(September 5, 1896): 7; 9(September 12, 1896): 6; 9(September 19, 1896): 8; Gay Daybook, April 17, August 10, 1896.
[141] *Dyers' Trade Journal* 1(May 1895): 85, 3(June 1897): 88–9; Wilson Kress, *Pennsylvania*

After a long delay, the suit came to trial in May 1895. The Dobsons alleged that they had ordered Dempsey to keep duplicate books of his color formulas for them, but Dempsey averred that no such arrangement had ever been called for, that it was contrary to customs of long standing in the craft. Dempsey showed that he had purchased the blank ledgers himself, and that of the 2,300 recipes in them, 1,800 were entered in England during his journeyman years. The defendants admitted as much, but argued that as Dempsey was their employee and the books were used in their business, they had believed them to be the firm's property as much as Dempsey's. In his charge to the jury, the Philadelphia judge focused more on the physical objects, the ledgers, than their contents and the issues surrounding Dobson's appropriation of Dempsey's trade knowledge through having the recipes duplicated. The verdict went to Dempsey; damages of $10,000 were awarded by a sympathetic panel. The millmen appealed, putting up a bond for one-half of the judgment as security.

The superior court, reviewing the case, determined that the penalty was disproportionate to the offense, and reduced the award to $5,000. This was not adequate; the Dobsons pursued an appeal to the state supreme court, which heard arguments on January 27, 1896. Focusing on the recipes, not their containers, the court viewed the dispute in the context of "master and servant" relations, not as a simple property trespass. The issue of who had title to the knowledge thus became central. Interestingly enough, the court did not discuss whether the Dobsons' claim might extend only to those formulas entered while Dempsey was their employee, the most recent five hundred, a step that would have opened the way to damages for copying the entire lot. Instead, it ruled broadly that the mixer's right to his recipes "was not an exclusive one as against his employers." The supreme court accepted the Dobsons' version of the contract with Dempsey (that he should make them duplicates) even though it had been rejected by the jury. This, together with errors perceived in the judge's charge to the jurors, led the court to order a new trial. The trade press, in celebrating "Victory for the Dobsons," omitted mentioning that four-fifths of the recipes predated Dempsey's term in their mills.[142]

The case went a second time before common pleas Judge Beitler in May 1897. Here the plaintiff's efforts stressed the weight of trade custom, upon which the Dobsons' actions were infringing. Testifying, Dempsey observed that: "Color mixers and dyers keep color books for their private use . . . I do not think that any color mixer in the United States or in England will give his books up, because they are the tools of his trade, and they guard them

State Reports, Volume 184, New York, 1898, pp. 588–9 (hereafter cited as 184 Pa., and Volume 174 as 174 Pa.).

[142]   174 Pa. 123–7; Manufacturer 9(March 14, 1896): 11; Textile World 9(March 1896): 23.

very secretly." To buttress his position, he called forward Lewis Longbottom, forty years a dyer first at John Crossley's famed mills in Great Britain and since 1881 at Kensington's Stinson Brothers. Longbottom and others were there to show that keeping formula books was a "known usage and custom in the trade" and that it was accepted that "the employer had no interest or title or property in them in any way." Beitler overruled this offer "to prove by anybody, or any number of people, the custom of the trade." Dempsey also had present John Forrest, "proprietor of the American Yarn Printing and Spinning Works of Philadelphia," prepared to argue the same point from the employers' side, affirming that it was the Dobsons who claimed property rights that violated long-established customs. This too was forbidden. Being "ruled and governed" by the supreme court's judgment on the issues in the first trial, Beitler directed the jury to find for the Dobsons. In its opinion, though case law was plainly divided on the ownership of knowledge question, the supreme court had used a strict interpretation of contract between master and servant to rule that as Dempsey was not an "independent contractor," he stood in the same relation to his employers as did spinners or watchmen. As to the recipes, "the processes and combinations they represented belonged for the purposes of their business" to the mill owners, whereas Dempsey was merely entitled to a copy for his own future reference.[143]

Dempsey by this time was residing and presumably working in Malden, Massachusetts, the location of the Cochrane carpet and calico printing companies. From there he sent off a circular to his fellow dyers, asking for funds with which to pursue an appeal of a decision that "affects every color mixer and dyer in this country, and if allowed to stand...no doubt will in the future operate seriously to their injury." Printed in the *Dyer's Trade Journal*, Dempsey's request evidently secured sufficient response, for the Pennsylvania supreme court again considered *Dempsey* v. *Dobson* in January 1898. His attorneys protested the directed verdict and offered eleven cases bearing on the force of trade customs, but their opponents argued only one point, that "a usage is never admissible to oppose or alter a general principle of law." With this the court agreed, claiming the custom to be both unreasonable and unlawful. Its reasoning was odd, as Justice Williams, writing for the court, referred to the custom as one "sought to be set up," one that "could not be sustained," rather than as a practice established and common on two continents for several generations. Nonetheless, its continuance would give the color mixer "power to inflict enormous loss on the manufacturer at any moment, and not merely to disturb, but to destroy his business."[144]

---

[143] 184 Pa. 589–91; *Dyers' Trade Journal* 3(June 1897): 89; 174 Pa. 130–1.
[144] *OATD (1898)*, p. 136; *Dyers' Trade Journal*, loc. cit., 184 Pa. 592–4.

Of course this was an exaggeration, but it touched the shift in power relations on the factory floor that lay at the heart of the case. The respect and authority dyers had long carried centered on their possession of craft knowledge that was their "special private property." This was their protection against arbitrary actions by proprietors, and as Forrest and others had been ready to testify, it played a balancing role in the social relations of production. With the Dempsey case, as with other business-related decisions in nineteenth-century American courts, the ground supporting customary practices was successively eroded to the advantage of entrepreneurs. The implications of *Dempsey* v. *Dobson* were quickly recognized. In its column on "this long contested case," the *Reporter* noted: "This decision will be a basis for the settlement of similar contentions in the future, and will be well to preserve." A dyer replied with keen apprehension and no little eloquence:

> Custom is one thing; justice is another... A dyer or color mixer is hired and paid for the work he does. The goods are sent to him to be colored, and the result of his efforts is what he is paid for, not how he does them. If his formulas are incomplete, or have not been compiled with skill, the result will be poor, and his services of no value. If, on the other hand, the colors are good, by his skillful mixing or his peculiar knowledge of process, he is of value to the concern employing him. These formulae and processes are often handed down (as in my case) from father to son (my grandfather having used some of them a hundred years ago). By what right should an employer demand these formulae to put into the hands of an inexperienced and cheaper man, after I had worked for some time?

This legal incursion on what Christopher Tomlins calls "the culture of control" threatened veteran, skilled dyers' proprietary knowledge, and strengthened their bonds with the men of the tub, the journeymen whose union became one of Philadelphia's strongest and most militant labor organizations.[145]

The Progressive Dyers' Union was active and visible throughout the depression. It greeted the 1894–5 trade recovery by sponsoring its first "masquerade ball" at the Labor Lyceum, attended by "over five hundred guests" and by opening a series of free classes for dyers, held every other Sunday under the direction of Edward Prag, editor of the *Dyers' Trade Journal* and "technical educator of the Union." The ball became an annual event, as did strikes at Dobsons'. A dye house hand there in the late 1890s observed

---

[145] *Dyers' Trade Journal*, loc. cit.; *AWCR* (1898): 431, 582; 184 Pa. 590; Morton Horwitz, *The Transformation of American Law, 1780–1860*, Cambridge, MA, 1977; Christopher Tomlins, *The State and the Unions: Labor Relations, Law, and the Organized Labor Movement in America, 1880–1960*, New York, 1985, pp. 16–20.

that "the men used to go on strike every time the blue birds came out in
summer," staying out for short periods either to enjoy a fair-weather break
or to express disapproval of the owners' hard-edged style. Yet within the
Dobson realm, even post-*Dempsey*, many customary practices remained intact. Youngsters got their first jobs by being taken to the mills by their fathers
and introduced to foremen, who did the hiring. Between tasks, they watched
their elders running cards or looms and when "permitted" could "practice"
a bit under their supervision. After a time, one could "request" to move up
the skills and pay ladder, again learning "by observation." However, a Dobson weaver, who had graduated from being elevator operator in the factory,
laid emphasis on outside, informal education: "I learned more in saloons,
hearing weavers talk, than I learned in the mill." Thus even as proprietary
authority was being extended in the courts, and unions were attempting to
build culture and education into their organizational bases, the older patterns
of shop relations continued their vitality, in networks within and outside of
the factories.[146]

John Dempsey's second disappointment at the hands of the state supreme
court coincided with the spring 1898 restoration of textile demand. Manufacturers commenced running full, but were cautious about attempts to
increase prices. Labor was equally conservative; steady work was gratifying
enough for the present. Thomas Dolan, after a conference with his workers,
did agree to a restoration of rates, advancing them 12 percent, but this had
no ripple effects in the region. The following spring, however, after a year
of increasing activity, petitions for new schedules began to percolate through
the system. With and without strikes, gains averaging 10 percent were made
at Kensington carpet mills and at Leedom's Bristol factory. As usual, success
energized other sections and sectors; by late summer advances of 5 to 10
percent were marked up in Manayunk and Spring Garden, in worsted,
spinning, and cotton specialty firms. However, George Campbell repeated
his 1895 tactic, firing all the weavers who struck for increases at his South
Philadelphia mills. It was not only merchants and trade rivals who could
smile at his embarrassment at the next year's end. In a sense, all this was
routine, a repetition of patterns ingrained in the Philadelphia textile trades.
However, late in 1899, organizations formed by proprietors and workers

---

[146] *Dyers' Trade Journal*, 1(April 1895): 26; 3(March 1897): 5; Philadelphia Labor Market
Studies, Works Progress Administration, Occupational History Schedules Nos. 1603,
1641, Urban Archives, Temple University. (Under the terms of deposit, the names of
informants for the W.P.A. project may not be individually mentioned by those consulting
its records.) On Dobson strikes, see *Manufacturer* 8(May 4, 1895): 5; *AWCR* 11(1897):
345.

during recent years underwent their first full-scale tests in the growing upholstery sector.[147]

Like the group of carpet men that the Gays joined, upholstery manufacturers in Philadelphia clubbed together in the late 1890s to set common terms for selling fabrics and coordinate movements in prices. In October 1899 as the spring season opened, they decided to raise all cotton upholstery goods 10 percent, partly due to upward movements in yarn prices, partly to take advantage of flourishing demand. A second meeting in mid-November produced a second advance, ranging from 10 to 15 percent. Aware of these machinations, the upholstery weavers drew up a new schedule of prices, which was submitted to the fifteen largest firms in the local trade. Their bill advanced rates "from 15 to 20 percent," included a ten cents per hour overtime supplement and called for a fifty-five-hour week, the last two provisions clearly aimed at spreading out the seasonal rush and/or making the long busy weeks proportionally more rewarding for weavers and more expensive for proprietors. Though some firms readily posted the rate advances, the first since 1893, they were reluctant to accept the whole schedule and the strike opened on December 1. Only the Orinoka Mills, whose "special line of goods" was exceptionally profitable, met the terms and continued in operation. Acknowledging that competition among manufacturers was intense and that yarn prices were gobbling a good portion of their price increases, the *Reporter* admitted that the workers had "some cause for complaint."

> The workman finds the price of all the necessaries of life advancing, and his former wages at this time do not go so far as when the grocer's and butcher's bills were less. The present strike is but the beginning of further trouble along this line unless there is a more thorough explanation of the situation.[148]

In the second week, one of the large Kensington mills tried opening with non-union workers, some of them brought in from Maryland. There were no disturbances, but within a few days these imports "joined the strikers." In West Philadelphia, George Brooks attempted to call in those of his weavers who were not unionists, but this too failed. His shop had been organized in 1896 by a longtime Kensington activist, and though Brooks had fired him for being "too radical," the organization held together. With nearly a thousand looms idled in late December, the struck upholstery mills recalled their

---

[147] *AWCR* 12(1898): 332; 13(1899): 655, 817, 827, 924, 961, 974, 991, 1060, 1075, 1173.
[148] *AWCR* 13(1899): 1226, 1405–6, 1420, 1438. *Textile Record of America*, though based in Philadelphia, continued its policy of refusing to cover strikes, except in general terms denouncing their foolishness.

road men "because they cannot get their orders filled." Concern mounted that the gap would be supplied by importers, and manufacturers intensified their efforts to staff the strikers' places without conceding their demands. Whereas the millmen by February claimed to have replaced half the weavers, production was negligible, as many of these new workers were "learners." Exhaustion of their resources brought the upholstery weavers to heel in late February; they secured the advance the proprietors had offered before the walkout, but not their rate schedule or the additional terms for overtime and a shorter week. Defections on either side had been few. In retrospect, the manufacturers' pricing alliance had served them better than the union had served the workers. The strikers knew the factories could not run effectively without them; upholstery work was near the top of the skills ladder. However, they were financially strapped after thirteen weeks on the pavement and had to concede. The defeat cost Upholstery Weavers Local 25 a portion of its membership and wrecked its treasury. Unable to meet its assessments and per capita payments to the National Union of Textile Workers, it suspended and was reorganized in fall 1900, the first of its reincarnations.[149]

Unfazed by their colleagues' misfortune, Philadelphia carpet weavers shortly proposed a new schedule of their own. The 1899 round of increases had brought rates back to 1895 levels at firms where reductions had later been installed. Now the Carpet Loom Fixers' and Weavers' Union proposed a 7 percent improvement as of June 1, 1900, pledging serious efforts "to avoid a general strike" as manufacturers were "busily engaged in dissecting" the proffered bill. Committees from the union and the Philadelphia Carpet Manufacturers Association met several times in late May. As the *Reporter* had urged, the mill owners provided a "thorough explanation" of the problems they were having with yarns. Their costs had risen 25 to 75 percent in six months, adding five to six cents to the expense for a yard of carpet whose price had with difficulty been raised three to four cents. With these figures in hand, an understanding was reached. A one-year extension of the 1895 schedule was adopted with the traditional provisos for thirty-day notice of intention to seek changes at the year's end and ratification by each group's membership. Satisfied at reaching a stable point without a walkout, the manufacturers commended the union in a fashion hardly imaginable ten or twenty years earlier. They "expressed themselves as favorably impressed with labor unions when conducted in a fair, business-like manner, and recognized the right of their employees to form such organizations."[150]

---

[149] Ibid., 13(1899): 1466, 1494, 1522; 14(1900): 71, 94, 127, 150, 213, 235, 262, 1333; W.P.A. Schedule No. 1642, Urban Archives, Temple University.

[150] *AWCR* 14(1900): 357, 434–5, 487, 622–3. The agreement covered the city ingrain mills only. A year later, replying to a questionnaire on "Plans for Strike Prevention" from

This opinion was subject to revision of course. Here the manufacturers had presented their case and had carried their point. In the context of the yarn-cost situation and upholstery loss, workers recognized that a strike had little hope of success and were satisfied to have a districtwide agreement from which to base later efforts. For their part, the proprietors had lost the horror of unions that surrounded their duels with the Knights of Labor. Unlike Local 25, most Philadelphia textile unions were independent, shop-based associations, prone neither to socialism nor to involving outside parties in their disputes with management. As such, their resources were modest, their cross-trade linkages weak. If they behaved themselves and respected proprietary prerogatives, if customary boundaries were maintained in a "business-like manner," unions could be tolerated and even faintly applauded. However, this mild approbation would be summarily withdrawn should labor attempt to dictate operating policies to mill owners. Reintroduction of the upholstery weavers' demand for shorter hours was viewed as just such an invasion. When it came, it was fiercely resisted, for it would fundamentally constrain the flexibility of firms faced with lumpy demand and seasonal peaks and valleys. As Philadelphia textile workers, and in time local civic figures and social scientists, focused their attention on addressing the irregularity of employment, relations between labor and capital swung back toward suspicion and hostility from this brief interlude of mutual backpatting.

The next several years were relatively quiet on the labor front. The market boom leveled off in 1901, but reductions were not attempted in Philadelphia mills. Lace workers organized yet another union in the city, embracing as well curtain and bobbinet firms in Chester and Scranton, Pennsylvania, but the national textile unions had little influence among Philadelphia's many separate locals. The National Association of Textile Operatives was a New England affair; the International Textile Workers, affiliated with the American Federation of Labor, concentrated on southern plants. When these two and three other Yankee textile unions banded together as the United Textile

the Pennsylvania secretary of internal affairs, a carpet man wrote:

nearly twenty years ago we had a strike in our mill [that] was a very costly affair both for the work people and ourselves...We have for many years since that time been in the habit of meeting a committee of our work people every six months, at the beginning of each season and before our prices are made for goods, at which time an agreement for prices of labor for the coming six months is established. We find this plan works admirably. Neither the men nor ourselves have ever failed to strictly comply with the terms, and we have gotten along very amicably, and with mutual respect ever since.

Pennsylvania Secretary of Internal Affairs, *Annual Report 1901, Part III: Industrial Statistics*, Harrisburg, PA, 1902, p. 655.

Workers of America in December 1901, Philadelphia labor was not represented on the national executive council. The key reason for the absence of interest in the emerging combine may have been the following constitutional provision: "that no strike can be ordered by any member of the organization unless ordered by the executive council." Philadelphians had their own regional body, the Central Textile Workers Union, expanded from the 1895 district council to embrace twenty-six area unions. Included were all the significant locals but the ingrain carpet weavers, who had withdrawn to full independence once more. As later events would confirm, Philadelphia labor's goals and concerns were distinct from those of the staple-mill unions, north and south. Moreover, area workers declined to take direction from or ask permission of central authorities, even at the regional level, when they chose to act. To be controlled by a national board was hardly appealing.[151]

In 1902 the upswing resumed, but Philadelphia remained calm. Labor turmoil visited American Woolen instead, as William Wood had determined to introduce the two-loom system into his fancy woolen and worsted mills, breaking an old custom in order to lower production costs. Beginning at Olneyville, Rhode Island, long a hot-bed of union activity, a "refusal" strike spread throughout the Blackstone Valley, silencing nearly 2,800 looms, 30 percent of the corporation's capacity and most of its fancy goods mills. While sympathizing with weavers' anger at intensification of their labors, the *Reporter* noted blandly that "all the world works harder than it did before," including corporate leaders. Wood, with his keystone Washington Mills only briefly affected, rode out the resistance, advertised for replacements, and tended to his public relations, claiming that the double-loom assignment was confined to "easily woven" fabrics, the sort of "neat, unobtrusive fancies which are often referred to as semi-staples." After three months, the strike faded away, allowing American Woolen "to weed out a number of operatives whose usefulness had become diminished and who had become habituated to antiquated methods." The struggle against the stretch-out was lost. The benefits of victory were sufficiently substantial that Wood's mill agents treated him to a complimentary banquet at Boston's Algonquin Club, May 14, 1903. Serenaded by the Orpheus Club's "50 male voices," he spoke of the "present prosperous condition of the business of the company" while the assembled managers enjoyed their "Salmon Cardinal" and "Saddle of Spring Lamb" with champagne "Brut Impérial." However, even as their toasts and cheers were ringing "to the echo," Lowell was in upheaval and the lines of struggle were hardening in Philadelphia.[152]

---

[151] *AWCR* 15(1901): 578, 581, 1488, 1606; *Philadelphia Record*, May 25, 1903.
[152] *AWCR* 16(1902): 361, 433, 457, 496, 799, 825, 863, 921; 17(1903): 623, 1586. The

If the American Woolen strike was a disorderly set of sympathy walkouts in response to a labor process issue, the confrontation in Lowell was a straightforward struggle for better pay. In early March 1903, the seven unions in the local textile council forwarded a request for a 10 percent advance to all the corporate agents in the city. An identical proposal the previous year had been rejected; indeed, the companies had in 1902 responded by announcing an indefinite shutdown, averted only when the unions backed away, withdrawing their demand and their "strike order." This time there would be no "postponement of controversies." The UTWA executive authorized a strike; the cotton mills again claimed they could not afford higher wages and suspended operations March 30 amid rumors that they were selling their baled raw stock profitably in a rapidly rising market.

Seventeen thousand cotton workers were locked out two days before the strike deadline, but neither Lowell carpet weavers nor knitters at the Lawrence Company were involved. Soon it was ominously reported that fewer than one-quarter of the strikers were union members, entitled to emergency benefits of five dollars weekly or less. "Hundreds of Canadians are returning to Canada, and the best operatives are seeking work elsewhere." Corporate leaders and their allies were in command throughout. A state investigative board visited the city and promptly reported that none of the cotton firms could sustain a wage advance, legitimizing the mills' refusal to budge. After two months, the corporations announced they were opening their doors June 1; their unity was unbroken. Resistance collapsed; over half the workers entered the factories immediately. The unions tried to renew the walkout a week later, but only 2,000 of the 12,000 operatives then at work heeded the call and these were chiefly union members, not the unorganized Quebecois, Portuguese, and Greek immigrants who formed the largest proportion of the workforce. The council abandoned the strike, completely defeated, two weeks later. The first important Lowell strike in thirty years revealed several things worth noting: durable corporate solidarity, the limits of craft leadership and organizational methods in integrated bulk-production mills, labor's inability to solve the ethnicity puzzle. Moreover, the cursory state inquiry showed how technically backward were several of the old cotton corporations. Only Tremont and Suffolk had made a commitment to large installations of the battery loom. The Lawrence Company was the only major firm that had paid substantial dividends in recent years, and it had given up weaving entirely in 1896, switching to knitting. Though they still had the power to

Washington was stopped for three weeks, in late April and early May, the strike having started in late March and breaking down in early July, 1902. Injunctions from the Rhode Island courts were used to break resistance in the original areas of opposition.

discipline the labor force through lockouts and the consequent privation, the Lowell cotton companies were suffering from internal dry rot as much as from southern plain-goods competition.[153]

Although the Lowell defeat was credited with balking planned strikes in other New England towns, it had only an ironic relation to developments in Philadelphia. On the day the corporations reopened and broke the Lowell strike, the CTUW inaugurated the largest walkout in Philadelphia's history, the general strike for a fifty-five-hour week in textiles. The *Reporter* immediately juxtaposed the two efforts:

> It is in the matter of the cause of the strike that the situation in Philadelphia differs most from that in Lowell. In Lowell the demand of the operatives was categorically for more pay. In Philadelphia... the bulk of the textile workers base their demand on a reduction from 60 to 55 hours, and express a willingness to accept the reduced pay which such a reduction naturally implies.

This goal had been established nearly a decade earlier in depression Philadelphia and had been cautiously but positively reviewed in the Manufacturers' Club journal at the time. Restated to no avail in the 1899–1900 upholstery clash, it was revived in January 1903 by the CTUW. In response to warnings from the "conservative element" among the delegates that it was "untimely" to raise the demand during "the present... dull season" in the trades, the group deferred any immediate action. Before they reconvened in April, a set of separate incidents indicated organized labor's growing influence in the area industry. Workers at Firth and Foster, one of the city's biggest dyeworks, stood out for an increase of one dollar weekly across-the-board, in order to "equal the schedules" in force at other shops where "the employees have some sort of an organization." At Dobson's, the Tapestry Carpet Weavers' Union returned from a short walkout to find non-union men assigned to some of their looms, and struck again until the owners conceded their right to their particular places. The Amalgamated Lace Curtain Operatives secured an 8 percent advance with hardly a murmur from the Bromleys and their fellow curtain mill operators. Though cotton was again running high, wool prices were moderate and markets begging for goods. The boom was back and the advantage appeared to lie with labor.[154]

On the second Saturday in April, "all the unions in the textile industries of Philadelphia, Pa., met in convention... at the Kensington Labor Lyceum"

[153] Ibid., 17(1903): 308, 365, 404, 419, 447, 475, 516, 522, 525, 589, 675, 785, 792–3; *PL*, June 2, 9, 1903. Total union membership at Lowell was reportedly 2,500, about 15 percent of the cotton-mill workers (*AWCR* 17[1903]: 848).

[154] *AWCR* 17(1903): 87, 209, 245, 312, 491, 695, 702; *Manufacturer* 7(May 12, 1894): 1–2; *American Carpet and Upholstery Journal* 21(April 1903): 75 (hereafter *ACUJ*).

and framed a call for fifty-five hours, thirty-nine trades ultimately joining the common front. However, it soon became evident that though all would stand for the five-hour reduction, there was division on the wage issue related to it. Thirty-six trades were willing to accept any loss in earnings the shorter week might entail. As most of the weavers, beamers, spoolers and such were paid piece rates, there was for them at least the potential of minimizing any real loss through close attention to their output levels. On the other hand, three important groups did not accept this consensus. Wool spinners, commonly paid by the week (except for those running mules), would not be able to avoid a cut in net earnings, and voted to ask sixty hours' pay for fifty-five hours' work. Under these terms, unless their frames were speeded up, spinning firms' labor cost per pound of yarn would escalate about 8 percent. Yarn dyers, fuming over the gradual degradation of their trade, demanded a general advance from twelve to thirteen dollars weekly, *plus* lopping off the five hours. This represented an 18 percent increase in their hourly wages, piece rates being unusual in dyeworks. The always independent ingrain weavers decided on fifty-five hours *and* a 10 percent rate hike in their price schedule. These three groups represented about one-sixth of the city's textile workers; their departure from the simple common demand was no trivial defection.[155]

The Kensington Labor Lyceum played a role for labor complementary to that which the Manufacturers' Club had for proprietors. It was the focal point for social and trade gatherings; unions, including the fractious skein

[155] *AWCR* 17(1903): 487, 607; *PL*, May 29, 30, June 1, 2, 1903; *Philadelphia Record*, May 28, 1903. Among the unions at the April convention were

Textile Union No. 8 (Germans-mixed), Art Square Weavers, Terry Weavers, Ingrain Carpet Weavers, Upholstery Weavers Union No. 25, Cloth Weavers' Union, Warpers and Warp Dressers, Tapestry Carpet Weavers' Unions Nos. 1, 2, and 3, Rug Weavers' Union No. 1, Beamers and Twisters, Skein Dyers [and Mercerizers], Germantown Textile Workers Union (mixed), Narrow Loom Fixers, Broad Loom Fixers, [Piece] Dyers, Tapestry Carpet Printers Unions Nos. 1, 2, and 3, Damask Weavers, Hosiery Workers, Upholstery Weavers of West Philadelphia, Plush Weavers, Amalgamated Lace Curtain Weavers, Weft Weavers, Spinners, and Blanket Weavers. [*AWCR* 17(1903): 487.]

Thus at least twenty-four unions and twenty-eight locals were present, each sending eleven delegates. Only two were nationally linked, the German union and Local 25. "Mixed" referred to unions making no craft distinctions, here an ethnic grouping carried over from the 1880s and a broad district association in Germantown. The mixed unions aside, craft organization, carried to quite fine extremes, was the template for labor activism in Philadelphia. Their very existence suggests the depth of laborist sentiments among local textile workers; their assemblies, parades, and shop-based democratic proceedings (delegates, et al.) indicate the continuity with practices from the 1870s and 1880s.

dyers, had their offices there. As the June 1 date for implementation of the shortened week neared, reporters would oscillate between the Lyceum and the Club, searching for signs of determination or weakening on either side. Though a few firms quickly granted the workers' demands and a few spinners struck for them early in May, spokesmen for the CTUW and the Textile Manufacturers' Association expressed nothing but confidence that their adversaries' wisdom would prevent a troublesome confrontation. No one from Central would "admit the possibility of a strike" in mid-May, referring to

> the fact that several firms have voluntarily reduced the hours ... and to the spirit of fairness to the employees which has characterized the manufacturers engaged in the textile industry. The manufacturers, on the other hand, assert there will be no strike and no reduction in hours because they will be able, when the proper time shall arrive, to convince their operatives that it would be suicidal to their combined interests to make the change under existing conditions.

Speak of peace, prepare for war. Certain that manufacturers would put up a bold collective front but quickly dissolve into individuals ready to make concessions, the CTUW chose an executive committee to coordinate labor's efforts and tuned up its connections with shop delegates from each trade. Aware of just this weakness in past performances, the TMA leadership quietly put together a "get tough" policy toward its members. During the strike it was revealed that to enforce solidarity, members had been pressed to deposit "forfeit" money with the association, $20 per loom for weavers, $500 per tub for dyers, and an undisclosed sum per spindle for the yarn mills. Should a firm flinch and agree to the workers' terms, these funds would be appropriated by the TMA. The scheme advanced in the 1886 Knights of Labor struggle was reactivated; this time it worked.[156]

---

[156] *AWCR* 17(1903): 515, 577, 637; *PL*, June 2, 4, 1903. The "ironclad" forfeit ploy was first revealed by a member of the dyers' union May 26, but he had the figures wrong ($40/loom). *Ledger* reporters pursued the matter with manufacturers and printed fuller details the following week, the final confirmation coming from a member of the TMA executive board. On the other side, W. T. Smith and Son, much involved in the 1880s fray with the Knights, issued this notice explaining its adoption of fifty-five hours:

> The firm of W. T. Smith and Son, Inc., being an incorporated company, incorporated not to sell stock, but to perpetuate the business and to give the deserving people in its employ a certain amount of stock to interest them in the business, have long contemplated putting the fifty-five hour week into execution, and previous to putting up this notice the firm called the heads of the departments together last November and discussed the matter. ... They (the firm) feel, with the large amount of new and improved machinery they have added to their plant, and the systematic method which they have of running their mill, that they can produce as much and as good work in fifty-five hours as heretofore in sixty,

The tactic split textile manufacturers into three groups. Most TMA members who were also members of the Manufacturers' Club reportedly sent checks to the association. A minority of this group and a majority of the 500 manufacturers not club members refused to do so, but individually pledged to resist the demand. A much smaller number thought the shorter week a reasonable notion and agreed to it before or in the first days of the shutdown. Whereas about eighty firms, including the Bromley lace mills, fell into this final category, profoundly encouraging the workers, most of the signers were small firms trying to keep running in their rush season. Four manufacturers admitted they agreed to reduce hours simply because they were in the process of moving their machinery from one mill to another and wanted to complete this while most of the industry was idle. As to the timing of the strike, it coincided far better with the production season for carpets, hosiery, upholstery, and lace than it did for woolens and worsteds. Though the former were producing on orders taken in April and May for the fall, the latter's fall rush was nearly over, for they had opened in February and by May were finishing duplicate orders before setting out their spring styles in August. Hence their suppliers, wool and worsted spinners and yarn dyers, were in their slowest period, having finished contracts for weaving mills' fall lines and waiting until late July for orders for the new season. Given the time spread of seasonal demands across sectors, there was no ideal moment for an industrywide strike. It may have been the relative strength of the carpet and upholstery locals that fixed the June 1 date, but it was surely not due to knit goods workers, for there the coalition was at its weakest. As principally "women and girls," hosiery workers drew little attention from organizationally minded male finishers and full-fashioned knitters. When several thousand female knitters joined the strike, both delight and surprise were expressed by workers in other trades.[157]

The general strike had a ragged beginning. By Friday May 29, thirty-seven firms had agreed to shortened hours. Workers at thirteen other firms, turned down in their request, jumped the gun and walked out. John Ledge, hearing his hosiery operatives discussing a strike, anticipated them and locked his doors at noon Friday. Nine more signatures were recorded Saturday, including Ivins, Dietz and Metzger, and the Bromleys, but here were some worrisome notes. The first firm granted the concession only to weavers and dyers, the second only to lace weavers. The auxiliary departments were not

besides saving coal bills and numerous other expenses. . . . In reference to paying the same amount of wages for fifty-five hours as sixty, this is a voluntary contribution of the firm to its employees, feeling that they will appreciate it in the spirit in which it is offered. (*ACUJ* 21[May 1903]: 65.)

[157] *PL*, June 3, 4, 1903.

affected (winders, spoolers, burlers, etc.). Were the companies' workers in other trades and unions to strike, effectively shutting the mill, or should they give up such leverage as they had and work as usual? In the rush toward Monday, no answer could be had, but this issue would prove to be one among many managerial wedges that would fracture labor's fragile unity.[158]

In a circular letter released by the CTUW's five-man executive to greet the strike's official opening, an appeal was made for press and public support. Memorably, the committee announced a "strike for lower wages in an effort to get shorter hours." Workers needed this change in seasonal trades "so that they may work more steadily." This was necessary "for the sake of the children and women" workers, to improve health, and enhance opportunities for family togetherness, education, and leisure. To these social concerns was added only one economic one: "to get some of the benefits from the use of machinery." The technical advances of the 1890s had made work more demanding and output more impressive, yet wages and hours had changed little. If workers could produce more in less time, they should have time as their reward rather than have production expectations expand limitlessly within a fixed sixty-hour frame. Noting that Monday was a holiday (Whit-suntide, observed at some predominantly English mills), the committee expected that the full impact of the strike and the rapid acceptance of the workers' terms would be apparent by Tuesday.[159]

The press quickly accepted quite fantastic estimates from the CTUW committee as to how many workers were involved in the general strike. The numbers started at 75,000, rose to 95,000, 102,000, and finally 125,000 within a week, even though the first figure was a high guess of total city textile employment and the last would have taken in every textile mill in the state. These figures were picked up by the trade journals, and proprietors made no efforts to counter them. More realistic data was buried in the manufacturing census volumes released the previous year, but no one in Philadelphia questioned the totals. It was enough that there were a vast mass of textile workers in the city and more of them were on strike than ever before.

Though the TMA board had imposed a gag order on its members, man-ufacturers were far from silent. Still, all but tough, crusty James Dobson spoke to newsmen anonymously. Views among those taking the strike were fairly uniform. With a fifty-five-hour week, Philadelphia mills could not compete with those in other states where statutory or customary hours were longer. Profits were already appallingly low; with fifty-five hours, mills would

---

[158] *AWCR* 17(1903): 710; *PL*, May 30, 31, June 1, 1903; *Philadelphia Bulletin*, May 30, June 1, 1903.

[159] *PL*, June 1, 2, 3, 1903; *Philadelphia Record*, May 31, 1903.

soon relocate. Worse, manufacturers doubted the truthfulness of the workers' sacrificial stance regarding lower earnings. Dobson firmly denied that workers had said anything of the sort. Others who had read or heard differently asserted with some plausibility that the ploy hid "a masked ulterior purpose." Strikers were already boasting that "once the reduction in hours is granted, ... they will agitate for another increase of wages." In scoring the role of professional "agitators," one proprietor showed he understood something about factory culture. "These strike promoters have renewed their war on us after wages in Philadelphia have been put upon a higher level than anywhere else in the country... Not one in ten of our people wanted to go out, but they went because they hated to be called scabs." His proportions may have been well off the mark, but he surely knew Kensington.[160]

The rowdy old factory district was a sight to behold on the first day of the general strike. A mood of celebration mixed with earnest calculation pervaded Kensington's streets and parks, and was captured with remarkable verisimilitude by a *Ledger* correspondent. Yet the same column showed indirectly how partial was this general strike. Some operatives went to work as usual, apparently indifferent to the hubbub. They were snubbed to be sure by their neighbors, who hoped the public silent treatment and private, after-hours pressure would have an effect. Outside Kensington, there were big gaps. Special efforts were made the first week to bring in the Spring Garden mills; but more encouraging words were said of Germantown. Committees were shipped out to rouse West Philadelphia; others crossed to bolster Manayunk, where young boys had walked out to the amazement of adult workers and overseers. Manayunk held about a thousand Polish workers at this time, immigrants chiefly from the textile district in and about Lodz. No effort had ever been made to organize them. A local was hurriedly formed, but what would hold it together? Though the CTUW claimed first 35,000 then 45,000 members among its affiliates, this was as exaggerated a figure as the press estimates of strikers. As with the Knights, the unorganized

[160] *PL*, June 2, 1903; *AWCR* 13(1903): 710. The *Ledger* was the paper of record; *AWCR* reproduced its lists of firms struck and signed verbatim, misspellings included. At least one proprietor complained vocally about the lack of effective manufacturers' publicity.

No side in a strike was ever successful without having public opinion with it. When the coal strike was on the mine owners and operators determined on a policy of silence. They lost because public opinion was with the strikers.... The manufacturers will lose this strike unless they are more open with the public. The strikers ... conceal nothing and everything they say and do is spread broadcast in the newspapers. The result is the public is with them.

This was a minority view; most millmen opposed publicity as it would "expos[e] ... the private business affairs of the manufacturers, which the public had no right to know." (*PL*, June 4, 1903.)

swelled the strikers' ranks, and even joined locals in a crisis, but like a shoddy fabric, the goods would pull apart under stress.[161]

By Wednesday, June 3, the strike had gathered momentum and enthusiasm; the big Southwark Mills, which now included Campbell's old plant, stopped work. Inroads were being made in the Spring Garden district and the hosiery girls were cheered as they came into the streets. Yet given the initial high estimates, these successes were merely tacked on to the totals for public consumption. What proportion of workers were actually out? How many had gained the fifty-five-hour concession? On the second point, a fair guess may be made from the published lists of mills signed up. Instead of the advertised 15,000, however, a generous estimate would place between 6,000 and 7,000 workers in the fifty-five-hour club. If we put the probable total 1903 workforce at about 65,000, a bit above the 1900 census level, my "educated" guess would be that roughly 36,000 workers struck June 1 or before, and that perhaps 10,000 more stopped their factories by the close of the first week. This would leave perhaps 20 percent of local textile workers unaffected, with 10 percent winning their demand and 70 percent striking to secure it. The strike was most effective in the carpet trade; sixty-two of the sixty-three ingrain firms were shuttered. It was least successful in knits; even the committee never put out a number representing much over half the city workforce in that sector. Nonetheless, fifty-five hours had magnetic appeal; the great strike was not as vast as its leaders imagined, but it was the most stunning effort yet made by Philadelphia labor.[162]

Everyone knew the strike pivoted around the militance of the dyers. It was dyers who policed Kensington and Port Richmond to prevent violence and avoid clashes with city blues. Without dyers returning to work, the big integrated mills and the middling and small specialists could little hope to resume. Yet manufacturers well knew that giving in to them would pave the way for the "ulterior purpose" in other crafts; the five hundred dollar penalty per tub reflected dyeing's centrality to the millmen's resistance. In the first days, one unionist spread the word that the dyers, spinners, and ingrain weavers would drop their wage planks in order that all could win the shorter week. Preserving its coordinating rather than managerial role, the CTUW committee immediately denied that any such plan was afoot. The consequence was a fatal stalemate. By Philadelphia standards the committee properly lacked the power to dictate terms to its constituent members, but this

---

[161] *PL*, May 31, June 1, 2, 1903. A problem that marked Manayunk as a painful weakpoint was that "one difficulty in effecting an organization in that part of the city is that no one will accept the responsibility of acting as officers" (*PL*, June 6, 1903).

[162] Ibid., June 2, 3, 4, 5, 1903; *Philadelphia Record*, June 3, 1903; *Philadelphia Bulletin*, June 3, 4, 5, 1903.

incapacity facilitated a demand spread that stiffened proprietary necks. In a test of endurance, the manufacturers could settle back and await splits among the strikers as the three crafts' tough stands inexorably shredded the coalition.[163]

Even facing a long battle, the textile workers were not without important resources. The *Ledger* asserted that many had been "thrifty," saving a portion of their earnings for several years in anticipation of an impending struggle. Some owned their homes, and "those who lease their dwellings get them at a small figure." Though neither Samuel Smiles nor Andrew Carnegie would have been pleased at this use of labor's capital, Kensington at least was prepared for the long haul. Beyond savings, textile workers had access to crucial sources of credit from their neighborhood "grocers and provision men." One of these corner-store merchants explained that most mill workers "deal on the book, . . . settling their account every week, or every two weeks, though some pay cash," adding, "It is from these persons that we make our living, and in this instance we must help those who helped us." The grocers had hardly been unaware of June first's significance.

> Anticipating the strike, many grocers had laid in a large stock before the strike was declared, and so will not feel the effects of the strike for some time. As the population of Kensington is not a floating one the grocers say they will not lose, whatever the outcome of the strike.

Butchers could not stock ahead like the grocers, but if strikers could stand tinned beef, bread, and beans as a diet, they would be well sustained by this petty bourgeois–labor alliance. However, inroads had already been made by the lower-price, cash-only stores, undermining to a degree this cultural linkage. The Philadelphia-based *American Carpet and Upholstery Journal* shrewdly commented on this shift in consumption patterns.

> [W]eavers have for some time past been buying their supplies from branches of a big grocery-store combination that sells only for cash. This feature has, of course, removed a source of strength which the textile weavers formerly banked on to a large extent. The stores at which they traded, in turn, obtained heavy credits from their wholesale houses and were thereby able to supply the most available aid.

John Kendrick, the *Journal*'s editor, may have overestimated the shift, but exchanging strike credit, "a feature of almost every corner in Kensington," for a few dimes' savings a week at a cash store was both modern, rational in the best neoclassical economic terms, and a terrible strategic bargain.

---

[163] *PL*, May 31, June 2, 3, 1903. Mr. Settle, a union president, said June 1 that "the dyers hold the key to the situation, for without them no mill can work and they are in a position to withstand a long siege."

Corner grocers only fed their regulars during walkouts, and the chains knew only the color of your money.[164] The TMA declined to meet with CTUW representatives throughout the strike, despite repeated pleas and union efforts to bring the mayor or other "disinterested" parties in as mediators. This, like the gag rule, was a departure from previous practice, a betrayal of tradition that was denounced to no effect. Philadelphia textile unions were no longer regarded as fair and businesslike; the TMA now treated them as though they were invisible. The threat to accumulation that short hours carried was ably, if naively, presented by another nameless spinning mill owner. Ignoring technological gains and seasonal surges and lags, he argued that cutting one-twelfth of the work week meant that mills essentially would be idle for a month every year, earning nothing on their operators' investments. The reduction of hours would seriously impair the manufacturer, "for he has steam up, machinery ready, and his fixed charges, and it is to his advantage to get as much out of his investment as he can each day." Marx could hardly have put it much better, though the distance between such thinking and Marshallian marginalism was considerable. Unwillingness to deal with the CTUW did not mean that proprietors were idle. When strikers arrived at the end of the first week to collect their pay for the last six days before the walkout, they were greeted with threats that unless they soon resumed the sixty-hour schedule the mills would close for the entire summer. James Dobson was prominent among these glowering figures, setting the pace for the entire Manayunk district where the notices were concentrated. There had already been a "break" in wool-centered Manayunk, "the weakest place in the strike." The threat produced "a general resumption of work" there on Monday, June 8.[165]

In Kensington, at James Doak's worsted spinning mill, the founder's son Charles was a year into his factory apprenticeship when the general strike arrived. In his journal, young Doak recorded the course of the affair at Standard Mills, providing an inside view of developments at the firm level. On the opening day, Doak's combers stayed home, but much of the rest of

---

[164] *PL*, June 3, 1903; *ACUJ* 21 (July 1903): 53. The chain Kendrick referred to was probably I.G.A., some of whose green-fronted corner stores still operated in Philadelphia neighborhoods in the 1970s. Kensington is the only area where "strike credit" is explicitly mentioned, but it would be surprising if it were not common throughout working-class districts of Philadelphia.

[165] *PL*, June 5, 7, 8, 9, 1903. A small number of "boys" had returned as early as June 4 to several mills; several hundred workers started in immediately upon hearing the Friday threat, and the whole district followed on the 8th. Dobson made no similar threats at his Falls of Schuylkill mills; there his workers would shortly experience a different tactical maneuver. See also *AWCR* 17(1903): 725, 733.

the workforce arrived at seven and left at ten in the morning to join the strike. On Friday, payday, a notice was posted to the effect that the mill would reopen Monday the eighth. It lacked the Manayunk addendum, stating only that "Any concessions made by the [Textile] Manufacturers Protective Association will be given by us." Since the association had announced it would make no compromises and was ignoring the CTUW committee, this was little more than an announcement of Doak's solidarity with the TMA. This attempt to "get the hands in" failed, as on Monday only "a few hands come [sic] in but not enough to start up the machinery, and at ten o'clock the engine was stopped again."

Charles Doak, then twenty-two years old, had started his tour through the rooms of his father's factory in 1902, after spending one year working with the wool sorters (whose tempers were as fabled as their skills) and three in technical school at Drexel Institute studying drafting, principles of the steam engine, and such. By the summer of 1903, he had progressed through the machine shop and carding rooms to the combing section, filling his journal with technical notes and comments on problem solving. During the strike, Charles and the room bosses circulated through the silent mill performing maintenance and repair jobs, for "there are a great many things that can be seen and need attending to when the machinery is stopped." Through this close contact with the set of supervisors, Doak became more intimately connected with the experienced overseers than he had previously been. In later months, his journal filled with appreciative passages on the "tricks" the "bosses" showed him; their full names disappeared as they became regular colleagues – George, Bill, and Tom. During the strike at Standard Mills, James Doak's son and eventual successor was integrated into the mill team, an important achievement that overshadowed lost business or the completion of overdue maintenance.

The Doak mills were one of the first Kensington firms to resume production. Rather than threatening to fire workers or idle them until the fall (James Dobson's tactic), the elder Doak sent his supervisors into the neighborhood to talk with operatives from their departments. The result: "On Monday June the fifteenth, a few hands were persuaded by J. Vogelman to come in. Each succeeding day of this week more came in, till on Monday the twenty-second a large majority started up." There was no hint of anger, but a spot of "trouble" appeared just as the strikers were beginning to pour back into the mill. When the firm had chosen to start its engine on June 8, Bill Anderson, the engineer, declined to report for work, exhibiting his solidarity with the spinners and combers. His assistant, the "fireman," had taken on the job and was rewarded by being promoted to the absent engineer's place. Upon Anderson's return, there was difficulty.

Trouble was just avoided at one stage. Bill Anderson came in on
Friday the nineteenth and was told that his job was given to the fireman,
but tha[t] he could work on the dryer. [H]e left and the combers who
had promised to come in Monday threatened to stay out. Anderson was
pacified, and promised his old job back, if he would take the dryer, till
everything was settled, at no monetary loss to himself. This brought
him in together with the combers.

With this compromise, forced by the comber's reciprocal solidarity, Anderson
was mollified, for his skilled worker's rate was assured during a face-saving
interval until the engine room would be his to manage once again.

   Crucially, the management option that was forgone must be stressed here,
for it indicates quietly the strength of workers' shop culture, even as a strike
was collapsing. Anderson, protesting, was not fired. Such an act would have
shut the mill again, wrecking a week's patient persuasion and demonstrating
bad faith on the Doaks' part. Anderson occupied that fuzzy middle ground
between labor and management, the foreman's realm. While other room
bosses had worked at routine tasks through the strike, accepting their bond
with the proprietor, Anderson had rejected this role and was punished with
a demotion in favor of the fireman who had broken ranks early on. This
action was rescinded, but in a fashion that minimized the social damage all
around. James Doak backed off in large part, but Anderson would spend
some penalty time away from his normal duties. The latter accepted this
once his pay was guaranteed at the old rate, leading to the combers' keeping
their "promise" and the full resumption Monday, June 22.[166]

   By that point, wider danger signs were accumulating. The flow of newly
signed fifty-five-hour firms had all but ceased. In Manayunk, the mills were
running solidly and elsewhere scattered "breaks" continued to surface, even
in Kensington. During the week of June 15, Mother Jones had toured the
city, making rousing speeches, asserting that "this great industrial war ...
will continue until the last capitalist shall surrender." Others were not so
certain. A monster parade was expected to draw 30,000 marchers, half of
them "toiling children." The result was hugely disappointing, as at least
nine-tenths of the strikers stayed home. "Several thousand" workers formed
at Independence Hall, carrying banners emblazoned "We Only Ask for
Justice" and "55 Hours or Nothing." At City Hall Plaza, where committee
members and Mother Jones spoke, the crowd of marchers and lunch-hour

---

[166] Charles Doak, Journal, 1902–06, Archives, Philadelphia College of Textiles and Science,
pp. 150–1. Doak's 300 workers held a general meeting on Tuesday, June 16 (*PL*, June
15, 1903), but did not vote then to return. Instead, workers trickled back later in the
week. No mention of intermediation surfaced at this point in press accounts.

onlookers numbered no more than five thousand. Given the banner's two options, it began to look as though "Nothing" was the more likely outcome.[167]

The several crafts demanding advances in conjunction with the hours reduction were becoming increasingly unpopular. On June 23, Mother Jones delivered a denunciation of their approach, in terms that curiously echoed the carpet manufacturers' 1900 statement. "You shouldn't come out with any demand for wages. There's where you made a mistake. You must learn to be more businesslike in dealing with problems of this kind. Wages should never have entered into this question. There is time enough for everything." The dyers and ingrain workers refused to budge; the spinners made no statement in reply. As the rest of the strikers witnessed breaks in Fairmount, South Philadelphia, and in knitting generally, manufacturers chuckled at James Dobson's artful manipulation of the scenario at the Falls of Schuylkill. The CTUW acknowledged that if Dobson gave way, the proprietors' coalition would sag. Dobson, at stage center, played his role with consummate skill.[168]

In their cloth, blanket, and carpet mills, James and John Dobson employed both workers calling for the straight fifty-five hours and dyers and spinners whose demands included wage increases. On June 19, James Dobson announced he would offer fifty-five hours to all, but pay increases to none, neatly dividing his strikers against one another. They wrangled for the best part of the next week. The dyers backed the "day workers" (those paid a flat hourly sum) in their reluctance to take the proportionate loss in earnings, while piece-rate hands urged acceptance of the proposal. Meeting with the strike committee on the twenty-fourth, the Dobsons withdrew their offer, returning to a no-compromise sixty-hour position. The committee returned the next day, cowed, and asked "if the strikers would be permitted to resume work at once." Replying that he had seventy-five "loyal" men "finishing up some work," James Dobson said he had no plans to open up until this was completed. "There is no use calling on me again for at least five weeks." Whipsawed by these tactics, the strikers were surely bewildered when the plant foreman spread word that the mills would reopen Monday, June 29. Nevertheless, their ranks closed; only 120 of the three to four thousand workers entered the mills. This reassertion of solidarity did not last very long. A week later, 1,400 workers joined the early defectors, imperiling resistance at the Falls.

The key to this shift was a symbolic but tiny concession to the Brussels carpet weavers union, the Dobsons having the largest assemblage of Brussels looms in the city. They were offered a fifty-eight and three-quarter hour

---

[167] *PL*, June 15, 17, 18, 1903; *AWCR* 17(1903): 762, 783, 793.
[168] Ibid., June 24, 27, 28, 30, 1903; *Record*, June 25, 1903; *AWCR* 17(1903): 832.

week on July 1 and within a few days voted to accept it and return to their looms. This separate peace both cracked the united front of the CTUW and sent masses of Dobson's strikers back into the plant. As the special call went out for a CTUW meeting to expel the Brussels weavers and news arrived that Mother Jones's children's crusade was disintegrating, the manufacturers coolly stated they were in no rush to reopen before September. "Affairs in Tangled Shape" read the *Ledger*'s headline July 13; thereafter, the strike deteriorated steadily. On the fifteenth, Dobson threatened to close until Christmas if the rest of his workers did not return. Within two weeks most, excepting half the dyers and all the loom fixers, had come in, but in their absence little serious work could be done. On July 29, the Falls mills stopped again, putting three thousand men and women on the street. The loom fixers soon gave up the fight citywide, but the dyers held out tenaciously, drawing growing hostility from their fellow workers. Brussels weavers were forced out of the carpet mills due to a shortage of colored yarns; they vowed to "get even at the first opportunity" with the dyers. Some of the latter were trickling back to their works, leading to outbursts of violence, as striking dyers clubbed them and were arrested by police on several occasions. In August unions began withdrawing from the CTUW; even in Kensington workers were deserting the strike in droves. Everywhere else production was moving toward normal levels, with dyed yarns being shipped in from New Jersey and Rhode Island and about half the city dyeworks operating with part or full complements. Dobson reopened at the end of the month, the ingrain weavers quit the struggle in mid-September, and the last third of the militant dyers finally gave it up October 12 after almost four and a half months. Whereas the ingrain union cautiously argued "the strike has shown our strength, our loyalty, and has taught us many lessons," one worker put it plainly: "We have lost the strike, and that is all there is to it."[169]

The 1903 general strike was only possible because textile labor in Philadelphia had adapted its institutions during the crisis of the 1890s, just as manufacturers had altered theirs. Independent unions, principally of skilled male workers, had reformed after the Knights' collapse and in time had

---

[169] *PL*, June 20, 21, 23, 24, 25, 26, July 1, 7, 8, 9, 11, 13, 14, 16, 19, 21, 25, 26, 29, 30, August 1, 17, October 13, 1903; *Philadelphia Bulletin*, August 10, 11, 14, 17, 27, 31, September 15, 26, 28, October 3, 5, 1903; *AWCR* 17(1903): 853, 883, 888, 917, 1015, 1191, 1251, 1286. About half of Dobson's dyers had returned by the end of July, so his July 29 shutdown may have been at least partly a revenge move. Reports of scattered rate cuts in Kensington also surfaced, and dyers were refused reemployment more often than any other class of workers. With regard to Dobson's maneuvers the *Ledger* noted July 25: "The determination of the owners of these mills to hold out against the demands ... and the methods employed to this end have met with the admiration of the strikers themselves, although detrimental to their interests."

federated under the CTUW banner. However, the system of delegates and shop committees that persisted in Philadelphia mandated that the CTUW would have few executive powers. As a miniature but independent version of the national AF of L, it attempted what the larger body rarely considered, a comprehensive mobilization of labor. Unable to dictate common terms, unable to manage any process of compromise on the core demands, its leaders instead rushed about the city speaking, cajoling, encouraging. This structural weakness was both perceived and exploited by the TMA, which refused to meet either with the CTUW executive or with individual union leaders, treating only as individual firms with their own shop delegations. Equally crippling, the separate unions had before the confrontation done little serious work among the unorganized. Both spatially and sectorally there were severe gaps – hosiery, Germantown, Manayunk. The gender line was barely crossed even in trades where union coverage was significant, and enrollment of the newer ethnic groups had been ignored. When women and girls abandoned the knit-goods mills, skilled male workers and their organizations had no idea what to do with or for them. No women's leadership roles were created or encouraged; Mother Jones was imported. The Polish textile workers in Manayunk and Port Richmond were tossed into new locals by organizers with Irish, English, or German backgrounds. Italians who were taking dyers' places, possibly lured from Paterson for the purpose, were either despised and assaulted or plaintively urged to go away. Organizational structure and the factory culture of skilled workmen were both critical handicaps in handling crisis tasks.

The strikers also came to their struggle in 1903 with fewer tools than they had possessed in nineteenth-century battles. Respectability haunted the strike; order, dignity, calm were the watchwords. Mother Jones brilliantly lampooned the millmen. They "tell you they cannot afford to give you shorter hours. But who built these big mills? If they make no money how were they erected? They stay at the seashore, yet they cannot afford it. I tell you what to do, start up a soup-house for them tomorrow." Yet the great firebrand, in concluding her speech, "warned the strikers to refrain from all violence, and be peaceable, but firm." They followed this advice, which was repeated daily. There were few disturbances, few attempts to intimidate defectors, no showers of rotten fruit. Even picketing was infrequent. Only the dyers, as the strike was crumbling, resorted to the older ways, battering Italian and Polish strikebreakers in desperate sallies that brought them rebukes and arrests. Fear of the police power *could* have contributed to this orderly pattern. The militia had helped to crush the 1902 Paterson strike. But whereas the Coal and Iron Police roamed the factory towns across Pennsylvania, they were forbidden entry to Philadelphia. Moreover, arrested strikers had long been released by politically sensitive magistrates' courts with small fines or on bond to behave themselves. Fear of force was not the key. Rather, in this strike, the CTUW believed the public held the balance of power, and played to public opinion and sympathetic press coverage. To achieve respectability, a lawful demeanor was essential. Hence the rationales for shorter hours stressed virtue and bourgeois sentiments: education, family togetherness, the frailty of women and children, as though five hours would yield social betterment and a demonstration that workers could control their tempers would secure the five hours. By all reports, the strikers were much admired for the moral tone of their demands and the absence of the customary rowdy tactics from years gone by. None of this made the slightest impression on the mill owners, for whom the issue was economic through and through. Exercising comparable discipline, which in the forfeit arrangement was even framed in money terms, and giving a little manipulative push here and there, they looked on with satisfaction as the strike self-destructed.[170]

Finally, in retrospect, the core demand was itself an indication of the unions' constituencies, and as such proved problematic for the strike. The CTUW held the best-paid section of the textile trades, skilled predominantly adult male craft workers, perhaps 20,000 strong. Two-thirds of them were willing to take the shorter hours and use their talents and piecework rates to restore any cash losses. The rest wanted shorter hours and the same or more money. Promulgating the fifty-five-hour line for the other forty to forty-five thousand city textile workers, many of them women and children working on flat hourly or weekly wages, virtually entailed defections and defeat. The skilled cadre earned from $9.00 to $20.00 weekly, but women "day workers" got $6.00 to $8.00 and children $3.50 to $5.00. Once the rhetoric faded, they recognized that they were going to lose about 8 percent of their much lower base ($.25 to $.50 per week) and that they had no means to recover this sum by working more intensively. The chance was that they would work harder anyway in the event the fifty-five-hour week was won, for they would have to keep up with the pace of the piece-raters. Though neighborhood pressure kept them out longer in Kensington than in Spring Garden or Manayunk, they broke everywhere in time. The fifty-five-hour demand had not been drafted with their interests in mind; morally satisfying, like the appeal to public opinion through respectability, it was materially deficient and it failed.

As the strike tide ebbed, and the CTUW faltered, representatives from the AF of L's United Textile Workers of America entered discussions with the skein dyers and other unions, arguing that national associations could better serve Philadelphia workers than their shattered regional assembly.

[170] *PL*, June 16, 1903.

When the strike finance committee filed its final report in December, the CTUW's tiny resource base was exposed. Only $25,000 had been raised and dispensed for strike support, a third of this coming from the United Mine Workers at Mother Jones's intercession. Those who had stayed out more than a few weeks had devoured savings and gone into debt. Moreover, the holdout dyers were confronted with a technological threat. In the course of the strike, both dyeworks and mills with attached dyehouses announced they had filed orders for the latest dyeing machines, each of which would do as much work with two or three men as had been possible with five or six before. In the fall of 1903, a number of questions became unavoidable. How many of the locals would survive this defeat? How many would join the UTWA? What was the future for industrywide action? Would women and the rest of the unorganized be drawn into the textile unions? How? These troubling matters hovered over Kensington as the great strike ended and winter approached.[171]

Manufacturers had reason for cheerfulness, to be sure, but their celebrations were tempered by concerns not vastly different from those that workers mulled over. Whereas knit-goods firms were pleased at the feebleness of the fifty-five-hour effort in their sector, the ingrain mills had lost a full season's trade. Would they ever recover? Tapestry carpets, straw mattings, even woven paper rugs were crowding the cheaper end of the business. Ingrain workers were broke, but they clung to their union with a stubbornness that was as infuriating as it was admirable. Would others do likewise, learn from the defeat and mount fresh challenges mill by mill, sector by sector? Or would the summer of 1903 erase the threat, confining labor organization to a handful of crafts? Would shop floor relations become more nettling and erratic or had conditions favorable to stability and successful accumulation been restored? Though divided on these issues, TMA members agreed that their association, assembled again in a crisis, should be perpetuated and extended beyond its core of Manufacturers' Club members. Labor would continue to search for an institutional form adequate to its needs, but capital seemed to have found one, refined it over the previous sixteen years and used it to forge an emergency alliance that stood the test of the 1903 general strike. With its whist tournaments and European excursions providing easy social intercourse, the Manufacturers' Club had developed as the focal point for Philadelphia industrialists' leisure activities as well as the operational center for their political and labor crisis mobilizations. In a sense, contin-

---

[171] *AWCR* 17(1903): 1230, 1601; PA Department of Internal Affairs, *Annual Report (1903), Part III: Industrial Statistics*, Harrisburg, PA, 1904, pp. 457–8; *Bulletin*, August 17, September 26, 1903.

uation of the TMA was of little moment, for so long as the club prospered, the base for its reconstitution was firmly established. No one would soon forget the manufacturers' decisive solidarity of 1903.

4.7. Conclusion

The decade after 1893 brought two crises in the Philadelphia textile industry, a long, grinding depression and a shorter, but intense confrontation between proprietors and textile workers. Viewed in the context of contemporaneous developments in Paterson, Fall River, Lowell, and Lawrence, the depression triggered a variety of reorientations, a blizzard of tactics devised to further accumulation in an environment of considerable constraint. In some cases, as at Paterson, the consequences both drove explosive wedges between millmen and workers and degraded their products, endangering the future of the trade. At Fall River, the innovative selling committee and the stretch out partly rebuilt profitability, but failure to exercise the technological option offered by the battery loom had similar negative implications. Meanwhile, at Lowell and Waltham, a set of venerable New England corporations abandoned the bulk staple orientation for mixed-output production or ventures into the burgeoning knitting sector. Their staple colleagues in cottons remained allied in strategy and had sufficient strength to obstruct labor's best efforts, but their dividends continued to slide toward unsettling levels. At Lawrence, William Wood employed marketing innovations, direct selling, and tactical pricing to establish the Washington Mills as the reference point in plain worsteds, then expanded its influence through the American Woolen merger. Not only did this combine substantially penetrate fancy-goods markets occupied by flexible firms, it also, through its financial strength and multiplant operations, had sufficient resources to stand a long strike against the stretch out, introduced to enhance productivity in its semistaple lines.

In Philadelphia, restructuring had production and distributional components. Major firms entered the manufacture of new novelties, lace and upholstery, full-fashioned hosiery, as others added more promising variations on their older specialties. (Park Mills started a shift toward tapestry and velvet carpets about 1900.) Doak and Dolan's successors dropped integrated production for specialization in worsted yarns, as did Dobson with the resuscitated Schofield mills. The 1903 strike pushed dyeworks toward technological change, and the ensuing mechanization further debilitated working dyers' control of a trade already bludgeoned by the Dempsey decision. In marketing their seasonal goods, firms moved toward leasing New York offices, hiring travelers, and in general sophisticating the means for selling direct and avoiding the loss of price control that went along with the use of commission houses. Attempts at common movements of pricing were undertaken, with some success, in carpets, upholstery, and spinning, adding to the interfirm links that contributed to the manufacturers' 1903 triumph. Skilled labor, recovering from the Knights' disaster, created in the 1890s a score of independent unions and a central body within which they could determine courses of action while preserving craft autonomy. The CTUW's failure in 1903 exposed the institutional weaknesses of Philadelphia textile unions, but did little to diminish the achievement their revival and development represented.

Yet just as in Lowell or Fall River, the decade's experiences illustrated the vulnerabilities of the Philadelphia production format. The shoddy maneuver degraded wool goods during the depression, and when firms sought thereafter to restore values and qualities, they met initially stiff price resistance from buyers. The trend toward sample and duplicate ordering added risk and stretched out the period for and costs of selling. Family firms faced succession tangles unlikely to cripple bureaucratically managed corporations. Technical advances, especially in simplifying knitting machines and speeding output, offered inducements for rural new starts as portions of the trade became relatively standardized in product, thus diminishing skill requirements. The emergence of American Woolen brought price leadership to bear on the worsted and fancy wool fabrics sector, duplicating the roles played by Smith and the Lowell Company in carpets. More broadly, the whole regional system was enormously dependent on the solidity of the tariff and the political dominance of protectionist Republicans in national politics. Like Paterson, Philadelphia's prowess had been shaped largely by immigrant workers and proprietors feasting on import substitution and a growing national market. If the tariff wall crumbled, or any of the above time bombs went off, prospects for accumulation could erode rapidly. Over the next fifteen years, from the great strike to the close of World War I, these concerns would provide a steady undertow to the more visible tides of advance and innovation in the Philadelphia textile trades.

5

Peace and war, 1904–1918

"Ten years – even five – have seen great changes in the Kensington mill district, – many old firms have outgrown their old quarters and the new tall mills show the advance of progress and time."

American Carpet and Upholstery Journal, April 1906, p. 73.

"In... these strikes considerable ill-feeling existed between the strikers and their respective employers, and in numerous instances clashes occurred, culminating in several cases in violence. At the [Dobsons'] Bradford Mills, Superintendent Mallison employed special officers and alleged detectives, who were aided at times by the city's policemen.... The Masland Mills are run and operated by the four sons of C. H. Masland... the eldest being the practical head of the concern.... Hitherto, these mills have rarely, if at all, had serious disputes with their employes [*sic*], almost all of whom have been in their service for many years,... not a few ever since the four Masland heads were boys toddling around the weavers' knees in the factories. Thus a feeling of mutual affection permeated the entire entourage, the workfolks and the Masland Boys usually hailing each other by their Christian names as they met in the mills or elsewhere. When, however, the employees and the Maslands differed on the points of wages and of unionization, the split was marked and for a time so bitter did those involved in the strike become, it seemed as if all of the old time friendly feeling had been wiped out,... Happily, your Commissioners were [instrumental] in ending the strike and reuniting the Masland workers and the Masland Boys in their old happy relations, both parties to the issue cordially thanking the Department of Labor for the success attending the efforts of your Commissioners."

Robert McWade and John Colpoys to William Wilson, Secretary of Labor, June 12, 1915, Federal Mediation and Conciliation Service Case File No. 33/78.

The decade between the end of the general strike and the onset of World War I featured two recessions, solid tariffs through 1913, significant expansion in the Philadelphia knitting trades, and relative calm in labor – capital relations in the regional textile industry. Whereas major upheavals stirred Lawrence and Paterson in 1912 and 1913, the only significant prewar textile walkout in Philadelphia was a 1910 sympathy strike in which Kensington mill workers supported city street railway carmen. Though the prospects for carpet firms eventually eroded, triggering the 1915 conflict at Masland Mills, technical advances deepened the city's position as the center

Figure 11. Carpet Row on Allegheny Avenue, Kensington, 1906, with Thomas Boggs and Sons' Model Carpet Mills in the foreground. (Courtesy of the Pennsylvania Historical and Museum Commission.)

of American hosiery production. Other sectors churned steadily along, dealing with seasonality and cyclical contractions in the course of "normal" business. Philadelphia textile earnings remained among the nation's highest, both for workers and proprietors, and in 1914 the Manufacturers' Club settled comfortably into new and opulent quarters on South Broad Street.

The war upset this "happy" picture. As in 1861, an initial panic gave way to intense activity. The 1913 recession and tariff alterations had induced fears of heavy importations. War declarations then spun off waves of cancelled orders and layoffs. Yet within months local mills were gearing to *export* acres of blankets and military cloths. Rumors of stunning profits circulated freely, but inflation and the necessity of conceding higher prices for work hopelessly muddled everyone's calculations. Supplies of German-made dyestuffs soon dwindled to a trickle, adding to the confusion. Overheated prosperity proved as problematic as depression had been. Relations between proprietors and operatives soured, each accusing the other of greedy self-ishness. Into this tangle plunged the federal government. Its conciliators nervously hovered over each conflict; time and again, Department of Labor administrators encouraged manufacturers to accept stablilization through formal union recognition. Proprietary resistance provoked the largest textile strike in fifteen years, as Kensington cloth weavers shut down production in the war winter of 1917–18. By the armistice, uncertainty had materialized in every quarter. Would there be a depression, a labor insurrection, a smooth transition to normal markets, a restoration of "mutual affection" between masters and hands? Would peace mean war on the home front? Were the war years an aberrant episode that would be followed by a return to older patterns and regularities, or was the ground shifting underneath the mills in some irreversible way?

This chapter is devoted to portraying the Philadelphia textile manufacture at the height of its power and prowess, and ultimately at the edge of decline. In a sense the very quietness of the decade after 1904 mirrors the steady rhythms of Lowell in the early 1850s or Detroit a century later, reflecting the assured workings of a mature industrial format. Disquieting notes were present but hardly dominant; they little prepared the "players" for the coming transformations in the rules and the boundaries of the "game." As in earlier sections, we will here move from aggregate information about the Phila-delphia industry, set against comparable data on other centers, to focus on the internal workings of enterprises. This will expose developing strategies of production and marketing, tensions within a father–son proprietary team, and the day-to-day mechanics of flexible manufacturing. A review of the 1910 transit strike will indicate the continuation of powerful nineteenth-century customs of solidarity, shaming, and collective violence which may be con-trasted with the character of contemporary outbursts in Paterson and Law-rence. Discussion of the flow of tariff revisions will suggest the slipping political force of staunch protectionism after the Taft Old Guard's debacle with T.R. and Wilson. Statistics drawn from 1914 and 1916 sources will then set the stage for war-era scenarios of gain and grasp, leading us toward the paradoxes of the 1920s and the global crisis that brought a weakened system of flexible production to its knees.

5.1. The Philadelphia system and its rivals in 1905

The most striking element in a 1905 freeze-frame of the Philadelphia textile industry (Table 5.1) appears only when it is viewed alongside a companion 1899–1900 portrait (Table 4.9). Whereas employment remained almost con-stant, overall capital invested in city mills rose $14.7 million in five years, a

Table 5.1. *Philadelphia textiles, characteristics by sector, 1905 (city only)*

	N_f	Capital (000)	Workers	Men (%)	Women (%)	Children (%)	Mean capital (000)	Mean workers	Cap./wrkr.
Carpets	91	20,566	12,618	53	38	8	$226	139	$1,629
Cottons	129	17,076	9,445	43	49	8	132	73	1,808
Dye-finish	97	5,098	2,882	81	10	9	52	30	1,769
Hose-knit	145	12,566	13,269	19	67	14	87	92	947
Silk & upholstery	49	7,425	3,344	34	57	9	151	68	2,220
Wool-worsted	130	30,357	16,552	43	44	14	233	127	1,834
Misc.[a]	87	6,077	2,285	59	31	10	70	26	2,660
Totals	728	$99,155	60,395[b]	42	48	10	$136	83	$1,641

N_f = number of firms.
[a] Includes jute and cordage, wool pulling, shoddy, etc.
[b] Includes 25,184 adult males, 28,754 adult females, and 6,457 children aged 12–16.
Source: Derived from Tables in Department of Commerce, Bureau of the Census, *Manufactures: 1905, Part 2: States and Territories,* Washington, D.C., 1907, pp. 978–83.

17 percent jump. Given Philadelphia firms' predilection for carrying large amounts of "live" capital, it might first be suspected that this could well represent reserves from earnings that had resulted from post-depression market surges. Alternately, since inventories are a component of this census category, it could indicate a heavy accumulation of goods, a significant departure from customary practice. Neither was the case; indeed, a simple comparison of sectoral fixed and working capital at the two dates indicates a different sort of reversal. Whereas in 1900, 54 percent of proprietary assets were held in liquid form, 56 percent of the gains through 1905 were spent on brick and iron ($8.3 million), divided about equally between buildings and machinery ($4.1 million vs. $3.8 million), the residual reflecting altered land values.[1] This penchant for expansion and replacement increased fixed assets by 22 percent, evidence of a drive to extend capacity that was visible in the Bromleys' new lace mills, expanded worsted factories, and $3.3 million worth of technology installed in knitting, carpet, and worsted operations. These machine expenditures in turn reflected the arrival of big-ticket, full-fashioned hosiery power knitters, the shift away from ingrains among carpet firms, and the general boom in worsteds, which steadily supplanted woolens in menswear. As ever, Philadelphia textile firms were reacting to the trends in fabric demand, plowing earnings at this juncture into hard assets that promised to keep the industry current technologically while deepening its flexible capacities.

The overall stability of the workforce totals, up only 6 percent since 1890, was also evident in their gender and age composition, little changed in fifteen years (Table 4.10). Within individual divisions, there were some shifts, however. A noticeable shrinkage appeared in dyeworks employment (-573, 1900–5, down 17 percent), stemming from the much-debated technological changes, but it was overshadowed by a sizable addition to the knitting total ($+1,325$, up 11 percent). As the trade that, more than any other in Philadelphia, engaged small numbers of skilled adult men and thousands of low wage women and children, and as, at this point, the trade with the lowest average per worker capital demands, knitting had become the sector of choice for budding entrepreneurs.[2] Though the cost of full-fashioned machinery was, and would remain, forbidding, the making of fancy seamless hose or

---

[1] Data drawn from United States Census Office, *Census Reports, Volume 8, Manufactures (1900), Part 2*, Washington, D.C., 1902, pp. 784–91, and U.S. Department of Commerce, Bureau of the Census, *Manufactures: 1905, Part 2: States and Territories*, Washington, D.C., 1907, pp. 978–83.

[2] Male knitters represented less than one-tenth of the area male textile workforce, though their sector accounted for over one-fifth of employment. By contrast, women in knitting were one-third of all females in area textile jobs and children represented 30 percent of the child labor total. For the wage differentials see Table 5.4.

knitted scarfs, caps, and cardigans involved modestly priced machines and could be commenced in a single room. For scores of eastern European Jewish immigrants, specialty knitting would replay the proprietary capitalist sequence followed earlier by English, Scots, Irish, and German shopmasters in Philadelphia's mid-nineteenth-century carpet, woolen, and spinning sectors.

Profitability in important Philadelphia sectors continued to slip, though relative to the performance of other urban textile centers, the city's advantages were still quite definite (Table 5.2). In most categories where New England contrasts could be developed, the Quaker City had retained the profitability lead it held in 1890. In cottons, only New Bedford's recent attention to finer-count staple goods brought it within reach of the returns harvested from Philadelphia's specialty work on coverlets and lace. Though Lowell in wool and Lawrence in worsteds surpassed Philadelphia's profits on sales, the higher capitalizations of plants in both cities brought their returns to investment below levels in the Pennsylvania metropolis. In wool or worsted, only Woonsocket, dotted with skill-intensive specialty mills, outperformed Philadelphia capital's productivity. Paterson was closely competitive in silks, as befitted the nation's hub of broadsilk output, and was superior in dyeing, understandable given its attention to this highest value textile versus Philadelphia dyers' broader range (from coarse carpet yarn to fine piece-goods coloring).

More significant, however, was the evidence that replication of Philadelphia-style manufacturing within the nearby region was showing greater returns than in the central city, for in woolens and knits, both Norristown and Reading were already presenting more robust figures than core city sectors could display. The threat from suburbanization of production seemed genuine, for the two satellite cities already counted 4,200 workers in these two sectors, over a fifth of Philadelphia's total. If their lower wage rates suggested that they could not attract the key skilled workers necessary to create the most stylish specialties, these outlying firms were nonetheless able to take rewarding advantage of negligible taxes and cheaper factory rents and/or constuction costs to sail forward on a base of generous profitability. In time they would be far more than an irritant, particularly in hosiery, as Reading, a city dedicated to the stocking business, became a nearby rival to Philadelphia's preeminence. On balance, the flexible system retained an edge over older bulk-production centers even as the rate of profit industrywide had fallen since 1890. However, the success of American Woolen in Lawrence and the solid performance of outlying Pennsylvania cities indicated that both mixed-output and suburban strategies were building challenges to Philadelphia's structure of linked specialist operations.

The wage situation had also changed significantly over the last decade

Table 5.2. *Profit and return to capital, Philadelphia textiles, by sector, 1905, with sectoral comparisons among eastern cities*

	Profit on sales (%)			Return to capital (%)		
	Phila.	Others		Phila.	Others	
Carpets	9	*		11	*	
Cottons	13	Fall River	3	14	Fall River	2
		Lowell	−2		Lowell	−2
		New Bedford	10		New Bedford	6
		Providence	9		Providence	6
Hose-knit	12	Lowell	6	15	Lowell	7
		Norristown	16		Norristown	19
		Reading	17		Reading	20
Dye-finish	15	Fall River	15	13	Fall River	5
		Lawrence	6		Lawrence	3
		Providence	9		Providence	5
		Paterson	15		Paterson	20
Silk	11	Paterson	8	11	Paterson	10
Wool	9	Lowell	13	11	Lowell	10
		Providence	8		Providence	6
		Woonsocket	6		Woonsocket	7
		Norristown	10		Norristown	11
Worsted	12	Lowell	4	16	Lowell	5
		Lawrence	18		Lawrence	14
		Providence	6		Providence	7
		Woonsocket	11		Woonsocket	20
All sectors	11[a]			13		

[a]Total product value, $117.8 million, profit $14.8 million, capital $99.1 million for Philadelphia 1905, representing 19% of all industrial capital in Philadelphia ($520 million) and 20% of its $591 million product value (*American Carpet and Upholstery Journal* 24 [August 1906]: 81).

Source: Calculated from sectoral data given in Bureau of the Census, *Manufactures: 1905, Part 2: States and Territories*, in tabular form for each city under state headings.

and a half (Table 5.3). In 1890, in only three of eleven eastern city sectors were average earnings higher than in Philadelphia textiles. By 1905, in over half the cases, the Philadelphia average trailed, and where it remained higher, the size of the gaps had often narrowed. Within Philadelphia, across six sectors, earnings had grown noticeably in four, whereas two sectors charted reductions from 2 to 4 percent. Meanwhile, in seven of the eight New

Table 5.3. *Index of average textile earnings, Philadelphia and eastern cities, by sector, 1890 and 1905*

	If Phila. 1890 = 100			Others, 1905,
	Others 1890	Phila. 1905	Others 1905	If Phila. 1905 = 100
Cottons	Lowell 83	109	Lowell 96	Lowell 88
	Lawrence 88		Lawrence 98	Lawrence 90
	Fall River 89		Fall River 95	Fall River 87
Hose-knit	Cohoes 114	109	Lowell 115	Lowell 105
Dye-finish	Lawrence 93	96	Lawrence 88	Lawrence 92
	Fall River 67		Fall River 85	Fall River 88
	Paterson 116		Paterson 104	Paterson 108
Silk	Paterson 118	98	Paterson 114	Paterson 113
Wool	Lowell 100	104	Lowell 113	Lowell 108
Worsted	Lawrence 98	106	Lawrence 112	Lawrence 106
	Providence 97		Providence 119	Providence 113

Source: Calculated from manufacturing census city tables, used for Tables 4.6, 5.1, and 5.2.

England city sectors, the compensation index had risen. Consistent with the spread of a more broadly integrated labor market, earnings levels were slowly converging between mid-Atlantic and New England production sites.[3] This phenomenon is however more complex than a labor-bidding model would expect. Beneath the aggregates, sector-specific details, technological changes and the gender composition of the workforce were all operative. In hosiery, at both points in time, sites far away from the technical center paid a premium for labor. At Paterson, competition among scores of proprietors for skilled workers pushed silk wages well above rates in Philadelphia, where silk was a small component of a much larger system. Even in "Silk City," however, machine dyeing had depressed earnings, displacing skilled men for "box" tenders. In wool and worsted, where Yankee earnings had surged ahead, a breakdown of wages by gender exposes the way in which male shop-floor customs in Philadelphia were allied profitably with the mill masters' interests. In these two sectors, adult *male* weavers and spinners in Kensington and

---

[3] Even if the anomalous Fall River dyers (1890 = 67) are excluded, the range of variations around Philadelphia's 100 Index decreases from 35 points in 1890 to 30 points in 1905.

Table 5.4. *Male–female textile earnings differential, Philadelphia and eastern cities, by sector, 1905*

	Philadelphia			Other cities			
Cottons	171	Fall River	117	Lowell	142	Lawrence	121
Dye-finish	179	Fall River	144	Lawrence	154	Paterson	168
Hose-knit	175	Lowell	132	Pawtucket	167		
Silk	181	Paterson	148				
Wool	143	Lowell	131	Providence	108		
Worsted	160	Lawrence	135	Providence	132		

Note: Male average earnings for each city sector divided by female average earnings gives the differential. All-sector averages for Philadelphia, 1905, men = $502, women = $319, index, 157, when carpets (index 132) are included. For Lawrence, all-sector averages, men = $447, women = $336, index, 133. Children's earnings are separate from these averages.
Source: Same as Table 5.1.

Manayunk earned as much as their counterparts in Lowell wool operations and more than worsted workers in either Providence or Lawrence ($504 vs. $496 and $450). However, the pay for *women* and *child* workers in the same sectors was substantially lower in Philadelphia, in wool, $301 and $194 versus Lowell's $343 and $250, in worsted, $317 and $195 versus $333 and $237 in Lawrence and $375 and $204 in Providence. Several contributory factors were interlaced to generate this differential. To be sure, spinning, with many low-wage "female" positions, was relatively more prominent in Philadelphia. More important, however, in weaving, New England firms had sent women to the loom, often on staple goods where income was above spinning levels yet below rates for fancies and specialties. Few staple goods were woven in Philadelphia, and skilled male weavers thus far had successfully resisted opening the top end of the trade to women. Specialty production, patterns of family labor, and kin hiring all combined in Philadelphia to enhance the earnings and prerogatives of adult men.

Indeed the definition of skill was "gendered" more in the Quaker City than in any other textile center (Table 5.4). In bulk-oriented districts where routine machine tending was more common than display of craft prowess, adult male wages were rarely more than half again the levels achieved by adult women. But in Philadelphia, only *one* of Table 5.4's six sectors showed less than this differential, as did the troubled carpet trade where the settling-in of women weavers had brought the gap down to New England levels (32 percent). For most men, Philadelphia textile wages remained satisfying at or near the top of the national scale, with few alternative complexes of fabric mills offering comparable possibilities. Textile women, on the other hand, had they been able to shed family and community ties and become market-sensitive, mobile workers, had cause to flee northward. Culturally and spatially bound, they did no such thing. In the new century's first decade, flexible production continued to make Philadelphia attractive for skilled workmen, a state of affairs secured to some degree at the expense of women and children employed in regional textiles.[4]

Once the tumult of the 1903 general strike abated, work for operatives of both sexes was plentiful in the Philadelphia districts. The general boom that had emboldened the craft unions in their shorter hours campaign continued through and past the 1905 benchmark of Table 5.1. Fancy goods reigned supreme in wool and worsteds. Hosiery and knit specialties sold heavily. Lace and decorative fabrics for the household burgeoned with the popularity of period stylings for middle-class homes (Gothic, Queen Anne, colonial, mission). The press of business at some local firms was so great that, as in earlier decades, they subcontracted work onto the looms of nearby mills. New firms at times reached extraordinary levels of specialization, as one small Kensington shop announced its devotion solely to printing fancy patterns on cotton hosiery. Meanwhile, experienced proprietors were impelled toward feats of design and production virtuosity. When the Oldham Mills brought out an extravagant fabric that contained 40,000 silk warp threads across its 50-inch breadth, the upholstery trade monthly outdid itself in applauding a superlative achievement.[5]

Yet there were two nagging worries that hovered at the edges of the city's general cheeriness: the problem of fabric quality among the wool-using sectors and the persistent dullness in ingrain carpets. Manipulation of fabrics through heavy adulterations with reprocessed wool ("shoddy") had been accentuated during the long depression. Now it had settled in as a continuing practice. The source of this durable problem lay in the spreading necessity of making for the price, particularly in menswear.

> Clothing, both suits and overcoats for men and boys, must be made to sell at certain ranges of prices. These have become fixed principles and cannot be altered, but the quality of the fabrics which enter into each suit varies each season. It is always the endeavor to keep the cost of making the fabrics ... for a $15 suit within a certain range, and where the cost of the raw material ordinarily used would make this price higher, manipulation is resorted to.[6]

[4] For related New England matters, see Tamara Hareven, *Family Time and Industrial Time*, Cambridge, UK, 1982, p. 428.

[5] *American Wool & Cotton Reporter* 19(1905): 1006, 1066, 1307, 1421 (hereafter *AWCR*); *American Carpet and Upholstery Journal* 24(April 1906): 64 (hereafter *ACUJ*).

[6] *AWCR* 19(1905): 30.

Not only was shoddy being added to new wool, but cotton fiber was being mixed with combed long-staple worsted tops "in order to supply the demand for goods at a certain price." Further, the convergence of clothing prices in fixed ranges (rather than along continuous, flexible lines) in turn yielded "a more general uniformity of price levels throughout the [fabric] market... than has been customary." The clothiers conscious of retailers' price levels, would pay no more than, say, one dollar per yard for the makings of their fifteen-dollar suit, inducing manufacturers to offer hosts of dollar goods, including by 1906, "many new lines of manipulated fabrics."[7] Here skill and versatility were becoming entangled in a degraded market as price standardization forced some Philadelphia firms toward a sleazy ingenuity that perversely mirrored the virtuosity of Oldham or the Bromley lace plants.

The impact of this trend was felt most directly in Manayunk, a wool district where silk, hosiery, and, outside of the Dobson Mills, carpets were virtually unknown. Responding to reports of a textile labor scarcity in Philadelphia, "Manayunker" wrote angrily to the *Reporter* in 1907:

> Another thing that is driving a great many more men out of the mill is the rotten work, as Manayunk for the most part is a shoddy and mungo district. For instance, a card feeder has to run two or more sets of camel-back cards and the work is so rotten that he has to be running around all the time like someone mad, trying to straighten out the choke-ups, broken webs... and one hundred and one things that go to make life miserable for a card feeder.

The goods and the weaving were equally dispiriting.

> The weaver... is supposed to make cloth... out of the above-named stuff whose grade is so low they cannot find a name in the dictionary suitable for it. The mill hands have a name for it. But that name would look bad in writing or print. Now some of this stuff is so rotten that it will not carry its own weight across the loom, and there are lumps in the yarn that will not go through the shuttle hole, and warp ends continually breaking out.[8]

"Manayunker" had known better times; his pride of craft was injured by mill conditions that resembled a "six-day race," but he could do little other than vent his spleen. The district was the city's weakest in labor militancy, and perhaps like many of its residents, "Manayunker" was possessed of a modest row home that further limited his options. In any event, spreading

---

[7] Ibid., 1218; 20(1906): 982.

[8] *AWCR* 21(1907): 240. "Mungo" is waste recycled from hard-finished woolens and worsteds, whereas "shoddy" refers to shredded soft-knitted and woven goods. See Isabel Wingate, *Fairchild's Dictionary of Textiles*, Sixth Edition, New York, 1979, p. 404.

price standardization had exercised a degrading feedback effect on the labor process in Manayunk mills. Worklife was dismal when you were making for the price.

This concern did not animate carpet manufacturers, for in their sector, depression-induced substitutions faded quickly. By 1906 a trade columnist could observe that "a few years ago the first question was one of price; now it is one of quality with the great majority of consumers." Carpet prices, led in most grades by the settings of Alexander Smith, were offered directly to dealers by the mills or their selling houses. Sizable post-depression advances were gradually accepted by retailers, permitting renewed use of virgin wools, which in turn enhanced the character and marketability of the goods. The carpet problem, acute for Philadelphia, lay within the ingrain division of the trade, whose products had been eclipsed by comparably priced and more attractive tapestry and velvet varieties. When a local proprietor, interviewed in 1905, announced the impending death of ingrain manufacturing, his bluntness touched off a furor. However, as half the city's ingrain looms were reported idle for want of orders, while other divisions were pouring out yardage, the implications of his pronouncement were plain.[9] Here then was a test of flexibility, for novel patterns and weaves would not revive ingrain demand. What would the ingrain men do?

The smallest shops simply folded; at least a half-dozen of them failed over the next three years. One significant operator, Thomas Bromley, Jr., went bankrupt two years after he succeeded to proprietorship upon his father's death. Although he had initially attempted a marketing focus on designing carpets for churches, this tactic proved an insufficient stimulus to sales. The firm went under early in 1906, owing $50,000 to its creditors. A year later, they recovered only 5 percent of the sums due when the mill's aged machinery was auctioned off.[10] Other ingrain proprietors were far more active, both individually and collectively. Between 1904 and 1907, Charles Cochrane, the Gays, the Maslands, Robert Dornan, and Ivins, Dietz and Metzger invested in tapestry, velvet, Axminster, and Wilton carpet machinery

---

[9] *AWCR* 20(1906): 182; *ACUJ* 23(April 1905): 72, (Dec. 1905): 57; *AWCR* 19(1905): 142.

[10] *ACUJ* 22(March 1904): 72–3; 23(May 1905): 85, (November 1905): 98; 24(February 1906): 71, (March 1906): 91; 25(July 1907): 73; *AWCR* 20(1906): 213, 255, 283. It is possible that this failure was "arranged" by Thomas Bromley, Jr. After his father's death, the two mills he had controlled were separated, Thomas's brothers operating the one devoted to yarn spinning. Then the mill building in which the ingrain weaving operation was housed was separated from the firm Thomas headed, he in turn leasing space from the family group controlling the buildings. Thus when the firm closed, its assets were confined to machinery, stock, and finished goods on hand, such accounts as were unpaid, plus his personal assets, which may also have been sheltered – hence the feeble return to creditors on liquidation.

while discarding some or all of their ingrain looms. The value of the latter was minimal; at one sale, five old Murklands brought only twenty-three to twenty-six dollars each as scrap. Another firm, James Hall, made a more radical shift, moving into production of hosiery and knits. Shifts within or across sectors were assertive moves consistent with a flexible production format, though a venture into knitting was appreciably more risky than switching to evidently rising carpet lines.

Moreover, as a group, the ingrain proprietors revived the selling committee and took the initiative of setting common prices by grade each season. Their advances for fall 1905 preempted their old nemesis, the Lowell Company, which shortly concurred with the level set by the united Philadelphians.[11] This strategy may have been aimed at preventing price-competitive losses on ingrains while many of the mills were expanding their commitment to more promising carpet products. It was successful enough that a proposal for merged selling, offered by New York agents W. & J. Sloane in 1907, was undersubscribed and withdrawn. The senior Masland, who was a Sloane client, had brought forward this logical extension of the pricing committee. If operators of 1,500 ingrain looms would agree to sell through Sloane for five years, the agency would handle all marketing, guarantee common pricing, insure receivables, etc. However, the loss of autonomy this plan entailed repelled most proprietors, whereas a gradual reduction in total ingrain capacity encouraged them in their present courses. The pricing committee was as far as they would go toward institutionalizing collective action.[12]

There were, in addition, technical developments that confirmed the carpet men in their independent shifts away from ingrains. In 1907, the Crompton and Knowles Loom Works, which had established a sizable Philadelphia plant near Kensington, announced it had devised a technique by which ingrain looms could be adapted to create pile carpets, a step taken largely in response to inquiries from Philadelphia firms. A modified Murkland was set up to run at their shops, and its inspection was invited. Moreover, Crompton also unveiled a new model loom for the trade's hottest selling line, the cut-pile Axminster. Its features included considerable versatility and an increase in daily output of roughly 20 percent over earlier models. Ingrain firms with small resources could thus have looms inexpensively modified, whereas those entertaining the notion of new equipment buying could take advantage of an advance in technical capacity. Recasting ingrain looms was not a monopoly of the local branch of the great Worcester machine works, however. Late in the year, William Caves, partner in a Kensington

[11] *ACUJ* 22(March 1904): 51, (May 1904): 53, (July 1904): 57; 23(May 1905): 63, (July 1905): 63, 87; 24(May 1906): 69, 98, (November 1906): 97; 25(November 1907): 78.
[12] *AWCR* 21(1907): 332, 434; *ACUJ* 25(March 1907): 53, (April 1907): 71.

ingrain mill, revealed that he too had converted a Murkland to weaving pile Wiltons. A practical manufacturer, Caves had "fitted up a miniature machine shop" on the third floor of his mill and worked through the summer engineering the transformation. Reportedly, he was considering performing the same service for other firms, "for a fixed sum."[13]

The intersection of these currents, together with an unexpected rise in demand for ingrains, generated a labor shortage when several hundred long-idle looms were called into service in the summer of 1907. One proprietor explained, "Many skilled ingrain weavers turned to other lines when this branch languished and no new ones have since been trained to take their places now that the ingrain industry has taken on renewed life."[14] Complaints about a persistent insufficiency in labor supply continued throughout the boom years, conditioning employers' willingness individually to shorten the work week, or collectively to accept advances in the schedule of prices, such as those the upholstery weavers presented them in 1907. General prosperity restored the fraternal relations between masters and operatives as well. Fred Dixon, secretary of the Art Square Weavers Union, reported "a good state of feeling between the mills and the weavers" in 1905. When the partnership agreement at Swire, Herring and Cairns was reshaped, and the proprietors arrived at the mill from their lawyer's office, they were met by a delegation of workers and conducted to the mill's second floor where "the assembled hands presented each of their employers with a superb floral tribute."[15] Departing room bosses were again feted; summer excursions to Atlantic City were coordinated, all the Kensington mills closing on late July Saturdays. At the larger factories, workers' beneficial associations sponsored outings, adding to their treasuries from the proceeds. Though accounts of twenty thousand textile workers pouring across the Delaware toward the seashore may have been fanciful, restoration of "the old time friendly feeling" was widely evident.[16]

At the same time, Philadelphia's preeminence in "specialty" textile production was proclaimed through the trade press, most signally in a series of articles published by the *American Wool and Cotton Reporter*, marking the

[13] *ACUJ* 25 (July 1907): 56, (November 1907): 99. Incidentally, southern competition was as yet not a factor in carpet circles. The only experiment in the South, a mill at Gaffney, S.C., had gone bankrupt in 1904, its equipment purchased by a Philadelphia machinery dealer and its stock by the Quaker City's Lit Brothers department store. (See *ACUJ* 22[October 1904]: 59; 23[January 1905]: 60.)

[14] *ACUJ* 25 (June 1907): 77. It is possible that retailers responded to the stock market slump (which began March 13) by ordering cheaper varieties for fall 1907.

[15] *AWCR* 19(1905): 1252, 1557; 20(1906): 14, 26, 1254; *ACUJ* 23(May 1905): 69, (November 1905): 95.

[16] *AWCR* 19(1905): 512; *ACUJ* 23(August 1905): 79; 25(August 1907): 62.

1907 convention of the National Cotton Manufactuerers' Association held
at the city's Bellevue-Stratford Hotel. The *Reporter*'s correspondent stressed
Philadelphia's reliance on skilled workers, its disintegrated system of production, and the constancy with which "new enterprises are being started
every week." He continued,

> There are no corporations, as mill corporations are classed up in
> New England, and there are but few large companies. The [incorpo-
> rated] companies are practically as closely held as the individual enter-
> prises, and no shares are offered the public... There is a refreshing
> lack of red tape in the conduct of the business, the proprietors often
> being found in overalls, running or directing the operations of looms
> or spindles, and personal knowledge and application to one department
> are believed by a majority of the manufacturers to be the sole cause of
> their success.... Pay of operatives is higher than ever before, and higher
> than in many other textile centres.... 57 hours is now a standard week's
> work.[17]

In a follow-up essay, he explored other aspects of the industrial format.

> As a matter of fact, a Philadelphian has a set purpose to have a business
> of his own, no matter how small, and young men are starting in business
> today with two or three looms, making worsteds or rugs particularly,
> and with one man or a boy, they are laying the foundations... for the
> future. The proprietor is the designer, operator and owner for a time,
> but before many weeks have passed, he has added some looms, increased
> his force to perhaps a dozen hands and then he becomes designer,
> selling agent and manager, as well as owner... [T]he character of the
> operatives is of the highest order, and almost without exception, they
> are consumers as well as producers... [T]hey are respected and take
> an active part in the social and political affairs of the city. Very few of
> the raw foreign help have reached here as yet.[18]

Nonetheless, immigrants remained a key element in the labor force, for in
woolens and worsteds, "the Philadelphia product has no superior, so far as
workmanship goes, as the expert English workman predominates."[19]

This contention was reaffirmed by a report on Philadelphia textile labor
released by the Pennsylvania Department of Internal Affairs (Table 5.5). As
these figures indicate, less than 5 percent of the city textile workforce was
drawn from the areas of the "new" immigration, southern and eastern Eu-

---

[17] *AWCR* 21(1907): 710.
[18] Ibid., 783. For the manufacturers' political activities, chiefly on the local level, see *ACUJ*
23(June 1905): 59, (July 1905): 83; 24(June 1906): 56, (July 1906): 72, 25(April 1907):
82; *AWCR* 21(1907): 399, 959, 1105.
[19] *AWCR* 21(1907): 783.

Table 5.5. *Birthplace of textile workers, Philadelphia, 1906, by sector*

	U.S.	England, Ireland, Scotland	Germany	"Poland"[a]	"Jews," "Hebrews"[b]	Other	Total	Foreign (%)
Cotton	4,229	709	207	80	32	38	5,295	20
Carpets	3,229	1,756	388	92	—	114	5,579	42
Dye-finish	1,154	505	280	54	—	66	2,059	44
Hose-knit	8,706	542	328	61	70	315	10,022	13
Spinning	3,965	623	128	289	2	163	5,170	23
Silk	1,160	75	150	—	—	108	1,493	22
Wool-worsted	5,887	1,638	433	343	46	328	8,675	32
Upholstery	1,479	788	244	34	—	131	2,676	45
Lace	474	439	42	—	—	—	955	50
Misc.	257	17	9	2	—	48	333	23
Totals	30,540	7,092	2,209	955	150	1,311	42,257	28
%	72	17	5	2	0[c]	3	99	

[a] Designated, because no Polish state existed at this date.

[b] Foreign-born Jews were listed separately from other nation-identified groups, as with Poles.

[c] Rounded down, as actual figure is 0.3%. In addition, among the U.S.-born were recorded 17 "Negroes," affirming the exclusion of the city's 60,000 black residents from access to textile employment.

Source: Pennsylvania Department of Internal Affairs, *Annual Report of the Secretary of Internal Affairs, Part III: Industrial Statistics,* Harrisburg, 1907, pp. 224–65 ("Textile Industries in Philadelphia").

rope ("Other" includes several hundred French and Nordic individuals). As a half-century before, the main immigrant connections were with Great Britain and Ireland (the American-born sons and daughters of postbellum immigrants were folded into the U.S. category). Of greater interest is the sectoral range of the immigrant proportions, highest in the wholly-imported lace trade and the recently expanding upholstery division, with significant English and Irish presences in wool and worsteds, carpets, and dyeing. Skilled workers from abroad, including textile veterans from the Polish Lodz district, continued to respond to the Philadelphia magnet, even as in-migrant natives and second-generation immigrant offspring increased their overall share of the workforce.[20]

In lace manufacturing, into which the Bromley family was gradually reinvesting two generations of carpet earnings, the link with Britain went well beyond the workforce. All machinery was English-made, installed by teams of British mechanics who accompanied crates of loom parts across the Atlantic. Moreover, the finest cotton yarns used in lace curtains and nets were purchased directly from British spinners. James Crawford's plea in 1820, that Americans could spin the highest counts were government disposed to lend a hand, had still not secured either a political or entrepreneurial response. However, heavy use of medium counts (up to two-ply 40s) by lace, upholstery, damask, and tapestry firms had made Philadelphia the center for distribution of southern yarn output. Indeed by 1907 there were "quite a number of mills in the South that run exclusively on lace curtain yarns." The Bromleys, in little over a decade, had become "the largest producers of lace curtains in the world, making everything from [medium-price] 6 points to the very finest effects that can be produced on a machine, that is, as high as 20 to 22 points." A varied range of designs and shades were created in response to regionally distinct markets, for "different sections of the country call for different kinds of goods," as the Bromleys' New York representative put it.[21]

---

[20] It is possible that the English and German workers were largely old veterans, a question that only extraction of worker households from 1900 census manuscripts by ethnicity would resolve. Sufficient resources to undertake this labor-intensive task were not available; however, the 1937 Palmer W.P.A. surveys of weavers and spinners present dozens of interviews with English workers who arrived in Philadelphia ca. 1895–1910, suggesting a perhaps narrowing but continuing flow from Britain.

[21] *ACUJ* 25(July 1907): 62, 74; *AWCR* 21(1907): 851. For James Crawford's statement, see Philip Scranton, *Proprietary Capitalism*, New York, 1983, p. 111. Yarn counts, here cotton, indicate the number of skeins of a standard length needed to weigh one pound. Net points indicate the number of twisted, openwork intersections per inch. For each, the higher the number, the finer the work. In 1912, Quaker Lace, the largest of the Bromley firms, purchased 64 percent of its curtain yarns from southern mills, the residual, fine counts (60s–80s) not reliably produced in the United States, being imported

The lace mills had little trouble marketing their products, as the demand for sheer curtains reached craze proportions. The sales of yardlace, which homemakers stitched into sash curtains, had quadrupled in the two or three years since 1904. However, to sell their carpet output, the Bromleys had to expand their road force, hiring the son of their recently deceased colleague, Louis Metzger, partner in Ivins, Dietz and Metzger. At the Park Mills, the Gays adopted a new distribution tactic, exclusive selling, whereby one retailer in each town and city would become the sole distributor of each season's styles in ingrain, tapestry, and velvet carpets. Other carpet firms pushed their marketing into institutional circles with greater success than Thomas Bromley, Jr., had had. Plush Philadelphia Brussels and Wiltons soon covered floors in new office suites, hotels, and fraternal and country clubs at sites as far distant as the Los Angeles Masonic hall, which was adorned with a massive Ivins, Dietz and Metzger Wilton measuring sixty by fifty-three feet. Though firms had routinely purchased display space in the trade press to command attention of distributors and store buyers, one fancy-goods firm, Philadelphia Tapestry, stepped onto the fast track by advertising its brand name directly to consumers. Flogging the "Artloom" line resolutely, Jacob Wasserman's firm bought columns in the *Ladies Home Journal*, other "popular magazines, . . . and women's favorite papers" beginning in 1904, becoming "pioneers" in mass advertising of upholstery, tapestry curtains, and drapes. The ads invited readers to write for a free color-illustrated "style book" that would instruct them in the tasteful use of Artloom finery. These consumer appeals were buttressed by trade journal displays featuring cuts of the magazine spreads with texts that urged dealers to load up on stock. Philadelphia Tapestry prospered mightily, perhaps having gained a leading edge, as no other sectoral competitor soon took this expensive plunge. Shortly, fearing a drift away from its pages, the *American Carpet and Upholstery Journal* responded editorially to those who would waste "thousands of dollars in mediums calculated to reach the buying public direct." The *ACUJ* asserted that manufacturers' prime market target should be dealers, who naturally recognize "the trade journals of America . . . as their guides and friends." Anyone who spends "$2,000 in the leading trade journal and secures ten replies from merchants . . . has accomplished a great deal more than if he had secured 2,000 replies from individuals whose eyes had been caught by catchy copy in some ephemeral publication."[22]

from Britain. All yarn for Levers lace was imported (100s–240s). See U.S. House of Representatives, Committee on the Ways and Means, *Tariff Hearings: 1913*, Washington, D.C., 1913, pp. 4023, 4025, 4032–1 (hereafter cited as *Tariff Hearings: 1913*).

[22] *ACUJ* 22(September 1904): 54; 23(February 1905): 91, (May 1905): 79, (October 1905): 61; 24(January 1906): 73, (May 1906); 97; 25(July 1907): 62, (October 1907): 52.

Figure 12. Advertising advertising: Philadelphia Tapestry Mills promoting its direct approach to consumers through mass market magazines by means of a parallel trade journal campaign targeting fabric dealers, 1905. (Author's collection.)

For Philadelphians, the *ACUJ*'s argument was apt, since the structure of the Philadelphia textile system militated against wide replication of the Artloom tactic. For small specialist firms, personal networks were the key to initial success. Thereafter, trade journal ads reached out to manufacturers in need of yarns or dyeing services and to buyers seeking a new source of novelties in knits or damasks. The *Journal* faithfully printed letters appreciative of its marketing value, framing them neatly in eye-catching boxes. One of these, from a Carlisle, Pennsylvania, carpet company, averred that "we find our advertisement...to be of great help to us, and [it] is undoubtedly one of the things which is aiding our steady growth."[23] That growth would soon lead E. C. Beetem, proprietor of the Carlisle Carpet Mill, to expand his operations by establishing a branch plant in the heart of Kensington and to send his son to the metropolis as manager of the enterprise. As an "incomer" at the low end of the trade, a father–son proprietary team, and a smallish firm whose Philadelphia start coincided with the unfolding

---

[23] *ACUJ* 23(February 1905): 71.

of the 1907 Panic, Beetem Carpets is triply interesting. Detailing its Philadelphia years and examining as well several facets of the Bromley lace companies' affairs will again bring us inside family firms here lodged in profoundly different sectors of the regional industry.

5.2.   Rags and riches: Beetem Carpets and Quaker Lace

In April 1907, the firm of E. C. Beetem and Son announced the opening of its branch mill in Philadelphia, an event duly reported in the carpet press. At a tiny Kensington shop on Hope Street, C. Gilbert Beetem would supervise the production of handwoven rag rugs, his father remaining in Carlisle to direct the company's main operations and oversee its overall finances. Following its 1875 start as one of the first textile furnishing stores in the Cumberland Valley, the partnership of Beetem and Stephens endured for a quarter-century until the latter's death in 1901. From beginnings as jobbers and retailers of "carpets, rugs, mattings, linoleum, hassocks, upholsteries, etc.," Beetem and Stephens had quickly moved into manufacturing cheap rag and jute piece goods, narrow rolls of carpeting sold regionally to retailers for cutting up on customer demand. At Stephens's death, with the firm turning over about $65,000 yearly, E. C. Beetem closed out his wholesale/ retail activities and created a fresh partnership with his foreman, William Johnson.

In its first year, the new team divided profits of $4,900, about 7.5 percent on sales, two-thirds to Beetem, the rest to Johnson, though nearly half the latter's share was returned to E. C. as part payment and interest on a loan made to the foreman at the inception of the partnership. Young Gilbert turned twenty-one in November 1902 and was shortly brought into the firm, receiving a half-share four years later, after Johnson's death. The firm's sales for 1906 reached $100,000 with the successful introduction of a new line of fringed rag rugs, each made separately on the loom, rather than being cut from rolls. A new sales house, Charles Young and Co. of New York, skillfully managed the marketing. Its principal also handled the rug lines of Bucks County's Eden Manufacturing Company, a firm in which he was financially interested. Slightly older than Gilbert's father, Charles Young formed an often tense but working alliance with E. C. Beetem and Son that lasted until his death in 1921.[24]

---

[24] *ACUJ* 25(May 1907): 69; E. C. Beetem and Son Collection, Hagley Library, Accession No. 1178, Series I, Box 9, "History of Business," n.d. (ca. 1926); C. G. Beetem to Whom It May Concern, March 25, 1930; "Yearly Settlement, 1902"; *Official American Textile Directory*: 1906–07, Boston, 1906, p. 303 (hereafter *OATD*). The firm records

Both the surge of sales and the Philadelphia venture, which separated rug from carpet weaving, were explained concisely by Gilbert:

> Some difficulty was experienced in weaving carpets and rugs in the same plant. The demand for rugs continued to increase; bungalows began to be built, the mission furniture craze came in; these rugs were considered ideal for all types of bungalows and cottages in preference to rooms entirely covered with carpets. Weavers preferred to weave rugs; they could cut [them] off the loom quicker and make weekly payrolls, whereas carpets running from 100 to 135 yards in the roll could not be cut from the loom till completed, and frequently weavers missed weekly pays. To obviate this it was decided the writer was to go to Philadelphia and locate a small rug carpet mill that could be purchased. …A mill was located up North Hope Street and its equipment purchased for $500.00. The weaving detail consisted of 16 hand looms.[25]

Although in retrospect Gilbert made this initiative seem cheap, simple, and logical, and claimed profitability for it from the start, his was a half-true tale. "Father" Beetem was dubious about securing a Philadelphia shop and Gilbert was reduced to pleading for his consent, which was ultimately given most reluctantly. After several years of operations, the Kensington mill *had* already repaid one-half of the $10,000 laid out from Carlisle in getting it under way. Still, the elder Beetem, as late as 1910, announced that "I wish more and more the rug business had been begun in Carlisle, and I regret the day I ever entered Philadelphia." By this point, the city factory had moved twice to larger quarters, had expanded its loom count to sixty, and was beginning to cast shadows over the original mill.

Tensions between father and son escalated, percolating through their exchanges of correspondence, straining bonds of blood and business that enmeshed them. With Young's support, Gilbert adapted to the market-sensitive demands of flexible production, taking what seemed to Edward Beetem dangerous risks while distancing himself from both his father's values and his business practices. These father–son dynamics suggest a range of nonmarket hazards that beset family firms, here enhanced by the hundred miles physically separating the two segments of the concern. As Gilbert grew into and expanded his role, Edward tried vainly to rein him in, an effort that would have been far simpler were they both resident in Carlisle. His "regret" in 1910 thus had as much to do with a sense of estrangement and loss as

will hereafter be cited as "Beetem Papers," Edward C. Beetem as "EB" and C. Gilbert Beetem as "CG."
[25] Beetem Papers, Series I, Box 9, CG to To Whom It May Concern, March 25, 1930, p. 2.

it did with the tiresome complexities of overseeing two mills in different cities.[26]

The Panic of 1907 and relocation to new Kensington mill space (on Jefferson Street) made the first Philadelphia year a trial for Gilbert. Edward paid all bills from Carlisle, exercising a crotchety financial control that required his son to file weekly reports of both business and personal spending. Gilbert, to justify eleven cents spent for New York newspapers, felt obliged to note that "I must watch N.Y. store ads." His attempt to purchase the equipment of John Diez's failed hand loom rug shop brought a quick rebuff, even though Diez had been hired by the Beetems, and the price for 14 looms, 7,000 spools, and a variety of other materials was but $125. Questioning Gilbert's eagerness, Edward Beetem wrote that he was "radically opposed to spending one dollar unnecessarily," adding with a Franklinesque pithiness, "Nothing is cheap that is not needed." On the definition of "cheap" and the boundaries of what was "needed," the two continued to disagree. Gilbert was anticipating rapid expansion, but his father counseled: "allow the business to grow with as little outlay as possible until you can demonstrate that you are making money." This conservatism riled the son. Claiming he had "tried to save expense every way," he took the offensive, pointing out that while other mills were idle during the slump, "our new mill's order book [was] always filled up." This success was due to the upper-middle-class, second-home market for his rug novelties, as "only the wealthiest people buy the kind of rugs we make, and they always have money – good times or bad times, a wealthy lady can get in her carriage and go down to Altman's and buy one of our Bungalow rugs."[27]

For the moment, Gilbert respected his father's judgment that the products should be strictly limited to "a small line of good things." But for every gesture of acquiescence recorded, one of defiance sprouted. Gilbert bought clothes at Jacob Reed's fashionable shop and had the bills sent to his father, schemed to erect a bungalow of his own, and adovcated opening a salesroom on Atlantic City's boardwalk (trial balloons that E. C. summarily popped). Production problems, however, brought the pair into a tentative harmony in

---

[26] Beetem Papers, Series II, Entry 91 – CG to EB (1908), Entry 92 – CG to EB (1909), Entry 93 – CG to EB (1910), Entry 112 – EB to CG (1908), Entry 113 – EB to CG (1909), Entry 113 – EB to CG (1910). In these letter books and bound packets may be found the correspondence; hereafter for letters, dates only will be used for simplicity. For the details here recounted, see CG to EB, January 12, 1908; EB to CG, May 6, 1908; CG to EB, November 18, 1909; EB to CG, March 11, 1910. The papers are voluminous and may well merit monographic treatment, but only those related to the Philadelphia "experiment" are referenced here.

[27] Beetem Papers Series II, Entry 91, personal accounts, May 7, 1908; also, CG to EB February 5, 1908; EB to CG, February 7, 1908; CG to EB, February 12, 1908.

1908. Though twenty-four looms were active in the larger Jefferson Street mill, poor-quality rugs were being woven. Bundles of them had been returned by disappointed dealers complaining that they were not up to the grade of work shown in the samples from which they had ordered. In order to save money, Gilbert had hired but one supervisor, Diez, who had been kept busy preparing warps and overseeing the winding of rag-based fillings. The weavers had been left to their own devices, as only when Gilbert himself toured the floor did they "hammer their carpets up tightly and make a proper selvidge [*sic*]." Rather than add a weave-room boss, young Beetem proposed naming one of the veteran loom men to the post, having him circulate to press for quality work, and paying him an extra fifty cents weekly as compensation. This thrifty solution was applauded by E. C., for it was a sign of sensible caution in contrast to Gilbert's other "extravagant" actions. The results were also satisfactory, for the son later reported that returns for "faulty workmanship" had become negligible.[28]

In making ordinary rag carpets, bales of secondhand fabrics, clothing, stockings, and scraps were purchased by the Beetems and delivered to women outworkers who cut them into strips and sewed the strips into tubular ropes ("chain") about one-quarter to one-half inch in diameter. This became the filling woven into jute or heavy cotton warps, a multicolored, variegated, nonpattern rug being the most common result. With color sorting of strips, all blue, brown, or tan rugs could be produced, though variations in shades were most likely given the heterogeneity of the raw materials. Whereas E. C. Beetem had direct relations with outworkers in Carlisle, Gilbert had engaged a South Philadelphia Italian contractor, Tony Vitale, for his city materials preparation. White or near-white rags were prized, for these could be bleached, then dyed, and used in truly monocolor rugs or, in multiple shuttle looms, to create stripe effects. The Carlisle plant had its own dyehouse for this work, but Gilbert quickly made a connection with Kensington's Brehm and Stehle works, thereby accommodating to the separate-establishments format basic to the Philadelphia textile system for both his chain sewing and his dyeing.[29]

For marketing, the firm had a blended system of travelers and Young's New York agency, plus the traditional, individual efforts of E. C. Beetem. Like the Gays in the 1880s, the elder Beetem twice yearly set out on sales tours, hauling samples through the coal valleys of central Pennsylvania and west to Johnstown and Altoona. The road men covered retail stores in other regions and E. C. Beetem handled mail orders, especially to the West, from

[28] CG to EB, March 7, April 15, 1908; EB to CG, April 24, May 5, 1908.
[29] CG to EB February, 1908 (n.d.); EB to CG, August 8, 1908; EB to CG, November 5, 1909.

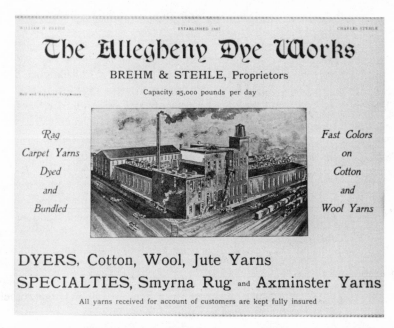

Figure 13. C.G. Beetem's specialty dyers, Brehm and Stehle's Allegheny Dye Works, 1904, with (at left) mention of a focus on coloring rag carpet yarns. (Author's collection.)

his Carlisle office. Young was responsible for the New York market, in which he expected to place Gilbert's rugs in the better stores and with buyers for Carson, Pirie, Scott or Filene's. Young encouraged Gilbert's enthusiasms, particularly directing him toward expanding the lines offered by the Raglin Rug Mill, as the Philadelphia shop was dubbed. Gilbert's key innovation was the introduction of the Poster rug, a picture carpeting with a log cabin at its center, rendered in various color combinations. This was jacquard-woven, requiring expenditures of three hundred dollars for designs and card cutting, a step that led to grumbling from Carlisle and heavy sales to the bungalow crowd. Fired by this success, Gilbert multiplied the picture designs in 1908–9, adding a windmill, a town pump, and other novelties that fed what may now seem an impossibly precious craze for pseudocolonial decoration. Raglin by late 1909 was producing eight lines of rugs, including several with simplified Oriental or Chinese motifs, to which Gilbert added pillow covers in fashionable Japanese figurings. Cheered by growing sales, he wrote his father of plans to extend yet further (into production of couch covers, draperies, and curtains), of ideas for adapting and recycling old Murkland ingrain looms to these ends, and of the need to engage part of the Carlisle mill on rug manufacturing, despite the aforementioned labor process difficulties this tactic had earlier caused.[30]

These advances generated problems in materials supply and mill capacity, brought copyist competition from other Kensington rug mills, and exacerbated relations between cautious Carlisle and progressive Philadelphia. Success with picture rugs called for large supplies of white rags for dyeing; but rising demand had lifted their prices, much to E. C.'s annoyance. Further, the original contractor and his South Philadelphia colleagues were overmatched by the expanding need for sewed chain and were tempted by other rug men's offers, as at least five local firms followed Raglin into the novelty craze in 1909. To deal with these matters, both Beetems wrote rag dealers and mills up and down the East Coast appealing for whites, either as secondhand goods or as factory waste. Meanwhile, Gilbert and Young quietly set up one George Smith in the chain-sewing business, pledging to supply him with stock and orders for Raglin and Eden Mills amounting to "several hundred thousand lbs. yearly." Carrying themselves the expense for raw stock, they guaranteed Smith 1 ½ cents per pound profit, or $3,000 on a turnover of 200,000 pounds at 7 ½ cents, this figure being a third below the 11 cents independent contractors were then charging. Homeworkers would be paid a pitiful one cent per pound for their sewing, evidently the going rate for such work. Despite the low pay, Smith within a few weeks had recruited "over 75 sewers." Gilbert commented, "I thank fortune that I have Geo sewing for me, I have every dealer in Town hunting whites..., and have written up East and have told Mr. Y to go to Boston, Chelsea, Providence, and Springfield this week....."[31]

By year's end these supply bumps had been smoothed out and the problem of mill capacity resolved with a second relocation to two floors of a three-story factory at Second and Norris Streets. Dissatisfaction with the Jefferson Street property was evident from early 1908, occasioning a plainly anti-Semitic father–son exchange concerning the shirt-manufacturing landlord who occupied the rest of the building. In the winter of 1908–9, heat was not supplied until Gilbert withheld the rent, a tactic forced by temperatures of 55 degrees in the office (where there was a small stove) and 40–45 degrees on the frigid shop floor. This condition, "cold, chilly, damp and absolutely unfit for men to cheerfully work in," particularly affected "some of the older weavers [who] are badly crippled up with rheumatism." As might be expected

[30] On father's trips see EB to CG, May 8, 1908, January 2, June 15, 1909. For salesmen and Young, see CG to EB, January 28, August 11, 1908, January 6, 1909. On expanding product lines, etc., see CG to EB, February 12, August 21, 1908, February 18, March 19, July 7, August 18, 1909.

[31] CG to EB, October 9, October 26, 1909; EB to CG, October 29, 1909; CG to EB, October 30, 1909.

given the decrepitude of hand loom weaving, many of Raglin's workers were aged carpet weavers successively displaced from other lines by the advance of power looms. These troubles, combined with the burst of sales activity in mid-1909, led Gilbert to seek a new workspace. Urged by his father to commit no more than $2,000 yearly to rental charges, 50 percent above the figure at Jefferson Street, Gilbert nonetheless offered $2,800 to the owners of the Norris Street mill. Grousing about wild spending, E. C. acquiesced, if only to balk his son's new scheme, building Raglin's own Philadelphia factory. The transfer was accomplished gradually, moving looms as their warps emptied and reerecting them as quickly as possible, for order books remained crowded. Gilbert estimated Raglin's 1909 sales at $50,000, five times the figure for the first eight-month year, and nearly double the 1908 total. At the same time, demand for rolls of ordinary rag carpets from Carlisle had stagnated; on one of his week-long 1909 trips E. C. Beetem sold only eighteen rolls (worth about seven hundred dollars). Taking risks, and thus far reaping the rewards, the son was threatening to surpass his father, a development viewed with deep ambivalence by the older man.[32]

Concern about competition revealed the widening gap between the two Beetems. In March 1908, acknowledging that it is "to be expected" that "others are going into the rug business," E. C. asked, "Do you and Mr. Young apprehend any trouble from Mr. Rump[f] as to breaking of prices. He is wealthy and unscrupulous and may be spiteful because Mr. Young turns him down." Frederick Rumpf operated an upholstery mill near the Eden plant in which Young was interested, and had evidently been refused the latter's marketing services when planning to venture into the rug trade. Partner as well in a new full-fashioned hosiery operation, Rumpf obviously was attuned to market openings and might cut prices on rug novelties to the Beetems' detriment. Gilbert, having investigated, asserted that "We have started the Phila mill on rugs not any too soon, Rump[f] means to go at them on a large scale." Both men were unsure of their ground and soon concurred on two moves that brought Raglin closer to the general practices of Philadelphia firms: to weave goods only on orders rather than running stock and to increase the wages paid several key employees to assure their retention as competition heightened.[33]

---

[32] For anti-Semitism see CG to EB, January 26, 1908; EB to CG, April 7, 1908. On heat see CG to EB, December 22, 1908; Paul Whiting to EB, February 2, 1909. For the new mill, see EB to CG, April 29, 1909, CG to EB June 29, 1909, and the move, CG to EB, September 5, November 18, December 8, 1909 (second letter of this date). Gilbert's estimate is given in CG to EB, October 7, 1909, and father's disappointing sales trip in EB to CG, October 6, 1909.

[33] EB to CG, March 9, 1908; CG to EB, April 16, October 1, 1908; EB to CG, October 3, 1908; CG to EB, November 20, 1908; EB to CG, November 27, 1908. For Rumpf,

This synchrony faded in 1909. When "the pressure brought to bear in New York City by our competitors" increased, E. C. expressed misgivings about the future of their rug venture. Gilbert saw the pressure differently; it called for "greater effort on our part in the way of enlargement if we are to eventually hold our trade." Noting that Altman's was demanding a thousand Log Cabins and that Young was "turning down orders... from the best Houses in New York City and Boston," he introduced the notion of expansion once more. Two weeks later, Gilbert worked a variation on this theme, explaining that, though rivals "eventually... will cut us out as to price on some of the low grades... in our New Mill we do not propose to compete with this sort of stuff." Properly wound up, he grew expansive:

> we will get on other fabrics such as you saw in New York which such people like Mawby and Myers and Jones will not be in competition with or could not make. The ordinary rag rugs are now about as perfect as they can be made, but the field for novelties is enormous and I have no fear in this line at all.

In mid-April, C. G. Beetem struck a nerve with an indirect restatement of his own confidence: "Mr. Young I find gets scared sometimes very easily (a little like yourself, at times), but I can not blame either of you, for you have been certainly longer in the trade than I." When this was followed by a further sally, the founder finally unburdened himself of his fears.

> Now let me advise you to use good judgment and don't be carried off your feet by promises and by Mr. Young.... I am with you so long as reason and good financiering is considered but don't count on me to do anything rash or to do any plunging.... You know I cannot stand owing too much money and I am afraid of debt and what is to be done in the way of advancement must be done judiciously and reasonably backed by common sense... It would cost me my life to meet failure at my age...
>
> You have a big future before you whilst I am on the decline so don't lose sight of the weakness of your Father who is always ready and willing to help his son who is deserving because of his energy and push but always remember that money is little good to any man without health to enjoy it.
> All well, with love. Yours etc.
>
> Father.[34]

An amalgam of anxiety, love, and pain, this letter signaled Edward Beetem's double fear, that his son would succeed mightily and grow ever more

see *OATD: 1906–07*, p. 303. Young is there listed as an agent for Rumpf's upholsteries and coverlets, but seems to have declined to take on the new line of rugs.
[34] CG to EB, March 19, April 1, April 16, 1909; EB to CG, April 29, 1909.

distant from him and closer to Young, a rival mentor, or that he would fail dismally and bring down the family and the firm through his excessive ambition. Gilbert continued to push against the boundaries of his father's authority, yet was locked in his arm's-length embrace. Within the family firm, neither could break free; beyond it, were the bond broken, lay a baffling unknown. Thus in the summer of 1909, E. C. harped on his son's personal spending ($160 in May "requires an explanation") or his going "gunning and fishing" on the Lord's Day. For his part, Gilbert commenced issuing directives and offering advice to his father, brash instructions on how to set up bookkeeping now that independent accounts for the two mills were to be established, yet another step toward separation. E. C. balanced defensive replies ("I never had a business college education") with injunctions to right behavior that nettled Gilbert. To one of these the son rejoined,

> You say you hope I am giving strict attention to business. That, coming from you, I think is a ridiculous remark. When was it that I ever failed to give business strict attention. You might explain this, for such things hurt, coming out of a clear sky and unwarranted. You must think I have gone "off."[35]

By the fall, barbs were mixed regularly with the flow of mundane account and payroll information. Gilbert frontally challenged his father's religiosity:

> You are a man who certainly from your religious belief and faith in providence (whatever that is) don't get near the courage and satisfaction that I do out of my belief... No religion should be all spiritual. It should be worldly... Prayers, offerings, sacrifices and communions in this tough old world are a waste of valuable time... When prayers give a man no more faith in work than you have, then I would cut them out and rely on myself. Or whatever causes these fears in you, I would cut out.... Understand I am not knocking you... [but] I suppose if I felt like you I would give up.[36]

Continuing by asserting that he and Young were working harder than E. C. at Carlisle, and were implicitly the heart and future of the business, Gilbert made plain the budding alliance, courageous New York and Philadelphia versus timid Carlisle, mentor and son versus father. By December, his peremptory manner and arrogation of decision-making authority in league with Young prompted a fresh explosion of patriarchal frustration.

Young's commissions were the proximate cause, but the pressure had been building for months. In expanding Raglin's rug lines, the New Yorker

---

[35] EB to CG, June 3, 1909; CG to EB, July 24, 28, 29, 1909; EB to CG, August 2, 1909; CG to EB, August 3, 4, 1909.
[36] CG to EB, October 7, 1909.

had introduced a novel nonrag weave for which new rug machinery was being installed at Carlisle, rather than in Philadelphia. Previously, Young earned a variable percentage on output of the Kensington mill only, for he did not handle roll carpets made in the main plant. Now that rugs based on his innovative weave were to be added there, Gilbert agreed to pay him 5 percent for selling them. This encroachment on E. C. Beetem's mill space, his prerogatives and authority, triggered an icy blast from Carlisle.

> I simply want to ask you if Mr. Young is to step in and control [the] Carlisle Mill as he does Eden and the Phila. Mill and I am to step down and out. I am growing a little tired in being dictated to by yourself and Mr. Young and used as a pack horse to furnish cash and carry the financial load. You have no right to offer Mr. Young 5% commission on anything woven at this Mill; . . . He has no investment in either of our Mills . . . If we keep on paying additional commissions his profit will be larger than ours, but this is only typical of New Yorkers who are always looking for big returns on no investments and without financial responsibility . . . very soon the meat will belong to others and we will have the bone left.
>
> Again it seems that you do not complete one thing and get in running order and demonstrate what can be done before you begin another, and the result is apt to be nothing completed. There is a limit to all things for safty [sic] and if you can not see this point, I can.

Expressing "disappointment" with his father's "short sighted" views, Gilbert replied with a detailed accounting of how Beetem's profitability would be enhanced by the new setup. Initially, the novel goods had been made on a subcontract with Eden, which had had idle looms suited to Young's design. The 50 to 53 cents a yard paid Eden for these goods would be reduced to 40.4 cents, Young's percentage included, were the work done at Carlisle, yielding a 10-cent savings that would allow wholesale pricing at 48 cents and deliver a hefty profit. Father's deeper grievance emerged in his response, that "you never fully inform me of facts when talking about such matters." This indeed was Gilbert's strategy, for he repeatedly presented E. C. Beetem with faits accomplis, evidence both of "push" and of his drive toward increased autonomy. The aging founder nursed his bruises, cavilled over tedious details, and expressed continuing concern over Gilbert's health, which under the strain had become understandably erratic. The son kept his distance, declining to travel up to Carlisle for the family's customary Christmas gathering, falling back for an explanation on the press of business and the completion of the Norris Street move-in. An unspoken truce had been established, but the longer-term question of authority within the family firm remained unsettled.[37]

[37] EB to CG, December 3, 1909; CG to EB, December 8, 1909; EB to CG, December 9, 1909; CG to EB, December 22, 1909.

Before addressing the way in which this stalemate was resolved, one final aspect of the Beetems' business practices raised in the preceding discussion may be fleshed out. Pricing goods for the market had long been done in a fashion that mirrored James Doak's calculations in the 1880s, the mill cost being figured, then 20 percent added, half for general expenses and the rest as profit. Gilbert's Philadelphia experience and his contact with surges in New York novelty rug markets led to opportunistic advances which he trumpeted as "asking a price considerably above any reasonable cost," another departure from his father's ingrained conservatism. On Carlisle's ordinary rag carpets, no such testing of what the market would bear was possible. How this aggressive pricing was structured is evident from 1910 documents in which Young reported how selling figures for new "Comme Il Faut" rugs had been calculated. As rugs were made in discrete sizes, rather than sold by the yard, gapped pricing, as in men's suits, was adopted instead of a flat price per square yard. Heavy demand for room-size rugs (9 by 12 feet) led Young to market them at $18.00 or $1.50 per square yard, whereas smaller, 6 by 9 feet rugs sold for $8.00 or $1.25 a yard, a 20 percent differential. Moreover, these selling rates were generated by a method far removed from E. C. Beetem's customary cost plus 20 percent standard. Now the cost of production was assessed, for a 3 by 6 foot "Comme Il Faut," $1.12; and a wholesale selling price at least twice this figure was established, here $2.50, providing a margin of $1.38 per rug. Then 10 percent of the selling price was allotted to mill expenses and 15 percent to commissions and discounts to retailers, leaving a net profit of 75 ½ cents per rug or 67 percent of production costs, a vast increment over the 10 percent profit model in which his father had schooled Gilbert.[38]

Three elements of this transformation of pricing practice are worthy of comment. First, it exemplifies the different market structures faced by producers of staple textiles (rolls of rag carpet) and specialty goods (novelty rugs), here within a single firm. Second, it illustrates how attention to fashionable lines in an environment of expanding urban retailing and emerging price ladders could offer manufacturers opportunity profits as they tailored their prices to sellers' expectations rather than relying on a production-cost-plus-percentage technique. The unit advantage of rugs over roll goods also helps account for the enthusiasm with which carpet mills shifted toward rug output. Last, it compresses into a single example the magnetism Young's commitment to specialty production held for Gilbert and the threat both he

---

[38] EB to CG, February 3, 1908; CG to EB, April 1, August 18, 1909; Young to EB, December 12, 1909, Young to CG, December 12, 1909 (both Young letters are in Entry 112, Beetem Papers). By EB's method, the selling price of the 3 by 6 foot rug would have been $1.35, for a unit profit of 11 cents, vs. the 75 ½ cents Young's pricing scheme realized.

and his sophisticated practices posed to E. C. Beetem's authority in firm and family. That the resented Raglin Mill was becoming the company's "profit center" galled Edward Beetem, but that Gilbert was taking this surrogate father's advice in preference to his own and making dramatic strides thereby struck at his pride and self-esteem, calling forth images of himself as a "pack horse" and Young as a "dictator."[39]

In March of 1910, Raglin's rug weavers went out in sympathy with the citywide transit strike. Expressing "surprise" that the Philadelphia mill "contain[ed] any such men" and chronicling his own ill health, E. C. Beetem indicated that these troubles showed "the necessity of seperating [sic] these two mills and [thus] relieve me of responsibility if we are to preserve the business and protect our family from disaster and loss in the future." Beetem encouraged his son to consider incorporating the Philadelphia firm as an independent concern, severing it and him from the Carlisle mill. This quiet threat Gilbert rejected immediately; but for the next three years, father and son fenced regularly over risk, expansion, Young, and the elder Beetem's health.

Raglin's sales continued to soar, reaching $94,500 in the 1912–13 business year. That summer a deal was struck that satisfied both Gilbert and his father and reunited the family team. E. C. feared his decaying energies and expanding trade demands would soon overmatch his ability to manage both Carlisle production and the financial affairs of the two mills. Gilbert wanted to build, now that the rug venture was a booming success. Build they did, not in or near the metropolis, but instead at Carlisle, to which Gilbert would relocate, "relieving you in every way."[40] Packing up his new family (wife May and two-year-old daughter), hiring a few key skilled men who would settle in Carlisle, arranging to ship equipment and supplies, Gilbert still battled his father's obsession with economizing. When told that he would no longer have need of membership in the Manufacturers' Club, Gilbert struggled to assert an independence never fully achieved and now again undercut by return to the patriarchal seat. He accused E. C. of wanting

> to deny his son all pleasant mingling with men whose equal he is in brains and business endeavour. As the mills get settled at Carlisle I will often come to Philadelphia, and I will want some place to stop and keep

[39] EB to CG, December 3, 1909. In closing this letter, Beetem described Young as "a dictator from outside who has not one dollar at stake; . . . "

[40] EB to CG, March 9, 1910; CG to EB, March 10, 1910; CG to EB, February 3, May 20, October 12, 1911, February 12, 1912, September 30, 1914; Raglin Mills sales reported in a typescript in Beetem Papers, Series I, Box 9, headed "Growth." Total sales since April 1907 had reached $356,00, over half of which were recorded in the two most recent business years, 1911–13. For an overview of Philadelphia's prominence in specialty rag rugs, see *AWCR* 25(1911): 667.

in touch with the cpt. trade all of which are Members, and also many
are my friends. You might as well get the idea out of mind that I propose
to totally bury myself in Carlisle when I live there, for I never proposed
to do anything of the kind...At my age [32] a man does not want to
disrupt his associations and that which he has worked hard to enjoy.... [41]

The 1914 consolidation had good business results for a time, however
much Gilbert may have had to wrestle at close quarters with his father.
Young secured nearly $400,000 in annual sales during the war years, but
his death in 1921 revealed how central he had been to the Beetems' prosperity. His successor was a dismal failure; sales dropped by two-thirds in
three years, in part a consequence of the wide acceptance of competing
Japanese imports. Incorporated defensively in 1923, with septuagenarian
E. C. Beetem as president, the firm lost all momentum; and two years later
its principal creditor, a Carlisle bank, engineered a stockholders' coup that
brought Gilbert's dismissal as head of production. Unable to succeed his
father, who hung on relentlessly, and equally incapable of separating from
him, Gilbert despite his brave words of 1914 was indeed "buried" in Carlisle.
Isolated from the fast-moving metropolitan swirl, he eventually suffered a
personal humiliation that was a consequence of product-line stagnation,
shifting trade currents, dependence on uninspired selling agents, and the
family compromise that ended the Philadelphia experiment. [42]

The distance that separated E. C. and Gilbert Beetem for eight years was
simultaneously physical, intergenerational, and in enterprise terms, structural. It triggered a correspondence that uniquely exposes the complex and
contradictory bonds and binds of proprietary capitalism, as what might be
seen as a struggle for individuation materialized in a business setting. Physical
distance created an open space for Gilbert's efforts at self-realization and
for his drive to diversify the company's production along lines that reflected
his enthusiasm for Philadelphia's flexible format of operations. Yet even within
Philadelphia, at firms that long exemplified its flexible style, fathers could
tighten their grip just as they were losing their grasp, as was clear in the
earlier Schofield case. (Clearly, bureaucratic-rational corporations, such as
Bigelow in carpets, had far narrower exposure to the hazards of family
succession.) Small-scale family firms operating in the twentieth century's
growing mass demand markets were increasingly handicapped by the poor

[41] CG to EB, May 1, 1914.
[42] For C. G. Beetem's several chronicles of post-1914 developments, see Beetem Papers,
Series I, Box 9, especially typescripts dated February 1, 1926, and March 25, 1930. By
1927, Gilbert was able to regain his post as general manager, at half his earlier salary,
as sales had slumped to $100,000. As ever, Gilbert advanced plans for recovery, but
they seem weak echoes of the ambitious projects conceived during his Philadelphia
years.

fit between their customary practices and the advances in delegation, cost finding, managerial recruitment, capital raising, etc., that have defined the Chandleresque "modern business organization." The Beetems "solved" this dilemma through a personalistic reliance on Charles Young, but Gilbert's learning (through constant association with Young, with Philadelphia rivals, and with New York buyers) was cut short in 1914, forcing yet heavier dependence on the firm's agent. At his death, the slide commenced.

By contrast, the adventures of the Bromley family dynasty in the new century suggest how an astute, extensive clan could redouble an earlier generation's successes through timely sector shifts and aggressive reinvestment of earnings in a series of nominally independent companies. Though Thomas Bromley's failure in 1906 removed one firm from the family constellation, eight others carried on. In carpets, John Bromley and Sons continued to turn out Smyrnas and Axminsters while James and George D. Bromley produced ingrains and art squares. Joseph H. Bromley manufactured lace curtains in a firm that bore his name, and owned outright or was partner with other family members in the Glenwood Lace Mills, the North American Lace Company, and the Lehigh Manufacturing Company. John Bromley and Sons also operated the National Lace Company, and the separate Bromley Manufacturing Company was involved in both lace and upholstery lines. Within the next several years, the original John Bromley and Sons added weaving of woolen and worsted menswear and dress goods to its vast one-thousand-loom plant at Front Street and Lehigh Avenue in Kensington. Thus in the two decades after 1890, the clan had shifted the bulk of its capital away from the sector to which it had been devoted for half a century, creating six lace firms and in time venturing into suitings and women's wear fabrics. In 1906, the *ACUJ* described the Bromleys thus: "the owners are all of them men of great financial strength and high personal integrity and all of unlimited credit." Though no firm-level employment figures were published regularly, in 1909 four of the Bromley factories alone reported a total workforce of 3,111.[43]

Created by the sons of immigrant carpet weaver John Bromley and managed by a cadre of third-generation cousins, the Bromley firms were separate entities linked by flows of information and advice among the family branches. Capital too may have been drafted at times from kin, but no available records verify this surmise.[44] Obviously, others followed the initial effort in lace-

---

[43] *ACUJ* 24(March 1906): 91; House of Representatives, Committee on the Ways and Means, *Tariff Hearings: 1909*, Washington, D.C., 1909, p. 4802 (hereafter cited as *Tariff Hearings: 1909*).

[44] Records of the Bromley lace concerns are privately held, stored in the basement of the still-active Quaker Lace Company in Kensington. The only documents to which access was approved were the Lehigh Manufacturing Company Invoice Book (1908–11) and

making and Joseph Bromley alone spun off three new firms as his success blossomed. Each of these was simultaneously a discrete entity and a functional subsidiary of the main Joseph Bromley plant, filling initial orders in large part through purchase of goods from its "parent" while adding to and perfecting its own manufacturing capacity. This strategy defended the main firm from potential market catastrophes during the early years of the "branch's" activity. The new operation might be confirmed as a separate entity in time, as was the case with North American Lace, or might be dissolved and reintegrated with its "parent," as happened with Glenwood and Lehigh in 1911–12, when in a paper merger they were joined with Joseph H. Bromley into a new unit renamed Quaker Lace.

These practices were documented in Lehigh's Invoice Book for the years preceding the establishment of Quaker Lace. During the period April 1908 to March 1909, the firm purchased $129,000 in yarns for use on its initial set of English Smith and Wass looms, running chiefly twelve- and fourteen-point Nottingham-style curtains. However, during that year, Lehigh was billed for $581,000 for merchandise made at Joseph H. Bromley and to a lesser degree at North American, purchases of Lehigh designs made on the other mills' equipment (Lehigh paid $7,250 for designing and jacquard cards in 1908–9). At the same time, the new factory was adding to its capacity, spending $22,000 for five more imported looms, and $9,000 in machinery duties charged at the then current 45 percent rate. When it is recalled first that new power carpet looms then sold for several hundred dollars each, that the Beetems haggled over used Murklands at one hundred dollars apiece, and second that the lace machines were over thirty feet wide and fifteen feet high, one understands why so few firms rushed into competition. Lace manufacturing's capital and space requirements far exceeded the resources of most specialty proprietors. New mills had to be built to deal with the verticality of lace weaving; only men with "unlimited credit" needed apply.[45]

a surviving sales register (1912–20) covering accounts alphabetically, A–E. It is hoped that these and other records will be preserved and in time made available to scholars, but this possibility is at yet only in the discussion stage. The limits of the ensuing presentation are thus plain, but without these two registers, no light at all could have been shed on the internal workings of this significant set of family enterprises.

[45] Calculated from entries in Lehigh Manufacturing Company Invoice Book, 1908–11, pp. 1–41 (hereafter cited as IB). Of $782,000 recorded in expenses, the $35,000 not accounted for above was allocated to mill supplies and office and general costs (shipping, heat, sundries). No wage or salary information was given in this ledger. Statewide, the value of lace and lace curtains rose from $3.0 million to $7.2 milliion, 1899–1909, whereas values of carpets and upholstery were stable, rising only 2–4 percent over the decade (*ACUJ* 30 [August 1912]: 66–7). On building requirements see *Tariff Hearings: 1913*, p. 4015.

During the ensuing twelve months, the additional looms were put to full use, as yarn costs mounted to $239,000 but total sales had so increased that merchandise billings from the related mills soared above $1.2 million. The firm's huge factory at Twenty-second and Lehigh was only partly filled as yet, but the demand for its goods very likely kept the main Bromley mill running busily while the proprietor readied himself for machinery purchases and transfers that would fully develop the potential of Lehigh Manufacturing. No new looms were purchased for over a year after February 1909, then in the second quarter of 1910 well over $300,000 was expended for fifty-nine lace machines that brought the North Philadelphia mill to full capacity.

Tariff politics were the key to this leap forward. In the summer of 1909, Congress, after the usual heavy lobbying, approved two duty changes that galvanized the lace sector. The ad valorem tariff on imported lace goods was increased from 60 to 70 percent, and at the same time, the 45 percent tax on machinery for lacemaking was suspended through January 1, 1911. Doubtless, Joseph Bromley swiftly cabled orders to Jardine and Company, for in the spring of 1910 crates of parts for forty-nine new Levers lace machines began arriving in Philadelphia, attended by teams of British mechanics who spent the summer erecting them in the Lehigh Avenue plant. Moreover, six low-point curtain machines (sixes and eights) were removed from the Kensington mill and installed at Lehigh Manufacturing, making room for additional new Levers machines ordered for use at Joseph H. Bromley. To these were added two experimental German Torchon lace machines (which made a coarse low-grade product), a warping mill, and a variety of ancillary devices, the final bills totaling $373,377 on Lehigh's accounts alone. During the seventeen months of tax-free machinery importing, 400 British looms worth $2.9 million were imported by American firms – nearly a third of them to Pennsylvania buyers among whom the Bromleys were by far the most prominent figures. At a stroke, the sector reached its full growth. A decade later only 590 lace looms were recorded in all U.S. plants, a number which, given the intervening war, reflects a sudden tripling of capacity in the tariff window months and only infrequent additions thereafter.[46]

As the Wharton School's Gladys Palmer observed in her dissertation (1925), this burst of capacity generated labor shortages, technical problems derived from the employment of thinly experienced workers, irregular output, and increased competition. As these difficulties were being endured, the ad

[46] IB, pp. 42–123; Gladys Palmer, *Labor Relations in the Lace and Lace-Curtain Industries in the United States*, U.S. Bureau of Labor Statistics Bulletin No. 399, Washington, D.C., 1925, pp. 22–3. On value of imported machines, see *Tariff Hearings: 1913*, p. 3960.

valorem duty on foreign laces was in 1913 reduced to 60 percent, a part of the sweeping revisions undertaken promptly after Woodrow Wilson's accession to the presidency. War soon shut off flows of French and English lace, but North American reported in the 1921 tariff hearings that widespread failures among the 1910 cohort of new starts meant that "one-third of the machines imported duty free have changed hands since 1913." Fresh competitors may have been flayed by tariff shifts and the slipping appeal of lace curtains during the late 1910s, but the Bromleys rolled along. The renamed Quaker Lace Company commenced issuing annual style books that were circulated to customers through retail outlets, maintained its street-level showroom in central Manhattan, and sold millions of dollars worth of yard goods, curtains, and trimmings annually.[47]

The survival of one volume of Quaker's sales ledgers for the period 1912–20 permits a rough sketch of the pattern of distribution and consumption of its specialty goods across the United States (Table 5.6). Clearly, lace was fed into a truly national market; indeed the proportion of sales to major cities exactly matches the segment of national population located in sizable urban centers in the 1910 census. However, disaggregating the totals shows a definite unevenness in the geography of distribution. Almost two-thirds of Quaker's urban markets were concentrated in the industrial belt from New York west to Milwaukee, accounting for 60 percent of all sales in two regions that numbered just over 40 percent of U.S. population. Though New England, the Plains, and the Far West took proportions of Quaker's output close to their share of population, the South lagged dramatically. None of these results should be terribly surprising. Laces and lace curtains were optional purchases for urban middle and working-class families, for farms and small-town commercial households. Where there was relatively ample disposable income, in the industrial belt's core cities and periphery, sales were five times higher per capita than in the southern states (4.6 cents vs. 0.9 cents per person, with the national average being 3.2 cents). Quaker had also reached firmly beyond the Mississippi, shipping a quarter of its output to distant buyers. Weaker direct links to retailers on the Pacific coast led the firm to trade with jobbers and wholesalers in San Francisco and Los Angeles, the only instance in which the bulk of regional sales went to urban outlets. By contrast, in Iowa alone, for the single ledger, Quaker sold directly to thirty-two stores in twenty-six communities, the value of goods amounting to some $180,000, 1912–20, equaling the entire Pacific edge trade.

Estimating beyond the available ledger (which was arranged alphabetically by client, A–E) to its three missing companions, it is plausible that Quaker

---

[47] Palmer, *Lace*, pp. 15, 22; *The Quaker Lace Book for 1913*, Archives, Paley Design Center, Philadelphia College of Textiles and Science. See also *ACUJ* 30(June 1912): 66.

Table 5.6. *Regional geography of sales, Quaker Lace Company, 1912–20, in thousands of dollars invoiced*

	N_f	Cities	Towns & rural	Total	% of sales	% of U.S. population (1910)
New England	33	$ 9	$ 162	$171	6	7
Mid-Atlantic	106	261	588	849	29	21
East North Central	117	249	654	903	31	20
West North Central	64	63	327	390	13	13
South & South Central	55	60	213	273	9	32
Mountains	26	51	105	156	5	3
Pacific	26	108	72	180	6	4
Totals	427	$801	$2,121	$2,922	99	100
Sales, cities *vs.* towns/rural		27%	73%			
U.S. population in 1910, cities *vs.* towns/rural		27%	73%			

N_f = number of client firms by region.

Notes: Cities here are those settlements with 50,000 + population 1910. Regions are those designated by U.S. Census Bureau; except South and South Central = South Atlantic, plus East and West South Central. U.S. population in 1910 = 92 million.

Sources: Sales figures from Quaker Lace Sales Ledger, Volume I, A–E, 1912; population data from Bureau of the Census, *Statistical Abstract of the United States: 1943*, Washington, D.C., 1944, Tables 6, 9, 10.

handled roughly 1,700 separate accounts in the 1910s with commercial sales totaling about $12 million. To this might be added its share of the war years' demand for military nettings, which Palmer notes took up the slack from faltering lace and curtain markets during the conflict. In 1920, the Bromley family's Philadelphia lace mills still dominated the sector statewide, as their collective output ($9.2 million in inflated dollars) represented 70 percent of total value generated in Pennsylvania laces and lace curtains. Evidently recognizing that further expansion in this trade was redundant, the Quaker Lace group's response to the sharp postwar depression was yet another lateral placement of capital, spawning the Quaker Hosiery mills to join the rising cadre of full-fashioned hosiery producers in the region's newest growth sector. Wealthy and resilient, alert to shifts in the industrial climate, the Bromleys were a model of the successful multigeneration proprietary family. Flexible, they accepted the lacemakers' craft unions transplanted from Britain, hewed to no single marketing approach, and steadily added to their array of designs. When the 1922 recovery brought lace sales only to 80 percent of the predepression peak, they had already branched off into hosiery, a sector into which virtually all new capital investment would be poured over the next two decades. Meanwhile, the Bromley firms gradually withdrew from the carpet trade.[48]

Taken together, the experiences of the Beetems and the Bromleys illustrate the workings of the Philadelphia format at the firm level. An aggressive incomer was stimulated by the heady environment of Kensington and the Manufacturers' Club and by his contact with New York commercial possibilities. He adapted to the creed of versatility and stylistic sensitivity preached locally, imagining new ventures beyond carpets into curtains and the like. Yet once the family compromise was activated, Gilbert Beetem was effectively cut off from the city's ferment. His dreams stagnated well before his business did. By contrast, immersed for generations in the flux of specialty production, the Bromleys forged carefully into new fields. Their timing of both the initiation and expansion of lace manufacturing was exquisite, as was their extension into full-fashioned hosiery. Yet their ability to make these departures depended on deep reserves of capital and credit, the retained profits of business achievement.

Novice entrepreneurs, the Philadelphia equivalents of Gilbert Beetem, could hardly expect to commence with six-thousand-dollar lace looms and new buildings, or with ten-thousand-dollar sets of full-fashioned frames. In

[48] Quaker Lace Sales Register, 1912–20, Volume I, A–E; Palmer, *Lace*, pp. 17, 23. For all its value, Palmer's study is weakened by virtually ignoring the textile trade journals, especially *American Carpet & Upholstery Journal*, the richest single source on lace manufacturing.

the 1910s, with the exception of knit specialties, the capital demands inherent in the new and flourishing textile subsectors dwarfed the entry costs of a generation earlier when hundred-dollar seamless and fancy knitters were all the rage. Never wide open, the door to innovative entrepreneurship seemed to be sliding shut just as the peculiar strengths of the Philadelphia system were being widely acknowledged within the industry. There still would be room for creative shifts after the Great War, but the time had indeed passed when onetime room bosses and salesmen could unite in cheaply begun firms at flexible production's cutting edge. The introduction of European-style decorative upholstery, ornamented hosiery, curtains and portieres, Smyrna and chenille carpets, fancy worsteds and damasks, had ended. An invigorating cycle of borrowing and development that filled the decades from the 1880s to the 1910s, a grand and profitable technical transfer, was completed before the war, but few of the "players" sensed it. From their commanding heights, the Bromleys could spend hundreds of thousands on the next generation of knitting technology; most others would have to rely on novelty, quality, and a healthy dose of good luck in order to extract profits from production in the perplexing climate of postwar "normalcy."

5.3. Textile labor, 1910–1914: Philadelphia, Lawrence, Paterson

In a vivid provocative essay, David Montgomery described the 1910s as "a decade of strikes of unprecedented scale and continuity," an era of "direct, mass-involvement challenge to managerial authority and contempt for accepted AFL practice." Three of the prewar struggles included in his treatment are directly relevant here: the 1910 Philadelphia general strike and the massive textile struggles at Lawrence (1912) and Paterson (1913). Their similarities well fit Montgomery's broad characterization, as the first and third of them featured the "workers' control" elements he details among machinists, miners, and railway workers.[49] More important however, their differences capture the distinctive industrial structures and sociopolitical cultures of the three cities. In Philadelphia, a naked exercise of transit management's power triggered a violent streetcar strike. Sympathy walkouts quickly spun off among Kensington textile hands, faded, then were reorganized and managed by the AFL Central Labor Union in an effort to break the impasse that an alliance between the Rapid Transit Company and city

---

[49] David Montgomery, "The 'New Unionism' and the Transformation of Workers' Consciousness in America, 1909–22," in *Workers' Control in America*, New York, 1979, pp. 93–5, 99.

authorities had produced. In Lawrence, an opportunistic wage cut by the dominant American Woolen Company set off an epic battle that yielded a temporary labor victory through the combined efforts of cross-ethnic solidarity, active women's networks, and the dramatic tactics of in-migrating IWW "leaders." At Paterson, stretch-out was the trigger, but despite the IWW's vitality, politicized and divided workers fell before the unanticipated solidarity of scores of mill proprietors, acting in a fashion mindful of the Philadelphia 1903 strike. In the Philadelphia case, textile labor's strength lay at the shop and sectoral level; once again citywide common action would prove maddeningly ineffectual. Moreover, the political polarization that mobilized all Lawrence against tyrannical William Wood fragmented into competing radicalisms in Paterson and only briefly dented the tough hide of Philadelphia's Republican machine or the consciousness of its shop and craft-focused supporters.

The 1910 Philadelphia confrontation stemmed from the city transit company's recent political-financial history and an organizing drive by the AFL's Amalgamated Association of Street and Electric Railway Employees. In 1901 "traction magnates" Peter Widener and William Elkins had consolidated ownership of all city streetcar lines through creation of a holding company. By 1906, Philadelphia Rapid Transit was a financial mess. Already accused of stock manipulations, the monopoly needed new investment capital to meet its commitment to "improved and expanded service" and to achieve a fast-vanishing potential for profitability. Balked in capital markets, in 1907 the PRT turned to city government, which delivered a long-term sweetheart contract confirming the monopoly, guaranteeing it control over all new construction (subways and elevateds), and essentially "surrender[ing] its regulatory powers over the transit system." Rather than transforming public transit into a municipal function, Philadelphia reaffirmed its support for private enterprise in public services (as it had done previously with the corruption-scarred city gas works). Stabilized, the PRT was not amused to discover AASERE buttons circulating among its drivers.

Second to raising capital, holding down costs seemed the key to realizing profits, but terrible working conditions (split morning–afternoon rush-hour shifts with unpaid "down time" between them) and low wages (20 cents per hour) were powerful stimuli toward organization. In 1909, declining to recognize the AASERE or discuss its demands, which included a 25 percent hourly raise, PRT took a strike. The public, disenchanted with the transit company's still-shabby performance, "sympathized with the strikers." Only after political pressure was brought to bear by the Republican machine, which feared a backlash against "organization" men in the spring primaries, did PRT come to terms. Though a 10 percent increase in hourly pay was secured along with full reinstatement and other minor gains, union recognition was refused. Denying contractual status to the AASERE was a tactical move, for within months PRT created a rival company union, using overt favoritism in job assignments to encourage and reward enrollees.[50]

Early in 1910, the AASERE pressed for a new agreement, asserting that the company had been lax in observing the 1909 settlement. "In no mood to dicker, the PRT belligerently fired 173 union men on February 19. The carmen launched another strike which was to become one of the bloodiest and most destructive in the city's history." The dismissal was neatly timed, for PRT had stalled the carmen until the Republican organization had scored a sweeping victory in municipal elections on February 15. Crushing the reformist challenge of the William Penn Party, using the specially created Workingmen's League as a stalking horse to draw Democrats away from the Penn slate, the Republicans also employed their usual "polling-place plan" through which hundreds of "Organization leaders assisted [voters] in marking the ballot."[51] When news of the firings and the carmen's walkout reached Central Labor Union chief John J. Murphy, he promptly raised the possibility that "all other labor organizations will be called out" to help win victory. Defiant, the company made good on its promise to run its lines regardless of the AASERE, using "loyal" members of its captive union. The PRT's provocation and the carmen's determination to shut down the system turned Sunday, February 20, into a day of mass violence.

> Cars were smashed, then burned. A score of riots in which policemen, mounted and on foot, used revolvers and clubs, sent more than 100 men and women to hospitals and impromptu infirmaries ... Almost simultaneously, in widely separated sections of the city, crowds of men and boys began a determined effort to aid the strikers ... Instances not unlike civil war marked the street disorders.[52]

The textile district, as ever, was the hub of militant outrage, as Lehigh Avenue became "the storm center from which disorderly crowds spread to all parts of Richmond and Kensington." Police had been stationed on the cars, and many were injured by flying bricks and sections of lead pipe. Communal violence was the order of the day, and of the days following. The crowds in Kensington alone, estimated at some ten thousand strong, far outnumbered the four to six thousand transit strikers systemwide. An ele-

---

[50] Lloyd Abernethy, "Progressivism, 1905–1919," in Russell Weigley, ed., *Philadelphia: A 300-Year History*, New York, 1982, pp. 547–9.

[51] Ibid., p. 549; *Public Ledger*, February 16, 1910, p. 1 (hereafter, *PL*). The independent Democratic candidate drew less than 5 percent of the 210,000 votes cast in the race for city receiver of taxes. Given the *Ledger*'s post-1900 expansion, page numbers will hereafter be provided for ease of reference.

[52] *PL*, February 20, p. 2; February 21, p. 1.

mental rage, rather than a political radicalism, targeted the cars of the hated PRT and the too-obvious alliance between company and city government, evident in the ubiquitous police presence.

Both the Republican machine and the PRT had reserve tactics intended to crush resistance. The mayor authorized enrollment of three thousand temporary police "specials," called in a troop of the State Fencibles to patrol Kensington, and jailed union leader Clarence Pratt. The company imported strikebreakers from New York in freight cars; rumors that "a large number of them were negroes aroused the indignation of strike sympathizers" who were as reliably racist as the rest of white Philadelphia. However, the troops were a walking disaster, as the *Ledger* headlined "Fencibles Routed by Rioters in Northeast." Spread out ten feet apart along six city blocks, the soldiers were first taunted then assaulted by hardened Kensingtonians. When their lieutenant was stripped of his saber, he rushed into a drugstore and phoned for police backup. A squad of mounted blues roared down Lehigh Avenue and rescued the beleaguered soldiers, whose campaign hats had been filched and torn into souvenir shreds by the delighted crowd. Questioned as to why he had not ordered his men to fire on the mob, the lieutenant, "white as a ghost, said he was not there to hurt anybody." As police cleared the streets, thrashing their billies, a group of six vocal women were driven back into the row house from whose steps they had contributed their insults to the wild scene. One of them tossed off a bit of instant political analysis, jerking open her front door to announce that "the whole trouble came about because the men had voted the Republican ticket." Doubtless, she was far from alone in perceiving the timing of the firings and the company's rigidity as related to the mid-February renewal of the organization's lease on city power. Their votes having been taken to the political bank, working-class Philadelphians vilified those whom they had just confirmed in office and communicated their sense of betrayal through escalating violence. Disappointed with the Fencibles, Mayor John Reyburn requested the governor to send four troops of Pennsylvania's famous "Cossacks," the state police.[53]

Pratt's arrest set off the first spontaneous sympathy strikes, as on February 22 an estimated 30,000 workers walked out of textile or clothing factories and off building sites "without waiting for an action by their locals." Pratt

[53] Ibid., February 21, p. 3; February 22, p. 1, 3; February 23, p. 2; February 24, p. 1. The rumored black strikebreakers were imaginary, it seems, but some of the new special police were Afro-Americans, and were pictured and lampooned as "Brownies" in the *Ledger* (March 6, p. 4; March 7, p. 3). John Golden of the UTWA rang the racist alarm as well, calling Kensington workers to consider "the most humiliating sight I ever saw ...an aged man elbowing his way thorugh the crowd was struck down by a negro policeman. I wondered then whether the Liberty Bell had proclaimed that kind of freedom" (*PL*, March 10, p. 3).

and Murphy promptly urged them to return; the former's release later that day eased the situation and his declaration that a general strike was not necessary deferred further action for a time. The state police, each armed with rifle, revolver, club, and a reputation for deadly efficiency, successfully intimidated Kensington and Frankford, though scattered incidents continued. Their introduction brought the CLU to issue a call for a decisive meeting, Sunday, February 27, at which unions both independent and affiliated would debate promulgating a general strike. Frank McKosky, "business agent" for nineteen Kensington textile workers' unions, only six of which were members of the CLU, signed the call for delegates with Murphy and representatives of the building trades, machinists, and other organizations. John Golden, national head of the UTWA, arrived in the city and spent the next day closeted with McKosky, Arthur McDonell of the Dyers Union, and leaders of other local independent textile unions. On Saturday even placid Manayunk boiled up, as 1,500 persons smashed windows in "a score of trolley cars," following the lead of men at the Pencoyd Iron Works who "amused themselves by throwing iron bolts at passing cars." When locally recruited specials were dispatched to the site, they proved as useless as the Fencibles had been, for "The crowd knows those fellows and won't hurt them, and they won't hurt the crowd." As the delegates gathered Sunday, the city held its collective breath.[54]

Sidelining calls by "radicals" for an immediate general strike, 142 union representatives offered both an olive branch and a rock to the PRT. Were the company to agree to arbitration during the coming week, no action would be taken. If not, the delegates pledged to bring out 75,000 union workers and cripple industry and construction throughout Philadelphia, commencing Saturday, March 5. Company president Charles Kruger sturdily rejected the notion of arbitrating the dispute after a Tuesday meeting with his board. The neighborhoods quieted; the state police were sent back to their barracks. Attention was riveted on what would happen come Saturday. Mayor Reyburn dutifully announced he would do nothing to promote arbitration, and forbade city councils from fooling with the risky proposition. Public Safety Director Henry Clay predicted a fiasco for labor, then struggled to cook up appropriately tiny figures once the shutdown gathered momentum. The UTWA's Golden, ever the compromiser, was forced to move beyond urging workers to join his union and vote scoundrel politicians out. At a Thursday night textile workers' session, he put the general strike question to a "cheering throng" whose "enthusiastic response" indicated Kensington's commitment to labor solidarity. On "The Day," labor claimed that 100,000 men and

[54] Ibid., February 23, p. 3; February 24, p. 2; February 25, p. 2; February 26, p. 2; February 27, pp. 1, 2.

women stood down from their quotidian tasks to back the carmen; organization man Clay muttered that only 20,000 were out. These vast reporting disparities continued throughout the three weeks of the general strike's duration; the actual numbers are from this distance indeterminate, though recent writers have accepted the unions' claim that 146,000 joined at the peak of the movement.[55]

What is important here is that Kensington closed shop. Led by dyers and carpet weavers, who had only recently settled price-of-work strikes, upholstery weavers and knitters, hosiery boarders and loom fixers hit the bricks by the thousands. The city association of hosiery manufacturers announced a one-week suspension of work, expecting the transit strike would soon be settled. The upholstery millmen posted an indefinite closure and the Dobsons shut several of their mills for three weeks "for repairs" normally undertaken in midsummer. McKosky said some 25,000 union and unorganized textile workers had come out the first day, but the *Ledger* established that outside textiles and the building trades the response initially was spotty. Glaring was the non-participation of employees at Philadelphia's giant enterprises: Baldwin Locomotive, Disston Saw, Atlantic Refining, Midvale Steel, the Navy Yard and Arsenals, Brill's car builders, and Cramps' Shipyards, together representing at least 40,000 workers. The walkout was surely immense, but it was far from general.

Reporters interviewed strikers about their reasons for supporting the sympathetic shutdown. Many responded plainly with statements of solidarity with oppressed union brothers, but some, like breweryman J. Lutz, were alert to the city's incestuous political dealings: "I'm for the strike because of what [Mayor] Reyburn is doing. They're running things as they please; the people have no say. Look at the thugs they're making special policemen. The Rapid Transit Company is in with the city ring, and we get our heads broken for nothing." Probably a veteran of the street clashes, Lutz viewed the great strike as a political statement, whereas others were performing a gesture of labor solidarity, and tens of thousands more were simply walking to work instead of riding scab streetcars, avoiding the whole controversy.[56]

With the addition of two to four thousand Baldwin workers late in the first week, the general strike stabilized, a bad sign, for the PRT stolidly ignored the whole proceeding. Press howling about the moral depravity of the sympathy effort was mounting. Lloyd Abernethy neatly summarized its later stages:

---

[55] Ibid., February 28, p. 1, 2; March 1, p. 1; March 2, p. 2; March 3, p. 1; March 4, p. 3; March 6, p. 1; Montgomery, *Workers' Control*, p. 93; Abernethy, "Progressivism," p. 549.

[56] Ibid., March 6, pp. 1–3, March 7, pp. 1–3; March 8, p. 1; March 9, p. 1, 2.

Public distaste for the "socialistic" general strike soon became apparent...as a flood of protests assailed the CLU's "unfair" tactics. Shaken by the massive criticism, the will of the sympathetic strikers weakened further as they saw much of the business of the struck plants going to non-union shops in Philadelphia and factories in other cities. When the Pennsylvania Federation of Labor decided not to support the Philadelphia union in a contemplated statewide strike, the CLU called off the general strike on March 27.

Having engaged the great syndicalist tactic, it became evident that Philadelphia craftsmen were far from syndicalists or socialists of any stripe. Their maneuver had been a calculated but bounded escalation, conceived as a means to ratchet up the pressure on the city government-PRT tandem, not as progress toward social revolution. Assaulted by charges of radical intent, appreciating that the outer limit of compliance with the strike call had been reached, rebuffed by initially supportive state-level AFL leaders, witnessing the classic 1903 drift back to the mills, Murphy, McKosky, and the rest of the leadership Committee of Ten pulled the plug, pledging financial support for the carmen but leaving them to go on alone.[57]

At the outset, textile workers had been viewed as the key to the general strike's expected impact, at least in the eyes of carmen organizer Pratt. The night before March 5, accompanied by Golden and McKosky, he circulated through Kensington labor halls thronged with thousands of hosiery and upholstery workers, urging that their enthusiasm for the sympathy walkout be accompanied by temperance and good order. "Be careful in your conduct," he begged. "Commit no overt act of destruction or menace that can be used against you. This is to be one great silent protest from the workers who make the city what it is." Arriving at the Dyers' annual dress ball, attended by 1,200, half the men "in evening dress" and the women "appropriately gowned," Pratt was announced as the orchestra burst into a rendition of the "Star Spangled Banner" (not the "Internationale"). Ending his speech with lines from Byron's "Battle of Waterloo," Pratt was mobbed

---

[57] Abernethy, "Progressivism," p. 550. Three weeks later, after sixty-six strike days, the PRT concluded an agreement with the AASERE that returned all the carmen to work, submitted the 173 dismissals to arbitration, and gradually elevated pay to 25 cents/hour over two years, but did not recognize the union. The result was a two-cheers victory for labor. The gains were small but tangible and the arrogant PRT management team was soon dismissed, as control of the transit system passed to E. T. Stotesbury of powerful Drexel and Company. Stotesbury replaced Kruger with Chicago's Thomas Mitten who deftly displaced the AASERE while improving both the PRT's service and its financial performance. Mitten's resourcefulness kept the carmen back on their heels for years to come.

by cheering celebrants. As the *Ledger* noted, "Kensington was going into this fight with a light heart and confident of victory for a just cause."[58]

Carpet and full-fashioned hosiery hands struck en masse, though in the woolen and worsted sectors (and outside Kensington generally), the response of textile workers was uneven. The mill owners reportedly were more "grieved and hurt than resentful at the strikers." One, confident that he could secure employees, distinguished sympathy strikes from the regular "grievance" walkouts. In the latter,

> workers are unwilling to take the places of men who have left their places because of a fancied injustice, but the case is different with the sympathy strike. The manufacturers up here have nothing to do with the Rapid Transit Company... and yet they are to be made the victims because some labor leaders think that is the way to win for the trolley men. It is absurd.

Commenting on the unity among Brussels carpet weavers, another less optimistic proprietor remarked, "That is one of the strongest unaffiliated unions in the country. When they strike, they generally lick us." Initially, unorganized textile workers who cared for neither the carmen nor the PRT bowed to community pressure and stayed away from the Northeast's factories. As one put the matter, "I do care for my hide and I don't like to be called a scab." However, the genuine difference between sympathy and grievance strikes and the textile unions' continuing inability to organize women and young workers soon led to scattered breaks. During the second week, Beetem's employees drifted back and hosiery mills were widely reported starting again. Manufacturers direly warned that April openings for the fall carpet trade were imperiled, that a full season's business might be lost unless samples were completed, helping to further a return-to-work movement that swelled on Monday, March 21. The next evening, the textile unions, which had been "the backbone of the local general strike," sent delegates to the Labor Lyceum for a joint session. With few dissenting murmurs, they voted an immediate cessation of the stoppage. The textile withdrawal triggered similar action by the building trades, eased the state AFL Executive Committee's refusal to endorse a wider callout, and doomed the general strike.[59]

Lacking an ideological base sufficient to bind persuasively the common interests of all labor, the general strike had foundered. Initial spasms of rage at the PRT and the organization could not be translated into a disciplined, sustained solidarity in the absence of a shared critique of capitalism and

[58] *PL*, March 5, p. 2.
[59] Ibid., March 7, p. 2; March 8, pp. 2–3; March 14, p. 2; March 15, p. 2; March 20, p. 1, March 23, pp. 1–2; March 24, p. 1.

machine politics. Crucially, the strengths of shop-centered craft practices and neighborhood militancy faded when pressed into service citywide. Able to time their initiatives with the patterns of seasonal demand, better placed to employ shop and community resources in direct engagements with proprietors, sectoral clusters of textile workers frequently managed to "lick" groups of millmen in battles over shop customs and the price of work. Yet, as in 1903, the scale boundaries to these efforts' efficacy were made clear when they were applied to the broader 1910 PRT controversy. Initiated to defend trade unionism rather than to advance the class struggle, dominated by personalities and local politics, the Philadelphia general strike illustrates the limitations borne by loosely federated craft organizations seeking to channel riotous enthusiasm into respectable pressure on stiff-necked businessmen and their political allies. As its course ill fits heroic models of working-class self-organization, the conflict has had but a marginal place in overviews of prewar labor history. This alone distinguishes the 1910 Philadelphia strike from its contemporaries, the mighty struggles at Lawrence and Paterson.

Other contrasts are more salient, however. In both cities, the textile labor force was far more generally populated by segments of "new" immigrants than was Philadelphia. Thousands of Italians and Russian Jews (at Paterson), Poles, Franco-Belgians, Quebecois, Syrians, and Italians again (at Lawrence) led the strike waves, as skilled English and American unionists held back, tried to avoid conflict, and jumped at compromise offers in a manner consistent with the cautious style of the AFL locals in which some of them were organized. In Philadelphia, alliances of skilled males were the core movers in 1910 (as in 1903). In both the 1912 and 1913 cases, the IWW, which had been locked in internecine conflict in 1910, emerged as the central militant focus for a radical industrial unionism foreign to the Philadelphia context. Talk of social revolution surely would have horrified the stylish crowd at the Dyers' Ball. In neither city was there the Philadelphia pattern of durable and effective union action, for Paterson organizations had been episodic and the Lawrence locals for Golden's UTWA were "somnolent" and "scarcely disturbed employers." Though Quaker City proprietors readily expressed their distaste for unions and their "fancied injustice[s]," they had long experience of the power craftsmen could bring to bear on individual firms. In Kensington, lines of continuity stretched back beyond the Knights to the rough democracy of factory committees in the 1870s. Local reliance on shop and craft autonomy blended uncomfortably with AFL practice after 1900; spontaneity and solidarity were tactical and based on custom and experience, not on an ideology of social transformation.

In terms of industrial structure, Lawrence and Paterson were cities dominated by the textile manufacture; each focused on one sector within the trades, worsteds and woolens versus silks, respectively. Neither displayed Philadelphia's diversity, in or outside of textiles. However, the presence of Wood's American Woolen company as the chief force in Lawrence served to target strikers' militancy in a fashion impossible at Paterson, where several hundred firms of all sizes were involved. When Wood relented in March 1912, the IWW scored its greatest triumph. By contrast, when the industrial union strategy was attempted at Paterson against a horde of separate establishments, the latters' crisis alliance, a panicky bond between small and large capitals, held long enough to exhaust labor's resources. Fractious political battles emerged between the syndicalist union and rival organizations and were enhanced by ethnic antagonisms of long standing. The ideological context in Paterson, which had had both socialist and anarchist movements of significance since the 1890s, was dramatically different from Philadelphia's squabbles between Republicans and reformers, despite the common proprietary form of specialty production in the two mid-Atlantic centers.

Indeed, at this juncture, the struggles of textile workers in the Northeast indicate that neither the industrial nor the craft approach to organization was broadly effective. Philadelphia's firm-based subsectoral unions (e.g., dyers, upholstery weavers) could pick and win small-scale fights, but were indifferent to the unorganized in other textile trades and were prone to making separate peaces in coalitions. The craft strategy, as codified by the UTWA, failed utterly in Paterson (where Golden bowed to manufacturers in a 1912 conflict) and had spawned spineless locals in Lawrence. In both places, the UTWA avoided commitments to strike-prone immigrant groups at the low end of the wage structure. On the other hand, the IWW's industrial efforts, alloyed with a revolutionary rhetoric, "worked" only briefly at Lawrence, where paralyzing a single massive firm was crucial, but were disastrous in Paterson. Dealing with Philadelphia's giant PRT, the carmen's union stuck to its craft approach rather than breach AFL divisional lines to mobilize powerhouse and maintenance workers, an "industrial" step that would have deepened the PRT's problems in operating lines with scab drivers. No single strategy transcended intra- and interregional differences in scale and the spatial distribution of work. Even where "appropriate" strategies were mounted, the organizational complexities of managing conflict bested the federated Philadelphia unions, whereas the challenges of sustaining a large industrial local defeated the Lawrence IWW soon after its initial success. Neither the respectable potential of pressure politics nor a radical vision of social transformation had sufficient magnetism to build upon the surges that outrage over short pay, stretch-out, or management arrogance had initiated. Given these constraints, durable victories, the marshaling of political influence, and the fostering of heightened class consciousness all proved elusive.[60]

Yet the labor battles of the 1910s continued, almost all failures, as Montgomery concludes. This decade featured both the dislocating impact of "rationalized industry" in bulk-production sectors where mergers were followed by throughput innovations or organizational tightening (e.g., work process restructuring, disciplinary firings), and intensified competition in batch sectors feeding an increasingly consolidated distribution system for consumer goods. In struggling against long odds, workers in these three prewar strikes called into service tactics rooted in "preindustrial" antagonisms between the powerful and the plebeian mass, tactics based on values and traditions shared among working people in their communities. Philadelphia's expressive rioting, the general utilization of public shaming, the critical value of women's networks at Lawrence, all employed in a context of skirmishing among complex organizations and interventions by "modern" state mediators, armed forces, and investigative commissions, suggest from another angle the seminal transformation of the political economy that was in process during the war decade.

Meanwhile, at the level of the firm, textile manufacturers with sufficient resources maneuvered to blunt the effect of these ancient tools of resistance, using locational flexibility as a powerful lever. Dubofsky reports that "the multi-plant companies operating in Lawrence would shut down their local mills, while running similar operations elsewhere full-time." The larger Paterson firms relied during and after the 1913 strike on the capacity of their Pennsylvania "annexes," whereas Philadelphia specialists like the Bromleys had built their new facilities outside the Kensington agglomeration. During the 1910 affray, the family's carpet factories in the district were shuttered, despite threats to fire all hands; but no trouble was experienced at their lace

[60] On Lawrence, see Donald Cole, *Immigrant City*, Chapel Hill, 1963; Charles Neill, *Report on [the] Strike of Textile Workers in Lawrence, Mass., in 1912* (Senate Document 870), Washington, D.C., 1912; Joyce Kornbluh, ed., *Rebel Voices*, Ann Arbor, 1964, ch. 6; Melvyn Dubofsky, *We Shall Be All*, New York, 1969, ch. 10 (quote from p. 234); and Ardis Cameron, "Bread and Roses Revisited: Women's Culture and Working-Class Activism in the Lawrence Strike of 1912," in Ruth Milkman, ed., *Women, Work and Protest*, Boston, 1985, pp. 42–61. For Paterson, see Kornbluh, ch. 7; Dubofsky, ch. 11; James Osborne, "Italian Immigrants and the Working Class in Paterson: The Strike of 1913 in Ethnic Perspective," in Paul Stellhorn, ed., *New Jersey's Ethnic Heritage*, Trenton, 1978, pp. 1–20, and Philip Scranton, ed., *Silk City: Studies on the Paterson Silk Industry, 1860–1940*, Newark, 1985. The third volume of the Commission on Industrial Relations' *Final Report and Testimony* (Senate Document 415), Washington, D.C., 1916, has considerable coverage of the 1913 strike. Two recent monographs are Anne H. Tripp, *The I.W.W. and the Paterson Silk Strike of 1913*, Urbana, IL, 1987, and Steve Golin, *The Fragile Bridge: Paterson Silk Strike, 1913*, Philadelphia, 1988.

mills west of Broad Street, well beyond Kensington's borders at Twenty-second and Lehigh. In the long run, capital restructuring across space could prove to be as potent a tactic as calling for the militia was in the short run.[61]

5.4. Troubled years: the state and/of textiles, 1913–1916

In late June of 1914, barely six weeks before the outbreak of the Great War, the Commission on Industrial Relations brought its traveling show to Philadelphia. Conceived amid a stubborn recession and the burgeoning labor battles of the period, and at this point headed by San Francisco liberal Harris Weinstock, the commission represented a federal intervention into what had chiefly been local questions of the relations between labor and capital. Arriving from New York, its representatives were respectfully but not warmly received. As the *Ledger* put it, the commissioners were in a "very awkward situation." President Wilson, who had appointed them, was insisting that the present hard times were only "psychological" and that "everything is all right in the world of industry." Nonetheless, the investigators were widely expected to show labor being so ill treated that "the strong arm of the Government must reach out to rescue the oppressed. Otherwise what use can hare-brained politicians make of [the] findings?" The commission's legislative concerns were clear, including advocacy of a federal employment exchange and mediation and conciliation services. In addition, Weinstock repeatedly expressed broad sympathy for the orderly processes of collective bargaining. On this issue, Special Counsel E. H. Busiek questioned a bewildered John Wanamaker, whose system of proprietary benevolent associations fell into neither of the keyword categories (individual vs. collective bargaining, open vs. closed shop) that would come to dominate twentieth-century discussions. Mutual noncomprehension characterized many of the exchanges during the Philadelphia hearings. Searchers for order struggled to compress the mosaic of Philadelphia relations into simple terms congenial to industrial rationalization, but witnesses described a production system laden with shop custom, erratic contests, shifting influences and alliances that reflected relationships basic to flexible manufacturing, rather than the routinized procedures of railway brotherhoods and managerial hierarchies.[62]

[61] Montgomery, pp. 94, 101–3; Dubofsky, p. 257; Steve Golin, "The Unity and Strategy of the Paterson Silk Manufacturers During the 1913 Strike," in Scranton, ed., *Silk City*, pp. 89–91; see *PL*, March 5, p. 2; March 20, p. 2; March 24, p. 2, for the Bromley details.

[62] *PL*, June 21, 1914, p. 4; June 24, p. 12; Commission on Industrial Relations, *Final Report and Testimony* (Senate Document No. 415), Vol. III, Washington, D.C., 1916, pp. 2669–71 (hereafter cited as CIR, *Report*).

Consider the commissioners' interest in strikes. When Busiek asked Arthur Spencer, managing director at Dobson's, how many strikes his firm had experienced, the response was simple: "We have constant strikes." William Turner of Quaker Lace, replying by letter to a question about "Labor Troubles," stated: "These are daily excepting Sunday, but we suppose you refer only to those that we find ourselves unable to adjust within 24 hours." In this category, there had been five shutdowns in the preceding sixteen months, two of which had lasted two weeks, closing the mills entirely. Major sectoral walkouts were, by contrast, infrequent; in upholstery, weaver Tobias Hall testified that only one, an eleven-week affair in 1913, had surfaced since 1904. Instead, constant contests were experienced in the mills, over prices to be paid for new styles, firings and hirings, machine assignments, and even, in the summer, provision of iced water. Such flareups were either quickly settled between shop delegates and proprietors or the affected section hit the pavement, a step that usually precipitated a compromise. In the case of new fabrics, when no agreement between delegates and the office could be reached (leading to walkouts at Dobsons'), controversies were settled either by two-week working trials at the office rate, followed by upward adjustments if weavers "can not make wages," or by putting weavers on "daywork" while calculating output against the new rate to evaluate its implementation's impact on earnings. Though the Dobsons' mills had had three sizable strikes in the past five years, Spencer discounted many other disputes, for when "the people were out for one day or two days, I would hardly call it a strike." Such stoppages were a "normal" component of the textile production process in Philadelphia. Ubiquitous and nearly invisible, their presence suggests that historians who count strikes and tally their "causes" may well miss the centrality of contest in everyday labor processes, its incorporation in the shared language of owners and workers, and the distance of their world from the organizing frameworks of emerging social-scientific labor relations, exemplified by the commission's conceptual conventions.[63]

In this light, consider the issue of "union recognition," another touchstone of modern labor organization. Quizzing Tobias Hall, a shop delegate in Upholstery Weavers Local No. 25, Weinstock was puzzled by Hall's assertion that the manufacturers "don't officially recognize" his union, though they had been dealing with it since the 1890s. The commissioner found it hard to fit this into his conception of recognition as a component of rational labor–capital relations. The following dialogue ensued:

[63] CIR, *Report*, Vol. IV, pp. 3041, 3053, 3057, William Turner to A. M. Daly, May 16, 1914, CIR Subject Files, "Industrial Relations: Philadelphia," Department of Labor, RG 174, National Archives.

```
┌─────────────────────────────────────────┐
│  ┌─────────────────────────────────────┐  │
│  │                                     │  │
│  │  Local Union No. 25                 │  │
│  │                                     │  │
│  │  ═══════════════════════════════    │  │
│  │                                     │  │
│  │  PRICE LIST                         │  │
│  │                                     │  │
│  │  FOR  WEAVING                       │  │
│  │                                     │  │
│  │  UPHOLSTERY                         │  │
│  │  GOODS                              │  │
│  │                                     │  │
│  │  ═══════════════════════════════    │  │
│  │                                     │  │
│  │           (emblem) 52               │  │
│  │                                     │  │
│  │  SPLANE & ARMSTRONG, PRINTERS       │  │
│  │  AMBER AND WESTMORELAND STS.        │  │
│  └─────────────────────────────────────┘  │
└─────────────────────────────────────────┘
```

Figure 14. Union price list for Upholstery Weaving, Philadelphia, 1911, cover. (Courtesy of the Philadelphia College of Textiles and Science.)

Weinstock: Well, I don't quite understand the distinction between unofficial recognition of the union and official recognition... Will you please explain?

Hall: The official recognition would be the getting together and agreeing with all our feet under the table on a scale of wages, and signing it.

Weinstock: Yes.

Hall: Unofficial recognition is the fact that after a contest with the employer and he having to come down from his original position, he then hands over a scale of wages to the employees, which is a compromise, generally, and he says, "This firm will pay that," and if the workers in the shop are then not strong enough to compel him, he evades living up to the conditions he has handed out.

Weinstock: You mean—

Hall: (interrupting) But where we have a sufficient number of union men, then we have a committee that demands recognition in the office.

At 2.5 ... per pk.

PICKS	1 or 2 Sheets	JUMBO 1 or 2 Sheets
8	1.8	2.5
9	2.1	2.8
10	2.3	3.2
11	2.5	3.5
12	2.8	3.8
13	3.0	4.1
14	3.2	4.4
15	3.4	4.7
16	3.7	5.1
17	3.9	5.4
18	4.1	5.7
19	4.4	6.0
20	4.6	6.3
21	4.8	6.6
22	5.1	7.0
23	5.3	7.3
24	5.5	7.6
25	5.7	7.9
26	6.0	8.2
27	6.2	8.5
28	6.4	8.9
29	6.7	9.2
30	6.9	9.5
31	7.1	9.8
32	7.4	10.1
33	7.6	10.4
34	7.8	10.8
35	8.0	11.1
36	8.3	11.4
37	8.5	11.7
38	8.7	12.0
39	9.0	12.3
40	9.2	12.6
42	9.7	13.3
44	10.1	13.9
46	10.6	14.5
48	11.0	15.2
50	11.5	15.8
52	12.0	16.4
54	12.4	17.1
56	12.9	17.7
58	13.3	18.3
60	13.8	19.0
62	14.3	19.6
64	14.7	20.2
66	15.2	20.9
68	15.6	21.5
70	16.1	22.1
72	16.6	22.8
74	17.0	23.4
76	17.5	24.0
78	17.9	24.7
80	18.4	25.3

157 cards for 1 cent

400 ... and Over At 2.5 ... per pk

PICKS	1 or 2 Sheets	3 Sheets	JUMBO 1 or 2 Sheets	JUMBO 3 Sheets
20	5.0	6.0	6.9	8.2
21	5.2	6.2	7.2	8.6
22	5.5	6.5	7.6	8.9
23	5.7	6.7	7.9	9.3
24	6.0	7.0	8.2	9.6
25	6.2	7.2	8.6	10.0
26	6.5	7.5	8.9	10.3
27	6.7	7.7	9.3	10.7
28	7.0	8.0	9.6	11.0
29	7.2	8.2	10.0	11.3
30	7.5	8.5	10.3	11.7
31	7.7	8.7	10.7	12.0
32	8.0	9.0	11.0	12.4
33	8.2	9.2	11.3	12.7
34	8.5	9.5	11.7	13.1
35	8.7	9.7	12.0	13.4
36	9.0	10.0	12.4	13.7
37	9.2	10.2	12.7	14.1
38	9.5	10.5	13.1	14.4
39	9.7	10.7	13.4	14.8
40	10.0	11.0	13.7	15.1
42	10.5	11.5	14.4	15.8
44	11.0	12.0	15.1	16.5
46	11.5	12.5	15.8	17.2
48	12.0	13.0	16.5	17.9
50	12.5	13.5	17.2	18.6
52	13.0	14.0	17.9	19.2
54	13.5	14.5	18.6	19.9
56	14.0	15.0	19.2	20.6
58	14.5	15.5	19.9	21.3
60	15.0	16.0	20.6	22.0
62	15.5	16.5	21.3	22.7
64	16.0	17.0	22.0	23.4
66	16.5	17.5	22.7	24.1
68	17.0	18.0	23.4	24.7
70	17.5	18.5	24.1	25.4
72	18.0	19.0	24.7	26.1
74	18.5	19.5	25.4	26.8
76	19.0	20.0	26.1	27.5
78	19.5	20.5	26.8	28.2
80	20.0	21.0	27.5	28.9
84	21.0	22.0	28.9	30.2
88	22.0	23.0	30.2	31.6
92	23.0	24.0	31.6	33.0
96	24.0	25.0	33.0	34.4
100	25.0	26.0	34.4	35.7
104	26.0	27.0	35.7	37.1
108	27.0	28.0	37.1	38.5
112	28.0	29.0	38.5	39.9
116	29.0	30.0	39.9	41.2
120	30.0	31.0	41.2	42.6
124	31.0	32.0	42.6	44.0
128	32.0	33.0	44.0	45.4

144 cards for 1 cent.

DAMASK At 2.6 ... per pk.

PICKS	1 or 2 Sheets	3 Sheets
20	5.2	6.2
21	5.5	6.5
22	5.7	6.7
23	6.0	7.0
24	6.2	7.2
25	6.5	7.5
26	6.8	7.8
27	7.0	8.0
28	7.3	8.3
29	7.5	8.5
30	7.8	8.8
31	8.1	9.1
32	8.3	9.3
33	8.6	9.6
34	8.8	9.8
35	9.1	10.1
36	9.4	10.4
37	9.6	10.6
38	9.9	10.9
39	10.1	11.1
40	10.4	11.4
42	10.9	11.9
44	11.4	12.4
46	12.0	13.0
48	12.5	13.5
50	13.0	14.0
52	13.5	14.5
54	14.0	15.0
56	14.6	15.6
58	15.1	16.1
60	15.6	16.6
62	16.1	17.1
64	16.6	17.6
66	17.2	18.2
68	17.7	18.7
70	18.2	19.2
72	18.7	19.7
74	19.2	20.2
76	19.8	20.8
78	20.3	21.3
80	20.8	21.8
84	21.8	22.8
88	22.9	23.9
92	23.9	24.9
96	25.0	26.0
100	26.0	27.0
104	27.0	28.0
108	28.1	29.1
112	29.1	30.1
116	30.2	31.2
120	31.2	32.2
124	32.2	33.2
128	33.3	34.3

139 cards for 1 cent.

BASIS: ONE OR TWO SHUTTLES

2 3-10 mills per pick for one or two shuttles under 4000 ends.
2 5-10   "   "   "   "   4000 ends and over.
2 6-10   "   "   Silk and Mercerized Damask Warps
2 9-10   "   "   Plain and Figured Goods for Moire

EXTRAS: 1c. per yard for each shuttle over 2.
        1c.   "   "   beam over 2.
        1c.   "   eight changes of shuttle.
        1c. per curtain for pulling fringe.
        2c.   "   "   tying cards on single machine.
        1c. per curtain or couch cover for each lift out of cards.
        2c.   "   "   "   "   rod for taking up slack ends.
        ¾c. per yard for rod for taking up slack ends on piece goods.
Curtains, Couch Covers and Table Covers to be paid by the number of cards.
        1 1-16 of price for 54 to 64 inches.
        1⅛ of price for 65 to 74 inches
        1 3-16 of price for 75 to 84 inches
        1⅜ of price for 100 inch or Jumbo.
        24c. per hour for Time Work.
        10c. per hour extra for each hour over 57 that the engine runs.

Figure 15. Schedules from the 1911 upholstery weavers' price list. Each of the three broad classes of goods has fifty-three subsections corresponding to the fineness of the individual fabrics, with separate columns for regular and wide (Jumbo) looms. The basic price per yard for a fabric may thus be located by specifying first its class, then the number of picks (filling yarns) per inch and the loom size (plus at center and right, the number of shuttles used in weaving). Thus a damask fabric running at 60 picks per inch with three shuttles earns the weaver 16.6 cents per yard completed. Extras for work on very complex goods, and the time work rate (24 cents hourly) for running samples or goods beyond the schedule are listed above. (Courtesy of the Philadelphia College of Textiles and Sciences.)

Weinstock: You mean that whatever collective bargaining may be done in your particular trade is done by the individual employers and the employees in his own shop?

Hall: No; I won't put it that way, Mr. Commissioner. He acts collectively with his fellow employers, and then tries to deal individually with his shops; respective shops.

Weinstock: You mean that the employers are a unity?

Hall: Yes, sir...

Weinstock: When this issue arises about wages and you finally come to an understanding is that understanding purely verbal, or do you enter into a regular written agreement with the employer?

Hall: No, the employer, after he and his fellow employers agree on something and we agree to accept it, he then tacks it up on the wall and signs his name to it.

Weinstock: There is no such thing, then, as an actual agreement between the employer on the one side and the workers on the other?

Hall: No; unofficial. You see, that was the unofficial part I stated a while ago.[64]

---

[64] CIR, *Report*, Vol. IV, pp. 3039–41.

What to make of this? First, there was no legal-rational system of contract bargaining and enforcement operative in upholstery or any other Philadelphia textile trade in 1914. Instead, the customary practices of the 1880s, themselves reflecting antebellum artisanal relations,[65] had survived virtually intact. Manufacturers signed a price of work schedule, not a contract; workers' vigilance was necessary to ensure its application. Second, upholstery firms had preserved a trade association to discuss scale fixing, an institutional continuity not shared by woolen or hosiery firms, sectors in which the numbers of local firms were far greater and union traditions less well rooted. Upholstery manufacturers convened as well to coordinate price movements for seasonal openings and, echoing the Alexander Smith carpet practice, had begun sponsoring an annual auction/liquidation of fabrics left over from cancellations and dropped styles. Though Hall glossed the point, Local 25 usually initiated scale contests by drawing up new schedules that were presented at mills where their representation was strongest. The millmen's association considered these schedules as a "unity" because hundreds of free-rider weavers, formerly or never union members, would refuse work unless the standard rate were paid to all weavers throughout the city. As 90 percent of American-made upholstery came from Philadelphia, and as manufacturers had to get their goods into seasonal markets or see imported fabrics fill the gap, Local 25 was strongly placed to contest rates and conditions, even though only half the city's upholstery weavers were paid-up members. With considerable leverage in this sphere of specialty production, official recognition and formal contracts were hardly essential. Without them, the Philadelphia weavers had pushed their rates to levels roughly 10 percent above those of 1893, though this fell a bit short of the increase in general price levels over the preceding twenty years. The relatively high labor cost of Philadelphia production in time would provide part of the incentive for the inauguration of Dixie competition. But for now, Philadelphia skilled workers were confident of their place in the flexible system despite the nervous ripples that recession and tariff reform were sending forth.[66]

Before moving away from the hearings and their clashes of concept and experience, one more example of the new model language and the implications of its implementation by experts will be offered. In the early 1900s, seasonality in industry came under attack. Once viewed as natural, the pattern of rush and slack was an obvious target for reformers seeking to stabilize

[65] See Melvyn Dubofsky. "Labor," in Glenn Porter, ed., *Encyclopedia of American Economic History*, Vol. II, New York, 1980, pp. 525–6.

[66] CIR, *Report*, Vol. IV, pp. 3035–42, 3062–3, 3077–8. For letters re schedule submissions by Local 25, see Selig Papers, Pastore Library, Philadelphia College of Textiles and Science. On auctions by the "United Upholstery Manufacturers of Philadelphia," see *ACUJ* 29(January 1911): 60.

the swings of capitalist production and ameliorate their impact on firms and workers. Championing the cause of steady work year round, critics of seasonality chose as models trades where product uniformity permitted production for stock in slack periods, yielding accumulations of staple goods that could be fed into rising demand when it returned. In the Philadelphia hearings, Morris L. Cooke, a "consulting engineer and [the city's] director of public works," was called upon for an evaluation of scientific management. Pleading "guilty to knowing very little about it," he spoke on "the intermittence of employment" instead. Drawing on Mary Van Kleeck's studies of women in seasonal sectors, Cooke stressed the wasteful disorderliness of fluctuating workforces, a point underscored by Joseph Willits in his University of Pennsylvania dissertation on seasonality and underemployment, completed and printed the following year. For a particularly "insidious" instance of the effects of insufficiency, Cooke referred to spare hands in Philadelphia textile factories, "men [who] are incapable of continuous employment...[T]hey have become so accustomed to working a few days, a few weeks, or a few months at a time, and then being laid off, that it gets on their nerves when they go to work as steadily as some of the rest of us are able to do."[67]

Cooke called on the commissioners not to regard seasonality as "something imposed upon us by Divine Providence," but instead as something amenable to detailed analysis and planning. The application of scientific management principles and practices (which, despite his disclaimer, Cooke knew thoroughly) would benefit labor, owners, and society alike. Unfortunately, labor unions had little positive to contribute to this stabilization process. The commissioners, citing Louis Brandeis's celebrated views in reply, argued that unionization was a prerequisite for scientific efficiency. The merits of the dispute are less important here than recognizing that a struggle was taking place for the conceptual high ground in industrial relations and that *both* positions were sublimely distanced from the dynamics of flexible production as practiced in Philadelphia textiles. Cooke and the commissioners alike sought to ram the characteristics of the local format through their ideological templates, shearing off the segments that did not fit their rival agendas. Here were the makings of a process of encroachment and marginalization different from that which would become manifest in production and markets. Terms were being set, lines drawn, for a generation of conceptual elaboration and policy debate that favored an orderly homogenization of industrial relations and a calculated standardization of the labor process. It would become gospel that piece rates were degrading, rather than objects of pride and subjects for ritual contest, gospel that shop disruptions were

---

[67] CIR, *Report*, Vol. III, pp. 2674–9; Joseph Willits, *Philadelphia Unemployment with Special Reference to the Textile Industries*, Philadelphia, 1915.

an indicator of irresponsibility, rather than signs of rude health in the daily give-and-take between labor and capital, gospel that formal negotiations and contracts showed maturity and achievement, rather than reflecting desperate attempts to codify and defend once-vital prerogatives and customs. As these "foreign" terms and meanings became conceptual staples, eventually embodied in statutory language and case law, the commissioners' assumption of a singular universe of industrial discourse and understanding became actualized, and the language of shop autonomy and factory culture withered and was forgotten.[68]

The relationship between tariff reform and recession, by contrast, was expressed in familiar language, but was no less contested for that. Philadelphia textile manufacturers had feared a repetition of the 1893 disaster should a rate-slashing Democrat be elected in 1912; James Gay penned the wry opinion that "things would be bad because of the injection in politics of college professors." As contraction and revision did come close together, protectionist pessimists again linked tariff-cutting Democrats with industrial depression. Arthur McDonnell, representing Philadelphia dyehouse workers before the commission, disagreed and pointed to the 1907 Panic's effects: "Talk about slack times. It was a cyclone . . . and not a Democrat in sight." In a letter to staff investigator A. M. Daly, McDonnell implied that manufacturers were making political hay rather than responding to a real crisis.

> At present there are not so many of our men out of work, but there are a few, and when our men ask for work, they are stabbed with the old gag – a Democratic Administration Tariff . . . And some of our employers are busy, never were more so, and still they will say, they are slack, just to run our men down a little. They seem to be sour and all their friendship for their fellows has disappeared.

Mayor Rudolph Blankenburg testified that the city had experienced "comparatively little . . . general suffering," largely "due to the fact that our working people . . . have saved money when they could save money, and they have something to fall back on." The recession was real, but not comparable to the disaster of the 1890s. As a reform Republican who triumphed on the heels of the transit strike fiasco, Blankenburg was independent of the organization and aimed no partisan shots at the Democrats. Silent on the tariff, he was confident that Philadelphia would soon again enjoy prosperity.[69]

---

[68] Ibid., pp. 2680–6. On Brandeis and scientific management, see Thomas McCraw, *Prophets of Regulation*, Cambridge, MA, 1984, pp. 92–4. The issues of language and industrial change deserve much fuller treatment than could be afforded here.

[69] CIR, *Report*, Vol. III, p. 2703; Vol. IV, pp. 3045, 3087; McDonnell to Daly, May 11, 1914, CIR Subject Files, "Industrial Relations: Philadelphia," RG 174, National Archives. After the Blankenburg reform interlude, the city would soon also enjoy another generation of machine Republican political dominance.

From an academic perspective, F. W. Taussig, the era's most persistent observer of tariff movements, thought the 1913 reductions and the establishment of duty-free raw wool imports would be a salutary test of the extent to which domestic textile firms were insulated from the stimulus of international competition. Discounting the recession, he expected that "readjustments" would be modest, that "a decade of experience under normal conditions" would show how riduculous were the fears of devout protectionists. However, Taussig wrote later, "as everyone knows, the years during which the tariff act of 1913 was in force were as far from normal as could be imagined. The war of 1914–18 turned everything topsy-turvy. To American manufacturing industries, it served as protection more effective than any tariff legislation could possibly be." Foreign imports dwindled whereas American goods once confined to home markets by price differentials (conditioned by the tariff) were readily exported "to neutral markets." The war was a shock initially, an annoyance through its entire span, yet an important stimulus nonetheless to mills seeking government contracts and export trade, to workers seeking organizing gains, and to the state, whose role in the economy reached unprecedented proportions after April 1917.[70]

Both the Taft and Wilson administrations undertook tariff restructuring, in 1909 and 1913 respectively. In the 1909 sequence, rates on specialty textiles were in spots advanced over the already high levels the 1897 Dingley tariff had provided. Commenting on this, Taussig observed that these were commodities "made by methods not adapted to American ways of efficiency," by which was meant "the use of highly-developed machinery, continuous operation, standardized processes, and interchangeable parts." Those sectors in which manufacturers used "much direct labor" and made "few goods of any [single] pattern" were vulnerable to competition from the "handcraft efficiency" of low-wage nations. It is in this context that the strident protectionism of Philadelphia industrialists and their allies (John Wood, Joseph Grundy, John Dornan, the Bromleys, Boies Penrose, et al.) is readily intelligible. High tariffs could insulate the flexible system from rival French, British, and German producers operating along similar lines, but only at the social cost of supporting selling prices of American specialties well above European levels for comparable goods.[71]

To reply to charges that protected manufacturers were gouging the public, Philadelphia's Theodore Justice had appeared at the December 1908 tariff hearings dressed in his "Exhibit A," an all-wool suit purchased off the rack

---

[70] F. W. Taussig, *The Tariff History of the United States*, Eighth Edition, New York, 1931, pp. 448–9.
[71] Ibid., p. 391.

on Chestnut Street for $12.50. Much cheaper than Justice's usual tailor-made garb, it was the durable sort of garment "such as a mechanic would wear." On the three and a half yards of fabric necessary for its manufacture, the mill cleared a 9 percent profit (28 cents on $3.19), whereas the clothier reaped a 10–18 percent return in wholesaling the suit to a retailer for about $8.00. The store marked the suit up over 50 percent, roughly half of the addition going to its operating expenses, leaving it a 21 percent profit on a net selling cost of $10.35. By Justice's calculation, each successive stage of making and marketing carved out greater profits than the weaving mill; yet even so, for roughly a week's wages, an adult worker could secure a ser-viceable suit made of all-new wool. In Europe, he averred, though the selling price of an identical garment would be appreciably lower, workers' earnings were so much inferior to American levels that two or more weeks' labor would be needed to fund its purchase. Cleverly done, Justice's stint at modeling carried the day. It was referred to repeatedly in later sessions; Wanamaker's promptly advertised in the Philadelphia *Record* that it was selling all-wool suits "equal" or "far superior in fabric" to Justice's for ten dollars. Most important, in 1909, except for some trivial alterations, "the wool and woolen duties were left intact."[72]

With Democrats in charge, the climate of the 1913 hearings was distinctly chillier for textile-industry witnesses. Representatives from Philadelphia specialty mills stressed their exposure to foreign fine-goods penetra-tion, bewailed the "fixed retail prices" for factory-finished goods (towels, hose, carpets), and tried to convince legislators of the complexity of their product markets, all to no avail. In one more example of the shifting conceptual climate, the committee members had bought whole-sale the notion of cost and price reductions achieved through Taussig's "continuous operations" and assumed its general applicability. Ques-tioned whether running "full time … would … materially decrease your cost [of] production," Quaker Lace's William Turner gave vent to his exasperation:

> Yes; but what would we do with the goods? We can not send them into any other market. We have investigated every channel. When the machinery production is larger than the uses of the domestic market, one of two things happens: You either have to restrict the production or you have the very closest kind of competition.

As Lamoreaux has indicated for the 1890s, batch specialists routinely chose Turner's first option in order to avoid the long-term, profit-killing impli-cations of the second. Few policymakers understood the limited relevance

---

[72] *Tariff Hearings: 1909*, pp. 5236–41, 5248–9, 5330; Taussig, *Tariff History*, p. 393.

of technical and organizational achievements in "throughput" sectors to the imperatives of flexible production.[73]

Regarding textiles, the New England corporate system was so fixed in the tariff revisionists' minds that Philadelphian John Wood had to field questions about his firm's capital stock and dividends (as a private partnership, it had neither), about mill directors owning selling agencies ("It is most unusual"), and about immigrants in the textile workforce ("Q: Is it not a fact that nearly all of them are foreign-born, except in the Southern States? A: It is not"). Unable to perceive the difference between proprietary and managerial firms, the legislators persisted in assuming that Wood's Philadelphia residence, as would be the case with a Boston address, indicated that his factory was elsewhere.

Q: Where is your mill?
A: Philadelphia, as I have three times said.
Q: I know that is where you live, but where is your mill?
A: In Philadelphia.

Pressed to affirm that the committee's goal, eliminating "excess" protection in order to establish a "competitive tariff," was well-founded, Wood agreed that "if . . . you can establish just and equal competitive conditions, we shall not raise any objection at all." However, he added, "because we know you can not do it, we ask for the present duties to remain . . . [T]he whole difficulty hinges upon making a classification that will have a rate that exactly fits each article." Given the vast diversity of textile products, Wood asserted that the effort was doomed, for neither value-based nor specific duties reflected the varying patterns of competition in different fabric lines with any exactness.[74]

Manufacturers had learned to live with the devil they knew, the 1897 Dingley system as slightly revised in 1909. Simple cuts in rate levels made no "scientific" contribution toward creating competition, yet the enormously more complex set of schedules necessary for precision in classification would take many man-years of work to assemble. Wood recognized that a vast gap existed between the rhetoric of a "competitive tariff" and the real dilemmas involved in specifying one. In substance, Taussig agreed with Wood's assessment. The competitive tariff principle did not "differ in essentials from . . . a tariff equalizing cost of production," the logic underlying traditional Republican protectionism. Moreover, neither principle offered reasoned support for the 1913 outcome, "sweeping" alterations in the duty structure. Tariffs on imported raw wool were eliminated, together with "compensating"

---

[73] *Tariff Hearings: 1913*, pp. 3609, 3670–2, 4031–2; Naomi Lamoreaux, *The Great Merger Movement in American Business*, New York, 1985.

[74] *Tariff Hearings: 1913*, pp. 4157, 4159, 4164–5, 4167–8:

duties on imported wool fabrics, political punishment for the long Republican alliance between western wool growers and eastern wool manufacturers. More critical for specialty firms, the system of specific duties, which had sheltered many of their lines, was virtually abrogated, while the value-based tariffs that remained were substantially reduced. These changes struck Philadelphians most severely. Taussig observed that they barely touched the market for coarse and medium-grade products of many New England and most southern mills, for "it was the finer grades of goods that were most likely to be affected." Having been the principal beneficiaries of "the specific duties of the earlier tariff acts," quality and specialty products faced rising importations "likely to be stimulated by the lower rates." The differential regional impact of these revisions in part accounts for the sourness McDonnell noted among Philadelphia millmen in 1914. They expected to be the hardest hit segment of the industry and were embittered by that "Democratic Administration Tariff."[75]

Despite Blankenburg's public statement that Philadelphia was bearing up well in the 1913–14 recession, the news from the textile districts was hardly cheerful. Industrial Commission researcher A. M. Daly reported the city statistician's estimate of spring 1914 textile unemployment at 15,000, a quarter of the workforce, and Quaker Lace's Turner wrote Daly that operations were at 60 percent of capacity. However, Local 25's W. T. Griffith observed that there was so much machinery in the city and so many staggered seasonal patterns that "normal" usage would be perhaps 75 percent. He figured current activity was 65 percent, a troubling dip but not a catastrophe. In this regard the limited relevance of the notion of "excess capacity" in accounting for trade difficulties must be stressed. Developed for analysis of capital-intensive bulk production, it ill fits the situation of textile specialists with their arrays of differently aged and variously used machines. As Howell Harris put it, "Every plant contains reserve battalions of veteran capital which doesn't eat and drink and is no trouble unless it's occupying space . . . that's wanted for something else." The ability to lay off and recall workers readily was a compensating element in a production format keyed to fluctuating demand, making nominal capacity use a measure of marginal significance. Thus, though Stanley Stager recalled the first half of 1914 as an exceedingly dull period, he was little distressed at running his spinning mill below half capacity for a time "to help pay some of the overhead and give employment to as many as possible." Gearing up and cutting back were routine matters, but the European mobilizations added new tremors to the spring's unsettled situation.[76]

[75] Taussig, *Tariff History*, pp. 413, 419, 428–9, 433.
[76] Daly Memorandum B.B. 8–27–14, p. 10; William Turner to Daly, May 16, 1914, CIR

The Gays' August 6, 1914, daybook entry promptly expressed two of the chief war-era concerns that would bedevil many textile mills: "This war practically stops all importation of aniline dyes and wools so manufacturers are making every effort to supply their requirements for at least [the] next 4 months so as to provide for a heavy advance in price and shortage of supply. We did very nicely in this respect." The dyestuffs issue stemmed from American reliance on German producers for the bulk of their synthetic colorants, whereas the raw materials question grew out of the refusal of the British (and later, Australian) government to permit general exports of wool. For carpet men, intervention in coarse-wool markets by the Russian state had a similar effect. The August shocks were brief, however; by October a rising wave of war-related orders sent scores of mills back on full schedules. Among others, the Dobsons began running an initial order of 100,000 blankets for the French army, and Kensington's Roxford Knitting Mill got down to fashioning a similar quantity of underwear separates. Civilian demand also seemed to be reviving; James Clarke of Orinoka relayed news of "a noticeable improvement in the upholstery trade . . . We are gradually filling up the ranks of our employees." In sum, the onset of war extended the slump into the early fall, but within sixty days, glimmers of a sustained recovery were perceptible. As the *Ledger* saw it, a "fair sign" of the shift was the return of "the nightly parade of mill operatives on Frankford, Allegheny and Kensington Avenues. The motion picture business is doing well."[77]

The war offered manufacturers chances to supply emergency demand among belligerents, eliminated their import threat, and opened appealing opportunities in neutral nations' markets, especially in Latin America. Though the *Reporter* began running an advertising section in Spanish and Portuguese, Philadelphia firms were generally indifferent to this drive, which was led by New England and southern staple-goods mills and their selling houses. It was the direct impact of the war on European rivals that interested Philadelphians. German advances flattened Belgium's Tournai tapestry district and overwhelmed the fine-goods cities of Roubaix and Lille. British mill forces were drained by enlistments, and output turned to military uses. Thus in textile specialties, mixing government work with supplying secure domestic demand seemed the keys to profitability. For cotton mills, the wool supply problem was initially irrelevant, and lace firms could disregard the

Subject Files "Industrial Relations: Philadelphia," RG 174, N.A.; Stanley Stager, "Autobiography," Accession No. 1154, Hagley Library, p. 15; *PL*, June 6, 1914, p. 3; Howell Harris to Philip Scranton, December 20, 1987.
[77] John Gay's Sons' Daybook, August 6, 1914, Archives, Historical Society of Pennsylvania; *AWCR* 28(1914): 1336, *PL*, September 3, 1914, p. 6; September 18, p. 10; September 21, p. 6; September 29, p. 10; October 7, p. 4; October 11, p. 6; November 15, p. 4; *Carpet and Upholstery Trade Review* 46(August 1, 1915): 75 (hereafter *CUTR*).

aniline curtailment. Hosiery makers had bright expectations, particularly for their quality full-fashioned lines, and basked in the *Ledger* headline, "Boom Expected for American Hosiery."[78]

For cloth and carpet proprietors, the wool and dyestuff supply derangements did become acute problems in 1915. Dye prices escalated rapidly; in late 1915, aniline oil and sulphur black, representative items, were offered at ten to fifteen times their prewar cost. The next year, alazarine red was available at eight dollars per pound versus fifteen cents in 1913. American dyemakers could in no way meet the call, for their natural and synthetic products were inadequate in quantity and regarded as inferior in quality to German dyes. When several hundred tons of the latter arrived by freight submarine in 1916, they generated tremendous publicity but in reality provided only a few weeks' normal supply for the industry. Thus Philadelphia dyers undertook to stretch materials by lowering vat concentrations, yielding fainter colors, and hiked their fees for services, on average tripling 1914 rates by 1916. Soon, fixed price lists were suspended, rates being figured by the job "according to the cost of dyeing same."[79]

The wool problem hit carpets hardest, for British colonial and Russian sources supplying 40 percent of demand were at an end. Soft domestic wools

---

[78] *AWCR* 28(1914): 1383–1437, *CUTR* 46(March 1, 1915): 87; *PL*, September 21, 1914, p. 6; October 7, p. 4; Patrick Hearden, *Independence and Empire*, DeKalb, IL, 1982, chapters 7, 8. The Textile Machine Works papers are Accession No. 1904, the Hagley Library. The firm's capital stock expanded from $60,000 in 1900 to $1.5 million in 1922. Its retained surplus, given in trial balances, rose from $271,000 in 1908 to $881,000 in 1917 and $1.24 million in 1918 (Boxes 9 and 22). As an example of the effect of the war in reserving the home market, consider the figures for imports of wool fabrics: January to July 1914, $29.2 million vs. Jan.–July, 1916, $9.6 million, a two-thirds drop in value at a time of sharply rising prices (National Association of Wool Manufacturers, *Bulletin: 1917*, Boston, 1917, p. 3). For an evaluation of the destruction wrought in the French and Belgian fine-goods centers see *CUTR* 49(November 15, 1918): 50–1. Cotton prices broke sharply upward once the full impact of the wool shortage was recognized, for manufacturers sought to run blended wool-cotton substitutes, increasing competition for available raw cotton supplies.

[79] For a Philadelphia perspective on the dyestuff crisis, see D. F. Waters (president, Master Dyers' Association) to Robert Lansing (Secretary of State), September 17, 1915, Federal Mediation and Conciliation Service File 33/100, RG 280, N.A. (hereafter cited as FMCS). Other information is drawn from *CUTR* 46(October 1, 1915): 93; 47(February 15, 1916): 64d; Dean Ivey, "Origins of the American Synthetic Dye Industry, 1865–1925," M.A. thesis, University of Delaware, 1963, pp. 37–41. The freight submarine's cargo consisted of dye concentrates from two to "twelve times the normal strength of the colors." These sold at from $5 to $70 per pound (*CUTR* 47[August 15, 1916]: 47). See also *ACUJ* 32(September 1914): 49, (December 1914): 56 and 33(May 1915): 30; *PL*, April 3, 1915, pp. 1, 10. An additional table showing the price increase in standard synthetic dyes by 1915 may be found in John Colpoys and Robert McWade to William B. Wilson (Secretary of Labor), August 17, 1915, FMCS File 33/91.

were unsuited to the heavy wear floor coverings endured, and were useless. Wool and worsted mills coveted Uruguay's 140–160 million pound clip as a replacement for Australian fleeces, but carpet men found coarse Chinese raws "practically the only source of supply left open," and one whose prices rose in successive 10 percent leaps. As British and Russian exports dropped by 90 percent, and total U.S. imports of carpet wool by two-thirds, production curtailments were general. Smith put its 7,600 workers on three-day weeks in April 1915, and auctioned 95,000 bales of warehoused rugs and carpets in a profit-taking coup. Though the British relented on their embargo and 1916 imports rebounded, the cost effects were staggering. By mid-1917 Chinese raws carried triple their prewar values, jute backing yarns quadrupled, and cotton filling for mixed goods merely doubled in cost. Goods prices followed the spirals of fleeces, yarns, and dyeing; inflationary pressures only intensified with American mobilization.[80]

Early war jitters were hardly confined to Philadelphia textiles, for both Amoskeag and American Woolen extended reduced operations into the autumn. By December, however, they were again running full, courting the same "business boom" that enlivened the Philadelphia trades.[81] On balance, 1914 was no banner year, an impression reinforced by profitability estimates derived from census returns for fiscal year 1913–14 (Table 5.7). When contrasted with figures for 1905 (Table 5.2), another reason for city millmen's sourness can be divined. Not only were recession returns down, they were particularly low in dyeing and wool/worsteds relative to the showings at Paterson and Lawrence, respectively. Whereas Paterson dyers matched earnings from 1905, Philadelphia profits on services had fallen three-fifths and returns to capital by half. In Lawrence, slack times thinned profits only to a respectable 12 percent, while Philadelphians had to make do with less than half their 1905 gains. "Pent-up" demand during the long early 1913 strike might account for busy times in Paterson dyeworks thereafter, but the Lawrence returns were notable, for American Woolen's mixed-output strategy seemed to have made the industry leader recession-proof. Single-factory independents were having to absorb most of the slack market's impact.

Philadelphia's dominance in cotton specialties gave it a solid lead over New England mill centers at both dates, in part a result of purchasing cheap southern yarns. Its fancy jacquard silk trade still held an advantage over Paterson's ribbon and broadsilk shops. However, in hosiery, even in hard times, Reading retained a cost and profit edge, and the new cluster of

---

[80] N.A.W.M., *Bulletin: 1917*, pp. 28, 349; *ACUJ* 32(October 1914): 50, (November 1914): 50; 33(January 1915): 55, (April 1915): 52; *CUTR* 45(March 1, 1915): 84; 46(February 15, 1916): 64d.

[81] *AWCR* 28(1914): 1093, 1639, 1743.

Table 5.7. *Profit and return to capital, Philadelphia textiles, by sector, 1914, with sectoral comparisons among eastern cities*

	Profit on sales (%)		Return to capital (%)	
	Phila.	Others	Phila.	Others
Carpets	7	*	6	*
Cottons	13	Fall River 1	12	Fall River 1
		Lowell 2		Lowell 2
		New Bedford 6		New Bedford 6
		Providence −3		Providence −2
Hose-knit	7	Reading 11	10	Reading 14
		Providence 8		Providence 12
Dye-finish	6	Paterson 21	7	Paterson 17
Silk	14	Paterson 10	18	Paterson 16
Wool/worsted*a*	5	Lawrence 12	6	Lawrence 9
		Lowell 7		Lowell 6
		Providence 5		Providence 5
All sectors*b*	7.7		8.5	

*a*Woolen and worsted products combined in 1914 classification.
*b*City of Philadelphia only, total product value, $140.8 million, profit, $10.8 million, capital, $127.3 million. For five-county metropolitan district, product value, $177.1 million, capital, $162.0 million; profit not calculable from available data. City thus represents 80% of regional output and 78% of area capital.
Note: Shifts in the content of "Miscellaneous expenses" category between 1905 and 1914 enumerations seriously underestimate these figures for the latter date, as rentals, interest, insurance, and other "sundry expenses" were excluded after 1905. To restore a rough comparability, the percentage of product value represented by "Misc. Expenses" in 1905 was calculated by sector and place, then multiplied by 1914 product value figures for the same sector and place. This figure, plus wages, salaries, and materials expenses, yielded an estimate of operating costs. As an example, in Philadelphia carpets, the narrowly defined "Misc." category included $479,000 for 1914, 2.3% of the year's $20.6 million output value. Had this been used without modification, profits on sales would have been 11% for the recession year, well above the 9% earned in a prosperous 1905. In 1905, however, "Misc." accounted for 5.9% of that year's product values; when this rate was applied to 1914, an estimate for all miscellaneous expenses totaled $1.2 million, yielding a more plausible 7% profit on sales. The 1905 rates clustered between 6% and 11%, not far from manufacturers' rule-of-thumb 10% for "mill expenses," with a low of 2.7% for Lawrence's integrated woolen/worsted complex and a high of 13.8% for Paterson silks, which were heavily reliant on outwork contracting.
Sources: Calculated from sectoral data given in Department of Commerce, Bureau of the Census, *Census of Manufactures: 1914, Volume 1: Reports by States with Statistics for Principal Cities and Metropolitan Districts*, Washington, D.C., 1918, in tabular form for each city under state headings.

Providence firms was operating a touch more comfortably than Quaker City producers. The carpet figures were especially depressing, for Alexander Smith and Company had retained price leadership, limiting profits on sales through their massive auctions and "barometer" settings of wholesale levels at each seasonal opening. Philadelphia carpet capital had been augmented by $5 million since 1905; to achieve that year's 11 percent return to investment, sales at 1914 unit profits would have to have reached above $38 million, nearly double the actual production ($20.6 million). Here as in wool/ worsteds, the emergence of a sectoral leader encroached mightily on the options individual flexible firms could exercise. Assessing the changed nature of the competitive environment, Bigelow and Hartford merged in 1914.[82] Philadelphia carpet mills essayed associational activity, but as we have seen, their individual masters were disinclined to pursue any comparably grand strategy. In consequence, during and after the war years, they were picked off, one by one, as major local nineteenth-century figures died (John Dobson, Thomas Boggs, Alex Crow, Jr., Pollock, Gay) and no one, given the sector's daunting prospects, stepped forward to take their places. The heralded success of area knitting, in which 1914 production was double that of 1905 ($31.3 million vs. $15.8 million) masked the decay for a decade longer; but the example set in carpets would indeed be repeated, with variations, in one sector after another.[83]

The role of labor in heightening Philadelphia proprietors' dilemmas cannot be overlooked. During the war period, in the three most troubled sectors – carpets, dyeing, and wool/worsteds – militance produced short-term gains that carried long-term liabilities, in both cost and cultural terms. Ultimately, labor's early wartime achievements set the stage for proprietary reprisals near the war's end and in the 1920s. Among the dozen sizable strikes in the initial war year, several highlight the range of issues raised by its impact on the system of shop autonomy and personalistic relations between workers and proprietors. At James Dobson's Bradford Mills, adapting looms for the huge blanket contract slowed output. Given the customary piece rate payment

---

[82] John Erving and Nancy Norton, *Broadlooms and Businessmen*, Cambridge, MA, 1955, ch. 10; on Smith's price leadership and auctions, see pp. 208, 212. For a worker's perspective, see CIR, *Report*, Vol. IV, p. 3045.

[83] These five carpet proprietors (and a number of lesser figures) all died between 1911 and 1918. Their obituaries were duly recorded in *ACUJ* and *CUTR*. In 1911, John Dobson left a fortune of $13 to $14 million to his daughter in trust (*ACUJ* 32[December 1914]: 56), whereas Gay died in 1918 just having been elected a member of the County Board of Commissioners (*CUTR* 49[October 15, 1918]: 53, 54b.). The hosiery output figures are given in Bureau of the Census, *Manufactures: 1905, Part 2: States and Territories*, Washington, D.C., 1907, pp. 978–83, and Department of Commerce, Bureau of the Census, *Census of Manufactures: 1914, Vol. 1: Reports by States...*, Washington, D.C., 1918, pp. 1348–57.

plan, weavers' wages dropped, leading to a winter 1914–15 walkout for rate increases that would restore expected levels of earnings. This dispute was amicably settled, but another surfaced in April, producing a two-month shutdown. The nominal issue was the weaving rate being paid on a contract for fine poplins, allegedly half the figure offered at Philadelphia's competing Saxonia and Prudential Mills. The core problem was, however, "the despotic and unjust treatment" workers received at the hands of Bradford superintendent Harry Mallison. Curt and peremptory, Mallison had no capacity for shop floor negotiating. When weavers asked for a one cent rise in their two and a half cent rate, he refused it completely, even though his assistant urged "the advisability and justice of granting at least ½ cent." When the operatives promptly struck, Mallison belatedly offered a quarter cent; too little, too late. After four weeks, the "super" hired strikebreakers and private police, precipitating rowdy street confrontations. At this juncture, a group of Germantown businessmen petitioned James Dobson to take the matter personally in hand.

Dobson was willing to match other mills' rates on the goods in question, but declined to fire the newly hired replacement weavers, thus partly backing his superintendent's actions. With this support Mallison announced that only his quarter cent offer would be implemented and that "he would drive out of Germantown all of the recalcitrant weavers." Commissioners from the U.S. Department of Labor's Conciliation Service faithfully documented Mallison's behavior, reporting to Dobson that his "language and manner were so vindictive as to convince [us] of the truth of the strikers' accusation of tyrannical misconduct." Dobson, after some deliberation, fired Mallison, replacing him with superintendent Frederick Eick from Saxonia. This news "so gratified" the weavers that they returned to work immediately, on June 7, without pressing for *any* rate increment. However, they had not forgotten the forty-five men and women whose looms were occupied by "scabs"; early the next week, the weavers demanded the displaced crew be returned to "their" looms, and stalked out again when this was rejected. As the situation worsened into street scrapping, arrests, and fines, Conciliation Commissioners Robert McWade and John Colpoys were called in again, arranging "almost continuous" conferences between the "strikers' committee" and Eick, with other company officials and the local police lieutenant attending from time to time. On June 24 an agreement was reached. Within three weeks, the "inefficient" replacements would be discharged, the "efficient ones" transferred to *other looms*, making room for return of the forty-five displaced weavers. If sufficient work for them all was not already booked, "available warps shall be divided in proportion," so that each would be able to run at least one loom, their second loom "kept in reserve." Once this was set, the five-person committee "guarantee[d] . . . the utmost harmony" would prevail, and penned their signatures, from Reba Rickenbaugh through James Sweeney, Chairman, alongside Eick's.[84]

As so often, personalized issues of right behavior dominated the second settlement at Bradford; the initial piece rate matter was not reopened, whereas weavers' entitlement to "their" places and "their" looms was central. The earnest entreaties of the federal commissioners, their efforts to draft and rephrase "various bases of settlement," facilitated the formulation of a livable compromise. Indeed, the conciliators' persistence and professional calmness suggested the injection of a "modern" alternative to traditional tests of will and strength, yet the federal team respected the values and boundaries of the factory culture that long antedated their appearance on the labor scene. Although an eager UTWA organizer circulated during the conflict, no effort was made to supersede the authority of the shop commit-tee, for the conciliators were laboring to establish their own legitimacy with owners and workers generally. This circumspection served McWade and Colpoys well, as they rapidly gained a reputation for fair dealing, which produced a steady stream of requests for assistance during wartime conflicts.[85]

Like the winter 1914–15 Bradford strike, the May 1915 fracas at C. H. Masland and Sons' carpet mills stemmed from wartime production adjust-ments. Facing a coarse wool shortage, Maurice Masland, the founder's eldest son, attempted to manufacture "a certain novel type of rugs" in which the filling yarn was composed of twisted paper. Again, production was slowed markedly and the weavers demanded a 40 percent advance over the rate initially posted. Pleading profitless operations, the firm refused; the weavers both struck and promptly "met in a nearby hall, where they decided to organize a local branch" of the UTWA. As the Maslands had never dealt with any formal labor organization, this step "intensified the apparent ug-liness of the situation." McWade reported Maurice's remarks:

> "We have tried to show them the actual facts and figures, but they refuse to be 'shown.' In all our experience we have never been confronted with such an ill-advised and unfair condition. And, mind you, those men are obstinate, for they are nearly all Scotch-Presbyterians, a lot of hard-headed workmen usually noted for their splendid fund of common sense." "Oh aye," retorted one of them when Maurice's words were quoted. "Oh aye, maybe we are dour as whinstanes, but it's no a' on the ae side."[86]

[84] McWade and Colpoys to Wilson, June 7, June 24, 1915, and "Agreement," June 24, 1915, FMCS File 33/79; McWade and Colpoys to Wilson, June 12, 1915, FMCS File 33/78.
[85] McWade and Colpoys to Wilson, June 24, 1915, FMCS File 33/79.
[86] Dour as whinstanes = hard as rocks, "but it's not all on the one side." See *Compact*

For two weeks, "British determination" was met by "Scotch dourness, each spelling OBSTINACY," but the conciliators squeezed out a compromise: a 10 percent hike in the rate, agreement to "confer with the local union's committee" (again, Hall's unofficial recognition), and all strikers rehired, "each given back his own looms."[87]

Both these conflicts reflected workers' defensive responses to incursions either on customary earnings expectations or established social relations of production. However, aggressive maneuvers by labor that took outrageous advantage of custom or the war urgency were far from uncommon. Two in the first class were disasters. At Overbrook Carpet, weavers had traditionally been paid the highest rates in the city, perhaps in part to attract them to the mill's isolated West Philadelphia site. When another firm matched Overbrook's scale, they demanded a raise to regain their preeminence, struck, and lost badly. At John Blood's hosiery mill, boarders, who stretched dyed stockings over leg-shaped forms, seized upon the occasion of the introduction of a new class of goods to call for a massive (68 percent) increase in their per dozen rate for finishing. Blood reluctantly dismissed the entire crew, many of whom had been with the firm for "15 to 20 years," and sent out his hose for boarding at an independent specialty shop. Again, defeat was complete. Dyers at the Buffalo Works fared better, as their firm was processing large orders of "gun cotton for the Allies." Their July demand for a 20 percent increase to thirty cents hourly was promptly met when the men consented to "be satisfied with the new rate . . . for at least one year." This success spun off appeals for a thirty cent wage in other dyeworks, none of which had gun cotton contracts. The August day the Buffalo agreement took force, dyers at Hardwick and Magee laid claim to the same increase. This firm, which had emerged alongside Dobson's as one of the city's largest carpet mills (1,100 workers), could ill afford the full closure that a dyeworks stoppage would entail. Moreover, superintendent Archibald Campbell had been trained as a "practical dyer" and expressed his "cordial sympathy" for his workers' "efforts to get a proper compensation for their skilled labor." Even though a concession would produce comparable demands from weavers, Campbell, "smiling," conceded the advance.[88]

Edition of the Oxford English Dictionary, Oxford, 1971, pp. 793, 3759; McWade and Colpoys to Wilson, June 12, 1915, FMCS File 33/78. My thanks to Howell Harris for help in rephrasing this dialect expression.

[87] McWade and Colpoys to Wilson, idem. For an earlier discussion of Masland's resistance to labor organization, see CIR, *Report*, Vol. IV., pp. 3046, 3050.

[88] FMCS File 33/81 (Overbrook), 33/72 (Blood), 33/113 (Buffalo; renamed the Anglo-American Cotton Products Corporation), 33/91 (Hardwick). Gun cotton is raw staple "treated with a strong solution of nitric acid and sulphuric acid" and used as an adjunct

Facing escalating supply costs and these signal successes by dyers, the independent shops panicked. The dyers' next target was Frankford's Daniel O'Keefe, who worked alongside his twenty employees. Known as an eminently fair proprietor, O'Keefe, were he to accept thirty cents, would fix the mark for every jobbing works in the area. Fearing economic disaster given the spectacular rise in dyestuff costs, O'Keefe appealed both to the conciliators and to the Master Dyers' Association. The latter had been active in pressing the federal authorities to recognize the severity of the sector's plight; its secretary urged O'Keefe to persuade his "help" that their demand was hardly warranted. McWade joined the chorus in conferences with dyers' union leaders, and citywide struggles for thirty cents were averted. "Captive" shops attached to weaving mills and firms with war contracts were differently situated than the independents; when this was acknowledged, the crisis abated in September. Ironically, the Buffalo dyers, whose tactically shrewd demand set off this spiral, became involved in a "freakish" fall 1915 strike that demonstrated the arrogance that embittered manufacturers and the quirky solidarity that baffled national trade unionists, yet cost the dyers their jobs and the much-prized increase.[89]

Emergency calls for gun cotton brought double shifting at Buffalo, but even with advanced pay, the eight-man night crew soon "began to shirk work." Remonstrances from the night boss, James Whalen, a union man temporarily appointed to the post, were useless. "On the morning of September 8, about half-past two o'clock, they told him that they'd have a snooze, as they thought they had done enough for that night." Reminded that the union would not stand for such a practice, "they laughed at him," lounged for three hours, and were discharged by their brother dyer. The company sustained Whalen's action, the union decried the night workers' indolence; but the sleepy eight called for shop support from the day shift. Without a qualm, fifty-five of their fellow workers struck in sympathy, *including Whalen*, who had cashiered them to begin with. Here was shop autonomy and craft solidarity with a vengeance. As the gun cotton work was simple, involving none of the dyers' usual skills, and was urgent to boot, the company hired "foreigners" at fifteen cents an hour to replace the entire workforce. Despite physical assaults on these Italian substitutes, the strikers were unable to force them out or dent the firm's resolve. Ultimately, seven of the union men,

to explosives (Wingate, *Dictionary of Textiles*, p. 280). No dyes were necessary for its processing.

[89] William Wall to Daniel O'Keefe, September 4, 1915, and McWade and Colpoys to Wilson, September 21, 1915, FMCS File 33/99; McWade and Colpoys to Wilson, October 4, 1915, FMCS File 33/113.

including Whalen, were selected by the firm manager to return as "bosses over ... the foreigners," with the rest abandoned by company and union alike to seek other positions.[90]

This sequence is little short of astonishing. Whether the night workers' stand-down grew out of a notion of completing a stint ("enough for that night"), was a gamelike ploy to test the mettle of their brother foreman, or expressed fatigue that had overwhelmed dyers inexperienced with staying up all night to work, the form of its presentation indicated their sense of effective control of the shop. No mention was made of negotiating a pay differential for night labor; in essence, by working seven rather than ten hours, they were directly claiming it. Straddling the labor–management divide, Whalen fired them, discharging his duty to the company, joined their strike, expressing his solidarity with his colleagues, be they right or wrong, then became one of the few taken back by the firm, perhaps in recognition of his sturdy attention to right behavior through the whole process. Arthur McDonnell and the UTWA Dyers' Union could not control the shopmen, could not *order* them back, though no financial support was forthcoming from the local or the international. At the shop level, here as in so many Philadelphia mills, solidarity was reflexive, not a result of permission given by bureaucratic institutions. Whether in or out of unions, skilled textile workers contested proprietary authority when it suited them, raked in their gains or took their lumps, and moved on with their work. In a sense this habitual style was a double-edged weapon, for workers seemed to be heedless of the shifting context that surrounded their machinations and would in time suffocate their industry. Enraging both harried proprietors and orderly minded union functionaries, they carried into the war years both the values and the erratic militance of the 1880s. Neither would serve them well in the decade to follow.

5.5.   Sectors and neighborhoods in 1916

By mid-1916, despite the complications of wool and dye supply, the Philadelphia textile manufacture was nearing full employment. Commenting on an investigation of mill conditions released by the Federal Reserve's Philadelphia district, the *American Wool and Cotton Reporter* observed that, regrettably, "Today there is no surplus of operatives. ... The operative knows that if he is discharged it will be almost impossible for the employer to secure

[90] McWade and Colpoys to Wilson, October 4, 1915, FMCS File 33/113; *PL*, September 24, 1918, p. 4.

a substitute, while it will be very easy for themselves [*sic*] to secure work."[91] Thus the spatial and sectoral summary of employment offered in Table 5.8 presents a portrait of the regional industry under boom conditions, and invites comparison with the turn-of-the-century situation (Table 4.7).

In 1916, Kensington remained the industrial pivot, as it had been for half a century at least, reporting over half the city's textile jobs, nicely spread across all the major divisions of manufacturing. Germantown, Frankford, Manayunk, and North Central districts each accounted for 8–10 percent of employment, with the remainder of Philadelphia from the downtown south and west holding the residual tenth. When contrasted with 1899 figures, a citywide employment increase of 17 percent is apparent. As the economy in 1899 had not fully recovered from the long depression, part of this advance is illusory, but substantial shifts in two sectors make it clear that structural changes were also afoot. The special troubles of the carpet sector are evident, for in busy 1916 employment was 15 percent below 1899 levels, even though many firms had shifted their looms to work on blankets, duck, and other military goods. The ingrain trade was nearly finished; high coarse wool prices made it senseless to continue manufacturing lines for the lowest end of the market. In March 1916, Park Mills scrapped and wrote off its last forty-eight ingrain looms, sold the old mill to Superior Yarn and Thread, and concentrated its efforts on tapestry and velvet varieties. On the other hand, hosiery employment had increased nearly 60 percent over 1899, indicating far more than a simple filling out of unused capacity. The new full-fashioned mills of Thomas E. Brown and William Meyer (whose German-American Hosiery Co. was soon patriotically restyled Apex Hosiery) and Wilson Brown's Continental Eiderdown, a knitted-fabric operation in Germantown, were packed with machinery and backed up with orders.[92]

Spatially, both Kensington and Germantown employment had expanded more rapidly than the city as a whole (26 and 27 percent), and Frankford was soaring, its net gain of 44 percent (1,500 jobs) reflecting the continuing northward drift of new-starting firms beyond crowded Kensington. The outlying mills in South and West Philadelphia had, by contrast, taken a sharp fall (employment down 40 percent), concentrated among older firms running woolen and worsted goods. There, as in the woven sectors of Delaware and Montgomery counties, major nineteenth-century companies, many integrated in response to locational constraints, had closed in the face of contemporary conditions. Nearly 4,000 fewer jobs were occupied in wovens in these three districts than in 1899, a net drop due to the absence of new

[91] *AWCR* 30(1916): 942.
[92] Gay Daybook, November 16, 1915; March 14, 1916; Stanley Stager, "Autobiography," pp. 15–16.

Table 5.8. *Employment in textiles by sector and district, Philadelphia and suburban counties, 1916*

	Woven goods	Carpets	Hose-knit	Dye-finish	Spinning	Misc.	Total	N_f Link	N_f Tot.
Kensington	12,086	5,217	9,710	2,448	3,148	1,247	33,856	331	407
Manayunk	2,644	1,693	0	73	1,799	150	6,359	43	50
Germantown	1,893	185	2,061	110	973	176	5,398	76	90
Frankford	2,244	78	885	640	192	1,108	5,147	69	100
North Central	1,780	237	1,363	69	1,165	550	5,164	48	64
S. & W. Phila.	746	314	319	16	412	472	2,279	25	33
Northern Liberties	1,218	8	466	157	109	104	2,062	27	35
Old City	341	90	1,416	18	182	154	2,201	44	65
City totals	22,952	7,822	16,220	3,531	7,980	3,961	62,466	663	844
% firms linked	(82)	(82)	(74)	(80)	(82)	(71)	(79)		
Bucks Co.	457	350	26	129	1,184	6	2,152	16	22
Chester Co.	424	0	905	14	47	0	1,390	13	20
Delaware Co.	3,842	0	110	770	2,105	217	7,044	43	58
Montgomery Co.	1,069	97	1,776	13	1,138	912	5,005	31	40
Suburban totals	5,792	447	2,817	926	4,474	1,135	15,591	103	140
% firms linked	(83)	(60)	(63)	(57)	(71)	(86)	(74)		
Region totals	28,744	8,269	19,037	4,457	12,454	5,096	78,057	766	984
% city	(80)	(95)	(85)	(79)	(64)	(78)	(80)	(86)	(86)

N_f = number of firms.
Sources: *Pennsylvania Industrial Directory for 1916*, Harrisburg, 1916; *Official American Textile Directory for 1916*, Boston, 1916.

starts comparable to those in lace, upholstery, curtains, damasks, etc., which had filled similar vacancies in the main city neighborhoods. Compensating for this decay was a rise in specialized suburban spinning mills, the most significant being the appearance of Courtauld's American branch, the American Viscose plant at Marcus Hook. Opened just before the war to create cellulose-based rayon fiber and yarns, the firm by 1916 held 1,178 employees, a quarter of all suburban spinning hands.[93] These nearly offsetting sectoral losses and gains stalled textile expansion in the surrounding counties, whereas restructuring in the city's agglomerated districts continued apace. As a result, Philadelphia contained 86 percent of all regional firms and 80 percent of area positions in 1916, each figure up two points from the 1899 proportions. Suburbanization of production as yet had no significant momentum; indeed, Kensington, Germantown and Frankford accounted for 57 percent of 1916 regional employment (vs. 51 percent in 1899). Concentration in Philadelphia neighborhoods and extension of operations within the structure of flexible manufacturing continued to be the order of the day well into the twentieth century's second decade.

5.6. Organization and inflation: labor and capital, 1916–1918

The hectic pace of conflict set in the 1915 strikes continued through the war's later progress, as inflation of living costs pushed textile workers into repeated calls for advances. After the April 1917 American entry into the European war, charges of unpatriotic behavior were constantly tossed back and forth by proprietors and workers, for it seemed that every afflicted mill was in some way involved in "government work." Manufacturers' associations along sectoral lines mobilized, or were convened in crisis fashion as decades earlier, to contend with labor militance in wovens, spinning, dyeing, and lace, among other trades. UTWA officials struggled to gain control over the shops, much as their Knights of Labor predecessors had, with success fully as mixed as in the 1880s. Examining several among the scores of cases documented in the Conciliation Service files will serve to portray a developing three-sided estrangement among mill hands, union leaders, and factory masters amid the hothouse environment of intense wartime controversy.[94]

---

[93] *Pennsylvania Industrial Directory: 1916*, Harrisburg, 1916, Delaware County, Marcus Hook, p. 986; *Tariff Hearings: 1913*, 4666–7; Jesse Markham, *Competition in the Rayon Industry*, Cambridge, MA, 1952, p. 9; Douglas Hague, *The Economics of Man-Made Fibres*, London, 1957, p. 26.

[94] For lace see FMCS File 33/611 (Quaker and North American); on hosiery, File 33/195 (Hancock), carpets, Files 33/297 and 33/566 (another Masland strike), blankets,

The Dyers' Union skillfully reined in its shopmen and outwitted the proprietary Master Dyers' Association in a series of maneuvers. Scattered strikes for the thirty cent hourly rate continued to surface early in 1916. To gain control of these brushfire outbursts, Arthur McDonnell gathered his shop delegates in April and presented the association with a formal call for a new general trade schedule, with the hourly demand as its key element. Closely advised by UTWA President John Golden and two Philadelphia-based vice-presidents, McDonnell on April 26 called out the dyers in fifty-eight plants, comprising forty-one independent shops and seventeen dyeworks incorporated within the mills of yarn, cloth, or carpet firms. Most of the free-standing job shops were members of the MDA. In order to get on with their pressing work, eleven of the mills with captive dyeworks capitulated within forty-eight hours, as did eight nonassociation independents. This neatly squeezed the Master Dyers as did the $10,220 in assistance provided by the UTWA for this authorized strike. After three weeks, the allied proprietors gave way, for the federal conciliators had enlisted the good offices of Wilson Brown and John Fisler, yarn spinners, and Nathan Folwell, president of the Manufacturers' Club, to reinforce the point that a dyed-yarn famine threatened to wreck trade commitments throughout the regional industry. As ever, no general contract was signed, but the dyers pledged themselves at each association firm to two years' service under the new rate.[95]

No such agreement had been made at the partly integrated firms with their attached dyeworks. Thus as inflation continued, early in 1917, Mc-Donnell approached these operators for a 10 percent advance, readily granted. McWade, relaying this news to Washington, noted that now members of the same local were working at two different scales. The thirty cent dyers "are growling, and insist that they ought to get 33 cents too; but the contract holds them until the expiration of another year ... " McDonnell kept his men in line, regardless of grousing, doubtless promising that 1918 would bring a rich harvest if discipline were maintained. The Master Dyers sensed what was coming; early in 1918, they voluntarily advanced rates to thirty-five cents, only to receive in April McDonnell's polite request for fifty cents, double the 1915 wages. Their gruff astonishment at this effrontery concealed their genuine fear of a stoppage. The industrial press was reporting

---

File 33/398 (Dobson). Quaker was making "nets" and both Dobson and Masland, blankets, for military use; indeed, the Dobson sales rep explained that "the entire mill is given over to government work" (James Kelly to Navy Department, August 1, 1917, File 33/398).

[95] FMCS File 33/160 has the general summary, additional details on some of the individual shop settlements may be found in Files 33/133, 33/161, 33/162, 33/164, 33/165, 33/167, 33/168, 33/261, 33/276, and 33/283.

the dyestuff crisis nearly over. DuPont had entered the trade, and other firms had expanded their capacity; tariff protection to secure the industry was on the horizon. Meanwhile, demand for their services was continuous; importunate manufacturers had already paid massive increases and could hardly blink at fresh advances. The Master Dyers offered forty cents on April 30. This was promptly rejected, and the day before the promised strike was to be launched, the proprietors crumbled. For one year after May 1918, fifty cents hourly would be the working dyers' wage. As in the 1916 fray, McDonnell was in steady contact with UTWA national officers, who had "conducted directly" the earlier battle "from its inception to its successful close." In 1918, the UTWA national secretary-treasurer, not McDonnell, notifed the Labor Department of its Philadelphia triumph. The dyers had become firmly lodged in the organizational networks of AFL craft unionism, which had certainly delivered the goods; but the proprietors were furious, pointing out that the settlement would put Philadelphia rates 30–40 percent above levels in other eastern cities. Early in the 1918 exchanges, the Master Dyers gave vent to their sense of being ill-used by labor in "a virile communication" to the newly formed Cloth Manufacturers Association, "professing moral sympathy and substantial financial support to aid the latter in the existing strike with their cloth weavers, male and female." In this larger fight, labor was far from successful.[96]

If any single confrontation can represent the clash of customary regional practices and rationalizing national forces that characterized the wider crisis and decay of Philadelphia textiles, it would be the twenty-one-week 1917–18 cloth-weaving strike. Inflation was the trigger, but the centerpiece of the drama consisted of struggles between old and new forms of organization and action, struggles that exposed a conscious effort to channel labor activism and proprietary defenses through authoritative, centralized management and thereby to void the traditional rituals of shop democracy and autonomy. In this effort, the interests of the national textile union leadership and the Cloth Manufacturers Association were complementary, while the conciliators became enmeshed in a thicket of accusations and manipulations. Ultimately, the local weavers, outmaneuvered, gained a pseudovictory from which they and their organizations never recovered.

At its core, the battle was an intralabor controversy. The main players on the "shop autonomy" squad were Morris Gorin, president of weavers' Local

---

[96] McWade to Wilson, February 10, 1917; McWade and Colpoys to Wilson, July 1, 1916, FMCS File 33/160. Master Dyers Association to McWade, May 8, 1918; McDonnell to Golden, May 16, 1918; Sarah Conboy (UTWA secretary-treasurer) to Hugh Kerwin (asst. secretary of labor), May 17, 1918; quote from McWade to Wilson, January 10, 1918, FMCS File 33/948.

72, members Samuel Bressler, Louis Gergots, and James Sweeney, chair of the shop committee in the 1915 Dobson strike, plus their allies, Tobias Hall and John Breen, of the upholstery and carpet weavers, both of whom had testified at the 1914 Industrial Relations hearings. Hall had then remarked on the level of organization among cloth weavers: "the percentage is so low you very near have to get a magnifying glass to find it." The war had changed this. Local 72 had grown to 1,100 members, who were joined in the strike by an independent "Franco-Belgium Union" about 250 strong. Together the two represented somewhat under half the 3,000 weavers who abandoned their looms October 2, 1917. The "business union" team was headed by John Golden, the UTWA national leader, Frank McKosky, locally resident vice-president, and Arthur McDonnell, the successful dyers' chieftain, seconded by Edward Keenen of the Philadelphia Central Labor Union and eventually by Gorin, who switched sides in the late going.[97]

Henry Morgan and H. H. Bosworth did the talking for the CMA. Morgan was the first full-time manager and strategist retained by any of the local textile alliances. Previously employed by the area Metal Manufacturers' Association, he doubled as operator of the CMA's "Labor Bureau," which supplied strikebreakers to members firms, and handled a string of paid observers "who continuously make stenographic reports for him of all meetings of the strikers." Bosworth, proprietor of the Delaine Mills in Manayunk, was president of the CMA and represented its sixty-one constituent firms in formal meetings. On behalf of the state, an early cluster of Labor Department conciliators was superseded by Robert McWade as the impasse dragged on. He in turn was joined by an assistant to the secretary of war, two staff men from the quartermaster general's office, two area congressmen, and a member of the Pennsylvania Board of Mediation during a February summit meeting at which the shop autonomists were subtly but thoroughly routed.[98]

Each of the four parties had distinct interests, material and ideological, that bore on the unfolding process. The shop militants wanted a higher price list, to be sure, reacting to what they claimed was a 90 percent increase in living costs, but they also struggled to restore working conditions that made for maximum employment (the one-loom rather than two-loom system) and to preserve the institutions and processes of shop democracy. The

---

[97] CIR, *Report*, Vol. 4, p. 3036; Transcript of Meeting between Local 72 Committee and Conciliators, October 15, 1917, FMCS File 33/731 (headed "In re matter of STRIKE of Cloth Weavers"); Telegram, McWade to Kerwin, February 22, 1918, File 33/731.

[98] McWade to Wilson, "Adjusting Cloth Weavers' Strike in Philadelphia," January 14, 1918, p. 11; "Report of Minutes: Conference between the United States Government, the Cloth Manufacturers' Association, and the Cloth Weavers' Union No. 72," February 19, 1918, pp. 2–3, FMCS File 33/731 (this file hereafter cited as FMCS 731).

UTWA officers affirmed the need for increased rates, but ignored the weavers' other concerns. They aimed instead to discipline the undisciplined, discredit local leadership, and get the mills running again in the national interest, thereby adding to the influence and power of the national union and establishing hierarchical authority over the locals. The association could agree with the first three points of this quintet, but its separate goals were to break the momentum of upward rate demands (which when made and granted at individual mills set off sequential echoes) and to forge a single sectoral policy toward labor that would supplant the individualistic practices of proprietors, thereby enhancing profitability for the longer term. Hostile to unionists of either camp, and to conciliation, the CMA drove toward establishing unilateral authority in the mills by cracking the customary forms without accepting the modern substitutes (collective bargaining, state-refereed compromises). If Golden's job was to subordinate the feisty locals for the general good of organized labor, Morgan's was to whip the mill owners into line, and keep them there, for the general welfare of capital.

For its part, the government wanted its woolen contracts fulfilled, whatever the character of the compromises necessary to that end. Beyond this however, the Labor Department's conciliators, committed to bureaucratic orderliness, deplored the CMA's stubbornness, the strikers' refusal to delegate authority to the UTWA, and the "anarchistic sophistries" of strike chairman Gergots, a former "Secretary of the Philadelphia Branch of the IWW." The UTWA and the CMA both used Gergots's ties with the antiwar Wobblies to account for the strike's long duration and to undermine the local bodies that had been so foolish as to fall under the spell of a subversive revolutionist. Marking Gergots as an ideological whipping boy served to obscure the deeper positional struggles in process, and in any event, had little impact on the strikers. Duly chosen their committee head in September 1917, Gergots retained that role through the finish of the conflict.[99]

The sequence commenced in typical fashion. In May 1917, Local 72 selected "a Committee to formulate a price list" that would increase piece rates and return complex work to single-loom assignments. Completed in early August, this document was printed and "transmitted to the international organization headquarters in New York." The national union stalled, for Golden was at a conference in Britain and his executive board was unwilling to "approve or endorse" either the schedule or any possible strike action. Certainly, as succeeding events showed, the Philadelphia weavers were not asking permission to act but instead were inviting the UTWA "to take notice"

[99] "In re matter of STRIKE," October 15, 1917; "Resolutions Adopted at the Textile Workers' Convention, January 19, 1918"; Golden to Wilson (secretary of labor), October 18, 1917; Morgan to McWade, January 30, 1918, FMCS 731.

of their stance, the formulation used in August communications with delegates to the local district textile council. In the last days of the month the list was presented to the mill owners, but the manufacturers stonewalled. The CMA made no response to the schedule and ignored as well a September 17th invitation to meet with a committee of workers, a request drawn up in a mass meeting held that day. Finally on October 1, at a second general session, the weavers assembled and voted to "leave their looms, wherever employed" the next morning at 11:00 A.M. if no response from the factory operators was received.

At 2:00 P.M. October 2, shop delegates reported only five firms granting the list. Promptly, each shop contingent elected two delegates to a general strike committee; they in turn elected a three-man executive committee chaired by Louis Gergots. These two groups had traditionally limited powers. While they were to oversee finances, picketing, and "legality," they had "no authority to make any compromise, or mediation or [to] decide anything" for the weavers as a body. The shopmen retained sole power to settle at their individual mills; indeed, "any shop wanting to return to work for less than the demands adopted by the mass meeting cannot be called off by the strike committee." All meetings were open both to Morgan's stenographic reporters and to the "Government representatives" who were directly invited to attend. Within ten days, thirty-seven mills were struck (four settled quickly). Overall, 3,000 weavers walked out, idling an estimated 2,500 ancillary workers (warpers, winders, burlers, etc.).[100]

The shutdown brought quick intervention by FMCS Commissioner Colpoys and E. E. Greenawalt, also a frequent mediator, who held eleven meetings with Gergots, Bosworth, Morgan, and the UTWA's Frank McKosky between October 6 and 17. On the eighteenth, Golden entered the fray by means of a confidential letter to Secretary of Labor Wilson. Denouncing Gergots as "the main cause of creating the present situation," the UTWA president offered a reprise of the troublemaker's IWW career in order to assist the department in "finally getting the goods on him." Golden assured Wilson that the strike was "in violation of the laws of our International" and would not be supported in any way. Further, he claimed that settlements thus far achieved had been secured by the UTWA's First Vice-President Jesse Walker, a strategic distortion of the actual process unfolding in Philadelphia. Golden and his minions sought to gain control of the situation, but were rebuffed by the CMA and the strike committee. When all parties were called to Washington for November meetings, the manufacturers, the

[100] Preliminary Report of Commissioner of Conciliation, October 17, 1917; "In re matter of STRIKE," October 15, 1917; McWade to Wilson, January 14, 1918, p. 3, FMCS 731.

weavers' committee, and the UTWA leaders conferred separately with Labor Department representatives. Several weeks later, through the conciliators, Golden tried to set up a direct session with the CMA, bypassing the local activists, but Morgan responded that his members had determined "no good purpose would be served" by this, for it "in fact might complicate matters." Instead they presented a separate price list that individual shopmen might accept. The CMA continued to refuse any direct contact with the strike committee or the national union. At this juncture, McWade noted, the conciliators "voluntarily gave up all efforts to arrange" a solution, a testament to "the remarkably unsatisfactory muddle in which the situation was abandoned" early in December.[101]

A number of separate complications had contributed to the stalemate. In their fall demands, weavers had notified the firms that they sought to install a special forty cents hourly rate "on all bad work." This was meant to regularize an old shop practice whereby piece rate schedules were temporarily suspended when poor-quality yarn was being run. In such cases, due to repeated yarn breaks, weavers could not earn their anticipated weekly totals. "Bad work" was designated situationally, through shop floor negotiations that depended on some degree of mutuality between weavers and bosses. These troubles were especially frequent in 1917 "on the government work which is shoddy, it breaks an awful lot. It doesn't run so good," as Gorin explained. Acceptance of the forty cent provision would confirm the centrality of flexible shop floor dealings to the relations of production in cloth mills. The CMA resisted firmly; Bosworth characterized it as a "flat rate . . . a so-called minimum wage" that had been "the large contention at the start" of the strike. Its adoption was "absolutely impossible," especially given the intention of CMA members to gain unilateral control over their mills. Other firms, those that settled in the first months of the walkout, were not so rigid. Where the forty cent rate was refused, shop committees secured compromises in which "the firms have agreed to pay on the average of the weavers' 4 previous pays," thus reaffirming the individuality of looms and mills as well as the weavers' right to expect normal earnings when bad work due to low-quality materials was under way. Thus the bad work claim had as much to do with ethics in production as with money, for it would force manufacturers to provide better yarns or suffer shrunken profits, for they not the weavers would carry the expense of slowed output.

The "shoddy trick," management inefficiency, and profitability were thus

---

[101] Preliminary Report, October 17, 1917; Golden to Wilson, October 18, 1917; Colpoys to Greenawalt, November 9, 1917; Morgan to Greenawalt, December 5, 1917; Edward Callaghan, District Council of Textile Workers, to Kerwin, December 20, 1917; McWade to Wilson, January 14, 1918, pp. 7–8, FMCS 731.

Table 5.9. *Cost estimate for one yard of government khaki, 1917, 16-ounce woolen fabric, Philadelphia*

	All new wool		One-third shoddy
Raw wool, 3 lbs. @ $1	$3.00	Raw wool, 2 lbs.	$2.00
Commission, spinning		Shoddy, 1 lb. @ .55	.55
to yield 1.1 lb. yarn	.22		2.55
Dyeing of same	.11	Spinning and dyeing	.33
Weaving, etc., labor	.21	Labor	.21
	3.54		3.09
Mill expense @ 10%	.35		.31
Total mill cost	3.89		3.40
Contract price/yard	4.08		4.08
Profit/yard	$ .19		$ .68

Note: Shrinkage of raw wool varies widely, but that three pounds of fleece would yield a bit over a pound of yarn was a fair rule of thumb. Waste in yarn during subsequent production estimated at 10%. All prices drawn from 1917 Philadelphia conditions. *Sources*: FMCS File 33–731; *AWCR* 31(1917): 1396; *CUTR* 47(February 1916): 64d.

quiet undercurrents that fed the controversy. Under piecework conditions, weavers bore the brunt of production delays, for they earned nothing while waiting for warps, supplies of filled bobbins or quills, or repairs. As Bosworth candidly admitted, "If a weaver is working piecework it is no loss to the firm if a delay comes up." On the other hand, profits could arise readily from manipulation, a returning, all too common practice in a period of astronomical wool prices. This was the root of the bad work squabble. Though manufacturers pleaded thin margins in opposing advanced rates, weaver Charles Sailer pointed out, "We are asking seven cents a yard; the government is paying $4 a yard for that stuff." What *were* the profits? The "stuff" to which Sailer was referring was wool khaki, weighing a pound per yard, the standard melton uniform cloth.[102] Table 5.9 offers an estimate of production costs, illustrating the power of the shoddy trick.

By mixing one-third shoddy with the new wool sent to a firm's commission spinners, a Philadelphia weaving mill could more than triple its per yard return (68 cents vs. 19 cents), yet take little chance that in the emergency, its manipulated product would be rejected by eager quartermasters. This tidy arrangement would be somewhat impaired were the CMA to accept a

[102] Callaghan to Kerwin, December 20, 1917; Report of Minutes, February 19, 1918, pp. 22, 26, FMCS 731.

Figure 16. The specialty lines of Folwell, Brother and Company's Colling-
wood Mills, Philadelphia, 1904. (Author's collection.)

time rate for bad work, but even if terrible yarn reduced production to half-
speed, the shoddy margin would only diminish from 68 cents to 65 cents
per yard. Firms agreeing to the time rate based on the average-pay substitute
recognized this, made an economically advantageous compromise, and went
back to work. However, as issues of ideology and control were the crux of
the CMA's hard-core resistance, the association negotiated nothing, sought
strikebreakers, and launched denunciations of Local 72's pro-German
obstructionism.[103]

A final complication had to do with the composition of the CMA itself.
Two of the great diversified family complexes (Dobson and Bromley) were
not CMA members, and had settled almost immediately on the list offered

[103] Report of Minutes, February 19, 1918, p. 33, FMCS 731. The calculations for the
reduction are as follows: per loom output in a week of 52–56 hours, roughly 200 yards,
or 4 yards per hour on good work, at 7 cents/yard, two-loom weekly earnings, $28.00.
At 2 yards hourly and a bad work 40 cents time rate, the per yard weaving expense rises
to 10 cents, taking 3 cents off the profit margin. This is in turn based on a 54 inch, 50
picks per inch fabric, running at 120 picks per minute or 15 minutes steady running
per yard. On good work, 10–15 percent of weekly hours were downtime for maintenance,
filling quills, inserting warps, hence the 200-yard estimate.

Table 5.10. *Cloth Manufacturers' Association and other firms involved in the 1917–18 strike, loom count, January 1918*

	Firms	Looms	Struck 10/17 firms	Struck 10/17 looms	Settled firms	Settled looms	Still Out 1/18 firms	Still Out 1/18 looms
CMA Members								
Narrow Division	30	5,333	2	680	2	680	—	—
Broad Division	31	3,880	29	3,499	9	611	20	2,888
	61	9,213	31	4,179	11	1,291	20	2,888
Independents								
Bromley and Dobson			2	700	2	700	—	—
Others			19	640	17	526	2	114
			21	1,340	19	1,226	2	114
Totals			52	5,519	30	2,517	22	3,002

Sources: McWade to Wilson, January 14, 1918, tables; Local 72, Official Report of Strike Situation, January 15, 1918; *OATD: 1916* (linked for loom count), pp. 270–301.

in October by Local 72. A number of small firms, likewise outside its ranks, acceded to the schedule, as did eleven CMA member firms. Was Bosworth's phalanx merely a papier-mâché front? Table 5.10 summarizes the situation at the outset of 1918. Within the CMA, the strike was largely confined to the broadloom division. Among its thirty-one firms, only Bosworth's Manayunk mill and that of Nathan Folwell, head of the Manufacturers' Club, failed to come out. Though the weavers soon reached terms with companies holding 46 percent of the affected looms, half of these were located at three firms, Bromley, Dobson, and Narrow Division member John Carruth, whose 600 looms represented the largest single operation in the CMA. The rest of the victories were generally at small operations averaging only forty-four looms. The secure big boys and the exposed dwarfs settled; but the center held, twenty substantial proprietary operations running with few exceptions from eighty to three hundred looms (mean: 145). In all, members with 83 percent of the CMA's idled broadlooms supported Bosworth, aided doubtless by Morgan's strikebreakers and perhaps by association funds supplementing the Master Dyers' pledged assistance. (By contrast, less than 10 percent of the struck looms held by independents remained idle three months into the conflict.) Neither indifferent giants nor nervous pygmies, Bosworth's hard-line cadre were optimally placed to gain from making a common stand, for they represented just the sort of midsize firms for whom trade associations and commitment to uncompromising shop control promised opportunities to build upon established success. Lacking the resources to match the Brom-leys' sectoral shifts, they banded together and fought where they stood, guided by the tactical shrewdness of Henry Morgan. An earlier cloth as-sociation had in the words of Folwell's general manager "died a natural death." This one would become the foundation for a revitalized Philadelphia Textile Manufacturers' Association in the postwar years.[104]

On January 4, 1918, ex-General Robert McWade "hustled to the Quaker City" to bring his considerable weight to bear on the "muddle." He spent the ensuing week interviewing and gathering documentation from the dozen principal figures before filing an extended evaluation of the stalemate. Though he denounced Gergots's "sinister" activities, McWade judged that "It is absurd to charge the striking weavers with disloyalty, for they have all along been ready and willing to confer with their employers on the issues involved, and to settle them in a friendly and mutually satisfactory way." In fact, full responsibility for the strike could be squarely laid to "the criminal folly, crass stupidity and censurable obstinacy and pride of the manufacturers' association members" who had since August refused every overture toward resolving the conflict. Instead of meeting the weavers' committee or embracing Golden's repeated initiatives, the firms had "engag[ed] an extra-ordinary number of boys and girls as learners" and were trying to run yardage on the nearly 40 percent of their looms committed to government contracts (1,114 of 2,888). Distrusting Gergots and the locals, plainly despising the CMA clique, McWade kept closely in touch with Golden and UTWA of-ficialdom as the final phase of the struggle opened with a call for a general sympathy strike from the District Council of Textile Workers.[105]

Chaired by Tobias Hall, the DCTW met January 19 in an open spe-cial convention and "pledged themselves to support the Striking Cloth Weavers to the utmost extreme." Strikebreakers at the twenty-two resist-ing mills were to be presented with the convention resolutions and urged to cease work; were this not done, the DCTW would reconvene to consider "further drastic action." Forwarding the resolutions to the secretary of labor, the DCTW's Edward Callaghan carefully observed that a prompt settlement would prevent any "further hinderence [sic] in Manufacturing of cloth for the soldiers." The day this politely threaten-ing communication was received, McWade telegraphed Golden to get down to Philadelphia: "I think your presence absolutely essential to avert imminent ugly menacing trouble."

Golden did not arrive, but McWade nonetheless scrambled to balk the

---

[104] CIR, *Report*, Vol IV, p. 3077.
[105] McWade to Wilson, January 14, 1918, pp. 1, 9, 11, FMCS 731.

anticipated general textile strike. At a Saturday, January 26, Labor Lyceum convention attended by "almost a thousand union textile workers," the general sidetracked a call for a Monday universal walkout by assuring the crowd that a joint meeting with the mill owners had been set at the insistence of President Wilson. The CMA left him with egg on his face three days later, as Morgan wrote rejecting the conference and chided McWade for "further stirring... a muddy pool." As the pool frothed, Golden wrote McWade a baffling letter announcing the initiation of a general strike movement and again blasting Gergots, a note that indicates the two had not been in direct contact for some time. When the UTWA president at last reached Philadelphia February 5, McWade found their exchanges disappointing. Golden "failed to keep his promises," he wrote, and "differed with me strongly, when I assured... him that the Cloth Weavers' strike would spread within a week and might become city wide!" Morgan too was indifferent to McWade's sense of crisis: "he insisted that 'the strike is over' and also that 'my presence in Phila was prolonging the strike' – two differing and contradictory assertions." Twelve hundred weavers remained out, but the manufacturers wanted only "a few" of these back and were unwilling to displace the "hundreds" of learners who after two to four months were turning out decent quantities of the simple, standard government goods.[106]

The results of the third DCTW convention, Saturday, February 9, showed textile labor's genuine reluctance toward risking a wartime general strike. Two weeks had passed since McWade's dramatic pledge, and nothing positive had happened. Yet the textile workers did not build patience into a broad militancy, as had been the case in 1910. Instead, they appointed Breen, Hall, and Gergots as a committee of three to travel to Washington and visit the War, Labor, and Justice departments in "a proper endeavor to arrange a proper mediation." Though the general conference was at last scheduled for February 19, the struggle was all but lost by the time McWade gaveled the attendees to order. Golden and Morgan had been right. By stringing out the strike, the CMA mills had adjusted successfully. By counseling order, the Local 72 leaders had sheathed the old weapons of intimidation and shaming. By refusing resources, supporting resolutions, but opposing wider allied action, the UTWA Philadelphia officers had set crippling boundaries around the cloth weavers' efforts. By holding out the promise of a just,

[106] "Resolutions Adopted at the Textile Workers' Convention," January 19, 1918; Callaghan to Wilson, January 22, 1918; McWade to Golden (telegram) January 24, 1918; *Philadelphia Press*, January 27, 1918, p. 1, 3 (clippings); Morgan to McWade, January 30, 1918; Golden to McWade, February 7, 1918; McWade to Kerwin, February 5, 1918, FMCS 731.

mediated settlement the conciliators had offered a fresh avenue for resolving disputes, but it proved to be a boulevard that narrowed to a dead-end alley as one traveled along it. By mid-February, the triple membrane of UTWA, CMA, and conciliators' organizations had fully sealed off the shopmen from direct access to proprietors for individual or committee-based clustered settlements. The end was drawing near, not simply for the strike, but as well for the autonomous shop pattern of labor conflict in Philadelphia's woolen textile industry.[107]

In this context, the February 19 summit meeting was a poignant anticlimax. Bosworth made it immediately clear that he did not attend "with power to act" for the CMA. When McWade's proposal for a six-member team to settle the strike (two each from Local 72, the CMA, and the Conciliation Service) was adopted, the Manayunk millman pledged only to "take it up with our colleagues and give it consideration," a deadly formulation. None-theless, the workers present elaborated on several issues that illustrated the conflict's unsatisfactory blending of old ways and new perspectives. Returning each striker to "his" or "her" place without discrimination was a perennial settlement term, here reiterated but left meaningfully untouched by the CMA spokesmen, as was the repeated and ever more empty threat of sympathy stoppages. Local 72 weavers expressed frustration that the CMA had made no effort to compromise, withdrawing from the give-and-take sequences Hall had described in the 1914 hearings. Again Bosworth was politely in-different. However, when the questions of efficiency and pay differentials between regions were broached, it became apparent that all parties were aware that American Woolen had become the sector reference point, the center firm pressing Philadelphians toward the margin. Gergots admitted that "We favor the American Woolen Company price list as a basis of settlement," and pointed out that Wood's mills were paying 7.65 cents per yard for "a 50 pick job" when the strikers were asking a raise to only a standard 7.5 cents for the same work. In one of the few rebuttals offered that day, Bosworth complained the analogy was in error, that no "flat rate" could be workable, for even "the American Woolen Company have nearly 1,000 rates on different classes of work." Weaver Charles Sailer then told of sitting down with "the United States Commissioner" and comparing "the price list of the American Woolen Company and our price list which he admitted on his figures was almost 25% less. If they can pay it in the New England States they can pay it here."[108] Philadelphia workers' claim to the

---

[107] Unidentified clipping, February 4, 1918; William Carr to A. Mitchell Palmer, February 11, 1918; FMCS 731.

[108] "Report of Minutes," February 19, 1918, pp. 9, 10, 22, 53–4 (Bosworth), 8 (Gergots), 33, 46 (Sailer), FMCS 731. These "minutes" are a 56-page verbatim transcript of the

industry's highest rates had long been an article of faith; the weavers were convinced that they were being exceedingly fair in posting a list a tad below the level of the Lawrence giant. Only blind stubbornness and greedy profiteering could explain the CMA's position.

There was of course another way of accounting for it. Surely wool manufacturers were trying to scoop as much profit out of government work and inflated civilian prices as possible, but they like the carpet men were beset by constraints that had intensified in recent years. Pricing pressures from the distribution end and American Woolen's semiannual opening lists created ceilings in semistaple and fancy goods above which Philadelphia goods could not be sold, unless superior novelty and quality were matched with quicker delivery and better credit terms than Wood's New York office could offer. This dismal prospect was further clouded by rampant and uneven inflation in costs of raw materials and dyeing services. Here Wood's global information sources and ability to buy wool in huge quantities represented organizational scale economies that midsize Philadelphia firms purchasing in smaller lots could not match. Integration permitted Wood to effect closer cost controls on dyeing, whereas the CMA core could do little but pay the steadily inflating charges of contract dyers and commission spinners. Declining wartime interest in stylish woolens and worsteds had intersected with massive demand for standardized government work and heightened the realization that flexible independents were far from cost-competitive on staple goods, as Table 5.10 suggests. For some firms, the short-term expedient was to manipulate fabrics, reap the shoddy profits, pay the scale increases, and get the goods out. But for the CMA, being tied to American Woolen's production rates in addition to being fenced in by its market power was the limit. Bewildered by inflation, unable to control either materials or markets, the members turned toward primitive efficiency measures: keep labor costs down and gain full sway over activity within the mill walls.

The strike committee gained nothing from the manufacturers in the February 19 conclave, but it did preserve its tattered autonomy from the UTWA's clutches. In a gesture that revealed his drift away from the cause, Gorin suggested that "someone representing the International should be present" at the six-person mediation session. Gergots's statement that "it would be bad policy to inject any more to it" was accepted by McWade as he showered

meeting. The CMA claim that Local 72 wanted a flat rate was false; no single rate for all varieties of weaving was proposed. Instead for two-loom work, the weavers list proposed a rate of 1.5 mills per pick, which would vary with the fineness of the goods. Fabrics warped at 50 picks per inch would run at 7.5 cents per yard; those at 60 picks, at 9 cents, etc. The weavers' effort was to introduce a single scale to achieve uniformity in *classes* of *goods* among firms, not a single "flat rate." On American Woolen's wage-rate leadership, also see *PL*, April 12, 1916, p.1; April 13, 1916, p. 5.

platitudes in all directions at the afternoon's close. The general concluded, "I will be delighted to see you again together." He never did. In the next three days, McWade twice telegraphed his superior in Washington that the strike was "petering out." On Saturday, February 24, the DCTW called off its general strike "pending the conference." On Monday, Bosworth notified McWade that "about sixty cloth manufacturers . . . voted unanimously that they did not wish to appoint representatives to the proposed conference." Many mills instead would put in effect on their own "a substantial increase in wages." Immediately, the general translated this news into a cheery message to Local 72: "We have the honor to congratulate you on the conclusion of your long and trying strike, and to inform you that as a result thereof you have secured a substantial increase in your pay . . . " Far from it, for the strike and the list were lost, along with the hope for a return to one-loom work. Gergots, in his final communication, asserted that forty-eight firms were discriminating, firing union operatives or declining to take strikers back, twenty "refuse to state what the increase is" and ten posted rates "from 5 to 10 percent less than our demands . . . This is rotten."[109]

Bernard Brogan, a weaver for thirty-nine years, agreed, and wrote President Wilson to complain of "the most brutal betrayal of trust and cold blooded heartlessness that I have ever know[n]." The settlement was a sham; hundreds of weavers had been discharged.

> This strike was prolonged much longer than it should have been. It looks as though John Golden . . . Arthur McDonald [*sic*] . . . and Frank McKosky . . . aided by some local followers were very anxious that it would be a failure. . . . The friends of Golden were always whispering we will never win with Louis Gergots Chairman. Gergots is an I.W.W., but I believe he is honest. I cannot say the same for some of the Union leaders, one of whom said to me we will have to call the strike of[f] reorganize and pull them out again in three mos. and have the International Officers settle . . . The scandal cannot be hushed up.[110]

But hushed up it was. In the following months, the triumphant millmen pressed their advantage, implementing "many tactics . . . to break the spirit and infuse distrust among the weavers," as Local 72's secretary complained in a pathetic fall 1918 telegram to the National War Labor Board. Union weavers were still being denied work, labor spies were now on factory payrolls, and when calls for advances resumed under the continuing inflationary pressure, Polish weavers had been told "that by remaining at work they could

---

[109] Ibid., pp. 55–6; McWade to Kerwin, February 21, 22, 25, 1918; McWade to Wilson, February 24, 1918; Bosworth to McWade, February 26, 1918; McWade to Local 72, February 26, 1918; Gergots to McWade, February 27, 1918, FMCS 731.

[110] Bernard Brogan to Woodrow Wilson, March 5, 1918, FMCS 731.

remain in the United States...let the Irish go out, they would be drafted for the trenches." This Local 72 appeal spoke volumes, for with its district base eroded and its UTWA relations soured, the Weavers' Union could do no more than beg for intervention from the state in the face of aggressive maneuvers to divide and control the workforce. Busy with more critical matters, the board did no more than acknowledge the communication from Local 72.[111] The war, which had seemed to promise a vital extension of shop authority into the woolen-goods mills, instead revealed the growing contradiction between customary forms and the evolving organizational environment. In the ensuing decade, one by one, the mainstays of autonomous activism by skilled Philadelphia textile workers went down in flames, as the carpet, upholstery, and hosiery unions were battered in turn. Only the last succeeded in partially and defensively challenging to the changing environment, a final beacon of vitality amid the lengthening shadows.

5.7. War's end

As exhausted German forces reeled in retreat during the fall of 1918, the Philadelphia textile trades faced their own battery of confounding circumstances. Inflation had hardly flagged; a government pegging of medium-count cotton yarns at nearly ninety cents a pound brought howls of discontent. Southern spinners were, local millmen claimed, making super-profits of twenty-five to forty cents a pound at the expense of their weaving and knitting clients. Beamers had just demanded a weekly raise of $5.75 beyond the $3.00 increase they had secured the previous spring. Influenza was reaching epidemic proportions, crippling many mills; and the diversion of wool to government use had led more carpet firms to experiment with paper substitutes. "For obvious reasons," spring lines of seasonal specialties were "restricted to smaller proportions than formerly."

Nonetheless, enthusiasm for the war and the home-front mobilizations remained intense. The textile section of the fourth "Liberty Loan" drive in Philadelphia oversubscribed its $12 million allocation by 190 percent, with James Dobson and his workers alone contributing a flashy $2.3 million. Quaker Lace heavily promoted its "Home Craft Week," during which women were entreated to buy curtains through slogans like "Women may not actually fight for their homes, but they make them worth fighting for." (The Bromleys also participated more directly in the war effort, as two of Joseph H.'s sons had joined the marines and the army's artillery branch.)

---

[111] Rhea Bucyk to Frank Walsh, telegram, September 27, 1918, Case File No. 580, National War Labor Board, RG 2, National Archives.

Figure 17. Pushing the Fourth Liberty Loan: patriotic messages in trade journals, here sponsored by Philadelphia's Alva Carpet and Rug Company, 1918. (Courtesy of the Philadelphia College of Textiles and Science.)

In carpets, though as little as 25 percent of machinery was estimated as being devoted to usual lines of output, shifts to massive production of cotton duck for tenting had taken up a good deal of the slack. In the meantime, firms devoted their regular trade advertising columns to bond-selling exhortations, featuring among others Rev. Billy Sunday excoriating the "Huns" and urging national harmony, echoing his triumphant revivals held in wartime Philadelphia.[112]

---

[112] *CUTR* 49(September 15, 1918): 25, 42, 56c, 60, 84–5, (October 1, 1918): 44, 55, (October 15, 1918): 52–34, 55, (November 1, 1918): 33, 37–9, 50, 58, (November 15, 1918): 38; Weigley, *Philadelphia*, p. 561.

At the first news of meetings between "envoys" from the contending great powers, Philadelphia was engulfed by premature peace celebrations. On November 7, "Wildest joy was rampant, . . . In less than an hour after the rumor had reached this city nearly every loom and machine in the textile sections was stopped and the workers were on the streets rejoicing along with the manufacturer[s] . . . in every trade."[113] Yet had these enthusiasts stopped for a moment to contemplate the near and long-term prospects of the regional industry, had they reflected on the changed context for its activity that had taken shape over the preceding fifteen years, their response to the conflict's impending close would have been far more equivocal. To be sure, protectionists had made major gains in that month's congressional elections, but all other signs were negative in their implications for specialty manufacturers.

In product terms, the war had created a powerful impetus toward combatting waste and inefficiency (politically potent concepts) and hence an urge to narrow the diversity of lines and styles that had long sustained Philadelphia's textile industry. Within days of the armistice, the *Reporter* explained that

> firms have learned many lessons from the production of a few fabric constructions. It is improbable that any extensive range of fabrics will be produced until such a time as the demand actually forces [it]. By keeping the constructions down, and by making staples largely, the costs of production may be held down, and it may be that the demand will be for staples for some years to come. . . . It is on the basis of conservatism that many are not going to branch out rapidly in the production of styles such as were formerly made.[114]

At the same time, dealers were being instructed on the folly of carrying too wide an array of styles, a practice that slowed turnover, and on the wisdom of selecting goods whose steady sales would spread fixed costs over four or more "turns" annually. From the design side as well came a frontal attack on seasonal novelty, which had "established an unsavory system of competition." Twice-yearly openings generated an "arbitrary concoction of styles, . . . one of the most wasteful procedures as to time, talent, materials, and money that can be found anywhere in the American manufacturing world."[115]

The war had provided an opportunity for an "American mode of expression" that would replace the serial "resurrection of dead styles" from European sources, a chance that would be lost were seasonal excesses resumed.

---

[113] *CUTR* 49(November 15, 1918): 38.
[114] *AWCR* 32(1918): 2237.
[115] *CUTR* 49(September 15, 1918): 66, (October 1, 1918): 58.

Is there anything constructive in the wilful "creation" of designs at such short intervals, when there is a premium on being "different," and when all agencies concerned (except the public, of course) consider each line of design a gamble? At least under war conditions, I cannot see Americanism in this procedure. I can only see waste and an economic whirlpool ahead.[116]

Alongside these nationalistic appeals to extend wartime simplification of products, trade journals published European stylists' denunciations of ornamental design, thus legitimizing the entire exercise in a traditional fashion. Arthur Wilcox, speaking to the British Designs and Industries Association, had dismissed elaborate styles as "rather harmful because they pandered to the whim and caprice of the public and thereby caused an enormous overproduction of patterns which were unnecessary and had the effect of increasing the difficulties of the distributors."[117]

This looming sea change of informed opinion would have had little weight had there not been over the preceding decades a gradual shift in the power relations between distributors and specialty textile manufacturers. Exemplified by retailers' gapped pricing and the constraints of "making for the price," this transformation narrowed flexible mills' ability to set and protect seasonal prices. As Wood's tariff testimony in 1909 suggested, distributors before the war had secured the largest share of profits on textile goods. Doubtless they would try in 1918 to displace onto manufacturers the effects of wringing out wartime inflation. Symbolic of this transition was buyers' effort to induce millmen to calculate their prices by figuring backward from retail levels rather than forward from materials and labor expenses. The days were gone (or going) when proprietors like James Doak or the Gays could assemble production figures, add so much for mill expense and so much for profit, and proceed to market. Now with the price-determining forces coalescing on the other side, they might have to respond to purchasers' demands by reflexively adjusting their expenses in a fashion that preserved some profit, an altogether more exposed, dependent situation.[118]

Within the larger industrial context, the rooting of price leadership in carpets and wool/worsteds together with the heavy war-era advances in wages, materials, yarns, and dyeing fees threatened to squeeze manufacturers in two of the city's core sectors. The greater scale and efficiency of Bigelow/

[116] *CUTR* 49(October 1, 1918): 66.
[117] Ibid., 68. Designers' contempt for "the public" on both sides of the Atlantic is noteworthy; education in "refined" tastes was the remedy urged.
[118] *AWCR* 32(1918): 2237; *CUTR* 46(March 1, 1915): 88. In the article cited, the *Reporter* stressed that "No decline in cloth quotations, even though large, can seriously affect such distributors." For an earlier comment on "standardization in fabrics" see *AWCR* 31(1917): 2044.

Hartford, Smith, and American Woolen, plus their ineffectual unions or open-shop operations, allowed these majors to set price levels that became ceilings or reference points for the rest of the trade. With price coming ever more to dominate markets for fashionable goods, and semistaples carving out chunks of the demand for, as Cole put it, "large quantities of homogeneous goods," the future was plainly uncertain for individual flexible firms. A correspondent for *Carpet and Upholstery Trade Review* nicely captured the problem. Manufacturers had to sell to middlemen, "and the middlemen's standard of appreciation, based on contour, color, and style, is a very puny thing compared to his standard as represented by the price of the article..."[119]

Only in knitting were prospects apparently bright. Not only had the full-fashioned hosiery manufacture become firmly planted in Philadelphia, but in addition, dozens of specialty firms in knitted outerwear had been launched to produce sweaters, scarves, bathing suits, knit caps, and puttees. The Bromleys' inauguration of Quaker Hosiery indicated where they thought favorable conditions for accumulation were developing, but their calculated escape from the troubled carpet and worsted sectors was cold comfort for those without the capital or venturesomeness to imitate such a strategy. Moreover, even if knitting continued to emerge as a powerful growth pole for the regional industry, how could proprietors evade the squeeze from distributors and the noose of intense, price-centered competition?

Equally disturbing, the Crompton and Knowles Loom Works, whose "relationship to the fancy woven industry was as important as that of the Draper Company... to the high-speed production of plain cloths," reduced the scale of its Philadelphia plant to consolidate machine building in Worcester and Providence,[120] as clear a sign as any that fresh expansion of the specialty weaving trades was considered doubtful in the Quaker City. In knitting technologies, the array of local mechanical innovators that sprouted in the 1880s had been superseded, especially in the critical full-fashioned division, by Thun and Janssen's Reading machine works. Furthermore, were one to gaze inside the mills in 1918, little trace of the "old happy relations" between workers and owners would still be visible. The war inflation had convinced each group that the other was relentlessly grasping for an unjust share of the returns from production. The cloth strike had shown how local, autonomous unions could be ground between the forces of na-

---

[119] Ewing and Norton, *Broadlooms and Businessmen*, pp. 179, 193–4; Arthur Cole, *The American Wool Manufacture*, Cambridge, MA, 1926, Vol. II, p. 271; *CUTR* 49(September 15, 1918): 66.

[120] M. D. C. Crawford, "The Textile Industry," in John Glover and William Cornell, eds., *The Development of American Industries*, revised ed., New York, 1941, p. 227.

tional labor organizations, federal authorities, and federated proprietors. While textile labor in Philadelphia girded itself to defend rates against cuts that were bound to be advanced once the expected deflation set in, manufacturers, who seemed to have the upper hand in this one aspect of their production relations, looked forward to curbing their workers' exaggerated appetites. Yet even here there ought to have been some disquiet in the owners' minds.

An excess of labor was one key to forcing rates down and snapping the influence of craft unions in textiles, but shortages had been more common in the war years than ever before, easing the upward movement of the price of work. Certainly learners had been slotted in during the cloth strike, but their thin experience ill suited them to meet any resumption of demand for fancy work, whereas continued production of wartime staple production lines (which they could manage) promised only the severest price competition. The immigrant flow that had been providing trained hands from Britain and Poland free of expense to the mills had been stopped for four years. War losses alone suggested that the British textile industry would have ample vacancies to discourage emigration, and a decline in regional wage rates would erode the magnetism Philadelphia once used to draw in-migrants from other northeastern centers. Would thousands of returning local textile workers-turned-doughboys form a surplus sufficient to sustain proprietors' determination to whack rates? Or would they contribute a military spine to the plotting of local Bolsheviki like Gergots? Nothing was as simple as it had been a decade earlier.

Had they soared far above Billy Penn's hat atop city hall to survey the national scene, Philadelphia textile manufacturers would have been assailed by thoughts far more chilling than the high-altitude temperatures. In the 1910s, Detroit had surpassed Philadelphia in the value of its industrial production, despite having a population little more than half its size.[121] This phenomenal expansion did more than testify to the spectacular value-added effects of Fordist throughput metalworking. It indicated that a generation-long transformation of American industrial structures was coming to full fruition. After the war, older industries in older cities would find capital and credit more difficult to secure and more expensive when secured, for the smart money moved heavily into the dynamic midwestern centers, or in the East, toward promising electrical, radio, and chemical sectors. To the extent these new industrial dynamos planted themselves in Philadelphia, and that extent was considerable in the 1910s and 1920s (GE, Westinghouse, Philco, Atwater Kent), they would offer additional problems, competing for the labor

---

[121] Olivier Zunz, *The Changing Face of Inequality: Urbanization, Industrial Development and Immigrants in Detroit, 1880–1920*, Chicago, 1982, p. 286.

of disgruntled textile workers and their offspring. More broadly, these heavily advertised, mass-produced items would successively beg for consumers' dollars, in a sequential rivalry that shoved textiles toward the periphery of public attention.

Of course, much of this was but dimly perceived in 1918, but the germs of the new wave had been evident even in the conceptual befuddlements apparent in the 1914 commission hearings. Terms and practices richly established in the Philadelphia context were poorly congruent with the new language of industry. Precious little was scientific about the management of flexible enterprises; Kensington schedules had a different texture and setting than those formalized by "collective bargaining," and the meaning of a "strike" was separately construed. Both costs and competition had distinctive connotations within specialty sectors that were consistent with their own histories but apart from the protean mainstream that Ford or DuPont represented and American Woolen, to a degree, mirrored. To adopt the language and techniques of industrial modernism necessitated the abandonment of a factory culture seasoned by generations of trial and error. To persist in following its mazeways in the 1920s, in the world of the Model T, the personnel manager, and the Pepsodent smile, was to court disaster. Though its contours had a different shape than he anticipated, the designer who envisioned an "economic whirlpool" ahead for "wasteful" flexible firms was profoundly and painfully accurate.[122] Although perils enough lay in the shop floor relations of flexible mills, the conflict that would crack their backs, undercutting their entire format for production and accumulation, came from the distribution side. Building on earlier trends noted above and spurred particularly by chaotic inflationary conditions, circa 1917–20, textile buyers altered their purchasing strategies fundamentally in the immediate postwar environment, applying modernist managerial techniques that exposed and exploited the weaknesses inherent in the personalistic, mill-centered proprietary system of flexible production.

[122] *CUTR* 49(October 1, 1918): 58.

6

The changing time, 1919–1933

"The social struggle [now] centers not on production but on distribution..."

American Wool and Cotton Reporter, July 29, 1920, 2754.

"The opinion most commonly expressed is that the hand-to-mouth buying policy to which the retailers seem to have definitely committed themselves is more responsible than any other single factor for the hard-sledding manufacturers... are experiencing... Nothing would go so far to restore confidence in the textile industry nor do more to revive business generally than a modification, if not an abandonment, of that policy."

Underwear and Hosiery Review 7 (May 1924): 66.

"The greatest factor of waste in distribution is in idle merchandise on retailers' shelves and in wholesalers' warehouses. [Hand-to-mouth buying is] scientific buying, or buying with information gained from analysis, facts and records, and it is a policy necessary to present-day business."

Carpet and Upholstery Trade Review 55 (July 1, 1924): 61.

As the foregoing chapters indicated, Philadelphia millmen had long fared far better in closing ranks against obstreperous demands by labor than they had in forging unity regarding the distribution of their goods to the nation's markets. Unlike companies in oligopolistic sectors of the industrial economy, textile firms generally, and those in specialty textiles to a marked degree, had proved to be uninterested in or incapable of integrating forward into distribution. This structural difference between Singer, Ford, or Standard Oil and the Philadelphia textile trades opened a window of vulnerability through which came a wintry blast in the aftermath of World War I.

In the seller's market of the war years, manufacturers had held the whip hand, readily passing inflationary pressures to their downstream clients. Wholesalers and retailers by 1918 expected sharp deflation would attend the close of the conflict, and guided by fashionable budget-management techniques, began to practice piecemeal or "hand-to-mouth" purchasing in place of the block or "sample and duplicate" patterns that had previously characterized relations in seasonal markets. This defensive innovation, designed to limit shelf stocks and increase turnover, proved its merit in the sharp

Hand-to-Mouth Buying Illustrated: A Merchant Securing His Week's Supply of Goods from His Jobbers at Little Rock, Ark.—a Trip of 43 Miles, which He Makes Each Week

Figure 18. The generalization of hand-to-mouth buying. By 1925, trade journals documented and bemoaned the diffusion of piecemeal purchasing throughout the distribution system. What had seemed a temporary response to postwar turmoil had become routine practice among wholesalers and retailers. (Courtesy of the Philadelphia College of Textiles and Science.)

1920–1 depression and became a permanent feature of the distributional scene. It served ultimately to shift costs from jobbers and retailers to the manufacturers, engendering an unrelenting profits squeeze for flexible mills. Demands for stock carrying at the factory increased the possibility of losses on "perishable" styles and also necessitated larger financial resources to cover the costs of enlarged mill inventories. Moreover, buyers kept pushing for ever lower prices while expecting wide pattern ranges would continue. Meanwhile, raw materials costs, which broke downward in the depression, climbed again, especially in wool, but the shift in market power relations made it difficult for mills to pass these expenses along. Hence, pressure intensified to hold or cut wages and gain fuller control of factory relations, to manipulate fabrics, or in other ways to reduce costs.

In the altered postwar environment, most flexible firms found they could no longer realize the above-average profits that their format for production had delivered for several generations. In consequence, millmen either tried to adjust to the new circumstances or simply ran down their capitals, liquidating on the death of the proprietor or when insolvency threatened. When general depression settled over the national economy after 1929, a process that had commenced a decade earlier was accelerated. By 1933, area textile employment was 60 percent of its 1925 peak levels; recovery in 1939 would indicate that some 30,000 jobs and 400 firms had permanently evaporated in fourteen years.

That the employment peak was reached in the mid-1920s suggests again a point raised previously: the decay of flexible production was lagged sector by sector. Price leadership in carpets and wool/worsteds had challenged proprietors in those trades before the war, but over the short term job losses in the two sectors were more than compensated for by the expansion of plush and upholstery mills and the rapid deployment of knitting firms in Philadelphia, especially in full-fashioned (seamed) hosiery and outerwear. Here alone did elements of a seller's market resume after the 1921 break; its effects temporarily overshadowed the broader problems of the regional industry. Shorter skirts and athleticism brought busy times to the knitting specialties, while in plushes and upholstery the automobile boom and the vogue for "all-over" fabric-covered furniture created openings for fresh accumulation. However, upholstery began to slip after 1925 as cheap copies of Philadelphia styles fed the market for low-price furniture and were increasingly made in southern mills moving away from glutted staple lines. Closed compartment cars brought in seating fabrics to replace leather, creating a basis for one local firm, Collins and Aikman, to mix long runs of staple goods for Detroit with seasonal specialties. As it became an industry major, Collins and Aikman soon discovered that for its mass-demand lines, location amid the urban skill nexus was hardly mandatory. By 1933, it had built plants in the far suburbs, North Carolina, and Quebec and had relocated its headquarters to New York. In hosiery, hand-to-mouth demand for ever cheaper lines and the relative standardization of products combined with the multiplication of regional and southern plants to generate a crippling spasm in the early months of the Great Depression. Thus the bright spots of the 1920s glimmered far too briefly to sustain a stabilizing reorientation of the flexible production system. Those sectors not squeezed dry by the post–1920 shift in market power relations were soon hammered by the Great Depression's global crisis. By 1933 it was all over but the shouting.[1]

---

[1] George Taylor, *Significant Post-War Changes in the Full-Fashioned Hosiery Industry*, Philadelphia, 1930; *Official American Textile Directory: 1934*, New York, 1934, p. 20 (hereafter cited as *OATD*); Gladys Palmer, "Economic Factors in the Decline of Philadelphia's Textile Industries," typescript, ca. 1932, Palmer Papers, Box 135, "Textiles: Miscellaneous Reports," pp. 14, 24–5, Urban Archives, Temple University (hereafter PP-135, TMR); Interviews with J. T. Ryan and Charles Tomlinson, High Point, NC, August 27, 1931, in ibid. (At this writing these papers have not been processed by the Urban

There was to be sure a good deal of shouting. Wrangles with buyers yielded quite bitter exchanges between millmen and dry goods, clothing, and retail merchants. Labor, generally defeated in postwar rate-cutting confrontations, launched at times sullen, at times exuberant, strikes and organizing drives after 1929. Manufacturers loudly repeated threats to relocate, but acted on them infrequently. Tariff politics continued to excite textile interests, but now second Industrial Revolution giants were seeking reciprocity formulas that would promote exports of autos, electrical equipment, or chemicals, sales which would keep their plants turning full bore. Moreover, the transformation of distributional relations within specialty textiles was but a part of a larger shifting context in the language, practices, and expectations of American business. As the 1914 Industrial Commission's conceptual contretemps suggested, the integrated, large-scale enterprise had been firmly installed as the prescriptive model for thought about and action in the national economy. The generalization of its methods, from promotion of standard cost-accounting procedures to the Hoover Commerce Department's obsession with waste, efficiency, and simplification, relegated producers to an industrial cul-de-sac. That the standards and, if you will, the image world of big business bore little relation to the necessities of differentiated, seasonal manufacturing was of little moment. In their stumbling efforts to overcome the postwar impasses, proprietary capitalists were strapped imaginatively and conceptually as well as financially and technically.

In his celebrated works on the evolution of the "modern business enterprise," Alfred Chandler has stressed the principle that structure follows strategy, that alterations in the scope or scale of oligopolistic corporations, stemming from the visions and analyses of acute managers, forced a reworking of organizational structures and the authority relations they indicate if not entail.[2] For Chandler's key industries, technological breakthroughs conditioned but did not determine corporate practices; the refrigerated railway car or the Bonsack cigarette machine opened avenues for exploiting entrepreneurial opportunity through articulation of long-term strategies that, often after some experimentation, were effectuated through varied production systems and managerial hierarchies and ultimately shaped sectoral structures beyond the firm. As they were rarely germane to the main themes of Chandler's project, being definitionally sidelined through the quest for the roots of "modern" enterprise, durably competitive sectors in which these

Archives, so no set of final inventory references is available. My thanks to Professors Ann Miller and Walter Licht of the University of Pennsylvania for offering information about and access to the Palmer materials.)
[2] Alfred Chandler, *Strategy and Structure*, Cambridge, MA, 1962; idem, *The Visible Hand*, Cambridge, MA, 1977.

practices and systems failed to thrive have held little interest for business historians.

Most of these competitive sectors, unlike the throughput, scale-economizing ones, were genuinely "old" industries (textiles, clothing, printing, furniture, tools, even toys) in which differentiated batch production once reflected regional skills and market limits. In the U.S., by or after the mid-nineteenth century, many of them segmented into expanding staple and flexible manufacturing divisions. Largely but not wholly concentrated in consumer goods (consider shipbuilding, tools, and machine building), these sectors shared structural positions that constrained the strategies that might be implemented by firm owners. Demand was both differentiated and discontinuous (seasonal, or in capital goods linked to longer investment cycles). Within each trade, flexible producers strove for quality and novelty, relied on skilled labor (which when female could be grossly underpaid), defended prices by cutting back output whenever possible, etc. Staple firms (sheetings, Bibles and textbooks, work clothes) sought cheap help and long runs, but faced intense price competition that made technological gains (the battery loom) ambiguous in their implications. Neither group, given the diversity of producers and products, could build lasting bridges to forward or backward integration. Thus, for example, reaching out toward a mixed-output blend of staples and specialties had appeal as a strategy, for structural obstacles confounded efforts to mirror developments in managerial, throughput industries. There is of course no simple uniformity among the histories of competitive sectors; Chandler as well takes pains to document and account for variations among his targets. Yet it is worth suggesting tentatively, as a starting point for a different line of industrial studies, that "strategy followed structure," from jewelry to jacquard, across a broad spectrum of American manufacturing sectors from the Civil War through the mid-twentieth century.

This formulation preserves the two senses in which Chandler has employed the term structure. Inventive corporate strategies shape both the particular organizational form of modern business and, historically, the larger sectoral structure of oligopoly. In persistently competitive sectors, the flow is reversed, as firms lodged within a low-concentration production system must derive strategies based upon their restricted abilities to influence outcomes and also must appraise the firm's internal structure (as given if not fixed) in contemplating the course ahead. From family loyalty to skill-centeredness, these structures are composed of settled relations: Factory proprietors surely had to question what gain could be expected from altering them in a larger environment where nothing like Rockefeller's coups or Duke's tobacco empire was imaginable. Hence, perhaps understandably, Philadelphia millmen fumed and dallied as the base for flexible production withered. Hence as well, the contention here that a lasting shift in relations of distribution deflated and defeated the city's textile specialists may be linked both with the interior routines of firms and factory districts and with the larger momentum of industrial transformation and the way this process has been conceptualized by scholars.

If it is helpful to visualize business management as a contingent, sequential effort to control or transfer risk, then a useful distinction between oligopolistic throughput and batch-based competitive sectors arises. The former, by incorporating distribution within their span of control, were deftly able to manage price and displace risk onto dealers (Ford agencies) or downstream manufacturers (steel fabricators). Competitive Philadelphia mills once had their own quite different means of approaching the same task. The network of separate establishments minimized the capital risked in enterprise and controlled the technical span across which owners' expertise had to be stretched. Production of samples for each season obviated the chanciness of running a stock of goods whose marketability was unknowable in advance. The "make-to-order" pattern of manufacturing and the practice of refusing returns (except for defects) shifted a measure of hazard onto purchasers, who had to judge well in advance what styles would "take" and were obliged to absorb their mistakes. (Balancing the scales between mill and merchant was the counterweight of cancellations, scotching orders not run or delivered when materials prices or the stock market broke downward.) Alternating busy and slack seasons shifted the wage/employment risk onto workers; piece-rate schedules made production expense dependent on the goods made, not on the length of the workday or the reliability of machinery in rush periods. Minimizing fixed costs maximized options for flexibility.

Each of these relations was conflictual and to a degree malleable. Positional advantage shifted back and forth between spinners and weaving firms, workers and masters, mill owners and merchants, each taking lumps and making gains periodically. The regional flexible production network had absorbed major shocks (the Knights, the 1890s depression, the 1903 general strike) and had recovered, adapting to shifts that changed rules without transforming the game (e.g., informal recognition of such unions as endured, the gradual displacement of block buying at seasonal openings by the sample and duplicate orientation). This network of social relations subtly (or clumsily, from a "modern" point of view) blended economic and personalistic considerations as actors managed risk over time. Surely calculation and reputation were mixed when mill owners and workers reached accommodations on work sharing in depressions, when spinners "carried" weaving mill yarn invoices overdue because of "slow pay" yard-goods clients, or when proprietors allowed returns of fabrics with trifling or imaginary defects to preserve a long-established account. If the accompanying rhetoric of honor and fair dealing fell short in practice, memories were long and betrayals painful. Workers damned the Dobsons and cherished the Bromleys; merchants' and manufacturers' satisfaction was general when George Campbell and William Browne sunk into bankruptcy.

Nevertheless, this supple structure could not endure the broad shift in distributional practice engendered by purchasers' reaction to wartime inflation and the peacetime crunch that followed. Baffled by the new doctrines of distribution, unable to adjust to their terms and prosper as before, manufacturers not surprisingly at first appealed to the values and sentiments of their now aggressive clients, receiving mild sympathy and great gobs of the new language of commerce in return. Based on "facts and records," the new policy was "scientific" and designed to eliminate "waste" and thereby increase efficiency. Unable to control either their market risks or a discourse that allowed no appeal from such pronouncements, most flexible textile enterprises entered an era of profitless prosperity, handling respectable volumes of business under conditions that realized pitiful returns. Thus, as we turn to considering the introduction and implications of "piecemeal" buying, Philadelphia dyer James Hulton's crisp contemporary comment is worth recalling: "Bad times have a faculty for showing up weaknesses."[3]

6.1 The advent and impact of hand-to-mouth distribution

Origins are elusive things, but it appears that the trend toward piecemeal purchasing of seasonal textiles had been initiated during the half-dozen years prior to the Great War. To cut down their transaction and information costs, millmen by 1900 had undertaken to bypass wholesalers and sell directly to the department store trade, securing chiefly sample and duplicate orders for current styles. Wholesalers, "in order to maintain their position as distributing agencies," eventually responded by encouraging retailers to make frequent, smaller purchases, which given the former's ample stocks, could be supplied with few delays, thus narrowing delivery lags and enhancing retail turnover. Wide adoption of this maneuver, circa 1911–12, intersected with the publication of "a great deal of literature in regard to the importance of buying in small quantities and buying often," a product of efforts to apply "scientific management" to retailing. "In 1911 the Harvard Bureau of Business Research started to study the costs of retailing and the whole movement

---

[3] For an evocative discussion of the advent of "waste" and "efficiency" as social and literary referents, see Cecelia Tichi, *Shifting Gears*, Chapel Hill, NC, 1987, pp. 63–96. Hulton's remark is given in *Textile Colorist* 43(1921): 169.

of hand-to-mouth buying began to spread very rapidly." In the articles that
circulated during 1913–14, emphasis was placed on quick stock turnover as
a key to financial management and on the value of close executive supervision
of store buyers' merchandise budgets.[4]

Such advocacy hardly created a national transformation overnight. Yet in
New York by 1913 there were clear signs that older patterns were being
displaced. Surveying the silk goods trade that year, James Chittick noticed
that wholesalers and jobbers had begun to adopt the retailers' tactics. "Recently," he wrote,

> another phase of jobbing distribution has arisen, which is shown in a
> disinclination to carry any reasonable stock and in trying to throw that
> burden on the manufacturers. A big silk jobbing house may send over
> several times in one day, to a [mill] commission agent, for one piece
> each time. . . . The advance orders from them have dwindled to miserable
> proportions . . . Thus does the jobber play the game of "heads I win,
> tails you lose," taking no chances himself and letting the mills sweat.

Cutters-up were pushing the limits of sample and duplicate ordering at the
same time. Buying sample pieces of a few styles from each of a number of
mills, clothing manufacturers would pointedly quote their likely yardage
needs, so as "to encourage the manufacturer to make up advance stock at
his own risk." Some months later,

> in come the cutters and want so many pieces of this, that, and the other
> thing for immediate delivery and if the manufacturer has not the stock
> on hand they profess great indignation. They will refer to what they
> told him as to their probable requirements, to the fact that they bought
> sample pieces of the goods, and will ask what kind of a way that is to

---

[4] James Fri, "Changes in Marketing Since 1900," *The Manufacturer* 11 (December 1929):
3–8, quotes from p. 6. The need for higher margins in department store operations and
the stress on competitive customer services suggest efforts to manage or avoid direct
price competition as a component in the logic of accumulation for retailers. Faster
turnover yielded increased velocity of capital and could ameliorate competition-induced
declines in per dollar returns on sales. Close budgeting of buyers installed controls on
the latter's enthusiasm and limited potential losses from markdowns on dead stock.
Such practices appeared first by the turn of the century, and were publicized ca. 1910
and generalized after World War I. As Chittick (below) noted, hand-to-mouth purchasing could increase the diversity of department store stocks without additional capital
being drafted, a tactic of value where specialty shops or chain stores threatened to
undercut the departmentalized generalists. Susan Benson, in her fine study of labor
relations in mass retailing (*Counter Cultures: Saleswomen, Managers, and Customers in
American Department Stores, 1890–1940*, Urbana, IL, 1987), cites a *Dry Goods Economist*
article from 1912 recommending hand-to-mouth purchasing (*DGE* 66 [February 3,
1912]: 41). Departmental buyers initially resisted managerial pressure to install this
practice (Benson, p. 50), but seem to have been tamed by the 1920s.

handle their trade, and in general will behave like very ill-used men, when really what they deserve is two swift kicks properly placed.[5]

Retailers were just as difficult. Advancing department store expenses for advertising, in-store amenities, delivery, and the like, which flowed from service competition in urban centers, now necessitated gross markups of 40–50 percent, double customary turn-of-the-century benchmarks. Departmental buyers were placed on budgets, "held strictly down to certain limits of capital by their principals," while the profusion of styles, steadily increasing, pushed them to carry a larger diversity of stock. The consequence was that buyers had begun to "spread [their] stock thinner," taking a single piece of a style or half a piece, which when sold had to be replaced "instanter." Hence the trend toward frequent tiny orders was gathering momentum, and as jobbers were backing away from holding stocks, stores expected that the mills would do it. In silk before the war,

> we now perceive that we have arrived at a point where the mills receive no advance orders worth mentioning from either jobbers, cutters, or retailers, but are expected to carry stock for all of them, stock paid for by money borrowed from commission houses at full rates of interest, and financed also by unduly long raw silk credits.... If today, a mill decides only to run on orders, it will run very few looms as it will not get the orders, and then, when the spot business comes, it will have no goods to sell, and if it runs on stock, it can get no profit sufficient to offset the certain losses [on styles that fail to sell].[6]

Here certainly are market-centered clues to the unusual proprietary unity and toughness in the 1913 Paterson silk conflict, as well as to the sources of the generalized installation of hand-to-mouth purchasing during the 1920s.

Before the new distribution pattern was fully implanted, however, there would be three full cycles swinging toward, then away from, advance ordering on seasonal goods. The first of these, early in the war, was most likely forced on buyers due to the substantial flow of export orders that simultaneously diminished the residuum of available goods and created a relative seller's advantage. Further, it should be remembered that throughout these years retailers in satellite cities and across the South and West remained disposed

---

[5] James Chittick, *Silk Manufacturings and Its Problems*, New York, 1913, pp. 285–6.

[6] Ibid., pp. 287–9. In a ten-part series on retailing during 1912–13, *American Wool and Cotton Reporter* estimated that selling markups in the last years of the nineteenth century added 16 percent to each cost-of-goods dollar to reach a break-even point, thus a 20–22 percent markup would yield about 4 percent net profit on a sales dollar. By 1913, Boston stores expected to mark up goods purchased by 42 percent in order to achieve a comparable return. See *AWCR* 26(1912): 1628–9, 1652–3; 27(1913): 93–4, 120, 142–3, 224, 401, 486–7, 566, 583.

to secure a season's worth of draperies, hose, lace, or carpets during a single trip to New York or to jobbing houses in regional metropolises. By 1917, expectations of U.S. entry into the war, and thus of further diversion of production outside normal channels, combined with advancing prices to induce intermediaries and retailers to return to repeated small orders for whatever goods they could secure. With inflation building, both groups were concerned to keep to modest inventories in order to limit damage once the price crest was passed. Moreover, "it was also considered more or less patriotic to hold down purchases to permit of as large production as possible for war purposes."[7]

In most lines, this practice continued through the end of the war, but hosiery proved an exception in 1918. With a general drabness among wartime stylings, fancy cotton hose had a vogue for they economized on materials while adding a decorative touch to clothing ensembles. Buyers stocked these lines heavily, ordering "as much as they could in 1918." To their chagrin, "not expecting the war to come to a sudden close, they were caught with quite an amount of merchandise on their hands" in November.[8]

The armistice created an opening for a self-fulfilling prophecy. All parties had expected a price decline once overheated war demand came to an end. Thus in November 1918 cancellations were sent out broadcast by purchasers who sought to run down current stocks and defer buying until mill prices had stabilized at lower levels. "There was chaos in the industry," especially in knits, where retail stocks were heavy. In the following months, "cotton hosiery was slaughtered; prices were not simply pared down, they were sliced down..." This sequence appeared to confirm the wisdom of piecemeal purchasing and the department store budgetary management systems that had set the pace for inventory control in retailing. Yet the panic that beset the hosiery trade was not generalized. True to form, flexible mills curtailed production in the winter of 1918–19, and at the new year's woolen/worsted openings 1918 prices were repeated, doubtless astonishing buyers. The mills stood fast; idle looms, which had been rare in the last war months, accounted for 40 percent of capacity early in 1919 and 58 percent by March.[9]

Philadelphia cloth manufacturers explained that the mass of warehoused wool in government hands, some 400 million pounds (a six-month supply for full national capacity), was overhanging the pricing situation. Were this dumped, values would collapse, and the state would absorb heavy losses. Until this issue was settled, proprietors would not backtrack from previous quotations and were closing bit by bit their factories in Kensington, Frankford, Manayunk, and Germantown as remaining orders were shipped or

[7] *AWCR* 34(1920): 458, 460, 470.   [8] Ibid., 494.
[9] Ibid., 470, 494; *Public Ledger*, February 3, 1919, p. 17 (hereafter *PL*).

cancelled. Added incentive to wait out buyers was provided by labor's revived demand for the forty-eight-hour week, an issue to which we will return. Widespread layoffs might both deflate this movement and protect prices. Were the government disposed to a gradual release of its raw materials, sharp deflations of the sort that were befuddling the hosiery millmen might be avoided entirely.[10]

The government did its part, scheduling a long, staggered series of raw wool auctions, handled by Philadelphia's Samuel T. Freeman & Co., which offered from one to three million pounds on each occasion and established minimum figures below which bids were refused. Cotton prices, which had fallen nearly a third from 1918 highs, turned upward again in February, helping reverse the momentum. In materials and cloths, after this point, "the advance was radical both in regard to prices and demand." By March, woolen purchasers' resistance was sapped. The depletion of their tactically reduced stocks "forced [them] into the market, machinery was started up" and the scare was ended. However, wholesale and retail buyers remained determined to retain the hand-to-mouth policy, keeping their orders frequent and tiny. At this juncture, "speculators" began active purchasing in a large way, accurately sensing a new inflationary wave being turned loose. Even hosiery firmed in April, as advances in yarn prices led millmen to stop the cycle of concessions.[11]

Though speculators had concentrated on quickly disposable staples, by early summer regular buyers abandoned their cautious approach across-the-board, calling for large blocks of style goods. When the "crush" came, "jobbers were not concerned with the prices any longer; it was a question of getting deliveries." As orders flooded selling agencies and mill offices, manufacturers found themselves overwhelmed, unable to get goods out fast enough "owing to inability to secure [sufficient] operatives ... late deliveries of yarn, etc." This kept production short of demand, and price offers continued to advance even as wool/worsted capacity use rebounded to 78 percent by August and 86 percent in November. To manage the overload, proprietors allotted available goods proportionally among buyers, further stimulating large orders as buyers hoped that they would yield partial deliveries adequate to meet a segment of runaway demand. Philadelphia firms, which had counted on a postwar return to stylish goods and had commenced running

[10] *PL*, January 16, 1919, p. 17.

[11] *Forbes* 18(September 15, 1926): 22. Freeman's sales realized a reported $250 million for the government. See also *AWCR* 34 (1920): 459, 470–1, 497; *PL*, April 16, 1919, p. 19; *Textile World* 67(1925): 887 (hereafter *TW*). Largely due to the gradual phaseout of controlled supplies, the wholesale price of wool in 1919 was on average only 2 percent below the 1918 level (Department of Commerce, Bureau of the Census, *Historical Statistics of the United States*, Series E–127, Washington, D.C., 1975, p. 208).

samples of fancies during the winter buyers' stalemate, reaped a bonanza. Strikes and threats of strikes were settled with wage advances ranging from 10 to 25 percent, even as area manufacturers undertook to build an organization that would better defend their interests when the craze flamed out and a slump materialized.[12]

By year's end, price movements had proved little short of spectacular. Fancy Philadelphia mercerized seamless cotton hose, which had fallen to $3.00 a dozen pairs in January 1919 and to $2.25 in March, bounced up to $5.00 in August and were opened at $6.50 after New Year's 1920, "with the mills sold up as far [ahead] as spinners will commit themselves" to yarn prices, about six months. Raw cotton had advanced from its low point through January roughly 50 percent (middling upland, N.Y. spot, 27–40 cents), whereas wholesale hose values had nearly trebled. In wool/worsted, "buyers were breaking their necks trying to get near deliveries, but manufacturers turned deaf ears . . . Deliveries for piece goods were booked for five and six months forward." The short-term profits accruing to local firms from this resurgence were rumored to be spectacular, one labor publication claiming that city mills had banked 1919 returns equivalent to half the entire capital invested in area textile production.[13]

This was fanciful, however. Textile output for the city that year was estimated at $358 million, but when inflation is taken into account, the value of goods in 1915 dollars was little changed from that of the first full war-demand year ($137.9 million in 1915, $143.2 million in 1919, deflated). In four years, if 1915 levels be taken as an index base of 100, wool had advanced to 251 in nominal prices, cotton to 318, and total product value to 250. Wages however had only roughly doubled, this lag being the source of sharp controversy and the key to hefty profits, though well below the 38 cents on every sales dollar that labor spokesmen charged. Less detailed publication of sectoral statistics in and after 1919 makes calculation of investment returns nearly impossible, but in Table 6.1 data from 1905 and 1919 are displayed to illustrate the shares in product value devoted to mill wages and materials, leaving a residual from which salaries, expenses, and profits must be derived. Both years were prosperous ones for the regional textile industry, but product value (in 1915 dollars) had risen 32 percent, 1905–19, while real wages were

[12] *AWCR* 34(1920): 471, 497; *PL*, February 20, 1919, p. 18; March 3, p. 3; March 12, p. 1; April 15, p. 5; December 20, p. 19.

[13] *AWCR* 34(1920): 444, 499; Evans Clark, *The Philadelphia Textile Industry: Labor's Viewpoint*, New York, 1921, p. 16, in Benjamin Barkas Collection, Acquisition No. 37, Box 38, Urban Archives, Temple University. Clark estimated profits at $133 million and capital at $140 million. Both figures were far off. The *Fourteenth Census* figures for 1919 capital in Philadelphia textile sectors total $244 million. Even generously estimated profits were not half the figure Clark calculated.

Table 6.1. *Wages, materials, and residual as proportions of product value,*
Philadelphia textiles, 1905, 1919, in percent

	1905			1919		
	Wages[a]	Mats.[b]	Res.	Wages	Mats.	Res.
Carpets	22	62	16	17	58	25
Cottons	19	52	29	16	53	31
Dye-finish	31	38	31	17	48	35
Knits	27	49	24	17	61	22
Silk	19	56	25	13	58	25
Woolens	18	66	16	17	58	25
Worsteds	15	65	20	13	69	18
All sectors	20	58	22	16	61	23

[a]Factory wages, not including salaries.
[b]Raw materials and power.
Sources: Bureau of the Census, *Bulletin No. 60, Census of Manufactures: 1905, Penn-sylvania*, Washington, D.C., 1906, pp. 68–73; Idem, *Fourteenth Census of the United States, Volume IX, Manufactures: 1919, Reports for States, with Statistics for Principal Cities*, Washington, D.C., 1923, pp. 1334–41.

virtually static and real materials costs had jumped 37 percent.[14] The larger throughput of materials kept the average residual from growing in share terms, but its size in both real and nominal dollars was augmented considerably.

In 1919, after paying for wages and materials, Philadelphia textile oper-ators had $82 million available from which to fund salaries ($14 million), taxes ($8 million in toto), and other miscellaneous expenses (at 8 percent of value, $30 million). This would leave estimated profits of about $30 million, or a healthy 14 percent return on investment (vs. 13 percent in 1905) (Table 5.2).[15] This is a conservative estimate, for miscellaneous ex-

[14] Textile products index for 1905 (with 1915 = 100) is 101. Product values in 1905 (nominal), were $107.3 million (real $108.5 million), and nominal 1905 wages were $21.9 million (real $22.1 million) vs. $55 million in 1919 (real $22.0 million). Materials expenses in 1905 (nominal $62.2 million, real $62.8 million) soared to $215 million in 1919, or $86 million in 1915 dollars. Calculated from census sources for Table 6.1 and wholesale textile price index (Series E–18) in *Statistical History of the United States*, Stamford, CT, 1966, pp. 116–17 (a commercial reprint and updating of the Commerce Department's 1960 edition). Meanwhile, the general cost of living had more than dou-bled since 1905 on either the Burgess (E–158) or Douglas (E–159) indexes (p. 127), accounting largely for labor's angry charges of unfair treatment and profiteering.

[15] Figures for these estimates were drawn from Bureau of the Census, *Fourteenth Census of the United States, Volume IX, Manufactures: 1919, Reports for States with Statistics for*

penses probably did not rise fully as much as did output and sales, and to evade taxation on "excess profits," chunks of the surpluses "were often distributed as salaries" to "officers in 'close' corporations where the stock is held by a few persons," the standard form in Philadelphia textiles.[16] By any measure, 1919 was a banner year for local millmen. Hand-to-mouth buying had collapsed; goods were demanded as fast as they could be manufactured and shipped. Yet these seasons of price setting and profitable accumulation soon ended in the market break and "inventory" depression that commenced in the spring of 1920.

Highly publicized attacks on the inflationary prices reached in 1919 were credited by many contemporary observers with generating a consumer's strike in 1920, a withdrawal from purchasing that was urged by newspaper editorialists among others. The first sign that textile markets were imperiled appeared March 1 in a carpet journal report that banks had begun to "curtail the facilities they have offered to merchandisers." Heavy stocking in 1919 had necessitated expanded short-term borrowing by distributors; financial cutbacks immediately prompted stores to begin "buying closer to their requirements." By April, the fabric trades had "taken on all appearances of a waiting game." John Wanamaker, nearing his eighty-second birthday, shortly broke the tension, personally announcing a gigantic stock liquidation sale, featuring 20 percent reductions in nearly all lines carried by his New York and Philadelphia stores. Wanamaker's promptly reaped "an enormous business" as customers poured through its doors. Other retailers rushed to match or better the old wizard's prices, and the drive to clear inventories gathered strength. Slow or late movers suffered, for after the first surge, consumers held back, anticipating deeper reductions. Factories that had been sold up through fall received cancellations by the bundle; prompted by the Wanamaker break, scratched orders "continue[d] to pour into the mills" of Philadelphia through late May. In June the local wool trade was dead, "curtailment of credits" was general, and money "very scarce." Throughout the regional textile districts, indefinite shutdowns mounted, "with more names being added to the list daily." At Lawrence, where American Woolen had continued to allot shares of spring production among the massive orders

---

Principal Cities, Washington, D.C., 1923, pp. 1334–41. In constant 1915 dollars, the residual in 1905 was $24 million vs. $33 million in 1919, a 38 percent increment. From these estimates, return on sales was about 9 cents per dollar, not the 38 cents Clark reported.

[16] Tax authorities' distress on this account was reported by the Philadelphia correspondent for *Carpet and Upholstery Trade Review* 51 (January 15, 1920): 42 (hereafter *CUTR*). Whereas nontextile Philadelphia manufacturing firms paid 3.6 percent of 1919 product value in local, state, and federal taxes, the city textile industry paid out only 2.4 percent of value in taxes (*Fourteenth Census . . . Manufactures: 1919*, pp. 133–41).

booked at its January openings, half the city's textile workers (15,000) were dismissed by mid-July.[17]

The fall brought no relief. Instead, Philadelphia's "prolonged dullness" became "greatly accentuated." Whatever quotes millmen offered, buyers demanded lower levels. Moreover, pacesetting purchasers were far more organized for common action than ever before. In 1919–20, the membership of the National Retail Dry Goods Association doubled to 1,362 businesses and included "most major stores" in the nation thereafter. A knitting manufacturer noted that his colleagues were blaming labor, overhead, government, and a host of other factors for their troubles, but the root issue was that "buyers have assumed the dominant position in the trade and are not disposed to give up this standing without a struggle." Retailers asserted that their immediate goal was to establish a general price benchmark at twice the trade's 1914 levels; manufacturers claimed that a multiple of two and a half or three was "only fair." In terms of the Bureau of Labor Statistics' wholesale textile products index, which had moved from 54 to 165 (1914–20), buyers were aiming for a fall of 35 percent to 108. They did rather better than this on average, for the 1921 index plummeted to 94.5, down 43 percent to 1.75 times the prewar level. In hosiery, which had a second time been heavily purchased, silk full-fashioned stockings, selling at $32.50 per dozen in mid-1920, dropped as low as $13.50 in October, off nearly 60 percent. By November, Philadelphia weaving and knitting mills had undertaken to cancel *their* contracts for yarn from local and southern spinners. These appeals were "in every case, refused by the yarn-seller, and where the customer refuses to take his yarn, his case is immediately put into court and he is forced to live up to his agreement." Unable in the short run to economize on the supply side, producers of yardage and finished goods had few defenses against buyers who felt themselves "badly deceived" the previous year and thus "not likely to purchase in anything but a hand-to-mouth manner for some time to come." Worse, amid this squeeze, "a great many retailers" were demanding rebates on goods already delivered and paid for. Outraged mill owners howled that the retailers "appear to want all the profits when an advance occurs but are unwilling to accept any of the corresponding losses when the market reversal comes." Replying, the managing director of the National Retail Dry Goods Association observed mildly that "all retail stores are carrying heavy stocks of goods purchased prior to the reductions." Losses incurred in liquidating these inventories, if not shared by the mills,

---

[17] *CUTR* 51 (March 1, 1920): 37, (May 15, 1920): 45, 52; *AWCR* 34(1920): 1494, 1975, 2228, 2291, 2754; *The Manufacturer* 2(June 1920): 26. A new series of *The Manufacturer* commenced October 1919, again as the organ of the Manufacturers' Club of Philadelphia.

would impair distributors' buying resources for quite some time. To keep major accounts open, many mills surely accepted such grim terms, which in time matured into new rules for distribution that helped solidify buyers' increasingly advantageous position.[18]

Having absorbed inventory losses in the 1920–1 deflation, textile buyers had returned to piecemeal purchasing and tried to extend the practice from main lines of yard goods, clothing, and hosiery into specialties like upholstery, carpets, and curtains. Jobbers and wholesalers soon adopted the same strategy. What manufacturers perceived at first as a crisis response became a durable feature of market transactions in the interwar decades. As its implications became clearer, the extent of the risk transfer from distributors to producers could be gauged. First, it should be understood that in staple textiles, hand-to-mouth buying had only a minor impact, that is, wholesalers and converters had to adjust staff and stock levels to deal with more frequent and somewhat smaller orders for basic shirtings and print goods. In a 1926 Harvard study, the size of the average 1924 order for staple prints (62,000 yards) was 45 percent of the 1920 average, yet was 75 percent of the 1915 figures, proportions that underscore the breadth of panic buying in 1920. Still when these reduced levels are contrasted with the size of 1924 orders for specialties (draperies, 5,500 yards; fancy prints, 9,900) and it is recognized that an indefinite number of styles comprised each of these smaller calls for seasonal goods, the far greater influence of hand-to-mouth buying on Philadelphia-type flexible mills comes into focus.[19]

Moreover, through the NRDGA, the managerial practices that would reinforce buyers' power were refined and disseminated. In February 1920, the association's Controllers Congress was formed, and shortly commenced coordinating its sales barometer reporting with the Harvard Bureau of Business Research. Supply market data was spread through a monthly *Confidential Bulletin*, and the controllers both developed a widely adopted "standardized system of accounting" and "propagated understanding of and faith in the Retail Inventory Method." In forming by 1925 the core of the Retailers' National Council, a group of ten national merchandising associations, the NRDGA promoted the generalization of budget buying and assertive price and terms-of-sale practices far beyond its two-thousand-plus member institutions. The association hired a permanent merchandise adviser, resident

---

[18] *AWCR* 34(1920): 3380, 3479–80, 3554–6, 3922–4, 3983, 4003. Mercerized cotton half-hose, mentioned above, reached $7/dozen at the peak, then collapsed to $3.50 in October 1920 (3604) and trended lower still with declines in raw cotton prices in 1921. On the NRDGA, see Benson, *Counter Cultures*, p. 313.

[19] Melvin T. Copeland, *Distribution of Textiles*, Cambridge, MA, 1926, pp. 171–6. Reflecting the larger numbers of smaller orders, the median order size for the three categories in 1924 was 8,000 yards for staple prints, 1,500 for draperies, and 2,800 for fancy prints.

in New York, to counsel visiting buyers; and its managing director coauthored *The Merchants' Manual*, the first comprehensive manual of modern merchandising. Published by McGraw Hill in 1924 and modeled on that firm's many engineering handbooks, the six-hundred-page guide, crammed with standard forms and tools for assessment and control of buying and turnover, went through three printings within a year. The NRDGA also published or distributed over a hundred pamphlets, mobilized trade resistance to manufacturers' early attempts at securing legislative authority to defend their battered prices (the Kelly price maintenance bill of 1925–6), and manipulated statistics cleverly to obscure retailers' returns on investment.

Preservation of buyers' market advantages thus stemmed not from a dramatic concentration of purchasing in ever fewer hands, though with the advance of chain stores, the continuing expansion of department stores, and the rise of independents associating in group buying through New York "resident buying offices," consolidation was proceeding gradually. Instead, it derived from the rapid adoption of techniques that rationalized and routinized business practice by retailers, all of whom were on different scales doing very much the same thing – moving goods, preeminently textile products, into consumers' hands. The NRDGA's members and the other thousands who forked over five dollars for the *Manual* were decisively strengthened in their dealings with specialty textile makers, who continued to talk of hand-to-mouth buying as if it were a short-term expedient rather than a transformation of purchasing methods. Relentlessly advertising the profitability benefits of the new methods through circulation of the Harvard statistics, and aided materially by the antiwaste fervor of Hoover's Department of Commerce (which distributed 55,000 copies of its first brochure on proper distributional trade practices), the NRDGA came to play in retail buying the leadership role that American Woolen had assumed in wool/worsteds production. As nothing was standard in flexible textiles but the need for orders, manufacturers were subject to perplexing dilemmas.[20]

As Copeland and his associates worded it,

> the prevalence of small orders for quick delivery has meant that if a
> manufacturer were to keep his plant in operation at full capacity he was
> likely to have to manufacture for stock, with the attendant risk of loss

---

[20] Lew Hahn and Percival White, *The Merchants' Manual*, New York, 1924, pp. vii–x, 311–97; *NRDGA Confidential Bulletin* 7 (January 1925): 32; (February 1925): 12–15; (March 1925): 8–9, 21; (April 1925): 38–41, 53; (June 1925): 6–10; (August 1925): 14–16; (December 1925): 5–7; 8 (January 1926): 2–3; (February 1926): 2–4. Chains and department stores were, according to retailing analyst Paul Nystrom, in 1925 responsible for 26 percent of all sales, up from 10 percent in 1915. Together with cooperative buying by independents, consolidated buying most likely represented about a third of purchasing in the mid-1920s (*NRDGA CB* 7 [June 1925]: 9).

from merchandise depreciation whenever prices dropped or style requirements were not accurately foreseen... [T]his change in buying
practice seems to have been a burden to the manufacturers, with few
offsetting gains.[21]

Full-capacity running was out of the question in seasonal sectors, but the
push for immediate delivery of multiplying, minuscule orders enhanced risks
and costs in several convergent ways. Transaction expenses for processing
ten lagged orders in the place of one or two large ones escalated dramatically,
as did the opportunities for error. Additional costs for office help and supplies
were reinforced by higher overall packing and transport charges. Small lots
cost proportionately more to ship than larger bundles, and it was no longer
clear that buyers would bear these costs. In addition, as Copeland noted,
atomized demand for "quick delivery" pushed mills to have seasonal styles
ready in advance. The normal production time for Philadelphia fancies
ranged from three to six weeks after receipt of orders. This would no longer
do; unless the item were sent within a week to ten days, orders were now
cancelled.

None of the options available to handle this pressure was especially attractive. Narrowing one's line of styles to ease stock carrying could lead to
missing the effect or color combination that proved to be the season's vogue.
Running stock of everything not only would cost a young fortune, but would
assure that some, perhaps sizable, quantities would be left at the season's
close as rapidly depreciating "dead stock." Nor would this tactic suggest
how much of any style to make up; a sudden rash of orders for any single
item would quickly exhaust shelf supplies unless mountains of each had
been prepared. Refusing to play the game at all was self-defeating. Unless
a mill had a reputation for stylistic brilliance or unsurpassed quality, it could
expect that delays in shipment (due to retaining the old pattern) would lead
it steadily toward the exit gate.

Ownership of machinery beyond the mills' average capacity needs provided
another avenue, but one with its own peculiar pitfalls. In prewar days the
bunching of orders in seasonal clumps had encouraged proprietors to hold
older weaving and knitting technology while adding new equipment, calling
into service the usually idle older machines in especially busy periods. It
would be theoretically possible to adapt to the new conditions by setting out
warp beams that spread the range of seasonal novelties across the full complement of equipment, then as needed activating those looms for which
orders materialized.[22] Yet while this might manage the stock risk, it would

---

[21] Copeland, *Distribution*, pp. 20–1.
[22] It is often forgotten that for patterned woven fabrics, warp beams frequently carry

demand that workers be free to move fluidly from loom to loom, a dimension of flexibility that contradicted shop floor customs that had endured from the nineteenth century. If workers retained "their" looms, there could be no guarantee of work under this or any version of tactical response. Were attempts made to keep favored workers and the most efficient looms busy, downtime for beam changes and pattern shifts could become forbidding, eroding earnings, morale, and profits. Ultimately, the structure of the labor process in Philadelphia's flexible textile trades inhibited decisive adaptation to the feedback effects of the new distributional relations.

Further, the disaggregated system of separate, functionally distinct establishments now became a liability, as short-term rather than seasonal timing became a priority. For mills that sought to evade carrying big stocks, "modification of the system of scheduling work" was critical to speeding turnaround on orders. Delays in spinners' provision or dyers' coloring of yarns now imperiled contract fulfillment, whereas a few days lost in a six-week production cycle had earlier been simply an annoyance. One could order up a season's yarn in advance of course, but this assumed a correct judgment of the array of counts needed, and among multifiber users, the likely balance among cotton, silk, rayon, and wool. Were this tried, how was one then to assess the relative balance of colors that would be required? Compression of the turnaround period as an alternative to making stock was fraught with perils. In a sense, the shift in distributional patterns and practices consequent on the installation of piecemeal buying turned former advantages of the flexible system into disadvantages. Routines that had long facilitated market responsiveness and product diversity were themselves insufficiently flexible to accommodate an acceleration in time demands on production (especially as this was not paired with a relaxation of the call for stylistic variation). Mills that had added their own dyeworks thus were in the 1920s more favorably placed than independent weavers and knitters. Fully integrated firms could perhaps exercise the greatest control over production timing,

multicolored components of the design and are thus not interchangeable except within narrow limits. To run the same design in blue and green vs. brown and tan usually necessitates a separate warp, unless all color effects are provided by filling yarns layered over concealed warps, as in some carpetings. On the mixing of new and old machinery in Philadelphia, see *TW* 77(1930): 3760. On higher transaction costs, see *Underwear and Hosiery Review* 5(February 1922): 70 (hereafter *UHR*). Adaptation to "excess capacity" by preparing large numbers of looms for anticipated orders and running only those for which pattern calls appeared, became common in Philadelphia upholstery weaving after 1925. This accounts for the ready sale of "surplus" looms at liquidations, as they fit cheaply into a flexibility strategy borne on decaying market relations (see Palmer, "Economic Factors," pp. 15–16, PP–135, TMR).

but in Philadelphia, this could be achieved only by risking additional capital, a far from magnetic idea.[23] Expedient reshuffling and a "this too shall pass" mentality appeared to hold sway through most of the 1920s; the general depression did not cause, but rather confirmed the marginalization of the regional industry.

The financial implications of hand-to-mouth buying must also be noted. At the level of the firm, the developmental logic of flexible textile manufacturing had been capital saving and skill using. Banking institutions created by area proprietors had underwritten calls for short-term seasonal working capital, but the distributional transformation entailed new capital needs in a more hazardous environment. These added demands struck hundreds of mills more or less simultaneously, would prove to be permanent, and went far beyond the resources of the Textile Manufacturers' Bank or the Ninth National. Before and during the war years, as one hosiery operator explained, there were "a great many mills... doing a large business on a very small capitalization." Making to order and selling on short terms (thirty days) narrowed their working capital needs considerably, for materials and stock inventories were kept modest. However, after 1920, buyers demanded far longer terms (sixty to ninety days) and post-dating, slowing the influx of cash, whereas the hardly avoidable necessity of carrying stock escalated the investment required to operate the factories. One thus either had to secure larger rollover credits as a manufacturer or introduce additional funds to sustain the stock burden, investments "which would have to earn dividends and be a perpetual charge for the rest of time against the profits of the mills." Since with banks, a knit-goods maker pointed out, "fixed assets are of no use as a basis for borrowing," and new investors could hardly look with enthusiasm at current accumulation prospects, proprietary or closely held firms would either have to find alternative credit sources, expend retained earnings, realize on other holdings to fill the capital gap, or achieve significant cost savings to offset the financial weight of creating a stock of goods and adjusting to slower payment of outstanding invoices.[24]

---

[23] Copeland, *Distribution*, p. 21. On the persistence of style variability in yard goods, see Reavis Cox, *The Marketing of Textiles*, Washington, D.C., 1938, chs. 15, 16. Trends toward stylistic simplification will be reviewed below. On yarns, see *Final Report to the Manufacturers and Union Members of the Philadelphia Upholstery Industry*, Industrial Research Department, University of Pennsylvania, 1931, ch. 4, pp. 2, 25, PP–135, TMR. (Hereafter cited as *FR-Uph*, this report is paginated by chapters.) The solution to the yarn problem tried by upholstery mills was to buy in small lots and deliver them to contract dyers who stored yarns until called on to color them as orders for specific goods materialized. In consequence, bankruptcy receivers for dyers were plagued by weavers' efforts to recover their yarn and send it to an active works.

[24] *AWCR* 35(1922): 395, 407. These capital demands may help account for the renewed prominence of specialized "factors" who bought accounts receivable from textile firms

As a different way to suggest the financial impact of the shift to piecemeal buying on Philadelphia textile producers, it may be useful to create a mock account set for a midsize firm, illustrating the effect of stock carrying and the shift to longer datings (payments due ninety days after shipment, rather than thirty days). Here we posit annual sales of $500,000, about average for Philadelphia, capital invested of $200,000 ($150,000 in plant and machinery, $25,000 cash, and $25,000 materials inventory), no finished stock carrying at the outset. In seasonal markets, four active sales months ($50,000) are followed by two slack months ($25,000) twice annually. For each dollar of sales, materials cost 60 cents, labor 20 cents, miscellaneous expenses including salaries 10 cents, and profit 10 cents. For simplicity it is assumed that: materials are replaced as needed each month, no discounts are involved, no new machinery is added or depreciated, borrowed funds may be had at 6 percent, and restoration of a January 1 cash balance of $25,000 is required. On these assumptions, Year One balances shape up as follows, before hand-to-mouth (000 omitted):

Month	Cash	Receipts[a]	Borrow/ payback	Material, labor, & misc.	Shipments
Jan. 1	25	25[b]	—	45	50
Feb.	5	25[b]	B. 20	45	50
Mar.	5	50	—	45	50
Apr.	10	50	—	45	50
May	15	50	P. 20	22.5	25
June	22.5	50	—	22.5	25
July	50	25	—	45	50
Aug.	30	25	—	45	50
Sept.	10	50	—	45	50
Oct.	15	50	—	45	50
Nov.	20	50	—	22.5	25
Dec.	47.5	50	—	22.5	25
		500	Debt 0	450	500

Jan. 1   75: (25 retained in cash): End of Year One – 50 to Profit
[a]Bills for January shipment due 30 days after end of month, hence March 1.
[b]Receipts from slack months, Nov. and Dec., of previous year.

during the 1920s, recycling needed cash minus a discount under longer-term selling conditions (Cox, *The Marketing of Textiles*, pp. 317–19). On draining retained surpluses, see *FR-Uph*, ch. 2, p. 6, table 6. With 1928 nominal-dollar surplus levels indexed at 100, war and postwar boom profits built retained earnings from 76 in 1919 to 109 in 1921, falling to 63 in 1922 and inching upwards through 1927, suggesting a substantial payout or plowback in 1922.

Here we have a delightfully profitable year, because returns to capital come in at 25 percent and borrowing is negligible (interest for three months would be just $300), only enough to cover seasonal drops in demand.

Now in January of Year Two, more suddenly than in reality, the quick-delivery, hand-to-mouth relations are installed. The mill must now carry a stock, conservatively put at just over one month's production ($50,000), must accept slower returns on invoices as ninety-day terms have been established, and faces the evening-out of sales. Again for simplicity, it is assumed that the production schedule is not initially altered, except for overtime work to generate the warehoused stock. The costs of additional material and labor must be borne through borrowing, and nominal profits will be used to reduce loan balances, as the proprietors will subsist on their salaries and there are no outstanding bonds or other instruments that have a privileged claim on returns (reasonable for Philadelphia). Prices of all inputs and finished goods remain stable and there is no depression. Under these conditions Year Two runs as follows:

Month	Cash	Receipts	Borrow/ payback	Material, labor, & misc.	Shipments	Inventory
Jan. 1	25	25	B. 25	65[a]	45	0
Feb.	10	25	B. 30	65	45	25
Mar.	0	0[b]	B. 45	45	40	50
Apr.	0	0	B. 45	45	40	50
May	0	45	—	22.5	40	50
June	22.5	45	—	22.5	40	50
July	45	40	—	45	45	50
Aug.	40	40	P. 30	45	45	50
Sep.	5	40	—	45	40	50
Oct.	0	40	B. 10	45	40	50
Nov.	5	45	—	22.5	40	50
Dec.	27.5	45	P. 25	22.5	40	50
		390	Debt − 100	540	500	

Jan. 1   25: End of Year Two − 0 to Profit
[a]Extra expense to accumulate stock in Jan. and Feb.
[b]Lags due to shift in payment dates from 30 to 90 days.

With the two changes due to the assumption of market power by buyers, the firm finds it necessary to borrow $155,000 to get through Year Two and, by devoting all profits to debt reduction, is able to lower its outstanding debt only to $100,000 at the year's end. Half of this is "covered" by inventory, but the payment lag due to the shifted terms of sale has cost the company $50,000, essentially wiping out the Year One profits. Moreover, interest charges on a balance that averaged about $120,000 for the year would amount to $7,200, yielding a loss on operations. The firm is most vulnerable to a failure in April, the fourth consecutive month in which new funds must be secured in order to keep running. Curtailment of "facilities" in the mythical spring of Year Two would derange its operations utterly.

Having cleared the transitional hurdles by absorbing losses and accumulating debt, the company is now set to seek stability in Year Three. It adjusts work schedules to reflect the less erratic swings of demand, reducing slack months from four to two and again undertakes to apply profit to indebtedness. Year Three:

Month	Cash	Receipts	Borrow/ payback	Material, labor, & misc.	Shipments	Inventory
Jan.	25	40	—	40	45	50
Feb.	25	40	—	40	45	(all
Mar.	25	40	—	40	40	year)
Apr.	25	40	—	40	40	
May	25	45	—	40	40	
June	30	45	—	25	40	
July	50	40	P. 30	40	45	
Aug.	20	40	—	40	45	
Sept.	20	40	—	40	40	
Oct.	20	40	—	40	40	
Nov.	20	45	—	40	40	
Dec.	25	45	P. 20	25	40	
		500	Debt – 50	450	500	
Jan. 1	25		End of Year Three – 0 to Profit			

Here the firm has taken giant strides toward regularization of its affairs. Debt is now fully offset by inventory holdings and could be eliminated in Year Four, though Year Five profits would have to be used to clear the $15,000 paid in interest overall. The end of seasonal demand has reduced the rush-slack amplitude for the workforce and the factory's cash position is much more stable than in Year One. This benevolent result was precisely what antiseasonality, efficiency reformers like Morris Cooke and Joseph Willits had in mind and fit well with the economic assumptions of journalists and distributors, progressive and Hooverite associationists of the 1920s. Yet if any of the conditions posited at the outset are altered to reflect "real time" shifts that were either implicit in the hand-to-mouth system or developed parallel to it, the happy portrait of a completed, if difficult, adjustment is no longer tenable.

First, stable prices have been presumed for materials, goods, and labor. The depression brought goods and materials levels down sharply, but wages were sticky, and a subject of fierce contention, as 1921 events demonstrated. More critically, in subsequent years raw materials costs for wool ranged from 30 to 60 percent above 1921 figures while the wholesale price index for textile mill products rose 18 percent from the depression trough then slid back gradually to below 1921 levels in 1929. Cotton fluctuated from 24 percent above the early nadir to 8 percent below it (1927), but increases proved difficult to cover whereas every fall occasioned buyer demands for lower goods prices. No simple adjustment was available for the manufacturers.

The example offered here also assumed stable values for inventories, and perfect clearance of them, rather than accumulations and periodic sacrifices without profits or below costs, as proved to be the case. If over the course of a year our firm's finished stock rose to $80,000, $30,000 of which was liquidated at two-thirds of its nominal value to close out the year, a $10,000 loss would be added to the burden of interest payments and debts. The model likewise presumes no cancellations, no refused shipments returned to the mill, no orders wrecked by delays, all of which would leave goods in the mill owner's hands. Further, it contains the expectation that orders would be regularized across the calendar and spread neatly across available machinery, facilitating more effective use of capital and labor, eliminating overtime, etc. Yet there is no reason why aggregate flattening should translate readily to individual mills. None could know what each day's mail would bring; with seasonal regularities gone, rush and slack could well continue with no cyclical pattern at all, and a single firm's orders degenerate from predictably erratic to unpredictably erratic. Unless stocks were optimally balanced in advance, orders would be delayed, under- and unemployment accentuated, etc.

Finally, the whole adjustment sequence depends on access to short-term credits which as profitability deteriorates have of necessity to be converted into longer-term obligations through renewal or consolidation. Placing several hundred Philadelphia firms in this situation alongside our single case would activate financial triage, forcing suspensions, loading "lucky" or well-placed firms with debt, and leading toward in-house expedients to reduce operating costs (wage cuts, manipulation of fabrics, narrowing of style ranges). Mills that have not distributed war-era surpluses will be insulated to a degree, but will find their reserves transformed into inventory or vanishing into carryover wages and materials expenses during Year Two. For debtors, interest charges add pressure to cut other costs. Downward price demands, inventory losses, together with disadvantageous terms of sale make it difficult to diminish principal. As this network of constraints persists, equipment renewal will be implausible and liquidation will become appealing for many proprietors; for most, new capital for restructuring or relocation will be difficult to secure. Finally, proprietors who "go public" through share or bond issues will of necessity sacrifice their cherished autonomy and risk being displaced by investors angered at the firm's lackluster performance (Gilbert Beetem's experience).

Though perception of and response to this portentous shift in the conditions for accumulation was lagged and uneven, Manayunk manufacturer G. T. Shepperd observed after a year of depression and deflation that "the little fellows have been living on hope."[25] Other, bigger players in Philadelphia textiles took a more aggressive stance. Through their newly christened Philadelphia Textile Manufacturers' Association, they promulgated a set of citywide wage reductions, employing a classic depression tactic clothed in the rhetoric of Americanism and open shop advocacy and voiced through the agency of a "modern" trade organization. Unhorsed by the buyers' ascent to market dominance, the millmen now sought to reassert their authority within factory walls.

6.2. Labor and capital, 1919–1925

The 1921 management offensive was directly linked to the general deflation, but must be understood in the context of postwar ebbs and flows in relations between Philadelphia textile workers and their employers. Gains made by the former in 1919 triggered a new phase in manufacturers' cyclical efforts to forge a united regional front. Apparent success in this regard during 1920 set the stage for common action in January 1921, but the results of the winter wage-cutting drive indicated how differently placed were the various divisions of the Philadelphia textile trade with regard to the immediate market crisis and, by extension, in relation to the longer-term constraints that a persistent buyers' advantage would establish.

The UTW opened the peacetime exchanges at its autumn 1918 convention, calling for renewed drives to establish the eight-hour day and the forty-eight-hour week in textiles. Under the guidance of Philadelphia's Frank McKosky, the national union's second vice-president, area locals ratified this stance in December and circularized the demand among the regional mills. Midway through January, Joseph Grundy, head of the Pennsylvania

[25] *AWCR* 35(1922): 2112.

Manufacturers' Association, denounced the maneuver and publicized the statewide group's refusal to entertain the proposal. As the UTW had mounted the short hours campaign in all regions, the national organizations of wool, cotton, silk, and knit-goods manufacturers assembled in Boston to promulgate a similar rejection. Locally, on January 24 McKosky's Textile Council responded with an ultimatum: either the mills would accept the forty-eight-hour week or workers would establish it by leaving their posts after eight hours' work, commencing February 3, accepting lower overall earnings if need be (an echo of the 1903 labor position).[26]

With this, the pace of events quickened and positions became clearer. Union spokesmen asserted that the demand was intended to "standardize the eight hour day," to regularize uneven employment patterns, and to install time-and-a-half pay for overtime so that hours would be lengthened "only when necessity calls for it." H. H. Bosworth, president of the Philadelphia Cloth Manufacturers' Association, replied that such a plan was "economically impossible." C. Stanley Hurlbut, a lawyer serving as counsel to and secretary of the Full-Fashioned Hosiery Manufacturers' Association, was named the official spokesman for a dozen local trade groups. He called attention to the industry's "very poor" selling conditions, discounting the forty-eight-hour proposal as not "a real controversy" since "the real matter of concern . . . is the question of being able to operate even thirty-five hours a week." As markets for and prices of goods were terribly uncertain, Hurlbut's constituents were unwilling to make commitments altering the length of the work day. Besides, they regarded the unions' lower pay statement as merely a ploy; demands for higher rates to offset any losses would surely follow acceptance of eight hours. Selection of a single voice did not however mandate a common response to the situation. News of firms accepting labor's terms filtered out. Significantly, four "large" full-fashioned firms not members of Hurlbut's association settled for forty-eight hours on January 31. Pressure on the millmen increased the next day, as firms in Fall River, New Bedford, Lawrence, and the Blackstone Valley all followed American Woolen's lead in adopting the new schedule. Moreover, George Wharton Pepper, representing the Council for National Defense, arrived in Philadelphia to add the government's weight to the drive for concessions. Resistance crumbled in all but eighteen mills, most of which were members of the Yarn Association of Philadelphia. As the overtime issue had been dropped, and as business was exceedingly slack, acceptance of the forty-eight-hour plan

---

[26] *PL*, January 14, 1919, p. 15; January 17, p. 15; January 24, p. 3. On the Textile Council, see Gladys Palmer, "History of the Philadelphia District Textile Council," *American Federationist* 39(October 1932): 1133–8.

appeared costless and could be characterized as bowing to the larger national interests Pepper epitomized.[27]

Parallel with these developments, a strike had materialized in full-fashioned hosiery, pitting two knitters' unions against Hurlbut's thirteen-firm association. This conflict, which commenced January 11, 1919, helps account for Hurlbut's high profile in the forty-eight-hour controversy, as he moved from being the visible "point man" in the knitting battle to a larger role in the wider affair. Contemplating the expiration of their 1918 agreement at the year's end, the hosiery workers' unions forwarded their employers a November demand for a 25 percent increase in piece rates and hourly wages. As full-fashioned hose were least affected by the post-armistice price slide, nonassociation mills shrewdly agreed to accept whatever settlement was reached with Hurlbut's FHMA and continued to operate. When the FHMA would concede no advance, 1,200 union men walked, idling several thousand others, "unorganized and out of work on account of [the] strike and mostly women." With the favorable resolution of the forty-eight-hour drive, this plank was added to the hosiery workers' platform.[28]

Following the tactical line set out at the December 1918 U.S. Chamber of Commerce Reconstruction Conference in Atlantic City, Hurlbut tabled a proposal for a joint "Men and Management" plan early in March 1919. Appealing directly to workers, he trumpeted the scheme as a "union of both employers and employes" which would protect their common interests while combatting the "interference" of Bolsheviks, Wobblies, and radicals. This "cooperative movement" would "put the textile industry on a basis where all will be prosperous, content and happy," as full-column advertisements in the *Ledger* explained. Directed at the hosiery workers, the Men and Management's Textile Council was something more than a strike tactic, being also a device intended to counteract the disunity that had been chronic among manufacturers. Its president (Hurlbut) had enlisted Bosworth as secretary, tough-minded C. W. Masland as treasurer, and John Snowden, of the prominent Stead and Miller upholstery firm, as vice-president. Among its members were representatives of eleven local mill associations and the unorganized silk sector. Though it received ample press coverage, "M and M" was rejected immediately by the unions. Conciliation Commissioner

---

[27] *PL*, January 31, 1919, p. 4; February 2, pp. 1, 12; February 3, pp. 1, 13; February 6, p. 10; *The Manufacturer* 1(October 1919): 7; John Golden to Hugh Kerwin, February 7, 1919, Department of Labor, Federal Mediation and Conciliation Service, Case File 170/120, Record Group 280, National Archives (hereafter cited as FMCS File…).

[28] *PL*, January 12, 1919, p. 5; Golden to Kerwin, February 7, 1919; Thomas Williams to Kerwin, April 14, 1919, FMCS File 170/120.

E. E. Greenawalt regarded it as an absurdity. In a March 13, 1919, letter, he remarked:

> Conditions in the textile industry in Philadelphia are greatly disturbed and the employers do not appear to be disposed to meet the situation in a concilatory spirit and are apparently determined to force a settlement of the matters in dispute upon terms dictated by themselves. In confirmation of this opinion it is only necessary to invite attention to the fact that employers... have formed what they are pleased to call the "men and management's Textile Council" through the operation of which they appear to believe they have found an open road to an industrial millennium in the textile world, although the workers have not been invited to participate in working out the rules and regulations to govern this high-sounding "fifty-fifty" cooperative profit-sharing scheme.[29]

Aimed at fellow millmen and the public as an organizing and legitimizing ideological sally more than as a live proposal for reshaping labor–capital relations, "M and M" was soon a dead letter. The FHMA's resistance to the knitters' demands proved similarly ineffectual.

As was suggested above, buyers' commitments to hand-to-mouth purchasing and lower prices flagged in March and April 1919. With a consumer boom in process, building demand provoked heavy ordering. Perceiving that they had misread the market signals, the FHMA commenced April 2 a series of conferences with the workers' "committee of fifteen" under the aegis of conciliator Thomas Williams. Agreement was reached on April 12, the manufacturers conceding the forty-eight-hour week, time work raises of 20 percent, and piece rate increases averaging 18 percent. Ten days later, the yarn mill lockout, which had followed on the February 3 refusal to work more than eight hours, ended with capitulation by the sixteen Yarn Association holdouts. Surging demand confirmed the wisdom of sacrificing principle to profits; a thousand UTW members and perhaps a thousand others unemployed due to the lockout returned to work April 22. Though it was a messy sequence, labor had its way in the spring of 1919; and textile capitalists, despite their intent to "dictate" settlement terms, were compelled to give ground.[30]

[29] *PL*, March 3, 1919, p. 3; March 9, p. 4; March 12, p. 1; March 18, p. 8; *Ledger* clippings in FMCS File 120/170; E. E. Greenawalt to Kerwin, March 13, 1919, and *Ledger* and *Record* clippings, in FMCS File 33/2870; *AWCR* 33(1919): 944.

[30] T. Williams to Kerwin, April 14, 15, 1919; McKosky to Kerwin, April 24, 1919, FMCS File 120/170; *AWCR* 33(1919): 1642; *PL* April 15, 1919, pp. 1, 5. Acceptance of eight hours came last in Manayunk, *PL*, June 17, 1919, p. 4. Philadelphia was not the only specialty textile center facing a rocky situation early in 1919. Providence mayor Joseph Geisner, at the White House Conference of Governors and Mayors, noted as well that

For the next year, with mills scrambling to fill orders, there was little evident static on the labor–capital wire. Such upward adjustments of rates as were pressed on manufacturers occasioned no public confrontations. When upholstery weavers' agreements expired in March 1920, uninterrupted production was maintained by the manufacturers' acceptance of the closed shop, a 16 percent schedule hike, and establishment of hourly pay of eighty cents for time work for a six-month term instead of the usual year. Rapid inflation had led workers to seek reopening in the fall, rather than be tied to commitments for twelve months. Dyers soon adopted the weavers' hourly figure as their benchmark, demanding eighty cents in April, a 14 percent rise. But in the intervening weeks, the previous year's momentum had faltered; job dyeworks in the Master Dyers' Association determined to take a strike rather than further augment their costs, rejecting the quick acceptance of the new level at thirteen weaving mills with integrated dyeworks. The walkout was a catastrophe for the workers; with markets collapsing, the little business that needed doing was handled at MDA firms by a few loyalists and green hands. The latter became permanent employees, learning to handle the closed-kettle technology over the next four months of low pressure, slack demand. By August the strike was broken; despite brave words from union leader Arthur McDonnell, individual dyers were being selectively rehired. Rising unemployment had aided the MDA members, for when the owner of the Nicetown Dye Works sought to "entirely replace" his operatives, he reported receiving 560 applications for less than a hundred learners' positions.[31]

If the dyers' challenge was ill-timed, so too was the fund-raising drive to finance construction of new facilities for the Philadelphia Textile School. Launched March 1, 1920, with a banquet and the unveiling of architectural drawings for a site along the Benjamin Franklin Parkway (near the planned Philadelphia Museum of Art), the two-million-dollar campaign was intended to siphon off a measure of the returns from current and recent prosperity. It suffocated in the blizzard of cancellations that swept across the industry that spring. Elsewhere, substantial 15 percent advances in wages at Fall

his city's "manufacturers are doing a hand-to-mouth business." See "Transcript of the Conference with the President of the United States and the Secretary of Labor by the Governors of States and Mayors of Cities in the East Room of the White House," March 3, 1919, p. 417, FMCS File 170/199. For information on relations among the knitters' unions, see Gladys Palmer, *Union Tactics and Economic Change*, Philadelphia, 1932, pp. 92–4.

[31] *CUTR* 51 (March 15, 1920): 46; (April 15, 1920): 62; (July 15, 1920): 42; (September 1, 1920): 60; *AWCR* 34(1920): 1352, 1493; *PL*, August 23, 1920, p. 3; *The Manufacturer* 2(July 1920): 18–20; Arthur McDonnell to FMCS, undated (1921?), FMCS File 170/1454; *FR-Uph*, ch. 6, pp. 15, pp–135, TMR.

River, duplicated by American Woolen and "a very large number of the foremost textile plants in New England," were rendered meaningless by massive layoffs. Sizable cuts were now anticipated generally "as soon as the textile business picks up," for when called back, workers would be offered lower rates. The only bright spot for Philadelphia labor was the September six-month renewal of the upholstery weavers' spring 1920 terms of work, a move that reflected Philadelphia's dominance of this specialty sector. Since city firms produced as much as 80 percent of domestic furnishing fabrics, manufacturers had refused to accept immediate delivery orders and declined to run stock. While buyers fumed at delays, the mills were able to defend terms if not prices, and to maintain the rate scale temporarily, while running part-time on such hand-to-mouth purchases as were booked.[32]

In other sectors the squeeze was intense, as a winter 1920 cost analysis for a Philadelphia wool tricotine fabric indicates. Expected to sell at $2.50 per yard wholesale, this cloth's materials and labor expense ($1.72 and $.38 respectively) comprised 84 percent of its value, leaving 16 cents on the dollar to cover mill overhead, salaries, taxes, insurance, and profit (vs. a 1919 woolens average of 25 cents: Table 6.1).[33] Were manufacturers able to reduce the wage bill by 20 percent and defend their prices, about three cents would be added to the residual in each sales dollar; or alternately, the selling price could be shaved by eight cents per yard without affecting already narrowed profits. As deflation was not uniform across the range of cost factors, and as some were clearly out of manufacturers' sphere of control, the general pressure for rate cutting did not precipitate immediate action. Even the victorious MDA retained the prestrike seventy-cent hourly pay level for dyers through the end of 1920. The main reason for the lag between market collapse and the institution of cuts, manufacturers asserted, was that they needed to know where the bottom was before they could estimate the adjustments called for in wage rates. In the meantime, idle mills in proprietary or closely held corporate hands cost little to keep in readiness and had none of the dividend

---

[32] *CUTR* 51(March 15, 1920): 46; (September 1, 1920): 60; (September 15, 1920): 54; *AWCR* 34(1920): 1887, 1902, 4068. Upholstery mills' resistance to hand-to-mouth pressures continued throughout the depression, as mills in Philadelphia were working "three fifths time" in summer 1921, with lags of "six to eight weeks to make up the goods" causing buyers "vexatious delays" (*CUTR* 52 [July 15, 1921]: 75). On Philadelphia's share of national upholstery output, see *FR-Uph*, ch. 3, p. 8, PP–135, TMR. The Textile School fund-raising effort netted less than $200,000 in pledges and was abandoned, then revived without success (*TW* 59[1921]: 3532.).

[33] *AWCR* 34(1920): 4124–6. Regrettably, this is the only mid-depression cost analysis of an identified Philadelphia fabric that I was able to uncover. As no single product is "typical" for this diversified industry, this example is meant only to be suggestive of price movements that led to efforts at wage cutting.

expectations that plagued the New England majors.[34] The long stretch of
short hours or shutdown had further value in softening up anticipated labor
resistance to reductions. Yet this "wait and see" posture did not indicate
total passivity on the part of local textile operators. C. Stanley Hurlbut was
busily assembling a new and grandiose coalition, the Philadelphia Textile
Manufacturers' Association.

Putting a novel, personalistic construction on the 1920 depression while
announcing the PTMA's goals in the Manufacturers' Club journal, Hurlbut
claimed that the "retarding of business had produced for the manufacturer
a period of relaxation and an opportunity... for some consideration of the
future." Reflection would show one and all that the preeminent question to
which they should "collectively apply their efforts" was "upon what general
principles their labor problems should be dealt with henceforth." The old
tests of strength whereby disputes were "adjusted by natural economic laws"
were outdated. Instead, in the language of the era, manufacturers should
rely on "standardization of ideas and principles," concretized in "a strong
centralized organization." To serve their interests, PTMA members would
sponsor a "free employment bureau" whose operation would reduce labor
turnover and eliminate the "floater" and the "professional agitator" from local
mills. The originators had already engaged J. Lewis Benton as a managing
director and created a twenty-four-man executive committee that included
both long-prominent Anglo-Saxon names (Bromley, Folwell) and representatives from the growing body of Jewish proprietors (Simon Miller, H. B.
Loeb). (See Table 6.2.) Recognizing that "firmness, strength and unified
action must take the place of fear and distrust" among manufacturers, the
PTMA executive committee regarded themselves as "agents" for individual
members, whom they would lead toward a brilliant future.[35]

There is much to learn from the composition of this core group. First
and most obvious, its officers were identical to those of the stillborn Men
and Management's Textile Council, and though Hurlbut did not acknowledge this to his fellow clubmen, the trade press noted the PTMA as its
successor. Having rejected the cooperative "millennium" and now focusing
on leading a new generation of owners in the struggle with labor, the PTMA
leadership included not the elder statesmen of the trade, but the sons of
Miller, Folwell, Rath, Holt, Bromley, and Masland family patriarchs. A

---

[34] In a fall 1920 letter, Robert McWade pointed out that some mills had gone so far as
to "part with their respective office staffs," so decisive was the curtailment. McWade
to Kerwin, November 30, 1920, FMCS File 170/120. Fall River-like sliding scales
might have eased adjustments to declining prices, but they would have given entirely
the wrong signals to buyers and workers – that downward movements in price could
readily be absorbed, and at labor's expense.

[35] *The Manufacturer* 2(September 1920): 20–1.

Table 6.2. *Executive committee, The Philadelphia Textile Manufacturers' Association, September 1920*

	Firm	Sector	District	Employment 1916	Employment 1925
Pres. C. S. Hurlbut	M. B. Laubach Co.[a]	Full-fashioned hosiery	Kens.	206	89
Treas. C. W. Masland	C. H. Masland & Sons	Carpets	Kens.	329	441
V.-Pres. John Snowden	Stead and Miller	Upholstery	Kens.	343	437
Sec. H. H. Bosworth	Delaine Mills	Cloth	Myk.	90	—
William Folwell	Folwell Bros. & Co.	Cloth	Kens.	1,031	551
Jos. Wasserman	Phila. Tapestry Mill	Upholstery	Kens.	374	370
William Wall	Nicetown Dye Works	Dye-finish	N. Central	65	37
Henry Rath, Jr.	Henry Rath, Inc.	Carpet	Kens.	30	20
William Meyer	Apex Hosiery	Full-fashioned hosiery	Kens.	468	698
R. A. Luken	Continental Mills	Knit goods	Grwn.	43	287
Edward Schloss	Roxford Knit Mills	Knit underwear	Kens.	870	ob
P. J. Masterman	Lafayette Mills	Cottons	Kens.	30	—
Simon Miller	Jacob Miller & Sons	Cloth	S. Phila.	—	ob
A. J. Gordon	A. J. Gordon & Co.	Cloth	Kens.	30	33

Name	Company	Product	Location		
M. G. Curtis	Collins & Aikman	Plushes	Myk.	230	1,149
H. M. Gwyn	Cadet Hosiery Mill	Seamless hose	Kens.	ny	488
G. R. Ayres	Wm. Ayres & Sons	Blankets	Kens.	307	ob
Henry Bromley	N. American Lace	Lace	N. Central	458	553
C. H. Hett	Gordon Bros.	Haircloth	Fkd.	91	ob
W. Rossmaessler	Sauquoit Silk Co.	Silk	N. Central	541	350
H. L. Thompson	Phila. Carpet Co.	Carpet	Kens.	125	203
H. B. Loeb	Rosenau and Loeb	Seamless hose	S. Phila.	162	ob
Will Holt	John P. Holt & Co.	Yarns	Myk.	129	209
William Dalton	William Dalton	Yarns	—	—	—
			Totals	5,952	5,915

[a]Name changed to No-Mend Hosiery, 1922.

Note: ny = not yet in business; ob = out of business; — = no data.

Sources: OATD, 1916, 1925; *Pennsylvania Industrial Directory*, 1916, 1925.

generation was indeed passing. James Dobson would shortly retire at eighty-four from direction of his sprawling empire. Theodore Search had died in 1920, and the estates of carpet men James Gay ($629,000), William Smith ($400,000), and spinner James Doak ($213,000) were in or through probate. In one of its first new-series issues, *The Manufacturer* had complained about the depletion of industrial leadership; Hurlbut and his associates seemed prepared to assume the mantle.[36] Absent however were representatives from important firms (like Hardwick and Magee) that had displayed an unhealthy tendency to put individual gain above the collective good by accepting labor's terms in tight spots while letting others bear the brunt of confrontations. Instead, hard-liners like Apex's William Meyer, the FHMA president, and the MDA's William Wall joined managerially assertive types like Collins and Aikman's Curtis, Sauquoit's Rossmaessler, and the younger Masland. The latter trio would all use up-to-date, cost-rational, branch-plant strategies to good effect in the 1920s, but others drawn to Hurlbut's flame epitomized the deeper troubles growing in the Philadelphia trades.

Five of the core twenty-four firms went out of business by mid-decade; they had represented over 1,500 jobs in 1916, about a quarter of those offered by PTMA executive committee enterprises. Roxford and Ayres were among the last of a fading cohort of nineteenth-century firms whose specialties were being undermined by secular changes. Schloss's knit goods plant had been a giant among underwear producers, but high materials' costs combined with mass cancellations and the advent of knitted outerwear to induce bankruptcy in the 1921 slump. Ayres had focused profitably on horse and car blankets, but the closed auto that boomed Collins and Aikman's upholstery sales devastated its market, leading to a 1922 offering of machinery and mill in liquidation. Southern competition in seamless hosiery flummoxed Rosenau and Loeb, which had not Cadet's resources to shift into expensive investments in full-fashioned technology. The Millers abandoned their cloth mill to buy fabrics for their clothing business, which stretched into retailing on Chestnut Street.[37] (Most likely, it proved cheaper to join the favored position of purchasers in the 1920s rather than follow the Folwells down the drain of steady contraction and minuscule profits.) Thus the Hurlbut aggregation included both the troubled and the "comers" within the local industry, and in that mixture exemplified the crossing paths of several of its sectoral constituencies. In one respect, however, the executive group was far from typical. Workforces at its 1920 member firms at both points

---

[36] *Annual Report of the Alumni Association of the Philadelphia Textile School* 19(1920): 12–13; *CUTR* 51(June 15, 1920): 80; (September 15, 1920): 54; 52(July 15, 1921): 58: (September 15, 1921): 57; *The Manufacturer* 1(November 1919): 29.

[37] *UHR* 5(January 1922): 79; *AWCR* 36(1922): 734; *OATD: 1925*, p. 471.

indicated in Table 6.2 averaged three times the scale of the mean Phila-delphia mill.[38] Though a few "little fellows" had been tapped, Hurlbut had gathered under the PTMA umbrella what he expected would be a dynamic core of sizable firms whose leadership initiatives would set the pace for the rest of the regional complex.

As the PTMA cadre recruited new members from area sectoral associ-ations (following an October organizing session that drew crowds of pro-prietors to the Manufacturers' Club), the subject of marketplace relations vied with labor discipline for center stage. "Putting an end to the cancellation evil" was the timely issue that led over a hundred textile activists to attend a November 8 gathering, again at the club. With Joseph Grundy in the chair and wool merchant and mill owner Charles Webb by his side, the assembled manufacturers issued a call for a national textile conference to establish standard contracts, means for their enforcement, and a mechanism to identify and punish bad-actor clients. Appointed to the continuing committee were Hurlbut, Bosworth, Folwell, Rossmaessler, Curtis, and Lukens from the PTMA executive committee, among others. The national meeting was duly held in New York during December, but proved fruitless. Despite rousing statements that "Americanism" should "stand for the belief that a contract is a contract," attendees acknowledged that however "outrageous and dam-aging to the nation" the mass of cancellations may have been, "the control of the market has passed into the buyer's hands." In a postmortem on the complete failure of this excited movement, a Philadelphian observed in *The Manufacturer* that the weakness and multiplicity of textile trade organizations was the chief obstacle to achieving a firm and uniform response to the commercial catastrophe. "The scattered energy, the divided effort, and the overlapping functioning inevitable with the numberless individual organi-zations which . . . too often hinder or actually defeat each other in the textile industry" stymied the unity drive. "Are businessmen – that is, industrialists – efficient in collective effort?" he asked. "There is but one answer, . . . it is NO; a plain but vigorously emphatic NO."[39]

To be sure, such a statement was but partly true. Short of illegal collusive

---

[38] Mean firm size in 1916 (from Table 6.2) was 307 workers, in 1925, 370 (standard deviations being 270 and 284, respectively). For the Philadelphia region generally, the comparable means and standard deviations were, for 1916, 100 and 169, and for 1925, 108 and 174. See Philip Scranton, "Beyond Anecdotes and Aggregates: The Pattern of Industrial Decline in Philadelphia Textiles, 1916–1931," *Antipode* 18(1986): 284–310 (Table II, 294).

[39] *CUTR* 51(November 1, 1920): 64; (November 15, 1920): 55–6; (December 15, 1920): 72; *AWCR* 34(1920): 4187; *The Manufacturer* 2(December 1920): 3; *PL*, November 8, 1920, p. 17; November 9, p. 17. The call for the national conference was issued from the PTMA headquarters (*PL*, November 13, 1920, p. 19).

price fixing, of dubious efficacy in a competitive industry, flexible manufacturers had to determine individually the mix of short-time work, concessions on price or terms of sale, and ventures toward novelty or manipulation that offered the best prospects for sustaining their firms. Given the variability of styles, not to speak of legal constraints, collective sharing of available orders along some quota model was impossible. Mills could no more force a sale than workers could force a place to be open for them in a shop. In this lay the vulnerability of each vis-à-vis those with funds to provide payment for services or products they chose to select. Yet this asymmetry had been one key to the exercise of power in those circumstances (1886, 1903, 1917–18) where manufacturers *had* been "efficient" collectively in breaking labor's thrusts. In a derivative form, it had at times worked to labor's advantage, as millmen crowded by rush orders had been poorly positioned to resist pressures from their operatives. In 1920, however, area textile proprietors' painful, fundamental exposure and isolation before the market was revealed to buyers. Short of state intervention to govern price falls, unimaginable following Harding's election, unmanageable and unenforceable even if attempted, what course was open? Merger and forward integration would be tried, brand name advertising urged as means to control costs or bypass dealers to stimulate consumer demand; but in the short run, manufacturers turned to exploit the asymmetry close to hand. Wages would be forced down.

Major New England firms led the parade. On December 9, 1920, officials from corporations representing 75 percent of Yankee capacity announced a 22 1/2 percent wage cut after a Boston meeting. PTMA managing director Benton shortly issued a statement indicating that similar cuts would be installed in Philadelphia, but no comparable unity or simplicity was evident when the news broke on December 21. Instead of the PTMA putting forth a flat and general reduction, four sectoral associations promulgated quite different cuts ranging from 25 percent in Brussels and Wilton carpets, 20 percent in seamless hose, 15 percent in full-fashioned, down to 10 percent for weavers of cotton terrycloth and towels. No common date for implementation had been arrived at, and eight other regional associations had not yet determined the level of reductions deemed necessary. By January 7, Benton had rounded up the groups of spinners (20–22 percent) and cloth manufacturers (12–22 1/2 percent), but dyers would only later bring forward a sixty-cent hourly rate (14 percent) and upholstery reductions would not come until fall. This ragged performance showed how far the sectoral assemblies in Philadelphia were from achieving Hurlbut's dream of a strong, centralized organization. Even the narrow Brussels and Wilton carpet association did not cover all local producers, as Dobson remained independent. Free riders, differential sectoral need assessments, and proprietors' customary unwillingness to cede authority to a more general body dramatically constrained the PTMA's effectiveness.[40] To no one's surprise, the labor response was equally differentiated. Terry weavers accepted the new scale promptly, noting its moderation, but full-fashioned knitters and carpet weavers vowed a fight. Indeed the outcomes of the 1921 confrontations offer another useful profile of shifting fortunes and power relations among Philadelphia's varied trade divisions. Employment in Philadelphia textiles was at remarkably low ebb in January 1920, as estimates of idle facilities ranged from 50 to 90 percent of capacity. The Federal Reserve Bank found only 8 percent of carpet looms running full-time, and Benton, while detailing the full roster of reductions, observed that mills would definitely resume "upon the slightest indication of there being any business in sight." In this context, those few at work could either accept the operator's terms or have no employment at all, whereas others, called back individually or in clusters as scattered orders were secured, were similarly pressed. Acquiescence was general in woolen and worsted weaving, for the 1917–18 defeat had never been overcome, and in seamless hosiery and knit goods, where labor organizations had been weak and ephemeral. In spinning, there was a brief strike by 3,000 Kensington and Manayunk workers (UTW estimate), perhaps emboldened by their 1919 triumph over the lockout attempt. This petered out with little incident, and spinners' unions became a negligible presence thereafter in Philadelphia. Older solidarities most likely contributed to scattered shop strikes that were numbered among the fifty-seven textile walkouts in the first half of 1921, often in mills where employees chose "to ignore the higher officials of the union." However, none of these had the weight and portent of the clashes in carpets and full-fashioned hosiery.[41]

The Power Loom Body Brussels Carpet Weavers' Mutual Defense and Beneficial Association, founded in 1891, had developed into an independent national union from its Philadelphia base, with five locals at New Jersey, New York, and New England mills holding half of its approximately 1,750 members. In 1921 it faced off against the Association of Wilton and Brussels Manufacturers of America, which comprised all but three of the trade division's important firms. Having achieved the closed shop, the Wilton weavers ran a classic craftsmen's union – conservative, focused on benefits, control

[40] *PL*, December 10, 1920, p. 1; December 15 p. 5; December 21, pp. 1, 3; January 7, 1921, p. 1; *CUTR* 54(January 1, 1921): 62. American Woolen was one of the last large firms to reduce, adopting the New England 22 1/2 percent standard in the second week of January (*AWCR* 35 [1921]: 99).
[41] *CUTR* 52(February 1, 1921): 64; (February 15, 1921): 59–61; (September 1, 1921): 71; *PL*, January 18, 1921, p. 5; January 21, p. 15; *AWCR* 35 (1921): 116.

Figure 19. Five-frame Brussels carpet weaving at Hardwick and Magee, Philadelphia, 1918. The five frames at left held hundreds of spools that fed yarn through the jacquard mechanism (whose cards and harness lines are at top right) for weaving into carpets taken up on the roll at lower right. (Courtesy of the Pennsylvania Historical and Museum Commission.)

over the supply of labor, shop conditions, apprenticeship rules, and defense of customary practices. By 1920, experienced weavers earned sixty to seventy dollars for a forty-eight-hour week, and the Wilton rugs they made were the highest-priced power loom carpets on the market.[42]

In their December 1920 proposal, the AWBMA cohort had added a "control" issue to the proposed 25 percent reduction, the reintroduction of "creeler boys" to the weaving floors, nominally to enhance production but practically to assert authority over determining the numbers of trainees present in their mills. Before 1914 these youthful assistants had graduated from helping several weavers to being "spare hands" on the way to securing their own looms as fully fledged craftsmen. They had been eliminated during the

---

[42] For additional background, see Palmer, *Union Tactics*, pp. 22–9. The nonmembers were the massive Bigelow-Hartford corporation (ca. 4,000 employees), Alexander Smith (ca. 6,000), and Dobson in Philadelphia. To my knowledge, Smith's Wilton weavers were not organized.

war. (Carpet demand had slackened, few new looms were likely to be installed to provide places for them, etc.) Now the association wanted them back, purportedly to have trained men available to replace aging veterans. Unionists suspected this move to have other intentions, namely to swell the available labor supply in a trade whose further expansion seemed doubtful. In a New Year's referendum, sponsored by the National Executive Board, 1,500 weavers voted against accepting either the cut or the creeler boys by a ratio of 58 to 1. The strike opened January 17, with no movement from the impasse for three quiet months. Late in April, the association moderated its reduction to 20 percent, and rather than letting each firm go its own way on the "boy question," fixed one assistant per four looms as a common proposition. In a second referendum, these terms were again overwhelmingly refused, with only a hundred votes shifting toward acceptance. On June 3, the association declared open shop conditions would prevail when members restarted their mills at midmonth under a 20 percent cut with one boy for every two or three looms. The union called the Labor Department for help.[43]

As usual in dull times, firms were better positioned to endure a long stoppage than were the workers, despite payouts from their rarely used strike fund. More discouraging than the lost earnings was the collapse of solidarity at non-ABWMA member Bigelow's factories. At one, weavers had never struck, accepting an early 20 percent compromise. In another, the largest plant, dyers joined Wilton weavers when they walked out in late February, after an exchange of unsatisfactory proposals and counter-offers. The dyers' action closed the entire operation, yet they and all others save the Wilton weavers returned April 8 on management's terms. Clearly isolated, striking carpet weavers saw the ABWMA team's determination stiffen rather than sag, as the June open shop resolution suggests. Mediator Robert McWade finally managed to convene a general conference between the two sides on July 28, but effected no conciliation and secured no concessions from the owners' stated terms. Despite union president John Mann's heated assertion that "We are not licked to a frazzle," defeat was soon beyond denial. The mills declined to guarantee any striker's place, and McWade rightly judged that protests over this discrimination would be little more than "an ineffectual kick." Each local on August 3 was given "freedom to act as it deems circumstances to justify." Both the cuts and the creeler boys were soon installed, and the remnants of the PLBBCWMDBA dissolved in factional squabbling within a year. Promptly after this August 1921 defeat, Philadelphia firms operating tapestry carpet looms secured a 20 percent rate concession from

---

[43] William Ingham (Weavers) to James Davis, Secretary of Labor, June 15, 1921, FMCS File 170/1458. See also from the same file the transcript of a meeting July 28, 1921, between conciliator Robert McWade and representatives of the two sides (29 pp.).

the weavers' union in that division, a prelude to its organizational collapse five years hence.[44]

The full-fashioned hosiery struggle was a prelude as well, but it instead led toward a series of spirited knitters' organizing drives that continued with mixed success through the last years of the Great Depression. The Full-Fashioned Hosiery Workers Union developed into one of textile labor's few dynamic bodies in the 1920s, after having been dramatically tested in the ten-month 1921 strike. The conflict was as well a watershed for the FHMA, as its member firms discovered that their tough resistance only encouraged others to enter the full-fashioned business or expand their capacity to meet sturdy and increasing demand for the seamed silk hose that became a style hallmark of the flapper era. As other sectors stumbled and fell, full-fashioned grew into the final great, skill-intensive section of the Philadelphia textile trades.

First organized in 1909, the knitters' union soon split into two sections, the larger of which was a UTW affiliate (Local 706) whereas the smaller operated as Branch 14 of the tiny Federation of Full-Fashioned Hosiery Workers. Together with a local organization of "boarders," who stretched dyed hose over finishing boards for shaping, the full-fashioned unions had enrolled about a third of the four to five thousand workers in the trade by 1921. The earnings of knitters (all men) were reported as averaging forty-five dollars weekly, boarders thirty dollars, and women working in inter-mediate steps of the production sequence drew between eighteen and twenty-four dollars, virtually all on a piecework basis. Non-union mills generally paid rates near the official schedule, and in some spots a notch above it to discourage unionization. Indeed this very point was raised by Local 706 president Gustave Geiges when the 15 percent reduction was publicized in December 1920. Geiges contested the logic of the FHMA reduction noting that rates in "shops of manufacturers not affiliated with the association" were 10–15 percent above those in their mills, yet these firms were seeking no cuts. A more fully developed account of the situation shortly appeared in the last 1920 issue of the union newsletter, *Hosiery Worker*, then a type-written broadsheet. Editor Ray Herflicker explained:

> The knitters have pointed out that a 15% reduction of wages could only bring down the price of hosiery less than 5 cents per pair ... The

[44] Transcript, July 28, 1921; Henry Magee to McWade, July 20, 1921, with McWade's July 31 annotations; Ingham to McWade, August 3, 1921, FMCS File 170/1458; *CUTR* 52(April 1, 1921): 75; (May 1, 1921): 57, 65; (May 15, 1921): 62; (July 1, 1921): 49; (August 15, 1921): 45; *PL*, March 17, 1921, p. 15; April 26, p. 2; August 8, p. 1; August 11, p. 2; Palmer, *Union Tactics*, pp. 26–7, 36–44; John Erving and Nancy Norton, *Broad-looms and Businessmen*, Cambridge, MA, 1955, pp. 218–19; *TW* 60(1921): 974.

manufacturers in several cases have replied that the jobber and retailer are continually asking them if they have reduce wages and when they are given a negative reply. Then the jobber and retailer come to the conclusion that the price of hosiery has not reached rock bottom and that they are going to wait until the price does touch bottom.[45]

From this perspective, the anticipated cost savings were of less significance than the proprietors' demonstration to buyers that, having pared labor rates, no further price concessions could be expected. This would put a floor under the market and lead purchasers to make commitments that would restore production and stabilize values. Workers rejected these arguments. In the 1920 slump, full-fashioned production had far outpaced seamless hosiery in terms of capacity utilization (58 percent vs. 42 percent); if any textile sector could hope for early revival with an advantage to the mills, it was theirs.[46] Moreover, as in carpets, a labor process demand had been wedded to the manufacturers' announced reduction. Hereafter, knitters would run two machines with the help of an assistant, again a return to prewar shop conditions. Since 1913, the organized knitters had been able gradually to establish single-machine assignments in the principal Philadelphia mills and to restrict the number of apprentices and helpers, who served a four-year term before being advanced to command of their own machines. In 1919, the FHMA had conceded that all new installations would be run as single-machine jobs and production on the remaining "doubles" would be compensated at the single rate, eliminating the labor cost savings incentive for double jobs. This arrangement was now to be swept away to economize in production and increase the flow of newly trained knitters, thus expediting expansion, or as labor expected, generating competitive downward bidding on rates.[47]

The fourteen FHMA firms were joined by six independents in advancing these demands (Table 6.3). Though twelve other full-fashioned mills stood aside, the central twenty represented 83 percent of sectoral employment, nearly 3,900 jobs, 959 of which were held by skilled knitters. From January through April there was a complete stalemate; but as workers had speculated, the withdrawal of some of the industry's largest mills from production intersected with reawakening demand. Two giant Reading full-fashioned plants (Berkshire, Nolde and Horst) began reaping a huge trade, "largely as a result of labor troubles in Philadelphia." Employment at Berkshire jumped from 1,000 to a record 1,400 as new equipment from the nearby

---

[45] Palmer, *Union Tactics*, pp. 78–83, 93–4, 220; McWade to Davis, June 15, 1921, FMCS File 170/1454; *Hosiery Worker*, December 31, 1920 (original text reproduced); *PL*, December 22, 1920, p. 4.
[46] *AWCR* 35(1921): 402.   [47] Palmer, *Union Tactics*, pp. 92–3.

Table 6.3. *Full-fashioned hosiery firms and employment in Philadelphia, 1921*

Not struck	Empl.	Struck, but conceded	Empl.	Struck, FHMA	Empl.
Cobert	19	Cambria	88	Aberle	462
Federal	49	Concordia	120	Apex	281
Gotham	243	Guenther	48	Bower & Kaufman	96
Hunt, R.	47	Largman, Gray	86	Brentmore	124
Lemuth	72	Lehigh	134	Brown, Henry	129
McCallum	72	Nickels & Lauber	115	Brown, Thomas	291
Mutual	66		591	Brown, William	205
Nebel	74			Cadet	111
Norma	33			Fidelity	369
Oliver	49			Glen	191
Peerless	30			Haines	77
Phila. Knit	64			Hancock	700
	818			Laubach	68
				Quaker	166
					3,270
Percent of empl.	17		13		70
Mean empl.	68		99		233

Source: McWade to Davis, June 15, 1921, Department of Labor, F.M. Conciliation Service, Case File 170/1454, Record Group 280, National Archives.

Textile Machine Works, owned by the Berkshire partners, was hurriedly set in place. By April the firm's monthly output had reached 100,000 dozen and was "sold up" through July. This was hardly enough to fill the gap however, for by May the shortfall in full-fashioned output was estimated at 600,000 dozen, and trade terms had shifted radically in the operating mills' favor ("cash in thirty days"). Seamless hosiery firms were running double shifts knitting "mock" full-fashioned stockings; in Philadelphia, this "rather sudden prosperity" had forced seamless mills into "bidding against each other for help," reversing the momentum for reductions. By June, the six independents had all settled on a return to production without alteration of previous pay rates or work rules, but the Hurlbut aggregation had declared its members would never again meet with union representatives and would install the open shop by hiring and training new hands. Thomas E. Brown baldly dismissed the need for long apprenticeships, claiming that a fully competent knitter could be schooled in six months. A belated sense of realism induced him to add that this would have to be a period of "intensive training" under the instruction of foremen and that the prospective knitter had to be "mechanically inclined" and the bearer of "machine shop experience."

Brown did not suggest what the cost of this preparation might be, what would be done with the seconds learners knitted from expensive silk, or how long it would take the firm to reestablish a reputation for quality products. Union workers doubtless saw Brown as a voluble, stubborn crank, but he could hardly hold a candle to Stanley Hurlbut.[48]

The FHMA's strategy was not working; this much was clear by June. Strikers were employed at active mills that were double shifting to get out production; only six hundred of them remained unemployed and these were "receiving double strike benefits," funded in part by 10–15 percent assessments on the earnings of those at work. As so often, Robert McWade arrived to attempt mediation, only to be on the receiving end of Hurlbut's fury. Declaring he would accept no third-party activities, Hurlbut asserted, "with emphasis," that

> The strikers are starving. I have beaten them and I'll keep them beaten until they submit to our terms. We have practically won this strike, but your official presence here will hearten these people and keep them out for two or three months longer. In addition you have lied about this situation through the newspapers and have misled the public as well as the strikers.

Appreciating that the ambitious lawyer "was in an ugly frame of mind," McWade managed only to arrange a meeting three days hence at which William Meyer of Apex, the FHMA president, would join in discussing the impasse. However, the June 9 session proved "remarkable for the grave discourtesy exhibited by Hurlbut," who denounced the union leaders as "crooks," rejected McWade's appeals to consider the "moral and material welfare . . . of the Nation," and claimed his group had already won the strike. At this, a nettled McWade scored a point by asking "Then, if you've won, have you and your organization colleagues started all your mills? If you have not begun to do so, when will you do it?" This enraged Hurlbut and relieved the conciliator's frustrations, but he well realized that his services were valueless in the present situation. The FHMA mills stayed shut for eighteen more weeks.[49]

The settlement was clumsy, but represented a compromise with a slight overall advantage to the workers. This in the 1921 context was tantamount to a victory, given the wrecked unions and wage rollbacks that dotted the textile landscape that year. It appears that separate trial solutions were worked out at Fidelity and Brentmore in late September, then generalized to all but

---

[48] McWade to Davis, June 15, 1921, FMCS File 170/1454; *UHR* 4(May 1921): 39, 77, 83; (July 1921): 40; *AWCR* 35(1921): 1548; *PL*, June 23, 1921, p. 17.
[49] McWade to Davis, June 15, 1921, FMCS File 120/1454; see also *UHR* 5(August 1921): 97.

three of the FHMA firms by November 1. These three, Thomas Brown, Henry Brown, and Glen, refused to enter into any agreement and sought to hire staff from Reading and other centers. The terms that labor had defended all along remained secure: the reduction was abandoned and two machine jobs would be permitted only when "all competent knitters in the trade are employed." The manufacturers' gains were more ambiguous. They could retain such strikebreakers as they had been able to hire, but all strikers were to be taken back either immediately or as vacancies arose. No crafts-man's stint or "limit on production" would any longer be accepted, though policing this was virtually an insoluble matter. More important, the firms established that hereafter their factories would be operated on an "open shop basis." Union leaders said this was meaningless "as the mills have always enjoyed the open shop," but something more was afoot. In the coming years, Apex and Aberle would become harsh territory for union members, as discriminatory firings, labor spies, and yellow dog contracts were intro-duced to increase the operators' control of the workplace, even as rates and overall earnings stayed high.

In a sense, the biggest loser was the militant Hurlbut, for his centralizing efforts fell short both in the PTMA and the FHMA during 1921. In reaching the settlement, his full-fashioned association had both to deal with unions and accept the assistance of mediators, its unity fragmenting before that of the unions did. After a fiery year in office, Hurlbut was replaced as the PTMA's president by the older and more circumspect Charles Webb in October 1921, surely a blow to his pride and very likely an evaluation of his performance. On the labor side, the two knitters' unions, having survived a ten-month shutdown without damage, entered into a merger in the winter of 1921–2, forming a single national organization for all full-fashioned work-ers. Led by Gustave Geiges, whose Local 706 became Branch No. 1 and the heart of the new UTW-affiliated union, the knitters were building their strength in an expanding trade. This happy prospect was shared by no other area textile labor organization.[50]

Over the next several years, Frank McKosky ritually announced revivals of interest in Philadelphia textile unionism at the UTW annual conventions, but nothing developed. McKosky resigned his office in May 1923. Mean-while, it was the American Federation of Full-Fashioned Hosiery Workers

---

[50] *Hosiery Worker*, September 20, October 3, November 28, 1921, May 3, 1922; *UHR* 4(December 1921): 66. See *PL*, October 10, 1922, p. 17 for Webb's reelection. The hosiery trade journal reported after the settlement that the unionists "were not working with the [former] strikebreakers smoothly and have been in many cases making it pretty disagreeable for them" (*UHR* 4[December 1921]: 38). This suggests just the sort of shop-floor harassment that might be expected after this long conflict, aimed at driving out scabs and creating vacancies for comrades.

who sent one-thousand-dollar donations to support New England textile workers during the great 1922 cotton strike.[51] Philadelphia labor's differential capacities to respond in the 1921 squeeze previewed the sectoral differentiation of the regional textile industry's course in the 1920s. Carpets, spinning, and woolen/worsted mills were drubbed; seamless hosiery and underwear firms slipped steadily. In the fall of 1923, for example, Notaseme, which had run two shifts and employed a thousand workers during the 1921 full-fashioned shortage, "discontinued" and sold its machinery to a merged seamless group, which in turn went bankrupt in six months.[52] In contrast, dyers, having displaced the union, held their own, being sustained as services demanded by the fast-growing full-fashioned mills offset the decline of former clients in other sectors. Upholstery, lace, and fancy weaving were solid as well, occupying niches that enabled them to defend older practices until late in the decade. When in October 1921 Local 25 and the upholstery operators at last worked out rate reductions, not only was the cut the smallest successfully implemented (9 percent), but it was also achieved in exchange for installing time-and-a-half rates for overtime and a 15 percent night work bonus that immediately affected earnings in "at least three mills" that had been "busy day and night for the past nine months." Here, as in full-fashioned, both mills and workers enjoyed prosperous years through much of the 1920s, as runaway demand or locally concentrated production of specialties permitted firm operators to contend successfully with hand-to-mouth purchasing, using profits to manage the transition to stock carrying or devising other more or less adequate reactive tactics.[53]

There were few strikes in Philadelphia textiles during the next seven years. In the older, troubled sectors a brief recovery (1922–3) did not last. As difficult seasons succeeded one another, resistance to proprietors' survival strategies was feeble. Under- and unemployment were ever more prevalent and persistent, the busy periods more frantic and the slack ones more dispiriting than anyone remembered. In the more prosperous sectors, sufficient work was available to keep resentments banked among dyers, whereas in upholstery annual bargaining became sufficiently routinized that 2,100 workers attended a grand 1927 banquet that their union sponsored to honor the mill owners and celebrate fourteen years of industrial peace. The hosiery union, for its part, worked to demonstrate its capacity to act responsibly and discipline its members, undertaking to eliminate the old pattern of spon-

---

[51] *Textile Worker* 9(1921–2): 278, 601–3; 10(1922–3): 339, 728; 11(1923–4): 83 (hereafter *TWkr*). This UTW monthly commenced new volumes each year in April.

[52] *PL*, September 23, 1923, p. 12; *UHR* 6 (November 1923): 94; 7(April 1924): 95; *AWCR* 35(1921): 1548.

[53] *CUTR* 52(October 1, 1921): 62.

taneous shop strikes over grievances and successfully establishing a standard set of local shop rules monitored by federation officers.[54]

In 1922 the full-fashioned and fancy weaving trades entered a period of renewed expansion in Philadelphia, whereas other sectors recovered toward previous levels of production. Manayunk's Shepperd noted in July that wool/ worsted firms were running about half speed, an improvement, but yarns were high and mills were having problems getting buyers' prices to match sellers' costs. In carpets, with the bottom having been reached and wages cut, area mills swung into motion as the year advanced and housing construction started its 1920s boom. Fears of an upward revision of the tariff on wool spurred demand in wool/worsteds and by fall both sectors had reached a healthy 80 percent capacity use. Despite quiet mutterings about low margins and the proliferation of piecemeal, express delivery orders, members of the PTMA seemed to have cause for celebration when they gathered for their autumn 1922 annual meeting. Charles Webb, association president, had led a highly successful membership drive that swelled representation from 78 to 215 firms, which together accounted for over a third of regional textile employment (Table 6.4). In addition, Webb had replaced fifteen of Hurlbut's original twenty-four executive committee members, retaining only one of the 1920 officers. Combative and ambitious plans for starting the PTMA's own worker training institute had been shelved; anti-Red rhetoric was dropped, but Hurlbut's employment bureau, intended to collate information on loyal workers and troublemakers, was continued. Comparatively, Philadelphia mills had been growing more active and trying out new styles while many New England staple cotton corporations had been idle for six months and longer due to effective and exhausting UTW resistance to a January 1922 20 percent wage reduction. With debate about the growing crisis in Massachusetts gathering steam, Philadelphia's difficulties seemed by contrast somehow less urgent.[55]

In appreciation of his "leadership and service," the PTMA membership presented Webb an engrossed resolution signed by representatives of each constituent mill, then settled back to enjoy a congenial talk by the general counsel of the National Association of Manufacturers. As he reliably stressed the value of plant level partnerships between capital and labor as an alternative to trade unionism, an atmosphere of mutual congratulation filled the

[54] *American Carpet and Upholstery Journal* 45(December 1927): 57 (hereafter *ACUJ*); Palmer, *Union Tactics*, pp. 82–3, 86, 106.

[55] *AWCR* 36(1922): 319–20, 726, 778, 967, 1943; *PL*, January 20, 1922, p. 1, February 7, p. 17, February 17, p. 22; September 8, p. 17; October 10, p. 17; October 20, p. 21; November 20, p. 17; *UHR* 5 (April 1922): 72; *CUTR* 52(March 1, 1921): 63; (April 15, 1921): 73; Tamara Hareven and Ralph Langenbach, *Amoskeag*, New York, 1977, pp. 296–300.

Manufacturers' Club. Yet the PTMA would sustain substantial losses in the next three years, failures that would vacate one in six of their comfortable chairs. Cumulatively, thirty-five PTMA 1922 member firms closed down by 1925. Some were frail creatures and trivial losses (Akmi Fabric Co., Supreme Thread), but others would leave ominous and significant gaps in the old edifice (John Wood's Pequa Mills, two of the Dobson companies). If the confident full-fashioned cluster kept close tabs on their trade journals, their brows might have knitted at the news that the Berkshire was doubling its capacity and North Carolina's Durham Hosiery Company had installed one hundred new machines, reinvesting its profits from seamless production in order to become the first full-fashioned plant south of Pennsylvania. There were ill tides ahead, despite the busy flush that was such a welcome change from the last two shaky, contentious years.[56]

Preservation of Webb's handsome scroll and linkage of its membership list with data on employment and location for 1922 and 1925 and with the full roster of Philadelphia regional textile firms for 1925 allows a rough analysis of the association group in the context of the larger industrial structure (Tables 6.4–6.6). (Unfortunately, no later membership counts or any general PTMA records have survived.) The first point to be drawn from Table 6.4 is that Hurlbut's early and Webb's more general recruitment had built the association into the most broadly representative organization of regional textile manufacturers yet achieved. In the two years from the formation of the executive committee core, its share of overall area employment had jumped from about one-twelfth to at least one-third. All sectors showed a significant presence except the scattered cordage twisters, asbestos weavers, waste reprocessors, and the like (grouped under Miscellaneous). Spatially, though Kensington and the other once-suburban nineteenth-century districts were well represented, both the central city areas and the twentieth-century suburban counties were but marginally active. The old downtown and the adjacent Northern Liberties were becoming homes for substantial numbers of small knitted outerwear firms, often run by "Russian" Jewish immigrants busily scrambling after orders in a relatively new trade. Their absence was most likely due more to the chaos of business than to any overt or latent anti-Semitism among the PTMA group, for fifteen or more clearly Jewish-surnamed proprietors signed the Webb resolution (Simon Berkowitz, Sol Dryfoos, Max Goldberger, et al.). More important was the thin participation among firms from the adjacent counties. Of 145 textile mills located

[56] "Resolution presented to Charles Webb," in possession of Charles Webb III, Chestnut Hill, Philadelphia; *PL*, October 10, 1922, p. 17; *OATD: 1925*; Pennsylvania Department of Internal Affairs, *Fifth Industrial Directory of the Commonwealth of Pennsylvania: 1925*, Harrisburg, 1926; *AWCR* 36(1922): 1267; *UHR* 5(April 1922): 72.

Table 6.4. *Member firms, Philadelphia Textile Manufacturers' Association, employment by sector and district, 1922*

	Sectors				Districts	
	N_f	N_l	Empl.		N_l	Empl.
Woven goods[a]	56	47	8,829	Kensington	94	12,591
Fancy wovens[b]	31	29	4,635	Manayunk	17	4,812
Carpets	20	18	3,958	Germantown	12	859
Hose-knit	46	40	5,954	Frankford	24	2,530
Dye-finish	26	25	1,857	North Central	19	3,066
Spinning	21	18	3,629	S. & W. Phila.	8	2,518
Miscellaneous	8	6	297	N. Liberties	1	19
Totals	208	183	29,159	Old City	4	557
No sector link	7			Suburbs	4	2,207
	215				183	29,159
				Regional empl. total[c]		87,500
				PTMA share		33%

Note: N_f = number of firms; N_l = number linked to location and employment.
[a]Weaving of wool, worsted, silk, and mixed-fiber suitings and dress goods, blankets, etc.
[b]Weaving of plushes, upholstery, lace, tapestries, damask, curtains, predominantly of cotton, silk, and rayon.
[c]For city of Philadelphia, from Biennial Census of Manufactures: 1923 – 68,923, plus a 1923 estimate for four suburban counties, ca. 18,500 (1925 actual: 21,224).
Sources: Webb Resolution, 1922; *Fourth Industrial Directory of the Commonwealth of Pennsylvania,* Harrisburg, 1922; *OATD: 1922.*

there, only 4 had joined the association, and one of these was Webb's own Kent Manufacturing Company. As the suburban proportion of regional textile employment would rise from a fifth to a third, 1916–34, this deficiency would assume an increasing significance. Third, the mean firm size among PTMA members remained well above the regional average (159 vs. 120 in 1922);[57] scores of small firms that had so often served to break efforts at a common front remained disproportionately outside the fold.

As suggested above, in three years the 1922 cohort was winnowed sharply. Following the survivors (Table 6.5) opens another vista on the cross-currents affecting the Philadelphia textile trades during the 1920s. The difficulties that beset the traditional woven goods division (wool/worsted suitings and dress goods, etc.) are readily apparent as fourteen member firms in this

[57] Philip Scranton, "Beyond Anecdotes," pp. 298–9.

Table 6.5. *1925 survivors, PTMA 1922 cohort, employment by sector and district, with shares of 1925 total regional employment*

	Sectors (City only)[a]				(Five-county region)			
	N_i^b	PTMA empl.	Total empl.	PTMA share (%)	N_i^b	PTMA empl.	Total empl.	PTMA share (%)
Woven goods	35	6,298	13,017	48	36	7,062	16,130	44
Fancy wovens	31	6,499	11,405	57	31	6,499	15,348	42
Carpets	18	4,212	9,143	46	19	4,265	9,554	45
Hose-knit	34	6,485	20,392	32	35	6,791	24,156	28
Dye-finish	22	1,773	3,511	50	22	1,773	4,380	40
Spinning	19	2,468	9,510	26	20	3,681	17,673	21
Miscellaneous	2	267	4,598	6	2	267	5,559	5
Totals	161	28,002	71,576	39	165	30,338	92,800	33
Not linked	15							
Total	176							

Table 6.5. (*continued*)

Districts	N_l[b]	PTMA empl.	Total empl.	PTMA share (%)	DSPE[c] (%)	DSTE[d] (%)
Kensington	88	14,776	34,763	43	49	37
Manayunk	18	4,324	7,292	59	14	8
Germantown	10	798	7,533	11	3	8
Frankford	18	1,917	6,522	29	6	7
North Central	18	3,184	5,100	62	10	6
S. & W. Phila.	6	2,808	5,211	54	9	6
N. Liberties	0	0	2,282	0	0	2
Old City	3	195	2,873	7	1	3
Suburbs	4	2,336	21,224	11	8	23
Totals	165	30,338	92,800	33	100	100

[a]All four 1922 suburban member firms persisted, one each in carpets, wovens, spinning, and knitting. Excluded here to allow focus on city distributions.

[b]N_l = number of member firms linked to industrial directories.

[c]DSPE = District Share of PTMA Employment (1925).

[d]DSTE = District Share of Total Employment (1925).

Sources: Webb, *Fifth ID of Pa.*, 1925; *OATD: 1925*.

Table 6.6. *PTMA knitting subsectors, 1922 and 1925; out-of-business PTMA firms, 1922–5, by sector and employment*

I. *Knitting*

	1922		1925		
	N_l	Empl.	N_l	Empl.	Empl. Change (%)
Seamless hose and knit goods	24	2,842	19	2,273	−20
Full-fashioned	16	3,112	16	4,518	+45
Total	40	5,954	35	6,871	+17

II. *Out of business by 1925, 1922 PTMA Cohort*

	N_f	N_l	1922 Empl.
Wovens	14	8	1,284
Fancy wovens	0	0	—
Carpets	1	0	—
Hose-knit	9	5	219
Dye-finish	4	2	11
Spinning	1	0	—
Miscellaneous	6	4	101
Totals	35	19	1,615

Note: N_f = number of firms; N_l = number linked to employment data.
Sources: Same as for Tables 6.4 and 6.5.

sector closed shop between 1922 and 1925 (Table 6.6., II) and mean employment for the rest slipped about 5 percent. Meanwhile none of the fancywork companies had fallen and their total employment had risen 40 percent, though half the gains were the product of Collins and Aikman's connection with auto upholstery users. PTMA carpet firms were in 1925 still enjoying the rebound from the depression; they would tumble shortly when the construction surge flagged. Little damage was evident among dyers and spinners, for they were in a sense insulated from the withering market pressures that final-product mills had to confront. Both sectors had a potentially vast range of clients and each had squashed labor organizations, giving them a short-range cushion. In knits, a disaggregation that separates full-fashioned firms from the rest of the trade shows anew the vitalizing currents that the silk hosiery craze set in motion (Table 6.6, I). While seamless hose and knit specialties producers among the 1922 PTMA membership experienced contractions in employment and the loss of nine firms, the full-fashioned group remained intact as demand-induced expansion increased available positions by nearly one-half. Overall, there were positive elements in the PTMA's course between 1922 and 1925. Surviving firms still held a third of all regional jobs, and according to one trade source, nearly a hundred new members in 1923 and 1924 more than filled the places of the lost firms. Yet it is clear that the distinctly different situations faced by the association's sectoral components predictably reduced the ground for common action. In 1924, the general meeting was devoted to considering ways to combat the "evils of unfair legislative proposals" brought forth by the Pinchot administration in Harrisburg. On the larger questions of the textile industry's future course, and the role of specialized, flexible firms within it, the association was utterly silent.[58]

The year 1925 stands as the apex of the Philadelphia textile manufacture, as some 92,800 workers were engaged among 1,054 firms in the five-county area, over 71,000 of them at nearly 900 companies within the city limits. In the nine years after 1916, full-fashioned hosiery work had quadrupled (from 2,545 jobs to 10,219), fine-woven employment had risen 50 percent, and American Viscose's burgeoning rayon fiber output (at nearby Marcus Hook) had helped spur a similar burst in spinning. Yet as the distributional squeeze persisted, as a once-hardy format for accumulation shriveled in an environment of risk-laden busyness, the stagnation and decay in carpets and wool/worsteds would quietly spread across the spectrum of Philadelphia textile expertise. Underneath the 1925 summit, the foundations were being or had already been nibbled away.

6.3. National shifts and regional strategies in the 1920s

At the national level, legislative, executive, and judicial actions helped structure the context for Philadelphia's decay as a new tariff statute was enacted, the Commerce Department advocated efficiency and simplification, and the Federal Trade Commission and the courts undercut a promising technique for defending prices. The Fordney-McCumber tariff of 1922 was a triumph for wool growers but a time bomb for their manufacturing allies. Levies on imported raw wools were raised near the 1909 levels, assuring domestic herders an above-world-market price for their fleeces, with compensating added duties on imported woolens to limit foreign penetration. As the price of raw wool rebounded from the 1920–1 lows toward wartime figures, manufacturers' weakened market power obstructed their capacity to hike fabric prices to offset these costs. In addition, substitutions for wool, especially in women's wear, proliferated, with increased demand for combed cottons, silks, rayons, and blends, a trend favored by the secular spread of central heating and closed cars and by the moderate and declining costs of these

[58] *PL*, May 16, 1924, p. 19.

raw materials. Philadelphia wool fabric makers seemed never fully to have comprehended these movements, and ritually blamed the modest flow of imports for all their troubles, appealing for yet more protection from "pauperized" European labor.

The tariff debates of 1921–2 were placid compared to their 1913 counterparts, as a Republican electoral triumph was reinforced both by a war-inspired determination to secure national self-sufficiency and an urge to prove Democratic complicity in establishing high rates on agricultural goods in the 1921 "emergency" tariff on behalf of their deflation-beleaguered rural supporters. The result was a statute "with rates higher than any in the long series of protective measures in the whole period" since the 1860s. Textile interests saw to it that wool and wool-goods duties returned to roughly their 1909 levels, though *ad valorem* rates on the finest goods were set at 50 percent, five points below the Taft-era percentage. When total 1923 textile imports jumped 20 percent over 1922 takings, manufacturers argued that the rates were inadequate, ignoring the general economic revival and the internal difficulties of the industry. With no changes in the schedules, imports leveled off, suggesting as Taussig had stated, that even specialty textiles "had ample protection" and that the source of dismaying circumstances lay elsewhere.[59]

However, the Fordney statute, by installing heavy duties on imported dyes (and other chemicals), both assisted the solidification of a tenuous "war baby" section of the chemical trades and made permanent the rise in dyestuffs costs. In the controversy, the job dyers and fabric manufacturers proved no match for the DuPont Company and the Chemical Foundation in an environment of continued anti-German sentiment. The waning political influence of the textile industry was also suggested by its inability to induce the Tariff Commission to exercise its authority and alter rates without further legislative action. Though a few voices spoke to the larger need for European states to sell goods here as a part of their effort to accumulate revenues that could retire war debts, Herman Blum, of Kensington's Craftex Mills, brushed this aside, asserting that "European workers don't spend their wages in America."[60] The millmen's unswerving commitment to protectionism was one point on which near-total solidarity was maintained across the decades,

---

[59] F. W. Taussig, *The Tariff History of the United States*, Seventh Edition, New York, 1923, pp. 451–66; U.S. Tariff Commission, *Textile Imports and Exports, 1891–1927*, Washington, D.C., 1929, pp. 302–22; idem, *The Cotton Cloth Industry*, Washington, D.C., 1924.

[60] John Hicks, *Republican Ascendancy, 1921–1933*, New York, 1960, pp. 58–9; George Soule, *Prosperity Decade, From War to Depression: 1917–1929*, New York, 1947, p. 131; *PL*, July 7, 1922, p. 17; *Textile Colorist* 43(1921): 309, 381–2; 44(1922): 643, 710; *The Manufacturer* 10(June 1928): 18–20.

but obsessive attention to this issue hindered their achieving a clearer vision of the implications of their growing dependence in specialty markets. While the exclusion of all imported goods would surely have sent tens of millions in additional sales their way, there is no reason to assume that buyers' terms and prices for handling these goods would have been any more rewarding for the mills, or that the risks of stock carrying, etc., would have been reduced.

A second federal policy thrust that affected Philadelphia textiles was the campaign for "the elimination of industrial waste by simplification" carried out by Herbert Hoover's Department of Commerce. Building on the War Industries Board's emergency efforts to streamline products and enhance efficiency in the use of manpower, machinery, and materials, Hoover created a Division of Simplified Practice within the National Bureau of Standards and charged it to deal with the "fact" that the nation was "suffering from too great variety in almost every article of commerce." A classic example of Hoover's associationist beliefs, the simplification project brought together voluntary groups of manufacturers (often based on trade organizations) to agree to eliminate from their lines such types and varieties of products as could be shown through statistical and engineering studies to be impeding smoother and more profitable operations. Chicago's A. W. Shaw, publisher of the influential trade journals *Factory* and *System* and former head of the WIB's Conservation Division, relentlessly publicized the benefits of narrowed product lines in his magazines, printing dozens of how-to-do-it articles and testimonials from luminaries like Harvey Firestone. Simplification was not simply standardization by a different name. Even in the absence of a more general trade agreement, individual firms could reduce waste and expense by declining to make just anything that a customer appeared to want, drawing his business instead by "convincing him that his service needs fall under certain well-defined headings." In this sense, simplification was a state-sponsored effort to provide ideological armor for a peacetime drive to eradicate "unnecessary diversity," relabeling what had earlier been the proud hallmark of flexible, skill-intensive manufacturing as an obstacle to progress and efficiency.[61]

---

[61] Department of Commerce, *Simplified Practice: What It Is and What It Offers*, Washington, D.C., 1924, pp. 1–2; Ernest L. Priest, *A Primer of Simplified Practice*, Washington, D.C., 1926; *Factory* 26(1921): 4513, 715–18, 952–3; 1175–7. The Firestone article may be found in *Factory* 27(1921): 739–43 (note that this journal published two volume numbers yearly). Educating the consumer was urged in Richard Landsburgh, *Industrial Management*, New York, 1923, pp. 171–2. Landsburgh, a Wharton School professor at the University of Pennsylvania, relied heavily on articles from *System* in his discussion of simplification, and on publications from the manufacturing department of the U.S. Chamber of Commerce. Its head, E. W. McCullough, served with Shaw and a Philadelphia consulting engineer (A. A. Stevenson) on the "planning committee" Hoover

The antiwaste and simplification hoopla hardly escaped the attention of textile interests. Efforts were undertaken to reduce the number of hosiery sizes and the varieties of boxes used in shipping, or to define simply a few basic types of staple cloths (i.e., cotton duck). The UTW monthly duly reported Hoover's public pronouncements, and the Manufacturers' Club journal published a glowing article on the movement. In this piece, Emmett Chapman characterized simplified practice as a business policy designed "to dispense with as many parts, as many types and varieties of products, as many price ranges, as many processes and methods as profitably can be eliminated," thus carrying on operations "with the minimum degree of elaborateness." Yet in specialty textiles it failed completely. Manufacturers well knew that narrowing style ranges could help them solve the stock-holding problem; one knitter estimated that reducing his product varieties from over a hundred to twenty would mean being able to run with an inventory of $25,000 in finished goods rather than $100,000–$150,000. However, buyers continued to demand wide style selections and they held the power over the mills. Indeed, trade observers throughout the 1920s would claim that never before had there been such marked differentiation of styles in hose, furnishing fabrics, and cloths for the apparel trade. Even the UTW called for constant alteration of "patterns... styles and constructions" so as to "force those... who are now choking the industry to supply the material the public will demand" and thus boost factory employment. By 1926, *Textile World* reported that the simplification drive had lapsed in the production end of the industry. Meanwhile, retailers had narrowed their "price ranges" as Chapman had suggested, to the point where "one-price" clothing shops were all the rage and department stores sold men's suits in three price lines, while offering hosiery (other than full-fashioned) at similar firm, gapped levels. In consequence, mills found it essential to find a way of "adapting [their] constructions to the new price ranges." Simplification applied to retailing meant further pressure on flexible manufacturers, who faced this trend as individuals.[62]

---

appointed to guide the effort. See also Soule, *Prosperity Decade*, p. 141; Ellis Hawley, "Herbert Hoover and Economic Stabilization, 1921–22," in idem, ed., *Herbert Hoover as Secretary of Commerce*, Iowa City, IA, 1981, pp. 46–51; and Robert Zieger, "The Wage Earner and the New Economic System, 1919–1929," in ibid., pp. 88–91.

[62] *UHR* 6(April 1923): 63, (September 1923): 111; *The Manufacturer* 6(January 1924): 7–8; *Factory* 31(1923): 445–7. On expanded style diversity see *UHR* 5(March 1922): 41, 7(December 1924): 68; *ACUJ* 41(September 1923): 52; *TW* 69(1926): 52; *TW* 69(1926): 181–2, 187, 277, and *PL*, April 7, 1924, p. 17. The union plea is in *TWkr* 12(April 1924): 13. For the failure of simplification, see *TW* 69(1926): 4241. On price lining, see *AWCR* 42(1928): 3748; *UHR* 6(February 1923): 87–8, 7(May 1924): 65 and *TW* 73(1928): 149.

Quasi-judicial rulings by the Federal Trade Commission, soon clarified by the Supreme Court, bludgeoned one potential means for these competing operations to stand collectively against buyers' encroachments. As Arthur Burns explained, in the postwar years diverse trade associations attempted to maintain market power through interlocking efforts to standardize cost accounting at the firm level, create common terms of and contracts for selling, and report throughout their membership the prices adopted by firms for each of their products. On the first count, manufacturers using traditional cost-finding methods might readily accept ruinous price offers because "they do not know their own costs," and such prices could quickly become the standard buyers demanded that other firms meet. This was especially the case for sectors in which "small producers" were prevalent, as one study indicated that in cottons, as late as 1926, only a quarter of all mills "used correct cost practices." Common terms and contracts, when established, could limit the depredations wrought by special deals and arrangements, and "open price" reporting might well deflect price competition and restore emphasis on quality, style, and service. However, these efforts could only be genuinely effective when they were ratified and administered by associations with a membership constituting a decisive majority of producers willing to press or punish backsliders in order to achieve uniform action. Such measures, insofar as they restrained interstate trade and competition, violated the Sherman Act, as the FTC ruled in its investigation of furniture manufacturers in 1921–2.[63]

The possibility of regulating competitive sectors by rule or persuasion was never as great in diversified product trades as it may have been in more staple lines (hosiery vs. maple flooring, for instance). Yet activity and interest in "open price" defenses against buyers' growing advantages was another straw briefly grasped by spinners, knitters, and others in the early 1920s. Far better focused on their slipping hold on the means to accumulation than were their tariff plaints, efforts to create a basis for a manufacturers' counteroffensive in the marketplace confronted insuperable structural and legal obstacles. The disintegrated character of most specialty textile production, the presence of contradictory spatially and sectorally organized associations, the unwillingness of firms to reach beyond crisis solidarities or to fund

---

[63] Arthur Burns, *The Decline of Competition: A Study of the Evolution of American Industry*, New York, 1936, pp. 48, 52–5, 60–3. Burns noted that of 139 associations operating on an open-price basis in 1921, only 33 continued some version of this activity by 1927. The key Supreme Court ruling was *Maple Flooring Manufacturers Association v. U.S.*, 268 U.S. 563 (1925). The furniture investigations were reported in Federal Trade Commission, *House Furnishing Industries*, 3 vols., Washington, D.C., 1923–5. For a detailed overview, see A. D. Neale, *The Anti-Trust Laws of the U.S.A.*, Cambridge, UK, 1960, pp. 40–5.

researchers and "efficiency men," all combined to render these attempts impotent. Indeed, Samuel Vauclain, head of the Baldwin Locomotive Works, "ridiculed the so-called 'efficiency experts' " in addressing one PTMA annual meeting and Simon Miller at another deplored the end of an era when master and man "stood shoulder to shoulder and established relationship[s] almost fraternal in character." With Vauclain deriding the new managerial rationality and Miller urging his colleagues to "cultivate personal contact with their workers," there was a cultural gap evident in Philadelphia textiles that further frustrated advocates of dispassionate costing and trade unity. Thus when the knitters' national trade body launched a 1923 drive to lobby for legalization of "resale price maintenance" as a way around the FTC rulings, it drew hardly a ripple of local support, despite the recognized "inability of a manufacturer to protect the price of his product" and the consequent "confusion which exists in many lines of business."[64]

In all, state actions highlighted the growing distance between administrators' and legislators' perceptions and appraisals of the manufacturing economy and those of regional textile proprietors. The former had digested the language of efficiency and mass production and assumed its universal relevance, whereas the latter clung to traditional shibboleths that composed something like a *mentalité* of proprietary business that was increasingly remote from the conceptual terrain of mainstream political economy. Preserving the family firm as a legacy, idealizing the tariff as the industry's Maginot Line, dismissing managerialism and close costing, mourning the decay of "almost fraternal" relations with workers, such behavior flowed from a mindset that sharply contrasted with the dominant Fordist/Hooverist trends of the era. Commitment to independence in all things essential blocked creation of any collective, regional response to the 1920s squeeze.

To set the diversity of Philadelphia reactions in the context of more general textile traumas, it will be useful briefly to scan the industry's wider landscape in the 1920s. The New England staple disaster is familiar enough, and Fall

---

[64] *AWCR* 36(1922): 27; *UHR* 5(January 1922): 50, (March 1922): 80; 6 (June 1923): 62; *PL*, April 14, 1922, p. 1; October 19, 1923, p. 19; *CUTR* 51(October 15, 1920): 58c. Even appeals to establish cost accounting at the individual firm level continued to have a rocky reception in Philadelphia late into the 1920. John Fisler, head of the yarn spinners' association, first cajoled his colleagues then threatened to resign unless they would abandon their privatism and help Wharton School researchers seeking to document spinning costs (*The Manufacturer* 10[June 1928]: 27–30). This study appeared as A. H. Williams et al., *An Analysis of the Production of Worsted Sales Yarn*, Philadelphia, 1929. Meanwhile, the Cotton Textile Institute had by 1932 assisted raising the proportion of mills using modern costing procedures to above three-fifths of the total (Burns, *Decline*, p. 48n.). For the CTI's activities, chiefly among staple mills, see Louis Galambos, *Competition and Cooperation: The Emergence of a National Trade Association*, Baltimore, 1966.

River's fate has long exemplified its wider course. Expansion in Fall River had to all intents ended before World War I, and modification of outputs to contend with southern advantages in coarse and medium-grade cottons had been slow. Textile corporations paid out war profits through heavy cash dividends (18, 15, and 29 percent on capitalization, 1918–20), but cutbacks during the inventory depression were quickly overcome by revived sales at lower margins, 1921–3. Profits reaped in part from a short-term rise in the price of cotton (which nearly doubled to about 30 cents per pound by 1923, before breaking downward again), permitted treasurers to reap gains on warehoused raw stock, and to pay dividends in cash of about 8 percent annually, plus stock bonuses totaling some $10 million. The bubble burst late in 1923. Sharp declines in staple goods prices evaporated profits, exposing weaknesses that had been latent for at least a decade. Within a year, dividends were suspended, mill employment dropped one-third (to 20,000), and the cycle of liquidation commenced. By 1932, half the city's cotton capacity had eroded; of its 101 factories (controlled by about 40 corporations), 27 were abandoned in 1929–30 alone. The 24 failed staple cloth corporations had in 1924 operated over 57,000 looms of which only 19 percent were automatic Northrops of any vintage. This technological lag had undercut productivity, for the bobbin-changing Northrops had set the standard for southern installations since the turn of their century. Similar stagnation was evident in equipment at New Bedford, despite its early attention to running fine grades of cotton goods. In 1928, an age analysis of machinery showed that 65 percent of looms, 76 percent of ring and 93 percent of mule spindles had been in place since before World War I. The New Bedford break came in 1928, when employment fell by almost half due to an extended strike against reductions, recovering only briefly before sliding steadily after 1929 through the Depression decade.[65]

In both cases, interlocked and unimaginative clans of treasurers and managers drew much of the blame for failing to adjust their rigid production systems to changing environments. Internal practices were often primitive. One study of several New Bedford corporations showed them to have taken no account of depreciation in figuring dividend payouts and selling prices. However, an element of flexibility that distinguished New Bedford from "the rest of the northern cotton textile manufacturing industry" was its "increased

---

[65] Thomas R. Smith, *The Cotton Textile Industry of Fall River, Massachusetts*, New York, 1944, pp. 122–4, 130; Seymour Wolfbein, *The Decline of a Cotton Textile City: A Study of New Bedford*, New York, 1944, pp. 156, 165–7. In a recent dissertation, William Mass traces Fall River's disdain for the automatic loom in part to attempts to widen the range of fabric constructions offered. For a summary of his work, "Technological Choice and Industrial Relations," Boston College, see *Journal of Economic History* 45(1985): 458–60 with a comment by Joel Mokyr at 473–4.

use of silk and rayon in combination with cotton goods," a tactic facilitated by the city's "skilled labor supply." This shift sustained its fine-goods mills through the later 1920s, but output of damasks, plushes, and other blends soon dropped by one-half to two-thirds (ca. 1929–33), ending the activities of a dozen major corporations. By the late 1930s, Fall River textile employment stood at 13,000 and New Bedford had slumped to below 10,000 jobs, whereas each had held over 35,000 positions at the war's end.[66]

At Lawrence, the news was hardly much better, for American Woolen both lost its founder to suicide in 1926 and began recording steady losses and rising inventories by the mid-1920s. Its earlier momentum reversed, the "big company" commenced selling off plants and suspended first common then preferred dividends. Price increases in 1924 and 1925, compelled by rising raw wool costs, were inadequate to offset them and still met resistance from buyers. In an attempt to hold the trade of large clothiers searching for bargains, American offered a 1926 program of bulk discounts and rebates for customers with million-dollar billings. Nothing seemed to work. At the nearby Pacific Mills, the city's preeminent cotton corporation, treasurer E. F. Green, in defending the 1922 20 percent wage reduction, had argued that his mill costs were two cents per yard above the market quotes for staple gray goods and had admitted that even if implemented, the cut would barely take one cent off the losses. Sales during the long 1922 strike relieved inventories at rising prices to be sure, but the cotton mills failed to secure the reduction (which however deep could in no way have solved the problem). Strikers pointed out that Pacific's long-term strategy was very likely tied to its development of southern branch plants, four of which were operating 4,800 looms near Columbia, South Carolina. This sort of capital restructuring within the textile industry, rare at New Bedford and Fall River, was more common elsewhere in New England. Pawtucket's Jenkes Spinning Company had purchased the later-famous Loray Mills at Gastonia, North Carolina, in 1919; similar branch plant and corporate acquisition steps were routinely reported in *Textile World*, though their extent

---

[66] Wolfbein, *New Bedford*, pp. 92–8, 102, 104, 156; Smith, *Fall River*, pp. 126, 132–3; *PL*, August 8, 1923, p. 17; August 7, 1925, p. 17; *TWkr* 12(November 1924): 459–65, a series of reprints from Fall River newspapers under the heading "What's the Matter with the Fall River Mills?" Here management deficiencies were stressed by Joseph Parks of the Massachusetts Industrial Accident board. Organized Fall River textile workers had left the UTWA in 1915 to form an independent union, chiefly of skilled operatives. Rivalry between the two organizations persisted through the 1930s, further weakening labor's position (see John Cumbler, *Working-Class Community in Industrial America*, Westport, CT, 1979, pp. 211–17). New Bedford's textile workers sustained a 25-week strike in 1928 against a 10 percent wage cut, leading to a compromise 5 percent settlement (*TW* 74 [1928]: 1949).

has not been carefully traced. In general, they reflected the attitude expressed by one Massachusetts board of directors that "voted to make no more capital expenditures" in the north. Few went so far as Manchester's Amoskeag, which created a separate holding company to manage the corporate surplus and protect it from accumulating distress in the operating division, but the crisis grew pervasive and resistant to the usual remedies. By 1926, Pacific passed its dividend and Philadelphia's *Public Ledger* estimated that half the textile capital in New England was earning no profits at all.[67]

Specialty districts in New England and the mid-Atlantic regions likewise had no smooth ride through the 1920s. Both Providence and Paterson faced the same buyers' pressure that Philadelphia firms squirmed to evade, and neither had a significant knitting or hosiery trade to buoy up flagging sectors. Though dyeing and finishing remained strong at both sites, their main lines, wool/worsteds and silks respectively, stagnated or decayed. In Providence, 95 percent of the mills reported short-time activities or complete shutdowns early in 1925, after having suffered through the previous year's slump. In Paterson the "cockroach" epidemic proceeded unabated, with scores of immigrant Jewish workers buying looms from collapsing firms to launch minuscule, self-exploitive broad-goods shops in screened-off sections of old mill floors. Following a short prosperity burst in 1918–20, Paterson's prewar miseries had returned. Hand-to-mouth buyers for basic broad silks created a curb market for commission weaving, gathering on the sidewalk outside the Paterson Trust Company to offer weaving contracts for a few pieces at tiny rates. As printed and finishing effects had become the key to cheapening the cost of rapid style changes, jacquards were displaced. Plain goods were now in demand for rapid delivery to the swelling dye/finish/print works and thence to New York cutters-up. In Paterson, manufacturers truly became appendages to the distribution network. Subcontracting relations and a rapid turnover of failed "mushrooms" confirmed the buyers' dominance and the worker-owners' debilitating dependence. In August 1926, seventy-two of these family shops shut down in an attempt to create "a scarcity in the silk market" and advance their rates, but as they represented only 10 percent of weaving firms and employed in toto only about a thousand workers, there was little hope. New York converters gradually established rosters of captive shops and moved rate levels in tandem; by the mid–1930s, the largest New

---

[67] For Wood's obituary, see *TW* 69(1926): 483. A.W.'s financial slide is reviewed in Frederick Zappalla, "A Financial History of the American Woolen Company," unpublished M.B.A. thesis, University of Pennsylvania, 1947. Other AW sources include: *The Manufacturer* 7(March 1925): 35–6; *TW* 69(1926): 2674–5; *PL*, January 23, 1923, p. 19; July 19, 1925, p. 1. For Green's statements and other details, see *AWCR* 36(1922): 319–20, 831, 1534; *TWkr* 10(January 1923): 596, *PL*, January 4, 1923, p. 19; February 13, 1926; p. 19; Hareven, *Amoskeag*, pp. 78, 302–3.

Figure 20. The curb market for silk weaving contracts, Paterson, NJ, 1920.
(Courtesy of the Philadelphia College of Textiles and Science.)

York agency alone controlled 73 of Paterson's 514 family enterprises through production contracts. With the distributors in command, Paterson's glory days were fast fading into memory.[68]

Southern prospects were surely more appealing in the early 1920s, but

[68] *PL*, February 4, 1925, p. 17; *American Silk Journal* 38(December 1919): 55–8; 39(July 1920): 45, 50; 40(July 1921): 73–4; 41(April 1922): 45–6; 42(March 1923): 61–2, (December 1923): 53–4; 59–62, this last the initial installment of a technical series on silk printing; 43(June 1924): 61, (December 1924): 63–4; *ACUJ* 44(August 1926): 56; David Goldberg, "The Battle for Labor Supremacy in Paterson, 1916–22," in Philip

the textile situation had a mix of pluses and minuses. On the positive side, Dixie mills were triumphant in all cotton staples and had steadily progressed along the skills continuum toward finer grades of yarns and fabrics. Moreover, the UTW's southern organizing campaign and been minimally successful and the region's knitting firms now dominated production of underwear and seamless cotton hosiery. Not only did southern firms supply the market for the cheaper grades of socks (retailing for 25 cents), but underwear mills were by 1924 installing sharp price cuts in order to run full while northern firms scrambled to hold their old clients. However, the staple crisis hardly bypassed the South. As Gavin Wright notes, "southern firms also went under during these years, many of them falling into the hands of northern creditors in the process." Though employment in cottons rose nearly 50 percent during the 1920s, jobs were more irregular and actual hours worked slumped under forty per week by 1928. Wright thus attributes the heavy labor turnover experienced by southern mills not to "the persistence of rural folkways" but to the fact that operatives "could not find steady work." Adding to the cotton sector's problems was the failure of wage rates to return to levels comparable to pay for agricultural labor (the prewar pattern), displaying a "stickiness" that was, in Wright's view, a consequence of the industry's "maturity" and the accumulation of ranks of experienced workers whose earnings could not be drastically cut without provoking a "labor revolt." These relations need further clarification, which more exacting research may yet provide, but it is evident that a persistent focus on low-value products in an environment of tariff-induced export blockage laid the foundations for future troubles in a regional industry "that never had a golden age."[69]

Yet with the accumulation of skills that two generations of textile production had generated came an opportunity for extension of investment into the provinces of specialty manufacture. While it was hardly sufficient to revitalize the regional industry, the doubling of southern knitting work during the 1920s (from 28,300 to 53,500 jobs) and the initiation of full-fashioned hosiery production posed a long-term threat to Philadelphia's most dynamic sector. In North Carolina, the sustained growth of furniture manufacturing, which neared 15,000 jobs in 1927, up 10 percent in two years, provided a demand node for a scattered set of upholstery ventures, making cheap knock-offs of Philadelphia patterns for the low-end furniture trade. Specialty dyeing

Scranton, ed., *Silk City*, Newark, NJ, 1985, p. 123; Philip McLewin, "Labor Conflict and Technological Change: The Family Shop in Paterson, New Jersey," in ibid., pp. 138–147; *TWkr* 9(November 1921): 369.
[69] *TWkr* 9(October 1921): 325; *UHR* 5(April 1922): 71, (October 1922): 105; 7(August 1924): 68; *PL*, August 31, 1922, p. 17; Gavin Wright, *Old South, New South: Revolutions in the Southern Economy since the Civil War*, New York, 1986, pp. 147–55.

services, notably the technologically progressive Franklin Process Company of Rhode Island, began to locate branches in the textile belt; and in 1928, Royal Little, formerly partner in a Philadelphia dyeworks, planted a comprehensive million-dollar cotton and rayon dyeing facility at Mt. Holly, North Carolina. Nearby Charlotte was gradually transformed into a regional center for specialty and fine-goods production, especially fancy knits and silks, a development local leaders regarded as insurance against the migration of staple sectors "from their midst to more remote sections." Massive rayon production plants were built in southern locations by domestic and foreign investors. Characteristically in 1924, American Viscose abandoned a plan to erect a second Philadelphia area complex for which land had been purchased at Holmesburg in the northeast quarter of the city. Future construction would be concentrated south of the Mason-Dixon Line. As Dixie advocates had expected, the South was creating a more diversified textile industry than ever before. Proceeding up the learning curve, some skilled workers were doubtless able to move laterally from dead-end jobs in staple mills to opportunities in new plants, or were recruited into the full-fashioned forces at mills that were shifting from seamless cotton into booming silks. Yet for Philadelphians, southern "maturity" would help bring to the local full-fashioned and upholstery sectors the general squeeze they had heretofore largely evaded. If the crisis of the 1890s had spurred New England's encroachment on segments of Philadelphia's cotton and woolen specialties, the staple goods crisis of the 1920s propelled a southern restructuring that menaced its remaining vital divisions.[70]

In design, a trend toward simpler forms failed to alleviate buyers' pressure for variation. Indeed, producers eager for orders now brought out new styles continually, further deranging the remains of the sample and duplicate system as both design piracy and cancellations increased. One observer summarized the situation:

> Today, fashion changes have not only moved into every nook and cranny of the industry, but have also increased in frequency ... and

---

[70] Wright, *Old South*, pp. 124–5, 153, 160; *Fourteenth Census, Volume VIII: Manufacturer: 1919*, pp. 408–11; *CUTR* 59(November 15, 1928): 99; *TW* 69(1926): 351; 73(1928): 130; 74(1928): 943; *UHR* 6(July 1923): 131, *PL*, July 21, 1924, p. 13; *ACUJ* 43(March 1925): 67, (June 1925): 50. On the physical relocation of northern machinery to southern sites, see *TW* 75(1929), 733, 809. *Textile World* estimated that in cottons, 1.35 million spindles were sold and relocated to the South (1921–8), 38 percent of the 3.55 million taken out of northern production. In 1928, over 600 knitting machines were shipped southward, but only 15 of these were full-fashioned devices. On the character of southern upholstery manufacturing shifts from staple lines, see Palmer, "Economic Factors," p. 16; Interview with Arthur Capper and John Fox, August 25, 1931, *FR-Uph*, ch. 3, p. 22, PP–135, TMR.

innumerable changes take place not only within a single year but within a single season ... Even such sturdy staples as ginghams and denims have felt the influence of fashion change ... Subtle changes in sheetings, draperies, curtains and upholsteries have made them subject to the same influences.

However, the severe pressure of frequent fashion change, especially in view of the lack of close relationship between the producer and distributor has served to increase instability in the industry.[71]

In the 1920s, ornamental designs popular in prewar days (elaborate florals and multicolor geometrics) were critiqued and replaced by simplified and more subtly toned Art Deco patterns. Monocolor broadloom carpetings were advocated as creating a neutral ground for interior decors; heavy draperies that overwhelmed the smaller spaces common to the new middle-class housing were rejected for openwork translucent curtains. In dress goods, weighty, elaborate woolen or jacquard silk fabrics gave way to sleek cotton, rayon, and silk prints. Yet none of these relative simplifications reduced the demand for wide stylistic variety within the constructions and price lines favored by buyers. Novelty became the cry even for fabrics long considered staples, as traditional trade definitions and boundaries collapsed.[72]

Given the cost and risk of stock holding, one path through this maze (followed in several sectors) combined standardization of semifinished goods with an increased reliance on generating diversity through dyeing, finishing, and printing. This pattern built on the old print cloth system, whereby mills, north and south, sold off-the-loom "gray" goods to "converters" who, attentive to market trends, had designs printed on them in varied color combinations on short notice. During the 1920s this sequence surfaced in upholstery, as heavy printed cottons (cretonnes) gained a vogue at the expense of fabrics whose color and design were dependent on yarn dyeing and fancy weaving. It materialized as well, as noted above, in silks and other women's wear and in hosiery, as full-fashioned *constructions* became relatively standardized (after a rush to diversification, 1922–5), with constantly shifting fashion hues being produced on demand in integrated or jobbing dyeworks. This trend helps account for the resilience of independent dyers generally and the solidity of large-scale dyer/printer operations.

The implications for skill-intensive weaving firms were grim, for producers

---

[71] Wolfbein, *New Bedford*, pp. 24–5.
[72] *FR-Uph*, ch. 1, pp. 2–3, ch. 3, p. 26. Evidence for continuing product flexibility in 1920s Philadelphia may also be drawn from John Shover, "Individual Production Rating: A Study of Measurement of Quantity and Quality of Individual Production Output in Two Textile Operations," printed Ph.D. dissertation, University of Pennsylvania, 1926. Investigating four local mills, Shover found them using yarns of 20–30 different counts and "from ninety to one hundred fifty varieties of yarn" in a season (pp. 33, 39).

of quite ordinary gray goods could through this mechanism limit risk and secure a share of fashion-sensitive markets. Were they to retain ownership of their fabrics through the printing and finishing stage, they might also capture timely profits normally available to fancy-goods makers only through running and holding finished stock. In a buyers' market, the lower prices of printed versus pattern-woven fabrics gradually gave them command of all but the fine and luxury trades, pressing fancy weavers toward the margins. By this means as well the skills of experienced weavers became less salient, less a key to a firm's viability. Like the advent of plain carpets, which had a similar effect on skill needs, this process was uneven in the timing and reach of its impact across sectors; an incremental adjustment to the permanent shift in style market relations, it took shape in the later 1920s and was widespread by the mid-1930s.[73]

The durability of piecemeal buying was of course reinforced by these adjustments. Assertive gestures by manufacturers' associations failed to offset the effects of hand-to-mouth purchasing and disadvantageous trade terms. For example, in a 1924 Philadelphia session, knitted outerwear mills sought to establish "a financial institution" to handle "the production and distribution of merchandise, in order to do away with the frantic dumping of distress stocks every time the retail buyers (smiling behind their hands) begin to cry 'Wolf!' " Nothing came of this, and panicky unloading of expiring styles at seasons' ends continued to hazard profits. As Chittick had warned a decade earlier, a firm selling five lines could have gains from four successful ones wiped out by stock losses on the fifth.[74] A reflective hosiery operator commented in 1926:

> There is nothing for the manufacturer to do but to make up his mind that he is up against a real gamble. If he plays safe and curtails his production, he is . . . going to be unable to give service to his customers and will eventually be out of business. If he piles up inventories in order to give adequate service, thus meeting competition, he is going to be sure to guess wrong at some time or other and take a tremendous loss as regards style fluctuations or costs of materials.[75]

The situation was no better two years hence. R. C. Huettig, head of a Philadelphia full-fashioned mill facing forceful price-cutting pressures, condemned "the retailers who have huddled together in groups and with their organized buying power are making raids on the market, [and] are committing the manufacturers to unequal propositions which are predicated on neither sincerity nor economic laws." Power struggles and not simple mutually ad-

---

[73] FR-Uph, ch. 1, p. 2; Cox, *Marketing of Textiles*, chs. 8–11; *TW* 77(1930): 634–5.
[74] *The Manufacturer* 6(September 1924): 20–1; Chittick, *Silk*, p. 289.
[75] *TW* 70(1926): 2232, in an article titled "Hand-to-Mouth Buying Here to Stay."

vantageous contractual relations lay at the core of this "unequal" exchange, a point NAM President John Edgerton stressed in his 1928 address to the Philadelphia Textile School alumni. In the face of market pressures,

> fratricidal competitions have developed [among manufacturers], mutual confidence has broken down, and cut-throat practices have crept in from various quarters. This has given the efficiently organized processes of distribution their opportunity to play one manufacturer or group against another, so as to render them almost helpless to protect themselves against destructive dictation.[76]

Stanley Stager, an incomer by marriage to the Ring family's Kensington wool spinning enterprise, eloquently summed up the market hemorrhages in a knitters' convention talk the same summer.

> [M]anufacturers have permitted the buyers to take one unfair advantage after another until many of the standards and ethics of business, or those basic principles upon which American industry has been founded, have been cast aside. When an industry reaches a point where an order ceases to be anything more than an indication of the probable requirements of the buyer, providing he cannot obtain a better bargain elsewhere; where merchandise must be sold with a guarantee against price declines; where orders may be cancelled at will whether [or not] the merchandise has been manufactured...; where merchandise may be refused by the buyer after shipment has been made on the pretext that he can purchase for less money, or... because of weather conditions or for some other equally fatuous reason; where the buyers' excess stock at the end of the season may be returned; where bills for merchandise may be paid at the convenience of the buyer and discount deducted which he is not entitled to receive;... then I say, gentlemen, that sort of trading is rapidly reaching a point where it is no longer worthy of the name of industry in the American definition of the term.

Trade associations had "failed miserably" in dealing with these "multitudinous abuses," as their individual members were in no way bound to common action. Stager proposed a probably illegal solution, a contractual alliance of producers, over a fixed term, with "penalties or fines" for violations of the organization's rules and regulations regarding standardization of business methods, ethics, and products, and provision of comprehensive statistical data. As Stager's profits had been "very lean" since 1921, and business so "spotty" that he and his partner had reduced their own salaries by a third, his denunciations of buyers' and his colleagues' associations stemmed from a typical old-sector Philadelphia experience. While such sentiments may well have prepared proprietors to embrace the corporatism of the NIRA, Stager's

[76] *The Manufacturer* 10(June 1928) 31, (July 1928): 14.

outrage at the "laissez-faire attitude[s]" common among businessmen suggests a deeper despair. Distributors were profiting as his mill foundered; other millmen were baffled, trying to save their own skins, or as in full-fashioned hosiery, were just beginning to be struck by the storm. The ebb and flow of positional advantage between mill owners and workers, mill owners and merchants, had ceased to oscillate. Now it seemed, buyers squeezed the mills, mills squeezed their employees, yet profit had been squeezed downstream. The state was indifferent, the tariff insufficient, the future bleak.[77]

Given all this, it bears asking why there was not a mass exodus from Philadelphia textile manufacturing, a radical scaling down of the sort that in a decade blotted out two-thirds or more of cotton production in New Bedford or Fall River? Second, and equally important, what strategies might flexible mills have adopted to reduce their disadvantages and to what extent were these paths chosen by regional producers? In dealing with both of these questions, the sectorally differentiated impact of the market power shift stands as a backdrop. On the first count, expansion in the local full-fashioned hosiery and fancy-weaving divisions prevented a rapid Yankee-style collapse, as these sectors'. troubles became acute only in and after 1929. On the second, it was in the relatively more solid sectors that aggressive strategies of response were mounted to some good effect, whereas accommodation and exit paths were more commonly charted among deeply troubled carpet, wool/worsted, and spinning mills.

Moreover, there were cultural rationales for Philadelphia proprietors to continue operating in unfavorable environments. At older firms, sons and grandsons carrying on family traditions and defending legacies had powerful incentives to hold out to the bitter end. Hopes that retailers would abandon hand-to-mouth purchasing and restore gentlemanly ethics in their dealings with mills never died out completely, and mills kept going so as to "preserve" their organizations for that happy day when a seller's market would reappear. Yet as these were not terribly plausible expectations, other more concrete "blind spots" must be invoked. One striking contrast with leading New England corporations was that Philadelphia firms with few exceptions were privately held and thus avoided that public failure to pay dividends that forced Fall River boards to assess their financial status and performance as stock prices plummeted, ultimately provoking liquidations. In addition, Philadelphia firms, at least from testimony presented in bankruptcy hearings, often had no familiarity with notions of return on investment (ROI) or cost analysis and rarely paid any attention to negative trends in asset/debt ratios

[77] TW 73(1928): 43–4; "Autobiographical Account by Stanley Ray Stager," Accession No. 1154, Hagley Library, p. 17.

until forced into receivership by creditors. This indifference to current industrial accounting practice was also reflected in the frequent failure to depreciate machinery values realistically (or at all) and by the tendency to retain ancient accounts receivable as assets rather than write them off as bad debts.

In one painful interrogation, a creditors' attorney quizzed John Schwehm, partner in the Buttonwood Worsted Mills and son of a proprietary weaving-mill family, about two dozen such accounts dating back three to seven years and amounting to $97,000. None was even remotely collectable, yet they had been carried on the plus side of the ledger, in part the attorney suspected to shield the firm's parlous financial state from suppliers who demanded occasional trial balances as a condition for continuing to offer trade credits. Had these sums been written off, the mill would have been sold out far sooner. As it was, the partners' business survived long enough to be bilked by the son of another local manufacturer. Eager for orders to reverse their slump in the later 1920s, Buttonwood hired Virgil Hughes, who advertised his connections with "two buying houses in New York who bought for a large number of retail stores all over the country." Hughes rapidly submitted about $100,000 in falsified blanket orders, invoices for fabrics whose style details would be filled in later, and collected $7,750 in commissions for his work. When the fraud was revealed, Hughes was arrested and indicted, but Buttonwood collapsed, holding $115,000 in overvalued inventory, chiefly of failed styles run in previous years.[78]

More positively, older firms could remain in business with negligible profits, for they had fully paid for their mills and machinery in better times. In woolens and wool/worsted spinning for example, where there were few significant technological breakthroughs during the 1920s, proprietors who could cover operating costs and salaries could stay afloat for years, while, like Buttonwood, accumulating uncollectables and dead weight inventories. In addition, the 1920s were not a decade of unrelieved slippage in demand. Periodically there were busy periods (for carpets in 1923, 1925, and 1927) when all the mills ran full for a time, encouraging their owners to stay the course. What few Philadelphians realized was that in wool/worsted and carpets, their firms had become the periphery and the northern price leaders (Alexander Smith, Bigelow-Hartford, American Woolen) the core of a restructured market system. When demand was flush they were active; but Philadelphians felt every sag quickly, while their powerful colleagues commanded the bulk of sales in contracted markets. Not surprisingly, no Phil-

---

[78] U.S. District Court, Eastern District of Pennsylvania, Bankruptcy Case File # 13884, Hearing Transcripts, pp. 53, 65–90, 200, NARS, Philadelphia Branch. For another example of similar practices, see BCF # 8409 (William Penn Knitting Mills), Hearing Transcript.

adelphia mill was drawn into the 1929 Bigelow merger and only one (Hardwick and Magee) proved able to establish its name brand on a national scale comparable to the northern giants.[79]

Finally, and obvious enough as to barely need mention, Philadelphia's diversity was a strong point even in decline. Some firms were lodged in niches sufficiently solid to endure through the post-World War II decades (e.g., lace, job dyeing, high-grade upholstery). Some were reaping gains from the full-fashioned hosiery surge that would carry them well into the 1930s; and a precious few had devised means by which they could cope successfully with the forces buyers had brought to bear. In a baroque fashion, the refusal of most proprietary capitalists to accept and implement the measurement and evaluative tools of modern management shielded them from the perception that the odds against them had grown ever longer during the 1920s. Had they been more short-term cost-rational, had they been able to abstract capital and investment from the activity of production, had their world been defined less personalistically, Kensington would have been far sooner silenced than was actually the case, and the Philadelphia textile industry would have succumbed to the marginalization of flexible manufacturing far more readily.

Like their workers, owners lacked unity of vision or purpose, and like them, they complained about "conditions" and scurried after elusive opportunities. Yet unlike labor, Philadelphia textile capitalists had the obligation to attack the distributional puzzle. What did they do? Consider three categories of possible reaction to the slowly building crisis that spread across the Philadelphia textile trades in the 1920s: aggressive, accommodation, and exit strategies. By aggressive I mean those strategies that aimed at reversing the imbalance vis-à-vis buyers and again securing a market advantage for producers of seasonal textiles. Accommodation moves suggested acceptance of the new terms of trade and adjustment for survival within them. There were as well a variety of ways to exit, once individuals or firms determined that their prospects were sufficiently gloomy to make suspending manufacturing unavoidable. Each of the three was well represented in Philadelphia.

Aggressive strategies theoretically could restore the profitablity the flexible trades once enjoyed. Though frequently discussed as the most potent format, collective action was rarely achieved. Collusive price fixing, which could have been tried for various grades of goods if not styles, was impractical and unlawful as were strictly governed open-price mechanisms. Collective financial institutions failed to gain support, like most of the parallel labor

[79] *CUTR* 53(November 1, 1922): 73; 54(February 1, 1923): 61; 55(October 1, 1924): 90; *ACUJ* 43(February 1925): 51; (June 1925): 30; 44(May 1926): 41; 45(March 1927): 55(October 1927): 55; Erving and Norton, *Broadlooms*, pp. 245–51.

banks of the period, and efforts to freeze out manipulative and slow-paying buyers through trade association credit and account reporting were of no value when nonmembers eager for sales dealt with them anyway. Campaigns to create standard contracts and terms were exposed to the same weakness. Collective national advertising was undertaken by full-fashioned hosiery firms in the early 1920s, in order to stigmatize seamless mills who were producing fake seamed stockings ("mock full-fashioned"), but this collaborative promotion of a quality line drew no imitators in other sectors.[80]

Individual firms could act assertively in several ways, through forward integration in selling, shifting to new markets, or engaging in mass advertising. The most basic maneuver was to bypass the distribution maze and seek direct sales to consumers, either for all or a price-defining portion of the mill's output. This route was denied to all service and most yarn providers of course (though Fleisher did manage retail placement of hand-knitting yarns), but hundreds of weaving and knitting mills could easily contemplate such a strategy. In the late nineteenth century numerous Philadelphia carpet firms had operated downtown retail outlets (McCallum, Hardwick and Magee, Dobson), yet all but Hardwick's had given way to comprehensive department stores by 1920. Within the sphere of manufacturing, no local fabric firms emulated James Doak's 1890s flirtation with garment manufacture, nor did any merge with clothing makers to integrate production across sectoral boundaries. Given their advantageous position, large established clothing firms had no incentive for such an alliance; and mills with no previous experience in the treacherous "rag trade" most likely saw ventures in that direction as more risky than stabilizing. Moreover, in the older sectors, there is no trace of fresh 1920s efforts to reach retail consumers.

However, in knit goods and specialty weaving, various direct sales schemes were attempted. For example, George Stein and Benjamin Lessner's Servis Hosiery Company sold to jobbers and operated its own shop in Philadelphia. The latter traded as Well-Knit Hosiery, using a different name "so that the jobbers . . . would not come back to us for selling . . . retail." Though evidence is extremely scanty, it is plausible that other small firms duplicated this practice, particularly the cohort of knitted outerwear operators that began to concentrate in the storefront row buildings that filled the declining commercial district north of Independence Hall at the eastern edge of Old City. On a much larger scale, Gotham Hosiery maintained retail stores in New York and Atlantic City, yet these shops could handle only a trickle of its

---

[80] *UHR* 6(March 1923): 79; 7(July 1924): 57–8, (December 1924): 93. The campaign cost $1.5 million over three years, raised by an assessment on association members of five cents per dozen pairs or roughly 0.5 percent of the wholesale value of silk full-fashioned hosiery.

thousand workers' full-fashioned output. Retailing allowed Gotham to discover "instantly what the consumer trend is – whether the leaning is toward one shade, one weight or another." This information together with daily sales reports from a hundred independent retailers guided the firm's much-touted "hand-to-mouth production" format, whereby a large stock of knitted stockings was kept ready for rapid dyeing and finishing across a wide range of colors in proportions set by current demand. Neither of these practices was genuinely aggressive, however, as Servis's shop was merely a covert means to secure a higher margin on a portion of its goods and Gotham's outlets were one component of a fairly creative and comprehensive adjustment, establishing an "elastic . . . manufacturing program" in order to cope with hand-to-mouth buying relations. Trade journals reported scattered attempts at direct-mail and door-to-door selling, but these quickly faded away.[81]

Only one firm in Philadelphia mapped out and implemented a direct alternative to the buyers' squeeze. Bernard Davis's LaFrance Textile Industries, founded at the close of the war, was a classic Philadelphia-style firm, manufacturing "plushes, velvets, tapestries, brocades, etc." for upholstery and decorative uses. It commenced as a partnership, became a closely-held corporation, and expanded incrementally through rental and purchase of additional facilities, all "done by reinvesting profits – and not by bringing in outside capital." After selling its diversified lines through road men and a New York office for some years, in the mid-1920s LaFrance initiated a "district distribution" plan, serially opening stores in twenty-six American and Canadian cities by 1929. Open to consumers as well as furniture makers and upholsterers, these shops carried light stocks of the firm's diverse patterns, making it possible to "guarantee quick delivery, so vital in these days of hand-to-mouth buying." Orders beyond an outlet's on-hand supply of a style were telegraphed to Philadelphia, where comprehensive inventory sheets for all stores were updated daily. Headquarters staff thus could rapidly identify which shop had sufficient additional yardage to fill the order, wire its manager to express it to the customer, and initiate production of replacement stock at the factory. By this means, inventory could be floated on a national scale. Jobbers and wholesalers were by-

---

[81] The McCallum firm went bankrupt in 1900 and was succeeded by H. G. Fetterolf; Dobson's downtown salesroom burnt down and its replacement was devoted to wholesaling, while most others suspended retail operations by 1910. On Servis, see Bankruptcy Case File # 8344, Hearing Transcript pp. 1–2, and for Gotham, *TW* 77(1930): 634–5. For a more extensive use of partial forward integration, see Charles Koepke's discussion of the Nunn-Bush Shoe Company in *Plant Production Control*, New York, 1941, pp. 70–2. This firm maintained 115 retail shops (or sections within department stores) accounting for 35 percent of its sales in the 1930s.

passed,and department stores ignored in major cities, whereas small-city retail accounts were readily serviced from the nearest district location. Using the New York office and road men, LaFrance recorded $3 million in 1925 orders. With the creation of its own chain of retail–wholesale outlets, 1928 sales neared $10 million, with net profits estimated at $1 million.[82]

Trained as an engineer and experienced as a furniture manufacturer, Davis had hired a full-time cost accountant at the outset of the new distribution program and installed a comprehensive inventory and cost-control system to track the firms' production and sales performance. Given these controls, "nothing is manufactured [simply] for the sake of artistic expression. Each item must pay its way." Beyond selling its own woven-pattern goods, LaFrance also initiated a "cretonne converting business" to deal with demand for the popular prints. By 1929 three Philadelphia mills were in operation, a New Jersey plant had been purchased, a Canadian subsidiary established along with a South Carolina branch and, echoing the practice of major nontextile corporations, a European factory was being started in Roubaix, France. Meanwhile, in Frankford, Davis, an avid amateur artist, inaugurated a free school of art and design that enrolled several hundred neighborhood students and sponsored annual gallery showings and prizes. Davis thus straddled the chasm between traditional proprietary practices and modern management techniques, reaching out to his community while defending prices and advancing accumulation through close costing and a deft distributional strategy. Yet his was a unique quest after blending "Art in Industry" with aggressive marketing.[83] Even in upholstery, other area firms took no such initiatives. Why not?

Reluctance to entrust their firm's basic financial controls to an expert outsider, or to take Davis-style risks in marketing without comparable experience in the furniture trade, simple inertia, all certainly played a role. However, equally important was the diversion of the Manayunk segment of the area plush/upholstery cohort away from furnishings fabrics and toward supplying the booming automobile demand (well before Davis's mid-decade

---

[82] *TW* 69(1926): 209–10; 75(1929): 712–14. To reach the centers of furniture making, outlets were situated in Grand Rapids, Michigan, and High Point, North Carolina, as well as in population concentrations like Chicago, San Francisco, Memphis, and Boston.

[83] Ibid. The South Carolina mill made simple lines of goods not competitive with the Philadelphia jacquard plants (*PL*, September 22, 1928, p. 19). On the school opening see *CUTR* 54(February 1, 1923): 96, and for other reports on LaFrance's upward course, *ACUJ* 41(October 1923): 47–8; 42(March 1924): 52; 43(June 1925): 52, (September 1925): 52, (November 1925): 41, (December 1925): 35; 45(April 1927): 48, (May 1927): 43, (October 1927): 43. LaFrance kept 700 patterns active in flat fabrics and 80 various velours, each in up to 20 color combinations (*ACUJ* 44 [October 1926]: 52). Profits in 1926 were $488,000 (net) on sales of $3.9 million and common stock issued of $850,000. (No full account of assets and debts has survived.)

Figure 21. LaFrance Textile Industries advertising its successful "Art Moderne" upholsteries, emphasizing that its branch warehouses relieve furniture makers of their inventory burden, 1928. (Courtesy of the Philadelphia College of Textiles and Science.)

innovations were publicized). This reduced temporarily the numbers of looms available for creation of fine upholsteries, enabling Kensington mills to process the flow of short-yardage orders without running stock. From roughly 1921 to 1926, buyers of Philadelphia upholstery had to accept four- to six-week lags between order and delivery, for southern capacity was slowly developing along with the style shift toward plainer, cheaper fabrics for interiors. Davis's strategy in this context appears to have been an effort to steal a march on his local rivals, by providing fast delivery at the quality end of the market. When the distributional crunch spread into upholstery in the later 1920s, LaFrance thus was nicely positioned to evade its strictures, whereas most of the Kensington crew resisted running stock even as their prospects and profits flagged. When the slide deepened early in the Depression, the associated Kensington upholstery mills joined the weavers' union in commissioning a Wharton School analysis of their situation, a study which indicated how thoroughly proprietors had clung to their traditional formats and how great was the gap between their relative passivity and Davis's systematic strategizing. The Wharton team's 1931 recommendations for installing cost accounting, strengthening the trade association, promoting quality goods through advertising, merging rival firms, improving equipment maintenance, and cutting executive salaries illuminated how rare was Davis's implementation of coordinated managerial practice in the city's most technically sophisticated weaving division.[84]

Meanwhile, Manayunk's market shifters had tied their fates to Detroit's mass-production star, reaping healthy advance orders for car seatings as fabric replaced leather in closed-cab vehicles. Meeting fast-rising industrial demand for long runs of semistaple goods reduced the importance of "short orders" in traditional channels. Chasing industrial demand was not confined to the plush and upholstery trade. Braiders turned to covering electrical cord for auto and appliance makers. A narrow fabric mill in Tacony (L. H. Gilmer) adopted double shifting in 1922 to supply Henry Ford with a million running feet of "brake bands" and 150,000 fan belts monthly, while continuing to make "soft collar cloth" and similar goods for apparel. By 1926, Manayunk weavers were heavily engaged in automobile supply, and the expansion of Collins and Aikman was supported by durable contracts with General Motors and Chrysler. (Half the 1928 output of its three mills was absorbed by GM alone.) Ford, however, began operating its own fabrics plant in 1926 and soon became self-sufficient in textiles, leading to a radical contraction at Gilmer and the mill's closing by 1930. Clearly, one of the risks entailed by becoming linked to the needs of mass-production corporations was that a boardroom decision to integrate further, or a managerial judgment to shift

[84] *FR-Uph*, "Suggestions," pp. 1–11.

purchasing or cut offering prices for goods, could swiftly precipitate a crisis for a specialist supplier. Nonetheless, connections with throughput giants insulated a segment of the local industry from the market miseries for most of the decade, served to sustain high wages and labor peace, and underwrote the growth of one firm (Collins and Aikman) toward national-scale diversification.[85]

Similar ties to other prosperous sectors were sought by local carpet manufacturers. For example, in 1924, Hardwick and Magee contracted with the Loews chain to provide floor coverings for its multiplying moving-picture theaters. Furthermore, the general surge in institutional building (hotels, offices, auditoriums, resorts) generated an attractive source for big advance carpet orders, ranging from 115,000 yards for the 2,268 rooms, corridors, and public spaces in Chicago's Palmer House (supplied by Hardwick and Magee) to 8,000 yards for Philadelphia's much smaller Ben Franklin Hotel (furnished by Germantown's H. G. Fetterolf). The appearance of hotel chains further concentrated this timely substitute for the frustrations of hand-to-mouth wholesale/retail demand. Thus Kensington's Pennsylvania Carpet Company happily trumpeted its agreement to provide eighteen of the American Hotel Corporation's properties with new floor coverings. Of course, competitive bidding against Bigelow, which won its share of this trade, might narrow profits in these deals, but they involved no flurry of tiny orders, no accumulation of devalued stocks, no dunning of slow-paying retailers. In fact, Fetterolf bet its future on contract carpeting, shifting entirely into this field, and lost when institutional construction dwindled steadily after 1927. As with the automobile trade, these efforts to bypass the piecemeal, wholesale/retail nexus were partially successful, but market shifting provided only a temporary respite. As contract opportunities ebbed, Philadelphia trade columnists again wailed: "Retailers – Have a Heart for the Manufacturers." The silence at the other end of the line was by then predictable.[86]

National advertising was another possible choice for an aggressive strategy. It genuinely annoyed retailers of textile products, for mass advertising had the capacity to establish brand recognition, thereby focusing demand and

[85] PL, August 8, 1922, p. 17; January 10, 1926, p. 19; February 9, p. 19; February 24, p. 17; CUTR 59(April 1, 1928): 82; ACUJ 42(November 1924): 47; TW 69 (1926): 1971–2.

[86] CUTR 54(June 15, 1923): 48–9; 59(March 1, 1929): 67; TW 73(1928): 227; ACUJ 42(July 1924): 44, (September 1924): 40; 45(April 1927): 65. Local carpet mills also landed contracts for small rugs to cover automobile floors, reportedly "hundreds of thousands of yards" in 1925 (ACUJ 43 [August 1925]: 42). In addition, some versatile fancy weavers provided large blocks of draperies to hotel and office complex builders, Kensington's Orinoka Mills being linked to the Biltmore chain (ACUJ 42[April 1924]: 54).

enabling manufacturers to defend prices and push retailers to maintain significantly larger stock levels than they preferred. In 1924 the chief of the National Retail Dry Goods Association complained that firms sponsoring national campaigns "desire...as a whole to dictate to retail merchants." They were seeking to "hog the situation" and make stores mere "depots of delivery." Repeat advertising in the *Saturday Evening Post*, general women's and household magazines, and even the upscale *Vanity Fair* and *Vogue* had the potential to level the playing field, or even tip it a bit toward high-recognition products. Though recent critics have called this magnetism into question, store managers in the 1920s evidently thought otherwise and re-sented direct appeals to consumers that would lessen their advantages vis-à-vis textile manufacturers. In any event, few Philadelphia firms followed Artloom (Chapter 4) into the practice of buying expensive glossy pages. The four that did so, Quaker Lace, Gotham, Hardwick and Magee, and Masland carpets, were already huge figures on the local scene and all made final goods that could be readily branded and identified in stores. Fabric producers whose materials went through clothiers' hands were poorly placed to profit from the strategy; even American Woolen had little luck in this regard. In 1927, the "big company" set out to build a consumer market for its "Ram's Head" trade name, marrying splashy monthly ads in the *Post* with distribution of woven labels by the hundreds of thousands to clothiers buying their goods. Sewn onto the sleeves of suits or dresses, the labels hopefully would identify "Ram's Head" fabrics to store browsers and raise public awareness of and demand for American Woolen lines. Unfortunately, the effort proved in-sufficient to stanch the corporation's losses (which rose from $1.2 million in 1928 to $4.2 million in 1929), even though advertising was expanded to include double-page color spreads in three publications plus mailings to 15,000 retailers. Major producers of ready-for-sale goods could make their presence felt, but upstream firms and the host of minor players in the Philadelphia carpet or knitting sectors stayed on the sidelines. Only Bigelow-Hartford could afford to erect a huge electric display on Broadway, showing a salesman unrolling a multicolor carpet and brightly illuminating the retail price it had established and was aggressively promoting. It was just such ploys that aroused retailers' indignation, but the "little fellows" were here clearly out of their league.

A final marketing tactic that was briefly tried by a sizable number of regional firms was shifting from direct selling to the use of agents, though this falls near the border between aggressive and accommodation ventures. In 1922, nearly 80 percent of firms (in employment terms) held to the direct selling style, with but 17 percent engaging commission agencies for distribution. By 1925, as pricing and marketing difficulties deepened, the "agency" pro-portion nearly doubled (to 31 percent); but these efforts to change channels evidently brought few satisfactory results. By 1928 agents commanded only 11 percent of the Philadelphia trade, and direct selling had rebounded to its previous four-fifths level. Nor, as suggested earlier, did the integration of production prove appealing, for the employment share of fully integrated companies never moved beyond 5 percent, roughly the same proportion observed in the late nineteenth century.[87]

In sum, across the spectrum of aggressive strategies that could have been implemented by Philadelphia textile firms to reverse the "wrongs" dealt them by the 1920s market-power shift, positional and resource constraints prevented all but a few firms from taking decisive action. The flight toward industrial and construction-based markets did generate (for some) just those advance orders that had become so fugitive, but success in these areas lured firms toward a different species of dependence, more transparent in retrospect than at the time. A fully self-contained strategy was only realized by the LaFrance operation, and its generalization was never plausible even among upholstery weavers. Advertising on a grand scale was the province of the affluent, a source of strength for the strong, and irrelevant for the rest. Thus, although calls to turn things around were frequent and strident among manufacturers, aggressive strategies were scattered, individual, and at best proved only partly successful where they were elaborated.

Accommodation strategies ranged from simple acceptance of the transformed market relationships to broad restructurings involving changes in organization and labor processes. The repeated nattering of proprietors about having to hold stock in anticipation of flurries of small orders represents an unquantifiable indication that this form of acquiescence was quite general. Indeed, it was barely a strategy at all, being largely a capitulation to buyers' terms. However, the implications of these new relations did generate shifts in manufacturing practice worthy of note. The plainest of these was the adoption of hand-to-mouth purchasing by manufacturers, as weavers and knitters attempted to reduce their supply inventories by making frequent calls on spinners for types and counts of yarns needed to replenish depleted

---

[87] *UHR* 7(December 1924): 93; *PL*, July 8, 1926, p. 19; July 9, p. 15; *CUTR*, 55(February 15, 1924): 57, (June 1, 1924): 61; *TW* 75(1929): 717–8; Zappala, "Financial History," p. 55. For works stressing advertising's force in the 1920s, see Stuart Ewen, *Captains of Consciousness*, New York, 1976, and Stuart and Elizabeth Ewen, *Channels of Desire*, New York, 1982. For a recent doubtful view, see Michael Schudson, *Advertising: The Uneasy Persuasion*, New York, 1984. The Bigelow sign had 5,700 electric bulbs and was 40 by 44 feet in dimension. Gotham's presence in the high-demand full-fashioned sector and its production/marketing adeptness paid off handsomely, as net profits were $2.2 million in 1925 and $2.9 million in 1926 (*PL*, February 21, 1927, p. 19). On marketing tactics and integration, see Philip Scranton, "Beyond Anecdotes and Aggregates," 295–7.

finished stocks. This backpassing of the problem demanded that spinning mills warehouse sizable stores of single-ply, double-ply, blended, etc., yarns of all numbers, rather than making to order in response to seasonal bookings by their clients. Although yarns were far less exposed to becoming dead stock, the financial commitments needed to create an on-call supply and the price risks that moving raw-materials costs entailed were far from welcome. Spinners in turn tended toward buying raws in small lots, though this brought corresponding price disadvantages and hiked transaction costs. To discourage this practice, which would complicate *their* agriculturally seasonal businesses, Philadelphia wool and yarn brokers seem to have extended larger and/or longer credits to wool/worsted spinners and users of southern cotton or regionally thrown silk yarns. Although detailed documentation for this pattern is not plentiful, such tactics would help explain the rise of Charles Webb, the city's premier raw wool agent, to leadership of the PTMA throughout the 1920s and for his brother Andrew's engineering of a merger uniting two outlying worsted yarn plants with the Fleisher family mills to form one of the city's largest textile enterprises (about two thousand employees). Where firms had once feared falling into the hands of selling agents who had suffered working capital loans and advances, they now drifted toward dependence on suppliers for credits to sustain inventories.[88] Mills that could not make such financial arrangements had a distressing predilection for accepting ruinous price quotes from buyers in order to raise cash by unloading stock, thereby providing benchmark figures that buyers quickly used to press for reductions by other producers.[89]

If the financial implications of hand-to-mouth buying permeated through supply transactions, the need to match a set of gapped and relatively inflexible buyers' price offers led to adjustments in production. The old reliable tactic, manipulating the goods, was quietly called again into service. As materials represented 50–60 percent of total costs, savings here could restore some measure of profitability, or at least compensate for downward price pressures far more readily than further piece-rate cuts. Both varieties of manipulation were practiced: adulteration of raw materials (the shoddy trick) and adjustments of fabric construction. This spread beyond woolens into hosiery, carpets, and by the late 1920s, fancy wovens (draperies). "Trashy hosiery" was reported as overloading markets for seamless cotton knits in 1923, "the inevitable result of distributors persistently hammering prices and the will-

[88] *PL*, September 9, 1924, p. 17; *ACUJ* 43(November 1925): 41; 44(July 1926): 36, (August 1926): 53; 45(April 1927): 47. *TW* 70(1926): 182, 2545. Another financial pressure stemmed from banks shifting their credit evaluations from " 'inventories' to 'receivables' in one form or another" (*TW* 70[1926]: 2231), as Federal Reserve Board member George James noted.

[89] *UHR* 5(December 1922): 62; 6(March 1923): 108.

ingness of too many manufacturers to sacrifice the reputation of their product for immediate business." In silk hose, knitters commissioned spinners to twist silk strands around a cotton or rayon core thread to save materials expense. For their part, carpet weavers objected to the "efficiency system" at Hardwick and Magee, which had brought the "introduction of light weight yarn and bad stock [that] made the work much harder." In drapery goods, Craftex Mills's Herman Blum complained that buyers' emphasis on slashing prices had encouraged "a definite tendency to lower the quality of fabrics." He explained,

> Fabrics of fine warps with plenty of ends and picks, designed in good taste and dyed with dependable ... colors, woven faultlessly and fairly priced have been imitated as to color and design, the yarns have been robbed, the picks have been reduced and the colors, instead of being fast, are of the cheapest, most fugitive kind.[90]

These tactics were self-defeating, for prices soon chased quality downward in a production variant of Gresham's Law.

On the labor front, tactical substitution of women workers for men was apparent only in hosiery finishing; the generality of piece rates made gender shifts valueless unless dual male–female schedules for the same work were implanted. Of this there is no evidence in Philadelphia textiles, though sex segregation of jobs was widespread. However, Hardwick and Magee did take advantage of the frequent surplus of weavers over active looms in the 1920s context of non-union employment relations. The tradition of weavers' "possession" of particular looms was abrogated. Instead, managers shifted those employed at any time from one loom to another, reflecting a practice of keeping different patterns set up throughout the mill and moving weavers around as shipments necessitated production of various styles for stock replenishment. The same plan was adopted generally among Kensington upholstery mills during the 1920s, though the unionized workforce brokered a more complex work assignment compromise once net sales dropped by a quarter, 1925–8, and to half their 1925 level in 1930.

In most cases, upholstery weavers could operate "their" looms, which were set up for a particular fabric, only when orders for that pattern were in hand. Lacking such orders, they were rotated to "spare" looms that rested prepared to weave other styles when called for. As it cost $7.50–$15.00 to change cards and tie in a new warp, and as average orders shrank to "half

---

[90] UHR 6(January 1923): 64, (February 1923): 121; 7(March 1924): 95, (June 1924): 91. Palmer, *Union Tactics*, pp. 140–1; *ACUJ* 45(October 1927): 76. In cotton hose, the trashy goods came from substituting lower-price carded yarn for knitting-grade combed yarn (*UHR* 7[February 1924]: 62). Overlaying a cheap core thread with more expensive surface silk was known as "plating" in trade parlance.

a piece" (about 25 yards), worth $40.00 to $75.00, this practice was a creative
means of cost saving that problematizes "excess capacity" as a simple way
of characterizing sectoral difficulties. The upholstery mills, unlike carpets,
held to high quality standards, and installed a production scheme whereby
the more looms held, the greater a firm's flexibility of response, though the
impact on workers was harsh and contributed to the determination with
which they fought a grim 1931 battle against piece-rate cuts. On the other
hand, a veteran carpet weaver argued that the rotation system "actually works
against the firm because the men lose interest in keeping their looms in
good condition. They become careless and lose interest in craftsmanship."
Both fiddling the fabrics and juggling technology and the workforce proved
to be accommodation strategies with real, if initially hidden costs, whatever
their short-term benefits.[91]

For a road not taken, we may offer the ubiquitous Charles Webb's anticipation of Lester Thurow. In 1923, Webb suggested "as an aid in the
present state of affairs, that employers establish an elastic salary list by profit
sharing all the way down to the office boy." This combination of wage and
bonus would generate "a deeper interest in the business" by workers, who
would come to feel "they were a part of the establishment instead of being
hired for a specific work for a given number of hours." Flexible payment
schemes, however, smacked too much of Taylorism to be appealing to workers, especially given the recent fakery of the Hurlbut "Men and Management" councils, and at the same time were invasive of proprietors' unfettered
right to profits. Webb's notion sank without a trace.[92]

Broader adaptive reorganizations might encompass mergers, branch planting and full-dress relocations, each potentially a means to gain better control
over costs and production flows. Yet in this area, mergers faced the same
obstacles that the Sloane plan for drawing together ingrain carpet producers
had encountered a generation earlier. "Weak sisters" were shunned as can-

---

[91] Palmer, *Union Tactics*, pp. 27–8, 44, 141. On the hosiery finishing shift, which followed
a technological innovation, see ibid., pp. 90–1. Rate cutting in besieged sectors was
problematic, given its small impact on overall pricing and the fact that women and
youthful workers were evidently being drawn toward the expanding electrical/radio
sectors, as Philco and Atwater Kent had plants in Kensington and North Central
Philadelphia. For a perception of this aspect of labor market competition, see *CUTR*
59(November 1, 1928): 92. For the upholstery situation see *FR-Uph*, ch. 2, p. 4; ch. 6,
pp. 11–12, and Palmer, pp. 67–75. Gender substitutions were not statistically obvious
even during the post-1929 depression. Workforce proportions remained at 47.8 percent
male, 51.2 percent female, 1929–31, and by 1933 reached 48.9 percent male, chiefly due
to failures of firms concentrated in sectors of predominantly female employment, hosiery
and spinning (data drawn from Pa. B.I.A. *Reports, 1929–33*, Philadelphia County Tables).

[92] *PL*, May 3, 1923, p. 21; Lester Thurow, *The Zero-Sum Solution*, New York, 1985,
pp. 160–3.

didates for merger and hardly had the momentum to win financial backing for spatial shifts. Stronger firms rarely sought alliances; indeed to do so violated proprietary independence and suggested vulnerability. Thus the 1920s mergers in Philadelphia textiles were either creditor-inspired rationalizations (Webb and Fleishers, in which the best machinery from three plants was consolidated) or built on apparent prosperity (Collins and Aikman's buyouts of three Manayunk plush mills). By contrast, the upholstery merger, urged by Wharton consultants to a flock of independent proprietors in 1931, never got past the discussion stage. Physical relocations within urban districts were common for knitting firms seeking larger quarters during the expansionary period, but movement to suburban counties or southern sites was unusual. Throughout the 1920s, fewer than 5 percent of roughly 1,400 active firms relocated outside Philadelphia, only two dozen of these to the South, half of which failed. When troubles came to the upholstery sector after 1927, only 100 of the trade's 2,400 local looms were shipped to new sites during the following four years. Further, in 1932, Herman Blum of Craftex noted the "recent elimination, via the bankruptcy courts, of at least three [upholstery] mills, who moved part or all of their equipment outside of Philadelphia," indicating that structural shifts in market relations and the character of demand could not reliably be overcome simply by a change of venue.[93]

However, strategic branch planting was fairly plausible as a lower-risk exercise in accommodation that preserved independence without plunging into all-or-nothing territorial shifts. It took shape along three axes: (1) as a part of genuine expansion; (2) as a means of spatially differentiating production of segmented product lines; and (3) as a defensive, stepwise test of the potential that withdrawing completely from Philadelphia held. In the first category lie Collins and Aikman's creation of first a West Philadelphia plant, expanded in stages, then its Doylestown and other mills, LaFrance's Canadian factory, and Masland's erection of a York, Pennsylvania, outlier. In the second are LaFrance and Stead and Miller's southern branches, targeted for running cheaper lines of upholstery to gain a share of the low-end furnishings business. By contrast, in establishing a Mt. Holly, New Jersey, branch, Royle and Pilkington first eluded Philadelphia's upholstery unionists then closed its city mill and leapfrogged to launch a Carolina operation whose success brought the subsequent shutdown of the Jersey mill. Boger and Crawford in fancy yarns, Powell in seamless, and Cadet in

---

[93] Scranton, "Beyond Anecdotes"; *UHR* 7(February 1924): 93; *ACUJ* 43(August 1925): 42; 44(July 1926): 36; 45(March 1927): 42, (April 1927): 47, (November 1927): 47, 61–2; *TW* 69(1926): 1971–2; *FR-Uph*, ch. 3, p. 11, Blum to Industrial Research Dept, November 2, 1932, in PP-135, TMR.

full-fashioned hose, each opened southern branches before pulling up their Philadelphia stakes. Though she did not pursue the sectoral details and thus overestimated the extent of its incidence, Palmer captured this sequence in the fabric trades:

> As in Paterson, many Philadelphia weaving mills established branch plants in other areas instead of expanding in Philadelphia. After a new labor supply had been trained, the outside plants were favored in the allocation of all orders which could be produced on a mass-production basis – the "bread and butter" of the industry. Philadelphia plants were left to make samples and short orders, and in some cases, eventually closed down completely.[94]

My estimates indicate that about 50 of the region's 1,100 textile firms in 1925 had branches beyond the metropolitan area (and 37 of 1,000 in 1928), comprising less than 10 percent of employment at each point. Indeed within this group, Gotham Hosiery was actually expanding *in* Philadelphia, buying in 1926 the full-fashioned mills of Oscar Nebel and Largman, Gray, both of which built new facilities in suburban counties only to fail during the Depression. Thus *some* rather than many companies tried spatial differentiation, running specialties in Philadelphia and staples elsewhere, but this option was not widely adopted. For small single-process operations, outlying or distant locations were unappetizing in that outside the city they would be compelled, as *Textile World* saw it, to maintain captive dyeworks which they "could not keep...sufficiently employed to make it profitable."[95] Overall, most Philadelphia proprietors lacked the resources, the analytical tools, or the subjective dispositions to pursue choices that might be appealing to modern business enterprises. They stayed put, stayed independent, and tried to keep afloat.

Accommodation to the 1920s market relations provided few virtuous opportunities for firm-level decision making in Philadelphia textiles. Efforts to shift risk to spinners, to gamble with product quality or labor tasking, or to play the location game involved an indeterminate mix of gains and gaffes. Standing pat and hoping for the best had the appeal of simplicity, especially

---

[94] Gladys Palmer, "A Footnote to the Industrial Revolution in Textiles," typescript, November 1939, p. 18, PP-135, TMR. Data analysis of a 30 percent sample of all textile firms in the five-county region showed 11.5 percent with two or more sites in 1925 (38 of 329) and 9 percent in 1928 (28 of 304). However, three-fifths of firms in this group had *both* their locations in the city, thus the effective rate of "outside" branch planting was 4.4 percent in 1925 and below 4 percent in 1928. These figures are drawn from the data analysis printouts, "Codebook, Scranton, Cross-sectionals," Rutgers Computer Center, October 15, 1985, based on *OATD* and *IDPa* entries. For an extended description of Powell's southern branch, see *TW* 69(1926): 429, 431.

[95] *TW* 70(1926): 3158–9.

in older sectors where firms had retrieved capital expended for plant and machinery. Yet for scores of mills, both active and passive, exit from the industry became increasingly unavoidable. For some, it was obligatory, sudden; others went quietly, having prepared for some time, while for a few, "angels" with open checkbooks appeared. As a proprietor realized that his remaining years would have to be spent outside the world of production, four possibilities were open. Bankruptcy was ugly, bordering on shameful. Voluntary liquidation was much to be preferred. Selling out to a successor firm was yet more dignified, as it preserved one's employees' positions, at least for a while. Finally, restructuring one's assets outside textiles avoided pouring money down a hole, even if it signaled a calculated abandonment of the factory as a legacy in favor of a portfolio of deeds and bonds. Like everything else in Philadelphia, departures were diversified.

In the century since Henry Korn had contemplated the "Horrors of Bankruptcy," there had been little change in the way Philadelphia textile operators regarded involuntary failures. When one "filed," outsiders soon probed the innards of one's lifework. Fault was found; squabbling over residual assets only drove the stake deeper. Little wonder that until the late 1920s, textile bankruptcies in Philadelphia were relatively infrequent. Whereas beyond three hundred firms exited, circa 1922–8, only about fifty textile failures are recorded in the federal court ledgers for those years, most often small operations that foundered due to unsalable stocks, hopeless pricing, self-delusion, or rotten bookkeeping. Voluntary liquidations predominated; many passed unremarked, as only veteran mills' suspensions usually rated coverage in trade journals. Without the intervention of referees and sheriffs, these companies went through a routine process of "winding up" their affairs, clearing trade debts, calling in open accounts (or selling their collectables to an agency), steadily reducing staff, then vending machinery and plant through a private sale or at auction under the auspices of Samuel Freeman and Company, specialists in textile liquidations. Thus, when the Griswold spinning mill (worsted yarns, thrown silk, and blends) closed in 1925, all its equipment was sold and shipped north to New York's Champlain Silk Company. However, when the Gays' Park Carpet Mills shut down two years later, only the factory and fifty-two looms remained for buyers to consider, as the proprietors had been deliberately shrinking their facilities for some time. (Like Fetterolf, the Gays had banked on contract work and plain carpetings as a last strategy before folding their cards.) Intrafamily battles, particularly after a patriarch's death, could in the 1920s context easily precipitate a liquidation, as was the case with the Boggs Model Carpet Mills. Such sales set off a good deal of machinery reshuffling; Cambria Carpet secured both Boggs's and Fetterolf's looms in 1929, surely for rock-bottom prices. Whether used for parts, removed to replace older machinery in the buyers's mill, or operated as needed *in situ* under a lease, such looms demanded tiny capital expenditures and could be used flexibly by firms hoping to ape Hardwick's and the upholstery mills' production strategy. On the negative side, as Stager and others complained, this recycling of machinery did nothing to undercut buyers' persistent advantages.[96]

Important because of their scale, the exits of the Dobson and Fleisher complexes also illuminate contrasts between proprietary and "modern" managerial techniques. By the early 1920s, James Dobson had reached his mid-eighties, presiding over a collection of nine factories in Falls of Schuylkill, Manayunk, Germantown, and Kensington. Having fathered no sons and evincing little confidence in his middle-aged nephew Dobson Schofield, the patriarch placed the "executive management" of production and marketing in the hands of the Margerison brothers, Kensington turkish towel manufacturers noted for being "unusually successful as sales organizers." The Margerisons, whatever their accomplishments in peddling towels, were overmatched by the need to market carpets, plushes, blankets, worsteds, yarns, and underwear. They also may not have been appreciative of Dobson's continued presence; the redoubtable founder continued to arrive daily at the mill offices as he had done for over half a century. Though the factories were reported running at full capacity early in 1923, within a year Germantown's Bradford worsted mill was closed and put up for sale. The Margerisons resigned at the close of a disastrous 1924; Dobson Schofield was at last elevated to president of the company. In April 1926, James Dobson died just after his eighty-ninth birthday. His underwear plant and a worsted factory had already been shuttered permanently and several tracts of vacant land owned by the firm were sold by July 1926. Six mills remained, but two of these were liquidated and the machinery removed before January 1927. By the time Dobson's $873,000 estate was probated that summer, rumors were flying that the end was near. Denied at first, they were confirmed early in 1928, when the remaining carpet, plush, and velvet mills at Falls of Schuylkill fell silent. The firm that had delivered 30,000 blankets weekly to the military during World War I and had achieved annual sales of $20 million at its peak laid off the last few hundred of its 6,000 employees and retired from the field. The gradual, painful orderliness of the Dobson liquidation suggests not a reaction to a sudden crisis, but instead a conscious attempt to prune loss-prone sections of the company, leading toward a

---

[96] Scranton, *Proprietary Capitalism*, New York, 1983, p. 118; U.S. District Court, Eastern District, Pennsylvania, Bankruptcy Case Ledgers, 1922–8, NARS, Philadelphia Branch; *ACUJ* 43(February 1925): 50; 45(March 1927): 42; *CUTR* 60(September 1, 1929): 60, (October 1, 1929): 48; *TW* 73(1928): 43–4. On scrapping looms from liquidating firms in staple sectors, see *TW* 70(1926): 885–6, an article which also stresses the competitive advantage that used equipment offered struggling firms.

decision to quit business before profitlessness overwhelmed the heirs' remaining assets. Even so, James Dobson's 1926 estate must have seemed a pittance compared with the $14 million left by his brother John, who died in 1911, well before losses began accumulating.[97]

By contrast, the Fleisher works' liquidation was quick and tidy. In early May 1930, the firm defaulted on a set of "first mortgage 6% sinking fund bonds" issued to facilitate Andrew Webb's 1924 merger. Fleisher had also failed to maintain "the proper ratio of current assets to liabilities" as stipulated in the "indenture" securing the bonds. Within two weeks, the South Philadelphia factory ended all spinning operations and dispersal of its assets commenced. In a 1929 attempt to tighten up operations, Andrew Webb had sold all of his wool-scouring and combing equipment, thereafter running Fleisher's 50,000 spindles on purchased "tops" (combed long-staple wool). This wage-saving expedient had done little to arrest the slide; once the bondholders formed a "protective committee," the finish came speedily.[98]

James Dobson had perhaps stayed too long at the helm, repeating a generation later his brother-in-law Sevill Schofield's proprietary doggedness. By the time he entrusted management to the incomer Margerisons, the market tide had turned. Dobson Schofield, whatever talents he possessed, was left with a nearly hopeless situation in 1925. Yet absent a clutch of stock- or bondholders perusing his balance sheets, Schofield could for three more years accumulate losses in competition with Bigelow and Smith in carpets or Collins and Aikman in plushes before retiring from the fray to manage the Manayunk spinning mill (Imperial Wollen) his father had built and his uncle had rescued. On the other hand, Webb's defensive merger had necessitated outside money, never an issue for the Dobsons. Hence, the businesslike, surgical strike of spring 1930 reflected a cool assessment that the bondholders' capital was imperiled, for there was no appeal from the slipping ratios. Piecemeal sell-offs for the Dobson properties and the fast action at Fleisher's drew upon different industrial mindsets, yet each served to protect capital from being further eroded while sending thousands of workers in search of new employers.

If workers were left high and dry by such exits, not all departures by experienced proprietors led to immediate job losses. In the decade after the 1920–1 depression, Marshall Field, Cleveland Worsted, and Collins and

[97] *The Manufacturer* 4(February 1922): 32; *CUTR* 53(January 15, 1922): 48, (March 1, 1922): 60, (October 1, 1922): 58; *ACUJ* 41(March 1923): 66; 42(December 1924): 45; 43(January 1925): 34; 44(April 1926): 44, (May 1926): 56, (July 1926): 50; 45(January 1927): 57, (June 1927): 44, (September 1927): 61; 46(February 1928): 79. The Falls of Schuylkill mills were sold to a wool dealer for storage uses later in 1928 (*ACUJ* 46(September 1928): 54).
[98] *TW* 77(1930): 3055–56; *ACUJ* 48(July 1930): 22.

Aikman bought eight Philadelphia firms, liberating their operators from the tangles of hosiery, carpet, worsted, and plush production. (It was, however, typical for the former owners to remain as managers.) Field had determined to integrate backward into production; Cleveland was attempting to amass facilities that would put it in American Woolen's league. Both had adopted problematic strategies; three of the five local mills thus acquired were disposed of by 1930. Direct manufacturing of specialties by distributors proved pointless in strong buyer's markets (though Field retained the southern mills acquired in the same integrative thrust), whereas Cleveland's vast capacity was more a burden than a boon in the struggling wool/worsted sector. Once Collins and Aikman diversified spatially, it simply unloaded its Pearson, Baker, and Bennett and Apsden facilities in Manayunk. Several local owners, not fortunate enough to be visited by acquisitions-minded corporations, sold out to partners who later went to the wall, or in one case, to managers and workers who bought and owned their jobs for the next decade. These were "half-exits," providing textile capitalists with the wherewithal to start new careers (as Stager did) or with funds to support a comfortable, if early, retirement. For a time, their mills continued, until Fleisher-like boards weighed the performance figures against their options and pulled out of Philadelphia.[99]

Finally, an exit strategy that allowed some local millmen to face ending production with equanimity was the reinvestment of accumulated profits outside the textile industry. Though it could well be viewed as a proprietary alternative to Amoskeag's holding company or a link back to the nineteenth-century pattern of buying row houses as a competence base for old age, this form of capital restructuring was surely encouraged by the flood of post-1900 incorporations, the rush of wartime profits, and the unsettled character of most textile markets thereafter. Whereas the Bromleys moved carpet money into full-fashioned hosiery, their colleague Thomas Develon invested in a downtown office building, a corner site he sold to Drexel and Company for $750,000 in 1923. Similarly, Clarence Taubel put his gains from seamless hosiery manufacturing into the construction of the Medical Arts Building, not far from Develon's property, and hosted its initial tenants, all of whom were "graduates of the recognized schools of medicine," at a welcoming

---

[99] *UHR* 6(June 1923): 93; *PL*, February 9, 1926, p. 19; July 11, p. 15; March 2, 1927, p. 19; *CUTR* 61(March 1, 1930): 43. The worker/manager buyout was at the William Horstmann company, active since the War of 1812 era in braid and trimmings [Scranton, *PC*, pp. 130, 187–8; *PL*, July 9, 1924, p. 15; *CUTR* 54(December 1, 1924): 75]. The specialty niche it occupied enabled Horstmann to continue through 1936, as the sale was precipitated by the death of William H. Horstmann, grandson of the founder, not by an immediate market crisis. On Collins and Aikman's dumping of one of its Manayunk acquisitions, see *ACUJ* 41(July 1929): 46.

Manufacturers' Club banquet. More modestly, Shepperd Royle, the upholstery millman, paid $70,000 in 1924 for a plot on Oxford Pike, then promptly leased it to "an oil company, who will erect a modern service station." Estates showed similar patterns. At his death in 1930, John Gay's $1.1 million holdings included substantial real property, whereas probate on Walter Blabon's assets of $4.2 million revealed $300,000 in real estate and a vast portfolio of "stock investments in many large companies." Two years earlier, George Cox, who ran a 400-loom haircloth factory (interlinings for suits), left over $2 million to his heirs, only a fraction of which could have been accounted for by the value of his ancient mill and its equipment. For older manufacturers in troubled sectors, taking asset diversification steps such as these surely eased acceptance of declining industrial prospects. As the mill came to represent an ever smaller part of their capitals and maintaining it threatened a lifetime's accumulation, exit from the trade could blossom into a prudent choice.[100]

Small firms had few opportunities to plow *their* returns into land, buildings, and stocks; such moves were the prerogative of veterans who had reached an optimal scale and voted for security over the hazards of further textile investments. Most "little fellows" liquidated quietly and sought jobs as managers or salesmen when their situation afforded no alternative, but a few took extreme measures. At fifty-six, Joseph Nicholas faced the collapse of his modest Frankford rug mill due to business reverses in the 1924 carpet slump. He shot himself in the head. In Kensington, Ben Lessner, anticipating the imminent bankruptcy of his partnership knitting business, cashed a $5,000 check to drain the firm's last liquid assets and disappeared, leaving his colleague to deal with creditors, lawyers, and the like.[101] Such drastic actions were quite rare; selling out, liquidation, even bankruptcy usually proved undramatic and often went unnoticed.

Aggressive responses to the decisive shift in market relations failed; accommodation strategies brought only low-profit business and the gnawing sense that one was playing out a losing hand. With the exception of full-fashioned, by 1928 it was plain in all sectors that the future was forbidding, that the vitality of the regional textile system was melting away. Exit attracted

[100] *CUTR* 54(February 15, 1923): 59; 55(August 1, 1924): 78A; *The Manufacturer* 8(March 1926): 20–1; *ACUJ* 46(February 1928): 56; 48(March 1930): 48. These various strategies could of course be combined. For example, this is the same Royle who moved his upholstery mill from Philadelphia first to southern New Jersey, then to Hazlewood, North Carolina (*ACUJ* 46[September 1928]: 73). Short of scanning thousands of probate records or sifting through mountains of deeds for real estate transactions, there is no way to assess how extensive was such restructuring of textile capital into other property.

[101] *CUTR* 55(February 1, 1924): 65; Bankruptcy Case File # 8344, Hearing Transcript, pp. 7, 17–18, 36–7, 46.

the aged, the insolvent, perhaps the shrewd, but until driven from business, most Philadelphia mill owners persevered, hoping for a fair trade wind or a war. The last thing the city's textile workers and proprietors needed was a global depression.

6.4. The hole in God's pocket: Philadelphia textiles in disarray, 1926–1933

The final sections of this treatment of the "changing time" for Philadelphia textile manufacturing will take up three related tasks. First, a variety of industrial statistics will be offered to document the character and course of decline from the mid–1920s peak to the ascent of the New Deal. Second, paralleling the preceding discussion, an overview of the range of worker initiatives in response to the growing crisis will be developed. Third, flowing from the first two, a portrait of the area's last dynamic sector, full-fashioned hosiery, will bring together questions of technological change, unionization, neighborhood power, local politics, interregional competition, and market relations as the last bright star in Philadelphia textile was brought low. A forty-year veteran of the trade expressed it well in 1931: "The full-fashioned hosiery industry has been carried around in God's pocket for many years. Now there is a hole in the pocket..."[102]

While it was true that full-fashioned had begun to slip through that hole, other Philadelphia sectors had preceded it, as the following data on employment, capital, and output values will indicate. Initially striking in the Table 6.7 figures is the loss of over 11,000 jobs before the market crash, especially in older sectors. Compared with 1925, carpet employment had dropped 50 percent, spinning 43 percent, and wovens generally, 22 percent. Overall, 17,000 jobs were vacated in older sectors, in part offset by 5,700 positions added in knitting. Irregular employment initially accentuated by piecemeal buying had matured into a permanent shrinking of the workforce. In 1928, Kensington mills reported being mired in a slump, full-fashioned excepted, as textile unemployment was estimated at 24 percent and factories ran at half capacity. The worsening of opportunities for even seasonal work had led carpet workers to seek other trades, a step doubtless hastened by a 10 percent wage cut early in 1928. While the mayor pledged increased relief allotments for the textile districts, Herman Blum urged all manufacturers to adopt/adapt the upholstery makers' rotation system. Firms employing their mills' full force half-time, rather than a half-force full-time, would

---

[102] *Knit Goods Weekly*, January 24, 1931, quoted in Palmer, "Economic Factors," p. 30, PP-135, TMR.

Table 6.7. *Employment by sector, Philadelphia textiles, 1925, 1929–33*

	1925	1929	1930	1931	1932	1933
Woven goods	13,017	10,611	9,375	7,429	5,452	6,051
Cotton	(4,331)	(5,343)	(4,293)	(3,284)	(2,560)	(2,435)
Wool/worsted	(7,443)	(3,334)	(3,354)	(2,782)	(1,734)	(2,373)
Silk/rayon	(1,243)	(1,934)	(1,728)	(1,363)	(1,158)	(1,243)
Fancy woven[a]	11,405	7,170	6,294	5,583	4,734	5,386
Carpets	9,143	4,554	3,856	3,293	2,603	3,393
Hose-knit	20,392	26,130	23,667	21,287	21,577	22,620
Hosiery	(16,064)	(21,827)	(19,330)	(16,792)	(16,697)	(17,493)
Knit goods	(4,328)	(4,303)	(4,337)	(4,495)	(4,880)	(5,127)
Dye-finish	3,511	3,370	3,121	2,795	2,537	3,042
Spinning	9,510	5,432	4,708	4,144	3,367	3,812
Miscellaneous	4,598	3,019	2,670	2,376	2,227	2,510
Total	71,576	60,286	53,691	46,907	42,497	46,814

[a]The RPI statistical categories understated *fancy wovens* by mixing upholstery, tapestry, and specialty woolens into the *cotton*, *wool/worsted*, and *silk/rayon* classes. For 1925, use of firm-by-firm trade and industrial directory entries enabled a correction to be made, which shows a more accurate balance and facilitates comparison with a similarly structured roster for 1934. Here, however, it suggests a more drastic dropoff in fancy wovens than was the case by 1929. In 1934 this sector retained 8,267 jobs (Table 7.1); roughly one-quarter of post-1925 woven goods decline was felt in the fancy division, rather than one-half as RPI categories infer.
Source: 1925, Table 6.5; 1929–33, Pennsylvania Department of Internal Affairs, *Report on Productive Industries, Public Utilities and Miscellaneous Statistics of the Commonwealth of Pennsylvania for the Year(s) 1929, 1930, 1931, 1932, and 1933*, Harrisburg, PA, 1931–4, Philadelphia County.

distribute earnings more widely and, equally or more important, preserve their organizations and deflect operatives, especially women, from seeking to shift sectors (to knitting) or industries (to expanding radio and electrical).[103]

The three-year slide after 1929 aggravated these already distressing conditions. As employment dwindled to just over three-fifths of its 1925 level, an additional 18,000 textile workers were idled by the general depression at its lowest point, nearly 5,000 of these in the knitting sectors. Full-fashioned work fell 24 percent from the 1929 high, but knitted outerwear expanded slightly, the only countervailing trend. The sweater/sportswear business's

[103] *CUTR* 59(February 1, 1928): 73, (April 1, 1928): 82, (June 1, 1928): 76, (November 1, 1928): 92; *PL*, April 29, 1928, p. 3, April 30, p. 4, *The Manufacturer* 10(June 1928): 18.

initial surge, doubling 1919–29 from a small start, was generally credited to the vogue for outdoor athletics among the middle classes. However, its depression advances may have had more to do with homeowners and landlords cutting down heating expenditures than with further extension of the market for letter sweaters and golf vests. In any event, other sectors were clearly harder hit than knitting, both carpets and wovens down another 43 percent since 1929, and spinning off 38 percent. Such numbers for all their starkness still conceal the extent to which part-time labor was standard. In hosiery, upholstery, and most other trades, workers were listed as employed, but, following Blum's model, actually could rely on two days' activity a week and not in all weeks, an observation reinforced by output data that will be revealed below. Job sharing became common, and procedures for its management were etched into several union agreements during the early 1930s. In 1933 the local press widely credited the NIRA with spurring recovery, and mentioned by name firms that returned to full running during the summer of hope, but the year-end figures were less than reassuring. Employment rose 10 percent over 1932, but almost four-fifths of the jobs lost since 1929 remained unreplaced.[104]

Firm closures combined with depreciation write-downs and an absence of reinvestment to reduce sharply both the capital sunk into city textile production, 1926–33 (Table 6.8), and textiles' share of all Philadelphia industrial capital. Overall, in seven years, investment slid by $73 million, 36 percent below 1926 levels. Half the first $20 million (1926–8) represented losses in carpets and wool/worsted spinning, long-troubled sectors now experiencing multiple exits. Through the end of 1930 there was little change, but in 1931, the second full year of depression, scores of firms running on air collapsed, wringing another $50 million out of the capital reports by Christmas 1932. Nearly a third of this shrinkage may be found on the hosiery line; the full-fashioned story had turned from a capitalist romance into a horror show in less than a decade. Further, textiles' share of Philadelphia industrial investment had fallen by 1933 from 20 to 15 percent, and contraction of the city's textile capital in real terms was proceeding steadily, whereas nontextile industries were holding their own. The indices show sectorally crossing paths quite neatly, with hosiery values actually reaching their apex in 1930, before dropping 20 percent in 1931, a year of full-fashioned write-downs, liquidations, and strikes. At the trough, half the real 1926 carpet investment had vanished, as had half the wool/worsted spinning capital, and the damage in dyeing and wool/worsted weaving was only slightly

---

[104] *PL*, June 29, 1929, p. 17; C. C. Balderston et al., *The Philadelphia Upholstery Weaving Industry*, Philadelphia, 1932, pp. 51–2, 68–9, 183–4; Palmer, "Footnote," pp. 17–18, PP–135, TMR.

Table 6.8. *Capital in Philadelphia textile manufacturing, selected sectors and all nontextile industries, 1926, 1928–33*

	Capital (in millions)						
	1926	1928	1929	1930	1931	1932	1933
All textiles	206.2	187.2	183.5	183.0	164.8	135.7	132.8
Hosiery	34.0	40.0	43.1	44.0	33.5	29.3	31.8
Carpets	30.8	24.4	22.2	20.9	19.3	15.9	18.4
Dye-finish	18.8	16.1	16.0	13.3	13.1	10.8	10.6
Wool/worsted goods	14.2	13.8	12.1	11.8	10.9	8.6	8.0
Wool/worsted yarns	26.4	18.2	22.6	21.3	15.7	13.0	12.2
PNTI[a]	820.5	786.8	846.0	834.5	808.1	766.4	736.8

	Index (corrected to 1929 dollars, 1929 = 100)[b]						
	1926	1928	1929	1930	1931	1932	1933
All textiles	129	109	100	100	95	84	87
Hosiery	91	99	100	102	82	77	89
Carpets	159	117	100	94	92	81	100
Dye-finish	135	107	100	83	86	77	80
Wool/worsted goods	135	121	100	98	95	81	80
Wool/worsted yarns	134	86	100	94	73	65	65
PNTI	111	99	100	99	101	103	105

[a]Philadelphia nontextile industries.
[b]Nominal figures corrected to reflect real 1929 dollars, using Series P-119, Capital in Manufacturing Industries, Real Net Value in 1958 Dollars (recalculated to base 1929), Department of Commerce, Bureau of the Census, *Historical Statistics of the United States*, Washington, D.C., 1975, p. 683.
Sources: Pennsylvania Department of Internal Affairs, *Report on Productive Industries*, 1926, 1928–33, Philadelphia County.

less drastic. Clearly, other than in hosiery fresh expenditure on plant or technology had become infrequent in Philadelphia textiles. There had been incremental improvements in the size, design, and speed of fancy looms, for example, but the advances were hardly the sort of breakthroughs that (as in full-fashioned) compelled proprietors to plow funds into their acquisition, especially when existing equipment was being ever more erratically used.

Having surveyed some 1,600 upholstery looms and their jacquard controls, the 1931 Wharton team noted:

> The looms are all old, broad looms of slow speed. A wide variety of fabrics can be woven on them but they are not adapted to the lighter weight fabrics [the cheap goods made in the South]... Many of the looms have been purchased from other companies which have gone out of business. The nature of a loom is such that it has an almost endless possible life. Adequate loom-fixing may keep it in good operating condition but the economy of old equipment is somewhat doubtful... [As to jacquard mechanisms,] little progress has been made in the design of these machines over the last twenty-five years.

Technology lags were not the source of the industrial doldrums; instead the market squeeze had led manufacturers to defer spending on sporadic updating that might add new dimensions of product flexibility in favor of niche hunting and product or labor manipulation. As there was no Northrop option, no technological fix, capitals were being run down, prior to being vaporized.[105]

This pattern can be made more vivid by examining several sectors a bit more closely. The capital drop might well conceal a pattern of concentration, if numbers of modest-scale firms were eradicated to leave behind a core of perhaps technically current, large operations. Quite the reverse took place. In hosiery, wool/worsted weaving, and spinning, to take examples from sectors where large enterprises had emerged in Philadelphia, the numbers of active firms were reduced by 13 percent (from 187 to 162), whereas overall capital declined substantially more, 1929–33 (Table 6.8, Index). Moreover, average capital per firm also fell in all three cases given, respectively by 13, 30, and 47 percent.[106] Put simply, large operations in Philadelphia textiles were prone in the crisis to downsize or depart, like Fleisher's yarns, and smaller ones more likely to persist.

A third indicator of the contours of the Depression's impact may be gleaned from data on production values. Table 6.9 mirrors its predecessor in giving nominal figures and an index; and to factor out price deflation and thus reflect declines in real values, the Bureau of Labor Statistics textile products price index was employed to recast reported figures into deflated or reflated 1929 dollars. This corrects for the double effect of lagging output

---

[105] FR-Uph, ch. 4, pp. 9–10, PP-135, TMR.

[106] The raw figures are: hosiery, 1929 average capital – $385,000, 1933 – $338,000; wool/ worsted weaving, 1929 – $336,000, 1933 – $235,000; wool/worsted spinning, 1929 – $587,000, 1933 – $313,000. Calculated from Philadelphia County tabulations in Pennsylvania Department of Internal Affairs, *Report on Productive Industries, Public Utilities, and Miscellaneous Statistics...for 1929*, Harrisburg, PA, 1931, pp. 232–9, and idem, *Report...for 1933*, Harrisburg, PA, 1935, pp. 284–9.

Table 6.9. *Product value for Philadelphia textiles, selected sectors, and all nontextile industries, 1926, 1928–33*

	Product Value (in millions)						
	1926	1928	1929	1930	1931	1932	1933
All textiles	334.9	334.8	344.4	241.9	179.3	126.8	142.4
Hosiery	89.3	95.9	103.4	65.1	45.7	38.4	35.3
Carpets	40.7	29.9	31.6	21.2	16.9	11.0	12.0
Dye-finish	20.8	23.2	21.4	16.1	13.4	8.9	9.5
Wool/worsted goods	26.1	25.6	23.3	21.8	16.9	7.8	10.8
Wool/worsted yarns	35.3	30.2	30.0	18.5	13.3	8.6	10.6
PNTI[a]	1,403.4	1,365.9	1,466.6	1,312.8	1,023.2	750.4	774.2

	Index (corrected to 1929 dollars, 1929 = 100)[b]						
	1926	1928	1929	1930	1931	1932	1933
All textiles	88	92	100	79	71	60	57
Hosiery	78	87	100	71	61	61	47
Carpets	117	89	100	75	73	57	53
Dye-finish	88	102	100	84	86	68	62
Wool/worsted goods	102	104	100	105	99	55	64
Wool/worsted yarns	107	95	100	69	61	47	49
PNTI	87	88	100	93	96	84	73
PNTI-2[c]	88	92	100	96	85	66	68

[a]Philadelphia nontextile industries.
[b]Nominal figures corrected to reflect real 1929 dollars, using Bureau of Labor Statistics Wholesale Price Index for Textile Products, Series E-29 of the Historical Statistics of the United States (1957 ed.), published as *Statistical History of the United States from Colonial Times to the Present*, Stamford, CT, 1965, p. 117. Price series figures were recalculated to a 1929 base 100.
[c]Second PNTI index corrects nominal totals through use of Series E-26, All Commodities other than Farm or Food Products, so as better to reflect the diversified output of city manufacturing, giving a slower initial drop and deeper bottom point, yet better performance than textiles in each post-1929 year. See *SHUS*, p. 117.
Sources: See Table 6.8.

and simultaneously falling price levels; the index shows actual contraction of production without the deflationary blurring. In real terms, textile values declined farther and faster than did those for other local industries, slumping one-fifth, 1929–30, and two-fifths by 1932 versus 7 percent for the rest in the first year and one-sixth by 1932. (In nominal prices, the textile fade was even more dramatic.) Sectorally, it appears that surging hosiery sales, in a context of generally declining prices, 1926–9, "carried" the industry to a 1929 production value high point, more than compensating for the mixed performance of the other trade divisions. However, in and after 1930, hosiery plotted a steady downward course and was one of three sectors that evidenced no "Blue Eagle" effect in 1933. The two woolen divisions touched lower bottoms and rebounded, but full-fashioned continued to crumble. As a result, hosiery's share in the city's textile output tumbled from 30 to 25 percent by 1933, below its 1925 portion, while the textile industry's segment of all Philadelphia manufacturing values, which hovered between 19 and 20 percent through 1929, quickly fell to 15 percent in 1932–3. These were ominous signs that the trade's "best" sector was weakening and now contributing to the industry's relative eclipse. Everything seemed to be slumping in the early 1930s, but Philadelphia textiles were plummeting disproportionately after a decade of discouragement.

Not all free-falling components of the textile system fell at the same rate. Neither employment, total wages, nor average earnings per worker (the latter pair set out in real terms parallel to output values) contracted as readily or as far as did real product value. Contrasting the wage and earnings indices in Table 6.10 with the output index from Table 6.9 is revealing. Though by 1932 real output had slumped 40 percent, real wages paid had been reduced only 30 percent. Worse, despite wage cuts and layoffs, the average work year of labor in textiles involved real dollar payouts in 1932 only 2 percent below the 1929 level. Two things were going on here. First, textile proprietors, lacking effective cost-accounting techniques and unable to gauge "market signals" with any accuracy, were the victims of a classic wage stickiness, itself a blend of blurs in gauging deflation, fears of decomposing the working group and of shedding key workers, and in spots, active resistance to rate cuts. Second, compared with area nontextile employers, though they dismissed proportionately more workers, 1929–32, textile firms were less able to adjust the gaps between real total wages and real output values. For nontextile operators, this lag was closed from seven and four index points in 1930 and 1931, to one and two points in 1932 and 1933. For the textile cohort, it expanded, from four and five points in the first two years, to ten and six in the latter pair. Moreover, in four of the five sectors analyzed, the 1926 textile output value index stood above the wage index, but this relation was completely reversed in 1933. Whether from ignorance,

Table 6.10. *Indices of employment, total wages and earnings per worker,*
Philadelphia, 1926, 1928–33, all textiles and selected sectors

Employment (1929 = 100)	1926	1928	1929	1930	1931	1932	1933
All textiles	106	100	100	89	78	70	78
Hosiery	80	91	100	91	81	83	87
Carpets	121	104	100	85	72	57	74
Dye-finish	100	110	100	93	83	75	90
Wool/worsted goods	128	109	100	101	83	52	71
Wool/worsted yarns	139	116	100	85	77	60	68
PNTI	95	96	100	92	84	74	80
Total Wages (adjusted, 1929 = 100)	1926	1928	1929	1930	1931	1932	1933
All textiles	88	92	100	83	76	70	63
Hosiery	67	85	100	76	62	67	52
Carpets	114	96	100	86	87	71	72
Dye-finish	85	110	100	103	97	92	81
Wool/worsted goods	113	106	100	104	111	66	73
Wool/worsted yarns	102	96	100	77	82	58	58
PNTI	85	88	100	100	100	85	75
Earnings Per Worker (adjusted, 1929 = 100)	1926	1928	1929	1930	1931	1932	1933
All textiles	85	92	100	93	97	98	81
Hosiery	84	76	100	85	81	88	64
Carpets	94	97	100	102	122	124	96
Dye-finish	86	91	100	111	117	124	90
Wool/worsted goods	88	107	100	104	129	128	102
Wool/worsted yarns	74	91	100	90	106	96	86

Note: Price index corrections made using Series E-2, BLS, as in Table 6.9, for *total wages* and *earnings per worker*.
Sources: See Table 6.8.

custom, anxiety, or benevolence, textile millmen failed to bring their real wage bills down sufficiently to compensate for the erosion of price and demand in tandem. Thus wages as a proportion of textile product values rose from a steady 23 percent (1926–9) to 27 percent in 1932, while in the rest of Philadelphia industry they represented a stable 17–18 percent across the entire period. Falling materials prices offered no opportunities, for they were routinely taken into account when buyers prepared price offers. Buffeted by ascendant purchasers and as baffled by deflation as they had been by the war-era inflation, Philadelphia proprietors surely sensed that if, outside a few favored sectors, profits during the 1920s had been dispiriting, current trends indicated that only losses could be expected in the coming years.[107]

Taken together, this melange of statistics and indices helps dramatize the plight of Philadelphia's textile trades as the pace of their unraveling quickened after 1929. Yet we have had thus far no hint of the profit slippage that accompanied decline. As mentioned earlier, both federal and state industrial surveys were so composed after 1919 as to shield information that would make even rudimentary estimates possible. However, in preparing the 1931 Wharton study of area upholstery mills, companies opened records for the preceding decade to scrutiny. Edward Wright, one of the researchers, was thereby enabled to generate data on cost and profit trends for the last prosperous weaving sector. Though average profit on net sales in 1921 stood at a healthy 18 percent, half again the level of depression 1920, the decade-long trend thereafter was downward, to 15 percent in 1923, 11 in 1925, and 5.6 percent in 1927. During the last two years of the 1920s, upholstery mills averaged a one percent return on sales, and in 1930 a net loss of 12 percent. Under the same piece-rate schedule for the ten years after 1921, labor costs comprised a high but stable 30 percent of each sales dollar, 28 percent in quite profitable 1921, 29 percent in a wretched 1929. The shifts that reflect falling margins were centered in Wright's "materials" category, which included inventories of finished goods, and in selling expenses. The former line moved from 23 to 35 percent of each sales dollar, 1921–9, which, given that raw materials costs were sliding, suggests the beginnings of stock holding or inventory losses late in the decade. In addition, advertising and related marketing expenses rose from about 6 to over 9 percent of all costs during the same years as firms tried to counter buyers' drift toward cheap and flimsy goods from rival localities. Even the 14 percent piece-rate cut installed in 1931 (after a long strike against an arbitrator's decision) lessened the labor share of the sales dollar only four cents, recovering only a third of the twelve

---

[107] That real earnings per worker remained near 100 for all textiles and above it for three sectors, 1929–32, is a statistical artifact which exposes wage rate stickiness and conceals widespread part-time or shared-work employment. Since this index is simply the result of dividing the real total wages index by that for employment, it makes it appear that the typical *working* textile operative was little hurt (or in three sectors actually advantaged) in real wage terms by the depression's effects. However, as employment figures were themselves reports of *average* annual workforces, they hid the extent to which jobs were shared on rotations, a practice quite general outside knitting. Had we figures for "total number employed" during the year, the real earnings index would be much lower, but this in no way alters the problematic relation between the total wages and product value indices. In fact, inefficiencies due to even a planned cycling of workers through the mill surely contributed to this evidently falling productivity, however much these provisions sustained workers' household economies and manufacturers' hopes.

cent loss on every dollar's worth of goods in 1930. Though they naturally varied from mill to mill across the city, it is reasonable to suggest that profits in those sectors unable to resist the pressure for stock carrying (and buyers' control over pricing and terms) faded sooner than in upholstery, indeed never recovered from the 1920–1 crunch. During the 1920s company earnings in carpets, cotton, silk, and wool/worsted weaving, spinning, and seamless hosiery were often negligible. Full-fashioned hosiery and knitted outerwear had longer profitable runs to be sure, but the market shifts sent the majority of the Philadelphia trades reeling well before the onset of the great contraction.[108]

To be sure, textile workers were less likely to be able to alter the conditions and relations that precipitated decline. However, they were far from idle in attempting to fashion strategies. By adding resistance to the three categories used in treating employers (aggressive, accommodation, and exit), the range of worker efforts can be surveyed. Alone among the remaining organized labor groups in Philadelphia, the full-fashioned hosiery workers met the late 1920s debacle with a determined attempt to organize their industry as a whole. If rival manufacturers could not reach a common basis on which to establish and defend prices, standardization of work rules, hours, and pay rates through aggressive extension of the union's sphere of influence could do the job. As *Hosiery Worker* explained editorially in 1930:

> No scheme of industrial regulation is feasible which does not include the organization of the labor force and a degree of cooperation between employer and employee ... The fact should be readily apparent that the best way to have regulation of production is through an agreement ... regarding the number of hours to be worked during a specified period. The employer making an agreement to slow down for a time would, under such a system, not have to fear that their competitors would go

---

[108] *FR-Uph*, ch. 2, pp. 5, 9, 12. Nationally, the share of manufacturing wages in sales dollars trended slightly downward during the 1920s, from 28 percent in 1921 and 1923 to 25 percent in 1929 (see National Industrial Conference Board, *Costs and Profits in Manufacturing Industry, 1914–1933* [N.I.C.B. Studies Number 213], New York, 1935, p. 6). It may also be added here that suburban patterns during the 1920s in the Philadelphia region cannot be analyzed with any confidence using the Pennsylvania Department of Internal Affairs *Reports*, as data on subsectors with fewer than three establishments were not separately printed. Whereas direct linkage between 1925 textile directories and the firm-by-firm employment tables from the 1925 *Pennsylvania Industrial Directory* revealed over 20,000 textile jobs in the four suburban counties (Table 6.5), the county tables for the 1926 B.I.A. *Report* numbered only 13,300 positions, excluding for example the giant Marcus Hook Viscose rayon plant since it was the sole rayon yarn producer in Delaware County. As a result, related B.I.A. capital, wages, etc., data from the suburban counties are of no immediate value. Linkage-based suburban employment information for 1934 will be presented in Chapter 7.

back on the bargain . . . The workers, to protect THEIR interests, would
see to it that the entire membership of the union would abide by whatever
agreement was entered into.[109]

To achieve this, full-fashioned workers would strive for efficiency in union
mills and simultaneously exercise themselves to organize non-union firms,
first in Philadelphia, then in the upstate Berks County district, and ultimately
in the South. Major "yellow dog" plants in the city would be initially brought
down (Aberle, Cambria, Apex) and the flagship Berkshire Mills just outside
Reading targeted. As more and more capacity was brought under contract,
a different species of worker control, benefiting the industry as a whole,
would come to be perceived as the essential, long-sought means of price
and product regulation in a sector whose rapid growth had handed market
power over to hosiery purchasers in 1928–9. Though this approach might
retrospectively be seen as near-utopian, it had a geographical plausibility at
the time. In 1929, 62 percent of the nation's full-fashioned machinery was
lodged in Pennsylvania factories, a third of national capacity in Philadelphia
alone. The South by contrast held only 11 of 111 mills with more than 25
machines (vs. 63 in Pennsylvania) and but 7 percent of all machinery. Timely
unionization starting at or near home, the workers' believed, was the best
hope for an industry that had doubled its capacity in four boom years (1924–
8) only to be bushwhacked by a trade depression. In advancing their ambitious plan, the hosiery workers demonstrated a clear understanding that
neither autonomous localism nor personalistic relations, watchwords for generations of area labor activists, were adequate tools with which to master
the situation. Adopting the language of efficiency and regulation, they began
practicing the labor equivalent of the modern business rationality so generally
rejected by Philadelphia manufacturers.[110]

More radically aggressive maneuvers based on socialist or communist
ideologies were nonstarters in Philadelphia, although some of the full-fashioned activists were Socialist Party members and would become more visible
as such during the New Deal years. Kensington textile workers did sponsor
and participate in the Unemployed League's challenges to city hall and its
defenses against evictions in the mill districts. Yet decisive socioeconomic
alternatives had little purchase on the industrial situation, circa 1926–33.
The full-fashioned union publicly distanced itself from those with "Com-

---

[109] *Hosiery Worker*, May 15, 1930, p. 1.

[110] *Cotton* 93(September 1929): 1309–15; George W. Taylor, *Significant Post-War Changes
in the Full-Fashioned Hosiery Industry*, Philadelphia, 1929, p. 60 On "yellow dog contracts" in hosiery see L. R. Thomas to H. L. Kerwin, January 26, 1927, FMCS File
170/3762, and *Hosiery Worker*, July 15, 1929, p. 1; July 31, p. 1, for use of an actual
yellow dog as a mascot in the Cambria organizing strike.

munistic tendencies" so as to clear ground on which to parade its moderate laborite collectivism as a unity strategy in hosiery. In a local context in which the head of the independent Beamers' and Twisters' Organization denounced UTW conservatives as "radicals... a bunch of reds," challenges to the capitalist system would fall on rocky soil.[111]

Resistance materialized periodically in the seemingly endless succession of wage and rate cuts. In all but a few cases, the results were predictably harsh. Tapestry carpet workers' futile resistance to a 1926 reduction brought collapse of their union, and later carpet mill strikes brought dismissals and replacements of disruptive operatives. Walkouts of three months and more early in the Depression against cuts at specialty weaving mills (F. P. Woll, Artloom) failed to prevent the slicing of rates.[112]

In upholstery, where an extended pattern of labor–proprietor collaboration existed, conferences on a sectorwide reduction in 1930 reached a stalemate, triggering implementation of a hitherto unused provision for binding arbitration. When Joseph Willits's report called for a 14 percent reduction of scales, Local 25 bolted, enraged at the result and at the pressure tactics of UTW national leaders encouraging acquiescence. The ensuing strike, which dragged on for four months, brought the local's expulsion from the UTW, while proprietors ran "looms where they were employed while learning the business," to fill a few scattered orders. Exhausted, the strikers returned to work in May 1931, accepting the cut at last, and joining with owners in requesting the aforementioned Wharton study, "a step quite unprecedented in the history of local industrial relations."[113] By contrast, no compromises stirred in the open-shop carpet sector. Late in 1930, all Philadelphia mills installed a 10 percent reduction, the third since 1925, but only at Hardwick and Magee was a committee elected and a strike begun. Enrolling in the UTW's shadow Carpet Weavers' Union, the strikers appealed for mediation, but company managers declined the option and asserted that none of the absent weavers would be rehired. In August the UTW considered the cause "hopelessly lost." At year's end, the weavers conceded after eleven months

[111] Hosiery Worker, March 30, 1929, p. 4; Palmer interview with William Thomas of the B.T.O., 1931, PP–135, TMR; Russell Weigley, ed., Philadelphia: A 300-Year History, New York, 1982, p. 610; Knitting Mill News 9(1930): 50 (hereafter cited as KMN).
[112] Palmer, Union Tactics, pp. 38–46; FMCS File 170/5406 (Barrymore), 170/5482 (Hardwick), 170/5537 (Woll), 170/5965 (Artloom).
[113] Palmer, Union Tactics, pp. 67–8, FMCS File 170/5749 (Primrose), Balderston et al., Upholstery Weaving, p. 4; Fred Keightly to Kerwin, February 4, 1931; March 3, 1931; April 9, 1931, April 17, 1931; Thomas McMahon, UTWA International President to Maurice Burns, Secretary, Local 25, April 16, 1931; Agreement between Upholstery Manufacturers and Local 25, April 30, 1931; Keightly to Kerwin, May 8, 1931, in FMCS File 170/6068; KMN 9(1931): 166.

only to find Hardwick bosses taking, in the conciliator's words, an "absolutely merciless attitude toward them," seeking to blacklist many of the weavers throughout the carpet industry.[114]

Resistance may well have helped moderate rate cuts, contributing to the real wage stickiness mentioned above, but most textile workers sought ways of accommodating to their straitened circumstances. So long as there were relatively vigorous sectors within the textile districts, workers could seek to transfer their skills from one trade division to another, shifting from coloring piece goods to hosiery dyeing, from winding carpet yarns to winding silk for knitting. As Gladys Palmer observed, "Many of the Philadelphia upholstery and tapestry weavers were formerly silk, woolen, or worsted weavers." The upholstery study bore this out, as 47 percent of some 700 workers reporting previous occupations had come to the furnishings trade from carpet, cloth, or chenille weaving, and another 16 percent from other textile jobs. However, it was far more difficult for knitters to shift from outerwear or seamless hosiery to full-fashioned, as the possible skill transfer was minimal. If the later WPA surveys of full-fashioned employees are any measure, few men managed this lateral move; one who did characterized the hurdle this way: "The difference between knitting on hosiery after knitting on sweaters was perhaps the difference between learning to pilot an airplane after having been able to drive a car." Women experienced as "loopers" in seamless hosiery had better chances, for "the looper's work isn't as different in the 2 types of stockings as some of the other operations." Two WPA informants who crossed over had both been employed at Buck Hosiery when "the firm began to get interested in Full Fashion" and thus learned the rudiments. Another coming from seamless spent three months as a "looper's apprentice" in 1931 before being promoted to a regular position.[115]

[114] Keightly to Kerwin, January 7, 1931; Strike Committee to Department of Labor, January 10, 1931, Keightly to Kerwin, March 5, August 10, 1931, January 5, 1932, FMCS File 170/6020. Interviews with textile workers conducted in the late 1930s (cited at n. 115) refer to dozens of other resistance strikes, 1925–32, not reported in the *Ledger* or involving federal conciliators. These recollections of strikes stretched back into the 1890s; indeed one weaver remembered in detail the cause and outcome of the 1915 walkout at the Dobson's Bradford Mill discussed in Chapter 5 (Philadelphia Labor Market Studies, Works Progress Administration, Schedule No. 1641, Urban Archives, Temple University). None of the accounts of the late 1920s and early 1930s strikes indicated any successes, though Schedule No. 1848 confirms the Hardwick blacklist.
[115] Palmer, "Decline of Weaving," p. 9; *FR-Uph*, ch. 6, Appendix, p. 7; Philadelphia Labor Market Studies, Works Progress Administration, Schedule No. 2199, Urban Archives, Temple University (hereafter WPA Schedules). For women shifters, see WPA Schedule Nos. 2593, 2598, and 2602. As these interviews were conducted in 1936–7 and as most women workers were then aged 18–25, only occasional views of the 1920–32 period are available. The three women here cited were 39, 40, and 39 years of age in 1936

As with firms, sector shifts by workers were far less common than fidelity to one's craft. In her 1930s studies, Palmer stressed "the tenacity with which textile workers seek to secure textile employment," particularly in their area of skilled experience.

> In some communities where shut-downs of major industries have oc-
> curred, the workers who have in later years drifted into other types of
> employment no longer report the declining occupation as their usual
> occupation. This does not appear to be true of weavers. They may not
> have worked at weaving for years, but this is their "trade," and, even
> if employed elsewhere at the time of study, they wish to return to weaving
> if possible and report this as their "usual" occupation.

In phrases familiar to students of recent deindustrialization, Palmer enlarged on this point.

> Most weavers who have tried other work after losing textile employment
> have found jobs only at levels of skill lower than weaving. Some of the
> older weavers have decided to try to get along on the inadequate income
> which is derived from highly irregular work at weaving rather than to
> attempt new work. In a city like Philadelphia where most textile workers
> own their homes, the possibilities of moving to other areas are greatly
> restricted. In any case, the problems of securing jobs in other areas and
> moving families are difficult.[116]

This stubborn individual refusal to behave as labor market signals ordered was collectively just as "irrational" as manufacturers' refusal to quit the trade and ease capacity and competition, for the labor pool remained brimming for two decades after the 1920–1 market power shift. Whereas WPA interviews with workers active throughout the 1920s indicate that many simply endured a succession of hirings and layoffs, some went to considerable lengths to retain their textile link. Two informants secured work after 1925 at Princeton Worsted in Trenton and drove back and forth daily as long as their jobs lasted, as did upholstery workers who commuted to Mt. Holly, New Jersey, (across the new Benjamin Franklin Bridge) until all nonresident weavers were dismissed in 1932, perhaps to stanch infiltrating union sen-

---

with at least ten years' experience in the trade. On the original schedules, which are organized by occupational category, the whole number sequence is inscribed in the upper right center, just *below* and *outside* the box labeled "schedule No." At the Urban Archives, the schedules are filed in this whole-number sequence, rather than by the original interview numbers, which reflect their chronological succession. Names of informants may not be revealed by researchers. Finally, "loopers" operated a machine that stitched a flat seam to draw together the underside of the foot portion in a fully knit fashioned stocking (see George Taylor, *The Full-Fashioned Hosiery Worker: His Changing Economic Status*, Philadelphia, 1929, pp. 187–8, hereafter cited as Taylor, *Hosiery Worker*).

[116] Palmer, "Decline of Weaving," pp. 21, 54.

timents. Some supplemented intermittent textile work with other jobs, specifically home repair and positions in the equally erratic radio industry. A Kensington weaver reported alternating between Follwells and RCA-Camden, for "as soon as the dress goods season was over, the radio production season began." Yet this crazy-quilt pattern of employment took its emotional toll. A veteran woman weaver felt by 1936 that she was a "JINX," as on three successive jobs after 1929 her employers had liquidated. A Lithuanian immigrant had even better cause to feel his resemblance to Al Capp's doomed cartoon character; five of his six employers since the war had shut down, sending him off to carry his black cloud to another mill. Overall, the sense of having a trade, part of the proud tradition of skill in Philadelphia, combined with the thin likelihood of transferring textile proficiencies to plants outside the industry to lock thousands of now surplus operatives into the exhausting routine of getting, losing, and seeking work.[117]

Trade unions chiefly accommodated to decline by attempting to limit wage reductions and secure orderly, rather than capricious, patterns of layoff, recall, and work sharing. They were generally unable to prevent stretch outs (of worsted and plush weavers to four looms or additions to the "sections" for which loom fixers were responsible), nor had they much impact on speedups, lowered materials quality, or the introduction of floating machine assignments. However, broader collaboration with owners was attempted in both upholstery and full-fashioned hosiery. The utter failure of Local 25's 1930 walkout yielded the joint approach to Wharton, but proprietors' indifference to the study's recommendations and the relatively high piece rates established in the 1932 contract negotiations augured poorly for the future. By the mid-1930s, Local 25 would still have contractual relations with only seven of the twenty-two firms struck in 1930, and four of these possessed branch plants at which it was claimed the bulk of their orders were woven.[118]

In full-fashioned, consistent with the "inside" portion of its aggressive organizing strategy, the knitters' union pressed members after 1926 to strive for elimination of waste and "bad work" at mills already in the fold and by 1929 achieved a uniform national agreement standardizing rates and con-

---

[117] WPA Schedule Nos. 1719–20, 1726, 1776, 1805, 1835, 1840, 1890–1, 1909.

[118] No mergers or collective marketing efforts appeared. The 1932 agreement was a straight hours, conditions, and rates document, ignoring issues of close-costing or product modifications. A joint technical committee without any genuine authority was created, and the hosiery trade's use of an impartial chairman to decide disputes over interpretation of the agreement was copied. As to piece rates, the 1932 schedule was in all major categories, and in time work pay, only 10 percent below the schedule in force during the 1920s (see Balderston, *Upholstery Weaving*, pp. 175–190, and for earlier price lists, Selig Papers, Pastore Library, Philadelphia College of Textiles and Science). On the union's decline, see WPA Schedule Nos. 1773 and 1906.

ditions in all union shops, then constituting just under 30 percent of total capacity. As both machinery in place and price pressure (particularly from Reading) had increased sharply, the parties to the September 1929 contract authorized a joint "Time and Effort Study," drew on clothing trade practice by installing an impartial chairman to settle disputes and prevent stoppages, and compromised on partial implementation of two-machine assignments. In the postcrash trade spasm, the contract was smoothly reopened and a June 1930 pact brought full "doubling" of machines plus an average 20 percent rate reduction. As the decline steepened, the full-fashioned union in October 1931 accepted further cuts of 35–45 percent on the major operations in return for a closed shop and "dues collection system" (checkoff), all the while pushing its organizing efforts relentlessly. For hosiery activists, "give-backs" made sense only in the context of intensive recruitment drives that could stabilize the industry. Thus acceptance of the 1930–1 retrenchments was a part of a larger dynamic strategy that sought to blend short-term accommodations with militant organizing that would lay the foundation for long-term "regulation." However, Wharton's George Taylor, selected as impartial chairman in 1931, cautioned that even that year's deep cuts would shrink total costs only 12–15 percent and that financial concerns could be far more crucial for individual firms that owed sizable sums for recently acquired machinery. These debts would have to be retired from such profits as could be harvested from deflated prices, an heroic problem whose solution hardly lay alone in piece-rate manipulations. Taylor's observation was crucial, for it highlighted the distance between even the most creative labor organization policies in 1930–1 and the development of a plausible strategy for reversing either the sectoral crisis or the decay of the whole system of flexible and specialized textile production. All the king's horses and all the king's men . . . [119]

For employees as for firms, exit was the terminal option, yet as Palmer noted, it was no more welcomed by workers than by proprietors, along either spatial or occupational lines. Few in either group behaved like "economic men." For young single males in full-fashioned, especially those discomfited by union membership, Reading was reportedly a magnet of sorts during the 1920s. As both men and women in this sector were markedly younger than workers in other textile trades, physical relocation was certainly a possibility. But for the rest, where would they go? Providence, Passaic, Paterson, Charlotte, all were hardly inviting venues in the later 1920s. Networks of contacts

---

[119] Taylor, *Hosiery Worker*, pp. 3, 11, 47–9; *UHR* 14(November 1931): 135–141; *Hosiery Worker*, October 1, 1927, p. 4; March 1, 1928, p. 4; January 31, 1930, p. 2, April 15, 1930, pp. 1, 3. See also *TW* 77(1930): 3003–6, for mill owners' comments on purchasing machinery "on tick," hand-to-mouth purchasing, and fashion shifts.

in the textile districts, homes paid for or nearly so, family ties, none would be abandoned by spinners, weavers, or dyers in any great numbers in the absence of some electrifying opportunity. A return to Europe was an option for only a few, as less than 9 percent of Philadelphia's textile workers in 1929 were foreign-born, and most of them were middle-aged or older. Sticking it out on their common ground was the general choice. As one veteran weaver later boasted, "I'm an old-timer in Kensington and I'm pretty well known. I don't have much trouble getting work." Still, even this networking adept admitted that he would rather not again "go through those years right after '29, when I'd make as little as a few hours a week." For those less well-connected, occupational change could become obligatory. Consider the thousands of Manayunk and East Falls workers cut loose by the sequence of Dobson closings. A displaced carpet weaver said, "the people here for the most part had their lives built around Dobsons and when it shut down things began to be very bad for them." Fortunately, for about a decade the rapid growth of Atwater Kent's famed radio-building plant (just atop East Falls near the Midvale Steel complex) provided hundreds of jobs for former Dobson operatives, especially women, as assemblers. Yet radio work was no less irregular than textile labor had been and disappeared entirely in a few years. Philco's cheap table radios displaced Kent's "cathedrals of sound" during the Depression, and the East Falls electrical plant went under in 1936.[120]

Among weavers and spinners who departed for other work yet retained the notion that textile employment was their "usual" trade, exit brought few satisfying experiences. Work in electrical factories (Philco, Exide) or at gas stations, painting houses, helping carpenters, or gardening for the rich was either numbing mass-production toil or undependable, servile outdoor labor. One blacklisted carpet weaver did become an activities leader at the Lighthouse, the sturdy settlement house not far from Hardwick that remained a rallying point for countless Kensington labor and community groups. Others started tiny restaurants, which failed, or cigar stores and taprooms, which

---

[120] The Reading drawing card was the chance to realize greater total income than could be achieved on one machine in union mills. This was done through operating two machines (with two helpers), despite lower per dozen piece rates. See Taylor, *Hosiery Worker*, ch. IV, for a fuller picture. Other sources used here, Pennsylvania B.I.A., *Report: 1929*, pp. 232–9, on foreign-born among textile workers, and WPA Schedule Nos. 1778 and 1610, respectively, for quoted matter. In 1936, the Palmer WPA team interviewed 130 immigrant Philadelphia textile workers. Their average age then, fifty, made most of them forty or older in 1929. The shift to radio among women textile workers has been uncovered by Patricia Cooper, as a part of work in progress on Philadelphia women's work during the Depression. It would be interesting to know whether perceptions that displaced textile workers would be available in significant numbers influenced the siting of the Atwater Kent plant, but no records currently available bear on this point.

brought them a living. Surely a few found ladders into other trades or out of the working class entirely; doubtless some women slid across into the needle trades or married, well or badly. But thousands remained poised for the big recovery that never came, husbanding their resources and harboring their grievances. This distraught summation vibrates still:

> I have been working at the weaving trade for 35 years, and I don't mean the time I was unemployed. I have 35 years of *experience*. I can't remember all the places I've worked in my lifetime... And look at me now! I'm no bum. I've got a trade, but where am I going to practice it?[121]

Insofar as workers' skills in textiles were industry-specific and, as Palmer found, thousands of veteran operatives clung to their trades, local mills' ability to endure was enhanced. The presence of a labor force in large part willing to accept part-time and erratic employment, aging in place rather than venturing into other fields, sustained the parallel commitment of manufacturers in older sectors. Each leaned upon the other as the horizon grew darker.

6.5. Full-fashioned hosiery from glamour to gloom, 1925–1933

The boom-to-bust sequence in Philadelphia's full-fashioned hosiery sector was more compressed than in any of its other specialty trades. The great fashion rush to silk that gathered force in the early 1920s burst forth in 1925 as runaway demand brought vast profits, encouraging both capacity expansion and new entries into the field. Only four years later, by the spring of 1929, buyers took command, moderating their stock levels, implementing piecemeal purchasing, and establishing in full-fashioned the array of advantageous practices that had become common across the rest of the style–goods spectrum. Within eighteen months, crisis conditions were plainly evident and were intensified when crash-panicked purchasers suspended buying in the winter of 1929–30. Yet the ensuing contraction was spatially differentiated; Philadelphia (and union mills within its full-fashioned complement) suffered acutely whereas the Reading district adjusted smoothly and southern activity barely flagged. In order better to understand the course of these events, it will help to review first the technical side of full-fashioned production, its capital costs, labor needs, and technological developments

[121] WPA Schedule Nos. 1623, 1631, 1708, 1730, 1752, 1806, 1817, 1859, 1865, 2028, 2046, 2053, 2058; Palmer, "Decline of Weaving," p. 55; Interview summaries, PP–135, TMR.

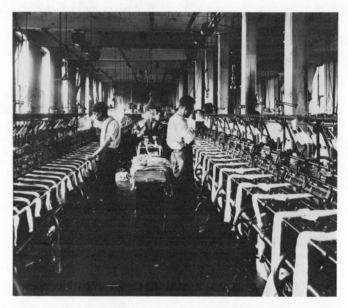

Figure 22. Full-fashioned knitting, twenty-section legging machines at Brown-Aberle, Kensington, 1922. Note that here one knitter attended each machine, rather than the "doubling" that was standard at Reading and a consistent issue between proprietors and workers in Philadelphia. (Courtesy of the Pennsylvania Historical and Museum Commission.)

during the 1920s. Then in turn, issues of style and product changes, financing, interregional competition, price leadership, and marketing will be highlighted in order to create an adequate context for the upheavals that early Depression organizing drives brought in 1930–1.

Making full-fashioned hosiery necessitated a battery of machines on which a flat fabric was first knitted then seamed to form a stocking that closely approximated the shape of a woman's leg. The flexibility of a knitted product and the silk that went into it combined with the design of the stocking, gradually narrowed from top to ankle, to yield a skinlike fit far superior to that of traditional seamless hose, which were essentially tubes shrunk on forming boards to the shape of a leg. In full-fashioned work, knitting was accomplished on two huge devices, known as leggers and footers, according to the part of the product they created. The first machine simultaneously knitted eighteen to twenty-eight stocking legs, each made in a separate section on a thirteen to fourteen inch bar, the knitting equivalent of multiple-shuttle ribbon looms common in narrow-goods weaving. The legger operated intermittently, for yarn breaks and the snapping of any of the eight to ten

Figure 23. Seaming the leg section of full-fashioned hosiery, Artcraft Hosiery Mills, Philadelphia, 1930. (Courtesy of the Pennsylvania Historical and Museum Commission.)

thousand knitting needles its sections held demanded instant repair. Moreover, the knitter hand-turned the stocking top (welt) to create a durable double thickness and controlled narrowing of the lower (boot) width manually. Hence the legger machine cycle involved an hour or more in order to finish its set of upper stocking segments, which were twenty-three to thirty-three inches long.

At the end of a cycle, skilled toppers disengaged the legs and slipped them onto a transfer bar for insertion into the footer, on which the knitting process was completed. As this was a comparatively shorter step, it was generally established that two or three operating leggers were necessary to feed one footer and keep it busy. A set of these three (or four) machines cost $15,000 to $35,000 in the 1920s; over two-thirds of those installed came from the Textile Machine Works in Reading, the dominant force in full-fashioned machine building. With the knitting at an end, looping and seaming were next. The first involved laying a flat seam forming the foot pocket from toe to heel, the second completed the enclosure of the leg section to the thigh top. These separate operations involved two more machines and delicate, skilled handling of the fabric. Finishing steps, unless the product was sold immediately "in the gray," included dyeing, boarding, pairing, inspection, and packing.[122]

Like all complex machines, the full-fashioned legger reflected intriguing tradeoffs between flexibility and rigidity. Its 5,000 parts, beyond the needles, had to be "in perfect order or the stockings will have a defect." Thus attention to precise operation and anticipation of or quick reaction to problems were the centerpieces of the knitter's skill. The machine itself was rigid along one crucial dimension, gauge. Stocking gauge numbers indicated the number of stitches knitted in every one and a half inches along the bar; a thirty-nine gauge thus meant twenty-six needles per inch. As the entire motive apparatus of the legger was geared to its gauge, this could not be altered, a fact of significance in a period of rapid technological response to fashion shifts. Nor could the speed of the machine be much accelerated, fifty-six to sixty-four courses per minute being the standard range written into piece-rate schedules. Still, within these constraints, a legger could run an enormous range of goods. Cotton, silk, or plated yarns posed no changeover problems technically. For example, silk hose often were made with cotton tops and/ or feet for durability and economy. Thrown silk, twisted from individual cocoon threads rather than spun from short fibers like cotton, both fine (three-thread) and coarse (eight- to eleven-thread), could be employed without difficult adjustments. Moreover, through the use of attachments, the stitch patterns could be altered, stripes, fancy heels, or ornamental details added, or lacelike fashion "inserts" built into the stocking. Each of these flexible possibilities was coded into the piece-rate schedule, which ran to several hundred lines in the 1920s and 1930s.[123]

---

[122] George W. Taylor, *Significant Post-War Changes*, ch. 1; idem, *Hosiery Worker*, pp. 184–9.

[123] Ibid., Gustave Geiges, "Waste Elimination in the Full-Fashioned Hosiery Industry," *Bulletin of the Taylor Society* 12(1927): 411; *UHR* 14(November 1931): 137–41; (December 1931): 121–2; (February 1932): 143.

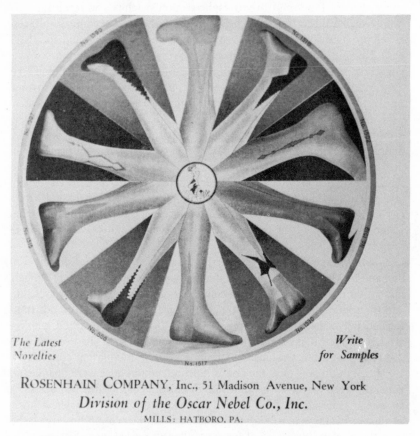

The Latest
Novelties

Write
for Samples

ROSENHAIN COMPANY, Inc., 51 Madison Avenue, New York
Division of the Oscar Nebel Co., Inc.
MILLS: HATBORO, PA.

Figure 24. Novelty heels, full-fashioned specialty designs from Oscar Nebel
Company, 1930. (Author's collection.)

Unlike most other textile sectors, full-fashioned experienced a fast pace
of technological change in the 1920s. As markets swelled, and finer, sheerer
hose became the "hot ticket," generations of ever higher-gauge leggers and
footers succeeded one another at a whirling, costly rate. Moreover, the
number of sections each new machine contained expanded at the same time.
Here was a case where "first-mover" advantages were quickly overwhelmed,
a pattern quite different from the Bonsack machine or the moving assembly
line, and one which may prefigure more recent experiences in electronics
or computers. Firms that in 1924 purchased eighteen-section, thirty-nine
gauge knitters, reliable machines with far fewer "bugs" than their war-era
prototypes, and depreciated them at the then standard 12 1/2 percent annually, found in three years that forty-two-, forty-five-, and forty-eight-

gauge, twenty-four- and twenty-eight-section machines were all the rage. Before their knitters were even half amortized, they had become obsolescent, lower-productivity machines, incapable of meeting the demand for sheerness. Mills in this situation seem to have responded by ordering scores of new knitters, much to the delight of the Textile Machine Works. Some 2,100 were installed in 1926 and 2,600 in 1929, increasing total capacity by one-third in the first year, another one-fifth in the latter. These replacements were financed by selling off thirty-nines, especially to southern mills, by drawing on surpluses thus far banked, or through using credit offered by machinery builders, especially TMW's eager competitors. New firms starting in the later 1920s, "late movers," were thus technically better positioned than veterans, but both would be driven by debt or high levels of sunk investment to secure maximum output from expensive capital goods of uncertain effective life. This perilous dynamic, which echoes imperatives that Lamoreaux detailed for the 1890s, helped set the industry up for the big drop.[124]

This bubble could not have inflated without the emergence of sharply rising demand for the full-fashioned product, a consequence as much of women's increasing role in service "white-collar" labor as of the shortening of skirts and the vogue for simpler silk and cotton garb. Three fashion trends transformed the market scale for full-fashioned hosiery. First, lifted hemlines eroded the appeal of seamless stockings, for they lost their shape and became "baggy" after a few washings, a fact long rued by women but concealed by ankle length dresses until the 1920s. Second, cotton hose were opaque, and generally were marketed in white and dark solid colors (the "fast blacks" of an earlier generation). This tended to make legs appear heavier, a horror as slim verticality was ruthlessly promoted. Lumpish cotton hosiery clashed with the modern sleekness of lustrous silk and rayon styles. Silk hose, and thus silk full-fashioned hose, rapidly displaced cotton in the early 1920s. Third, only silk, through variations in yarn twists and knit gauges, could create the illusion of transparency and sheerness that caught fire about 1925 and underwrote the technological successions of the later 1920s. Moreover, silk hose dyed readily as color changes proliferated, were cool in summer wear yet retained body heat in winter, and were sufficiently fragile to need regularly to be replaced. Indeed the sheerer the knit, the sooner they "lad-

---

[124] Taylor, *Significant Post-War Changes*, ch. 5; *UHR* 12 (January 1929): 65, 13(March 1930): 183–4, (June 1930): 172, (September 1931): 48; Naomi Lamoreaux, *The Great Merger Movement in American Business, 1895–1904*, New York, 1985, chs. 2, 3. Machines purchased and in place rose from 2,400 in 1919 to 5,500 in 1924, 7,100 in 1925, 9,200 in 1926, and 12,600 in 1928 (Taylor, p. 60). About 700 of these had been scrapped by 1929, making the active total early that year 11,900, to which 2,600 were added in 1929 (ibid., p. 90; *TW* 77[1930]: 2168).

dered" and expired, to the certain glee of manufacturers. Thus, from 1919 to 1927, output of full-fashioned hose nearly quadrupled from 6 million to 23 million dozen pairs; and, whereas about half the 1919 production was cotton, silk represented above 95 percent of the 1927 total. Meanwhile output of women's seamless stockings contracted sharply, by early 1929 to little more than half the level reported in 1925.[125]

In the early 1920s, silk full-fashioned hose had been essentially a luxury good, costing above three dollars a pair retail, an appendage to the larger cotton hosiery market. They were fairly plain as well, shiny thirty-nine-gauge stockings made in black and a few colors, easy enough to stock and sell to the upscale trade. For all their structural complexity, they represented something like a luxury staple, a narrow market commodity. With the demand surge came a wave of product differentiation along three lines of development: construction, composition, and style. In construction, a range of thread categories developed according to the fineness of the yarns used (from two- to twelve-thread) and the machine gauges (as they emerged on the scene). Heavier weight (usually six to eleven thread, thirty-nine gauge) hose were more durable and less stylish, coming to be known as "service" lines, distinct from the fancy "chiffons" (two to five thread, forty-two gauge and up). Second, a composition spectrum developed, ranging from all-silk (top to toe) to cotton welt, silk leg, to cotton welt and foot, silk boot, with variants in yarn makeup (silk plated over cotton, rayon-silk and even silk-wool blends) adding to the stew. Finally, styles simply spun off geometrically, up to sixty colors by the late twenties in plain service and chiffons, an indefinite range of machine effects (the "extras" noted above), and embroidered add-ons at the high-fashion end of the trade. With heavy demand and growing capacity still inadequate to meet it, hand-to-mouth buying could not be practiced, for full-fashioned was a seller's market in the mid-1920s. The proliferation of stocking types and the ability of makers to defend prices swelled store stocks and frustrated price lining. Big advance orders were necessary to command a share of mill product, concentrated in the middling price ranges ($1.50–$2.50), with color details following as sales patterns indicated the trends. Overloaded mills reserved the right to allot output, one of the clearest of all signs of producers' envied position. Forward contracts permitted mills to run full, holding spoken-for stock only until dyeing instructions were received. Mills also could regulate returns and set up machines for long, profitable runs based on order style book totals. Fancies were made to order for big-city shops and department stores, where they sold in relatively modest quantities to the carriage trade at $3.50–$10.00 a pair.[126]

[125] Taylor, *Significant Post-War Changes*, pp. 1–2, 12, 22–3, 35.
[126] *UHR* 6(February 1923): 57, 87–8, (May 1923): 85; 7(December 1924): 67–8; 8(February

The luxury layer thus having been redefined, mass demand for modest-priced full-fashioned hose gradually created nodes of more or less staple concentration, chiffons at about $2.50 retail and service hose at $1.40–$1.50 in 1925. As in other textile lines, retail prices became one of the key benchmarks by which goods were described and compared (e.g., a $2.50, four-thread, forty-two-gauge all-silk). As elsewhere, buyers sought to secure lower prices in seller's markets by offering volume contracts, a practice doubly enhanced in the mid-1920s by the centralized purchasing of chain stores and the leaguing together of retailers for "group buying." Yet this lure was soon replaced with an increasingly forceful drive for price reductions after 1926. Raw silk, which had averaged six to eight dollars per pound, 1923–6, fell below five dollars, 1927–9, just as mill capacity was escalating to record heights. Further, department stores, chains, and a host of independent hosiery shops had become engaged in retail stocking wars, particularly at the lower end of the trade. At first, seconds and odd lots appeared on the market fringes as specials sold for a dollar retail, but by 1928 this price had become virtually fetishized. Chains took up the gauntlet and pledged big orders to mills that could fiddle construction, cheapen dyeing, etc., in order to build the dollar trade, which it was imagined would expand demand to poorer women still wearing cheaper seamless hose.

Competition for all contracts tightened in 1927–8, with prices for finer goods also chasing staples downward as total output rose. New firms with old 39s whether in the South, or run by knitter entrepreneurs in Philadelphia, battled to harvest the low-end business, whereas older firms with state-of-the-art technology needed to keep running full to recover their capital expenditures or retire their debts as fast as possible. As buyers became more exacting, sensing the shifting climate, they began moderating the scale of their stocks and purchases and commenced "price-chiseling" (by 1928), the old round of taking one mill's quote to another to invite a reduction. A direct indicator of full-fashioned producers' inability to arrest the momentum of their activities as the market advantage was slipping from them is the dramatic rise of mill inventories. From mid-1926 to mid-1928, they nearly tripled (from 1.1 million to 2.9 million dozens) which even with extended capacity meant an increase from one month's to two months' worth of production lying in factory stockrooms.[127]

Looking back from 1931, full-fashioned hosiery manufacturers regarded

1925): 75; (August 1925): 103; (September 1925): 60; *TW* 69(1926): 1022–3. Early five-thread silk chiffons (39 gauge) sold for $20/dozen wholesale in 1921, giving a retail price of $2.75–$3.00 *after* the sharp deflation (*UHR* 13[June 1930]: 147).

[127] H. E. Michl, *The Textile Industries: An Economic Analysis*, Washington, D.C., 1938, p. 245; *UHR* 12(January 1929): 65, 215, (February 1929): 50, (June 1929): 184, (October 1929): 67; (November 1929): 207; Taylor, *Significant Post-War Changes*, pp. 119–120.

1928 as the year when things began to go sour; the troubles familiar to woolen and carpet men gathered force and a 20 percent increment to machine capacity in 1929 finished the game. Scores of mushroom firms, financed both by machinery "on tick" and by six-month to a year materials credits from silk dealers, flooded the market with decently made hosiery at "What will you offer?" prices, accelerating the deteriorating market environment for all but top-end and novelty goods. When the crash caused wholesalers and store buyers to pause and run down currently held stocks, a step taken with conscious reference to 1920, the director of the National Association of Hosiery and Underwear Manufacturers quickly urged mills to cut back to 75 percent of capacity. He was abused from every quarter for his effrontery. The president of Philadelphia's Lincoln Hosiery Corporation rejoined, "Profits are so small that it is necessary to get capacity output. If we do not, then the overhead cost goes up and profits down. They are at rock bottom now." No one curtailed, demand continued to ebb, and inventories soared to above 5 million dozens by February 1930 before the millmen got the message. Many of them, especially in Philadelphia, were soon to discover that "rock bottom" was not the bottom at all.[128]

Competition on price-sensitive lines of relatively standardized service and chiffon stockings, sold unbranded, rapidly intensified in 1930. Buyers exerted strong pressure on mills to meet their bid offers. Major purchasers like Macy's, which normally sold 360,000 dozens of full-fashioned yearly, or chains like J. C. Penney (600,000 dozens at the one-dollar price alone) held a privileged position, able virtually to dictate terms given the vastness of overhanging inventories. Over the next two years retail prices broke through the dollar level for service class full-fashioned, slipping to eighty-nine cents, then seventy-five, and chiffons trended toward $1.25. Philadelphia manufacturers soon faced three interlocked problems. First, they could not capture profits from the declines in raw silk values (down to one-third their 1929 levels by 1932) or from rate cuts implemented before and after 1930. Buyers' power entailed that cost reductions were passed along in the competitive struggle for survival. Second, debts for silk and machinery purchases had to be paid off during a deflationary spiral. Each dollar for liquidation of such obligations was dearer and harder won than at the time the debts had been contracted. Third, interregional cost differentials became for the first time a decisive element in the quest to secure business. Though average earnings per hour for Philadelphia leggers and footers fell by half or more, 1928–32, wide gaps persisted even after several rounds of wage cuts, most critically between the two Pennsylvania centers. In 1932, Reading district leggers

---

[128] *UHR* 12(December 1929): 75, 183, 210; 13(June 1930): 60–1, 171–2, (October 1930): 60; 14(January 1931): 53, (August 1931): 42.

averaged fifty-nine cents per hour and Philadelphians, eighty cents, with the developing North Carolina complex paying about fifty cents. Although a part of the elevated Philadelphia rate was due to the city's prominence in high-style novelties, George Taylor attributed the bulk of the gap to the "difference in rate per dozen" in standard lines. Matching Reading prices could be handsomely profitable for southern mills, but ruinous for Philadelphia.[129]

Some area firms recognized this and rushed toward style specialties in 1930–1, particularly into the market for fashionable openwork mesh hosiery. This was far from a cost-free evasion strategy, for retooling each full-fashioned legger or footer to knit nets and meshes involved an estimated expense of $1,200. More commonly, local firms met the lower prices and took losses on every dozen, a step eased by their still rudimentary approaches to cost finding. Charles Scott, superintendent at Philadelphia's Howard Hosiery, circulated among twenty area full-fashioned mills in a 1930 attempt to discover how his colleagues could quote prices "too low to show a profit."

> One ... when asked if he had figured machinery depreciation in his costs, said "No, not at the present time." He was leaving out that item to meet the price. Another manufacturer said he had made no allowance in his costs for interest on the money invested, because he had inherited the business and had no money invested. Such a folly in figuring costs! Another said that, at a time like this he did not see why he should not leave out depreciation and interest on his investment, so that he could keep his plant in operation and keep the organization together. Another mill had made no allowance for waste, and still another figured nothing for loss on hosiery returns.

Strikes, another "evil" besetting the trade, were in Scott's view likewise "caused by the manufacturers who do not know how to figure cost," for they cut rates to get an edge, found it quickly absorbed by buyers, and infuriated their workers in the bargain. "Show me a mill that is having labor trouble," he concluded, "and I will show you a mill that is selling hosiery very low." The debt pressure that induced running for stock and price slashing was also plain.

> Any manufacturer who makes up stock and figures that if he does not move it before his silk bills come due, he will sacrifice it to get the money, is doing a great wrong. This is the chief cause of conditions in

---

[129] Michl, *Textile Industries*, p. 245 (average raw silk prices in 1929, $4.77/pound vs. $1.47 in 1932); *UHR* 12(October 1929): 56; 13(February 1930): 63; 14(April 1931): 50; 161; (November 1931): 136; 15(February 1932): 56; 16(February 1933): 101–6. In spring 1931, 50 percent of full-fashioned hose were selling at or under $1.00, 13 percent below 90 cents; by fall 1931, the latter proportion had risen to 25 percent (*UHR* 14[February 1932]: 56).

the industry today... The practice of some manufacturers of full-fashioned hosiery machinery who offer to install machines in plants at no cost whatsoever, not even a down payment, is another glaring evil in our industry... This policy puts men in the hosiery business who have no right to be in it... [T]hese mill men often obtain their silk in the same way, and when they are pushed to make payments or must meet their bills, they are forced to give away their hosiery.[130]

What the manager of Quaker Hosiery called the "mad desire for volume" had undermined prosperity and put buyers in control as producers strove to pick one another's pockets. Yet Scott's impassioned plea for the national trade to "unite as a body" and end these manifestly destructive practices was launched into a void. Interregional cost advantages soon had a direct and differential impact on capacity use. After the slaughter of 1930, Philadelphia full-fashioned mills in 1931 were operating at 40 percent of capacity, Reading at 80 percent, and southern mills at 90 percent. Hence the incentives for unity were minimal. Moreover, stylish novelties represented only 12 percent of full-fashioned sales, far too little to sustain more than a fraction of the city's 4,500 machines, and staple markets had become agonizingly profitless for local firms. The crisis was more severe in the Quaker City then elsewhere, but area manufacturers remained hopelessly divided. Giant Gotham had devised a hand-to-mouth production system for its trademarked goods; Haines held to the luxury trade for specially made "ingrain" stockings. Quaker moved into mesh novelties. Aberle, Apex, and other big mills struggled to elude the mainstream price squeeze, while dozens of ten-machine shops enhanced it, running full to meet notes due, taking buyers' "low-ball" offers, flailing to stay in business. In this chilling context, the hosiery workers' union set about the task of stabilizing prices through establishing wage uniformity and defending its members' jobs through aggressive organizing. Though the odds against them may have been formidable, no other agent had a comparably broad vision or a snowball's chance of realizing it.[131]

Having launched the first drives in its mobilization campaign, the union

[130] See *UHR* 13(March 1930): 183–4 for Scott's full review, and for a similar evaluation by the manager of Philadelphia's Owen Osborne mills, *UHR* 13(December 1930): 155. On mesh, see *UHR* 14(April 1931): 147–8, (September 1931): 48, (October 1931): 56, 15(January 1932): 60–2, (February 1932): 143. The resort to manipulation of goods under severe price pressure was widely remarked upon (*UHR* 13[June 1930]: 70, 147; 14[January 1931]: 53, [August 1931]: 42).

[131] *UHR* 13(March 1930): 184, 14(September 1931): 48, 138–9, (November 1931): 158; 15(February 1932): 59–60. Manufacturers' attempts at defensive cooperation included efforts to create a national trade association separate from N.A.H.U.M., to establish a Hosiery Exchange to handle distress stocks and cast-off machinery, and to secure passage of a federal resale price maintenance statute (The Capper-Kelly bill, 1930). All failed (*UHR* 13[February 1932]: 192, [April 1930]: 70, 173, [October 1930]: 159).

showed its full awareness of the market power shift that rapid growth had precipitated and the crisis that had ensued. *Hosiery Worker's* editorialist explained in January 1930:

> The full-fashioned hosiery industry has reached the stage today where the union worker can no longer uphold the standards of the non-union workers... At one time unfilled orders were greater than stock on hand in the majority of mills and prices were uniformly good for the manufacturer. Today, when stock on hand is usually greater than unfilled orders, the buyer has the advantage and the temptation of the employer to cut wages, in a fruitless effort to grab business, is very great, even though entirely mistaken... Unless there is a trade union in the industry that will make it possible for employers and employees jointly to regulate production... nothing in the world will prevent the... full-fashioned hosiery industry from going the way of cotton textiles and bituminous coal.

A few weeks later a simple headline – "Organization or Chaos" – bluntly reinforced the point. Widespread organizing had not been the central feature of the union's activities in the mid-1920s. Instead, defense of ground already won through an emphasis on the exemplary efficiency of union workers overshadowed generally unsuccessful unionization sallies in Durham, North Carolina, Philadelphia, and Reading, circa 1925–7. Though it once bragged that 95 percent of Aberle knitters were signed up, no agreement was achieved. Apex (and Brownhill and Kramer) met the local head on, successfully engineering individual acceptance of yellow dog contracts specially drafted by A. D. McDonald of the hated Allied Manufacturers League, open-shop promoters. Reading was a desert, despite creative use of billboards and a weekly ninety-minute radio show in which "short speeches on trade unionism" were "sandwiched in between the musical numbers." A 1928 Berks County campaign yielded only a much publicized but futile walkout at Noe-Equl. As in similar battles in Kenosha, Wisconsin, and Buffalo, New York, the union learned that other open-shop employers in Reading were processing the struck firm's orders so as to preserve their common front against labor organization.[132]

These 1928 initiatives did, however, signal a growing awareness that partial coverage of the full-fashioned workforce, which once had set the standard that Philadelphia non-union rates had to meet, was no longer sufficient. The transfer that spring of all production in one Kensington union mill to its new open-shop branch in suburban Phoenixville provided a disturbing object

---

[132] Editorial from *Hosiery Worker*, January 31, 1930, p. 4. Other material from ibid., January 12, 1926, p. 1; May 14, p. 1; December 2, p. 1; January 24, 1927, p. 1; May 15, 1928, p. 1; July 2, pp. 1, 4; July 15, pp. 1–2; February 15, 1929, p. 1.

lesson. The move had been made so that Ajax Hosiery could adopt the two-machine system (resolutely fought in the city but securely in place for years at Reading), and thus improve productivity and counter declining margins. Other gloomy events followed swiftly. The defeat of the Reading maneuvers in fall 1928 forced the spring 1929 concession of partial doubling in union mills, a step which seems to have provoked the resignations of Gustave Geiges both as president of the American Federation of Full-Fashioned Hosiery Workers and as leader of Branch No. 1 in Philadelphia. Within weeks, unionized Gotham's personnel department hired Geiges as a welfare and efficiency manager; meanwhile two other union firms, which had changed ownership, dismissed their workers and offered reemployment at deeply cut rates and longer hours (fifty-four vs. the union agreement's forty-eight).

Milwaukee's Emil Rieve, chosen as Geiges's successor, called a special convention to ratify the reductions and adopt "new policies and methods regarding the organization of the unorganized." A general membership vote proved necessary before resistance was overcome and the pact took hold, August 1, 1929. Both troublesome Philadelphia firms were brought back into the fold, one only after it changed hands a second time, and simultaneous recruitment drives were set off in all regions. By the October stock market break, these ventures began to bear fruit in the form of autumn organizing strikes for union recognition at sizable firms in Nazareth, Pennsylvania, and Paterson, New Jersey. In Philadelphia, scores of mill gate meetings broadcast unionism "with the aid of the amplifying system," a timely use of new technology. Yet a far better aid was the round of rate reductions booked by non-union plants in Philadelphia, for they galvanized resistance, most visibly among the 1,400 workers at H. C. Aberle in Kensington.[133]

The Aberle strike, which began in January 1930, was the first salvo in a two-year barrage of organizing strikes whose focal point oscillated between the industry's two chief centers, Kensington and Reading. Winter 1930 battles in Philadelphia were succeeded by a Berks County revival and an upstate "general strike" in the fall. In January 1931, Kensington was the hub of another "general strike" at non-union mills followed by a second summer attempt at rallying Reading workers to labor's standard. Results in Philadelphia were mixed, on the whole disappointing, whereas at Reading the sequence of failures that traced back to 1912 remained unbroken. Thun and Janssen's Berkshire mill rested unruffled, its docile workers accepting

---

[133] *PL*, April 18, 1929, p. 23; April 28, p. 2; June 25, p. 2; June 28, p. 2; *Hosiery Worker*, April 15, 1929, pp. 1, 4; April 30, p. 1; May 15, pp. 1, 3; June 15, p. 1; July 15, pp. 3, 13; July 31, pp. 1, 2; October 30, pp. 1, 2; November 15, pp. 1, 2; January 31, 1930, p. 1.

drastic rate cuts that helped the massive enterprise engineer "stunning" price reductions that reasserted its leadership among northern producers. In 1932 the full-fashioned union shelved strenuous organizing in order to devote its energies to political action, but, distrusting Roosevelt and the Democrats, endorsed Norman Thomas and Pennsylvania's Jim Maurer on the Socialist ticket. Like British textile workers of the 1890s, confronted by major parties that "can't" or "won't" represent labor's needs, the full-fashioned leaders placed their hopes in a workers' party but secured none of the gains realized by their transatlantic counterparts.[134] As financial disarray festered during the postelection interregnum, hosiery workers wondered what Roosevelt might do, and as liquidations spiraled in Philadelphia, whether anything done would make much of a difference.

The H. C. Aberle Company was a pioneer in the full-fashioned trade. Formed in 1900 by two immigrant German brothers with thirty years' experience in local knitting mills, it was in 1930 formally headed by the survivor, Frederick Aberle, eighty-two years of age. Daily operations were governed by his three sons, H. C., George, and Gustave, the last being general manager of the Kensington plant. Near the peak of the craze for sheer silk stockings, the Aberles ran 250 leggers and footers of recent vintage (worth roughly $1.5 million) and engaged well over a thousand operatives.[135]

From Gustave's perspective, the firm leaders were gentlemen well regarded in their community.

> As far as friends are concerned, we have always been very friendly with anyone in Kensington. There have been three generations [of Aberles] there – there is no animosity with our employees. I have learned the industry, and I learned to run the machines with these boys here [gesturing toward workers present] . . . We have grown up with them; we know the situation entirely.

The family team had run their mill as a typical Philadelphia open shop, rejecting both formal union agreements and dictatorial antilabor practices, dealing instead with the customary shop committees long recognized by local textile men.

> We . . . have always bargained with the employees in our own shop and the only exception to this was during the War years, 1917–18–19, when the Union gained control and we were forced through economic pressure to submit to Union rules and regulations. This became unbearable and we were unable to sell our product late in 1919, and during 1920

---

[134] On British textile workers and the Labor Party, see J. A. Jowitt, "Textile Workers, Trade Unions and Politics in Bradford and Lawrence, 1880–1920," in Robert Weible, ed., *The World of the Industrial Revolution*, North Andover, MA, 1986, pp. 145–68.

[135] *OATD: 1916*, p. 270; *OATD: 1928*, p. 463; *KMN* 10(1932): 389.

we had an 11-month strike, at which time we again instituted an open shop.

Though others, notoriously Apex's William Meyer, employed labor spies to identify unionists for dismissal, the Aberles were genuinely indifferent to their employees' affiliations; they simply would not negotiate with the federation over rates, hours, or conditions. In 1929 the firm was paying union scale on footing, nearly scale on auxiliary and finishing operations, and, depending on styles and constructions, from 5 to 15 percent below for leggers.[136]

Openness in relations between the family and shop committees at times reached levels remarkable even for Philadelphia. Earlier in 1929, the firm had proposed an 11 percent reduction across-the-board, a response to slipping market prices. This was refused by the shop delegates, who were "mostly . . . union members"; a strike vote affirmed their stance when the Aberles declined to rescind the cut. The evening before the strike was to begin, a last-ditch meeting was held. It "lasted four hours and the manager [Gustave] offered to open up his books to the union, permitting them to examine them and put an engineer in the plant for a time study to prove that he was making more than 8% profit. If this could be proved, the workers would get everything over 8%." This was accepted, the study undertaken, and its findings both canceled the cut and "brought a 5% increase for the 45-gauge knitters." However, by December the firm had recorded losses for four consecutive months. The Aberles posted reductions for 1930 on knitting and topping ranging from one to nine percent, together with larger cuts in other departments. Two shop ballots rejected the proposition. When the mill committee chairman then tried to arrange a compromise without authorization from the workers, he was cashiered for violating the procedures of shop democracy. The Aberles at first believed the changes in force as of January 1 had been accepted, for workers had come in during the week that ended January 3. However, the knitters had throughout the week been formulating a position reflecting the Federation's drive to add to its base of union contract mills. Completed during weekend meetings, it was presented in the form of a demand for withdrawal of the reductions *and* assent to "the union shop, with union rules and union wages" on Monday the sixth.[137]

Gustave Aberle became furious at what he felt to be betrayal, double

---

[136] H. C. Aberle and Co. to Keightly, January 9, 1930; and Transcript of Conciliation Session, January 11, 1930, p. 37, FMCS File 170/5452; L. Griggs Pierce, "The H. C. Aberle Company Strike," in Palmer, *Union Tactics*, p. 153.

[137] Pierce, "Aberle Strike," p. 154–8; "Transcript," January 11, 1930, pp. 7–8; Aberle to Keightly, January 9, 1930, FMCS File 170/5452.

dealing. As Griggs Pierce, a knitter and versifier who contributed regularly to *Hosiery Worker*, recalled it:

> Mr. Aberle said, "You can have a union shop; I don't care what kind of shop you have, but this is the rate of wage you are going to work for here," pointing to the wage scale that included the cut. He said, "You are going to pull the shop, all right, but remember I will always be one step ahead of you." He went out of our presence into the outer office, swearing as he left, for he was somewhat in a fit of rage.

The next morning, everyone reported for work as usual, then at ten o'clock, January 7, the workers rolled out of the mill "like they were going to a picnic, laughing and kidding each other." The union had prepared armbands for pickets, telegraphed President Hoover to deplore the Aberles' rejection of his appeal to hold back wage reductions and preserve workers' buying power, and scheduled a mass parade of strikers past all the major non-union full-fashioned plants in the city. Gustave Aberle invited "loyal" workers to return, sought new hands, and when Kensington's traditional jeering crowds assembled to make their lives miserable, successfully petitioned Judge "Injunction Harry" McDevitt for a broad restraining order.[138]

True to form, strikers observed the terms of the injunction in letter but not in spirit. As only eight strikers were permitted to picket, and were not to shout "scab" or otherwise cause trouble, an octet of Aberle workers performed this duty daily, joined by hundreds of rowdy, freeborn Kensingtonians not covered by the decree. In reply, McDevitt banned all picketing with a fresh order early in February, and the police refused permits for protest marches. Wild disorders were the result. Pierce explained:

> We could maintain order on the picket lines when our pickets were there, but shortly after their removal, riots started. Homes were stoned, doors broken, mobs in the streets; people from all classes marching to destroy. "Scabs" [and] . . . innocent people . . . were the victims of attacks by people who took it upon themselves to avenge. Sympathizers on a wild rampage and strikers! Yes, strikers were among them. Strikers who had been warned against violence by union officials.

After a series of nasty incidents, one police sergeant declared, "There's bound to be a killing before this is over." And there was.[139]

[138] Pierce, "Aberle Strike," pp. 158–61; *Union Labor Record* (Philadelphia), January 10, 1930, pp. 2, 14; *Philadelphia Record*, January 19, 1930, p. 2; "Bill of Complaint," H. C. Aberle Company to Judge McDevitt, December Term 1929, No. 8969, Philadelphia Court of Common Pleas, January 14, 1930, in FMCS File 170/5452. The "Bill" listed by name over a thousand Aberle employees who were enjoined from interfering with company operations.

[139] *Philadelphia Record*, February 8, 1930, p. 1 (second news section), March 1, p. 1; Pierce, "Aberle Strike," pp. 161–2.

In February and March of 1930, thousands of Kensington residents, men and women, chiefly but not exclusively textile workers, vented the resentments accumulated during a decade of decline, besieging the few score locals and imports who dared to accept both employment at Aberle and police escorts to and from the mill. Salutory clubbings, hundreds of arrests, nothing balked the fuming crowds. Some strikebreakers sped away from the mill each day in cars, to distance themselves quickly from the melees. One such group, on March 6, was pursued by several vehicles, one of which cut in front of the strikebreakers' auto and was hit by a burst of gunfire that killed Carl Mackley instantly and wounded two others. Police rescued the shooters from menacing onlookers and 500 bluecoats shortly occupied the mill district. Though their intentions had hardly been peaceable, the victims were unarmed. Mackley, twenty-two, had been a hosiery union member but, characteristically, was not an Aberle employee. Sensing a shift in the strike's political climate, Philadelphia Mayor Harry Mackey promptly blasted the company for refusing his call for an arbitrated settlement, and placed the responsibility for further violence at its door. To no one's surprise, four days of rioting followed Mackley's funeral, attended by 35,000 mourners (and 700 police) in Kensington's MacPherson Square. On that fourth afternoon, when an estimated 7,500 men and women were, among other things, bricking trolleys carrying strikebreakers, Gustave Aberle consented to outside intervention. Arbitrators would decide the case. After fierce debates, the union accepted the city police superintendent's request for assistance in patrolling the district; a hundred men began circulating with federation badges and credentials and the neighborhood at last quieted on March 14.[140]

Everyone involved had gotten more than they had bargained for in the winter 1930 confrontation. The Aberles, far from the worst characters among Philadelphia textile employers, had been trying to end operating losses through wage cuts that would soon seem immoderately tiny. Yet their workers had whipsawed them, turning their mill into the focal point for the federation's larger strategy and ultimately into a symbol of all the reversals, dismissals, and cuts that Kensingtonians had been enduring since the sea change of 1920–1. The union had unleashed forces that often had played a tactical role in bringing community power to bear on recalcitrant millmen, but here they raged out of control once state coercion escalated and were driven forward by Mackley's death. Strikers broke the customary rules of

[140] *Philadelphia Record*, March 7, 1930, p. 1, 4; March 8, pp. 1, 2; March 9, pp. 1, 11; March 10, pp. 1, 11; March 11, p. 1, 2; March 12, pp. 1, 2; March 13, pp. 1, 2; March 14, pp. 1, 2; March 15, p. 1, 2; Pierce, "Aberle Strike," pp. 162–5; *Union Labor Record*, March 7, 1930, pp. 1, 5, 14; March 14, pp. 2, 19; *Hosiery Worker*, February 15 and 28, 1930 (double issue), pp. 1, 3, 4; March 15 and 31, pp. 1, 3; *PL*, March 11, 1930, pp. 1, 15; March 12, pp. 1, 6.

combat, while the police were overmatched and the mayor danced on a political razor blade. The government of Philadelphia was deeply divided, even paralyzed. Ward-based magistrates rapidly released those arrested without bail, handing them "a copy of the charge," infuriating higher-court judges like McDevitt. Mackey hardly thought it wise to bring the militia into the neighborhood's solid Republican wards, and could not be certain that liberal governor Gifford Pinchot would send state troopers if asked. For its part, depressed Kensington was revealed as a powder keg again, as capable of spasms of responsive violence as it had ever been. Workers still cradled the rituals of shaming and the rocks of revenge that could wreak local havoc but were utterly impotent in the larger context. When Aberle gave in (if only to arbitration) and the outcome of the immediate arm-wrestling match seemed clear, when unionists switched roles and blurred meanings by a "peace patrol" alliance with the police, Kensington's fury stilled in an exhausted blend of satisfaction and regret. For many, concerns about the outcome of the arbitration were overshadowed by the tragedy and violence that had been necessary to place the dispute before a technically informed panel. An unmistakable whiff of decay was replacing the aroma of factory smoke throughout the district.[141]

The three arbitrators sifted documents and testimony for the next several weeks. At their instruction, most strikers returned to work alongside the hated "scabs" while the final decision was being prepared. The team consisted of the familiar Morris Cooke, former Philadelphia public works director and later a prominent New Dealer, Morris Leeds, the progressive and respected owner of Leeds and Northrup, precision equipment makers, and Chicago's Benjamin Squires, impartial chairman of the men's garment trades and a veteran arbitrator. In their award, released April 14, they rejected both the union shop and most of the firm's broad reductions. Instead, Aberle was ordered to reinstate all strikers (146 had been refused reentry) and of its eight classes of cuts, only one was fully and three partially allowed. A local rabbi active in community affairs was appointed continuing arbiter to evaluate the firm's complaints against the excluded workers (all but eleven were reinstated), creating a post to which Wharton hosiery expert George Taylor soon succeeded.

Although another step had been taken toward devising institutional means for resolving conflicts, the Aberle strike did little to advance the Hosiery Workers' larger program. Spinoff organizing strikes appeared at only three of the city's forty-odd non-union mills, and none was successful. With layoffs and short-time multiplying, union members in non-union plants simply could not mobilize their colleagues for action. When, later that summer, the 20

---

[141] On the confusion the "peace patrol" caused, see Pierce, "Aberle Strike," p. 166.

percent schedule reduction was negotiated with unionized mills, Aberle secured approval for instituting it, on condition that a union contract be signed. The firm dawdled over details for six months, until in March 1931 the pact was finally inked. The strike's enormous expenditure of effort had, after a year of struggle and delicate prodding, added one firm to the roster of unionized mills. In the interim, the American Federation of Full-Fashioned Hosiery Workers turned its attention to Reading.[142]

In the aftermath of spring 1930 reductions in rates and hours, a "spontaneous" revival of interest in unionism bubbled forth in Berks County. A federation organizer returned to Reading in May to chair meetings of men and women workers who seemed prepared to defy the "intimidation" that so long had been "the check on union growth." As the big mills operated double jobs with one knitter and two low-paid helpers, skilled positions were never plentiful enough to allow ready promotion of well-versed helpers to their own set of machines. However, if a knitter advanced union ideas, a helper informing on him could secure his machines once the offending agitator was shown the gate. This tidy control system appeared to be breaking down, as Emil Rieve and his aides canvassed Berks County, attempting particularly to make inroads on the Berkshire fortress. Whether unwittingly or to force labor's hand, Berkshire managers precipitated an October outburst, slashing rates by 30 percent, more than the union mills' August reduction and the third there in a year. Simultaneously, the firm lowered selling prices by twenty-five to seventy-five cents per dozen, shocking the full-fashioned trade. As other mills duplicated the Berkshire's rate cut, feverish meetings culminated in a general strike vote, to commence when mill activists blew "shrill toy whistles" at 10 A.M., Monday, November 17. Though walkouts at small firms and lockouts at larger mills were initially heartening, the Berkshire fired a score of suspected unionists first thing Monday and the effort there fizzled. With state police monitoring the plant's gates, Berkshire continued production, and the operators of idle mills soon announced they would reopen, some rescinding part of their cuts. What

---

[142] For the full text of the award, see Palmer, *Union Tactics*, pp. 187–94. The three other strikes were at mills totaling about 300 workers (Rodgers, Artcraft, and Tulip), *Hosiery Worker*, February 15 and 28, 1930, pp. 1, 4; March 15 and 31, p. 1; April 15, p. 4. For other details, see Pierce, "Aberle Strike," pp. 167–9, *KMN* 8(1930): 191, 193, 243, 279, 281, *Union Labor Record*, March 20, 1931, p. 1. For reports on the jury verdict freeing the gunman in the Mackley case, see *Hosiery Worker*, May 15, 1930, p. 2; *KMN* 8(1930): 295, 303. The market collapse produced at Aberle a work sharing scheme in which two shifts each labored three days weekly for five hours, keeping 1,000 of the firm's 1,400 employees active. However, total worker hours weekly were thus only 15,000 compared with 67,000 when the firm was running full in late 1929 (*KMN* 8[1930]: 297).

little momentum had been achieved quickly lapsed, and as workers rushed back, the strike was abandoned after eleven days. Though "stool pigeons" and foremen had urged a return, *Hosiery Worker* admitted the first day's disappointment was crippling: "workers in almost every mill were banking on a considerable walkout at the Berkshire, and when this did not occur at once the undercover agents were able to make cleavages in the ranks."[143]

The Reading debacle had an immediate impact on Philadelphia. Within a week, the secretary of the unionized proprietors' group, the Full-Fashioned Hosiery Manufacturers of America, sent out an open letter to his members, reading in part:

> I am informed that the union's activities in Reading. . .have failed. . .On account of the failure to enforce maintenance of higher wage rates in this important section. . .and. . .the continued adverse business conditions, it would seem that the schedule of union wage rates paid elsewhere in the industry becomes a subject of pertinent importance.

Though Joseph Haines, Jr., here made no overt threats, the implication was plain. The union either had to make a breakthrough and roll back deep cuts that were undercutting attempts at price stabilization or be faced with the need to meet the open shops' radical reductions. Spot strikes and occasional gains would no longer be sufficient. The union's response surfaced in January 1931: all Philadelphia full-fashioned shops would be organized immediately. Any not adopting union contracts by February 16 would be struck, whereas those acquiescing would run unimpeded.[144]

Serial rate cuts in non-union mills set off scattered strikes near the turn of the year, as firms chasing falling prices revised rates again and again. To arrest this slide by bringing the whole Philadelphia full-fashioned complex into formal acceptance of the 1930 general agreement (which would expire August 31, 1931) was the primary goal of the federation campaign. "Stabilization through unionization" captured this intention in an organizing slogan, though industry critics scoffed at labor's ambition to halt deflation, a

---

[143] *Hosiery Worker*, May 15, 1930, p. 3; October 15, pp. 1–3 (published late or misdated, has full strike reports); *KMN* 8(1930): 530–1, 545, 555, 591, 593; *Evening Public Ledger*, November 19, 1930, p. 3 (hereafter *EPL*); *Union Labor Record*, October 17, 1930, p. 4. Federal mediators were refused by both sides, according to *KMN* 8(1930): 530. Berks County mills regularly used Pinkerton and Cummings agents to track organizers, monitor workers, and break up picketing. See *Violations of Free Speech and Assembly . . . : Hearings before a Subcommittee of the Committee on Education and Labor*, April 10–23, 1936, U.S. Senate, 74th Congress, 2nd Session, Washington, D.C., 1937, pp. 186–91, 196–202, 209–19.

[144] *KMN* 8(1930): 583, 597; 9(1931): 10; *Hosiery Worker*, February 14, 1931, p. 1, 2; Keightly to Kerwin, January 13, 1931, January 19, FMCS File 170/6040; *Union Labor Record*, December 19, 1930, p. 4.

task neither business nor government had been able to accomplish. On February 16, given that no firm had volunteered to join the union fold, federation members struck thirty-nine open-shop mills in and near Philadelphia. With them came sufficient sympathizers to bring the strikers' numbers to about three thousand, though others were idled when several large firms (Quaker, Blue Moon) locked out their whole staffs. Indeed, Quaker Hosiery's Charles and John Bromley closed their factory "and left for Florida, leaving instructions with the Superintendent to keep it shut down until they returned" in mid-March. This was hardly a promising note. Worse, at Apex, which with 2,000 employees was the largest open-shop mill in the city, only 100 workers joined the struggle – Berkshire all over again. Furthermore, aiming to prevent a repitition of the previous year's disorders, city Public Safety Director Lemuel Schofield issued a February 18 order banning all picketing and blasted the unionists:

> Whoever called this strike at a time like this, with 150,000 people out of work and starving for bread, should have his head examined. Anyone who strikes today is plain foolish. He ought to be glad to have a job...I am going to stop all picketing. I am going to keep the streets of Kensington as clean as this floor. There will be no assemblages allowed, no demonstrations, no parades, and no protest meetings.[145]

Criticism of Schofield's draconian edict flooded the mayor's office, from the District Textile Council, the Central Labor Union and, significantly, from Governor Pinchot, who asserted that neither state police nor the militia would be sent to Philadelphia. One magistrate quickly released arrested pickets, claiming Schofield had exceeded his authority. On February 22, Mayor Mackey hosted a meeting of labor leaders, acknowledged Schofield had overreacted, and pledged to rein in his excitable appointee. Still, flooding the textile districts with police kept the number of "outrages" to a minimum. Never would the 1931 strike conflicts reach the explosive levels achieved in the Aberle confrontation. As the weeks churned by, settlements were reached and signatures gathered, thirteen firms in the city and twenty-one overall in the area by the end of March. A mayor's commission, led by Rabbi Fineshrieber and including Leeds and Taylor, held hearings during March to gather testimony that might reveal the true condition of the industry and lead toward compromise settlements. Yet three elements in the panorama

---

[145] *Hosiery Worker*, February 14, 1931, pp. 1–2; *KMN* 9(1931): 57–9, 61–2; *EPL*, February 19, 1931, p. 2; *PL*, February 20, 1931, p. 3; Keightly to Kerwin, December 9, 1930, FMCS File 170/5991; idem, January 10, 1931, FMCS File 1701/6021; idem, January 21, 1931; FMCS File 170/6039; idem, February 23, 1931, February 27, February 28, FMCS File 170/6100; see *Philadelphia Record*, February 19, 1931, p. 1 (for Schofield's statement).

of contracts won and repression moderated were genuinely distressing. First, the mayor's investigators were powerless to impose a solution; the Aberle mess had taught open-shop firms to resist arbitration absolutely. Second, mills shut down were, as in earlier situations, filling their orders by sub-contracting to active firms elsewhere, a further sign of relative standardization. One Philadelphia proprietor dropped into the *Knitting Mill News* office to explain that he had "no orders that he cannot fill by buying from mills that are operating . . . [S]o long as he can get along in this fashion, it were needless to enter into any agreement with anybody." Third and most critical, the big mills, Quaker, Apex and such, were unmoved, Apex running steady despite repeated attempts to bring the rest of its force into the streets. The victories, as in so many Philadelphia textile strikes historically, had come disproportionately at small firms eager to get back into production for the spring trade and fearing fatal consequences if they missed the seasonal tide. After April 1, additions to the contract roster were insignificant; the mobilization drive had realized gains under trying depression circumstances, but had failed to overcome the resistance of the major open-shop players in the Philadelphia district.[146]

Shortly after the federation's Philadelphia campaign ground to a halt, a new gauntlet was flung from ninety miles away. The Berkshire released a startling price list (five-thread, forty-two-gauge all-silk chiffons for $6.50 a dozen, etc.) that met buyers' demands and promised to lure sufficient orders to keep its machines running steadily. Preceded as usual by another round of rate shrinkages, and launched in an environment in which many Philadelphia firms could not alter union labor costs through the end of August, it was a perfect bombshell. On June 4, the FFHMA served notice on the union that it would terminate all agreements at their expiration date. Then what? Desperate to avoid total catastrophe, the federation adopted a two-track approach to this crisis – build toward a revitalization of the balked

---

[146] *Union Labor Record*, February 27, 1931, pp. 1, 10; March 6, p. 1, 2; March 13, p. 1; March 27, pp. 1, 2; May 1, pp. 1, 2; May 29, p. 1 (hosiery workers were picketing the Chestnut Hill mansion of the reluctant Bromleys, who controlled Quaker Hosiery and two other mills); June 5, pp. 1, 12; *KMN* 9(1931): 109, 115, 137, 139, 141, 143, 212, 213; *PL*, March 5, 1931, p. 3; March 27, p. 2; April 16, pp. 1, 16; May 29, p. 2; *Hosiery Worker*, February 28, 1931, pp. 1, 2; March 16, pp. 1, 2; March 31, pp. 1, 2; April 30, p. 2; *EPL*, March 28, 1931, p. 24; Keightly to Kerwin. March 22, 1931, March 25, March 26, March 28, March 31, April 2, FMCS File 170/6100. On March 9, McDevitt granted Apex the standard injunction limiting picketing, but accepted the union's claim that there was a strike at the plant, against the firm's contention that all was serene and that therefore there was "no reason for any picketing" (Keightly to Kerwin, March 9, 1931, in ibid.). For the mayor's commission hearings, see "Proceedings of the Fact-Finding Committee," March–April 1931, Record Group 60.9, City Archives of Philadelphia, a full transcript of the sessions.

Reading drives while dealing quietly with the union firms for to-the-bone cuts that would preserve the union contracts. With trumpets and fanfares, rather than ground-level organizing, a new "general strike" was promised for Berks County in August. The response was so brutally feeble that *Hosiery Worker* did not shrink from dubbing it a "complete, amazing failure," though this may have been a way of preparing members for the savage cuts (35–45 percent) ultimately negotiated with the FFHMA.

The root of this ghastly situation was not simply the rushed, expansionary overequipping of the industry, but more precisely the narrowing of the predominant style structure to a relatively few constructions in the context of mass demand and buyers' powerful price chiseling. As many mills were now making much the same goods, as Berkshire rose to a price leadership position, and as the Depression furthered the erosion of style flexibility as a viable production target, genuine price warfare on staple goods intensified, inflicting on most manufacturers just that sort of near-perfect competition that the entire twentieth century oligopolistic mechanism was designed to evade. The full-fashioned sector now confronted conditions similar to those that had shattered other flexible sectors by establishing a price-obsessed market that eradicated or ignored differences in product or quality, drumming out skill and versatility in a rage for cheapness and volume. The full-fashioned union, appreciating this self-immolating trend, had neither the resources nor the statutory backing to confront it successfully. In the Depression context, partial successes were almost valueless; the second Berks County embarrassment mandated acceptance of humiliating reductions in exchange for confirmation of the spring Philadelphia victories through checkoff and full unionization among FFHMA signatories.[147]

The hosiery workers' union was wracked by the side effects of the 1931 contract; ratification was tortured and reports of membership dropouts followed. Little wonder that the union soon veered toward "labor party" politics, running its leader for mayor of Philadelphia in 1931 and backing the Socialists' national ticket in 1932. Workplace exertions had been keenly disappointing in a political economy of injunction rule, steady deflation, and flaccid solidarity (outside disturbingly riotous Kensington). Norris-LaGuardia and the New Deal enactments might in time shift the power balance labor's way, triggering new waves of organizing militancy, but they would not alter the distributional relations that now trapped all of Philadelphia's textile trades, nor would they mandate the machinery wrecking that overcapacity analysts stressed. Neither the NIRA nor Wagner's brain child would do

[147] *KMN* 9(1931): 218–19, 247, 270–1, 374–5, 407, 411, 426–7, 451, 478–9; *Hosiery Worker*, March 31, 1931, pp. 1–2; July 31, pp. 1, 3; August 15, pp. 1, 3; *UHR* 14(October 1931): 127–9, (November 1931): 135–7.

much more than bring a contentious Indian summer to Philadelphia textiles.[148]

By 1932, trade observers relayed the claim that Reading had become the full-fashioned hub and that Philadelphia's sputtering complex was on the wane. Contemporary statistics reinforced this evaluation. Not only had Philadelphia capacity use dipped as low as 20 percent, but in every category covered by the commonwealth's reports on "Productive Industries," Berks County was more resilient in depression and outperformed the Quaker City (Table 6.11). Though Reading had its share of two- and three-day work weeks, employment there on balance was more stable than in Philadelphia, and earnings in real terms shrank far less through 1932. Despite the fact that Philadelphia piece rates were generally higher, its lower capacity use brought earnings (in current dollars) down to or below Reading levels in three of the four years after 1929. Similarly with capital and product values (nominal or real), Berks County contracted more slowly and less severely than did Philadelphia. In part the latter's showing reflected real losses of firms to closure or relocation. Yet shifting sites was hardly a reliable strategy. Though tiny Mammoth Mills resettled capably in upstate Stroudsburg, other movers fared badly. Cadet, aided by generous local financing, relocated to Tennessee and promptly went bankrupt, as did Charles Lehmuth after transplanting his operations to Glassboro, New Jersey. Fidelity, Lehigh, U.S. Silk Hose, Olympia, Signature, Nomend, Siliko, Hancock, and Weber, Friedrich and Weil all liquidated, voluntarily or otherwise, between mid-1930 and FDR's inauguration, as did James O'Connell, "the last Philadelphia manufacturer of women's seamless silk stockings." Early in 1933, a group of accountants who "professionally" investigated the books of seventy-one local full-fashioned firms, most likely for credit reporting, found only twelve showing any profits for 1932 and warned that there were a number of "concerns who will be forced to a showdown by creditors" shortly. In the 1920s, the Philadelphia full-fashioned trade had gone up like a rocket; now it was coming down like a rock.[149]

6.6. Conclusion

Overall, the textile industry of Philadelphia, remarkable for its flexibility in product terms and its resilience across three generations, showed a fun-

---

[148] Keightly to Kerwin, June 25, 1933, FMCS File 170/9044; *Hosiery Worker*, July 15, 1931, p. 1; March 11, 1932, p. 1; July 8, 1932, p. 3; October 14, 1932, p. 1; November 4, 1932, p. 1.

[149] *KMN* 8(1930): 585, 613; 9(1931): 10, 35, 341, 353, 385; 19(1932): 123, 385, 428, 526; 11(1933): 64, 67, 92, 169, 170, 181.

Table 6.11. *Employment, capital, product value, and average earnings, silk hosiery, Berks County and Philadelphia, 1928–33*

Employment	1928	1929	1930	1931	1932	1933
Berks	10,661	12,587	13,304	12,593	13,977	13,281
Philadelphia	17,264	19,286	17,447	15,210	15,463	16,344
Index (1929 = 100)						
Berks	85	100	106	100	111	106
Philadelphia	90	100	90	79	80	85
Capital (millions)						
Berks	22.4	26.1	27.5	27.8	27.7	22.9
Philadelphia	35.8	39.3	41.3	31.3	28.0	30.5
Index (adjusted, 1929 = 100)[a]						
Berks	91	100	105	112	121	106
Philadelphia	91	100	102	82	77	89
Product Value (millions)						
Berks	54.6	60.2	49.4	39.6	31.0	24.9
Philadelphia	88.3	95.4	59.4	42.2	36.4	33.7
Index (adjusted, 1929 = 100)[a]						
Berks	86	100	92	90	84	57
Philadelphia	84	100	70	61	62	49
Average Earnings/Worker						
Berks	$1,388	1,390	1,210	1,052	801	753
Philadelphia	1,602	1,610	1,209	940	847	734
Index (adjusted, 1929 = 100)[a]						
Berks	91	100	98	104	94	75
Philadelphia	91	100	85	80	87	65
Berks/Phila. (%)	86	87	100	112	95	103

Note: Silk hosiery classification includes seamless and full-fashioned, but seamless was by the later 1920s a small part of the industry in both counties.
[a]Adjusted to show real values for capital, product, and earnings; see Tables 6.8 and 6.9.
Sources: Same as for Table 6.8.

damental inability to overcome the structural shifts in market relations that settled in place during the 1920s. Underneath the versatility of its skill-intensive production format lay a set of settled practices, among both proprietors and workers, whose lack of fluidity enfeebled the regional industry's capacity to respond to the reigning buyers' supremacy. There had been "hard times" before, and losses of mills due to general contractions or credit crunches. But this time, textile buyers had implemented an array of institutionalized management controls devised in the prewar years, adapted by mass distribution leaders like Macy's and Marshall Field from the pioneering efforts of transportation and industrial corporations. Detailed cost accounting, budget management, and accentuation of inventory reduction in the service of heightened turnover, all spread from giant department stores throughout the retailing trades. The novel techniques were heavily publicized by trade associations advocating scientific attention to cost and flow, and the crisis of 1920 confirmed their value. Soon wholesalers and jobbers joined in displacing risk and expense for stock holding back onto producers of seasonal goods. Terms of trade were reshaped and further concretized buyers' privileged status, while price lining pressed mills to create goods to meet retail target levels, goods for which price homogeneity dominated distinctiveness in quality or style. Meanwhile, a secular trend toward lower materials prices reinforced buyers' incentives to ratchet prices downward and capture the benefits of deflation, while resisting upward revaluations that occasional increases in materials costs led producers to attempt.

As the make-to-order system broke down, few Philadelphia textile mills found themselves able to adopt similar managerial practices vis-à-vis their internal operations or their upstream suppliers. Like Samuel Vauclain, they distrusted experts and outsiders, prized their independence, and were wary of being dictated to by statistical indicators. Previous cycles of relative disadvantage had evened out, so too would this one. They placed their faith as always in skill, theirs and their workers, in adjusting piece rates and hours of operation, and in the tariff. Their organizations were better at banqueting and battling labor than they were at promoting tight costing, group purchasing, or the wisdom of restructuring labor processes and technology to facilitate hand-to-mouth production.

An array of proprietary dispositions that had well served the Philadelphia textile industry for generations ceased to have its old potency, and the categorical shifts in practice and perception that might have adapted mills to the new conditions were rarely achieved. Millmen screened market signals through cultural filters and translated them into personalistic terms ("have a heart for the manufacturers") rather than regarding them as cues for a decisive reorientation of approaches to production. Whereas the most far-seeing of labor unions had a notion of the necessary scale and direction of actions that might yield stabilization, it lacked the resources, legally, financially, and ideologically, to establish its claims. Neither labor nor the state would reverse the negative trends. Yet proprietors, given the centrality of the factory, the partnership, the family firm to their way of life, hung on doggedly. Unable to mimic the adaptive resilience of a set of exemplary, well-heeled families and firms, most manufacturers viewed the mergers, managerialism, and impersonal mathematics of business modernism with distaste. The very blinders inherent in their self-image as "practical textile men," together with their durable machinery and paid-for buildings, led hundreds of them to stay in business even as silent looms and empty rooms proliferated in the textile districts. Philadelphia proprietors were commonly as bound into the fabric of their industry as were the weavers Gladys Palmer studied with such care. Against all reasoning in strictly economic terms, few on either side would abandon the mills until the day when death or disaster drove them out.

7

Long nights, false dawns,
1933–1941

"The rising tide of price fetishism is sounding the death knell of high standard producers . . . Present methods of retail merchandising are retarding and hampering the consumer's natural desire to buy through fear that prices will be lower. . . . Business is being destroyed by the theory that price is the basis of all barter."

American Wool and Cotton Reporter, January 26, 1933, p. 36

"The poor seller, who for three years has been at the mercy of the voracious buyer, has become timid, is living in a buyer's age, and this poor seller has got to operate on himself, extract the jelly and put in the back-bone."

Underwear and Hosiery Review, April 1934, p. 129

The New Deal briefly revived the hopes of mill owners and textile workers. As all efforts by organized labor and trade groups had failed to reverse the flow of market power to distributors, eager unionists and discouraged manufacturers embraced the activist state, the former taking heart from Section 7(a) of the National Industrial Recovery Act and the latter viewing its promise of industrial self-governance as the only imaginable means to stabilize prices. In textiles, at least, and especially in Philadelphia, all parties were to be keenly disappointed. With the deterioration of the National Recovery Administration, millmen struggled vainly in their enfeebling dealings with buyers while fending off labor militancy. Passage of the Wagner Act renewed organizers' energies, but its contested constitutionality encouraged proprietary resistance even as the toll of broken firms mounted. Focused more on production than on exchange relations, the New Deal industrial program did little to alleviate the suffocating forces that bore on flexible and bulk-oriented textile firms. Still, from the NIRA to the Fair Labor Standards Act, state authority over economic behavior steadily advanced. When after 1939 war preparations brought the first seller's market in two decades, federal regulation of materials, prices, and products obstructed surviving mills' opportunities for sudden gains. To be sure, the war did extend many firms' lease on life, but it did not alter the basic trends in motion since the early 1920s. Once the postwar burst of domestic consumption petered out,

Figure 25. Sit-down strikers settled in, occupying the Artcraft Hosiery Mills, Philadelphia, April 1937. (Courtesy of the Historical Society of Pennsylvania.)

hundreds of battered firms (and 20,000 more jobs) expired in Philadelphia's factory districts, reducing the industry to below a third of its 1925 size.

The final stages of this regional decay will be here summarized in four sections. Contemporary diagnoses of textiles' troubles will lead toward a statistical portrait of Philadelphia's course through 1941. Then in separate, related discussions, the evolution of market relations and the impact of labor organizing will be profiled. Last, the war crunch and postwar downswings will be briefly characterized, carrying the story in compressed fashion into the 1950s.

7.1 Scholars and data: textiles in the 1930s

Textile manufacturing's persistent doldrums led sectoral associations and the Textile Foundation to support a series of scholarly investigations of trade problems, involving academics from the Harvard Business School and Wharton's Industrial Research Department. These studies recognized that eroded profits and lost momentum had yielded stagnation, sought its sources, offered tentative solutions, and considered the obstacles to their implementation. In so doing, both Melvin Copeland's Cambridge crew and Hiram Davis's Penn team assessed current explanations of the industry's ills against their developing understanding of trade structures and relationships. Their work provides an in-depth portrayal of the transfer of risk to producers and buyers' capture of the benefits and mechanisms of flexibility.[1]

Five industrial fault lines were most often noted: excess capacity, poor management, technological backwardness, weak distributional and disjointed industrial structures, all frequently contrasted with the heralded success and consolidation of the auto trades (particularly the benchmark progress of General Motors). Using this reference, Copeland quickly dismissed the argument from excess capacity, finding that since the war cotton mills showed capacity use comparable to "other industries that were more prosperous." George Taylor agreed, asserting that "the overcapacity situation has been greatly exaggerated." He continued:

> Data relating to over-capacity commonly pre-suppose full-time operation of all equipment no matter how old and decrepit, and without making allowance for style-changes, breakdowns, adjustment of machinery, etc. Prevailing industrial capacity has been built up by the construction of additional plant facilities whenever a prospect of profitable operation has appeared. This leads in most industries to a capacity that is sufficient to meet a peak demand rather than an average demand...

Copeland reinforced the point in his study of silk and rayon weaving. Cross-industry comparisons showed that more salient than the quantity of ma-

Three "Harvard" studies are of the greatest relevance here: Melvin Copeland and Edmund Learned, *Merchandising of Cotton Textiles: Methods and Organization*, Boston, 1933; John Madigan, *Managing Cloth Inventories in the Cotton Textile Industry*, Boston, 1934 (a dissertation Copeland supervised); and Melvin Copeland and Homer Turner, *Production and Distribution of Silk and Rayon Broad Goods*, New York, 1935. The "Penn" group includes: Jeremiah Lockwood and Arthur Maxwell, *Textile Costing*, Washington, D.C., 1938; Reavis Cox, *The Marketing of Textiles*, Washington, D.C., 1938, H. E. Michl, *The Textiles Industries: An Economic Analysis*, Washington, D.C., 1938 (these three designed as text/reference volumes); Hiram Davis, *Vertical Integration in the Textile Industry*, Philadelphia, 1938; Hiram Davis, *What to Do About Denim Stocks*, Washington, D.C., 1941; Robert Armstrong, *Managing Inventory Losses in the Men's Wear Division of the Wool-Textile Industry*, Washington, D.C., 1941; George Taylor, *Inventory Guides in Cotton Fine Goods Manufacture*, Washington, D.C., 1941; G. Allan Dash, Jr., *Inventory Management in Rayon Weaving*, Washington, D.C., 1941; Hiram Davis, *Controlling Stocks of Cotton Print Cloths*, Washington, D.C., 1941; George Taylor and G. Allan Dash, Jr., *Stock and Production Policies in the Full-Fashioned Hosiery Manufacture*, Washington, D.C., 1941; and Hiram Davis, *Inventory Trends in Textile Production and Distribution: An Appraisal of Experience During the 1930s*, Washington, D.C., 1941. Taylor's articles in trade journals, based on IRD studies, will be cited below as appropriate.

chinery relative to demand was the way that machinery was regarded and used by managers.[2]

The Harvard analyst similarly rejected the claim that textile managers were incompetent; he judged them about average. Indeed, New England staple cloth mills had adopted the costing practices Philadelphians long ignored but had botched an opportunity to build flexibility and more realistic assumptions into their quantitative measures.

> Had the older mills been willing to operate at less than capacity, the manufacturing margins on cloth perhaps need not have declined so much. The lower...margins were a logical result of volume mania, which was motivated by an illogical principle of accounting for overhead costs...the practice of loading overhead into cost of products on the assumption of 100 percent capacity as normal... Unless a mill operates at night and at the same time loads overhead on a single shift basis, it cannot earn 100 percent of its overhead, because it is physically impossible for a plant to be 100 percent efficient in operation.[3]

Here, in another Gresham's Law variant, bad practice drove out good sense. Once any mill created prices based on 100 percent loading, any other using a lower basis would generate higher per yard costs and be driven from staple markets. Excess capacity thus was a foggy shorthand for managerial practices whose unreal assumptions mandated full-bore production. Standard costing rules called for the pragmatic spreading of the overhead burden, as with GM's "standard volume" base,[4] but in staple textiles these guidelines were disregarded, generating self-blocking expectations and losses. By contrast, specialists' primitive cost finding, with its idiosyncrasies and flat percentages for "mill expense," contained different illusions, but given their diversity, did not lead to a collective logic.

What of technology? Here the academics were at their weakest, for, other than Taylor, none displayed familiarity with the course of technical change. Perhaps thinking of the assembly line, he observed that textiles had experienced no "revolutionary change in method of operations, which quickly reduces the cost of production to a striking extent." The balkiness of materials, the range of goods and demands, and the dubious promise of throughput in a labor-intensive, competitive trade made the prospect of a single

---

[2] Copeland and Learned, *Merchandising*, p. 1; *Underwear and Hosiery Review* 17 (November 1934): 118 (hereafter *UHR*); Copeland and Turner, *Silk and Rayon*, p. 5.

[3] Copeland and Learned, *Merchandising*, p. 80. For the hosiery sector's use of the same "loading," see *UHR* 17 (January 1934): 95.

[4] Cox, *Costing*, pp. 79, 235; Howell Harris to Scranton, December 20, 1987. As Southern staple-goods mills tended toward regular double-shifting both in and after World War I, it would be interesting to know whether they calculated overhead beyond 100 percent single-shift expectations, enabling a further spread and yet lower pricing.

fiber-to-fabric machine a technocracy addict's dream, not a plausible goal. In general, textile machinery and production practices were not "rendered obsolete" at a rapid rate, but this might represent a major problem only if one was already committed to the excess capacity line and ignored the multiple, incremental technical advances after World War I (in rayon alone *Textile World* once devoted twenty pages to reviewing them). Millmen did not rush to incorporate new devices, layouts, and process techniques because their operating returns were fast fading, except in full-fashioned; and even there, after 1929 Textile Machine Works' new models found few takers. The first three "causes" inadequately captured the dynamics of decline. Whether viewed as a case of failed institutional evolution or as the fruit of contradictions between industrial and merchant capitals, the crux of the problem lay in relations between production and distribution.[5]

The antagonism between textile mills and distributors was as elemental as that between Ford and its dealerships, yet Ford could compel its agencies to accept goods in quantities and at prices determined by corporate leaders, a capacity absent in textiles. This contrast indicates that distributional issues are entwined with matters of industrial structure, a linkage evident in the 1930s studies' repeated discussions of inventory, merchandising, integration, and flexibility. Copeland scored the durable "separation of the production and merchandising function" as the root of "a division of interest in and responsibility for the final product" that spawned relations "susceptible to the intrusion of abuses and the development of chaotic market conditions." Converters' "intimate acquaintance" with demand and style shifts afforded them considerable "flexibility in adjusting merchandising plans to varied and changing market requirements." As staple cotton mills had great difficulty "reconciling large scale production with flexibility in merchandising," merchant-finishers, before World War I, seized the flexibility initiatives, setting a pattern echoed in other trades.[6]

Similarly, alert buyers had forced weavers of semistaples "into a stock-carrying position" even though such goods could not "safely be produced unless the mill knows that a demand will arise and has some idea of its

---

[5] Copeland and Learned, *Merchandising*, p. 1; *UHR* 18 (February 1935): 122; on textile technology, see *American Wool and Cotton Reporter* 47 (January 26, 1933): 11 (hereafter *AWCR*). Textile Machine Works' knitting machine production series moved from whole number 2,000 to 9,000, 1920–28, but did not reach 10,500 until 1933 and 12,000 until 1941 (Textile Machine Works Correspondence File, Quaker Hosiery, in Quaker Lace Papers, Philadelphia).

[6] Copeland and Learned, *Merchandising*, pp. 2–3. On Ford, see David Hounshell, *From the American System to Mass Production, 1800–1932*, Baltimore, 1984, chs. 6, 7; Richard Tedlow, "Automobile Marketing in the Context of American Business History," unpublished paper, Harvard Business School, 1988.

strength and size." In fancies, buyer/converters either finished drapery and curtain cloths or demanded "control of the designs" and "exclusive distribution" of fabrics. Thus, when a seasonal style took off, dealers could invite various mills to bid downward for duplicate orders. Styling progressively became a New York activity, and flexibility was transferred from the manufacturer's to the distributor's toolbox in exchange for inventory risk or the status of dependent commission producer.[7] It was this situation that illuminated the structural vulnerability of textiles and informed proposals for comprehensive integration. In 1933, Copeland stressed that the "close coordination" necessary in "modern business" mandated central control over production, finance, and marketing, and urged comprehensive subsectoral mergers. Though earlier integrated corporations had demonstrated an "inflexibility" that had hampered their ability "to adjust to new conditions," Copeland wistfully imagined this could be avoided if managers adopted "the right point of view in the perception of their problems." This vague appeal for mental housecleaning in no way dealt with providing incentives or coercion sufficient to draw marketers into such cartel-like giants, nor did it consider their dubious legal status.[8] Integration was also the panacea urged in Copeland and Turner's 1935 study of silk and rayon weaving. Again the steady capture of flexibility by fabric buyers and converters was documented, as style-leading manufacturers of the 1910s were transformed into staple-goods appendages of downstream specialists, who were "most likely to profit," given their "freedom from fixed investment," from commission buying and finishing. Declines in silk and rayon yarn prices generated further pressure on styling mills; for as "more hand-to-mouth buying" developed in response, "inventory losses had to be absorbed" and market quotes "tended continually to be below the cost price." Just as a decade later in full-fashioned, larger mills commenced gray-goods contracting with tiny "family shops" as a tactical reply, but witnessed the styling initiative pass fully to merchandisers whose "dominant position" allowed them to demand pass-through reductions reflecting lower materials prices. As elsewhere, buyers were "the masters of the industry."[9]

Put simply, "the transference of the marketing problem has removed from the producer the control of production." Once-successful fancy-goods proprietors "who failed to manufacture goods at a profit... now subsist simply by the sale of weaving services," running "cockroach" commission shops. Buyers' 1920s extensions of prewar experiments with piecemeal purchasing and inventory displacement had pulverized the structure of Paterson's silk

[7] Madigan, *Managing*, pp. 10, 16, 21.
[8] Copeland and Learned, *Merchandising*, pp. 5, 82.
[9] Copeland and Turner, *Silk and Rayon*, pp. 2, 3, 49–50.

trades and shattered its format for accumulation. Now "desperate" tiny shops were recycling depreciated machinery in devalued space to create price-depressed goods and subsistence earnings for demoralized owners and degraded workers. In contrast to oligopolistic sectors in which smaller firms depart or are absorbed as consolidation proceeds, here with distributors dominant, larger units dissolve as tiny, marginal enterprises proliferate in what might be termed the "lemon capitalism" phase of flexible manufacturing. In textiles, "the general subordination of the individual entrepreneur" materialized not through the rise of technically and organizationally superior, grand-scale firms as it had in steel, auto, or glass. Instead, proprietors were brought to heel before the textile trade's pacesetting nexus of New York buyers, who had institutionalized the practices spawned in the preceding decade.[10]

More attuned to Philadelphia conditions, Hiram Davis and his Wharton collaborators were skeptical of the value of integration, pointing out in 1938 that the "variety barrier" frustrated integration in seasonal lines due to "the pyramiding of style risks" as one proceeded from yarn to garment. Moreover, attempts to do one's own merchandising in staple lines, where merchant converters ruled, brought the unappetizing prospect of "competing against [established] specialists at every turn." Of various schemes to take charge of marketing, none held much promise. Compelled to deal with the lack of incentive for distributors to vacate their preferred place in the textile system and the multiple difficulties for mills intruding on their turf, the Penn group asked, "If integration requires a weaver ... to deal with all the problems raised, why should he not maintain his specialized position rather than borrow trouble?" Their honest, if feeble, reply: "There is much to be said for this point of view."[11]

Like their Cambridge colleagues, the Philadelphia scholars stressed flexibility, but none of their three means to achieve it would sustain accumulation. Contract/commission operations simply accepted "the policy which nearly all retailers and wholesalers ... followed" and market shifting (from yarn to gray or finished goods as opportunities afforded) demanded information flows that would "not always work out in practice." Product diversification, the

---

[10] *Ibid.*, pp. 3, 50, 51, 74, 76. On the family shop, see Philip McLewin, "Labor Conflict and Technological Change: The Family Shop in Paterson, New Jersey," in Philip Scranton, ed., *Silk City*, Newark, 1985, pp. 135–8. In New Jersey silk and rayon during the 1920s, 964 new firms started business and 921 liquidated. By 1935, Paterson commission weavers accounted for 60 percent of the city's 480 firms vs. 23 percent in 1924. Similarly, family shops or commission mills held 60 percent of Paterson looms surveyed in 1935 (Copeland and Turner, *Silk and Rayon*, p. 1; McLewin, "Labor Conflict," pp. 140–1).

[11] Davis et al., *Vertical Integration*, pp. vii, 7, 19, 21, 67, 112.

third, had been the hallmark of the very mills wrecked by the collapse of advance orders, inventory losses, and the transfer of savings on materials and labor to purchasers. Though they struggled to evade it, the implicit conclusion was that integration was a chimera and flexibility an exhausted resource for specialist mills.[12]

As all efforts to "minimize inventory hazards" had fallen short, the Textile Foundation soon commissioned six Wharton sectoral studies of the inventory question. Assertive strategies had been found vacuous; seeking survival accommodations was now the fallback priority. Published in 1941, these studies confirmed manufacturers' well-known disabilities. Staple mills had entered "the warehouse business" and were unable to resist reductions in contract prices. Consolidated purchasing had advanced, intensifying negative trends; no relief was in sight.[13] Print cloths offered "an example of how theory frequently goes awry in practice." Advocates of industrial stabilization and efficiency through standardization had ignored market relations and sectoral structures. No fabrics were more standardized than print cloths, yet output and stocks "fluctuated... violently" and mills "not only suffered losses from inventory depreciation but... also experienced higher costs from intermittent operations." In seasonal/styled goods like hosiery, advance orders only appeared when "the price outlook makes such a step seem profitable." Otherwise, hand-to-mouth practices were general. Further, big contracts with later detailing (from chains or sizable distributors) contained one-way ratchets – if materials or labor costs rose, the price was firm, but if they receded, "substantial concessions" were guaranteed purchasers. Were mills to run their own style choices for stock, buyers, in Taylor's phrasing, would predictably say:

> Well, it's a good 45 gauge construction, but I really wanted merchandise with about 1450 courses instead of the 1550 courses you have made and the extra [features] do not mean anything to me. If you want to sell at the price of the construction I have in mind, I might be able to take the goods to help you out.[14]

Here was a tidy double bind. Without inventory, hosiery mills could not provide quick delivery; with it, they were open to squeeze plays. This "lose-lose" situation made mill styling chancy and emphasized the lesser risks of gray-goods production, to which many mills "confined" themselves after 1933. "In a sense they 'solved' the inventory problem by selecting a type of operation that require[d] the carrying of little hosiery in stock," and conserved working capital. The step to commission knitting for distributors or

---

[12] *Ibid.*, pp. 118–20.

[13] *Ibid.*, p. 116; Davis, *Denim Stocks*, pp. 4, 8, 12.

[14] Davis, *Print Cloth*, p. 1; Taylor and Dash, *Full-Fashioned*, pp. 2, 3, 5.

chains was easily taken, as the implications of buyers' control over price and styling percolated through the specialty trades. The remaining make-to-order segments had become completely disheveled. In menswear, orders with later detailing and ratchets were routine. Yet "clothing manufacturers, through cancellations, deferment [of detailing], price adjustments and returns" were able to make even these orders "indefinite," exposing mills to losses on unusable materials, finished goods canceled or sent back, or on fabrics "for which the full purchase price is never received." Making to order now put "the buyer in the driver's seat" and differed from commission work only in "that the mill bears the risk on materials."[15]

Though Davis, in his overview and summation to the sectoral reports, proposed another "program of flexible production," it both supposed mills to be far freer and more knowledgeable agents than they were in fact and evaded existing power relations. As if realizing just this point, he closed by stressing buyers' "dominant role" in the industry's fluctuations. Asking "Who are these buyers?" Davis wondered whether this " 'merchant' class" controlled business conditions generally or just in textiles.[16] Reflecting on the New Deal, he noted that if buyers hold sway, "it may be questioned whether any public policy is wise which seeks to minimize business fluctuations by regulating production." It was deplorable that a purchaser could order goods up to a year ahead at fixed prices in rising markets (the case in 1940) "without tying up any of his funds." Davis urged that federal power be used to alter relational asymmetries between mill and market, to end predatory practices and reduce buyers' advantages. The government should create "tighter" trade rules, and act "to shorten terms, to eliminate dating, to establish

[15] Taylor and Dash, *Full-Fashioned*, pp. 22, 24; Armstrong, *Men's Wear*, pp. 1, 2, 16–17 (especially for price pressures by big clothiers and chains); Davis, *Inventory Trends*, pp. 28–9. The Davis team investigated proportions of inventory to output or sales among 106 classes of textile manufacturing and distribution. Producers clustered at the high end and distributors at the low end of the range. In the lowest two quartiles ($6.20–$17.70 of inventory per $100 of output or sales), 50 of 53 classes represented distribution; in the third quartile ($18–$22/$100), 17 of 27 were distributors, whereas mills predominated in the top quartile ($22–$40/$100) by 15 classes to 11. Two-thirds of the distributional classes fell in the lower half of the roster, over half the textile-making classes in the top quartile (Davis, *Inventory Trends*, pp. 4–5). The figures were calculated from unpublished returns to the 1939 censuses of manufacturing and business, and were consistent with less complete data for 1937 (p. 7). Inventory data was gathered erratically prior to 1937.

[16] Davis, *Inventory Trends*, pp. 31–2, 50–1. On buyers' power and unspecified orders, see *American Carpet and Upholstery Journal* 53 (April 1934): 17 (hereafter *ACUJ*); *Textile World* 89 (Annual 1939): 91, 96 (hereafter *TW*); *UHR* 18 (February 1935): 88, (May 1935): 112; 20 (November 1937): 23. In 1938 *TW* switched to issue pagination. The annual was a thirteenth "monthly" issue, reviewing the previous year and present prospects, published in late February.

warehouse service charges and in particular to require advance payments on forward orders." However brilliantly perceptive, this political proposition was never viable. Distributors could promptly raise the specter of higher consumer prices, rattle the sacred bells of competition, and mobilize their lobbyists, whereas producers remained profoundly divided regionally and sectorally. Unable to view markets as power contests, unable adequately to conceptualize the structured diversity of production itself, academics and politicians framed programs whose generality and uniformity assured their irrelevance to specialty trades or whose interventionist specificity (Davis) made their adoption quite implausible. Neither academic inquiry nor state action would arrest the tides of decline.[17]

In Philadelphia, the corrosive effect of the long-term power shift may be gauged through data that first contrast the situation in 1934 with that of 1925, the peak year for employment, before looking ahead to the later 1930s. Table 7.1 presents the net change in workforce and the shifting sectoral shares of total employment. In the city, three-quarters of the jobs in "Woven Goods" (chiefly wool/worsted and mixed-fiber semistaples) had vanished in nine years, accounting for 40 percent of total employment lost. Another 40 percent came from carpet mill closings and the slippage among yarn spinners who had supplied the weaving sectors. However, fancy goods (plush, lace, etc.) held up relatively well, whereas dyers and miscellaneous operations (waste, cordage, etc.) sustained moderate declines. Knitting showed the sole gain, with full-fashioned work firmly displacing seamless manufacturing. Clearly contractions were not evenly distributed, as the shift-share column suggests. Used by geographers, these figures express the deviation of each group from the "expected" mean loss, were decline uniform. [18] The sizable negatives for spinning, carpets, and woven goods indicate that these sectors were especially hard hit, whereas those insulated from the miseries of the wool-using trades (fancy wovens) or able to contract for work from knitters (dyeing) actually gained a share point or two despite shrinkage in absolute terms. Most striking is the city industry's increasing reliance on knitting employment as the last bastion; nearly half the remaining places for workers were in 1934 concentrated in hosiery and knitted specialties. Regionally, though spinning was fast fading in Philadelphia, it remained important in suburban counties hosting silk throwers and the Viscose rayon plants. Second, nearly as many outlying full-fashioned jobs had been added since 1925

[17] Davis, *Inventory Trends*, p. 51.
[18] T. W. Buck, "Shift-Share Analysis: A Guide to Regional Policy," *Regional Studies* 4(1970): 445–50; Graham Gudgin, *Industrial Location Processes and Regional Employment*, Farnsborough, UK, 1978; Edward Soja et al., "Urban Restructuring: An Analysis of Social and Spatial Change in Los Angeles," *Economic Geography* 60(1984): 195–230.

Table 7.1. *Philadelphia regional textile industry, employment by sector and district, 1934, with 1925 comparisons*

	$N_i{}^a$	Sectors (City Only)				Sectors (5-County Region)			
		1934 Empl.	Loss/Gain Since '25	% '34	Shift Share^b	1934 Empl.	Loss/Gain since '25	% '34	Shift Share
Woven goods	40	3,011	− 10,006	6	− 12	5,563	− 10,567	8	− 9
Fancy wovens	94	8,267	− 3,138	18	+ 2	10,609	− 4,739	15	− 2
Carpets	27	3,820	− 5,323	8	− 5	4,165	− 5,389	6	− 4
Hose-knit	156	21,012	+ 620	46	+ 18	28,690	+ 4,534	42	+ 16
(Full-fashioned)	67	(14,816)	(+ 5,119)	32	(+ 16)	(19,789)	(+ 9,740)	27	(+ 16)
(Seamless)	13	(1,555)	(− 3,912)	3	(− 6)	(2,348)	(− 4,474)	3	(− 4)
Dye-finish	67	2,749	− 762	6	+ 1	3,529	− 851	5	0
Spinning	50	4,263	− 5,247	9	− 4	12,743	− 4,930	18	0
Miscellaneous	42	2,913	− 1,685	6	0	3,729	− 1,830	5	− 1
Totals	476	46,035	− 25,541	99	0	69,028	− 23,772	99	0

Districts	N_l[a]				Shift share[b]		
Kensington	228	21,429	− 13,334	47	− 2	31	− 6
Manayunk	25	1,267	− 6,025	3	− 7	2	− 6
Germantown	73	7,883	+ 350	17	+ 7	11	+ 3
Frankford	63	6,109	− 413	13	+ 4	9	+ 2
North Central	21	4,259	− 841	9	+ 2	6	+ 1
S. & W. Phila.	19	2,712	− 2,499	6	− 2	4	− 2
Northern Liberties & Old City	45	2,376	− 2,779	5	− 2	3	− 3
				100	0		
Bucks County	29	2,853	+ 785			4	0
Chester County	11	2,277	+ 811			3	+ 7
Delaware County	19	8,565	− 2,590			12	
Montgomery County	62	9,298	+ 2,763			14	+ 7
Totals	597	69,028	− 23,772			99	0

[a]N_l = Number of firms from trade directory linked to employment figures from the state industrial directory. Overall for the city, 476 of 548 firms were linked, and 121 of 136 for the suburbs, or an 87 percent linkage rate.

[b]Shift share is a rough measure of the unevenness of change in proportions of employment held by sectors or districts. If all sectors or areas grew or shrank at the same rate, all figures in this column would be zeroes. A gain in share indicates here relative growth vis-à-vis the shares of other units; a negative figure shows a faster decline than the category as a whole, thus in general expressing deviation from the mean.

Sources: Data in Table 6.5; Seventh Industrial Directory of Pennsylvania., 1934; OATD: 1934.

as in the city. Perhaps 10 percent of these positions were the fruit of re-location, but the rest represented on-site expansion of older mills and the appeal of non-union sites for new starts. As the district distributions show, three suburban counties, even in depression, retained a net expansion of 4,300 jobs over 1925, but the bulk of the increment was offset by losses in southernmost Delaware County, where wovens collapsed and knitting failed to root. Meanwhile full-fashioned work soared tenfold, as the broad north-west corridor toward Reading supported twenty-seven full-fashioned mills in 1934 where only three had stood in 1925.[19] Overall, the suburban share of textile labor rose from a fifth to a third of the regional totals.

In the city, decay was again uneven yet patterned. Kensington suffered more than half the area's job losses, but remained the site for about half of Philadelphia textile work, retaining its traditional diversity. Manayunk was a wreck; 80 percent of its textile positions were gone, as only a cluster of spinning mills, including Schofield's Imperial Woolen, still operated. In the center, south and west, 50 percent losses were common, but Germantown experienced a resurgence, partly from relocators fleeing Kensington clashes or pushed out of commercializing downtown fringes, and especially from the Bromleys' expansion of a full-fashioned mill that came under their control. Bulk ordering high-gauge machines, both in the late 1920s and promptly after the NRA was activated, they tripled employment at Rodgers Hosiery to 600. Meanwhile Frankford, a late bloomer, half of whose workers were involved in fancy wovens or full-fashioned, held its own to become a relatively larger presence on a contracting stage.[20]

The depth of the post-1925 slide can also be assessed from another angle, using a components of change portrait (Table 7.2) that illustrates the balance between losses and new starts by 1934. The results are stark; over half the 1925 cohort disappeared in nine years, whereas in 1916–25 less than a third of active firms liquidated or removed, despite the hazards of shortages, inflation, and the postwar depression. Sagging new starts after 1925 yielded a net loss of nearly 300 companies by 1934. Moreover, whereas survivors

---

[19] These figures are drawn from worksheets for Table 7.1. Original information for 1934 compiled from *Official American Textile Directory: 1934*, New York, 1934, pp. 285–351, and Pennsylvania Department of Internal Affairs, *Seventh Industrial Directory of the Commonwealth of Pennsylvania*, Harrisburg, 1935, county listings by firm, and for 1925, *OATD:1925* and *Fifth ID*.

[20] For example, on September 15, 1933, the Bromleys ordered two new footers from the Textile Machine Works and nine more footers and leggers on September 20 (total cost – $103,000) as a part of joint orders that totaled twenty-nine machines by early 1934. Eighteen of these were installed at Rodgers. See Memoranda, September 20, 1933, and June 4, 6, 1934, Textile Machine Works Correspondence File, Quaker Hosiery, in Quaker Lace Papers, Philadelphia (hereafter cited as TMW File, Quaker Hosiery).

Table 7.2. *Components of change, textile firms and employment, Philadelphia and Manayunk, 1925–34*

Philadelphia

Firms

	N	%
Total 1925	843	100
Lost 1925–34	437	52
1934 survivors	406	48
Active new starts (25–34)	142	
Total 1934	548	

Employment

	1926			1934		
	N_f	N_l	Empl.	N_f	N_l	Empl.
1934 Survivors	406	313	41,221	406	313	36,508
1925–34 lost	437	294	27,187	NS[a]		
				142	103	6,860
Totals	843	607	68,408[b]	548	416	43,368
Survivors' contraction			4,713			
Lost jobs less new starts			20,327			
Net loss			25,040			

Manayunk

Firms

	1925			1934		
	N_f	N_l	Empl.	N_f	N_l	Empl.
1934 survivors	22	19	1,623	22	19	1,098
1925–34 lost / New starts	27	22	4,559	5	4	160
Totals	49	41	6,182	27	23	1,258
Survivors' contraction						525
Lost jobs less new starts						4,399
Net loss						4,924

[a] NS = New-starting firms after 1925 still active in 1934 and number of replacement jobs at these firms.

[b] Employment figures will not match those in Table 7.2, because in order to measure expansion or contraction of employment at survivor firms, workforce data for both 1925 and 1934 must be available. This requirement excluded some firms, and totals here are thus lower, as are linkage rates.

Sources: Same as for Table 7.1.

among a 320 member 1916 sample group posted 1925 employment figures
17 percent above the total for the whole sample in 1916, by 1934 persisting
firms had suffered net losses of 11 percent since 1925. Only a fifth of the
32,000 dropped positions were replaced by new or successor firms. In Manayunk, the death of weaving and Collins and Aikman's disinvestment left
only small firms growing smaller (mean employment in 1925, 85, in 1934,
55). The handful of new ventures huddled in portions of largely vacant mills
and were able to resurrect only 4 percent of the district's lost jobs.[21]

What happened to these once-valued, vacated industrial spaces? The flagging Philadelphia Textile Manufacturers' Association conducted a 1936
industrial postmortem that provides an answer. Surveying the status of 212
buildings emptied by closures (covering virtually all the larger firms) across
the previous decade, they found 97 of them (46 percent) either vacant or
demolished. Of those again in use, a fifth had been converted to service
sector activity (laundries, storage, sales) while the rest had new manufacturing
occupants, chiefly quite small firms (164 total) renting but part of the available
space. For the 185 failed textile companies, only 65 replacements had appeared, a fifth of these being pre-1925 firms trading down to cheaper quarters. Nontextile occupants clustered in trades for which low rentals in aged
buildings keyed minimizing overhead (apparel, novelties, waste reprocessing). Spatially, the vacancies were concentrated in Kensington (63 percent),
with nearly half the district's failures finding no successors versus only one
in eight in again-popular Germantown. The Manayunk pattern, shutdowns
without replacements, now closed in on the old focal point of both production
and contest in Philadelphia textiles.[22]

----

[21] Data for 1916–25 drawn from printouts "Codebook:Scranton," September 30, 1985,
and "Outbus:25 Scranton, " October 15, 1985, Rutgers University Computer Systems
and Information Service. A fuller components-of-change analysis would include all
interim starts and closures with yearly employment gains and losses, plus more thorough
breakdowns on the sources of new starts (in-movers, branch plants) and "departures"
(bankruptcies, liquidations, mergers, relocations). The data sources were not rich enough
for this effort; trade directories that had regularly reported details about departures
largely ceased to do so after 1930. For the 1916 sample (30 percent, 320 firms in the
five-county region) of 303 active in 1916, 207 were still in the area and operating in
1925. By 1931, 73 more of these veteran firms were gone. Of the 167 lost over 15
years, 150 liquidated voluntarily or otherwise, 8 burnt down and did not restart, and 9
moved outside the region (whereas 124 changed locations within it at some time). For
more components-of-change studies, see K. C. Bishop and C. E. Simpson, "Components of Change Analysis," *Regional Studies* 4(1970): 59–68; P. E. Lloyd, "The Components of Industrial Change for Merseyside Inner Area, 1966–1975," *Urban Studies*
16(1979): 45–60; P. N. O'Farrell, "Components of Manufacturing Employment Change
in Ireland, 1973–1981," *Urban Studies* 21(1984): 155–76; Michael Taylor, "Industrial
Geography," *Progress in Human Geography* 8(1984): 263–73.
[22] Philadelphia Textile Manufacturers' Association, "Textile Mills That went Out of Busi-

Table 7.3. *Employment by sector, Philadelphia textiles 1935–6, 1938–9, 1941*

	1935	1936	1938	1939	1941
Woven goods	6,431	6,199	5,077	5,450	4,981
(Cotton)	(2,181)	(2,134)	(1,556)	(1,656)	(1,728)
(Wool/worsted)	(2,858)	(2,915)	(2,591)	(2,930)	(3,391)
(Silk/rayon)	(1,391)	(1,140)	(930)	(864)	(862)
Fancy wovens*a*	5,243	5,756	4,893	6,605	7,672
Carpets	3,063	3,387	3,373	3,744	4,247
Hose-knit	22,917	22,579	16,885	15,938	12,778
(Hosiery)	(17,691)	(16,099)	(11,717)	(10,617)	(7,205)
(Knit goods)	(5,226)	(6,480)	(5,168)	(5,321)	(5,573)
Dye-finish	3,770	4,026	3,962	4,343	4,926
Spinning	4,573	4,227	3,216	3,789	3,856
Miscellaneous	2,625	2,761	2,604	2,933	4,367
Totals	48,622	48,935	40,010	42,802	43,827

a Fancy woven figures, 1936–41, do not compare directly with 1934 firm-by-firm tabulations (Table 7.1), because state categories mixed upholstery, fine woolens, and other specialties into their general woven goods classes. Within the terms of the commonwealth's designations, comparison of 1936–41 totals with figures in Table 6.5, 1929–33, reflects consistent categories, even though they understate the scale and resilience of fancy weaving.

Note: Sectoral totals for 1937 and 1940 omitted for simplicity. They were, for the city as a whole, 48,699 in 1937 and exactly 39,000 for 1940, as reported in the *RPI* volumes for these years.

Source: Pennsylvania Department of Internal Affairs, *Reports on Productive Industries, Public Utilities and Miscellaneous Statistics of the Commonwealth of Pennsylvania for the Year(s) 1935, 1936, 1938, 1939, and 1941*, Harrisburg, PA, 1937–42, Philadelphia County.

Overall, in employment terms, the false recovery drew employment up to 48,000 by 1935, but the 1937 relapse forced it back to 40,000, below the 1932 trough (Tables 7.3 and 6.7). War fever brought expansion in 1939, war nerves a new low (39,000) in 1940, and war procurement a flush of demand in 1941. Calls for military goods again spurred conversions for

ness from 1926 to 1936 in the City of Philadelphia," typescript, July 1936, Archives, Pastore Library, Philadelphia College of Textiles and Science. In the survey both Kensington and Germantown closings were reported as a slightly but symmetrically higher proportion of all shutdowns than were the districts' shares of 1925 employment (Kensington = 55 percent of closures vs. 49 percent of employment, Germantown = 11 vs. 10). Yet 21 of 24 Germantown mills had been put to new uses compared with only 65 of 117 Kensington facilities.

Table 7.4. *Capital in Philadelphia textile manufacturing, selected sectors and all nontextile industries, 1929, 1935, 1937–9, 1941*

| | Capital (in millions) | | | | | |
	1929	1935	1937	1938	1939	1941
All textiles	183.5	111.9	101.0	91.5	85.8	76.1
Hosiery	43.1	26.4	22.3	16.5	14.9	8.4
Carpets	22.2	11.9	8.7	11.4	10.3	7.0
Dye-finish	16.0	10.6	9.4	8.6	8.6	9.0
Wool/worsted goods	12.1	7.0	6.5	6.4	5.8	6.8
Wool/worsted yarns	22.6	12.3	10.6	9.9	8.4	7.0
PNTI[a]	846.0	720.0	636.8	641.7	638.3	613.7

| | Index (corrected to 1929 dollars, 1929 = 100)[b] | | | | |
	1935	1937	1938	1939	1941
All textiles	80	71	66	62	50
Hosiery	81	66	50	46	23
Carpets	71	50	67	62	38
Dye-finish	87	75	71	72	68
Wool/worsted goods	76	69	70	64	68
Wool/worsted yarns	72	60	58	50	37
PNTI	112	97	100	101	87

[a]PNTI = All manufacturing other than textiles in Philadelphia.
[b]Index based on Series P-119, Capital in Manufacturing Industries, in Bureau of the Census, Department of Commerce, *Historical Statistics of the United States*, Washington, D.C., 1975, p. 683.
Sources: Pennsylvania Department of Internal Affairs, *Report on Productive Industries*, 1929, 1935, 1937–9, 1941, Philadelphia County.

remaining mills in cloth and carpets; dyeworks and knit outerwear goods expanded healthily. However, the critical hosiery sector was in sad shape, shrinking relentlessly to half its 1935 workforce levels in five years. Lagged a decade behind their woolen and carpet colleagues, full-fashioned mills were liquidating with dull regularity. Once the 1925 pinnacle passed, textile employment slumped more deeply with each economic tremor and recovered to ever lower peaks before decline resumed. The newest "healthy" clusters (dyeing, outerwear) had little of the generative power that carpets and specialties displayed in their glory years or hosiery carried in the 1910s and 1920s.

Data on capital and product values for the later 1930s confirm this unhappy picture (Tables 7.4 and 7.5). In real terms, 1941 textile capital was but half

Table 7.5. *Product value for Philadelphia textiles, selected sectors and all nontextile industries, 1929, 1935, 1937–9, 1941*

	Product value (in millions)					
	1929	1935	1937	1938	1939	1941
All textiles	344.4	173.1	202.2	136.9	176.5	246.5
Hosiery	103.4	41.4	42.6	27.1	25.4	29.5
Carpets	31.6	14.2	19.0	11.1	17.4	28.7
Dye-finish	21.4	13.6	15.8	12.9	17.0	24.7
Wool/worsted goods	23.3	15.7	20.3	14.7	20.6	30.3
Wool/worsted yarns	30.0	15.4	20.7	11.2	15.2	24.3
PNTI[a]	1,466.6	1,026.4	1,319.3	1,079.5	1,231.5	1,845.7

	Index (corrected to 1929 dollars, 1929 = 100)[b]				
	1935	1937	1938	1939	1941
All textiles	64	70	54	65	76
Hosiery	51	49	35	32	30
Carpets	64	72	47	72	97
Dye-finish	81	88	81	103	123
Wool/worsted goods	86	104	85	115	138
Wool/worsted yarns	61	82	50	66	88
PNTI – a	89	107	99	109	134
PNTI – b[c]	82	97	83	94	130

[a]Philadelphia nontextile industries.
[b]Nominal figures adjusted to reflect real 1929 dollars, using Bureau of Labor Statistics Wholesale Price Index for Textile Products. See notes to Table 6.9.
[c]The first PNTI index uses the textile series as an inflator, the second – to mirror better Philadelphia's diversified trades – employs the BLS All Commodities Other than Farm or Food Products wholesale series. See notes to Table 6.9.
Sources: Same as for Table 7.4.

the 1929 investment, whereas city-based nontextile industries slipped only 13 percent. Hosiery had collapsed, more rapidly after 1935 than any other trade division. Dyeing and wool/worsted did stabilize, evidently replacing depreciated assets with some fresh equipment and deferred repairs, but by 1941 each was employing a 1929-scale complement of workers on a real capital base a third smaller. The few firms updating their machinery or refurbishing their mills were outnumbered by the majority that stood pat, dodging liquidation and awaiting revived demand. When this materialized, as real product values jumped by half, 1938–41, area hosiers did not share in the wartime largesse that raised dyers and wool/worsted firms to performance levels comparable to area nontextile companies. Indeed, the returns from increased sales of stockings, 1939–41, were outpaced by inflation, as the index indicates. In general, the textile system was so depleted that even with war-spurred expansion it could reach in constant dollars only three-quarters of its 1929 output. By contrast, nontextile trades leapt over earlier benchmarks, far less damaged by the Depression than textiles had been by two decades of misery. Philadelphia's 1941 textile survivors were not a saving remnant poised to revitalize the industry, but rather a cohort of hardy left-overs who could gratefully parlay war opportunities into another decade of operation on the fringe.[23]

7.2. Production, distribution, and regulation

In those first terrible years after 1929, Philadelphia millmen well knew their weaknesses. When "voracious" fabric and knit-goods buyers, aided by "Dame Rumor," circulated the news that business could only be gotten at such and such a price, the jelly-spined individualists among them quailed. Cutting their lists to grasp at orders, "timid" proprietors handed their profits to distributors, chiseled their workers' rates, and, sucked into the game, competed with one another for the right to an early liquidation. It was the rush of this whirlpool that the NIRA and its code authorities aimed to reverse. As George Taylor put it, "The code idea is to prevent certain types of individual behavior for the benefit of the industry, while allowing for complete freedom of individual initiative in those directions that will not react to the detriment of the industry as a whole." Yet the NRA, as Ellis Hawley has shown, was never able to reconcile the strain between collectivism and in-dividualism. Interests in conflict could not be harmonized without some parties losing latitude for action or advantages they had held, and without a legit-imate, effective coordinating force with adequate tools for enforcing deci-sions. Though price and jobs drew the most attention, position and power were profoundly at issue in competitive industries where trade practices were crucial and more difficult to alter. After all, labor was weakened but pur-chasers remained in the ascendant.[24]

---

[23] It should be noted that the apparently healthy showing of wool/worsteds' real product value is measured against a 1929 base, by which time the sector had already declined considerably. Even so, this performance was, due to stretch-out and overtime operations, better in real value than any year since 1921.

[24] *UHR* 17(January 1934): 93, (April 1934): 129; Ellis Hawley, *The New Deal and the Problem of Monopoly*, Princeton, NJ, 1966, chs. 3–5, Conclusion, especially pp. 36–50, 97–103, 472–6. See also John K. Ohl, *Hugh S. Johnson and the New Deal*, DeKalb, IL, 1985, ch. 7–10, especially pp. 178–87.

Promulgation of the cotton code, largely designed by the Cotton Textile Institute, led the parade in June 1933. It aimed to end price cutting in brutally competitive staple lines, and it set the pattern for trade "policing" by manufacturers' associations that was followed closely by woolens in July and dozens of textile sectors and other industries later in 1933–4.[25] Though Apex chief William Meyer greeted the NIRA with murmurs about Russian parallels for "government operation of industry," less reactionary figures hastened to create a hosiery code on the CTI model. Echoing cotton's hours and minimum wage figures, the hosiery code went much further in detailing and forbidding onerous trade practices: price guarantees and ratchets, kickbacks of "bonuses, commissions, unearned credits or discounts," consignment sales, "commercial bribery," and the all-important "selling below cost." Only if such marketing practices ended could increased production costs be supported by enhanced returns for hosiery.[26]

When activated in September, the hosiery code had already been overtaken by earlier events. Though trade leaders and large mills had tried to blame "mushroom" firms operated by former "foremen and superintendents" for prices typically 10 percent below production costs, seasoned observers responded that it had been industry majors desperate to run full-bore who had led "the vanguard" of low price taking. Hence "many of the leaders are directly responsible for the situation they deplore." With May 1933 prices at historic lows as the NIRA swept through Congress, buyers rapidly placed the largest advance orders in five years, trying to dodge the expected, unavoidable advances that would flow from reflationary legislation. Successful in this they settled back to await deliveries. When code implementation brought a September spike in mill prices, buyers sat on their hands, working off their cheaply gotten stocks. Within sixty days the market softened; retailers held to their forty-nine, fifty-nine, and eighty-nine cent price lines, confident of their power to secure resupply with "'low-ball" offers to frazzled firms.[27] Thus the Code Authority confronted at its start the aftereffects of "pre-buying," as buyers' machinations prevented prices from elevating to profitable levels. In December it decreed a universal curtailment (40 percent

---

[25] Ohl, *Johnson*, p. 115. See on cotton textiles, Louis Galambos, *Competition and Cooperation*, Baltimore, 1966, as well as Sidney Fine, *The Automobile under the Blue Eagle*, Ann Arbor, 1963, and Norman Nordhauser, *The Quest for Stability: Domestic Oil Regulation, 1917–1935*, New York, 1979. Ohl (pp. 324–5) cites additional articles and dissertations on steel, coal, and lumber.

[26] *TW* 83(1933): 941, 1470, 1614–15, 1650; G. Allan Dash, Jr., "The Hosiery Code," unpublished MA thesis, University of Pennsylvania, 1935, pp. 37–9.

[27] *TW* 83(1933): 1301, 1615, 1852, 2030–1, 2216; *Knitting Mill News* 11(1933): 5, 73 (hereafter *KMN*); *UHR* 18(March 1935): 118; *AWCR* 47(March 9, 1933): 32.

for three weeks) which helped move mill inventories, but 1934 prices hovered at least 20 percent below the optimistic fall postings buyers had ignored.[28] Apex manager Elwood Struve blamed buyers' summer "speculation" for the autumn mess.

> They bought so heavily so as to encourage mills to speed up, and most of us really overproduced during May, June, July and August. Now, as we made up hosiery in proportion as many of the retail units bought, we are in a position in which it is ridiculous to quote [list prices] to dealers who do not want merchandise.[29]

The enthusiasm for a return to full running led full-fashioned mills to build inventories that in turn exposed them to purchasers' fall demands for concessions. One millman appreciated that buyers had outmaneuvered the NRA. Before the code, "mills had to manufacture to a price and ... in spite of the Code they still have to manufacture to a price."[30]

A spring 1934 attempt to set and enforce a livable minimum price for silk hosiery was a complete fiasco. Though the code board and the hosiery trade association joined posting a break-even price for basic forty-two gauge stocking with release of a standard costing manual and a pledge to punish "chiselers," within moments of the announcement there was a rush to the telephone banks. "Big distributors" reported a "stream" of calls from mills quoting lower rates.

> There were offers to pre-date orders, to ship at the low price without orders, and even to add a zero to the figure designating the quantity already on order ... These suggestions ... came from the big producers, not from the same fellows who have often been charged with disturbing the price situation.[31]

In staple hosiery lines, as in cottons, non-union majors like Apex and Berkshire sought to use price concessions and labor cost advantages to achieve full capacity operations. Though one wag suggested the trade substitute the chisel for the Blue Eagle emblem, the Code Authority abandoned price management, simply dropping "the entire project after realizing the difficulties in the way of enforcement."[32] Buyers cheered, and were soon booking

---

[28] UHR 18(February 1935): 32; TW 84(1934): 118; Dash, "Hosiery Code," pp. 73–4.

[29] KMN 11(1933): 461. [30] UHR 17(January 1934): 49.

[31] UHR 17(May 1934): 17, 111. For a direct account of this rush to undercutting deals, given by the buyer for John Wanamaker, see KMN 12(1934): 157.

[32] UHR 17(May 1934): 17; Herbert Taggart, Minimum Prices Under the NRA, Michigan Business Studies, Volume 7, Number 3, Ann Arbor, 1936, p. 48. Taggart's 300-page monograph is a remarkable survey of price-elevating efforts that considers the experience of over a hundred code authorities. His conclusions were that no unproblematic basis for price setting could be shaped, and that enforcement without comprehensive statist regulation of supplies and production was impossible.

orders at five dollars a dozen, seventy-five cents below the "official" rate. Though full-fashioned prices had risen nearly a third over their 1932–33 lows, Taylor estimated that minimum wages and increased materials costs consumed virtually all the gains, leaving average mill profits of less than one percent on basic constructions.[33] With its fair-trade practices a dead letter and a second curtailment plan "withdrawn" after "determined" resistance, the limits of the NRA's impact were plain by mid-1934. Neither distributional power relations nor the pacesetting ties between big mills and chains/ group buyers had been altered. Moreover, the two forty-hour shift limit on operations had set in motion structural shifts that hastened the degradation of the trade.[34]

In and beyond Philadelphia, hosiery firms' response to the hours restriction accelerated the expansion of the gray-goods market. Its emergence helped transform flexible specialists into staple-goods producers little different from their dependent cotton colleagues. Starting in 1930–2, hard-pressed mills eager to cut the time working capital was sunk in inventory hosiery began booking distributors' orders for hose knitted but not dyed and finished. Takers contracted independently for these steps, replicating in a sense Gotham's hand-to-mouth production system by holding gray stock that could be quickly colored to meet retail demand trends. The NRA machine-hours limit gave a solid push to this budding gray-goods trade. Fearing on-hand machinery would be inadequate to fill anticipated demand given shortened hours, large Philadelphia mills snapped up bargains at liquidation sales. Unwilling to build new space for these machines, such firms closed their finishing departments, ending the partial integration once a sign of company maturity, relied on "outside" dyers for "detailed" orders, and sold the rest of their goods as gray hose. This restructuring sustained area dyers whose trade from other sources was diminishing, and, in union knitting mills, eliminated higher-paid AFHW members for the services of unorganized outside dyers, a probable cost saving. Both gray-goods converters and knitting mills stood to gain, but the new relations entailed two peculiar tradeoffs.[35]

[33] *KMN* 12(1934): 157; *UHR* 18(March 1935): 118. Wage provisions of the hosiery code had increased southern and non-union costs for auxiliary as well as knitting labor, narrowing previous gaps, stiffening resistance to continued drastic reductions without by any means assuring livable profits (Dash, "Hosiery Code," pp. 49–51 and Table 19).

[34] *UHR* 17(November 1934): 136; *TW* 83(1933): 1418, 1615.

[35] *KMN* 12(1934): 6, 40, 135, 186. All sources agreed that there was no gray-goods market in hosiery before 1930, but such operations became sufficiently common by 1934 that the 97-member non-union trade group established a "clearing house" service for information on sources of and outlets for "hosiery in the unfinished state" (ibid., 174). For background, see Irving Kravis, "A Study of the Commercial Finishing of Full-Fashioned Hosiery with Special Emphasis on Labor Relations," unpublished MA thesis, University of Pennsylvania, 1939.

Gray hosiery was as near a staple item as the stocking trade produced, and the fast cash realized was usually, at rock-bottom prices, survival money, a drawing card for marginal, mushroom firms. Distributors finishing gray goods to match style trends were positioned both to score timely profits and to outflank full-process manufacturers by achieving a comparable flexibility. Mills that had dropped finishing were middled. In selling gray goods they had to match prices the desperate would take; in pricing finished goods they had to meet levels converters operating in parallel would set. Firms that had retained captive dyeworks were no less troubled. "Inside" finishing, unless done cheaply, became a liability, for non-union contractors held a 20–40 percent cost advantage. Further, code jurisdictions had placed independent finishers with all textile processing, not hosiery, despite union and trade protests. Instead of providing solutions, the NRA had greased the slippery slope.[36]

Three developments provided a temporary resolution to the tangle. Buyers discovered the price-battered grays from marginal mills were uneven and unreliable in quality, leading them to favor purchasing from old-line firms after 1934. These companies stopped haunting auctions and commenced contracting for gray goods with peripheral mills, closely specifying constructions, checking quality, and at times sending out their own silk yarns to create a true commission shop relation. This "tapered capacity" approach modified older capital-saving strategies common among flexible firms, now adapted to the new dependency. Finally, the hosiery union, ever battling for wage uniformity and stabilization, set about organizing independent finishers with fair initial success. Like the adjustment of the 1920s, these manuevers bought time, being means to manage decline, not innovations to avert it.[37]

The Schechter decision was anticlimactic, for by 1935 all faith in the NRA had dissipated. At the April trade meetings, hosiers bitterly assailed buyers

[36] Kravis, "Commercial Finishing," pp. 17–8, 28–36. By 1938 contract operations had sufficient capacity to finish every pair of full-fashioned hose made in the United States (p. 39). See also J. D. deHaan, *The Full-Fashioned Hosiery Industry in the U.S.A.*, The Hague, Netherlands, 1958, pp. 72–3, and George Taylor and G. Allan Dash, Jr., *Stocks and Production Policies in the Full-Fashioned Hosiery Manufacture*, Washington, D.C., 1941, pp. 17–22. In 1933, some seventy-one independent finishers were slotted under the Textile Processing Code Authority (Kravis, p. 29), beyond the reach of Taylor, Constantine, and the hosiery crowd and enjoying lax oversight that preserved differentials. Gray goods were sold without terms, discounts, or datings, with payment due on receipt of shipment.

[37] Taylor, *Stocks*, pp. 5, 18, 22–4; *KMN* 13(1935): 195, 342; *UHR* 18(May 1935): 112, (November 1935): 115; Kravis, "Commercial Finishing," pp. 46–56. On "tapered capacity," see Hiram Davis et al., *Vertical Integration in the Textile Industry*, Philadelphia, 1938, p. 17.

and "chiseling finishers" without appealing to the codesmen. Proposing a mill holiday, echoing the bank and farm varieties, one operator asked:

> Why not end shipments from all mills for two weeks? ... Shut off this supply of finished hosiery. Call it a week of Sundays if you like. All of the burden of the distributor and dealers is on the back of the mill at present because of this lack of advance buying.[38]

Purchaser's organizations were meanwhile calmly disseminating formal classifications of mills (through the Wholesale Dry Goods Institute), according to how favorable their selling practices were for members' interests. When buyers pounced after the court ruled, attempts to secure mill operators' commitments to retain NRA hours and wage limits proved fruitless in both full-fashioned and seamless divisions. In durably competitive industries, manufacturers' associations could not restrain the race to laissez faire. Buyers, cemented in control, would purchase ahead only when it suited *their* interests, and played the "how low can you go" game until the war intervened.[39]

Outside hosiery, Philadelphia fabric manufacturers were likewise facing narrowed options for adjustment. Three survivors will here be considered, the Bromleys, the Artloom Corporation, and Bernard Davis's LaFrance mills, being in turn mid- and late-nineteenth-century stalwarts and a hugely successful 1920s firm. The Bromley carpet mills had become peripheral; their protests against code provisions concerning grade and quality standards and sales below cost both suggested a scrambling at the market's edges and were ignored by the Carpet Institute leadership. However, the family lace and hosiery firms worked in tandem to reposition Bromley investments in the later 1930s.[40] Accumulated reserves at Quaker Lace and North American Hosiery funded purchase of full-fashioned equipment from liquidating firms, creating in 1935 Bromley and Company as another of the clan's spinoff

---

[38] *UHR* 18(May 1935): 112.

[39] *UHR* 18(June 1935): 94; 19(June 1936): 44; *KMN* 13(1935): 201. In August *KMN* reported that "there is still a great deal of $4.50 a dozen hosiery in the market ... and some buyers whose patronage is generally much sought after, are reported manifesting a bearish attitude, in line with which orders are being withheld" (270). Even the usually rabid anti-union *KMN* by September admitted, through the persona of Joe Pliers, its fictional knitter-turned-proprietor, that "the union is the best friend the manufacturer has and he does not know it. If he did not have to pay union wages he would be first of all cutting his own throat with low prices and then he would start in on his competitors' throats and then finally when he got all prices so low he would start cutting the help. All this would be ruinous ..." (308). The Supreme Court's revocation of the NRA came May 27, 1935.

[40] *ACUJ* 52(October 1933): 19, 23.

firms. Bromley full-fashioned mills then had a two to two and a half million dozens annual capacity, half the size of the Berkshire and 5 percent of national capacity. Having quietly accepted the AFHW at Quaker Hosiery in 1934, the Bromleys moved steadily to restructure investments outside the city, first in nearby New Jersey then in 1936 at Athens, Georgia. Two Kensington mills closed in 1937, and two years later Quaker Hosiery ordered new Reading knitters for a Tennessee subsidiary, Smoky Mountain Mills. Product diversity continued, as the firms' maintained twenty-one lines of silk stockings as well as silk-wool blends for winter. However, such profits as were secured were now for the first time being invested outside the region. With this restructuring, the city's most successful textile proprietors signaled their recognition that an era was ending.[41]

The Bromleys' self-financing abilities insulated them from external threats that disrupted Artloom and LaFrance, which had "gone public" with bond and share offerings in the 1920s. Artloom descended from an 1892 immigrant partnership among three Wassermans and John Zimmerman, who had earlier worked for the Bromleys. Zimmerman's technical inventiveness spurred their success with three firms running jacquard Wiltons, tapestries, and plushes before they were merged to form the Artloom Corporation in 1925. The original team retained a controlling interest when common and preferred shares were sold to raise added capital, but the Depression triggered readjustments. The firm gave up direct selling of carpets and hired a New York design firm to revitalize its drapery and upholstery lines, yet by 1934 annual losses mounted above $200,000. More important, with the post-1929 deaths of several founders, their holdings were divided among heirs and also depreciated in value (common shares fell from $42.00 in 1928 to $2.50 in 1933 and $3.75 in 1935). Small wonder that when a group of Detroit-connected investors offered to buy 80,000 shares at $14.00 each in 1936 a deal was quickly struck. The new interests indirectly "represented the Chrysler Corporation" and planned a mixed-output emphasis on automotive fabrics and consumer specialties, hiring the J. Walter Thompson Company to focus on brand visibility.[42] Though Artloom had been shoved

---

[41] *KMN* 11(1933): 361; 15(1937): 105; *TW* 86(1936): 2133: *UHR* 18(April 1935): 2–3, 18(September 1935): 2–3: 19(December 1936): 2; *Union Labor Record*, May 18, 1934, pp. 1, 7 (hereafter *ULR*). *Davidson's Knit Goods Trade: 1937*, New York, 1937, pp. 116, 148; Memorandum, September 19, 1939, and R. J. Ryan to John Bromley, January 8, 1941, TMW Files, Quaker Hosiery.

[42] *AWCR* 42(1928): 213, 1069; 47(March 2, 1933): 33; *ACUJ* 54(April 1935): 25; 55(February 1936): 14, 55(March 1936): 7, 55(June 1936): 31, 55(November 1936): 10, 55(December 1936): 39; *Carpet and Upholstery Trade Review* 65(October 15, 1934): 34; 66 (April 15, 1935): 33, 66(October 16, 1935): 3; 67(March 1, 1936): 15, 67(March 15, 1936): 25, 67(December 15, 1936): 38; *TW* 86(1936): 905.

onto the corporate fast track, the results hardly thrilled the new leaders. After a spurt to $22.00, common stock slumped below $5.00 in the 1937 recession. Mounting losses brought dismissal of the company president, a holdover from the old regime, but this purge did little good. Preferred dividends were suspended, and only redeemed during World War II. Except as a captive supply source for auto upholstery, Artloom proved to be a dubious acquisition. Few other takeovers were ventured in the 1930s, and those that materialized after the war soon led to liquidations.[43]

LaFrance, darling of the upholstery trade in the 1920s, became entangled with New York financial houses and barely escaped a forced liquidation. In 1932, while losing $282,000 on operations, Bernard Davis managed to place $1 million in 7 percent mortgage bonds to raise capital for reorganization. However, losses in 1934–5 (over $500,000) and a fire at its Frankford mills derailed LaFrance's recovery. Davis sold part of his stock and committed receivables (to New York's Textile Banking Company) to raise funds, but at last filed for bankruptcy reorganization in July 1936, precipitating four years of legal wrangling. After Manufacturers Trust, which held the largest minority share of LaFrance common stock, torpedoed three restructuring plans, a $600,000 Reconstruction Finance Corporation loan in 1940 at last ended the controversy. LaFrance survived to make military duck, serges, and shirtings during the war, only to close shop locally and consolidate production at its South Carolina and Ontario plants by 1949.[44]

From the NIRA through the Robinson-Patman and Miller-Tydings acts, New Deal legislation did little to aid Philadelphia's battered mills. Moves toward tariff reciprocity and the government's 1941 assumption of control over silk supplies only added to general demoralization. Early expectations among flexible mills that the activist state would redress their grievances and improve their prospects dissolved. Further, in labor relations, the NIRA and the Wagner Act offered unions a conditional legitimacy and provided the state with a decisive role in setting and enforcing rules of conduct, displacing older localist, individualistic practices and patterns. Few firms were in a

---

[43] *ACUJ* 56(March 1937): 10; (November 1937): 12; 57(February 1938): 18, 57(November 1938): 11; 58 (August 1939): 16; 60(January 1940): 13. Wasserman heirs attempted to regain control in 1941 but failed (*ACUJ* 60[March 1941]:4), as a TWOC-organized union backed the corporate directors, a nice alignment of a "modern" labor organization with bureaucratic managers.

[44] *ACUJ* 53(April 1934): 26; 54(March 1935): 22; 55(April 1936): 24; 55(August 1936): 24; 55(October 1936): 21; 55(November 1936): 26; 56 (March 1937): 29; 57(January 1938): 23; 57(August 1938): 13; 58 (April 1939): 25, 58(May 1939): 32; 58(October 1939): 24; 59(May 1940): 17; *Davison's Textile Blue Book: 1943*, New York, 1943, p. 173; Pennsylvania Department of Internal Affairs, *Twelfth Industrial Directory of Pennsylvania*, Harrisburg, 1950, pp. 464–83.

position, like Quaker Hosiery, to accept unionization and plot a spatial shift. Most fumed, delayed, and fought back. Workers had by 1933 already endured from five to a dozen years of underemployment and rate cuts. Yet their demands for a better deal exasperated millmen unable to defend their prices. Another "lose-lose" situation beckoned.[45]

7.3   Grinding defeats and empty victories: textile labor, 1933–1941

Symbolizing the passing of a generation, the union press reported Tobias Hall's death during the first week of the New Deal. Emigrating from Britain in 1863, Hall had been a Knights of Labor stalwart, fifty years a militant socialist, and "a leader in every struggle of the Upholstery Weavers' Union." It was "Toby" Hall who had enlivened the Commission on Industrial Relations sessions with tales of shop-floor squabbling with proprietors, his talk of "unofficial" recognition, and his obvious pride in skill. He was gone, scarcely a decade after the mill relations he epitomized had begun to deteriorate. Deeply troubled, his beloved Local 25 spawned no successor to Tobias Hall, but if any Philadelphia labor leader did fit the new era, Emil Rieve was the man. Heading the AFHW, Rieve appreciated the power shifts that localist, shop-based unionists rarely perceived. He moved easily between Washington hearings and city labor halls, brokered job-conserving concessions and pressed national organizing efforts, allying his union with Sidney Hillman's Textile Workers Organizing Committee to seek stabilization of the hosiery trade. Manager more than militant, Rieve held to the terms of contracts and the language of efficiency, recoded visions of workers' community into achieving federal backing for union-sponsored public housing (the Carl Mackley Homes), and kept his eager Philadelphia forces out of the disastrous 1934 general textile strike. The world of Tobias Hall no

---

[45] For textile manufacturers' response to the price discrimination (R-P) and price maintenance (M-T) statutes, see *UHR* 20(March 1937): 37–8, 135; 20(September 1937): 27; *KMN* 14(1936): 411; 15(1937): 69. On tariff reciprocity fears, see *TW* 88(March 1938): 46–7, 88(December 1938): 44. For chains, see Federal Trade Commission, *Chain Store Inquiry*, 5 vols., Washington, D.C., 1932–5. On the transition and continuities between the NIRA and the Wagner Act, see Christopher Tomlins, *The State and the Unions*, New York, 1985, and James Gross, *The Making of the National Labor Relations Board*, Albany, N.Y., 1974. For reactions to the FSLA, see *TW* 88(October 1938): 44; 89(February 1939): 33, 89(Annual 1939): 95, 89(April 1939): 62–3, 89(September 1939): 62; *KMN* 17(1939): 198, 273, 305. Its primary impact initially seems to have been to raise southern textile wages generally and rural women's earnings as well in northern areas. See also A. S. Neale, *The Anti-Trust Laws of the U.S.A.*, Cambridge, UK, 1960, chs. 9–10.

longer existed. Only occasional glimpses of its fierce neighborhood loyalties and mill-centered solidarities appeared on a landscape crowded with labor boards, federation vice-presidents, and earnest academics.[46]

The 1934 general strike's failure must be set against the backdrop of NRA-inspired expectations. For Philadelphia AFHW members, creation of the first codes coincided with demands by the union mills' group, the Full-Fashioned Hosiery Manufacturers of America, for a 20 percent cut in National Labor Agreement rates at its expiration on August 31, 1933. Rieve, William Leader and Alex McKeown, the union's most active officers, had to contend with a welter of crosscurrents. Everyone prayed that codes would yield wage advances and wider employment, but such effects had not yet been realized. Drastic reductions accepted in 1931 had yielded only a short period of "steady full-time operations" before open-shoppers installed their own cuts and regained the favor of price-mad buyers. Gaining approval for another round of reductions would be an unwelcome challenge, but collapse of the NLA and its standard-setting measures would be a far greater setback and the contents of the hosiery code were in June 1933 unknowable.[47]

Taking an aggressive stance, the AFHW kindled a triple-threat organizing drive under the banner of Section 7(a), targeting Reading for a fresh assault, reviving the 1931 tactic of striking all non-union Philadelphia mills, and pressing firms in the intermediate counties as opportunities afforded. Seven Reading strikes for raises and recognition were quickly mounted, but the intervention of Secretary of Labor Frances Perkins brought postponement of the city walkouts until the hosiery code could be finalized. As the June Reading walkouts swelled to include over five thousand workers, millmen threatened mass dismissal and offered rate hikes without recognition, to no avail. At month's end, seventeen hundred knitters idled three factories in suburban Lansdale, just as Perkins's "personal representative," Benjamin

[46] *ULR*, March 10, 1933, p. 1; *Textile Worker* 21(1933): 78. For Rieve's contemporaneous activities, see *ULR*, February 2, 1933, p. 3; June 16, p. 1; October 27, p. 1. On the union apartment complex, see ibid., October 13, 1933, p. 3; November 10, pp. 1, 3; November 24, p. 4, and February 9, 1934, pp. 1, 6. For a brief overview of textile labor's experience in the 1930s, see Emil Rieve, "Introduction," in Richard Kelly, *Nine Lives for Labor*, New York, 1956, pp. 3–7. *Union Labor Record*, which commenced publication in 1928, was initially a textile workers' weekly ("Every Member, Upholstery Weavers' Union, A Subscriber") endorsed by the Textile Workers' District Council. Its social democratic viewpoint and later enthusiasm for the CIO were not shared by the conservative, craft-led Philadelphia Central Labor Union, which declined to join the Amalgamated Clothing Workers, the International Ladies' Garment Workers, United Hatters, et al., in supporting it.

[47] Fred Keightly to H. L. Kerwin, June 25, 1933, Department of Labor, Federal Mediation and Conciliation Service, Case File 170/9044, Record Group 280, National Archives (hereafter FMCS File . . .).

Squires, was dispatched to Reading to negotiate a settlement at its twenty-four struck plants. So far, so good.[48] Squires's July 4 announcement that managements would meet workers' representatives once "the mills are operating" and that unresolved issues would be arbitrated did not bring the strikes to an end. Suspicious unionists soon discovered, in their first joint "conference" with manufacturers, that the latter's lawyers rejected workers' signatures on union cards, demanding the "the employees ... be questioned in small groups by the employer and his counsel" to verify their commitments. Condemning this intimidation, Rieve declared the drive would be expanded; and within three days, the kingpin Berkshire, Nolde and Horst, and Rosedale mills were emptied. Strikers' numbers mounted to twelve thousand by mid-month. Eight other walkouts commenced in and near Philadelphia, as management duplicity at Reading helped build the regional movements.[49]

The non-union Association of Full-Fashioned Hosiery Manufacturers counterattacked by decreeing a forty-hour week and rate increases throughout its 108 member companies, with, naturally, no mention of union recognition. Two weeks after this July 20 move, the Reading cohort agreed at last to hold "secret ballot" elections for representation, and this brought strikers back to their machines. Though workers voted for the AFHW in thirty-six of forty-four plants that fall, company attorneys used the ambiguities of statute language to make the "Reading formula" a dead letter. Union spokesmen were either ignored or enmeshed in empty bargaining; the NIRA had said nothing about *signing* contracts. Elsewhere strikes dragged to desultory conclusions, though violent clashes at Philadelphia's Cambria Company did climax with two killings when a terrified strikebreaker emptied his revolver at menacing picketers. Again, as in the Aberle case, bloody dues brought a contract, but in general, hosiery firms, through deft lawyers or sheer stubbornness, successfully fought the AFHW and preserved their open shops.[50] Following the August return to work at Reading, Rieve pledged

[48] Ibid.; *ULR*, June 16, 1933, p 1; June 23, p. 1; June 30, p. 1; *KMN* 11(1933): 102, 241, 395, 399; *Public Ledger*, June 22, 1933, p. 1; June 25, p. 3; June 29, p. 3; July 1, p. 20; July 4, p. 2 (hereafter *PL*); *TW* 83(1933): 1301, 1470.

[49] *PL*, July 5, 1933, p. 2; July 7, p. 4; July 8, p. 2; July 12, p. 1; July 15, p. 2; July 17, p. 6; July 29, p. 2; *ULR*, July 7, 1933, pp. 1,3; July 14, p. 1; July 21, p. 1; *Evening Public Ledger*, July 24, 1933, p. 1 (hereafter *EPL*). The *Public Ledger*, a morning newspaper, closed at the end of 1933, the *Evening Public Ledger* continuing.

[50] *PL*, July 21, 1933, pp. 1, 6 (a full list of the 108 firms is given on p. 6); July 22, pp. 1, 4; August 2, pp. 1, 5; August 3, p. 1; August 4, p. 9 (union leaders agree to keep order, as in the Aberle strike); August 20, p. 4; September 1, pp. 1, 4; September 2, p. 1; *KMN* 11(1933): 276, 278, 357; *EPL*, August 1, 1933, p. 1; August 10, p. 17; August 25, p. 2; August 31, p. 1; September 1, p. 1. A week before the shootings, strikebreakers or company agents had paint-bombed the homes of strike committee leaders, restarting the cycle of violence that ended with the August 31 deaths. Other sources include *ULR*,

that all disputes would be laid before the president's "Peace Board" for resolution, but demanded that renewal of the NLA be conditional on union mills doing more than matching the AFHM's July terms. A brief effort to restore the revered 1929 schedule, followed by a briefer general strike threat, made no headway; and the AFHW needed federal help to mediate a far less ambitious settlement with the FHMA. Fall distress succeeded the summer's promise. Buyers who had loaded up in the pre-NIRA rush were resolutely resisting mills' price list increases. Strike settlements were either disappointing or deferred, and the Berkshire was vigorously contesting orders from the National Labor Board. Though Rieve, as a newly appointed member of the Hosiery Code Authority, applauded when Senator Wagner ordered a December 5 percent hike in full-fashioned rates, the teeth of the NRA were already being pulled. By spring 1934, the AFHW would lodge bitter complaints about wholesale violations of Section 7(a). Having sheathed the strike weapon to cooperate with federal authorities, it found little other than frustrations accumulating.[51]

If the strongest segment of Philadelphia textile labor was balked in 1933, it should be no surprise that other union buds were snipped as well. A ten-week Collins and Aikman strike against the four-loom system yielded only a vague compromise that the company soon disregarded. Of forty other firms struck outside hosiery, thirty-five refused union recognition, with most settlements reflecting rate increases offsetting hours reductions to preserve overall weekly earnings. Recognitions secured at one wool-weaving and two knitted outerwear mills held some promise, but efforts in dyeing, plush, and carpets all stalled. Overall, Philadelphia proprietors were more willing to take long shutdowns than to accept formal union relations. After six to twelve weeks, local textile strikes petered out, most having achieved either loosely worded pledges to comply with the NIRA or nothing at all.[52]

July 21, 1933, p. 1 (Guards shoot two pickets in a nasty Lansdale exchange); July 28, p. 1; August 4, pp. 1, 3 (Reive asked police "if they want another murder, like that of Carl Mackley"); August 11, p. 1; August 25, p. 1; September 1, p. 3; September 8, p. 1; *TW* 83(1933): 1650, 1952 (on Reading votes and mills' refusal to endorse agreements). For an inclusive overview of federal labor relations policy, see Howell Harris, "The Snares of Liberalism," in Steven Tolliday and Jonathan Zeitlin, eds., *Shop Floor Bargaining and the State*, Cambridge, UK, pp. 148–91.

[51] *EPL*, August 7, 1933, p. 23; *PL*, August 8, 1933, p. 2; August 15, p. 1; August 25, p. 2; September 2, p. 1; *ULR*, September 1, 1933, p. 1; September 8, pp. 1, 3; October 27, p. 1; December 12, p. 10; March 2, 1934, pp. 1, 3.

[52] FMCS Files 170/9184 (Artloom), 170/9024 (Collins and Aikman), 170/9315 (Hellwig Dye Works), 176/310 (Concordia Silk), 176/369 (Delta Finishing), 170/9399 (Kaufman Plush, Philadelphia Pile Fabric), and 176/679 (Monarch Silk); on wool/worsted, see *ULR*, May 19, 1933, p. 1, June 23, p. 1; August 18, p. 3, and for knit goods, *ibid.*, June 9, 1933, p. 1; June 30, p. 1; July 14, p. 1; July 21, p. 1; August 25, p. 1; *PL*, August 25,

Until March 1934, the textile labor scene was quiet. Union full-fashioned mills at last ratified a standstill agreement with the AFHW in January, and, despite worrisome prices, demand and employment gradually rose. A spring knitwear campaign created quite a stir, but no victories. The TWU Knit Goods Workers presented forty-eight firms with a full price list and calls for recognition and a thirty-five-hour week. Only half the mills' four thousand workers struck in late March, leading to wild frays in Germantown and Kensington between strikers, refusers, and police. Largely Jewish and/or Socialist, knit-goods strikers loudly sang the "Internationale" at factories and in police stations, intensifying political and ethnic hostilities, but six weeks on the line proved fruitless. The KGWU did rebound quickly, borrowing six organizers from the International Ladies' Garment Workers after a July agreement for joint action in Philadelphia, but few other area unions shared the "When shall we strike?" fever that soon coursed through the UTW's August convention.[53]

Assembled in haste and intended both to channel southern enthusiasm and force acceptance of liberal interpretations of the NIRA, the 1934 general strike was a desperate, losing gamble. Its three demands – union recognition, a thirty-hour week without earnings loss, and an end to stretch-out – were fantasies in the current context, unless labor demonstrated such *force majeure* as to humble its foes in business and government. Threatened thus, millmen and politicians were far more prone to call for troops, as they did, than to bargain over contract language. Instead of stopping the wheels of industry to establish labor's rights, the strike became a three-week fiasco with multiple deaths, both of workers and of the labor movements in southern textiles, and closed with a worthless, face-saving return-to-work compromise.[54]

1933, p. 2. Though Collins and Aikman pled poverty in its summer claims for the necessity of stretch-out, corporate net profits for the first six months of 1933 turned out to be $634,000 vs. a loss of $438,000 for the same period in 1932 (*TW* 83[1933]:2025).

[53] *TW* 84(1934): 682, 883; *KMN* 12(1934):21, 81, 125; *EPL*, March 22, 1934, p. 2; March 23, p. 27; March 26, pp. 1, 17; April 12, pp. 1, 21; April 13, p. 1; April 20, p. 1; April 23, p. 1; April 24, p. 21; April 26, pp. 1, 21; May 1, p. 35; *ULR*, March 9, 1933, p. 1; March 16, p. 6; March 30, p. 3; April 20, p. 1; May 25, p. 1; June 15, p. 1; June 29, p. 1; July 6, p. 1; July 13, p. 4; July 20, p. 1; August 16, p. 1. On upholstery and Viscose conflicts, see respectively National Labor Relations Board Papers, Case Files 222 and 659, Record Group 25, National Archives (hereafter NLRB File...).

[54] On the general strike nationally, see Irving Bernstein, *Turbulent Years*, Boston, 1970, pp. 298–315, and for the South, James Hodges, *New Deal Labor Policy and the Southern Cotton Textile Industry, 1933–1941*, Knoxville, TN, 1986. Information on Philadelphia used here also drawn from *Evening Bulletin*, August 30, 1934, pp. 1, 2; August 31, p. 1; September 1, p. 1; *EPL*, August 30, 1934, p. 1; August 31, pp. 1, 21; September 1, p. 1.

Emil Rieve's actions that summer opened some distance between the AFHW and the direction Thomas McMahon and Francis Gorman charted for the UTW. Rieve was busily working on damage control at Reading, where the 1933 organizations had faltered and ever-reasonable George Taylor's disgust with mill owners' defiance triggered his resignation as arbitrator. Recognizing that another rout was on in Berks County, Rieve coolly returned from the UTW convention to initial a year's renewal of the NLA August 29, three days shy of its expiration. The contract kept his hardy militants at work when the strike commenced, and only in its second week did the AFHW invite walkouts at non-union plants, a proclamation rescinded the day it was to take effect. When knitters vacated forty-three mills anyway, Rieve ordered them back, substituting a one-day solidarity "holiday" for any wider participation. Ten thousand unionists shouting "their readiness to join the strike" grumblingly accepted the switch, and thereafter Philadelphia hosiery workers' activity was negligible. Though Rieve loyally sent organizers south, in mid-September he emphasized that his union's "economic objectives . . . can more readily be obtained by direct collective bargaining . . . than by any other method."[55]

Instead of risking everything on a September miracle, the AFHW understood that recognition, like checkoff and the closed shop, waved red flags at which millmen stiffened. Though the federation sought written agreements, arbitration, etc., it at first crafted documents that only provided union wages and conditions, then worked toward incorporating additional provisions at organized mills. Accepting "unofficial" status provided a base for building, but from the federation's perspective, the UTW's far broader demands surely seemed quite mad. Once the great surge had ground to a halt, further damaging the NRA, the AFHW returned to its own agenda with speed. On September 28, Leader announced a new organizing target, the non-union finishing works whose involvement in the gray-goods trade was harming full-process NLA scale firms. There was much to be done, and none of it would be any easier after "McMahon's folly."[56]

[55] *Hosiery Worker*, March 9, 1934, p. 5; March 30, p. 4; May 18, pp. 1, 8; May 25, pp. 1, 2, 8; August 17, pp. 1, 3; August 23, pp. 1, 3; September 14, p. 3 (hereafter *HW*); *TW* 84 (1934):1096, 1238, 1296, 1846; *EPL*, September 10, 1934, p. 1; September 12, p. 1; September 13, p. 1; Ohl, *Johnson*, pp. 210–12.

[56] *HW*, September 28, 1934, pp. 1, 4; Ohl, *Johnson*, pp. 247–52. These documents were carefully called "agreements," not "contracts," until later successes in securing closed shops, when the latter term was more freely used. The thirty-hour week provision was derived from the labor-supported Black bill of 1933 (*ULR*, February 2, 1933, p. 3; April 14, p. 1; April 21, p. 5), and continued to reappear in other strike and legislative proposals. UTW leaders focused stubbornly on production limits; unlike the AFHW chiefs, they failed to sense the structural and distributional constraints that made simple, formulaic solutions untenable.

With hosiery on the fringes, the general strike turnout in Philadelphia's wool/worsted, cotton, silk, and rayon sectors was little short of pitiful. Twenty-thousand to twenty-four thousand city operatives worked in these trades, perhaps a third of them at fifty firms the UTW identified as prime sites whose stoppage would induce smaller concerns to tumble into line. Yet on day one, September 4, the strike was marked by "considerable confusion," and the union could report only eight mills shuttered (a thousand workers). UTW national officer William Kelly admitted he was "not satisfied with the progress in this city," as flying squadrons of strikers trucked from mill to mill in Kensington were either ignored or jeered by those remaining at work. Ten days later, at most twenty-five mills had suspended, leading defensive UTW leaders to claim that Philadelphia was "not an especial textile center." A generous estimate might place three to four thousand workers from the targeted city sectors on strike at some point. Why was the effort such a bust in Philadelphia?[57]

Three factors surely conditioned this dismal showing. First, the UTW's key sectors had been badly battered in the city. Once-great firms were on their last legs, shrinking year by year, and millhands' hopes for revival were at a low ebb. Thus, second, a sustained program of educational work was mandatory if such workers were to view the strike as the first step toward rebuilding their trades. Nothing of the sort was undertaken; the 1920s crunch had broken the UTW's continuity in Philadelphia, unlike New Bedford where locals remained resilient enough to bring out most of the workforce. It would take more than Gorman's urgent rhetoric to restore the solidarities of 1903. Finally, nothing about this general strike resonated with the ways local workers had made gains through shop vigilance and incrementalism, long the guiding principles at the firm or sectoral level. Head-on contests with proprietors were readily comprehensible, but pounding the pavement for grandiose demands in order to speed activity by the federal government was not. The general strike in Philadelphia demonstrated only how poorly

---

[57] *EPL*, September 1, 1934, p. 20; September 4, p. 29; September 5, pp. 1, 21; September 7, p. 21; September 10, p. 21; September 13, p. 21; September 14, pp. 1, 25; September 15, pp. 1, 20; September 18, pp. 1, 21; September 20, pp. 1, 25; September 24, p. 1. Failing to secure effective walkouts at most of their original Philadelphia targets, the UTW encouraged sympathy strikes in dyeworks, carpet mills, etc., adding a half-dozen firms briefly thereby. See also *ULR*, September 7, 1934, pp. 1, 5, where a list of eleven closed mills and three partly struck was given near the end of the first week. Together twelve of the fourteen in this group reported a total of 1,386 workers to the 1934 state industrial directory, or less than 20 percent of the 7,500 Philadelphia strikers claimed in the *ULR* article. Three sizable Norristown mills were shut; adding them would still leave the regional total at half the figure asserted for the city. (Workforce data drawn from Pennsylvania Department of Internal Affairs, *Eighth Industrial Directory*, Harrisburg, 1935, Philadelphia and Montgomery County listings.)

local conditions meshed with the plans of the national union and how ill prepared area workers were for broad-gauge confrontations with their bosses.[58]

The neighborhood factory culture that had supported Kensington mobilizations since the 1880s had eroded profoundly.[59] The 1930–1 organizing strikes may have been its last gasps, but general strike threats and solidarity appeals had grown fainter and less galvanizing ever since 1920. It was the Hosiery Workers' genius to draw on still meaningful shop-level associations and to build through them an organizational loyalty that channeled gut militancy into more disciplined sectorwide alliances. Neither the economic nor the institutional base for any comparable achievement existed any longer in the rest of the regional trades. The hosiery union was the local late bloomer, maturing in a war and postwar political and ideological context distinct from the Knights-era roots of the district's other craft unions, and advantaged by the initial concentration and terrific prosperity of the 1920s full-fashioned mills. That it remained intact to fashion a "modern," at times visionary, unionism can be credited to its lasting ties with a cohort of organized firms, its alertness to the larger market and structural hazards besetting the trade, its tactical marriage of concessions with vigorous organizing, and its willingness to experiment with every device that might preserve or extend existing contracts. The absence of this combination of continuity,

[58] *EPL*, September 5, 1934, p. 21 (18,000 of New Bedford's 20,000 textile workers struck); September 7, p. 25 (United Press estimate, 50,000 of Pennsylvania's 124,000 textile workers on strike). The hosiery workers' William Leader said two years later that the PTMA's Manufacturers' Protective Association, headed by Marlin Bell, was active in providing strikebreakers and guards to local mills (*HW*, September 25, 1936, unpaged). The PTMA also went to court for an injunction to limit pickets, but only seven mills were appealing for this action (*KMN* 12[1934]:314). The Norristown strikes were prolonged by management's refusal to take back 1,800 workers at Lees' woolen mill. Violence ensued when the company brought in scabs to restart a portion of its factories and used armed thugs, reportedly from Philadelphia and possibly from Bell's agency, to escort them. In an October 3 melee, a guard's wild shooting killed a worker returning home from a rubber plant near the Lees' mills. No union agreement was achieved (*EPL*, September 8, 1934, p. 22; September 12, p. 1; September 24, p. 1; September 28, p. 1; October 3, p. 6; October 4, p. 1; October 6, p. 2). For a later look at the Norristown textile industry and its community, see Sidney Goldstein et al., *The Norristown Study*, Philadelphia, 1961.

[59] As one example, pickets pursuing strikebreakers during the 1933 Cambria walkout had to chase some of them twelve miles north of the city to Willow Grove before being able to run them off the road (the strikers were jailed). The 1930 Mackley killing was the end result of a car chase, and proprietors' use of auto convoys and even buses to ferry scabs gained a vogue in the 1930s. Thus did the car culture help dissolve spatial boundaries and further impair weakened solidarities. (See *EPL*, August 10, 1933, p. 17; October 4, 1934, p. 1.)

settled purpose, and flexibility severely hampered the rest of the area textile labor movement. Yet even the AFHW found itself unable to manage the industry's larger trends.

Outside knitting, Philadelphia textile unions languished. In a humiliating vignette, striking Paterson dyers complained that their employers were securing scabs from the Quaker City, once an unimaginable maneuver. Meanwhile, the AFHW was busily strengthening bonds among its members, fostering dozens of shop association Christmas fests at which labor leaders, bosses, and industry friends like George Taylor exchanged toasts, sponsoring a federation soccer league, and expanding its free workers' education curriculum. By January 1935, the Mackley apartments began receiving union tenants. In matters cultural the AFHW became a hub for social intercourse; membership enriched workers' lives while defending their pocketbooks. In politics, Rieve's organization lobbied for progressive state and federal bills and kept weekly track of their status. Responding to an emergency appeal to back the Wagner Act, the Gotham shop alone sent Congress fourteen hundred postcards in April 1935. With the demise of the NRA, the federation added ten staffers, each assigned to an open-shop mill, carrying the message that workers "now have no measure of protection other than the union." Last, in negotiating with the FHMA, Rieve pledged a fall 1935 effort to establish the union in commission-finishing works. Methodically, shop autonomy was being commingled with managerial responsiveness and planning, erecting a democratic union with both an industrial and a social vision.[60]

Returns on these investments came first in a trickle, then after another Berks County setback, in a rush. Two weeks after the shop-assigned staffers began work, a series of one-at-a-time Philadelphia contests opened, yielding a bare-bones NLA parity settlement at Lucille, and a model closed-shop contract at Opal Hosiery. The latter was especially savored, for Opal's owner, Howard Pike, had once headed union Local 706 before he left the union, in the old phrase, to commence on his own account. His open-shop practices

---

[60] *ULR*, November 3, 1934, p. 2; December 21, p. 1; December 28, p. 4; January 4, 1935, p. 6; January 11, p. 1; March 8, p. 1; April 5, p. 3; April 19, p. 3; M̄y 24, p. 5; June 6, pp. 1, 3; June 21, p. 1; August 2, pp. 1, 6. There were other facets to the AFHW program, including a fervent anti-Nazi stance, important given the German backgrounds of many members who remained socialists and as a rod with which to beat the hard-line Reading millmen, who were openly pro-German and whose chief attorney, Arno Mowitz, was the Nazi government's consul in Philadelphia (*ULR*, November 16, 1934, p. 1; August 7, 1936, p. 4; January 15, 1937, p. 1 [Headline – "Berky Hitlers Threaten Reading with Storm Troopers"]). For other perspectives on the AFHW, see *UHR* 18(September 1935):37; *TW* 8(1935): 1680; *Textile Worker* 22(1934): 451; *KMN* 13(1935):221, 231.

were a betrayal most foul, but shaming, an equally ancient tactic, was used effectively when Pike's ex-wife joined the picket line to back the union. New and upgraded agreements at the Bromleys' Quaker and Windsor Mills soon followed without a strike, introducing dues checkoff. With test flexings in Philadelphia completed, the AFHW turned to the finishers. October strikes brought thirteen city agreements by November l, the first sizable dent in the gray-goods problem. At the same time, a UTW strike against reductions at a worsted spinning mill failed to secure union recognition or to deflect the cut.[61]

Hosiery unionists spent most of 1936 being political activists, as contract battles went on the back burner. Said Rieve in April: "Until the constitutionality of the Wagner Act is settled by the Supreme Court, the National Labor Relations Board will be able to do little or nothing for the workers of this country." In the interim, while fighting company union charters in the courts, testifying before the LaFollette Committee on labor spies, and running Bill Leader for Congress, the AFHW heads prepared for another try at Reading's antiunion citadel, the Berkshire. Diligent spadework paid off when two-thirds of Berkshire's employees struck in October, including over 85 percent of its skilled knitters. However, the resilient company shifted orders to subcontractors and a Buffalo mill in which it was interested. Picket "lie-downs" blocked gates and generated a Wobby-style "fill the jails" flood of arrests, but local lawmen soon farmed out their charges to lockups in adjacent counties. A national boycott followed, replete with prolabor film stars denouncing scab hosiery and picketing F. W. Woolworth stores to pressure the mill's most important account. Washington trips to corner congressmen, testify before LaFollette, and offer a "memorial" to FDR were undertaken, but the drive dissipated. Strikers crawled back or sought other jobs by February. The castle still stood, unyielding.[62]

---

[61] *ULR*, July 12, 1935, p. 1; July 26, p. 1; August 2, p. 6; August 9, p. 5; August 23, p. 1; September 20, p. 1; October 11, p. 5; October 18, p. 1; October 25, p. 1; November l, pp. 1, 6; *HW*, October 11, p. 1; October 18, pp. 1, 4; November 8, pp. 1, 5; *UHR* 18(November 1935):115; *KMN* 13(1935): 224, 262, 309, 342; *TW* 85(1935): 2288, 2493. On Opal, see NLRB File 924.

[62] *ULR*, April 24, 1936, p. 1; August 8, pp. 1, 3, 5; October 2, pp. 1, 3; October 9, pp. 1, 3; October 16, pp. 1, 6; October 30, p. 1; November 13, pp. 1, 8; December 4, pp. 1, 3; December 18, pp. 1, 3; December 25, p. 1; January 8, 1937, p. 1; January 15, p. 1; February 19, p. 5; *HW*, December 6, 1935, p. 1; January 2, 1936, p. 1; September 25, unpaged; November 27, p. 1; December 18, p. 1; *KMN* 14(1936): 380, 416; 15(1937): 20. Leader and the other AFHW witnesses testified before LaFollette on April 16–17, 1936. Interestingly, the PTMA used spies to track union meetings in Philadelphia and identify sympathizers, but the most flagrant employment of thugs from Railway Audit, Cummings, etc., was in Berks County. See *Violations of Free Speech and Assembly and*

Within the labor movement, during 1936 the AFHW stood with Sidney Hillman and John L. Lewis's industrial unionism forces and ran Rieve against McMahon for the UTW leadership. Internally, delegates authorized a universal 3 percent assessment to raise a million dollars for organizing. When renewal of the NLA came around, the FHMA again pressed for reductions, based in part on Sears chairman Lessing Rosenwald's 1935 report on marginal profitability at union firms. Accepting cuts would undermine the big organizing drive planned for 1937, as would striking FHMA firms. Thus the union gambled, letting the NLA lapse, and invited shop associations to police each firm's fidelity to the 1935 terms. It worked; the FHMA was equally strike-shy and vigilance prevented scattered, opportunistic cuts.[63] Two sour notes were sounded, however. Eager to show its constant surveillance of industry conditions, the federation began publishing a detailed city-by-city "barometer" of hosiery capacity use. This was quickly employed by hosiery buyers to indicate where there were mills running slack and likely to accept low-ball offers. Reporting its discontinuance, a trade journal explained: "New York hosiery buyers ... equipped with ... figures gleaned from the 'Hosiery Worker' began to work on mill owners, working at partial capacity, and demanded unreasonable concessions in price." Nevertheless, the owners' association continued to issue similar monthly reports, which had the same effect, adding another weapon to buyers' crowded arsenals. Second, during the Berkshire clash, the company leaked the news that it would soon open a southern unit in Albany, Georgia. Though this was a feint (after the war, a branch was placed in North Carolina), it struck an exposed nerve. Southern relocations were few and risky, as Taylor documented in a 1936 study, but southern capacity grew yearly through new starts and expansion. Still before the South could be mobilized, the North had to be organized.[64]

The hosiery workers almost pulled it off. Using "sitdowns" and aided by the Supreme Court's confirmation of the Wagner Act, the AFHW rolled up an unprecedented series of 1937 victories. Copying Flint and Philadelphia's Exide Battery workers, knitters occupied two Kensington mills in January, successfully preventing transfer of equipment to suburban sites. In

---

Interference with Rights of Labor: Hearings before a Subcommittee of the Committee on Education and Labor, April 10–23, 1936, U.S. Senate, 74th Congress, 2nd Session, Washington, D.C., 1937, pp. 159–241.

[63] *ULR*, July 19, 1935, p. 3; August 9, p. 5; August 30, pp. 1, 6; October 18, p. 3; April 24, 1936, pp. 1, 7; May 1, pp. 1, 7; September 18, pp. 1, 3; *HW*, June 11, 1937, p. 1; June 18, p. 8; *KMN* 14(1936): 112, 192; *TW* 86(1936): 1884, 2132, 2351.

[64] *KMN* 14(1936):192; HW, April 3, 1936, p. 4; TW 86(1936):867 (Taylor), 2351; *Davison's Blue Book: 1943*, p. 514; *Davison's Textile Directory for Executives and Salesmen: 1954*, Ridgewood, NJ, 1954, pp. 220, 332–3.

March, mass strikes hit twenty Berks County firms, generating a fifteen-company rates and conditions pact and several broader individual settlements within a month. The spring offensive in and near Philadelphia netted twenty closed shops, as strikers demanded tighter terms, and in the Midwest, break-throughs were made at Wisconsin's Allen-A, Minnesota's Strutwear, and Indiana's Real Silk plants, each a long-term source of frustration. On May 6, after a violent exchange in which owner William Meyer was injured, workers seized the hated Apex and shut it down. There had never been anything to match it. Following this sweep, the FHMA firms, untouched throughout, signed a new national agreement in late June, providing 6–12 percent rate increases.[65] An appeals court ruling ended the Apex sitdown on June 23, but mass picketing kept the plant idle until a July 29 settlement was inked, after eighty-four days. A masterpiece of tortured prose, the text provided that after seven months a closed shop would take effect if the AFHW enrolled a "substantial majority" of Apex workers, with the unionists having two hours daily to solicit registrations. Apex had been taken; but Meyer filed a federal suit for triple damages under the Sherman Act, charging that violence and the occupation had restrained interstate commerce and cost the firm over $1 million in wreckage and lost business. Ignoring the litigation, thousands of celebrants nonetheless ringed the mill and roared their delight at toppling Philadelphia's prince of the open shop.[66]

Three questions arise. How was it that such massive gains were achieved in hosiery after so many lean years? Given the TWOC had the same spring launched area organizing drives, how did they fare? Did hosiery unionization stabilize or further demoralize Philadelphia's largest remaining textile sector?

[65] *ULR*, January 8, 1937, pp. 1, 5; January 22, pp. 1, 7; February 19, pp. 4, 5; March 5, p. 1; March 26, p. 1; April 30, p. 1; May 21, pp. 1, 6; May 28, p. 1; June 11, p. 5; June 28, pp. 1, 4; July 30, p. 1; *HW*, February 26, 1937, p. 5; March 12, p. 1; March 19, p. 1; March 26, p. 1; April 2, p. 1; April 16, pp. 1, 5; April 23, p. 1; May 7, p. 1; May 14, p. 1; May 21, pp. 1, 5; May 28, p. 1; June 4, pp. 1, 4; June 11, pp. 1, 4; June 18, pp. 1, 5, 8; July 2, p. 1; July 30, p. 1; *EPL*, May 25, 1937, pp. 1, 21; *TW* 87(1937):755, 993, 1199, 1630. At Apex, management discovered that workers planned to pull the shop with a huge march on the mill, giving the signal for activists inside to start a sitdown. Meyer thus closed and cleared the factory before the AFHW mass parade reached it. After verbal exchanges with guards and firm officials, workers broke into the plant, expelled Meyer and his crew after a hand-to-hand battle, and occupied the mill. For a concise account, see Memoranda, P. W. Chappell to Kerwin, May 10, 1937, and May 12, FMCS File 182/2625.

[66] *ULR*, May 23, 1937, p. 1; May 28, p. 1; June 11, p. 5; June 28, pp. 1, 4; July 30, p. 1; *KMN* 15(1937):192, 230; *HW*, July 30, 1937, p. 1; *EPL*, May 7, 1937, p. 23; May 24, pp. 1, 14; June 3, pp. 1, 25,; June 5, pp. 1, 24; June 7, p. 3; June 22, pp. 1, 10; June 23, pp. 1, 19; July 1, pp. 1, 23; July 2, p. 19; July 24, p. 20; July 29, pp. 1, 8, 17. Full text of the Apex agreement may be found in FMCS File 182/2625, along with P. W. Chappell's running commentaries on settlement efforts.

To be sure, the radical tactics and confirmation of the Wagner Act, plus the AFHW's diligent preparations, must be credited with forming a phalanx of forces not previously brought to bear. Yet, another political item must be stressed. In 1933 the city's Vare machine had fallen before a "fusion ticket" that placed Democrats and maverick Republicans in important city posts. One of these, S. Davis Wilson, accepted the machine's mayoral nomination in 1935 and slipped into office by a narrow, possibly manipulated margin. Wilson then shocked his promoters by securing WPA funds the organization had scorned, appointing a permanent labor board, hiring the AFHW's attorney as city solicitor, and, crucially, terminating the police's provocative, probusiness role in strikes. Police were on duty when knitters stormed and seized Apex, but they stood aside, infuriating Meyer and his fellow operators. Federal mediators spelled out the Wagner Act's requirements to them, the mayor urged accepting the new era, the governor reined in unlawful use of police powers in outlying districts, and the millmen capitulated. Not only had the rules of the game changed, the political will to enforce new ones seemed to exist at all levels of government.[67]

However, this meshing of law, tactics, organization, and politics was of no value to TWOC in the Philadelphia region. Of 132 agreements nationally, covering 83,527 workers enrolled by July 1937, just one stemmed from city organizing (181 at a worsted mill). Regionally, only the participation of 3,000 Marcus Hook Viscose workers in a TWOC national pact prevented a suburban shutout. In accounting for this, it is crucial to reflect on the weavers' and spinners' work histories gathered by the WPA Palmer team. Such workers well knew the liquidation sequence, the struggle to find new jobs at ever fewer mills, and accepted owners' claims that union agreements would bring the end of many an enterprise. TWOC also had understandably directed its energies at large national concerns; twenty of the above contracts brought in two-thirds of its new members. Philadelphia's fragmented and shrinking fabric sectors were now poor prospects for organizers, peripheral to TWOC's agenda. Though a few firms did sign over the next five years, later blaming unions when they closed, their ultimate fates owned more to the shifts of the 1920s than to the entry of the CIO.[68]

Further, labor's hosiery victories were terribly flawed. Costs rose, union coverage of the industry was inadequate, legal tangles abounded, and reces-

---

[67] *Violations of Free Speech Hearings*, pp. 166–71, 206; Russell Weigley, ed., *Philadelphia: A 300-Year History*, New York, 1982, pp. 621, 623–5; *ULR*, September 18, 1936, pp. 1, 3; FMCS File 182/2625

[68] Interoffice Memorandum No. 6, "TWOC Agreements," FMCS File 196/46; *HW*, March 12, 1937, p. 1; FMCS File 199/6770 (James Doak, Jr.); *ACUJ* 60(March 1941): 4.

sion loomed. By early 1938, three Philadelphia mills struck by the AFHW collapsed. In recession, others followed. The Berkshire fought NLRB rulings until, in a changed political climate, unfavorable late-1930s decisions were set aside. In its suit, Apex convinced a jury that Branch No. 1 leaders had engineered the May 1937 mill assault and was awarded three times $237,000 in damages. The federal appeals court reversed, finding the Sherman Act inapplicable (a judgment affirmed by the Supreme Court); but the AFHW, facing a state court retrial, paid Apex $110,000 to settle the case in 1941. More immediately salient in 1937–8, the NLA that newly organized firms had signed had hiked labor costs, making price increases imperative, for fiddling the goods invited buyers' rejection of "substandard" stockings. Purchasers ably fought such advances and squeezed union mills instead for reductions, using both the faltering economy and the spatial unevenness of unionization to supplement their "hand-to-mouth buying policy." The roughly 125 firms observing the NLA's terms had generated 63 percent of northern full-fashioned output (1936), but as the South now made 30 percent of the national total, union mills "controlled" only 45 percent of all production. It was just not enough.[69]

In consequence, 1938 was ugly. In recession, mill inventories jumped 25 percent, buyers stalled, orders collapsed. Union firms promptly appealed for rate reductions, but three arbitrators cut the list only on the finest gauges and fancies. As this was chiefly Philadelphia work, Branch No. 1 rebelled; President Bill Leader called a defiant strike, a challenge to Rieve that misfired. On its first day, Rieve swayed a mass meeting of knitters, vanquishing Leader and sending those who had work back to their jobs. Even so, half the city's sixty full-fashioned mills shut down from lack of business. If "sane and clear-headed action prevailed," stopping the wildcat, the federation's troubles were far from over.[70] Reading arbitrators soon approved another set of partial list reductions, pleading uselessly with distributors not to demand that "the decrease [be] passed on to them." Renewed southern organizing beckoned, but as full-fashioned workers' earnings there rested well above incomes in other southern textile sectors, incentives to join the AFHW were few. One observer put it simply: "Why should a [knitter] join a union when he is making wages as high as the average mill foreman or section boss in the cotton mill?" The southern campaign flopped in hosiery, and

[69] On Apex, see *KMN* 16(1937): 183–4; 270, 283, 320; 16(1938): 162, 357; 17(1939): 11–12, 125; 18(1940): 161, 163, 254; 19(1941): 83, 162. For the Berkshire, see *KMN* 17(1939): 154, 206, 387; 18(1940): 156, 193; 19(1941): 281. On unionized share of the workforce, see *UHR* 20(August 1937): 128 and deHaan, *Full-Fashioned*, pp. 98–9.

[70] *KMN* 16(1938): 40, 59, 69; *TW* 88(March 1938): 89; W. H. Davies to Dr. Steelman, February 28, 1938, and March 1, FMCS File 199/1299.

TWOC's early achievements there dissipated as 40 percent of its 1937 enrollees departed in two years. Organizing drives would not provide relief.[71]

In this context, to retain the NLA the AFHW negotiated what now might be called a "competitiveness" package. Signatories to a three-year renewal of the 1937 rates seeking to replace older machinery could secure below-scale special terms. George Taylor and the union would monitor the reinvestment of wage savings in new technology, a tactic adopted by November 1938 in twenty firms' "retooling programs," the reductions averaging 14 percent. Individual mills concealed their involvement, fearing that as soon as the "news" spread, "their selling agents and customers will realize they they are now paying lower wages and jump on their respective necks for lower hosiery prices." Secrecy failed, buyers behaved as expected, and the federation's imaginative "rehabilitation" program proved disappointing. J. D. deHaan explained: "Although it may have postponed the liquidation of some mills, it did not result in a considerable improvement [in] competitive position."[72] Ironically, instead of firming the center, the project promoted lemon capitalism at the periphery. Eager to raise cash, retooling mills sold rather than scrapped old machines. Scores of Philadelphia workers bought them, starting minifirms just as Paterson silk weavers had done twenty years earlier, and fed the gray-goods market.

Both two- and four-machine shops as well as larger, cooperative mills surfaced. One of the latter, Germaine Hosiery, drew the savings of sixteen unemployed AFHW knitters into restarting a liquidating company. Promptly expelled from Branch No. 1 for becoming capitalists, they soon faced picketing by union men formerly employed at the defunct mill, demanding their jobs back. All work stopped, for in the political/cultural confusion, the "equal shares" owners could not bring themselves to cross their erstwhile brothers' line. A Germaine spokesman wrote Leader for help.

> We have orders, which if not promptly filled may cause the loss of our market. This will result in the loss of our investment, and the consequent loss of our livelihood, since it is practically impossible for an unemployed hosiery worker to obtain work at his trade, at the present time.

Condemning the sixteen, who "have really bought their jobs," Leader backed the pickets and Germaine folded within a month. Aided by community

---

[71] *KMN* 16(1938):92, 146; Gavin Wright, *Old South, New South*, New York, 1986, ch. 7, especially pp. 216–25; Philip Wood, *Southern Capitalism*, Durham, NC, 1986, pp. 90–3, 133–53; deHaan, *Full-Fashioned*, p. 110. DeHaan points out that in 1935 Philadelphia leggers earned $1.02 hourly on average vs. $.72 in North Carolina and $.70 elsewhere in the South, halving the gap that had existed in 1929.

[72] *TW* 88(August 1938): 52, *KMN* 16(1938): 326–7; deHaan, *Full-Fashioned*, pp. 25, 123. The agreement included a no-strike clause and employers' assurances that they would neither relocate nor buy gray stockings for finishing (*KMN* 17[1937]: 10).

figures like Kensington's Rev. David Colony, at least four other sizable co-op shops tried the gray-goods route in 1938–9, but scraps with the union on one side and buyers on the other bankrupted them all by the end of 1940.[73]

Leader's tough stance indicated that he recognized the paradox that proliferating lemon capitalism shops presented the union. If these operations were ignored they would work below scale and help depress prices for unionized mills' hosiery. If they were unionized, they would go broke, being unable to sustain union scale, returning their worker-owners to the ranks of the unemployed. The AFHW hard line made it impossible for mushrooms to root in Philadelphia, or for echoes of the Knights' cooperative imagery to undercut already strained union–management collaboration. However, beyond its reach, ministarts arose throughout rural Pennsylvania and the South, as the proportion of firms with ten or fewer machines jumped from a quarter to half of all full-fashioned mills, 1936–40. A trade journalist commented in 1941:

> Carolina hosiery mills disappear and reappear too rapidly for yarn sales-men to keep accurate records ... The story told is, these salesmen slow down their cars, stick their heads through the car window and listen for the rhythmic sound of knitting machines in operation. If heard, they get out to sell, if not they drive on. [74]

As in silk and rayon, neither trade associations nor alert unionists could arrest the structural dissolution; the war only slowed its tempo.[75]

The struggle to conserve the Philadelphia full-fashioned trade was lost by 1940. Flexibility and resourceful adaptation were in distributors' hands. "The buyers generally work out to the best advantage, as they make money as prices rise, and crawl out through the cancellation route at times when prices take a flop. It seems to be something that manufacturers cannot guard

---

[73] Arthur Hughes to William Leader, October 21, 1938; Rose Forrester to Director of Conciliation, November 5, 1938, and December 12, FMCS File 199/2575; Kravis, "Commercial Finishing," pp. 50–1, 92–7, 116–20; *KMN* 17(1939): 315, 172, 382; 18(1940): 81–2, 157, 265–6, 303. Between 1936 and 1940, at least twenty Philadelphia full-fashioned mills liquidated, cutting the city machines in use by one-half (to 1,700). In 1930, 4,500 leggers and footers had been in place, 29 percent of national capacity; in 1940, the remaining equipment accounted for 11 percent (national totals, 1930 – 15,600, 1940 – 16,000). See John Roughan, "The Movement of the Full-Fashioned Hosiery Industry Out of Philadelphia," unpublished MBA thesis, University of Pennsylvania, 1950, pp. 30, 110.

[74] DeHaan, *Full-Fashioned*, p. 66; *UHR*, 23 (October 1940): 20; 23(October 1941): 120.

[75] *KMN* 17(1939): 341. In 1939, indicating the enduring extent of buyers' gains, full-fashioned hosiery retailing at $12 a dozen pairs could be purchased from mills for $6.50–$7.25 vs. $8.00–$9.00 in the late 1920s. This moved the ratio of markup to store wholesale cost from 25–33 percent to 63–85 percent (*TW* 89[January 1939]:38).

against." If for want of better options, many workers and mill masters stayed to the end, clinging to their jobs and red-inked ledgers, no one was any longer "kidding themselves about the future." In as good a symbolic gesture as any, George Taylor left the knitting trades in January 1941 to become "permanent arbitrator" for General Motors and the UAW.[76]

7.4 Aftermath

In the two decades after Taylor's departure for Detroit, nothing altered the course of decay. The war again brought government contracts and postwar civilian buying sustained some weaving mills through the latter 1940s. In knitting, firms shifted to cotton and rayon, but machinery in place steadily eroded. By 1946, fewer than a thousand full-fashioned machines remained, a fifth of the 1930 complement. In 1950–1, Gotham and Apex employed two-thirds of the city's 3,200 full-fashioned workers. When Apex, the larger, went bust in 1954, little was left in hosiery.[77] Employment, which had hovered above 35,000 after the war, dropped sharply in the early-1950s recessions (Table 7.6). By 1960, only the expansion of knitted outerwear, in tandem with exploding demand for "leisure goods," kept the aggregates from being more meager; and knitwear tailed off soon thereafter. Dyeing, which had

[76] *KMN* 17(1939): 341; 19(1941): 4. Taylor in 1939 predicted accurately that full-fashioned would "be predominantly a southern industry within ten years." In 1938, of 88 new starts, 56 were southern, whereas of 42 closures, 39 were in northern locations (*KMN* 17[1930]: 18). A few months after Taylor took up his new position, Hanes Hosiery Mills of Winston Salem, North Carolina, announced the first seamless nylons were ready for sale. Though of no immediate importance, this innovation took advantage of nylon's great elasticity and brought low-skill seamless hose to the fore in the 1950s, leading to the demise of virtually all full-fashioned production wherever located (*KMN* 19[1941]: 122; deHaan, *Full-Fashioned*, pp. 174–6).

[77] Rachel Maines, "Textiles for Defense," unpublished Ph.D. dissertation, Carnegie-Mellon University, 1984; Roughan, "Movement," pp. 33–8; deHaan, *Full-Fashioned*, pp. 123–4; Aaron Ellis, "A Study of the Raw Materials Problems Caused by the War in the Women's Full-Fashioned Hosiery Industry," unpublished MBA thesis, University of Pennsylvania, 1943, chs. 3, 4; Pennsylvania Department of Internal Affairs, *Thirteenth Industrial Directory*, Harrisburg, 1953, pp. 451–2; idem, *Fourteenth Industrial Directory*, Harrisburg, 1956, p. 852; Gladys Palmer, *Philadelphia Workers in a Changing Economy*, Philadelphia, 1956, pp. 33–9. Two fairly pathetic state-level studies of the textile collapse, far too late to matter, are: Textile Study Committee, "The Textile Industry in Pennsylvania," typescript, March 24, 1954 (the outcome of a charge by Governor John Fine to investigate "a growing threat to Pennsylvania's textile industry") and Edwin Roscoe and George Thuerling, *The Textile Industry in Pennsylvania*, Engineering Research Bulletin B–74, The Pennsylvania State University, May 1958 (a contextless, social science questionnaire and interview pastiche).

Table 7.6. *Textile employment, Philadelphia and region, 1945–60, with selected sectors, Philadelphia and Berks County*

	City	Suburban counties	Total region
1945	38,280	17,933	56,213
1951	36,239	19,701	55,940
1954	27,166	13,469	40,635
1957	24,133	10,054	34,167
1960	22,389	8,747	31,136

	Philadelphia			Berks County
	Knit goods	Dye-finish	Hosiery	Hosiery
1945	3,820	5,828	4,993	7,373
1951	5,605	5,823	4,281	7,847
1954	6,824	3,883	1,137	5,584
1957	7,583	2,050	1,118	4,123
1960	8,573	1,991	1,029	2,697

Sources: Pennsylvania Department of Internal Affairs, *Eleventh–Sixteenth Industrial Directories*, Harrisburg, PA, 1947–62. County listings by firm and sector.

feasted on the hosiery gray-goods transition, faded steadily once seamless nylons came to the fore, largely southern-based under the sway of chain mills like Hanes and Burlington. Among Philadelphia's mill districts, Manayunk fronted a silent riverside, Germantown's main shopping street was haunted by abandoned stores, its mills turned into warehouses or windowless ghosts. Across factory-packed Lehigh Avenue to Kensington, in-migrant black residents arrived to find textile mill doors tightly closed against them when not closed forever. Collapsing opportunities for industrial jobs reinforced among adversity-worn whites a defensive racism that the 1964 North Philadelphia riots only deepened. Kensington was never a garden, but the long, agonizing decline made life there ever more harsh and brittle by steps and stages.[78]

[78] Pennsylvania Department of Internal Affairs, *Sixteenth Industrial Directory*, Harrisburg, 1962, p. 33; Peter Binzen, *Whitetown*, New York, 1970; Weigley, ed., *Philadelphia*, pp. 668–72, 675–9, 720–5; Peter Muller, Kenneth Meyer, and Roman Cybriwsky, *Philadelphia: A Study of Conflicts and Social Cleavages*, New York 1976. In full-fashioned, the explosion of now scattered Paterson-like tiny shops continued after World War II, assisted by federal small-business loans to returning GI's. In 1945–8, 406 new firms were started, one-third by veterans with government assistance; by the opening of 1954, 825 entries accumulated along with 425 failures and withdrawals to give a national total

Rather than pull a cliché from "Prufrock," it may be more apt to end with Veblen. In his customary, convoluted prose, the great maverick considered the implications for *The Instinct of Workmanship* of businessmen's "trained inability to apprehend any other than the immediate pecuniary bearing of their maneouvres." In consolidated "mechanical industries" a "somewhat thoroughgoing standardization of processes and products in mechanical terms" had become manifest "in terms of price, and so made subject to accountancy in terms of price." Obsession with price and pecuniary valuation engendered an environment in which "workmanship comes to be confused with salesmanship," degrading the notion of efficiency as a service to the common good. Indeed, "under the canons of . . . pecuniary valuation the test of efficiency in economic matters has come to be not technological mastery and productive effect, but proficiency in pecuniary management and the acquisition of wealth."[79]

Philadelphia textile workers and proprietors, masters of technology and productive versatility, had not the capacity to overcome the power accumulated by those who appreciated the virtues of accountancy, stock control, program budgeting, and "pecuniary management." Among distributors, skillful merchandizing based on numerical analysis yielded a timely capture of flexibility's advantages, leaving producers immobilized among its hazards. Veblen, realizing that the dispiriting process he despised had by 1914 matured only in the "big business" parts of the economy, concluded by noting the price/efficiency mania's encroachment on yet vital "workmanship" segments of manufacturing. Rationalizing, predatory practices created profits for some businessmen "proportioned to the magnitude of the disturbance" their implementation caused, "rather than to [their] industrial productiveness."[80]

However logical in the abstract, buyers' relentless hammering contributed nothing to the common good, except under the most meretricious constructions. Instead, it generated an intranational dissolution process that demoralized an industry and imperiled cities, and at the same time unwittingly previewed the price-governed, politicized, global restructuring process with which the bellwether industries of Veblen's era have now to contend. Lowell's

---

of 757 firms, 60 percent above the 1940 total. In 1954, 71 percent of all firms had ten or fewer machines. In 1954–5, as the seamless incursion took effect, 244 of these collapsed. Leader's 1938 strategy had worked, however, for of 189 tiny full-fashioned firms in the eight-county Philadelphia SMSA (including by 1954 three southern New Jersey counties), only 24 located their operations in Philadelphia (deHaan, *Full-Fashioned*, pp. 66–7; *Davison's Textile Directory: 1954*, pp. 128–59, 286–346).

[79] Thorstein Veblen, *The Instinct of Workmanship*, New York, 1914, pp. 218–19, 347, 349.

[80] Ibid., pp. 350, 353–55. For a recent echo, see Seymour Melman, *Profits Without Production*, New York, 1983.

rebound from economic despair may have excited advocates of a high-tech, postindustrial transformation, but Kensington's attenuated decay offers a far more chilling template, already copied at dozens of sites from New Britain to Youngstown and South Chicago and available for frequent, future use. The faint noise you may hear is Veblen, laughing sardonically.[81]

[81] See Jeremy Brecher, *Brass Valley*, Philadelphia, 1982; Robert Reich and Ira Magaziner, *Minding America's Business*, New York, 1982; Robert Reich and John Donahue, *New Deals*, New York, 1985; David Bensman and Roberta Lynch, *Rusted Dreams*, New York, 1987; and Stephen Cohen and John Zysman, *Manufacturing Matters*, New York, 1987.

8

Conclusion

"To anticipate the demand is dangerous, to await it is fatal."

Textile World 70(1926):1299.

"Combat Reductionism."

Political button, Philadelphia, 1980.

This book and its predecessor have been concerned to document and analyze a form of industrial capitalism that emerged and flourished in the nineteenth century, then decayed and dwindled after World War I. Reconstituting the contours of its evolution and success led readily toward evaluating the character of its vulnerabilities and the course of its decline. Whereas in large part the conclusion will summarize central themes from the preceding chapters, it will also consider the implications of this study for research in industrial history and its bearing on recent debates over the revival of flexible manufacturing.

In an effort to present a multidisciplinary narrative, this study has interlaced two sorts of space with several kinds of relationships. Both national and regional contexts thus helped frame the political and spatial environments for industrial change and the dimensions of the textile manufacture's structure and shifts. As the tariff, the NRA, American Woolen, and the Paterson silk trades were more than background stage props, they have been depicted as involved in a continuing interaction with Philadelphia millmen and workers. Further, though relations between capital and labor have often been considered so pivotal to industrial processes as to obscure other bonds and binds, here they have been portrayed as but one component of a larger network of contests and connecting tissues. Links and fracases among proprietors, and similar ties and tears within workforces, exposed the strains within individualism, the paradoxes of collective action, and the difficulty of bridging contradictions institutionally. Relationships inside firm-owning families carried their own contingencies, as did crisis encounters with agents of the state. Finally and critically, relations between producers and distributors provided a key to accumulation and clues to the dynamics of decay. The resulting "figured tapestry" has expressed in prose my conviction that

Figure 26. Tieing-in harness lines on a massive jacquard loom at LaFrance, Frankford, 1937. (Courtesy of the Pennsylvania Historical and Museum Commission.)

complex phenomena like industrial change may best be appreciated through inclusive narratives that reject the temptations of ready-made theory and the reductionism of "other things being equal" simplification.

The Philadelphia textile manufacture took shape by the mid-1800s, alongside but counterposed to bulk textile enterprises meeting fairly homogeneous demand for staple goods. Erected on a base of urban demand for seasonal and specialty lines rivaling imported fabrics, flexible, batch production was both protected by war tariffs and sustained by war contracts, proving to be resilient in the 1870s depression and profiting from the Gilded Age vogue for ornamental styles. However, in and beyond textiles, the economic difficulties of the 1880s and the 1890s created crises for more capital-intensive bulk divisions, leading, as Lamoreaux has suggested, first to profit-wrecking competition (full running to cover high fixed costs) then toward ameliorative mergers and forward integration into distribution to increase control over pricing. Bulk textile producers, obstructed from similar solutions for reasons Chandler has stressed, moved either to shave unit costs through cuts and stretchouts, adoption of Northrop looms, etc., or to lessen their dependency on staple lines through product diversification, a maneuver effectively combined with mergers at American Woolen. Such "mixed-output" strategies both encroached on the terrain of some Philadelphia specialists and neatly intersected with consolidating demand among clothiers and retailers in the decade before World War I. Batch operators had (like Lamoreaux's specialty paper makers) cut back production and employment to defend prices in the 1890s and had adapted to sample and duplicate ordering, battling periodically with labor over shop control issues, yet enjoying substantial profitability through the war years. However, the decisive shift in market power relations in and after 1920, the institutionalization of practices that undercut flexibility and erased profits, and the harsh effects of general depression combined to block virtually all efforts to preserve the vitality of batch firms. By the late 1930s, liquidations spiraled and the region's once-vigorous full-fashioned hosiery sector was following Paterson's silk manufacture into the dead end of lemon capitalism, devolving into ever smaller, marginal units.

What had gone wrong? Examining each of the relations noted above helps identify the pattern of the net that closed around batch specialists. In distribution, merchandisers fighting rising operating costs adapted tools of budget control, cost analysis, and inventory management from model transportation and industrial corporations to displace risk and expense onto producers while rationalizing their own capital use and authority lines. Chain store and group purchasing, together with timely information dissemination by retail/wholesale trade associations, consolidated these gains and encouraged elaboration of a battery of predatory practices that added to buyers' advantages. Further, through price lining, retailers and clothiers alike made quality and diversity take second place to price considerations, as "pecuniary valuation" and "accountancy" joined to create a singular, quantitative standard against which differentiated, subjective criteria had no appeal. The producers' inability to craft an effective response to this durable power shift demoralized flexible batch manufacturing.

In undertaking to deal with these changed market conditions, relations among manufacturers were triply frustrating. Their trade associations were ill designed for collective market actions and unable either to mandate or cajole members' unity regarding price defense, terms of exchange, curtailments, or installation of inventory and cost control systems. Regionally distinct cohorts of mills with differing patterns of specialization, unionization, etc., entailed a spatial fragmentation of batch sectors as well. Moreover, free riders were a constant concern, including both large veteran and new mushroom firms, hampering any initiatives for collective strategizing. Within the Philadelphia industry, relations between capital and labor remained laden with expectations whose rationality was in no way congruent with the logic of bureaucratic modernism. Few firms accepted either the abstractions of standard costing or the agency of union representatives ("outsiders") with any ease. Among labor's ranks, conflict between independent craft organizations and national union leaders was endemic from the Knights through the UTW, and hardly absent in later Branch No. 1 hosiery squabbles with the AFHM's Emil Rieve. Coordination among trade divisions was just as elusive as for manufacturers and the spatial limits just as profound, even for the keenly analytic full-fashioned union. Inside the firm, relations, routines, and values inherited across generations involved commitments to autonomy and perseverance, leading millmen often to hold the helm far too long, or to reject liquidation, recapitalization, or relocation for stubborn struggles in place. Scorning experts and efficiency men, they, in the words of a yarn millman's grandson, "made the best stuff they could for as long as they could," and then gave it up.

For both workers and proprietors, relations with the state were problematic and at times utterly bewildering. Conflict managers from the conciliation service operated from an orderly process agenda and spoke the language of collective bargaining, formal contracts, and union recognition. They much preferred treating with the UTW hierarchy to dealing with Philadelphia's mutated artisan republicans, and clearly preferred McMahon and Rieve over "Toby" Hall and Bill Leader's localist traditions. For batch manufacturers, antitrust law obstructed efforts to fix a floor under prices, whereas the NRA proved a weak reed, the Wagner Act a horror. After 1920, the tariff no longer worked its vaunted magic, though millmen clutched it like a talisman, and Pennsylvania Republicans began to behave like Democrats or radicals.

New Deal policy so focused on reviving industry's bulk-production segments that it seemed no one noticed the suffocating effects uniform programs had on its batch components. Meanwhile the reduction of operators' influence with local politicians gave Philadelphia labor access to pressure points that deepened the damage inflicted by buyers, particularly in hosiery.

Batch firms' basic capacity for flexibility, in products and use of labor and facilities, was insufficient to deliver sustained returns once the practices working to distributors' advantage were institutionalized and generalized, a process that sharply revealed the long-hidden rigidities and vulnerabilities of the proprietary, specialist format. Only in a logic of retrospective determinism was this outcome natural or inevitable, for indeed state-sponsored policies have been implemented to support or rescue sectors or firms deemed important to industrial nations across the last century. However, in the 1920s and 1930s, the conventions of economics and politics alike inhibited perception of the decay of batch manufacturing as a problem of any sort, much less one amenable to public policy initiatives. Moreover, advocates of that quantitative efficiency Veblen abhorred would shed few tears over the fate of these personalistic, specialty enterprises, celebrating instead the achievements of standardization and mass production in other segments of the economy. Yet both the scale and duration of their presence in American industry and the now-dawning awareness of rigidities and vulnerabilities within the seemingly triumphant core sectors raise significant questions. Our understanding of industrialization has long been conditioned by a linear attention to the development of great firms and oligopolistic sectors, peripheralizing the extension of batch and custom production in the post-Civil War generations. How has our vision of industrial process been foreshortened by this reduction, this selection of a past to fit the contours of a mid-twentieth-century landscape? If millions of workers and thousands of entrepreneurs were active in batch sectors from jewelry to apparel, tool making to shipbuilding, how did their activities intersect, advance, supplement, or contradict the parallel drive to throughput? Is the "modern business enterprise" really a solution to the dilemmas of strategy and structure or, rather, another self-limiting restatement of them, possessed of conjunctural advantages over proprietary forms in Hoover's era but also of internal fault lines that have surfaced to perplex contemporary managers? Do recent calls for a return to flexibility and quality-centered management offer a means to revitalize manufacturing and restore global competitiveness?

To be sure, the form of these questions immediately suggests in large measure the shape of *my* answers to them. I suspect that once the broad array of batch-oriented manufacturing sectors is surveyed critically, our sense of how industrialization happened will be more than a bit altered. Once we acknowledge that multiple formats for production coexisted and prospered in nineteenth-century America, the matter of their interrelations becomes magnetic, as do issues of technological change, homogeneous versus heterogeneous demand, locational patterning, the sources and uses of capital and labor, and the language of production, management, and politics. As this inquiry proceeds, representing "industries" by their staple divisions, as has so long been the case in textiles, will give way to disaggregating them both spatially and sectorally to assess their batch and bulk components, their markets and trade practices, the collective institutions of workers and owners and their individual operating assumptions, customs, and rules. From such a perspective, the rise of oligopoly and managerialism may seem less inexorable and more contingent and contested when set in a moving context of shifting labor, market, and political relations than is evident in current organizational/technological formulations, and hence more historical and mutable. Attention to the interactive diversity of work and business cultures might as well suggest that American industrial vitality derived from the *mix* of batch and bulk forms, of routinizing and flexible rationalities (which Burton Klein evokes provocatively),[1] rather than from a single-track drive to mass production.

In rethinking the dynamics of industrialization, what was lost when the regime of "accountancy" was established will become more apparent, as will the formidable obstacle it poses to those who would rebuild the industrial base along flexible lines or transform vast hierarchies into centers of mutualistic exchange. The difficulties of adapting authoritarian and number-driven corporations to accept the uncertainties and qualitative dimensions of flexibility are well known, but the fate of the Philadelphia textile trades, if mapped onto a global competitive scene, is equally disconcerting to those who would let a thousand new starts bloom. As much as at the turn of the century, political determinants are crucial to enterprise success, and the political clout of small operators is itself minuscule, especially given the internationality of the problem. The costs of new-generation flexible technology are formidable, and sources of venture capital far too thin to generate much optimism.[2] National trade associations and unions are as ill suited to shape global developments as regional and local ones were in 1920; distributional and pricing concerns are equally problematic and complicated by exchange-rate fluctuations and international trade policies. It may be possible to draft programs for renewal that would redress the self-blocking weaknesses flexible producers displayed historically, to differentiate state pol-

---

[1] Burton Klein, *Dynamic Economics*, Cambridge, MA, 1977, pp. 23–4, 233, 259.

[2] Lester Thurow, *The Zero-Sum Solution*, New York, 1985, p. 165. See also idem, "Creating a World-Class Team," in David Obey and Paul Sarbanes, eds., *The Changing American Economy*, New York, 1986, pp. 169–79.

icies to address distinctive needs (though the political contests between segments of the business community and reformers might be ferocious), and as well to reeducate managers to regard workers as resourceful. Yet it is far from clear that any of this, from the coining of new managerial buzz words to the most imaginative schemes, has the capacity to offset the triumph of quantity over all the qualitative components of relations in production and distribution.

Promoters of "flexible specialization" thus place little faith in the workings of contemporary markets, for its articulation "requires a fusion of competition and cooperation that cannot occur in the model of market transactions."[3] Indeed, industrial districts built through exploiting a version of that "fusion" were silenced as the dominion of price and the institutionalized practices to support it dissolved personalism into a calculating diffidence. Market operations are unlikely to restore such antique relations, hence the turn toward politics, that relentlessly subjective, qualitative sphere, as the location for strategic action. However, in the United States, the political prospects seem bleak.

> We do not develop strategic aims [for industrial policy] in part because we do not want to, in part because we have never had to, in part because we are quite unprepared intellectually, institutionally, and politically to take on the task, and in part because we assume that domestic interventions simply serve to advantage some groups rather than others and that they advance the particular rather than the general interest.[4]

Nor is it likely that some great general catastrophe, another depression, would somehow generate the political will to foster "dynamic flexibility," given that ad hoc scrambling rather than planning is the the classic American response to emergencies.[5] Like the proprietors and workers of Philadelphia, American industry may now possess values and capacities that in a specific context brought profits and prosperity and in an altered environment prove both ineffectual and a source of profound immobilization. Perhaps as in Philadelphia, the weight of settled practices and the cultural inability simply to discard them make acceptance of decline and peripheralization seem more "sensible" than radical restructuring of our ways of being and doing. Perhaps several of this nation's proudest features, its giant corporations and centrist politics of balance, have become millstones that cannot be set down in order to rebuild swiftly and decisively. Certainly, the course of a regional industry's

---

[3] Michael Piore and Charles Sabel, *The Second Industrial Divide*, New York, 1984, p. 298. See also Michael Piore, "Beyond Social Anarchy," in Obey and Sarbanes, pp. 155–68.
[4] Stephen Cohen and John Zysman, *Manufacturing Matters*, New York, 1987, p. 235.
[5] Piore and Sabel, pp. 91–103.

development and decay cannot, except speculatively, mirror the national experience, but in its achievements and failings lie both clues to a larger history of industrialization and cautions against underestimating the challenges of restoring productive flexibility.

Index